WordPress®

ALL-IN-ONE

4th Edition

by Lisa Sabin-Wilson

for dummies®
A Wiley Brand

WordPress® All-in-One For Dummies®, 4th Edition

Published by: **John Wiley & Sons, Inc.**, 111 River Street, Hoboken, NJ 07030-5774, www.wiley.com

For general information on our other products and services, please contact our Customer Care Department within the U.S. at 877-762-2974, outside the U.S. at 317-572-3993, or fax 317-572-4002. For technical support, please visit https://hub.wiley.com/community/support/dummies.

Wiley publishes in a variety of print and electronic formats and by print-on-demand. Some material included with standard print versions of this book may not be included in e-books or in print-on-demand. If this book refers to media such as a CD or DVD that is not included in the version you purchased, you may download this material at http://booksupport.wiley.com. For more information about Wiley products, visit www.wiley.com.

Library of Congress Control Number: 2019933834

ISBN: 978-1-119-55315-1 (pbk); 978-1-119-55318-2 (ebk); 978-1-119-55322-9 (ebk)

Manufactured in the United States of America

V10010757_060419

Contents at a Glance

Table of Contents

Introduction

WordPress is the most popular online content management software on the planet. Between the hosted service at WordPress.com and the self-hosted software available at WordPress.org, millions of bloggers use WordPress, and to date, WordPress powers 30 percent of the Internet. That's impressive. With WordPress, you can truly tailor a website to your own tastes and needs.

With no cost for using the benefits of the WordPress platform to publish content on the web, WordPress is as priceless as it is free. WordPress makes writing, editing, and publishing content on the Internet a delightful, fun, and relatively painless experience, whether you're a publisher, a designer, a developer, or a hobbyist blogger.

About This Book

The fact that WordPress is free and accessible to all, however, doesn't make it inherently easy for everyone to use. For some people, the technologies, terminology, and coding practices are a little intimidating or downright daunting. *WordPress All-in-One For Dummies*, 4th Edition, eliminates any intimidation about using WordPress. With a little research, knowledge, and time, you'll soon have a website that suits your needs and gives your readers an exciting experience that keeps them coming back for more.

WordPress All-in-One For Dummies is a complete guide to WordPress that covers the basics: installing and configuring the software, using the Dashboard, publishing content, creating themes, and developing plugins. Additionally, this book provides advanced information about security, the WordPress tools, the Multisite features, and search engine optimization (SEO).

Foolish Assumptions

I make some inescapable assumptions about you and your knowledge, including the following:

- » You're comfortable using a computer, mouse, and keyboard.
- » You have a good understanding of how to access the Internet, use email, and use a web browser to access web pages.
- » You have a basic understanding of what a website is; perhaps you already maintain your own.
- » You want to use WordPress for your online publishing, or you want to use the various WordPress features to improve your online publishing.

If you consider yourself to be an advanced user of WordPress, or if your friends refer to you as an all-knowing WordPress guru, chances are good that you'll find some of the information in this book elementary. This book is for beginner, intermediate, and advanced users; there's something here for everyone.

Icons Used in This Book

The little pictures in the margins of the book emphasize a point to remember, a danger to be aware of, or information that you may find helpful. This book uses the following icons:

TIP

Tips are little bits of information that you may find useful — procedures that aren't necessarily obvious to a casual user or beginner.

WARNING

When your mother warned you, "Don't touch that pan; it's hot!" but you touched it anyway, you discovered the meaning of "Ouch!" I use this icon for situations like that one. You may very well touch the hot pan, but you can't say that I didn't warn you!

TECHNICAL STUFF

All geeky stuff goes here. I use this icon when talking about technical information. You can skip it, but I think that you'll find some great nuggets of information next to these icons. You may even surprise yourself by enjoying them. Be careful — you may turn into a geek overnight!

REMEMBER

When you see this icon, brand the text next to it into your brain so that you remember whatever it was that I thought you should remember.

Beyond the Book

On the web, you can find some extra content that's not in this book. Go online to find

- The Cheat Sheet for this book is at www.dummies.com/cheatsheet. In the Search field, type **WordPress All-in-One For Dummies Cheat Sheet** to find the Cheat Sheet for this book.
- Updates to this book, if any, are at www.dummies.com. Search for the book's title to find the associated updates.

Where to Go from Here

From here, you can go anywhere you please! *WordPress All-in-One For Dummies* is designed so that you can read any or all of the minibooks between the front and back covers, depending on what topics interest you.

Book 1 is a great place to get a good introduction to the world of WordPress if you've never used it before and want to find out more. Book 2 gives you insight into the programming techniques and terminology involved in running a WordPress website — information that's extremely helpful when you move forward to the other minibooks.

Above all else, have fun with the information contained within these pages! Read the minibooks on topics you think you already know; you might just come across something new. Then dig into the minibooks on topics that you want to know more about.

1 WordPress Basics

Contents at a Glance

IN THIS CHAPTER

» Discovering content publishing

» Publishing and archiving content

» Interacting through comments

» Syndicating through RSS

» Using WordPress as a content management tool to create different types of sites

Chapter 1

Exploring Basic WordPress Concepts

Blogging gives regular, nontechnical Internet users the ability to publish content on the World Wide Web quickly and easily. Consequently, blogging became extremely popular very quickly, to the point that it's now considered to be mainstream. In some circles, blogging is even considered to be passé, as it has given way to publishing all types of content freely and easily with WordPress. Regular Internet users are blogging, and Fortune 500 businesses, news organizations, and educational institutions are using WordPress to publish content on the web. Today, 30 percent of all sites on the web have WordPress behind them.

Although you can choose among several software platforms for publishing web content, for many content publishers, WordPress has the best combination of options. WordPress is unique in that it offers a variety of ways to run your website. WordPress successfully emerged as a favored blogging platform and expanded to a full-featured content management system (CMS) that includes all the tools and features you need to publish an entire website on your own without a whole lot of technical expertise or understanding.

In this chapter, I introduce you to such content basics such as publishing and archiving content, interacting with readers through comments, and providing ways for readers to access to your content through social media syndication

(RSS technologies). This chapter also helps you sort out the differences between a blog and a website, and introduces how WordPress, as a CMS, can help you build an entire website. Finally, I show you some websites that you can build with the WordPress platform.

Discovering Blogging

A blog is a fabulous tool for publishing your diary of thoughts and ideas. A blog also serves as an excellent tool for business, editorial journalism, news, and entertainment. Here are some ways that people use blogs:

- **Personal:** You're considered to be a personal blogger if you use your blog mainly to discuss topics related to you or your life: your family, your cats, your children, or your interests (such as technology, politics, sports, art, or photography). My business partner, Brad Williams, maintains a personal blog at `http://strangework.com`.
- **Business:** Blogs are very effective tools for promotion and marketing, and business blogs usually offer helpful information to readers and consumers, such as sales events and product reviews. Business blogs also let readers provide feedback and ideas, which can help a company improve its services. A good example of a business blog is on the Discovery Channel site at `https://corporate.discovery.com/discovery-newsroom/`.
- **Media/journalism:** Popular news outlets such as Fox News, MSNBC, and CNN are using blogs on their websites to provide information on current events, politics, and news on regional, national, and international levels. *Variety* magazine hosts its entire website on WordPress at `https://variety.com`.
- **Government:** Governments use blogs to post news and updates to the web quickly and to integrate social media tools as a means of interacting with their citizens and representatives. In the United States, the White House is using WordPress to power its official website at `https://whitehouse.gov`, where the executive branch of the government provides policy statements and updates on the economy, national security, the budget, immigration, and other topics. (See Figure 1-1.)
- **Citizen journalism:** Citizens are using blogs with the intention of keeping the media and politicians in check by fact-checking news stories and exposing inconsistencies. Major cable news programs interview many of these bloggers because the mainstream media recognize the importance of the citizen voice that has emerged via blogs. An example of citizen journalism is Power Line at `https://www.powerlineblog.com`.

» **Professional:** Professional blogs typically generate revenue and provide a source of monetary income for the owner through avenues such as advertising or paid membership subscriptions. Check out Darren Rowse's ProBlogger blog at `https://www.problogger.net`. Rowse is considered to be the grandfather of professional blogging.

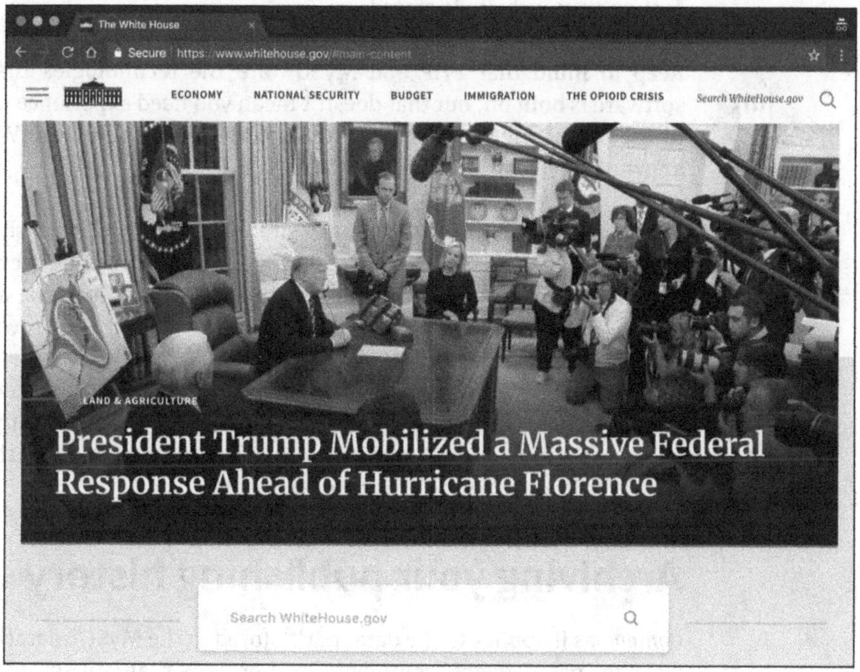

FIGURE 1-1: The official White House website is powered by WordPress.

The websites and blogs I provide in this list run on the WordPress platform. A wide variety of organizations and individuals choose WordPress to run their blogs and websites because of its popularity, ease of use, and large and active development community.

Understanding WordPress Technologies

The WordPress software is a personal publishing system that uses a PHP-and-MySQL platform, which provides everything you need to create your blog and publish your content dynamically without having to program the pages yourself. In short, with this platform, all your content is stored in a MySQL database in your hosting account.

TECHNICAL STUFF

PHP (which stands for *PHP Hypertext Preprocessor*) is a server-side scripting language for creating dynamic web pages. When a visitor opens a page built in PHP, the server processes the PHP commands and then sends the results to the visitor's browser. MySQL is an open-source relational database management system (RDBMS) that uses Structured Query Language (SQL), the most popular language for adding, accessing, and processing data in a database. If all that sounds like Greek to you, think of MySQL as being a big filing cabinet where all the content on your website is stored.

REMEMBER

Keep in mind that PHP and MySQL are the technologies that the WordPress software is built on, but that doesn't mean you need experience in these languages to use it. Anyone with any level of experience can easily use WordPress without knowing anything about PHP or MySQL.

Every time a visitor goes to your website to read your content, she makes a request that's sent to your server. The PHP programming language receives that request, obtains the requested information from the MySQL database, and then presents the requested information to your visitor through her web browser.

TIP

Book 2, Chapter 1 gives you more in-depth information about the PHP and MySQL requirements you need to run WordPress. Book 2, Chapter 3 introduces you to the basics of PHP and MySQL and provides information about how they work together with WordPress to create your blog or website.

Archiving your publishing history

Content, as it applies to the data that's stored in the MySQL database, refers to your websites posts, pages, comments, and options that you set up in the WordPress Dashboard or the control/administration panel of the WordPress software, where you manage your site settings and content. (See Book 3, Chapter 2.)

WordPress maintains chronological and categorized archives of your publishing history automatically. This archiving process happens with every post you publish to your blog. WordPress uses PHP and MySQL technology to organize what you publish so that you and your readers can access the information by date, category, author, tag, and so on. When you publish content on your WordPress site, you can file a post in any category you specify; a nifty archiving system allows you and your readers to find posts in specific categories. The archives page of my business partner's blog (`http://strangework.com/archives`), for example, contains a Category section, where you find a list of categories he created for his blog posts. Clicking the Blog Updates link below the Categories heading takes you to a listing of posts on that topic. (See Figure 1-2.)

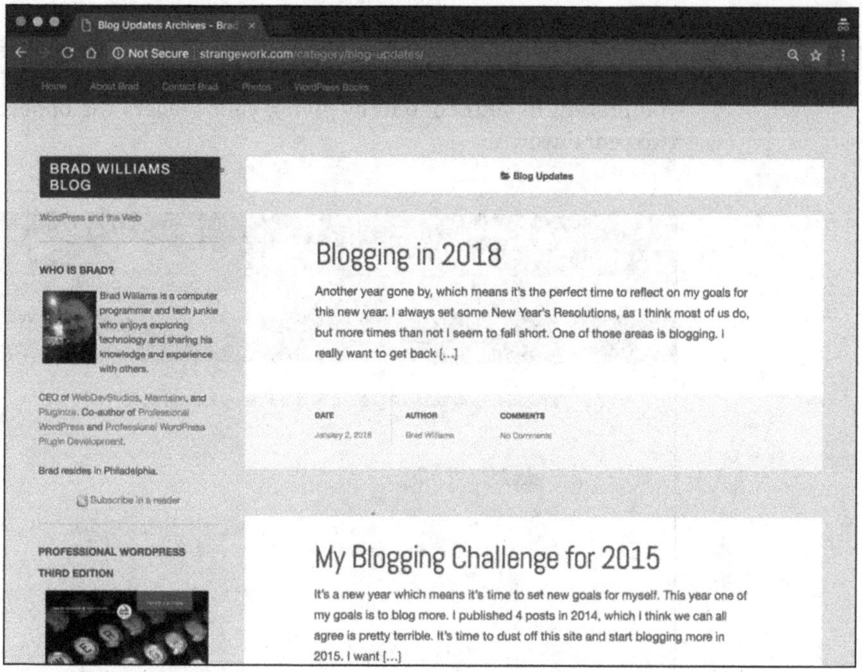

FIGURE 1-2: A page with posts in the Blog Updates category.

WordPress lets you create as many categories as you want for filing your content. Some sites have just one category, and others have up to 1,800 categories. When it comes to organizing your content, WordPress is all about personal preference. On the other hand, using WordPress categories is your choice. You don't have to use the category feature if you'd rather not.

TIP

When you look for a hosting service, keep an eye out for hosts that provide daily backups of your site so that your content won't be lost if a hard drive fails or someone makes a foolish mistake. Web hosting providers that offer daily backups as part of their services can save the day by restoring your site to a previous form.

REMEMBER

The theme (design) you choose for your site — whether it's the default theme, one that you create, or one that you custom-design — isn't part of the content. Those files are part of the file system and aren't stored in the database. Therefore, it's a good idea to create a backup of any theme files you're using. See Book 6 for further information on WordPress theme management.

Interacting with your readers through comments

An exciting aspect of publishing content with WordPress is receiving feedback from your readers after you publish to your site. Receiving feedback, or *comments*, is akin to having a guestbook on your site. People can leave notes for you that publish to your site, and you can respond and engage your readers in conversation. (See Figure 1-3.) These notes can expand the thoughts and ideas you present in your content by giving your readers the opportunity to add their two cents' worth.

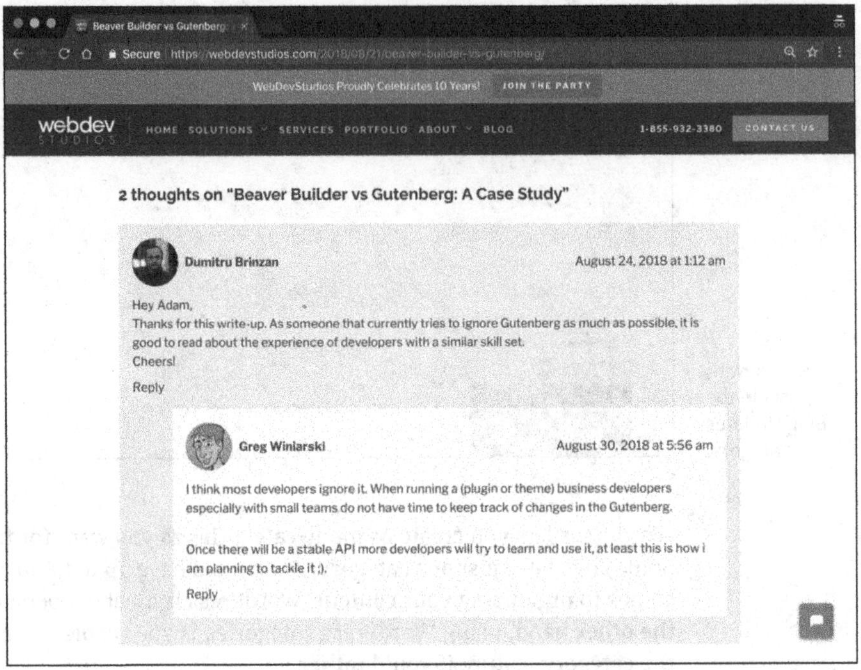

FIGURE 1-3: Blog comments and responses.

REMEMBER

The WordPress Dashboard gives you full administrative control over who can leave comments. Additionally, if someone leaves a comment with questionable content, you can edit the comment or delete it. You're also free to not allow comments on your site. (See Book 3, Chapter 4 for more information.)

Feeding your readers

RSS stands for *Really Simple Syndication.* An *RSS feed* is a standard feature that blog readers have come to expect. So what is RSS, really?

RSS is written to the web server in XML (Extensible Markup Language) as a small, compact file that can be read by RSS readers (as I outline in Table 1-1). Think of an RSS feed as a syndicated, or distributable, autoupdating "what's new" list for your website.

TABLE 1-1 Popular RSS Feed Readers

Reader	Source	Description
Feedly	`http://feedly.com`	RSS aggregator for websites that publish an RSS feed. It compiles published stories from various user-chosen sources and allows the Feedly user to organize the stories and share the content with others.
MailChimp	`https://mailchimp.com`	MailChimp is an email newsletter service. It has an RSS-to-email service that enables you to send your recently published content to your readers via an email subscription service.
dlvr.it	`https://dlvrit.com`	Use RSS to autopost to Facebook, Twitter, LinkedIn, Pinterest, and other social media sites.

Tools such as feed readers and email newsletter services can use the RSS feed from your website to consume the data and aggregate it into a syndicated list of content published on your website. Website owners allow RSS to be published to allow these tools to consume and then distribute the data in an effort to expand the reach of their publications.

Table 1-1 lists some popular tools that use RSS feeds to distribute content from websites.

For your readers to stay up to date with the latest and greatest content you post, they can subscribe to your RSS feed. WordPress RSS feeds are autodiscovered by the various feed readers. The reader needs only to enter your site's URL, and the program automatically finds your RSS feed.

WordPress has RSS feeds in several formats. Because the feeds are built into the software platform, you don't need to do anything to provide your readers an RSS feed of your content.

Tracking back

The best way to understand *trackbacks* is to think of them as comments, except for one thing: Trackbacks are comments left on your site by other sites, not people. Sounds perfectly reasonable, doesn't it? After all, why wouldn't inanimate objects want to participate in your discussion?

Actually, maybe it's not so crazy after all. A trackback happens when you make a post on your site, and within the content of that post, you provide a link to a post made by another author on a different site. When you publish that post, your site sends a sort of electronic memo to the site you linked to. That site receives the memo and posts an acknowledgment of receipt in the form of a comment to the post that you linked to on the site. The information contained within the trackback includes a link back to the post on your site that contains the link to the other site — along with the date and time, as well as a short excerpt of your post. Trackbacks are displayed within the comments section of the individual posts.

The memo is sent via a *network ping* (a tool used to test, or verify, whether a link is reachable across the Internet) from your site to the site you link to. This process works as long as both sites support trackback protocol. Almost all major CMSes support the trackback protocol.

REMEMBER

Sending a trackback to a site is a nice way of telling the author that you like the information she presented in her post. Most authors appreciate trackbacks to their posts from other content publishers.

Dealing with comment and trackback spam

The absolute bane of publishing content on the Internet is comment and trackback spam. Ugh. When blogging became the "it" thing on the Internet, spammers saw an opportunity. If you've ever received spam in your email program, you know what I mean. For content publishers, the concept is similar and just as frustrating.

Spammers fill content with open comments with their links but not with any relevant conversation or interaction in the comments. The reason is simple: Websites receive higher rankings in the major search engines if they have multiple links coming in from other sites, like trackbacks. Enter software like WordPress, with comment and trackback technologies, and these sites become prime breeding ground for millions of spammers.

Because comments and trackbacks are published to your site publicly — and usually with a link to the commenter's website — spammers got their site links posted on millions of sites by creating programs that automatically seek websites with open commenting systems and then hammer those systems with tons of comments that contain links back to their sites.

No one likes spam. Therefore, developers of CMSes such as WordPress spend untold hours trying to stop these spammers in their tracks, and for the most part, they've been successful. Occasionally, however, spammers sneak through. Many spammers are offensive, and all of them are frustrating because they don't contribute to the conversations that occur on the websites where they publish their spam comments.

All WordPress systems have one important thing in common: Akismet, which kills spam dead. Akismet is a WordPress plugin brought to you by Automattic, the creator of the WordPress.com service. I cover the Akismet plugin, and comment spam in general, in Book 3, Chapter 4.

Using WordPress as a Content Management System

A *content management system* (CMS) is a platform that lets you run a full website on your domain. This means that WordPress enables you to create and publish all kinds of content on your site, including pages, blog posts, e-commerce pages for selling products, videos, audio files, events, and more.

A *blog* is a chronological display of content — most often, written by the blog author. The posts are published and, usually, categorized into topics and archived by date. Blog posts can have comments activated so that readers can leave their feedback and the author can respond, creating a dialogue about the blog post.

A *website* is a collection of published pages with different sections that offer the visitor different experiences. A website can incorporate a blog but usually contains other sections and features. These other features include

- **Photo galleries:** Albums of photos uploaded and collected in a specific area so that visitors can browse through and comment on them
- **E-commerce stores:** Fully integrated shopping area into which you can upload products for sale and from which your visitors can purchase them
- **Discussion forums:** Where visitors can join, create discussion threads, and respond to one another in specific threads of conversation
- **Social communities:** Where visitors can become members, create profiles, become friends with other members, create groups, and aggregate community activity
- **Portfolios:** Sections where photographers, artists, or web designers display their work

» **Feedback forms:** Contact forms that your visitors fill out with information that then gets emailed to you directly

» **Static pages (such as Bio, FAQ, or Services):** Pages that don't change as often as blog pages, which change each time you publish a new post

The preceding list isn't exhaustive; it's just a listing of some of the most common website sections.

Figure 1-4 shows what the front page of my business blog looked like at the time of this writing. Visit `https://webdevstudios.com/blog` to see how the site displays the most recent blog posts. Although our blog doesn't publish the dates of each blog post, I can personally attest that it is a chronological listing of our most recent posts.

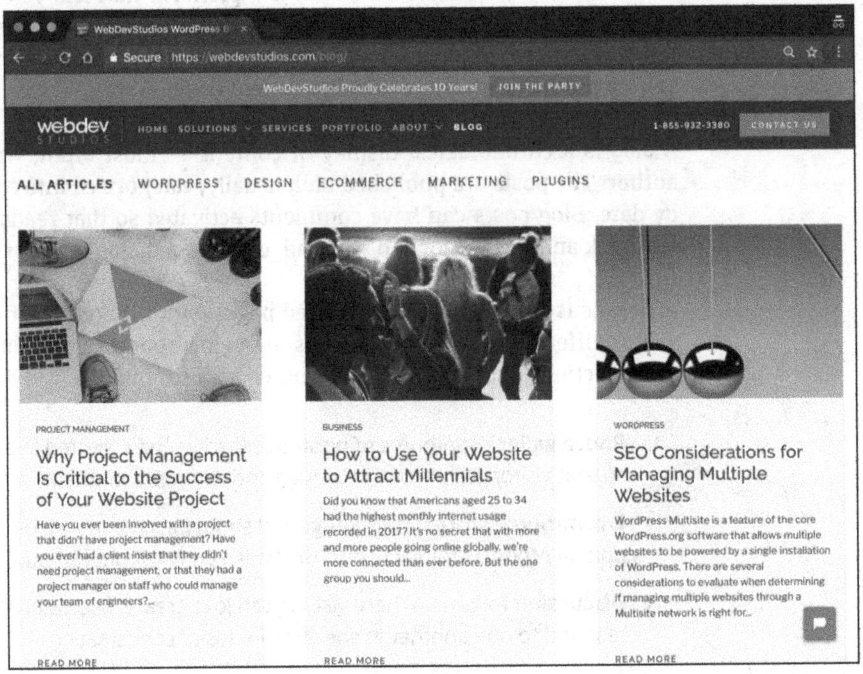

FIGURE 1-4: Visit my business blog at `https://webdevstudios.com/blog` to see an example of a chronological listing of blog posts.

My business website at `https://webdevstudios.com` also uses WordPress. This full site includes a static front page of information that acts as a portal to the rest of the site, on which you can find a blog; a portfolio of work; a contact form; and various landing pages, including service pages that outline information about the different services we offer (`https://webdevstudios.com/services`). Check out Figure 1-5 for a look at this website; it's quite different from the blog section of the site.

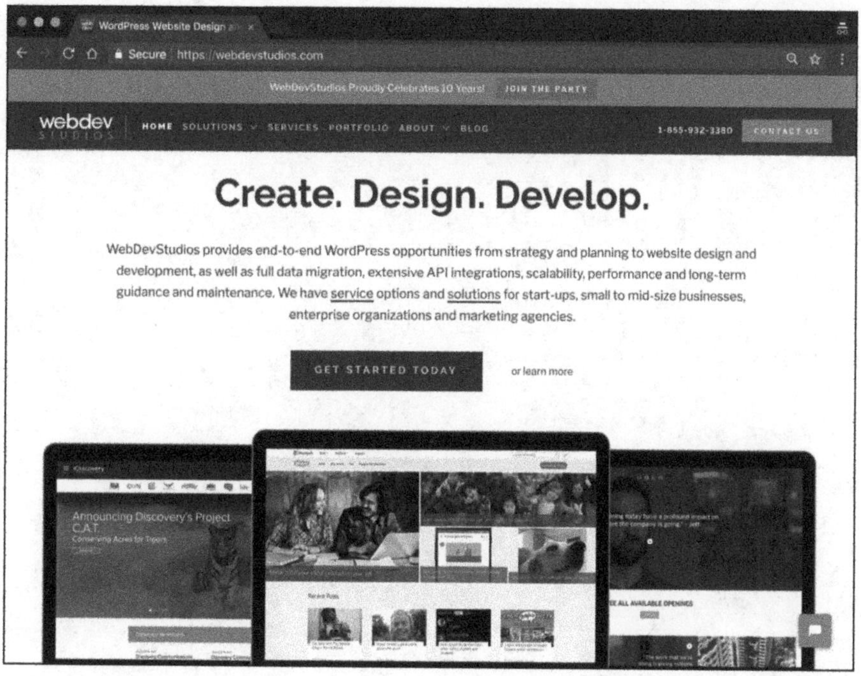

FIGURE 1-5: My business website uses WordPress as a CMS.

Using WordPress as a CMS means that you're creating more than just a blog; you're creating an entire website full of sections and features that offer different experiences for your visitors.

IN THIS CHAPTER

» Exploring open-source concepts

» Discovering examples of open-source projects

» Understanding WordPress licensing

» Applying WordPress licensing

Chapter 2
Exploring the World of Open-Source Software

Open-source software is a movement that started in the software industry in the 1980s. Its origins are up for debate, but most people believe that the concept came about in 1983, when a company called Netscape released its Navigator web browser source code to the public, making it freely available to anyone who wanted to dig through it, modify it, or redistribute it.

WordPress software users need a basic understanding of the open-source concept and the licensing upon which WordPress is built because WordPress's open-source policies affect you as a user — and greatly affect you if you plan to develop plugins or themes for the WordPress platforms. A basic understanding helps you conduct your practices in accordance with the license at the heart of the WordPress platform.

This chapter introduces you to open-source; the Open Source Initiative (OSI); and the GNU General Public License (GPL), which is the specific license that WordPress is built upon (GPLv2, to be exact). You also discover how the GPL license applies to any projects you may release (if you're a developer of plugins or themes) that depend on the WordPress software and how you can avoid potential problems by abiding by the GPL as it applies to WordPress.

REMEMBER

IANAL — *I Am Not a Lawyer* — is an acronym that you often find in articles about WordPress and the GPL. I use it here because I'm not a lawyer, and the information in this chapter shouldn't be construed as legal advice. Rather, you should consider the chapter to be an introduction to the concepts of open-source and the GPL. The information presented here is meant to inform you about and introduce you to the concepts as they relate to the WordPress platform.

Defining Open-Source

A simple, watered-down definition of open-source software is software whose source code is freely available to the public and that can be modified and redistributed by anyone without restraint or consequence. An official organization called the Open Source Initiative (OSI; `https://opensource.org`), founded in 1998 to organize the open-source software movement in an official capacity, has provided a very clear and easy-to-understand definition of open-source. During the course of writing this book, I obtained permission from the OSI board to include it here.

Open-source doesn't just mean access to the source code. The distribution terms of open-source software must comply with the following criteria:

1. **Free Redistribution**

   The license shall not restrict any party from selling or giving away the software as a component of an aggregate software distribution containing programs from several different sources. The license shall not require a royalty or other fee for such sale.

2. **Source Code**

   The program must include source code, and must allow distribution in source code as well as compiled form. Where some form of a product is not distributed with source code, there must be a well-publicized means of obtaining the source code for no more than a reasonable reproduction cost preferably, downloading via the Internet without charge. The source code must be the preferred form in which a programmer would modify the program. Deliberately obfuscated source code is not allowed. Intermediate forms such as the output of a preprocessor or translator are not allowed.

3. **Derived Works**

   The license must allow modifications and derived works, and must allow them to be distributed under the same terms as the license of the original software.

4. **Integrity of the Author's Source Code**

   The license may restrict source-code from being distributed in modified form only if the license allows the distribution of "patch files" with the source code for the purpose of modifying the program at build time. The license must explicitly permit distribution of software built from modified source code. The license may require derived works to carry a different name or version number from the original software.

5. **No Discrimination Against Persons or Groups**

   The license must not discriminate against any person or group of persons.

6. **No Discrimination Against Fields of Endeavor**

   The license must not restrict anyone from making use of the program in a specific field of endeavor. For example, it may not restrict the program from being used in a business, or from being used for genetic research.

7. **Distribution of License**

   The rights attached to the program must apply to all to whom the program is redistributed without the need for execution of an additional license by those parties.

8. **License Must Not Be Specific to a Product**

   The rights attached to the program must not depend on the program's being part of a particular software distribution. If the program is extracted from that distribution and used or distributed within the terms of the program's license, all parties to whom the program is redistributed should have the same rights as those that are granted in conjunction with the original software distribution.

9. **License Must Not Restrict Other Software**

   The license must not place restrictions on other software that is distributed along with the licensed software. For example, the license must not insist that all other programs distributed on the same medium must be open-source software.

10. **License Must Be Technology-Neutral**

    No provision of the license may be predicated on any individual technology or style of interface.

The preceding items comprise the definition of open-source as provided by the OSI. You can find this definition (see Figure 2-1) at `https://opensource.org/osd`.

Open-source software source code must be freely available, and any licensing of the open-source software must abide by this definition. Based on the OSI definition, WordPress is an open-source software project. Its source code is accessible and publicly available for anyone to view, build on, and distribute at no cost anywhere, at any time, or for any reason.

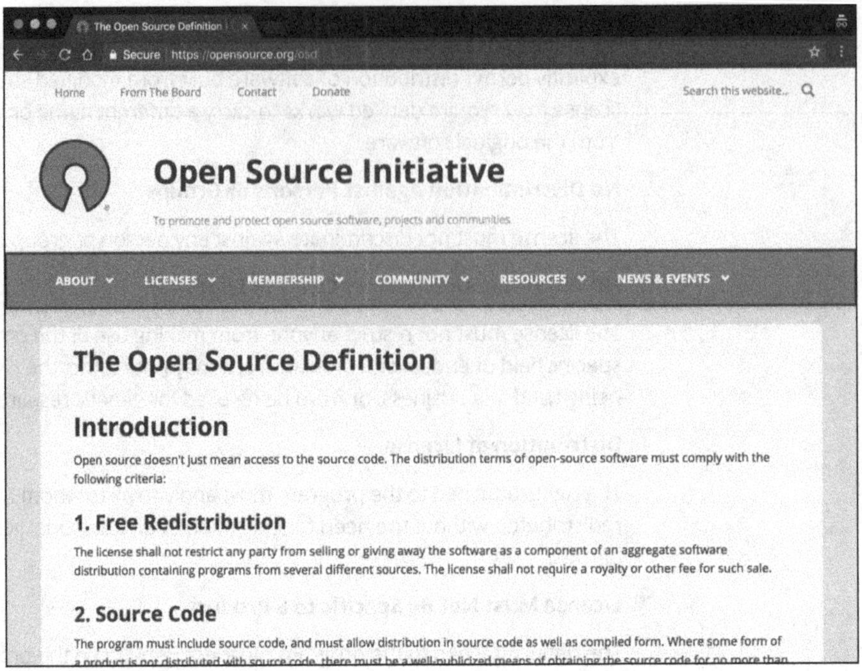

FIGURE 2-1: Definition of open-source from the OSI.

Several examples of high-profile software enterprises, such as the ones in the following list, are also open-source. You'll recognize some of these names:

- **Mozilla (**`https://www.mozilla.org`**):** Community whose projects include the popular Firefox Internet browser and Thunderbird, a popular email client. All projects are open-source and considered to be public resources.
- **PHP (**`http://php.net`**):** An HTML-embedded scripting language that stands for PHP Hypertext Preprocessor. PHP is popular software that runs on most web servers today; its presence is required on your web server for you to run the WordPress platform successfully on your site.
- **MySQL (**`https://www.mysql.com`**):** The world's most popular open-source database. Your web server uses MySQL to store all the data from your WordPress installation, including your posts, pages, comments, links, plugin options, theme option, and widgets.
- **Linux (**`https://www.linux.org`**):** An open-source operating system used by web hosting providers, among other organizations.

As open-source software, WordPress is in some fine company. Open-source itself isn't a license; I cover licenses in the next section. Rather, open-source is a movement — some people consider it to be a philosophy — created and promoted to provide software as a public resource open to community collaboration and peer review. WordPress development is clearly community-driven and focused. You can read about the WordPress community in Book 1, Chapter 4.

Understanding WordPress Licensing

Most software projects are licensed, meaning that they have legal terms governing the use or distribution of the software. Different kinds of software licenses are in use, ranging from very restrictive to least restrictive. WordPress is licensed by the GNU General Public License version 2 (GPLv2), one of the least restrictive software licenses available.

If you're bored, read the GPL text at `www.gnu.org/licenses/gpl-2.0.html`. Licensing language on any topic can be a difficult thing to navigate and understand. It's sufficient to have a basic understanding of the concept of GPL and let the lawyers sort out the rest, if necessary.

TIP

A complete copy of the GPL is included in every copy of the WordPress download package, in the `license.txt` file. The directory listing of the WordPress software files shown in Figure 2-2 lists the `license.txt` file.

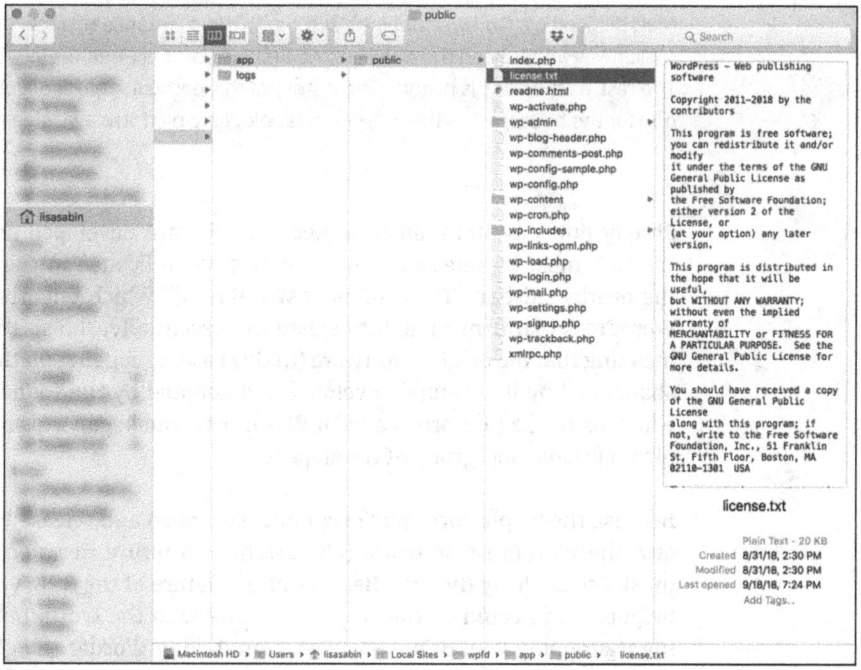

FIGURE 2-2: The GPL text is included in every copy of WordPress.

THE ORIGINS OF WordPress

Once upon a time, there was a simple PHP-based blogging platform called b2. This software, developed in 2001, slowly gained a bit of popularity among geek types as a way to publish content on the Internet. Its developer, Michel Valdrighi, kept development active until early 2003, when users of the software noticed that Valdrighi seemed to have disappeared. They became a little concerned about b2's future.

Somewhere deep in the heart of Texas, one young man in particular was very concerned, because b2 was his software of choice for publishing his own content on the World Wide Web. He didn't want to see his favorite publishing tool become obsolete. You can view the original post to his own blog in which he wondered what to do (`https://ma.tt/2003/01/the-blogging-software-dilemma`).

In that post, he talked briefly about some of the other software that was available at the time, and he tossed around the idea of using the b2 software to "to create a fork, integrating all the cool stuff that Michel would be working on right now if only he was around."

Create a fork he did. In the absence of b2's developer, this young man developed from the original b2 code base a new blogging application called WordPress.

That blog post was made on January 24, 2003, and the young man's name was (and is) Matt Mullenweg. On December 26, 2003, with the assistance of a few other developers, Mullenweg announced the arrival of the first official version of the WordPress software. The rest, as they say, is history. The history of this particular piece of software surely is one for the books, as it's the most popular blogging platform available today.

Simply put, any iteration of a piece of software developed and released under the GPL must be released under the very same license in the future. Check out the nearby sidebar "The origins of WordPress," which tells the story of how the WordPress platform came into existence. Essentially, the software was *forked* — meaning that the original software (in this case, a blogging platform called b2) was abandoned by its original developer and adopted by the founders of WordPress, who took the b2 platform, called it WordPress, and began a new project with a new plan, outlook, and group of developers.

Because the b2 platform was originally developed and released under the GPL, by law, the WordPress software (all current and future iterations of the platform) must also abide by the GPL. Because of the nature of the GPL, you, your next-door neighbor, or I could do the very same thing with the WordPress platform. Nothing is stopping you, or anyone else, from taking WordPress, giving it a different name, and rereleasing it as a completely different project. Typically, open-source projects are forked when the original project development stalls or is abandoned (as was the case with b2) or (in rare cases) when the majority of the development community is at odds with the leadership of the open-source project. I'm not suggesting that you do that, though, because WordPress has one of the most active development communities of any open-source project I've come across.

Applying WordPress Licensing to Your Projects

Regular users of WordPress software need never concern themselves with the GPL of the WordPress project at all. You don't have to do anything special to abide by the GPL. You don't have to pay to use the WordPress software, and you aren't required to acknowledge that you're using the WordPress software on your site. (That said, providing on your site at least one link back to the WordPress website is common courtesy and a great way of saying thanks.)

Most people aren't even aware of the software licensing because it doesn't affect the day-to-day business of blogging and publishing sites with the platform. It's not a bad idea to educate yourself on the basics of the GPL, however. When you try to be certain that any plugins and themes you use with your WordPress installation abide by the GPL, you have peace of mind that all applications and software you're using are in compliance.

Your knowledge of the GPL must increase dramatically, though, if you develop plugins or themes for the WordPress platform. (I cover WordPress themes in Book 6 and WordPress plugins in Book 7.)

The public licensing that pertains to WordPress plugins and themes wasn't decided in a court of law. The current opinion of the best (legal) practices is just that: opinion. The opinion of the WordPress core development team, as well as the opinion of the Software Freedom Law Center (`https://www.softwarefreedom.org/services`), is that WordPress plugins and themes are derivative works of WordPress and, therefore, must abide by the GPL by releasing the development works under the same license that WordPress has.

A *derivative work*, as it relates to WordPress, is a work that contains programming whose functionality depends on the core WordPress files. Because plugins and themes contain PHP programming that call WordPress core functions, they rely on the core WordPress framework to work properly and, therefore, are extensions of the software.

TECHNICAL STUFF

The text of the opinion by James Vasile from the Software Freedom Law Center is available at https://wordpress.org/news/2009/07/themes-are-gpl-too.

To maintain compliance with the GPL, plugin or theme developers can't release development work under any (restrictive) license other than the GPL. Nonetheless, many plugin and theme developers have tried to release material under other licenses, and some have been successful (from a moneymaking standpoint). The WordPress community, however, generally doesn't support these developers or their plugins and themes. Additionally, the core WordPress development team considers such works to be noncompliant with the license and, therefore, with the law.

WordPress has made it publicly clear that it won't support or promote any theme or plugin that isn't in 100 percent compliance with the GPL. If you're not 100 percent compliant with the GPL, you can't include your plugin or theme in the WordPress Plugin Directory hosted at https://wordpress.org/plugins. If you develop plugins and themes for WordPress, or if you're considering dipping your toe into that pool, do it in accordance with the GPL so that your works are in compliance and your good standing in the WordPress community is protected.

Table 2-1 provides a brief review of what you can (and can't) do as a WordPress plugin and theme developer.

TABLE 2-1 **Development Practices Compliant with GPL License**

Development/Release Practice	GPL-Compliant?
Distribute to the public for free with GPL.	Yes
Distribute to the public for a cost with GPL.	Yes
Restrict the number of users of one download with GPL.	No
Split portions of your work among different licenses. (PHP files are GPL; JavaScript or CSS files are licensed with the Creative Commons license.)	Yes (but WordPress.org won't promote works that aren't 100 percent GPL across all files)
Release under a different license, such as the PHP License.	No

The one and only way to make sure that your plugin or theme is 100 percent compliant with the GPL is to do the following before you release your development work to the world:

- Include a statement in your work indicating that the work is released under the GPLv2 license in the `license.txt` file, which WordPress does. (Refer to Figure 2-2.) Alternatively, you can include this statement in the header of your plugin file:

```
<?php

 This program is free software; you can redistribute it and/or modify it
   under the terms of the GNU General Public License, version 2, as
   published by the Free Software Foundation.

 This program is distributed in the hope that it will be useful,
 but WITHOUT ANY WARRANTY; without even the implied warranty of
 MERCHANTABILITY or FITNESS FOR A PARTICULAR PURPOSE. See the
 GNU General Public License for more details.

 You should have received a copy of the GNU General Public License
 along with this program; if not, write to the Free Software
 Foundation, Inc., 51 Franklin St., Fifth Floor, Boston, MA 02110-1301 USA
*/
?>
```

- Don't restrict the use of your works by the number of users per download.
- If you charge for your work, which is compliant with the GPL, the licensing doesn't change, and users still have the freedom to modify your work and rerelease it under a different name.
- Don't split the license of other files included in your work, such as CSS or graphics. Although this practice complies with the GPL, it won't be approved for inclusion in the WordPress Plugin Directory.

IN THIS CHAPTER

» Delving into WordPress release cycles

» Exploring betas, release candidates, and final release versions

» Navigating WordPress release archives

» Tracking WordPress development

» Using bleeding-edge builds

Chapter 3
Understanding Development and Release Cycles

If you're planning to dip your toe into the WordPress waters (or you've already dived in and gotten completely wet), the WordPress platform's development cycle is really good to know about and understand, because it affects every WordPress user on a regular basis.

WordPress and its features form the foundation of your website. WordPress is a low-maintenance way to publish content on the web, and the software is free in terms of monetary cost. WordPress isn't 100 percent maintenance-free, however, and part of maintenance is ensuring that your WordPress software is up to date to keep your website secure and safe.

This chapter explains the development cycle for the WordPress platform and shows you how you can stay up to date and informed about what's going on. This chapter also gives you information on WordPress release cycles and shows you how you can track ongoing WordPress development on your own.

Discovering WordPress Release Cycles

Book 1, Chapter 2 introduces you to the concept of open-source software and discusses how the WordPress development community is primarily volunteer developers who donate their time and talents to the WordPress platform. The development of new WordPress releases is a collaborative effort, sometimes requiring contributions from more than 300 developers.

The public schedule for WordPress updates is a goal of roughly one new release every 120 days. As a user, you can expect a new release of the WordPress software about three times per year. The WordPress development team sticks to that schedule closely, with exceptions only here and there. When the team makes exceptions to the 120-day rule, it usually makes a public announcement so that you know what to expect and when to expect it.

Mostly, interruptions in the 120-day schedule occur because the development of WordPress occurs primarily on a volunteer basis. A few developers — employees of Automattic, the company behind WordPress.com — are paid to develop for WordPress, but most developers are volunteers. Therefore, the progress of WordPress development depends on the developers' schedules.

REMEMBER

I'm confident in telling you that you can expect to update your WordPress installation at least three, if not four, times per year.

Upgrading your WordPress experience

Don't be discouraged or frustrated by the number of times you'll upgrade your WordPress installation. The WordPress development team is constantly striving to improve the user experience and to bring exciting, fun new features to the WordPress platform. Each upgrade improves security and adds new features to enhance your (and your visitors') experience on your website. WordPress also makes the upgrades easy to perform, as I discuss in Book 2, Chapter 6.

The following list gives you some good reasons why you should upgrade your WordPress software each time a new version becomes available:

- **Security:** When WordPress versions come and go, outdated versions are no longer supported and are vulnerable to malicious attacks and hacker attempts. Most WordPress security failures occur when you're running an outdated version of WordPress on your website. To make sure that you're running the most up-to-date and secure version, upgrade to the latest release as soon as you can.

- **New features:** Major WordPress releases offer great new features that are fun to use, improve your experience, and boost your efficiency and productivity. Upgrading your WordPress installation ensures that you always have access to the latest, greatest tools and features that WordPress has to offer. (I discuss the difference between major and minor, or point, releases later in this chapter, in the sidebar titled "Major versus point releases.")
- **Plugins and themes:** Most plugin and theme developers work hard to make sure that their products are up to date with the latest version of WordPress. Generally, plugin and theme developers don't worry about backward compatibility, and they tend to ignore out-of-date versions of WordPress. To be sure that the plugins and themes you've chosen are current and not breaking your site, make sure that you're using the latest version of WordPress and the latest versions of your plugins and themes. (See Book 6 for information about themes and Book 7 for details about plugins.)

Understanding the cycles of a release

By the time the latest WordPress installation becomes available, that version has gone through several iterations, or *versions.* This section helps you understand what it takes to get the latest version on your website and explains some of the WordPress development terminology.

The steps and terminology involved in the release of a new version of WordPress include

- **Alpha:** This phase is the first developmental phase of a new version. Alpha typically is the "idea" phase in which developers gather ideas, including those from users and community members. During the alpha phase, developers determine which features to include in the new release and then develop an outline and a project plan. After features are decided, developers start developing and testers start testing until they reach a "feature freeze" point in the development cycle, at which all new features are considered to be complete. Then development moves on to perfecting new features through user testing and bug fixes.
- **Beta:** This phase is for fixing bugs and clearing any problems that testers report. Beta cycles can last four to six weeks, if not longer. WordPress often releases several beta versions with such names as WordPress version 5.0 Beta, WordPress version 5.0 Beta 1, and so on. The beta process continues until the development team decides that the software is ready to move into the next phase in the development cycle.

- **Release candidate:** A version becomes a release candidate (RC) when the bugs from the beta versions are fixed and the version is nearly ready for final release. You sometimes see several RC iterations, referred to as RC-1, RC-2, and so on.
- **Final release:** After a version has gone through full testing in several (ideally, all) types of environments, use cases, and user experiences; any bugs from the alpha, beta, and RC phases have been squashed; and no major bugs are being reported, the development team releases the final version of the WordPress software.

After the WordPress development team issues a final release version, it starts again in the alpha phase, gearing up and preparing to go through the development cycle for the next major version.

REMEMBER

Typically, a development cycle lasts 120 days, but this figure is an approximation, because any number of things can happen (from developmental problems to difficult bugs) to delay the process.

Finding WordPress release archives

WordPress keeps a historical archive of all versions it has ever released at `https://wordpress.org/download/releases`, as shown in Figure 3-1. On that page, you find every release of the WordPress software for which a record exists.

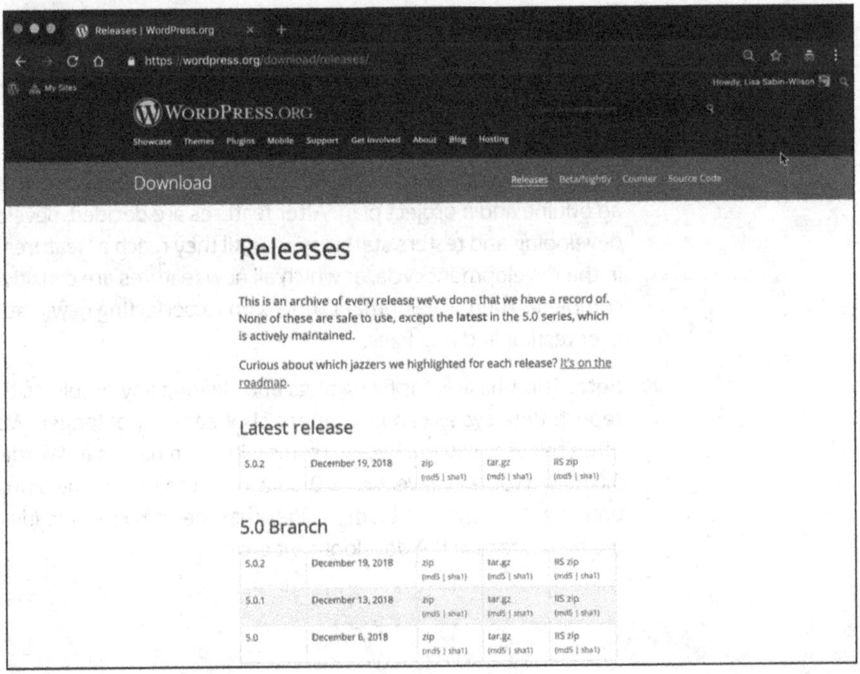

FIGURE 3-1: The archive of every WordPress release on record.

MAJOR VERSUS POINT RELEASES

You may have noticed that WordPress versions are numbered. These numbers show the progress of the development of the software, and they also tell you something else about the version you're using. *Software versioning* is a method of assigning unique numbers to each version release. Generally, the two types of versioning are

- **Point release:** Point releases usually increase the numbered version only by a decimal point or two, indicating a relatively minor release. Such releases include insignificant updates or minor bug fixes. When the version number jumps from 4.9.7 to 4.9.8, for example, you can be certain that the new version was released to fix minor bugs or to clean up the source code rather than to add new features.
- **Major release:** A major release most often contains new features and jumps by a more seriously incremented version number. In 2016, when WordPress went from 4.6.12 to 4.7 (release 4.6 versioned into 4.6.12 before jumping to 4.7), that release was considered to be a major release because it jumped a whole number rather than a decimal point. A large jump is a sign to users that new features are included in this version, rather than just bug fixes or cleanup of code. The bigger the jump in the version number, the more major the release is. A release jumping from 4.5 to 5.0, for example, would be an indication of major new features.

WARNING

None of the releases on the WordPress website is safe for you to use except the latest release in the 5.0.x series. Using an older version leaves your website open to hackers. WordPress just likes to have a recorded history of every release for posterity's sake.

Keeping Track of WordPress Development

If you know where to look, keeping track of the WordPress development cycle is easy, especially because the WordPress development team tries to make the development process as transparent as possible. You can track updates by reading about them at various spots on the Internet and by listening to conversations between developers. If you're so inclined, you can jump in and lend the developers a hand, too.

You have several ways to stay up to date on what's going on in the world of WordPress development, including blog posts, live chats, development meetings, tracking tickets, and bug reports, just to name a few. The following list gives you a solid start on where you can go to stay informed:

- **WordPress development updates (**`https://make.wordpress.org/core`**):** The WordPress development team's blog, Make WordPress Core, is where you can follow and keep track of the progress of the WordPress software project while it happens. (See Figure 3-2.) You find agendas, schedules, meeting minutes, and discussions surrounding the development cycles.

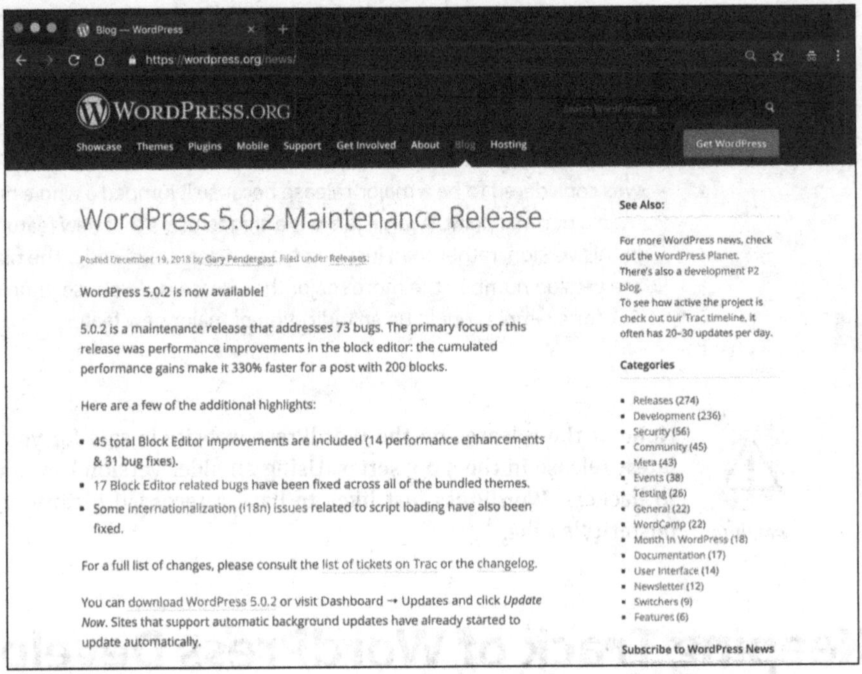

FIGURE 3-2: The WordPress development blog.

- **WordPress developers' chats (**`https://make.wordpress.org/chat`**):** Developers who are involved in development of WordPress core use a real-time communication platform called Slack (`https://slack.com`). You can easily participate in any of the scheduled meetings listed on `https://make.wordpress.org/core`. Regular scheduled chats are listed on the right sidebar of the site.
- **WordPress Trac (**`https://core.trac.wordpress.org`**):** Here are ways to stay informed about the changes in WordPress development:
  - Follow the timeline: `https://core.trac.wordpress.org/timeline`
  - View the road map: `https://core.trac.wordpress.org/roadmap`

- Read reports: `https://core.trac.wordpress.org/report`
- Perform a search: `https://core.trac.wordpress.org/search`

» **WordPress mailing lists (**`https://codex.wordpress.org/Mailing_Lists`**):** Join mailing lists focused on different aspects of WordPress development, such as bug testing, documentation, and hacking WordPress. (For specific details about mailing lists, see Book 1, Chapter 4.)

Downloading Nightly Builds

WordPress development moves pretty fast. Often, changes in the software's development cycle occur daily. While the developers are working on alpha and beta versions and release candidates, they commit the latest core changes to the repository and make those changes available to the public to download, install, and test on individual sites. The changes are released in a full WordPress software package called a *nightly build.* This nightly build contains the latest core changes submitted to the project — changes that haven't yet been released as full and final versions.

WARNING

Using nightly builds isn't a safe practice for a live site. I strongly recommend creating a test environment to test nightly builds. Many times, especially during alpha and beta phases, the core code breaks and causes problems with your existing installation. Use nightly builds in a test environment only, and leave your live site intact until the final release is available.

Hundreds of members of the WordPress community help in the development phases, even though they aren't developers or programmers. They help by downloading the nightly builds, testing them in various server environments, and reporting to the WordPress development team by way of Trac tickets (shown in Figure 3-3; check out `https://core.trac.wordpress.org/report`) any bugs and problems they find in that version of the software.

You can download the latest nightly build from the WordPress repository at `https://wordpress.org/download/beta-nightly`. For information about installing WordPress, see Book 2, Chapter 4.

REMEMBER

Running the latest nightly build on your website is referred to as using *bleeding-edge* software because the software is an untested version, requiring you to take risks just to run it on your website.

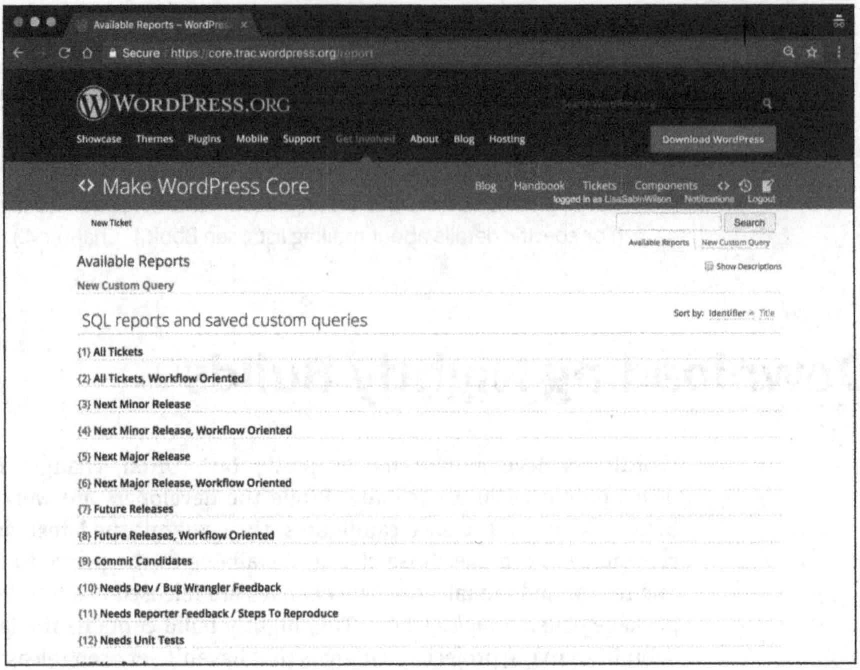

FIGURE 3-3: WordPress Trac tickets.

TIP

WordPress Beta Tester (`https://wordpress.org/plugins/wordpress-beta-tester`), by Peter Westwood, is a super plugin that enables you to use the automatic upgrade tool in your WordPress Dashboard to download the latest nightly build. For information about installing and using WordPress plugins, check out Book 7, Chapter 2.

IN THIS CHAPTER

» Finding WordPress users

» Locating users on social networks

» Getting help in the support forums

» Participating in testing and bug squashing

» Discovering professional consultants and services

» Attending and organizing local WordCamps

Chapter 4

Meeting the WordPress Community

Allow me to introduce you to the fiercely loyal folks who make up the WordPress user base, better known as the WordPress community. These merry ladies and gentlemen come from all around the globe, from California to Cairo, Florida to Florence, and all points in between.

Early on, in March 2005, Matt Mullenweg of WordPress proudly proclaimed that the number of WordPress downloads had reached 900,000 — an amazing landmark in the history of the software. By contrast, in 2019, the download counter for WordPress version 5.0 had exceeded 18 million times in the first month after its release in December 2018. The World Wide Technology Surveys (`https://w3techs.com`) published results showing WordPress to be the most popular content management system (CMS) being used on the web today. An astounding 32.7 percent of all sites on the Internet that use a CMS use WordPress. This popularity makes for a large community of users, to say the least.

This chapter introduces you to the WordPress community and the benefits of membership within that community, such as finding support forums, locating other WordPress users on various social networks, getting assistance from other users, participating in WordPress development, and hooking up with WordPress users face to face at WordPress events such as WordCamp.

Finding Other WordPress Users

Don't let the sheer volume of users intimidate you: WordPress has bragging rights to the most helpful blogging community on the web today. Thousands of websites exist that spotlight everything, including WordPress news, resources, updates, tutorials, and training. The list is endless. Do a quick Google search for *WordPress*, and you'll get about 1.6 billion results.

My point is that WordPress users are all over the Internet, from websites to discussion forums and social networks to podcasts and more. For many people, the appeal of the WordPress platform lies not only in the platform itself, but also in its passionate community of users.

Finding WordPress news and tips on community websites

WordPress-related websites cover an array of topics related to the platform, including everything from tutorials to news and even a little gossip, if that's your flavor. The Internet has no shortage of websites related to the popular WordPress platform. Here are a few that stand out:

- **WP Tavern (`https://wptavern.com`):** A site that covers everything from soup to nuts: news, resources, tools, tutorials, and interviews with standout WordPress personalities. You can pretty much count on WP Tavern to be on top of what's new and going on in the WordPress community. WP Tavern is owned by Automattic, the parent company of WordPress.com.
- **Smashing Magazine (`https://www.smashingmagazine.com/category/wordpress/`):** A very popular and established online design magazine and resource that has dedicated a special section of its website to WordPress news, resources, tips, and tools written by various members of the WordPress community.
- **Make WordPress Core (`https://make.wordpress.org/core`):** A website that aggregates content from all the "Make WordPress" websites built and maintained by the WordPress.org community. It includes resources for contributing to WordPress core, making plugins and themes, planning WordPress events, supporting WordPress, and more.

Locating users on social networks

In addition to WordPress, many bloggers use microblogging tools such as Twitter (https://twitter.com) and/or social-media networks such as Facebook (https://www.facebook.com) to augment their online presence and market their blogs, services, and products. Within these networks, you can find WordPress users, resources, and links, including the following:

- **WordPress Twitter lists:** Twitter allows users to create lists of people who have the same interests, such as WordPress. You can find a few of these lists here:
  - *Twitter:* https://twitter.com/search?q=WordPress
  - *Google:* https://www.google.com/#q=WordPress+Twitter+Lists
- **Facebook Pages on WordPress:** Facebook users create pages and groups around their favorite topics of interest, such as WordPress. You can find some interesting WordPress pages and groups here:
  - *WordPress.org:* https://www.facebook.com/WordPress
  - *Advanced WordPress:* https://www.facebook.com/groups/advancedwp
  - *Matt Mullenweg* (founder of WordPress): https://www.facebook.com/matt.mullenweg

TIP

You can include Twitter lists on your site by using the handy Twitter widget for WordPress at https://wordpress.org/plugins/widget-twitter.

Users Helping Users

Don't worry if you're not a member of the WordPress community. Joining is easy: Simply start your own website by using the WordPress platform. If you're already publishing on a different platform, such as Drupal or Tumblr, WordPress makes migrating your data from that platform to a new WordPress setup simple. (See Book 2, Chapter 7 for information on migrating to WordPress from a different platform.)

WordPress support forums

You can find the WordPress Support page (shown in Figure 4-1) at https://wordpress.org/support. This page is where you find users helping other users in their quest to use and understand the platform.

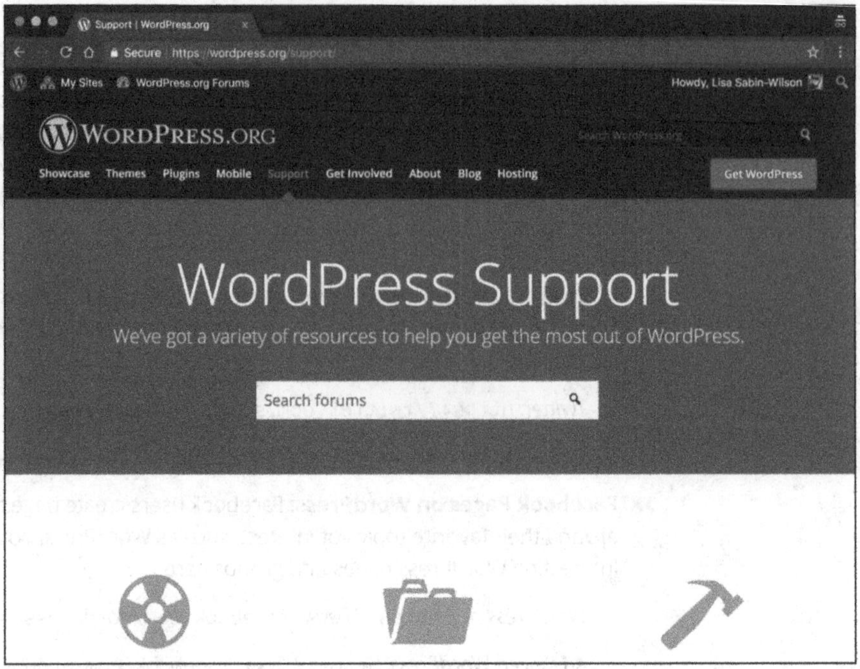

FIGURE 4-1: WordPress Support page.

REMEMBER

The support forums are hosted on the WordPress.org website, but don't expect to find any official form of support from the WordPress developers. Instead, you find a large community of people from all walks of life seeking answers and providing solutions.

Users from beginner and novice level to the most advanced level browse the forums, providing support for one another. Each user has his or her own experiences, troubles, and knowledge level with WordPress, and the support forums are where users share those experiences and seek out the experiences of other users.

REMEMBER

It's important to keep in mind that the people you find and interact with on these official forums are offering their knowledge on a volunteer basis only, so as always, common-courtesy rules apply. "Please" and "Thank you" go a long, long way in the forums.

TIP

If you find solutions and assistance in the WordPress support forums, consider browsing the forum entries to see whether you can help someone else by answering a question or two.

WordPress user manual

You can find users contributing to the very helpful WordPress Codex (a collection of how-to documents) at `https://codex.wordpress.org`. *Codex*, by the way, is Latin for *book*.

The WordPress Codex is a collaborative effort to document the use of the WordPress software. All contributors are WordPress users who donate their time as a way of giving back to the free, open-source project that has given them a dynamic piece of software for publishing freely on the web.

Make WordPress

If you'd like to get involved in the WordPress project, Make WordPress is the place to go. The Make blogs in this community offer you the opportunity to become involved in various aspects of the WordPress community as well as future development of the software. All the available WordPress Make blogs are on the WordPress website at `https://make.wordpress.org`. The most popular ones include

- **Core** (`https://make.wordpress.org/core`): Subscribe and participate on the Make Core blog list to interact and talk to the WordPress core development team — keep up to date on the status of the project, and get involved in discussions about the overall direction of the project.
- **Accessiblity** (`https://make.wordpress.org/accessibility`): The Make WordPress Accessible blog is an area to get involved in if you're interested in helping improve the accessibility of WordPress to (among others) people who can't see or use a mouse, people who can't hear and/or use sign language as a primary means of communication, users and visitors whose primary language isn't your primary language, people who use special assistive devices to access the Web, and people who are color-blind.
- **Support** (`https://make.wordpress.org/support`): The Make WordPress Support blog is where you should go if you have an interest in helping other users. Answering questions in the Support Forum is one of the easiest ways to contribute to the WordPress project.

Discovering Professional WordPress Consultants and Services

Meeting the WordPress Community

You have big plans for your website, and your time is valuable. Hiring a professional to handle the back-end design and maintenance of your website enables you to spend your time creating the content and building your readership on the front end.

Many website owners who decide to go the custom route by hiring a design professional do so for another reason: They want the designs/themes of their website to be unique. Free themes are nice, but you run the risk that your blog will look like hundreds of other blogs.

A *brand* (a term often used in advertising and marketing) refers to the recognizable identity of a product — in this case, your website. Having a unique brand or design for your site sets yours apart from the rest. If your website has a custom look, people will associate that look with you or your company. You can accomplish branding with a single logo or an entire layout and color scheme of your choosing.

Many consultants and design professionals put themselves up for hire. Who are these people? I get to that topic in a second. First, you want to understand what services they offer, which can help you decide whether hiring a professional is the solution for you.

Here are some of the many services available:

- Custom graphic design and CSS styling for your website
- Custom templates
- WordPress plugin installation and integration
- Custom WordPress plugin development
- WordPress software installation on your web server
- Upgrades of the WordPress software
- Web hosting and domain registration services
- Search engine optimization and site marketing

REMEMBER

Some website owners take advantage of the full array of services provided, whereas others use only a handful. The important thing to remember is that you aren't alone. Help is available for you and your website.

Table 4-1 pairs the three types of blog experts — designers, developers, and consultants — with the services they typically offer. Many of these folks are freelancers with self-imposed titles, but I've matched titles with typical duties. Keep in mind that some of these professionals wear all these hats; others specialize in only one area.

I wish I could tell you what you could expect to pay for any of these services, but the truth is the levels of expertise — and expense — vary wildly. Services can range from $5 per hour to $300 or more per hour. As with any purchase, do your research and make an informed decision before you buy.

TABLE 4-1 Types of WordPress Professionals

Title	Services
Graphic Designers	These folks excel in graphic and layout design using software like Adobe Photoshop for the purpose of creating a unique visual design for your website.
Developers	These guys and gals are code monkeys. Some of them don't know a stitch about graphic design, but they pair up with a graphic designer to provide custom code to make your website do things you never thought possible. Usually, you'll find these people releasing plugins in their spare time for the WordPress community to use free.
Consultants	If you have a website for your business, these folks can provide you a marketing plan for your site or a plan for using your site to reach clients and colleagues in your field. Many of these consultants also provide search engine optimization to help your domain reach high ranks in search engines.

Listing all the professionals who provide WordPress services is impossible, but Tables 4-2 through 4-4 list some of the most popular ones. I've tried to cover a diverse level of services so that you have the knowledge to make an informed decision about which professional to choose.

TABLE 4-2 Established WordPress Designers

Who They Are	Where You Can Find Them
WebDevStudios	`https://webdevstudios.com`
eWebscapes	`https://ewebscapes.com`
Pixel Jar	`https://www.pixeljar.com`

TABLE 4-3 Established WordPress Developers

Who They Are	Where You Can Find Them
WebDevStudios	`https://webdevstudios.com`
eWebscapes	`https://ewebscapes.com`
Covered Web Services	`http://coveredwebservices.com`
Voce Communications	`http://vocecommunications.com`

TABLE 4-4 Established Blog Consultants

Who They Are	Where You Can Find Them	Type of Consulting
Kaplan Marketing	`www.kalpanamarketing.com`	Search engine optimization (SEO), digital marketing
Pam Ann Marketing	`https://pamannmarketing.com`	SEO
WordPress 101	`https://www.wp101.com`	WordPress training

WordPress designers

WordPress front-end designers can take a simple website and turn it into something dynamic, beautiful, and exciting. These people are experts in the graphic design, CSS styling, and template tagging needed to create a unique theme for your website. Often, WordPress designers are skilled in installing and upgrading WordPress software and plugins; sometimes, they're even skilled in creating custom PHP or plugins. These folks are the ones you want to contact when you're looking for someone to create a unique design for your website that's an individual, visual extension of you or your company.

Some website designers post their rates on their websites because they offer design *packages*, whereas other designers quote projects on a case-by-case basis because every project is unique. When you're searching for a designer, if the prices aren't displayed on the site, drop the designer an email and ask for an estimate. Armed with this information, you can do a little comparison shopping while you search for just the right designer.

The designers and design studios listed in Table 4-2 represent a range of styles, pricing, services, and experience. All of them excel in creating custom WordPress websites. This list is by no means exhaustive, but it's a nice starting point.

Developers

The WordPress motto sits at the bottom of the WordPress home page:

> Code is poetry.

No one knows this better than the extremely talented developers in the core WordPress development team. A developer can take some of the underlying code, make a little magic happen between PHP and the MySQL database that stores the content of your website, and create a dynamic display of that content for you. Most likely, you'll contact a developer when you want to do something with your site that's a little out of the ordinary, and you can't find a plugin that does the trick.

If you've gone through all the available WordPress plugins and still can't find the exact function that you want your WordPress blog to perform, contact one of these folks. Explain what you need. The developer can tell you whether it can be done, whether she's available to do it, and how much the job will cost. (Don't forget that last part!) You may recognize some of the names in Table 4-3 as developers/authors of some popular WordPress plugins.

Consultants

Website consultants may not be able to design or code for you, but they're probably connected to people who can. Consultants can help you achieve your goals for your website in terms of online visibility, marketing plans, and search engine optimization. Most of these folks can help you find out how to make money with your website and connect you with various advertising programs. Quite honestly, you can do what website consultants do by investing a little time and research in these areas. As with design and coding, however, figuring everything out and then implementing it takes time. Sometimes it's easier — and more cost-effective — to hire a professional than to do the work yourself.

Who hires website consultants? Typically, businesses that want to take their websites to the next level through expert consulting and new businesses that want to launch new websites and need some help with marketing, branding, and search engine optimization (SEO). Table 4-4 lists some people and organizations that offer this kind of consulting.

Contributing to WordPress

Contributing code to the core WordPress software is only one way of participating in the WordPress project. You don't need to be a coder or developer to contribute to WordPress, and it's easier than you might think. Here are several ways you can contribute to the project, including (but not limited to) code:

- **Code:** One of the most obvious ways you can contribute to WordPress is providing code to be used in the core files. The WordPress project has several hundred developers who contribute code at one time or another. You submit code through the WordPress Trac at `https://core.trac.wordpress.org`. Within the Trac, you can follow current development and track changes. To contribute, you can use the Trac to download and test a code patch or look at reported bugs to see whether you can offer a fix or submit a patch. Required skills include, at the very least, PHP programming, WordPress experience, and MySQL database administration. (That list isn't exhaustive, mind you.)

» **Testing:** You can join the WordPress Test Make Blog (`https://make.wordpress.org/test`) to test beta versions of WordPress and report your own user experience. WordPress developers monitor this Make Blog and tries to fix any true bugs or problems.

» **Documentation:** Anyone can submit documentation to the WordPress Codex (the user documentation for WordPress). All you need to do is visit `https://codex.wordpress.org`, create an account, and dig in!

TIP

Be sure to check out the article titled "Codex: Contributing" (`https://codex.wordpress.org/Codex:Contributing`), which provides good tips on how to get started, including guidelines for documentation contributions.

» **Tutorials:** Do you feel that you have a few tips and tricks you want to share with other WordPress users? Take them to your blog! What better way to contribute to WordPress than sharing your knowledge with the rest of the world? Write up your how-to tutorial, publish it on your website, and then promote your tutorial on Twitter and Facebook.

» **Support forums:** Volunteer your time and knowledge on the WordPress support forums at `https://wordpress.org/support/forums`. The involvement of the WordPress users who donate their time and talents in the support forum is an essential part of the WordPress experience.

» **Presentations:** In the next section of this chapter, I discuss live WordPress events where users meet face to face. Consider offering to speak at one of those events to share your knowledge and experience with other users — or hosting one in your area.

Participating in Live WordPress Events

You can not only find out about WordPress and contribute to the project online via the Internet, but also get involved in WordPress offline. Live WordPress events, called WordPress Meetups and WordCamps, are where users and fans get together to discuss, learn, and share information about their favorite platform. The two events are somewhat different:

» **WordPress Meetups:** Generally, these events involve small groups of people from the same geographical location. Typically, these speakers, organizers, and attendees enjoy gathering on a monthly or bimonthly basis.

You can find a WordPress Meetup near your community by visiting the Meetup website at `https://www.meetup.com` or by performing a search, using the keyword *WordPress* and your city or zip code.

- **WordCamps:** These annual events are usually much larger than Meetups and are attended by people from all over the country. WordCamps are hosted in almost every major city in the United States and abroad. Usually, WordCamps cost a small amount to attend, and speakers at WordCamps are well-known personalities from the WordPress community.

  You can find a WordCamp event close to you by visiting the WordCamp website at `https://central.wordcamp.org` and browsing the upcoming WordCamps.

TIP

If there isn't a Meetup or WordCamp scheduled in your area, consider getting involved and organizing one! You can find some great tips and information about organizing WordCamps at `https://central.wordcamp.org`.

IN THIS CHAPTER

» Getting hosted with WordPress.com

» Self-hosting with WordPress.org

» Running a network of blogs with the Multisite feature

» Exploring enterprise options and VIP services

Chapter 5

Discovering Different Versions of WordPress

Website publishers have a wealth of software platforms to choose among. You want to be sure that the platform you choose has all the options you're looking for. WordPress is unique in that it offers two versions of its software. Each version is designed to meet the various needs of publishers.

One version is a hosted platform available at WordPress.com that meets your needs if you don't want to worry about installing or dealing with software; the other is the self-hosted version of the WordPress software available at `https://wordpress.org`, which offers you a bit more freedom and flexibility, as described throughout this chapter.

This chapter introduces you to both versions of the WordPress platform so you can choose which version suits your particular needs the best.

Comparing the Two Versions of WordPress

The two versions of WordPress are

- The hosted version at WordPress.com
- The self-installed and self-hosted version available at WordPress.org

Certain features are available to you in every WordPress site setup, whether you're using the self-hosted software from WordPress.org or the hosted version at WordPress.com. These features include (but aren't limited to):

- Quick, easy installation and setup
- Full-featured publishing capability, letting you publish content to the web through an easy-to-use web-based interface
- Topical archiving of your posts, using categories
- Monthly archiving of your posts, with the capability to provide a listing of those archives for easy navigation through your site
- Comment and trackback tools
- Automatic spam protection through Akismet
- Built-in gallery integration for photos and images
- Media Manager for managing video and audio files
- Great community support
- Unlimited number of static pages, letting you step out of the blog box and into the sphere of running a fully functional website
- RSS capability with RSS 2.0, RSS 1.0, and Atom support
- Tools for importing content from different content management systems (such as Blogger and Movable Type)

Table 5-1 compares the two WordPress versions.

TABLE 5-1 **Exploring the Differences between the Two Versions of WordPress**

Feature	WordPress.org	WordPress.com
Cost	Free	Free
Software download required	Yes	No
Software installation required	Yes	No
Web hosting required	Yes	No
Custom CSS control	Yes	Available in the Premium or Business plan up to $96/year
Template access	Yes	No
Sidebar widgets	Yes	Yes
RSS syndication	Yes	Yes
Access to core code	Yes	No
Ability to install plugins	Yes	Available in the Business plan up to $300/year
WP themes installation	Yes	Available in the Business plan up to $300/year
Multiauthor support	Yes	Yes
Unlimited number of site setups with one account (multisite)	Yes*	Yes
Community-based support forums	Yes	Yes

**Only with the Multisite feature enabled*

Choosing the hosted version from WordPress.com

WordPress.com (see Figure 5-1) is a free service. If downloading, installing, and using software on a web server sound like Greek to you and are chores you'd rather avoid, the WordPress folks provide a solution for you at WordPress.com.

WordPress.com is a *hosted solution*, which means that it has no software requirement, no downloads, and no installation or server configurations. Everything's done for you on the back end, behind the scenes. You don't even have to worry about how the process happens; it happens quickly, and before you know it, you're making your first blog post.

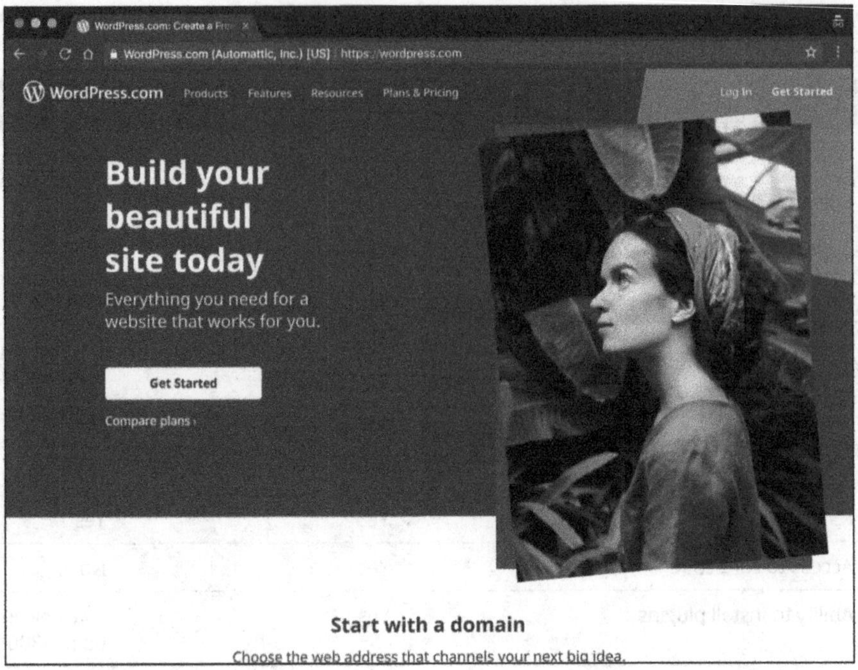

FIGURE 5-1: The WordPress.com website.

WordPress.com offers several upgrades (see Figure 5-2) to help make your publishing life easier. Here's a list of package upgrades you can purchase to enhance your WordPress.com account, with prices reflecting the annual cost:

- **Personal:** This plan allows you to add your own domain name to your WordPress.com account; see Book 2, Chapter 1. This service also provides you email and live chat support, basic design customizations, and 3GB of storage space. For the additional fee, your site also becomes ad-free. (With the free plan, WordPress.com advertisements are part of your experience.) This plan costs $2.99 per month, billed annually at $35.88 per year.
- **Premium:** This plan provides you everything included in the Personal plan and also includes more advanced theme customization (full control of the CSS), increased storage space at 13GB, the ability to monetize your site, and VideoPress support. This plan costs $8 per month, billed annually at $96 per year.

  TIP The VideoPress service is described in the "Discovering WordPress VIP Services" section at the end of this chapter.
- **Business:** This plan provides you everything included in both the Personal and Premium plans. In addition, you have access to premium themes, unlimited storage space, live courses, Google Analytics integration, and the removal of all WordPress.com branding — all for the cost of $25 per month, billed annually at $300 per year.

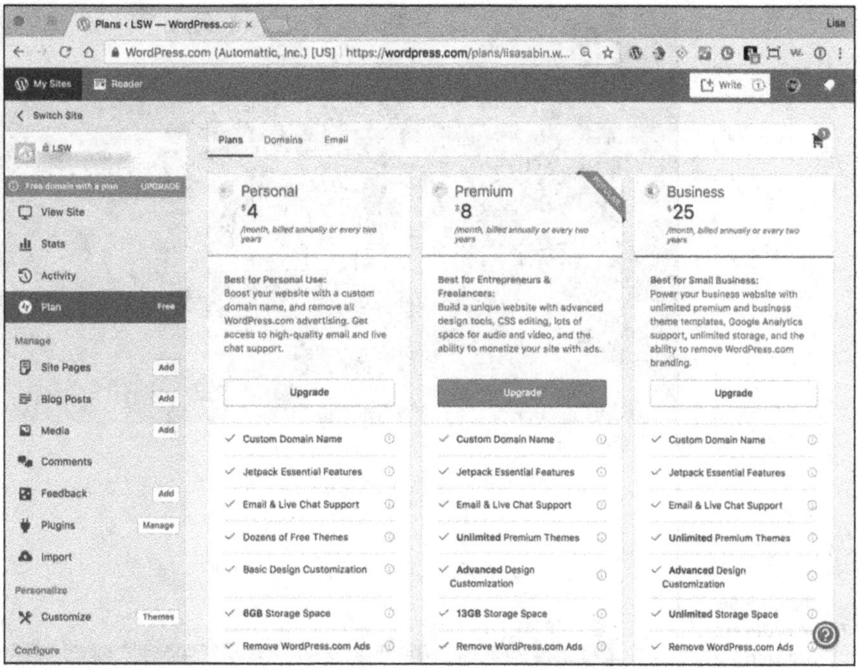

FIGURE 5-2: Several paid upgrades available on the WordPress.com free service.

TIP

WordPress.com has some limitations. You can't install plugins or custom themes, for example. Neither can you can customize the base-code files, sell advertising, or monetize your site without upgrading to a paid plan. But even with its limitations, WordPress.com is an excellent starting point if you're brand-new to Internet publishing and a little intimidated by the configuration requirements of the self-installed WordPress.org software.

The good news is that if you outgrow your WordPress.com-hosted site and want to move to the self-hosted WordPress.org software, you can. You can even take all the content from your WordPress.com-hosted site with you and easily import it into your new setup with the WordPress.org software. The makers of WordPress.com also provide you with a handy guide on how to move off the hosted platform onto your own self-hosted version using the software available at WordPress.org. You can find the guide at `https://move.wordpress.com`.

Therefore, in the grand scheme of things, your options aren't really that limited.

Self-hosting with WordPress.org

The self-installed version from WordPress.org is the primary focus of *WordPress All-in-One For Dummies.* Using WordPress.org requires you to download the software from the WordPress website at `https://wordpress.org` (shown in Figure 5-3); then you need to install it on a server from which your website operates.

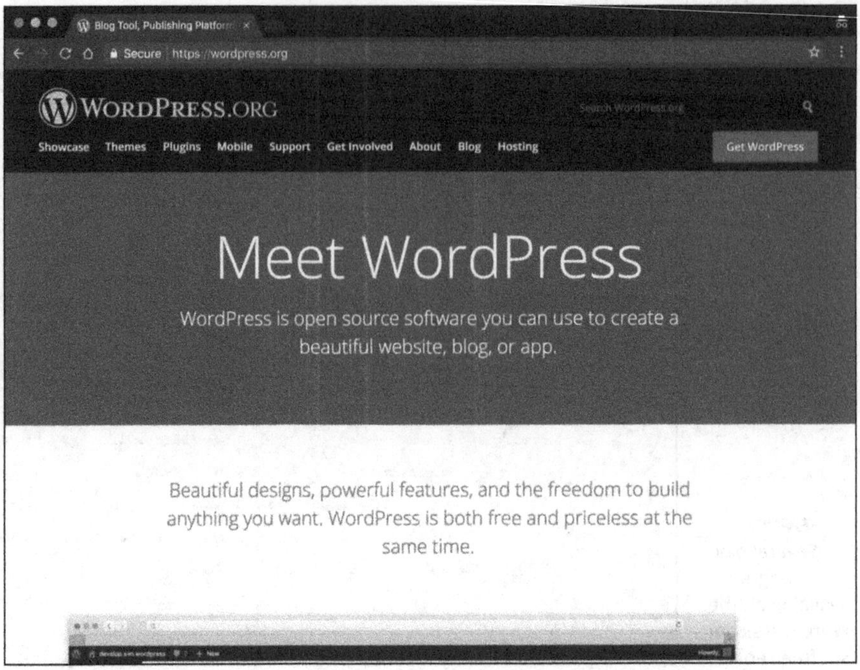

FIGURE 5-3: The WordPress.org website.

The WordPress.org website is an excellent repository of tools and resources for you throughout the lifespan of your WordPress-powered website, so be sure to bookmark it for future reference! Here's a list of helpful things that you can find on the website:

- **Plugins (`https://wordpress.org/plugins`):** The WordPress Plugins page houses a full directory of plugins available for WordPress. You can search for and find the plugins you need for search engine optimization (SEO) enhancement, comment management, and social media integration, among many others.
- **Themes (`https://wordpress.org/themes`):** The Theme Directory page, shown in Figure 5-4, is a repository of WordPress themes that are free for the taking. In this section of the WordPress.org website, you can browse more than 6,000 themes to use on your site to dress up your content.
- **Codex (`https://codex.wordpress.org`):** Almost every piece of software released comes with documentation and user manuals. The Support section of the WordPress.org website contains the WordPress Codex, which tries to help you answer questions about the use of WordPress and its various features and functions.

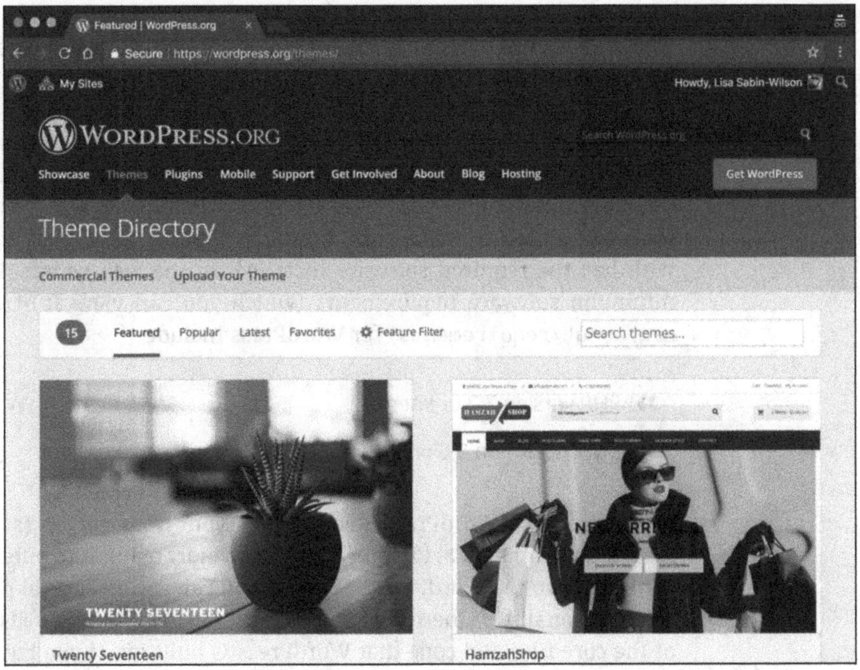

FIGURE 5-4: Theme Directory on WordPress.org.

- **Forums (`https://wordpress.org/support/forums`):** The support forums at WordPress.org involve WordPress users from all over with one goal: finding out how to use WordPress to suit their particular needs. The support forums are very much a community of users (from beginners to experts) helping other users, and you can generally obtain a solution to your WordPress needs here from other users of the software.
- **Roadmap (`https://wordpress.org/about/roadmap`):** This section of the WordPress.org website doesn't contain support information or tools that you can download; it offers an at-a-glance peek at what's new and upcoming for WordPress. The Roadmap page gives you a pretty accurate idea of when WordPress will release the next version of its software; see Book 1, Chapter 3 for information about versions and release cycles.

  Click the version number to visit the WordPress Trac and see what features developers are working on and adding.

TIP

WordPress.org is the self-installed, self-hosted software version of WordPress that you install on a web server you've set up on a domain that you've registered. Unless you own your own web server, you need to lease one. Leasing space on a web server is *web hosting*, and unless you know someone who knows someone, hosting generally isn't free.

That said, web hosting doesn't cost a whole lot, either. You can usually obtain a good, basic web hosting service for anywhere from $10 to $15 per month. (Book 2, Chapters 1 and 2 give you some great information on web hosting accounts and tools.) You need to make sure, however, that any web host you choose to work with has the required software installed on the web server. The recommended minimum software requirements (which you can view at `https://wordpress.org/about/requirements`) for WordPress include

- PHP version 7.2 or later
- MySQL version 5.6 or later *or* MariaDB version 10.0 or later

After you have WordPress installed on your web server (see the installation instructions in Book 2, Chapter 4), you can start using it to publish to your heart's content. With the WordPress software, you can install several plugins that extend the functionality of the software, as I describe in Book 7. You also have full control of the core files and code that WordPress is built on. If you have a knack for PHP and knowledge of MySQL, you can work within the code to make changes that you think would be good for you and your website.

You don't need design or coding ability to make your site look great. Members of the WordPress community have created more than 1,600 WordPress themes (designs), and you can download them free and install them on your WordPress site. (See Book 6, Chapter 2.) Additionally, if you're creatively inclined, like to create designs on your own, and know Cascading Style Sheets (CSS), you have full access to the template system within WordPress and can create your own custom themes. (See Book 6, Chapters 3 through 7.)

Hosting Multiple Sites with One WordPress Installation

The self-hosted WordPress.org software also lets you run an unlimited number of sites on one installation of its software platform, on one domain. When you configure the options within WordPress to enable a multisite interface, you become administrator of a network of sites. All the options remain the same, but with the multisite options configured, you can add more sites and domains, as well as allow registered users of your website to host their own sites within your network. For more information about the Multisite feature in WordPress, see Book 8.

The following types of sites use the Network options within WordPress:

- **Blog networks,** which can have more than 150 blogs. The tech giant Microsoft uses WordPress to power thousands of tech sites at its TechNet portal: `https://blogs.technet.microsoft.com`.
- **Newspapers and magazines,** such as *The New York Times,* and universities, such as Harvard Law School, use WordPress to manage the blog sections of their websites.
- **Niche-specific blog networks,** such as Edublogs.org, use WordPress to manage their full networks of free sites for teachers, educators, lecturers, librarians, and other education professionals.

TIP

Extensive information on running a network of sites by using the Multisite feature in WordPress is available in Book 8. The chapters there take you through everything: setup, maintenance, and the process of running a network of sites with one WordPress installation.

With the Multisite features enabled, users of your network can run their own sites within your installation of WordPress. They also have access to their own Dashboards with the same options and features you read about in Book 3. Heck, it probably would be a great idea to buy a copy of this book for every member of your network so everyone can become familiar with the WordPress Dashboard and features, too. At least have a copy on hand so people can borrow yours!

If you plan to run a few of your own sites with the WordPress Multisite feature, your current hosting situation is probably well suited to this purpose. (See Book 2, Chapter 1 for information on web hosting services.) If you plan to host a large network with hundreds of sites and multiple users, however, you should consider contacting your host and increasing your bandwidth and the disk space limitations on your account.

The best example of a large site network with hundreds of blogs and users (actually, more like millions) is the hosted service at WordPress.com, which I discuss earlier in this chapter. At WordPress.com, people are invited to sign up for an account and start a site by using the Multisite feature within the WordPress platform on the WordPress server. When you enable this feature on your own domain and enable the user registration feature (covered later in this chapter), you invite users to

- Create an account
- Create a site on your WordPress installation (on your domain)
- Create content by publishing posts and pages
- Upload media files, such as photos, audio, and video
- Invite their friends to view their blogs or sign up for their own accounts

WARNING

In addition to the necessary security measures, time, and administrative tasks that go into running a community of sites, you have a few things to worry about. Creating a community increases the resource use, bandwidth, and disk space on your web server. In many cases, if you go over the allotted limits given to you by your web host, you incur great cost. Make sure that you anticipate your bandwidth and disk-space needs before running a large network on your website! (Don't say you weren't warned.)

REMEMBER

Many WordPress network communities start with grand dreams of being large and active. Be realistic about how your community will operate to make the right hosting choice for yourself and your community.

Small Internet communities are handled easily with a shared-server solution; larger, more active communities should consider a dedicated server solution for operation. The difference between the two lies in their names:

- **Shared-server solution:** You have one account on one server that has several other accounts on it. Think of this as apartment living. One building has several apartments under one roof.
- **Dedicated server:** You have one account on one server. The server is dedicated to your account, and your account is dedicated to the server. Think of this as owning a home where you don't share your living space with anyone else.

A dedicated-server solution is a more expensive investment for your community; a shared-server solution is more economical. Base your decision on how big and how active you estimate that your community will be. You can move from a shared-server solution to a dedicated-server solution if your community becomes larger than you expect, but starting with the right solution for your community from day one is best. For more information on hosting WordPress, see Book 2, Chapter 1.

Discovering WordPress VIP Services

The company behind the Automattic WordPress.com service is owned and operated by the WordPress cofounder, Matt Mullenweg. Although Automattic doesn't own the WordPress.org software, Automattic is a driving force behind all things WordPress.

REMEMBER

As an open-source platform, WordPress.org is owned by the community and hundreds of developers that contribute to the core code.

Have a look at the Automattic website at `https://automattic.com` (shown in Figure 5-5). The folks behind WordPress own and operate several properties and services that can extend the features of your WordPress site, including

- **WordPress.com (**`https://wordpress.com`**):** A hosted WordPress blogging service, discussed previously in this chapter.
- **Jetpack (**`https://jetpack.com`**):** A suite of plugins that can be installed on a WordPress.org self-hosted site.
- **VaultPress (**`https://vaultpress.com`**):** Premium backup and restoration service for your blog.
- **Akismet (**`https://akismet.com`**):** Spam protection for your blog. This service comes with every WordPress.org installation, but there are different levels of service, as discussed in Book 3, Chapter 4.
- **Polldaddy (**`https://polldaddy.com`**):** A polling and survey software that easily plugs into the WordPress platform.
- **VideoPress (**`https://videopress.com`**):** Video hosting and sharing application for WordPress.
- **Gravatar (**`https://gravatar.com`**):** Photos or graphical icons for comment authors (discussed in Book 3, Chapter 2).
- **Longreads (**`https://longreads.com`**):** Great examples of storytelling on the Internet.
- **Simplenote (**`https://simplenote.com`**):** An easy way to keep notes across various iOS, Android, Mac, and Windows devices.
- **WordPress.com VIP (**`https://vip.wordpress.com`**):** Enterprise-level web hosting and WordPress support starting at $15,000 per year (usually reserved for heavy hitters such as CNN, BBC, and *Time* magazine, for example).
- **Cloudup (**`https://cloudup.com`**):** Easy sharing of media including videos, music, photos, and documents.

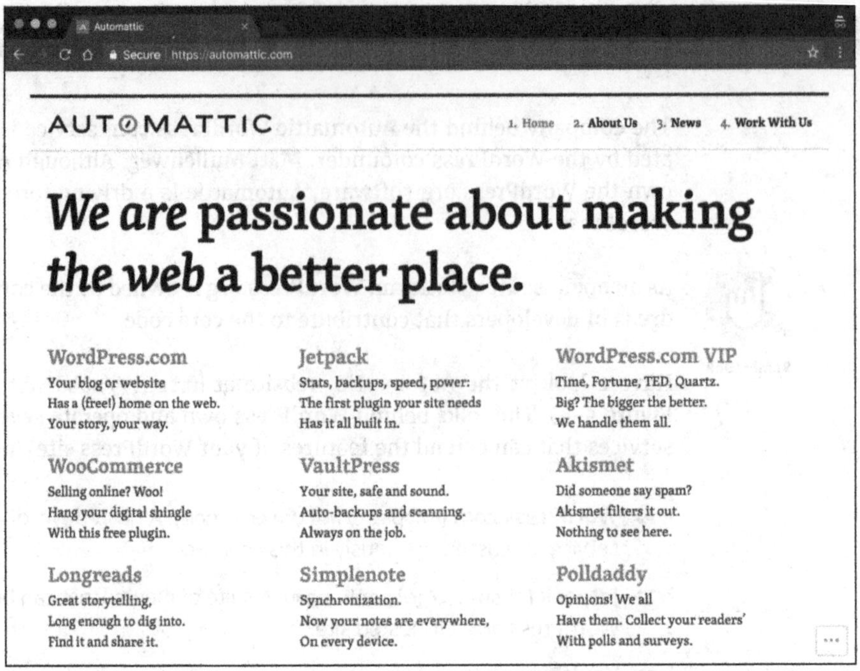

FIGURE 5-5: The Automattic website.

2 Setting Up the WordPress Software

Contents at a Glance

IN THIS CHAPTER

» Registering a domain name

» Exploring web hosting environments

» Knowing the basic requirements for PHP and MySQL

» Getting web hosting recommendations for WordPress

» Understanding bandwidth and disk space needs

Chapter 1
Understanding the System Requirements

Before you can start creating content with WordPress, you have to set up your foundation. Doing so involves more than simply downloading and installing the WordPress software. You also need to establish your *domain* (your website address) and your *web hosting service* (the place that houses your website). Although you initially download your WordPress software onto your hard drive, you install it on a web hosting server.

Obtaining a web server and installing software on it are things you may already have done on your site, in which case you can move on to the next chapter. If you haven't installed WordPress, you must first consider many factors, as well as cope with a learning curve, because setting up your website through a hosting service involves using some technologies that you may not feel comfortable with. This chapter takes you through the basics of those technologies, and by the last page of this chapter, you'll have WordPress successfully installed on a web server with your own domain name.

Establishing Your Domain

You've read all the hype. You've heard all the rumors. You've seen the flashy websites powered by WordPress. But where do you start?

The first steps in installing and setting up a WordPress site are making a decision about a domain name and then purchasing the registration of that name through a domain registrar. A *domain name* is the *unique* web address that you type in a web browser's address bar to visit a website. Some examples of domain names are `WordPress.org` and `Google.com`.

REMEMBER

I emphasize *unique* because no two domain names can be the same. If someone else has registered the domain name you want, you can't have it. With that in mind, it sometimes takes a bit of time to find a domain that isn't already in use.

Understanding domain name extensions

When registering a domain name, be aware of the *extension* that you want. The `.com`, `.net`, `.org`, `.info`, or `.biz` extension that you see tagged onto the end of any domain name is the *top-level domain extension.* When you register your domain name, you're asked to choose the extension you want for your domain (as long as it's available, that is).

A word to the wise here: Just because you registered your domain as a `.com` doesn't mean that someone else doesn't, or can't, own the very same domain name with a `.net`. Therefore, if you register `MyDogHasFleas.com`, and the site becomes hugely popular among readers with dogs that have fleas, someone else can come along, register `MyDogHasFleas.net`, and run a similar site to yours in the hope of riding the coattails of your website's popularity and readership.

DOMAIN NAMES: DO YOU OWN OR RENT?

When you "buy" a domain name, you don't really own it. Rather, you're purchasing the right to use that domain name for the time specified in your order. You can register a domain name for one year or up to ten years. Be aware, however, that if you don't renew the domain name when your registration period ends, you lose it — and most often, you lose it right away to someone who preys on abandoned or expired domain names. Some people keep a close watch on expiring domain names, and as soon as the buying window opens, they snap the names up and start using them for their own websites, in the hope of taking full advantage of the popularity that the previous owners worked so hard to attain for those domains.

If you want to avert this problem, you can register your domain name with all available extensions. My business website, for example, has the domain name webdevstudios.com, but we also own webdvstudios.net just in case someone else out there has the same combination of names.

Considering the cost of a domain name

Registering a domain costs you anywhere from $5 to $300 per year or more, depending on what service you use for a registrar and what options (such as storage space, bandwidth, privacy options, search engine submission services, and so on) you apply to your domain name during the registration process.

REMEMBER

When you pay the domain registration fee today, you need to pay another registration fee when the renewal date comes up again in a year, or two, or five — however many years you chose to register your domain name for. (See the nearby "Domain names: Do you own or rent?" sidebar.) Most registrars give you the option of signing up for a service called Auto Renew to automatically renew your domain name and bill the charges to the credit card you set up on that account. The registrar sends you a reminder a few months in advance, telling you that it's time to renew. If you don't have Auto Renew set up, you need to log in to your registrar account before it expires and manually renew your domain name.

TIP

When choosing a domain name for your website, you may find that the domain name you want isn't available. You know if it's available when you search for it at the domain registrar's website (listed in the next section). Have some backup domain names prepared just in case the one you want isn't available. If your chosen domain name is cutepuppies.com, but it's not available, you could have some variations of the domain ready to use, such as cute-puppies.com (notice the dash), mycutepuppies.com, or reallycutepuppies.com.

Registering your domain name

Domain registrars are certified and approved by the Internet Corporation for Assigned Names and Numbers (ICANN). Although hundreds of domain registrars exist, the ones in the following list are popular because of their longevity in the industry, competitive pricing, and variety of services they offer in addition to domain name registration (such as web hosting and website traffic builders):

- **GoDaddy:** https://www.godaddy.com
- **Register.com:** https://www.register.com
- **Network Solutions:** https://www.networksolutions.com
- **NamesDirect:** http://namesdirect.com

No matter where you choose to register your domain name, here are the steps you can take to accomplish this task:

1. **Decide on a domain name.**

   A little planning and forethought are necessary here. Many people think of a domain name as a *brand* — a way of identifying their websites or blogs. Think of potential names for your site and then proceed with your plan.

2. **Verify the domain name's availability.**

   In your web browser, enter the URL of the domain registrar of your choice. Look for the section on the registrar's website that lets you enter the domain name (typically, a short text field) to see whether it's available. If the domain name isn't available as a `.com`, try `.net` or `.info`.

3. **Purchase the domain name.**

   Follow the domain registrar's steps to purchase the name, using your credit card. After you complete the checkout process, you receive an email confirming your purchase, so be sure to use a valid email address during the registration process.

The next step is obtaining a hosting account, which the next section covers.

REMEMBER

Some of the domain registrars have hosting services that you can sign up for, but you don't have to use those services. Often, you can find hosting services for a lower cost than most domain registrars offer. It just takes a little research.

Finding a Home for Your Site

After you register your domain, you need to find a place for it to live: a web host. Web hosting is the second piece of the puzzle that you need to complete before you begin working with WordPress.org.

A *web host* is a business, group, or person that provides web server space and bandwidth for file transfer to website owners who don't have it. Usually, web hosting services charge a monthly or an annual fee — unless you're fortunate enough to know someone who's willing to give you server space and bandwidth free. The cost varies from host to host, but you can usually obtain quality web hosting services for $10 to $50 per month to start.

REMEMBER

When discussing web hosting considerations, it's important to understand where your hosting account ends and WordPress begins. Support for the WordPress software may or may not be included in your hosting package.

Some web hosts consider WordPress to be a *third-party application*. This means that the host typically won't provide technical support on the use of WordPress (or any other software application) because software support generally isn't included in your hosting package. The web host supports your hosting account but typically doesn't support the software you choose to install.

On the other hand, if your web host supports the software on your account, it comes at a cost: You have to pay for that extra support. To find whether your chosen host supports WordPress, ask first. If your host doesn't offer software support, you can still find WordPress support in the support forums at `https://wordpress.org/support/forums`, as shown in Figure 1-1.

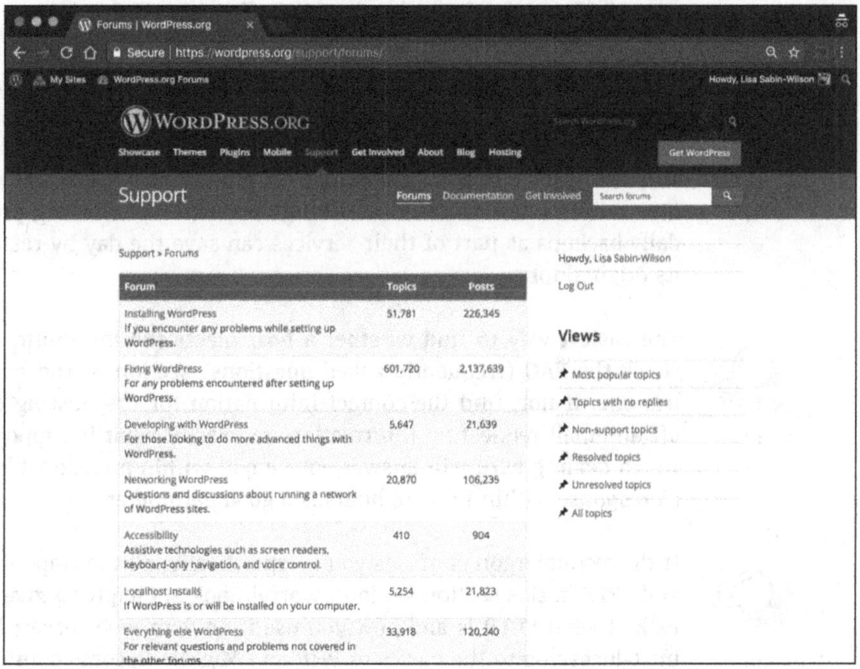

FIGURE 1-1: The WordPress support forums.

TIP

Several web hosting providers also have WordPress-related services available for additional fees. These services can include technical support, plugin installation and configuration, and theme design.

Generally, hosting services provide (at least) these services with your account:

- Hard drive space
- Bandwidth (transfer)
- Domain email with web mail access

- Secure File Transfer Protocol (SFTP) access
- Comprehensive website statistics
- MySQL database(s)
- PHP

Because you intend to run WordPress on your web server, you need to look for a host that provides the *minimum* requirements needed to run the software on your hosting account which are

- PHP version 7.2 (or later)
- MySQL version 5.6 (or later) *or* MariaDB version 10.0 (or later)

TIP

You can view the requirements for WordPress at `https://wordpress.org/about/requirements`.

You also want a host that provides daily backups of your site so that your content won't be lost in case something happens. Web hosting providers that offer daily backups as part of their services can save the day by restoring your site to its original form.

TIP

The easiest way to find whether a host meets the minimum requirement is to check the FAQ (frequently asked questions) section of the host's website, if it has one. If not, find the contact information for the hosting company and fire off an email requesting information on exactly what it supports. Any web host worth dealing with will answer your email within a reasonable amount of time. (A response within 12 to 24 hours is a good barometer.)

TIP

If the technojargon confuses you — specifically, all that talk about PHP, MySQL, and SFTP in this section — don't worry! Book 2, Chapter 2 gives you an in-depth look at what SFTP is and how you use it on your web server; Book 2, Chapter 3 introduces you to the basics of PHP and MySQL. Become comfortable with these topics, because they're important when using WordPress.

Getting help with hosting WordPress

The popularity of WordPress has given birth to web services — including designers, consultants, and (yes) web hosts — that specialize in using WordPress.

Many web hosts offer a full array of WordPress features, such as an automatic WordPress installation included with your account, a library of WordPress themes, and a staff of support technicians who are very experienced in using WordPress.

Here are some of those providers:

- **Pagely:** `https://pagely.com`
- **WP Engine:** `https://wpengine.com` (shown in Figure 1-2)
- **Pantheon:** `https://pantheon.io`

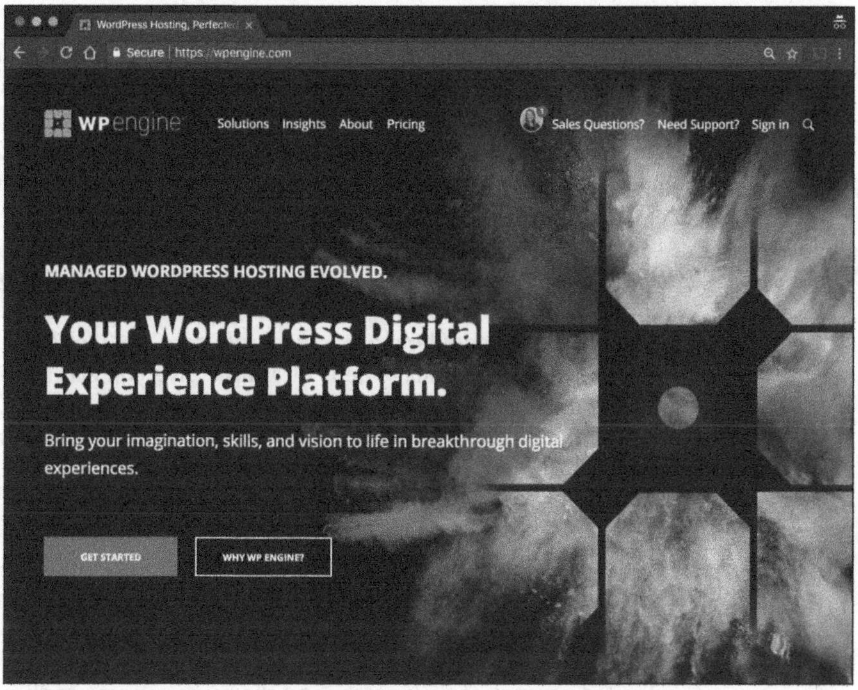

FIGURE 1-2: The WP Engine WordPress hosting provider.

WARNING

A few web hosting providers offer free domain name registration when you sign up for hosting services. Research this topic and read the terms of service, because that free domain name may come with conditions. Many clients have gone this route only to find out a few months later that the web hosting provider has full control of the domain name and the client can't move that domain off the host's servers, either for a set period (usually, a year or two) or for infinity. You need control in *your* hands, not someone else's, so stick with an independent domain registrar, such as Network Solutions.

Dealing with disk space and bandwidth

Web hosting services provide two very important things with your account:

- **Disk space:** The amount of space you can access on the web servers' hard drive, generally measured in megabytes (MB) or gigabytes (GB).
- **Bandwidth transfer:** The amount of transfer your site can do per month. Typically, traffic is measured in gigabytes.

Think of your web host as a garage that you rent to park your car in. The garage gives you the place to store your car (disk space). It even gives you the driveway so that you, and others, can get to and from your car (bandwidth). It won't, however, fix the rockin' stereo system (WordPress or any other third-party software application) that you've installed — unless you're willing to pay a few extra bucks for that service.

TIP

Most web hosting providers give you access to a hosting account manager that allows you to log in to your web hosting account to manage services. cPanel is perhaps the most popular management interface, but Plesk and NetAdmin are still widely used. These management interfaces give you access to your server logs, where you can view such things as bandwidth and hard disk use. Get into the habit of checking those things occasionally to make sure that you stay informed about how much storage and bandwidth your site is using. Typically, I check monthly.

Managing disk space

Disk space is nothing more complicated than the hard drive on your own computer. Each hard drive has capacity, or space, for a certain amount of files. An 80GB hard drive can hold 80GB of data — no more. Your hosting account provides you a limited amount of disk space, and the same concept applies. If your web host provides you 10GB of disk space, that's the absolute limit you have. If you want more disk space, you need to upgrade your space limitations. Most web hosts have a mechanism in place for you to upgrade your allotment.

Starting with a self-hosted WordPress website doesn't take much disk space at all. A good starting point for disk space is 20GB to 50GB. If you find that you need additional space, contact your hosting provider for an upgrade.

Choosing the size of your bandwidth pipe

Bandwidth refers to the amount of data that's carried from point A to point B within a specific period (usually, only a second or two). I live out in the country — pretty much in the middle of nowhere. The water that comes to my house is provided by a private well that lies buried in the backyard somewhere. Between my house and the well are pipes that bring the water to my house. The pipes provide a free flow of water to our home so that everyone else can enjoy long, hot showers while I labor over dishes and laundry, all at the same time. Lucky me!

The very same concept applies to the bandwidth available with your hosting account. Every web hosting provider offers a variety of bandwidth limits on the accounts it offers. When I want to view your website in my browser window, the bandwidth is essentially the pipe that lets your data flow from your "well" to my computer. The bandwidth limit is similar to the pipe connected to my well: It can hold only a certain amount of water before it reaches maximum capacity and won't bring the water from the well any longer. Your bandwidth pipe size is determined by how much bandwidth your web host allows for your account. The larger the number, the bigger the pipe. A 50MB bandwidth limit makes for a smaller pipe than a 100MB limit, for example.

Web hosts are pretty generous with the amount of bandwidth they provide in their packages. Like disk space, bandwidth is measured in gigabytes. Bandwidth provision of 50GB to 100GB is generally a respectable amount to run a website and/or a blog.

WARNING

I've found that if your website exceeds its allowed bandwidth, the web host won't turn off your website or limit traffic. The host will continue to allow inbound web traffic to your site but will bill you at the end of month for any bandwidth overages. Those charges can get pretty expensive, so if you find that your website is consistently exceeding the bandwidth amount every month, contact your web host to learn whether you can get an upgrade to allow for increased bandwidth.

REMEMBER

Websites that run large files — such as video, audio, or photo files — generally benefit from higher disk space compared with sites that don't involve large files. Keep this point in mind when you're signing up for your hosting account. Planning will save you a few headaches down the road.

Be wary of hosting providers that offer things like unlimited bandwidth, domains, and disk space. Those offers are great selling points, but what the providers don't tell you outright (you may have to look into the fine print of the agreement) is that although they may not put those kinds of limits on you, they will limit your site's CPU usage.

CPU (which stands for *central processing unit*) is the part of a computer (or web server, in this case) that handles all the data processing requests sent to your web servers whenever anyone visits your site. Although you may have unlimited bandwidth to handle a large amount of traffic, if a high spike in traffic increases your site's CPU use, your host will throttle your site because it limits the CPU use.

What do I mean by *throttle?* I mean that the host shuts down your site — turns it off. The shutdown isn't permanent, though; it lasts maybe a few minutes to an hour. The host does this to kill any connections to your web server that are causing the spike in CPU use. Your host eventually turns your site back on — but the inconvenience happens regularly with many clients across various hosting environments.

TIP

When looking into different web hosting providers, ask about their policies on CPU use and what they do to manage a spike in processing. It's better to know about it up front than to find out about it after your site's been throttled.

IN THIS CHAPTER

» Discovering SFTP

» Understanding secure file transfer

» Exploring easy-to-use SFTP clients

» Making sense of SFTP terminology

» Editing files by using SFTP

» Changing file permissions

Chapter 2 Using Secure File Transfer Protocol

Throughout this entire book, you run into the term *SFTP*. SFTP (Secure File Transfer Protocol) is a network protocol used to copy files from one host to another over the Internet. With SFTP, you can perform various tasks, including uploading and downloading WordPress files, editing files, and changing permissions on files.

Read this chapter to familiarize yourself with SFTP; understand what it is and how to use it; and discover some free, easy-to-use SFTP clients and programs that make your life as a WordPress website owner much easier. If you run across sections in this book that ask you to perform certain tasks by using SFTP, you can refer to this chapter to refresh your memory on how to do it, if needed.

Understanding SFTP Concepts

This section introduces you to the basic elements of SFTP, which is a method of transferring files in a secure environment. SFTP provides an additional layer of security beyond what you get with regular FTP, as it uses SSH (Secure Shell) and encrypts sensitive information, data, and passwords. Encrypting the data ensures that anyone monitoring the network can't read the data freely — and, therefore, can't obtain information that should be secured, such as passwords and usernames.

TIP

I highly recommend using SFTP instead of FTP because SFTP provides a secure connection to your web host. If your web hosting provider doesn't provide SFTP connections for you, strongly consider switching to a hosting provider that does. Almost all hosting providers these days provide SFTP as the standard protocol for transferring files.

The capability to use SFTP with your hosting account is a given for almost every web host on the market today. SFTP offers two ways of moving files from one place to another:

- **Uploading:** Transferring files from your local computer to your web server
- **Downloading:** Transferring files from your web server to your local computer

You can do several other things with SFTP, including the following, which I discuss later in this chapter:

- **View files.** After you log in via SFTP, you can see all the files that are located on your web server.
- **View date modified.** You can see the date when a file was last modified, which can be helpful when trying to troubleshoot problems.
- **View file size.** You can see the size of each file on your web server, which is helpful if you need to manage the disk space on your account.
- **Edit files.** Almost all SFTP clients allow you to open and edit files through the client interface, which is a convenient way to get the job done.
- **Change permissions.** You can control what type of read/write/execute permissions the files on your web server have. This feature is commonly referred to as CHMOD, which is the command that you use to change the permissions.

SFTP is a convenient utility that gives you access to the files located on your web server, which makes managing your WordPress website a bit easier.

Setting Up SFTP on Your Hosting Account

Many web hosts today offer SFTP as part of their hosting packages, so confirm that your hosting provider makes SFTP available to you for your account. In Book 2, Chapter 1, I mention the hosting account management interface called cPanel. cPanel is by far the most popular hosting account management software used by hosts on the web, eclipsing other popular tools such as Plesk and NetAdmin. It's cPanel, or your hosting account management interface, that allows you to set up an SFTP account for your website.

TIP

In this chapter, I use cPanel as the example. If your hosting provider gives you a different interface to work with, the concepts are still the same, but you need to refer to your hosting provider for the specifics to adapt these directions to your specific environment.

Mostly, the SFTP for your hosting account is set up automatically. Figure 2-1 shows) the User Manager page in cPanel, where you set up user accounts for SFTP access.

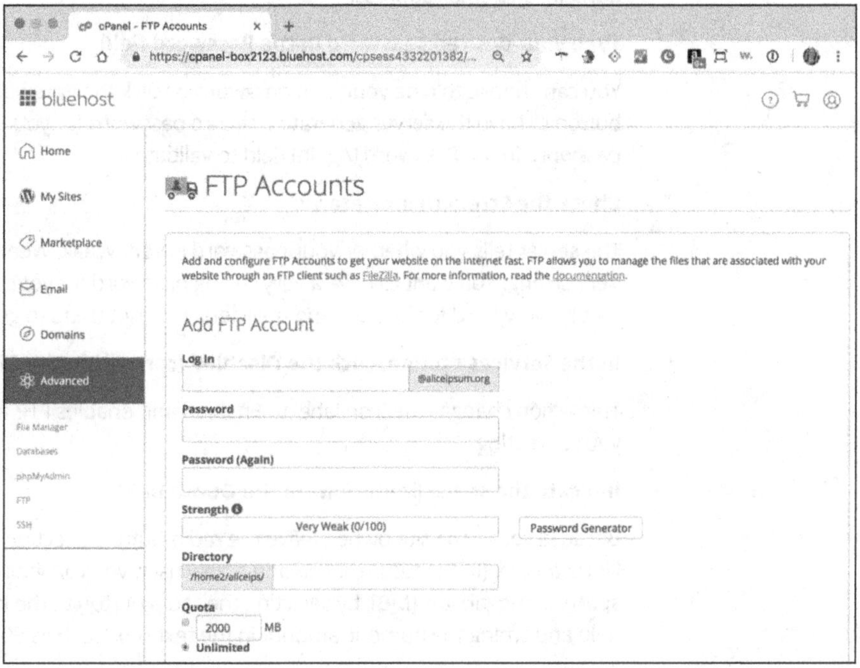

FIGURE 2-1: The User Manager page within cPanel.

Follow these steps to get to this page and set up your SFTP account:

1. **Log in to the cPanel for your hosting account.**

   Typically, you browse to `http://yourdomain.com/cpanel` to bring up the login screen for your cPanel. Enter your specific hosting account username and password in the login fields, and click OK.

2. **Browse to the User Manager page.**

   Click the Add User button in your cPanel to open the User Manager page (refer to Figure 2-1).

3. **View the existing SFTP account.**

   If your hosting provider automatically sets you up with an SFTP account, you see it listed on the User Manager page. Ninety-nine percent of the time, the default SFTP account uses the same username and password combination as your hosting account or the login information you used to log in to your cPanel in step 1.

If the SFTP Accounts page doesn't display a default SFTP user in the User Manager page, you can create one easily in the Add SFTP Account section:

1. **Fill in the provided fields.**

   The fields of the User Manager page ask for your name, desired username, domain, and email address.

2. **Type your desired password in the Password field.**

   You can choose to type your own password or click the Password Generator button to have the server generate a secure password for you. Retype the password in the Password (Again) field to validate it.

3. **Check the Strength indicator.**

   The server tells you whether your password is Very Weak, Weak, Good, Strong, or Very Strong. You want to have a very strong password for your SFTP account so that it's very hard for hackers and malicious Internet users to guess and crack.

4. **In the Services section, click the Disabled icon within the FTP section.**

   This action changes the icon label to Enabled and enables FTP for the user you're creating.

5. **Indicate the space limitations in the Quota field.**

   Because you're the site owner, leave the radio-button selection set to Unrestricted. (In the future, if you add a new user, you can limit the amount of space, in megabytes [MB], by selecting the radio button to the left of the text field and typing the numeric amount in the text box, such as 50MB.)

6. **(Optional) Type the directory access for this user.**

   Leaving this field blank gives this new user access to the root level of your hosting account — which, as the site owner, you want, so leave this field blank. In the future, if you set up accounts for other users, you can lock down their access to your hosting directory by indicating which directory the user has access to.

7. **Click the Create button.**

   You see a new screen with a message that the account was created successfully. Additionally, you see the settings for this new user account; copy and paste them into a blank text editor window (such as Notepad for PC or TextEdit for Mac users). The settings for the user account are the details you need to connect to your web server via SFTP.

8. **Save the following settings.**

   Username, Password, and SFTP Server are specific to your domain and the information you entered in the preceding steps.

   - Username: *username@yourdomain.com*
   - Password: *yourpassword*
   - Host name: *yourdomain.com*
   - SFTP Server Port: 22
   - Quota: Unlimited MB

TIP

Ninety-nine point nine percent of the time, the SFTP Server Port will be 22. Be sure to double-check your SFTP settings to make sure that this is the case, because some hosting providers have different port numbers for SFTP.

REMEMBER

At any time, you can revisit the User Accounts page to delete the user accounts you've created, change the quota, change the password, and find the connection details specific to that account.

Finding and Using Free and Easy SFTP Programs

SFTP programs are referred to as SFTP *clients* or SFTP *client software*. Whatever you decide to call it, an SFTP client is software that you use to connect to your web server to view, open, edit, and transfer files to and from your web server.

Using SFTP to transfer files requires an SFTP client. Many SFTP clients are available for download. Here are some good (and free) ones:

- **SmartFTP (PC):** `https://www.smartftp.com/download`
- **FileZilla (PC or Mac):** `https://sourceforge.net/projects/filezilla`
- **Transmit (Mac):** `https://panic.com/transmit`
- **WinSCP (PC):** `https://winscp.net`

In Book 2, Chapter 1, you discover how to obtain a hosting account, and in the previous section of this chapter, you discover how to create an SFTP account on your web server. By following the steps in the previous section, you also have the SFTP username, password, server, and port information you need to connect your SFTP client to your web server so you can begin transferring files. In the next section, you discover how to connect to your web hosting account via SFTP.

Connecting to the web server via SFTP

For the purposes of this chapter, I use the FileZilla SFTP client (`https://sourceforge.net/projects/filezilla`) because it's easy to use and the cost is free ninety-nine (open-source geek speak for free!).

Figure 2-2 shows a FileZilla client that's not connected to a server. By default, the left side of the window displays a directory of files and folders on the local computer.

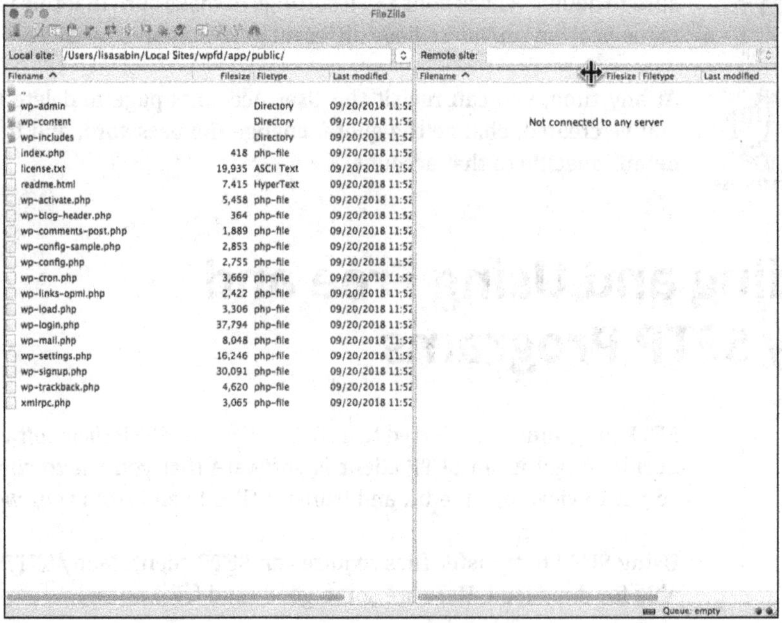

FIGURE 2-2: Mozilla FileZilla SFTP client software.

The right side of the window displays content when the FileZilla client is connected to a web server; specifically, it shows directories of the web server's folders and files.

REMEMBER

If you use different SFTP client software from FileZilla, the steps and look of the software will differ. You need to adapt your steps and practice for the specific SFTP client software you're using.

Connecting to a web server is an easy process. The SFTP settings you saved from step 8 in "Setting Up SFTP on Your Hosting Account" section in this chapter are also the same settings you see in your cPanel User Manager page if your SFTP was set up automatically for you.

- Username: *username@yourdomain.com*
- Password: *yourpassword*
- Server: *yourdomain.com*
- SFTP Server Port: 22
- Quota: Unlimited MB

This process is where you need that information. To connect to your web server via the FileZilla SFTP client, follow these few steps:

1. **Open the SFTP client software on your local computer.**

   Locate the program on your computer and click (or double-click) the program icon to launch the program.

2. **Choose File ➪ Site Manager to open the Site Manager utility.**

   Site Manager appears, as shown in Figure 2-3.

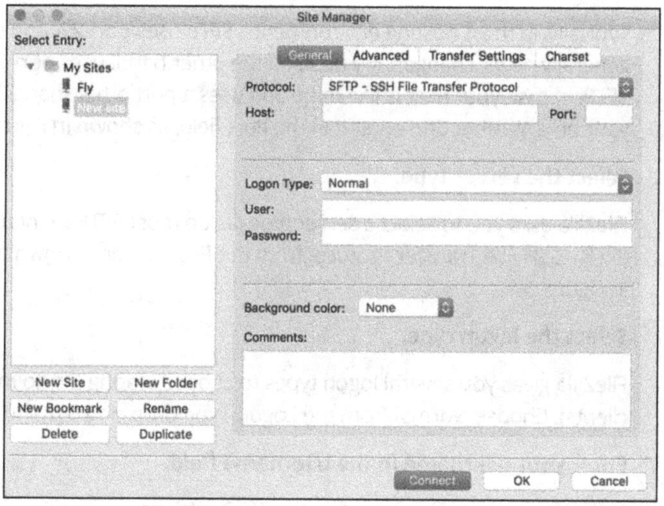

FIGURE 2-3: The Site Manager utility in the FileZilla SFTP client software.

3. **Click the New Site button.**

4. **Type a name for your site that helps you identify the site.**

   This site name can be anything you want it to be because it isn't part of the connection data you add in the next steps. (In Figure 2-4, you see Fly — which is the name I chose to name the site.)

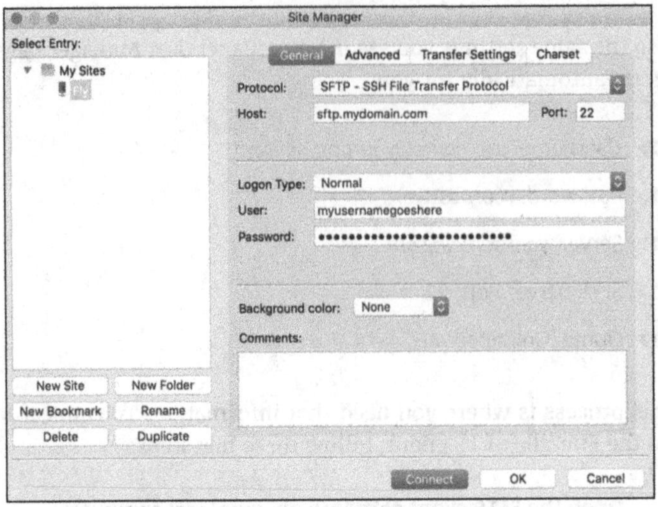

FIGURE 2-4: FileZilla Site Manager utility with SFTP account information filled in.

5. **Enter the SFTP server in the Host field.**

   Host is the same as the SFTP server information provided to you when you set up the SFTP account on your web server. In the example, the SFTP server is `sftp.mydomain.com`, so that's entered in the Host field, as shown in Figure 2-4.

6. **Enter the SFTP port in the Port field.**

   Typically, in most hosting environments, SFTP uses port 22, and this setting generally never changes. My host, on the other hand, uses port 2222 for SFTP. In case your host is like mine and uses a port other than 22, double-check your port number and enter it in the Port field, as shown in Figure 2-4.

7. **Select the server type.**

   FileZilla asks you to select a server type (as do most SFTP clients). Choose SFTP – SSH File Transfer Protocol from the Protocol drop-down menu, as shown in Figure 2-4.

8. **Select the logon type.**

   FileZilla gives you several logon types to choose among (as do most SFTP clients). Choose Normal from the Logon Type drop-down menu.

9. **Enter your username in the Username field.**

   This username is given to you in the SFTP settings.

10. **Type your password in the Password field.**

    This password is given to you in the SFTP settings.

11. **Click the Connect button.**

This step connects your computer to your web server. The directory of folders and files from your local computer displays on the left side of the FileZilla SFTP client window, and the directory of folders and files on your web server displays on the right side, as shown in Figure 2-5.

Now you can take advantage of all the tools and features SFTP has to offer you!

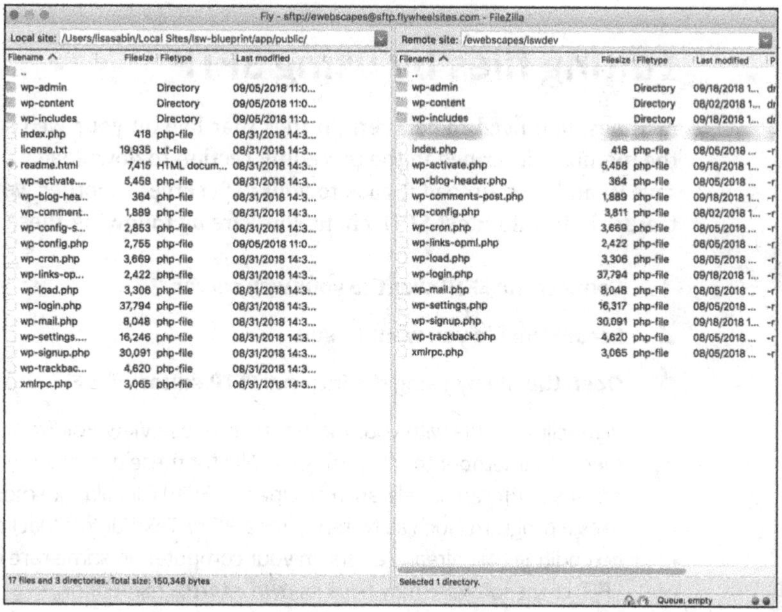

FIGURE 2-5: FileZilla displays local files on the left and server files on the right.

Transferring files from point A to point B

Now that your local computer is connected to your web server, transferring files between the two couldn't be easier. Within the SFTP client software, you can browse the directories and folders on your local computer on the left side and browse the directories and folders on your web server on the right side.

SFTP clients make it easy to transfer files from your computer to your hosting account by using a drag-and-drop method. Two methods of transferring files are

» **Uploading:** Generally, transferring files from your local computer to your web server. To upload a file from your computer to your web server, click the file you want to transfer from your local computer and then drag and drop it on the right side (the web-server side).

» **Downloading:** Transferring files from your web server to your local computer. To download a file from your web server to your local computer, click the file you want to transfer from your web server and drag and drop it on the left side (the local-computer side).

TIP

Downloading files from your web server is a very efficient, easy, and smart way of backing up files to your local computer. It's always a good idea to keep your files safe — especially things like theme files and plugins, which Books 6 and 7 cover.

Editing files by using SFTP

At times, you need to edit certain files that live on your web server. You can use the methods described in the preceding section to download a file, open it, edit it, save it, and then upload it back to your web server. Another way is to use the edit feature built into most SFTP client software by following these steps:

1. **Connect the SFTP client to your web server.**
2. **Locate the file you want to edit.**
3. **Open the file by using the internal SFTP editor.**

   Right-click the file with your mouse, and choose View/Edit from the shortcut menu. (Remember that I'm using FileZilla for these examples; your SFTP client may use different labels, such as Open or Edit.) FileZilla, like most SFTP clients, uses a program (such as Notepad for a PC or TextEdit for Mac) designated for text editing that already exists on your computer. In some rare cases, your SFTP client software may have its own internal text editor.
4. **Edit the file to your liking.**
5. **Save the changes you made.**

   Click the Save icon or choose File⇨Save.
6. **Upload the file to your web server.**

   After you save the file, FileZilla alerts you that the file has changed and asks whether you want to upload the file to the server. Click the Yes button. The newly edited file replaces the old one.

That's all there is to it. Use the SFTP edit feature to edit, save, and upload files as you need to.

WARNING

When you edit files by using the SFTP edit feature, you're editing files in a "live" environment, meaning that when you save the changes and upload the file, the changes take effect immediately and affect your live website. For this reason, I strongly recommend downloading a copy of the original file to your local computer before making changes. That way, if you happen to make a typo in the saved file and your website goes haywire, you have a copy of the original to upload to restore the file to its original state.

TECHNICAL STUFF

Programmers and developers are people who generally are more technologically advanced than your average user. These folks typically don't use SFTP for editing or transferring files. Instead, they use a version-control system called Git. Git manages the files on your web server through a versioning system that has a complex set of deployment rules for transferring updated files to and from your server. Most beginners don't use such a system for this purpose, but Git *is* a system that beginners can use. If you're interested in using Git, you can find a good resource to start with at SitePoint (`https://www.sitepoint.com/git-for-beginners`).

Changing file permissions

Every file and folder on your web server has a set of assigned attributions, called *permissions,* that tells the web server three things about the folder or file. On a very simplistic level, these permissions include

- **Read:** This setting determines whether the file/folder is readable by the web server.
- **Write:** This setting determines whether the file/folder is writable by the web server.
- **Execute:** This setting determines whether the file/folder is executable by the web server.

Each set of permissions has a numeric code assigned to it, identifying what type of permissions are assigned to that file or folder. There are a lot of permissions available, so here are the most common ones that you run into when running a WordPress website:

- **644:** Files with permissions set to 644 are readable by everyone and writable only by the file/folder owner.
- **755:** Files with permissions set to 755 are readable and executable by everyone, but they're writable only by the file/folder owner.
- **777:** Files with permissions set to 777 are readable, writable, and executable by everyone. For security reasons, you shouldn't use this set of permissions on your web server unless absolutely necessary.

Typically, folders and files within your web server are assigned permissions of 644 or 755. Usually, you see PHP files — files that end with the `.php` extension — with permissions set to 644 if the web server is configured to use PHP Safe Mode.

TIP

This section gives you a very basic look at file permissions because usually, you won't need to mess with file permissions on your web server. In case you do need to dig further, you can find a great reference on file permissions from Elated.com at `https://www.elated.com/articles/understanding-permissions`.

You may find yourself in a situation in which you're asked to edit and change the permissions on a particular file on your web server. With WordPress sites, this situation usually happens when you're dealing with plugins or theme files that require files or folders to be writable by the web server. This practice is referred to as *CHMOD* (an acronym for Change Mode). When someone says, "You need to CHMOD that file to 755," you'll know what that person is talking about.

Here are some easy steps for using your SFTP program to CHMOD a file or edit its permissions on your web server:

1. **Connect the SFTP client to your web server.**
2. **Locate the file you want to CHMOD.**
3. **Open the file attributes for the file.**

   Right-click the file on your web server, and choose File Permissions from the shortcut menu. (Your SFTP client, if not FileZilla, may use different terminology.)

   The Change File Attributes window appears, as shown in Figure 2-6.
4. **Type the correct file permissions number in the Numeric Value field.**

   This number is assigned to the permissions you want to give the file. Most often, the plugin or theme developer tells you which permissions number to assign to the file or folder — typically, 644 or 755. (The permissions in Figure 2-6 are assigned the value 644.)
5. **Click OK to save the file.**

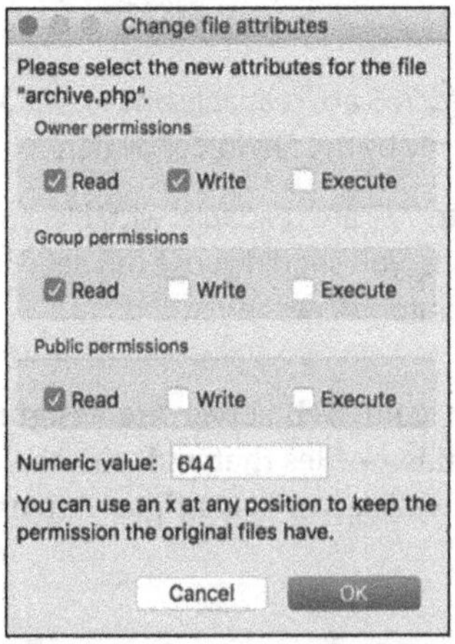

FIGURE 2-6: The Change File Attributes window in FileZilla.

IN THIS CHAPTER

» Working with PHP and MySQL

» Creating a page with PHP

» Managing a database with MySQL

Chapter 3

Getting to Know PHP and MySQL

In Book 6, you dig into the code necessary to create functions and features on your website. Many, if not all, of these functions and features use Hypertext Preprocessor (PHP) tags. When combined with the WordPress code, these tags make things happen (such as displaying post content, categories, archives, links, and more) on your website.

One of the reasons WordPress is the most popular content management system (CMS) is that you don't need to know PHP code to use it. That's to say, you can use WordPress easily without ever looking at any of the code or template files contained within it. If, however, you want to tweak the settings of your WordPress theme (flip to Book 6) or the code of a particular plugin (see Book 7), you need to understand the basics of how PHP works. But don't worry; you don't need to be a PHP programmer.

This chapter introduces you to the basics of PHP and MySQL, which is the database system that stores your WordPress data. After you read this chapter, you'll understand how PHP and MySQL work together with the WordPress platform to serve up your website in visitors' browsers.

REMEMBER

This book doesn't turn you into a PHP programmer or MySQL database administrator, but it gives you a glimpse of how PHP and MySQL work together to help WordPress build your website. If you're interested in finding out how to program PHP or become a MySQL database administrator, check out *PHP, MySQL & JavaScript All-in-One For Dummies*, Richard Blum (John Wiley & Sons, Inc.).

Understanding How PHP and MySQL Work Together

WordPress uses a PHP/MySQL platform, which provides everything you need to create your own website and publish your own content dynamically without knowing how to program those pages. In short, all your content is stored in a MySQL database in your hosting account.

TECHNICAL STUFF

PHP is a server-side scripting language for creating dynamic web pages. When a visitor opens a page built in PHP, the server processes the PHP commands and then sends the results to the visitor's browser. MySQL is an open-source relational database management system (RDBMS) that uses Structured Query Language (SQL), the most popular language for adding, accessing, and processing data in a database. If all that sounds like Greek to you, just think of MySQL as a big file cabinet where all the content on your blog is stored.

Every time a visitor goes to your site to read your content, she makes a request that's sent to a host server. The PHP programming language receives that request, makes a call to the MySQL database, obtains the requested information from the database, and then presents the requested information to your visitor through her web browser. PHP doesn't require a MySQL database to perform some functions, but for the purposes of this chapter, understand that PHP is making requests for data stored in the MySQL database.

Here, *content* refers to the data stored in the MySQL database — that is, your site posts, pages, comments, links, and options that you set up on the WordPress Dashboard. But the *theme* (or design) you choose to use for your website — whether it's the default theme, one you create, or one you've custom-designed — isn't part of the content in this case. Theme files are part of the file system and aren't stored in the database. Therefore, it's a good idea to create and keep backups of any theme files that you're currently using. See Book 6 for further information on WordPress theme management.

REMEMBER

Make sure your web host backs up your site daily so that your content (data) won't be lost in case something happens. Web hosting providers that offer daily backups as part of their services can save the day by restoring your site to its original form. Additionally, Book 2, Chapter 7 covers important information about backing up your website.

Exploring PHP Basics

WordPress requires PHP to work; therefore, your web hosting provider must have PHP enabled on your web server. If you already have WordPress up and running on your website, you know that PHP is running and working just fine. Currently, the PHP version required for WordPress is 7.2 or later.

Before you play around with template tags (covered in Book 6) in your WordPress templates or plugin functions, you need to understand what makes up a template tag and why, as well as the correct syntax, or function, for a template tag as it relates to PHP. Additionally, have a look at the WordPress files contained within the download files. Many of the files end with the `.php` file extension — an extension required for PHP files, which separates them from other file types, such as JavaScript (`.js`) and CSS (`.css`).

As I state earlier, WordPress is based in PHP (a scripting language for creating web pages) and uses PHP commands to pull information from the MySQL database. Every tag begins with the function to start PHP and ends with a function to stop it. In the middle of those two commands lives the request to the database that tells WordPress to grab the data and display it.

A typical template tag, or function, looks like this:

```
<?php phpinfo(); ?>
```

This example tells WordPress to do three things:

- **Start PHP:** `<?php`
- **Use PHP to get information from the MySQL database and deliver it to your website:** `phpinfo();`
- **Stop PHP:** `?>`

In this case, `phpinfo();` represents the tag function, which grabs information from the database to deliver it to your website. The information retrieved depends on what tag function appears between the two PHP commands.

Getting to Know PHP and MySQL

REMEMBER

Every PHP command you start requires a stop command. For every `<?php`, you must include the closing `?>` command somewhere later in the code. PHP commands that are structured improperly cause ugly errors on your site, and they've been known to send programmers, developers, and hosting providers into loud screaming fits. You find a lot of starting and stopping of PHP throughout the WordPress templates and functions. The process seems as though it would be resource-intensive, if not exhaustive, but it really isn't. You can read all about PHP tags at the official PHP docs site at `https://secure.php.net/manual/en/language.basic-syntax.phptags.php`.

WARNING

Always, always make sure that the PHP start and stop commands are separated from the function with a single space. You must have a space after `<?php` and a space before `?>`, because if you don't, the PHP function code doesn't work. Make sure that the code looks like this

```
<?php phpinfo(); ?>
```

and not like this:

```
<?phpphpinfo();?>
```

Trying Out a Little PHP

To test some PHP code, follow these steps to create a simple HTML web page with an embedded PHP function:

1. **Open a new blank file in your default text editor — Notepad (Windows) or TextEdit (Mac) — type `<html>`, and then press Enter.**

   The `<html>` tag tells the web browser that this file is an HTML document and should be read as a web page.

2. **Type `<head>` and then press Enter.**

   The <head> HTML tag contains elements that tell the web browser about the document; this information is read by the browser but hidden from the web-page visitor.

3. **Type `<title>`This Is a Simple PHP Page`</title>` and then press Enter.**

   The `<title>` HTML tag tells the browser to display the text between two tags as the title of the document in the browser title bar.

Note: All HTML tags need to be opened and then closed, just like the PHP tags that I describe in the preceding section. In this case, the `<title>` tag opens the command and the `</title>` tag closes it, telling the web browser that you're finished dealing with the title.

4. **Type `</head>` to close the `<head>` tag from step 2 and then press Enter.**
5. **Type `<body>` to define the body of the web page and then press Enter.**

   Anything that appears after this tag displays in the web browser's window.
6. **Type `<?php` to tell the web browser to start a PHP function and then press the spacebar.**

   See "Exploring PHP Basics" earlier in this chapter for details on starting and stopping PHP functions.
7. **Type `echo '<p>Testing my new PHP function</p>';` and then press the spacebar.**

   This function is the one that you want PHP to execute on your web page. This particular function echoes the text *Testing my new PHP function* and displays it on your website.
8. **Type `?>` to tell the web browser to end the PHP function and then press Enter.**
9. **Type `</body>` to close the `<body>` HTML tag from step 5 and then press Enter.**

   This tag tells the web browser that you're done with the body of the web page.
10. **Type `</html>` to close the `<html>` tag from step 1 and then press Enter.**

    This tag tells the web browser that you're at the end of the HTML document.

When you're done with steps 1 through 10, double-check to make sure that the code in your text editor looks like this:

```
<html>
  <head>
    <title>This Is a Simple PHP Page</title>
  </head>
  <body>
    <?php echo '<p>Testing my new PHP function</p>'; ?>
  </body>
</html>
```

After you write your code, follow these steps to save and upload your file:

1. **Save the file to your local computer as `test.php`.**
2. **Upload the `test.php` file.**

   Via Secure File Transfer Protocol (SFTP), upload `test.php` to the root directory of your web server. If you need a review of how to use SFTP to transfer files to your web server, look through the information presented in Book 2, Chapter 2.
3. **Open a web browser, and type the address `http://`*`yourdomain`*`.com/test.php` in the web browser's address bar (where *yourdomain* is your actual domain name).**

   As shown in Figure 3-1, a single line of text displays: `Testing my new PHP function`.

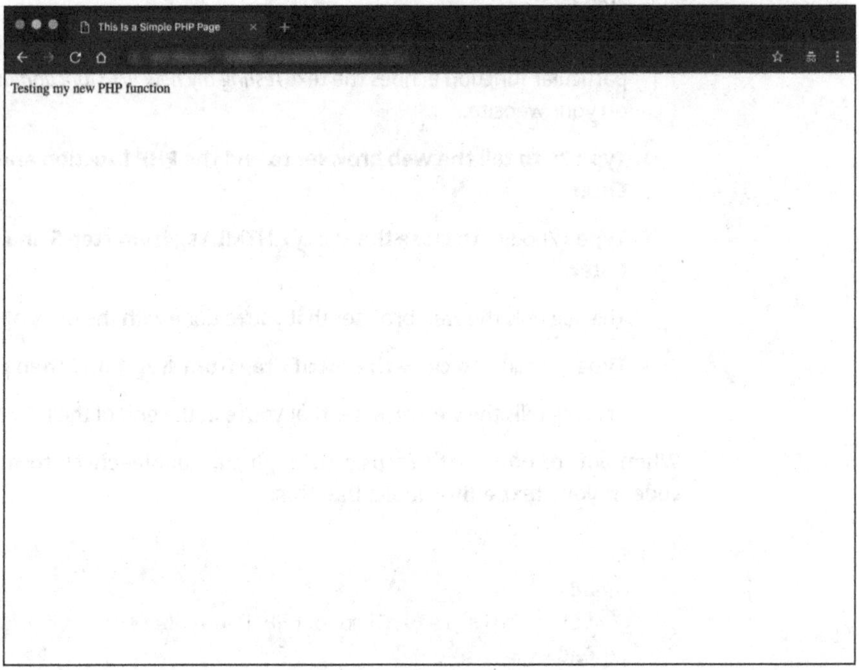
This Is a Simple PHP Page
Testing my new PHP function

FIGURE 3-1: A basic PHP page in a browser window.

If the `test.php` file displays correctly in your browser, congratulations! You've programmed PHP to work in a web browser.

TIP

If the `test.php` file doesn't display correctly in your browser, a PHP error message gives you an indication of the errors in your code. (Usually included with the error message is the number of the line where the error occurs in the file.)

Managing Your MySQL Database

Many new WordPress users are intimidated by the MySQL database, perhaps because it seems to be way above their technical skills or abilities. Truth be told, regular users of WordPress — those who use it just to publish content — don't ever have to dig into the database unless they want to. You need to explore the database only if you're dealing with theme or plugin development, or if you're contributing code to the WordPress project.

This section gives you a basic overview of the WordPress database stored in MySQL so that you have an understanding of the structure and know where items are stored.

TIP

Currently, WordPress requires MySQL version 5.6 or greater to work correctly. If your web hosting provider doesn't have version 5.6 or later installed on your web server, kindly ask to upgrade. WordPress can also use MariaDB version 10.0 or later, but the typical use is MySQL.

After WordPress is installed on your server (which I discuss in Book 2, Chapter 4), the database gets populated with 12 tables that exist to store different types of data from your WordPress blog. Figure 3-2 displays the structure of the tables, as follows:

- **`wp_commentmeta`:** This table stores information, or *metadata,* for every comment published to your site and includes:
  - A unique comment ID number
  - A comment meta key, meta value, and meta ID (unique numerical identifiers assigned to each comment left by you or visitors to your site)
- **`wp_comments`:** This table stores the body of the comments published to your site, including
  - A post ID that specifies which post the comment belongs to
  - The comment content
  - The comment author's name, URL, IP address, and email address
  - The comment date (day, month, year, and time)
  - The comment status (approved, unapproved, or spam)
- **`wp_links`:** This table is no longer actively used by the latest version of WordPress, it exists for backward compatibility from a time when WordPress used to have a Link Manager feature. This table stored the name, URL, and description of all links created by using the WordPress Link Manager. It also stored all the advanced options for the links created, if any.

- **`wp_options`:** This table stores all the option settings that you set for WordPress after you installed it, including all theme and plugin option settings.
- **`wp_postmeta`:** This table includes information, or *metadata,* for every post or page published to your site and contains metadata that includes
  - The unique post ID number. (Each blog post has a unique ID number to set it apart from the others.)
  - The post meta key, meta value (unique numerical identifiers for each post created on your site), and any custom fields you've created for the post.
- **`wp_posts`:** This table features the body of any post or page you've published to your website, including autosaved revisions and post option settings, such as
  - The post author, date, and time
  - The post title, content, and excerpt
  - The post status (published, draft, or private)
  - The post comment status (open or closed)
  - The post type (page, post, attachment, or custom post type)
  - The post comment count
- **`wp_termmeta`:** This table stores the metadata for terms (taxonomies, categories, and tags) for content.
- **`wp_terms`:** This table stores the taxonomies and categories you've created for posts, as well as tags that have been created for your posts.
- **`wp_term_relationships`:** This table stores the relationships among the posts, as well as the taxonomies, categories, and tags that have been assigned to them.
- **`wp_term_taxonomy`:** WordPress has three types of taxonomies by default: category, link, and tag. This table stores the taxonomy associated for the terms stored in the `wp_terms` table.
- **`wp_usermeta`:** This table features information, or metadata, from every user with an account on your WordPress website. This metadata includes
  - A unique user ID
  - A user meta key, meta value, and meta ID, which are unique identifiers for users on your site
- **`wp_users`:** The list of users with an account on your WordPress website is maintained within this table and includes
  - The username, first name, last name, and nickname
  - The user login
  - The user password

- The user email
- The registration date
- The user status and role (subscriber, contributor, author, editor, or administrator)

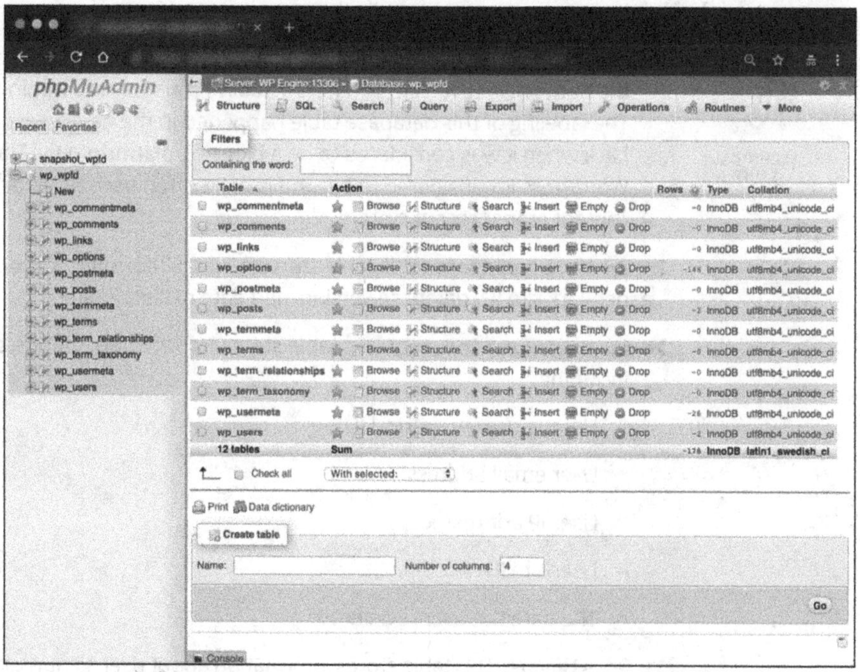

FIGURE 3-2: The WordPress database structure.

Most web hosting providers give you a *utility*, or an interface, to view your MySQL database; the most common one is phpMyAdmin (refer to Figure 3-2). If you're unsure how you can view your database on your hosting account, get in touch with your hosting provider to find out.

When the Multisite feature in WordPress is activated (check out Book 8 for information about the Multisite feature), WordPress adds six additional tables to the database:

» **wp_blogs:** This table stores information about each site created in your network, including
  - A unique site numerical ID
  - A unique site ID number (determines the ID of the network site to which the site belongs)

    - The site domain
    - The site server path
    - The date the site was registered
    - The date the site was updated
    - The site status (public, private, archived, or spam; see Book 8 for more information on site status)

TECHNICAL STUFF

Although the database table that contains information about each site within the network is called `wp_blogs`, it actually refers to sites within the network. The labeling of this database table happened in the early years of WordPress, back when it was considered to be a blogging platform only. These days, WordPress is considered to be, and is most often used as, a full website content management system.

- **`wp_blog_versions`:** This table stores general information about each network site ID, database version, and date of last update.
- **`wp_registration_log`:** This table stores information about registered users, including
    - Unique user numerical ID
    - User email address
    - User IP address
    - User site ID
    - The date the user registered
- **`wp_signups`:** This table stores information about user signups, including all the information from the `wp_registration_log` table, the date the user account was activated, and the unique activation key the user accessed during the signup process.
- **`wp_site`:** This table stores information about your main installation site (or network site), including the site ID, domain, and server path.
- **`wp_sitemeta`:** This table stores all the information about the multisite configurations set after you install the Multisite feature. (See Book 8.)

IN THIS CHAPTER

» **Discovering preinstallations by your host**

» **Manually installing WordPress**

» **Running installation scripts**

Chapter **4**

Installing WordPress on Your Web Server

This chapter takes you through two installation methods for WordPress: automatic installation with an installer provided by a managed web hosting service, which is available from your web hosting provider, and manual installation.

I also show you how to set up a MySQL database by using the cPanel web hosting management interface. By the time you're done reading this chapter, you'll be logged in to and looking at your brand-spanking-new WordPress Dashboard, ready to start publishing content right away. (If you already have WordPress installed, go ahead and skip to Book 2, Chapter 5, which contains great information about configuring WordPress for optimum performance and security.)

REMEMBER

Before you can install WordPress, you need to complete the following tasks:

- Purchase the domain-name registration for your account (Book 2, Chapter 1).
- Obtain a hosting service on a web server for your website (Book 2, Chapter 1).
- Establish your hosting account username, password, and Secure File Transfer Protocol (SFTP) address (Book 2, Chapters 1 and 2).
- Acquire an SFTP client for transferring files to your hosting account (Book 2, Chapter 2).

If you omitted any of the preceding items, flip to the chapters listed to complete the step(s) you're missing.

Exploring Preinstalled WordPress

The WordPress software has become such a popular publishing tool that almost all hosting providers available today provide WordPress for you in a couple of ways:

- Already installed on your hosting account when you sign up
- A user dashboard with a utility for installing WordPress from within your account management

TIP

If your hosting provider doesn't give you access to an installation utility, skip to "Installing WordPress Manually" later in this chapter for the steps to install WordPress manually via SFTP.

One of the most popular web hosts for managed WordPress hosting is a service called WP Engine, which you can find at `https://wpengine.com`. The service provides a handy, easy-to-use installation utility that's built right into your account dashboard at WP Engine to allow you to get up and running with WordPress right away.

You may not be using WP Engine, so your host may have a slightly different utility, but the basic concept is the same. Be sure to apply the same concepts to whatever kind of utility your hosting provider gives you.

To install WordPress from within the account dashboard of WP Engine, follow these steps:

1. **Log in to the WP Engine user dashboard.**

   (a) *Browse to* `https://my.wpengine.com` *to bring up the login screen.*

   (b) *Enter the email address you used to sign up, enter your password, and then click Log In. The page refreshes and displays the dashboard for your account.*

2. **Click the Sites link on the top menu.**

   The Sites page displays in your browser window, as shown in Figure 4-1.

3. **Click the Add Site button.**

   A small window labeled Add Site opens.

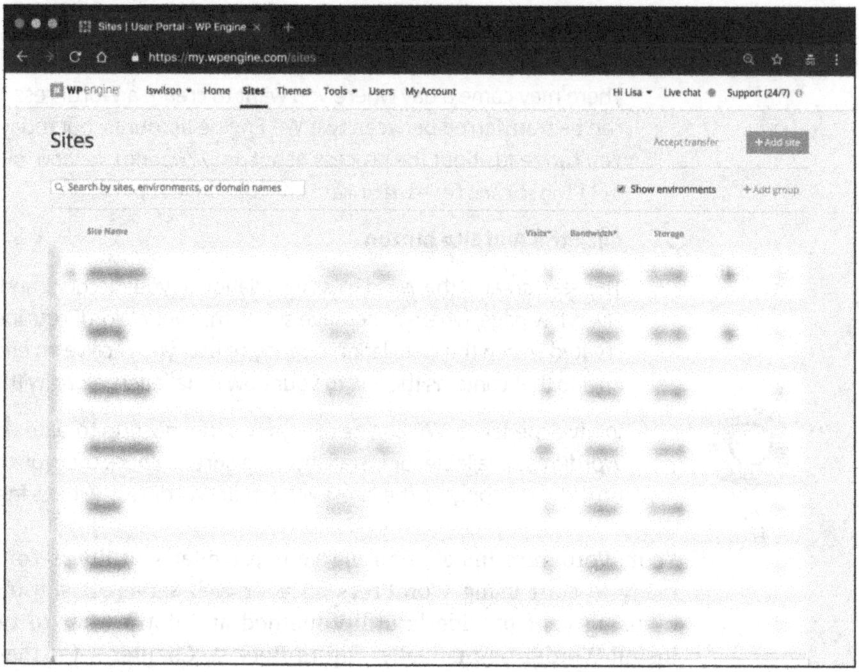

FIGURE 4-1: The Sites page at WP Engine.

4. **Type the name of your new WordPress installation in the Site Name field.**

   This name is the temporary domain name of your new website. As shown in Figure 4-2, I'm using *wpfd*, which stands for *WordPress For Dummies*. This step creates the domain name `wpfd.wpengine.com`.

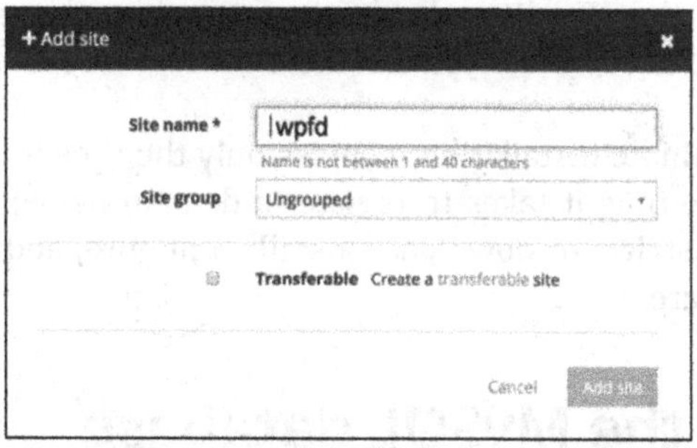

FIGURE 4-2: The Add Site window at WP Engine.

5. **Choose Ungrouped from the Site Group drop-down list.**

   This step ensures that your new WordPress installation isn't associated with any other sites that you may already have set up within your WP Engine account.

6. **Leave the Transferable check box unselected.**

   There may come a day where you want to create a WordPress installation that can be transferred between two WP Engine accounts, but today isn't that day. You can read about the process at `https://wpengine.com/support/billing-transfer-information-for-developers`.

7. **Click the Add Site button.**

   This step creates the WordPress installation in your account and takes you to the Overview page, where a message states that your WordPress installation is being created. When the installation is ready to use, you receive an email from WP Engine that contains the link to your new installation, along with login information.

   TIP

   In my experience, WP Engine always has the most up-to-date version of WordPress available for installation. Be sure to check that your hosting provider is supplying the latest version of WordPress with its installation utility.

Your WordPress installation via your provider's utility is complete, and you're ready to start using WordPress on your web server. If you installed WordPress by using your provider's utility method and don't want to review the steps to install WordPress manually, flip to Book 2, Chapter 5 for the steps to optimize your WordPress installation for performance and security.

Installing WordPress Manually

If you install WordPress manually, here's where the rubber meets the road — that is, where you're putting WordPress's famous five-minute installation to the test. Set your watch, and see whether you can meet the five-minute goal.

REMEMBER

The famous five-minute installation includes only the time it takes to install the software — not the time it takes to register a domain name; obtain and set up your web hosting service; or download, install, configure, and figure out how to use the SFTP software.

Setting up the MySQL database

The WordPress software is a personal publishing system that uses a PHP/MySQL platform, which provides everything you need to create your own website and publish your own content dynamically without knowing how to program those pages. In short, all your content (options, posts, comments, and other pertinent data) is stored in a MySQL database in your hosting account.

Every time visitors go to your website to read your content, they make a request that's sent to your server. The PHP programming language receives that request, obtains the requested information from the MySQL database, and then presents the requested information to your visitors through their web browsers.

Every web host is different in how it gives you access to set up and manage your MySQL database(s) for your account. In this section, I use cPanel, a popular hosting interface. If your host provides a different interface, the same basic steps apply, but the setup in the interface that your web host provides may be different.

To set up the MySQL database for your WordPress site with cPanel, follow these steps:

1. **Log in to the cPanel for your hosting account:**

   (a) *Browse to* `http://`yourdomain`.com/`*cpanel* *(where* yourdomain.com *is your actual domain name) to bring up the login screen for your cPanel.*

   (b) *Enter your specific hosting account username and password in the login fields, and then click OK.*

   The page refreshes and displays the cPanel for your account.

2. **Locate the MySQL Databases icon.**

   Click the MySQL Databases icon to load the MySQL Databases page in your cPanel.

3. **Enter a name for your database in the Name text box.**

   Be sure to make note of the database name, because you need it to install WordPress.

4. **Click the Create Database button.**

   A message appears, confirming that the database was created.

5. **Click the Back button on your browser toolbar.**

   The MySQL Databases page displays in your browser window.

6. **Locate MySQL Users on the MySQL Databases page.**

   Scroll approximately to the middle of the page to locate this section.

7. **Choose a username and password for your database, enter them in the Username and Password text boxes, and then click the Create User button.**

   A confirmation message appears, stating that the username was created with the password you specified.

TIP

For security reasons, make sure that your password isn't something that sneaky hackers can easily guess. Give your database a name that you'll remember later. This practice is especially helpful if you run more than one MySQL database in your account. If you name a database *WordPress* or *wpsite,* for example, you can be reasonably certain a year from now, when you want to access your database to make some configuration changes, that you know exactly which credentials to use.

WARNING

Make sure that you note the database name, username, and password that you set up during this process. You need them in the section "Running the installation script" later in this chapter before officially installing WordPress on your web server. Jot these details down on a piece of paper, or copy and paste them into a text editor window; either way, make sure that you have them handy.

8. **Click the Back button on your browser toolbar.**

   The MySQL Databases page displays in your browser window.

9. **In the Add User to Database section of the MySQL Databases page, choose the user you just set up from the User drop-down list and then choose the new database from the Database drop-down list.**

   If the user and/or database you created in the earlier steps don't display in these drop-down lists, you've done something wrong and should start over from step 1.

10. **Click the Add button.**

    This step displays the Manage User Privileges page in your browser window.

11. **Assign user privileges by selecting the All Privileges check box.**

    Because you're the *administrator* (or owner) of this database, you need to make sure that you assign all privileges to the new user you just created.

12. **Click the Make Changes button.**

    The resulting page displays a message confirming that you've added your selected user to the selected database.

13. **Click the Back button on your browser toolbar.**

    You return to the MySQL Databases page.

The MySQL database for your WordPress website is complete, and you're ready to proceed to the final step of installing the software on your web server.

Downloading the WordPress software

Without further ado, get the latest version of the WordPress software at `https://wordpress.org/download`.

TIP

WordPress gives you two compression formats for the software: `.zip` and `.tar.gz`. Use the `.zip` file because it's the most common format for compressed files and because both Windows and Mac operating systems can use the format. Generally, the `.tar.gz` file format is used for Unix operating systems.

Download the WordPress software to your computer and then *decompress* (unpack or unzip) it to a folder on your computer's hard drive. These steps begin the installation process for WordPress. Having the program on your own computer isn't enough, however. You also need to *upload* (or transfer) it to your web server account (the one discussed in Book 2, Chapter 1).

Before you install WordPress on your web server, you need to make sure that you have the MySQL database set up and ready to accept the WordPress installation. Be sure that you've followed the steps to set up your MySQL database before you proceed.

Uploading the WordPress files via SFTP

To upload the WordPress files to your host, return to the `/wordpress` folder (shown in Figure 4-3) on your computer, where you unpacked the WordPress software that you downloaded earlier. If you need a review on using SFTP (Secure File Transfer Protocol) to transfer files from your computer to your web server, see Book 2, Chapter 2.

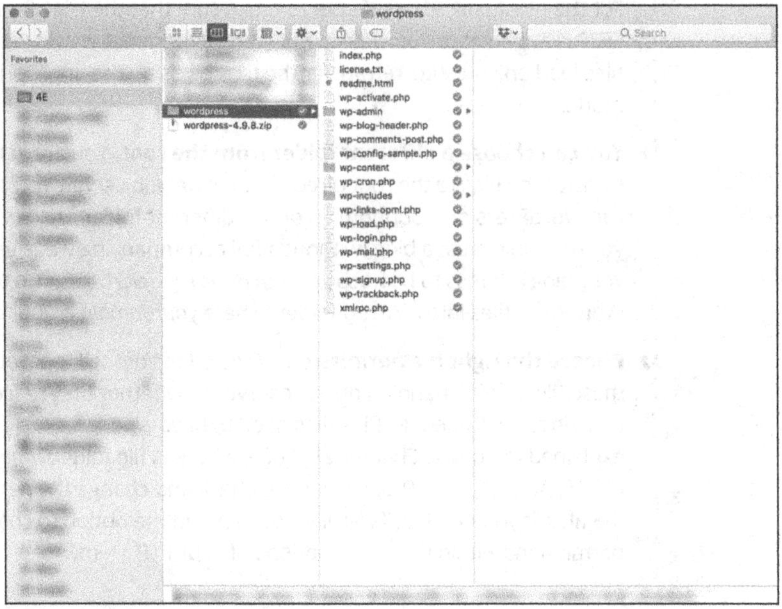

FIGURE 4-3: WordPress installation files to be uploaded to your web server.

Using your SFTP client, connect to your web server and upload all these files to the root directory of your hosting account.

TIP

If you don't know what your root directory is, contact your hosting provider and ask, "What is my root directory for my account?" Every hosting provider's setup is different. The root directory is most often the `public_html` folder, but you may find an `httpdocs` folder. The answer depends on what type of setup your hosting provider has. When in doubt, ask!

Here are a few things to keep in mind when you upload your files:

- **Upload the *contents* of the `/wordpress` folder to your web server — not the folder itself.** Most SFTP client software lets you select all the files and drag and drop them to your web server. Other programs have you highlight the files and click a Transfer button.
- **Choose the correct transfer mode.** File transfers via SFTP have two forms: ASCII and binary. Most SFTP clients are configured to autodetect the transfer mode. Understanding the difference as it pertains to this WordPress installation is important so that you can troubleshoot any problems you have later:
  - *Binary transfer mode* is how images (such as JPG, GIF, BMP, and PNG files) are transferred via SFTP.
  - *ASCII transfer mode* is for everything else (text files, PHP files, JavaScript, and so on).

  For the most part, it's a safe bet to make sure that the transfer mode of your SFTP client is set to autodetect. But if you experience issues with how those files load on your site, retransfer the files by using the appropriate transfer mode.
- **You can choose a different folder from the root.** You aren't required to transfer the files to the root directory of your web server. You can choose to run WordPress on a subdomain or in a different folder on your account. If you're running just a blog (without a full accompanying website) and want your blog address to be `http://`*`yourdomain.com`*`/blog`, you transfer the WordPress files into a `/blog` folder (where *yourdomain* is your domain name).
- **Choose the right file permissions.** *File permissions* tell the web server how these files can be handled on your server — whether they're files that can be written to. Generally, PHP files need to have a permission (CHMOD is explained in Book 2, Chapter 2) of 666, whereas file folders need a permission of 755. Almost all SFTP clients let you check and change the permissions on the files, if you need to. Typically, you can find the option to change file permissions within the menu options of your FTP client.

TECHNICAL STUFF

Some hosting providers run their PHP software in a more secure format: *safe mode.* If this is the case with your host, you need to set the PHP files to 644. If you're unsure, ask your hosting provider what permissions you need to set for PHP files.

Running the installation script

The final step in the installation procedure for WordPress is connecting the WordPress software you uploaded to the MySQL database. Follow these steps:

1. **Type the URL of your website in the address bar of your web browser.**

   If you chose to install WordPress in a different folder from the root directory of your account, make sure you indicate that in the URL for the install script. If you transferred the WordPress software files to the `/blog` folder, for example, point your browser to the following URL to run the installation: `http://`*`yourdomain.com`*`/blog/wp-admin/install.php`. If WordPress is in the root directory, use the following URL to run the installation: `http://`*`yourdomain.com`*`/wp-admin/install.php` (where *yourdomain* is your domain name).

   Assuming that you did everything correctly, you should see the first step in the installation process that you see in Figure 4-4. (See Table 4-1 for help with common installation problems.)

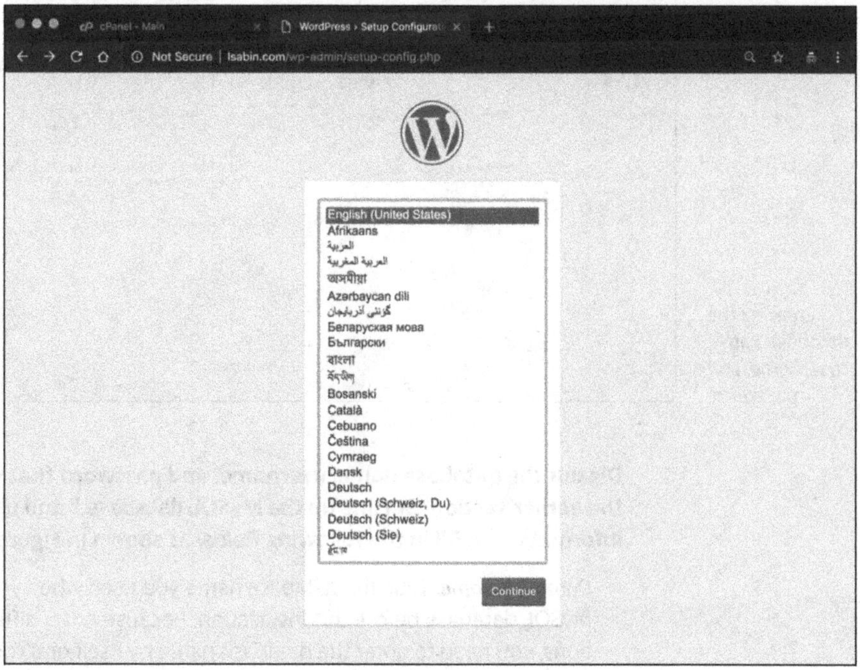

FIGURE 4-4: Choose the language for your installation.

2. **Select your preferred language from the list provided on the setup page, shown in Figure 4-4.**

   At this writing, WordPress is available in 116 languages. For these steps, I'm using English (United States).

3. **Click the Continue button.**

   You see a new page with a welcome message from WordPress and instructions that you need to gather the MySQL information you saved earlier in this chapter.

4. **Click the Let's Go button.**

   A new page loads and displays the fields you need to fill out in the next step, shown in Figure 4-5.

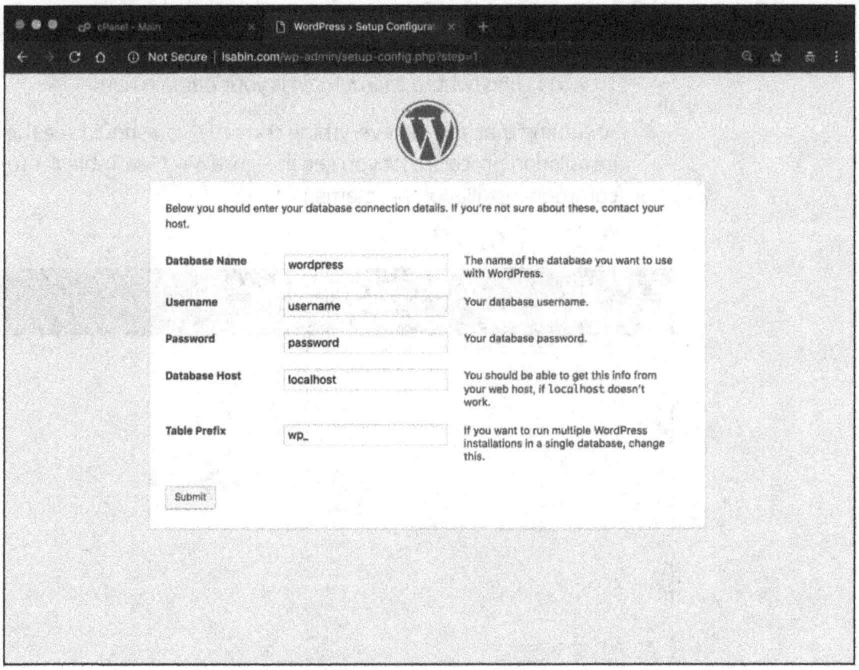

FIGURE 4-5: Entering the database name, username, and password.

5. **Dig out the database name, username, and password that you saved in the earlier section "Setting up the MySQL database," and use that information to fill in the following fields, as shown in Figure 4-5:**

   - *Database Name:* Type the database name you used when you created the MySQL database before this installation. Because hosts differ in configurations, you need to enter the database name by itself or a combination of your username and the database name, separated by an underscore (_).

If you named your database *wordpress,* for example, you enter that in this text box. If your host requires you to append the database name with your hosting account username, you enter ***username*_wordpress**, substituting your hosting username for *username.* My username is *lisasabin,* so I enter **lisasabin_wordpress**.

- *Username:* Type the username you used when you created the MySQL database before this installation. Depending on what your host requires, you may need to enter a combination of your hosting account username and the database username separated by an underscore (_).
- *Password:* Type the password you used when you set up the MySQL database. You don't need to append the password to your hosting account username here.
- *Database Host:* Ninety-nine percent of the time, you leave this field set to `localhost`. Some hosts, depending on their configurations, have different hosts set for the MySQL database server. If `localhost` doesn't work, you need to contact your hosting provider to find out the MySQL database host.
- *Table Prefix:* Leave this field set to `wp_`.

  You can change the table prefix to create an environment that's secure against outside access. See Book 2, Chapter 5 for more information.

6. **After you fill in the MySQL database information, click the Submit button.**

   You see a message that says, `All right, sparky! You've made it through this part of the installation. WordPress can now communicate with your database. If you're ready, time to run the install!`

7. **Click the Run the Install button.**

   Another page appears, welcoming you to the famous five-minute WordPress installation process, as shown in Figure 4-6.

8. **Enter the following information:**

   - *Site Title:* Enter the title you want to give your site. The title you enter isn't written in stone; you can change it later, if you like. The site title also appears on your site.
   - *Username:* Enter the name you use to log in to WordPress. By default, the username is *admin,* and you can leave it that way. For security reasons, however, I recommend that you change your username to something unique. This username is different from the one you set for the MySQL database in previous steps. You use this username when you log in to WordPress to access the Dashboard (which is covered in Book 3), so be sure to make it something you'll remember.

- *Password:* Type your desired password in the text box. If you don't enter a password, one is generated automatically for you. For security reasons, it's a good thing to set a different password here from the one you set for your MySQL database in the previous steps; just don't get the passwords confused.

  TIP

  For security reasons (and so other people can't make a lucky guess), passwords should be at least seven characters long and use as many different characters in as many combinations as possible. Use a mixture of uppercase and lowercase letters, numbers, and symbols (such as ! " ? $ % ^ &).

- *Your Email:* Enter the email address you want to use to be notified of administrative information about your blog. You can change this address later, too.

- *Search Engine Visibility:* By default, this option isn't selected, which lets the search engines index the content of your website and includes your site in search results. To keep your site out of the search engines, select this check box. (See Book 5 for information on search engine optimization.)

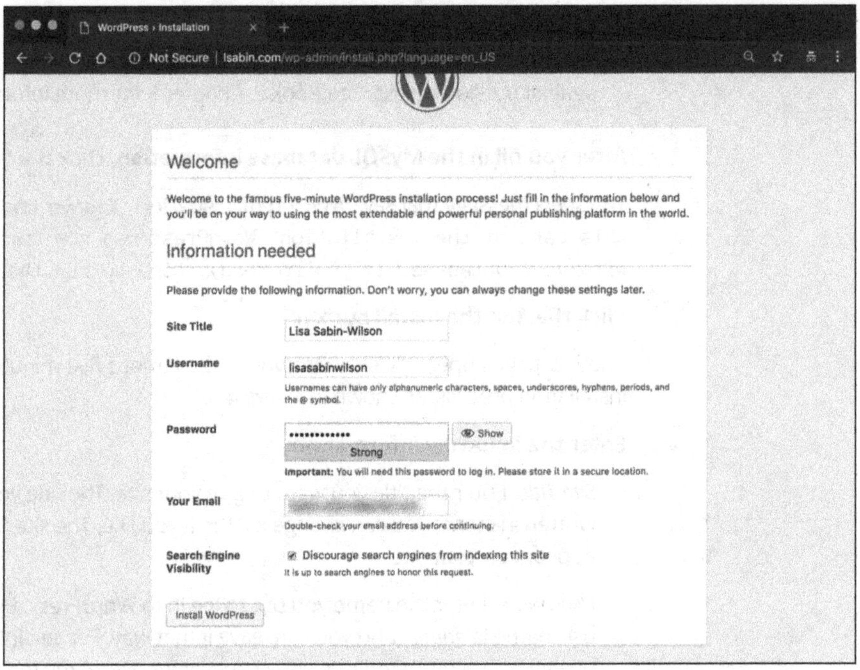

FIGURE 4-6: Finishing the WordPress installation.

9. **Click the Install WordPress button.**

   The WordPress installation machine works its magic and creates all the tables within the database that contain the default data for your blog. WordPress displays the login information you need to access the WordPress Dashboard. Make note of this username and password before you leave this page. Scribble them on a piece of paper or copy them into a text editor, such as Notepad.

REMEMBER

After you click the Install WordPress button, you're sent an email with the login information and login URL. This information is handy if you're called away during this part of the installation process. So go ahead and let the dog out, answer the phone, brew a cup of coffee, or take a 15-minute power nap. If you somehow get distracted away from this page, the email you receive contains the information you need to log in to your WordPress blog.

10. **Click the Log In button to log in to WordPress.**

TIP

If you happen to lose this page before clicking the Log In button, you can always find your way to the login page by entering your domain followed by the call to the login file (such as `http://`*`yourdomain.com`*`/wp-login.php`, where *yourdomain* is your domain name).

You know that you're finished with the installation process when you see the login page, shown in Figure 4-7. Check out Table 4-1 if you experience any problems during this installation process; it covers some of the common problems users run into.

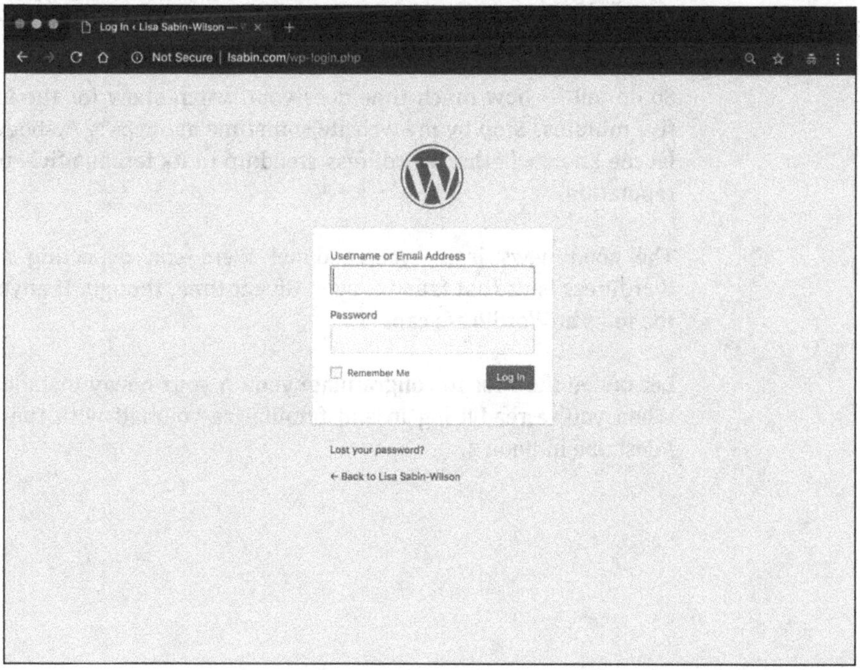

FIGURE 4-7: You know you've run a successful WordPress installation when you see the login page.

TABLE 4-1 Common WordPress Installation Problems

Error Message	Common Cause	Solution
Error Connecting to the Database	The database name, username, password, or host was entered incorrectly.	Revisit your MySQL database to obtain the database name, username, and password and then reenter that information.
Headers Already Sent	A syntax error occurred in the wp-config.php file.	Open the wp-config.php file in a text editor. The first line needs to contain only this line: <?php. The last line needs to contain only this line: ?>. Make sure that those lines contain nothing else — not even white space. Save the file changes.
500: Internal Server Error	Permissions on PHP files are set incorrectly.	Try setting the permissions (CHMOD) on the PHP files to 666. If that change doesn't work, set them to 644. Each web server has different settings for how it lets PHP execute on its servers.
404: Page Not Found	The URL for the login page is incorrect.	Double-check that the URL you're using to get to the login page is the same as the location of your WordPress installation (such as http://*yourdomain.com*/wp-login.php).
403: Forbidden Access	An index.html or index.htm file exists in the WordPress installation directory.	WordPress is a PHP application, so the default home page is index.php. Look in the WordPress installation folder on your web server. If an index.html or index.htm file is there, delete it.

So do tell — how much time does your watch show for the installation? Was it five minutes? Stop by my website sometime at https://webdevstudios.com and let me know whether WordPress stood up to its famous five-minute installation reputation.

The good news is — you're done! Were you expecting a marching band? WordPress isn't that fancy . . . yet. Give it time, though. If anyone can produce it, the folks at WordPress can.

Let me be the first to congratulate you on your newly installed WordPress blog! When you're ready, log in and familiarize yourself with the Dashboard, which I describe in Book 3.

IN THIS CHAPTER

» Introducing web security

» Understanding today's web threats

» Reducing the risk of attack

» Using sources you can trust

» Cleaning up to avoid a soup-kitchen server

» Hardening WordPress

Chapter 5
Configuring WordPress for Optimum Security

In this chapter, you deal with web security and how it pertains to WordPress. There are a lot of scary threats on the Internet, but with this chapter — and WordPress, of course — you'll have no problem keeping your website safe and secure.

TIP

Always have a reliable backup system in place so if something goes wrong with your website, you can reset it to the last version that you know worked. Book 2, Chapter 7 shows you how to back up your website.

Understanding the Basics of Web Security

Information security is the act of protecting information and information systems from unwanted or unauthorized use, access, modification, and disruption. Information security is built on principles of protecting confidentiality, integrity, and availability of information. The ultimate goal is managing your risk.

REMEMBER

No silver bullet can ensure that you're never compromised. Consider your desktop: The idea of running an operating system (whether it be Windows or Mac OS X) without antivirus software is highly impractical. The same principle applies to your website. You can never reduce the percentage of risk to zero, but you can implement controls to minimize impact and to take a proactive approach to threat preparedness.

You need to be familiar with six distinct types of risk (or threats):

- **Defacements:** The motivation behind most defacements is to change the appearance of a website. Defacements are often very basic and make some kind of social stance, such as supporting a cause or bringing attention to your poor security posture. If you visit your website, and it doesn't look anything like you expect it to, contact your host to find out whether it has been defaced, and if so, ask for assistance in restoring it.
- **Search engine optimization (SEO) spam:** This kind of attack sets out to ruin your search engine results; search engines can warn viewers away from your website. The most popular one is the Pharma hack, which injects code into your website and search engine links to redirect your traffic to pharmaceutical companies and their products. If you find that your website listing disappears from major search engines, such as Google, you should be concerned that your website has been a victim of SEO spam and contact your hosting provider for assistance.
- **Malicious redirects:** Malicious-redirect attacks direct your traffic somewhere else, most likely to another website. If your domain is `http://domain.com`, for example, a malicious redirect might redirect it to `http://adifferentdomain.com`. Malicious redirects are often integrated with other attacks (SEO spam being one). If you visit your website and discover that your domain redirects to a different domain that you don't recognize, your website has been a victim of a malicious-redirect attack, and you should contact your hosting provider for assistance.
- **iFrame injections:** This kind of attack embeds a hidden iFrame in your website that loads another website onto your visitor's browser (like a pop-up ad). These embedded websites or ads can lead to malicious websites that carry a multitude of infections.
- **Phishing scams:** Phishing scams used to belong only to the world of email: You get an email from your bank asking you to confirm your login information, but if you follow the instructions, your information actually goes to the attacker's servers rather than the legitimate site.

  WordPress websites are sometimes used for the distribution of these attacks. Attackers develop malicious files and code that look like plugins and themes and then exploit credentials on a server or WordPress site, or the attackers use a known vulnerability to infect the plugins and themes. Then they use the bait-and-hook approach through ads or emails to redirect traffic to these fake pages stored on legitimate websites. Keep an eye out for abnormal behavior on your website, such as the display of ads that you didn't insert yourself or the redirect to domains you're not familiar with. If at any time you suspect that your website and underlying files have been tampered with, contact your web hosting provider for assistance.

- **Backdoor shells:** With a backdoor shell, an attacker uploads a piece of PHP code to your website, which allows him to take control of it, download your files, and upload his own. This kind of attack is more difficult to discover because it doesn't always change the appearance of your site or your experience with it. You typically discover this kind of attack by noticing new files in your file system or notice a marked increase in your bandwidth use.

The rest of this chapter shows you how you can prevent any of these nasty attacks against your WordPress website so that you can keep yourself and your visitors safe.

REMEMBER

Part of being a website owner is keeping your website and subscribers safe from hackers.

Preventing Attacks

You can't ever be 100 percent secure. But with a WordPress website, you're in good hands. The WordPress developers understand the importance of security, and they built a highly effective system to address any vulnerabilities you'll run across.

Updating WordPress

The first way to prevent hackers is to keep your WordPress website up to date. The quick-and-easy way to do so is through the automatic update feature. Book 2, Chapter 6 takes you through the process of updating WordPress step by step.

REMEMBER

The beauty of applying updates is that they often introduce new streamlined features, improve overall usability, and work to patch and close identified or known vulnerabilities.

As technology and concepts evolve, so do attackers and their methods for finding new vulnerabilities. The farther behind you get, the harder it is to update later and the more your risk increases, which in turn affects how vulnerable you are to attacks.

Installing patches

All WordPress updates are not created equal, but you should pay special attention to a few updates of the WordPress core software.

Updates include *major releases,* which contain feature additions, user interface (UI) changes, bug fixes, and security updates. You can always tell what major release you're on by the first two numbers in the version number (as in 5.0). See Book 1, Chapter 3 for more information about the difference between major and minor releases.

Then you have *point releases,* which are minor releases that can be identified by the third number in the version number (as in 5.0.1). These releases contain bug fixes and security patches but don't introduce new features.

TIP

When you see a point release, apply it. Point releases rarely cause issues with your site, and they help close off vulnerabilities in a lot of cases.

Using a firewall

A firewall builds a wall between your website and the much larger Internet; a good firewall thwarts a lot of attacks.

Your web server should also have a good firewall protecting it. Every day, countless visits, good and bad, are made to every website. Some visits are by real visitors, but many are by automated bots. A web application firewall (WAF) helps protect your WordPress installation from those bad visitors.

REMEMBER

WAFs don't offer 100 percent protection, but they're good deterrents for everyday attacks.

TECHNICAL STUFF

If you plan to manage and administer your own server, install and configure a tool such as ModSecurity (`www.modsecurity.org`), an open-source, WAF-like solution that lives at the web server level as an Apache module.

If you're using a managed hosting solution, you're probably in luck, because most of these solutions offer built-in WAF-like features.

As a user, you can also install a WordPress plugin called Cloudflare, which you can find in the official WordPress Plugin list at `https://wordpress.org/plugins/cloudflare`. Cloudflare (see Figure 5-1) provides the best available WAF-like features for your WordPress website on a managed hosting solution. If you'd like to use the Cloudflare plugin on your WordPress website, you need to have a Cloudflare account at `https://www.cloudflare.com`. You can open a free account or upgrade to a paid account that includes more features. After you've installed the plugin on your website, follow the instructions on the Cloudflare configuration page to connect your WordPress blog to your Cloudflare account.

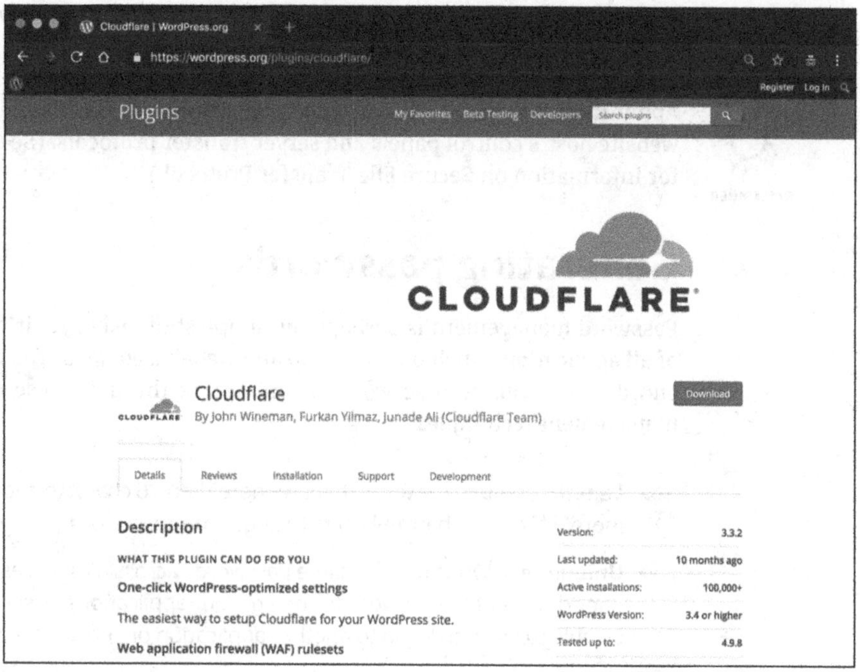

FIGURE 5-1: The Cloudflare plugin for WordPress.

Using Trusted Sources

One of the simplest things you can do to keep your website secure is vet all the people who work on your website: website administrators, website designers, developers, and web hosts. Also be sure to use trusted plugins, themes, and applications. If you're running a self-hosted WordPress website, this could be quite a few people.

If you're using themes or plugins, use the WordPress.org Theme and Plugin directories (`https://wordpress.org/themes` and `https://wordpress.org/plugins`, respectively). Each plugin and theme you find in those directories has gone through a documented review process, which reduces the risk of your downloading dangerous code.

Engage the WordPress user community. The WordPress forums (`https://wordpress.org/support/forums`) are great places to start. Ask for community references, and identify the support mechanisms in place to support the theme or plugin over the long term.

Managing Users

The concept of *least privilege* has been in practice for ages: Give someone the required privileges for as long as he needs it to perform his job or a task. When the task is complete, reduce the privileges.

REMEMBER

Apply these safeguards not just to your WordPress Dashboard, but also to your website host's control panels and server transfer protocols. (See Book 2, Chapter 2 for information on Secure File Transfer Protocol.)

Generating passwords

Password management is perhaps the simplest of tasks, yet it's the Achilles' heel of all applications, including desktop and web-based apps. You can keep your files and data on your web server safe and secure through these simple password-management techniques:

- **Length:** Create passwords that are more than 16 characters long to make it more difficult for harmful users to guess your password.
- **Uniqueness:** Don't use the same passwords across all services. If someone does discover the password for one of your applications or services, she won't be able to use it to log in to another application or service that you manage.
- **Complexity:** A strong password contains a minimum of 8 characters and is made up of upper- and lowercase letters, numbers, and symbols, making it hard to guess.

TIP

Use password managers and generators. Two of the most popular products right now are LastPass (`https://www.lastpass.com`) and 1Password (`https://1password.com`).

Limiting built-in user roles

Not all users of your website need administrator privileges. WordPress gives you five user roles to choose among, and those roles provide sufficient flexibility for your websites.

You can find detailed information on each of the roles in Book 3, Chapter 3. You can also discover more information on users and roles in the WordPress.org Codex at `https://codex.wordpress.org/Roles_and_Capabilities`.

TIP

Create a separate account with a lower role (such as Author) and use that account for everyday posting. Reserve the Administrator account purely for administration of your website.

Establishing user accountability

The use of generic accounts should be the last thing you ever consider because the more generic accounts you have, the greater your risk of being compromised. If a compromise does happen, you want to have full accountability for all users and be able to quickly answer questions like these:

- Who was logged in?
- Who made what changes?
- What did the users do while logged in?

Generic accounts preclude you from doing appropriate incident handling in the event of a compromise. In Book 3, Chapter 3, you find all the information and step-by-step details on how to create new users in your WordPress Dashboard. Keep the principles of least privilege and user accountability in mind as you're creating users.

Staying Clear of Soup-Kitchen Servers

Among the regular issues plaguing website owners are soup-kitchen servers. A *soup-kitchen server* is one that has never been maintained properly and has a combination of websites, old software, archives, unneeded files, folders, email, and so on living on its hard drive.

The real problem comes into play with the "out of sight, out of mind" phenomenon. A server owner can forget about software installations on a server that may be outdated or insecure. Over time, this forgetfulness introduces new vulnerabilities to the environment:

- Disabled installations or websites that live on the server are as accessible and susceptible to external attacks as live sites.
- When a forgotten installation or website is infected, it leads to *cross-site contamination* — a wormlike effect in which the infection can jump and replicate itself across the server.
- In many instances, these forgotten installations or websites house the backdoor and engine of the infection. This means that as you try to rigorously clean your live website, you continuously get reinfected.

Figure 5-2 demonstrates what a soup-kitchen server looks like. `$wp_version` indicates the version of WordPress that is currently installed in the directory. The many listings for `$wp_version = 2.9` (at this writing, the most recent version of WordPress is 5.0) show how many out-of-date installations of WordPress this particular soup-kitchen server has.

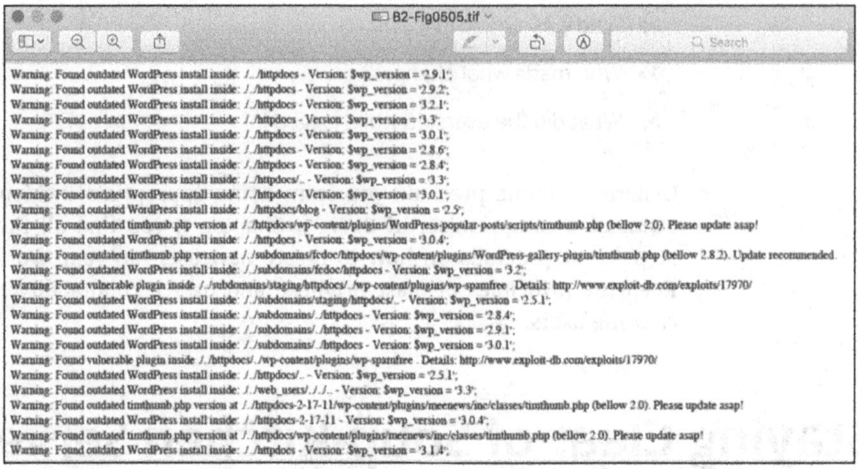

FIGURE 5-2: A file-server listing from a typical soup-kitchen server.

TIP

If you have more than one installation of WordPress on your current hosting account, try the following techniques to reduce your risk of running a soup-kitchen server:

- **Isolate each installation with its own user.** This action minimizes internal attacks that come from cross-site contamination.
- **Keep your installations up to date, and remove them when you no longer need them.** This action lessens the risk of attacks that result from outdated software on your server.

Hardening WordPress

When you *harden* (or, secure) your WordPress installation, you reduce your risk of being hacked by malicious attackers.

Hardening your website involves following these five steps:

1. **Enable multifactor authentication.**
2. **Limit login attempts.**
3. **Disable theme and plugin editors.**
4. **Filter by IP (Internet Protocol) address.**
5. **Kill PHP execution.**

I cover each of these steps in the following sections.

REMEMBER

Hardening your website doesn't guarantee your protection, but it definitely reduces your risk.

Enabling multifactor authentication

Authentication, in this case, refers to confirming the identity of the person who is attempting to log in and obtain access to your WordPress installation — just like when you log in to your WordPress website by using a username and password. The idea of multifactor authentication stems from the idea that one password alone isn't enough to secure access to any environment. *Multifactor authentication* (also called *strong authentication*) requires more than one user-authentication method. By default, WordPress requires only one: a username with password. Multifactor authentication adds layers of authentication measures for extra security of user logins.

WEBSITE HARDENING RESOURCES

I recommend a few website resources to follow for your WordPress hardening and security needs:

- **Hardening WordPress:** `https://codex.wordpress.org/Hardening_WordPress`
- **The Ultimate WordPress Security Guide:** `https://www.wpbeginner.com/wordpress-security`
- **Sucuri:** `https://blog.sucuri.net`
- **WordPress Security – 19+ Steps to Lock Down Your Site:** `https://kinsta.com/blog/wordpress-security`

To enable multifactor authentication, you can use a free plugin called Google Authenticator for WordPress, which provides two-factor user authentication through an application on your mobile or tablet device (iPhone, iPad, Android, and so on). For this plugin to work, you need the following:

- **Google Authenticator app:** Find it at the App Store for iOS devices or the Google Play Store for Android devices.
- **Google Authenticator plugin:** You can find this plugin in the Plugin list at `https://wordpress.org/plugins/miniorange-2-factor-authentication`. See Book 7, Chapters 1 and 2 for details on finding, installing, and activating plugins.

Configuring Google Authenticator

When you have both of those tasks accomplished, you can configure the plugin for use on your website. Follow these steps to configure the plugin for each user on your site:

1. **Click the 2FAS link on the Settings menu on your Dashboard.**

   The 2FAS — Two Factor Authentication Service page opens.

2. **Download the authenticator app to your smartphone (Android or iPhone).**

   The authenticator app on your phone is required to complete the two factor authentication. I've chosen the Google Authenticator app, downloaded to my iPhone.

3. **Click the Show QR Code button.**

   This button displays on the 2FAS page in your WordPress Dashboard (see step 1) and when you click the button, the QR code displays.

4. **Scan the QR code in the Google Authenticator application on your phone.**

   Point your device camera at your computer screen, and line up the QR code within the camera brackets of your mobile device. The application automatically reads the QR code as soon as it's aligned correctly and displays a six-digit code identifying your blog. The six-digit code refreshes on a time-based interval. After you scan the QR code is scanned, you receive a message on your mobile device that contains a unique numeric code.

5. **Enter the six-digit code generated by the Google Authenticator app in the Token field.**

6. **Click the Add Device button.**

   You see a notice at the top of the 2FAS page that the tokens are configured.

7. **(Optional) Click the Add Another App/Device button.**

   Perform this step if you want to add more than one smartphone device for authentication. (See Figure 5-3.)

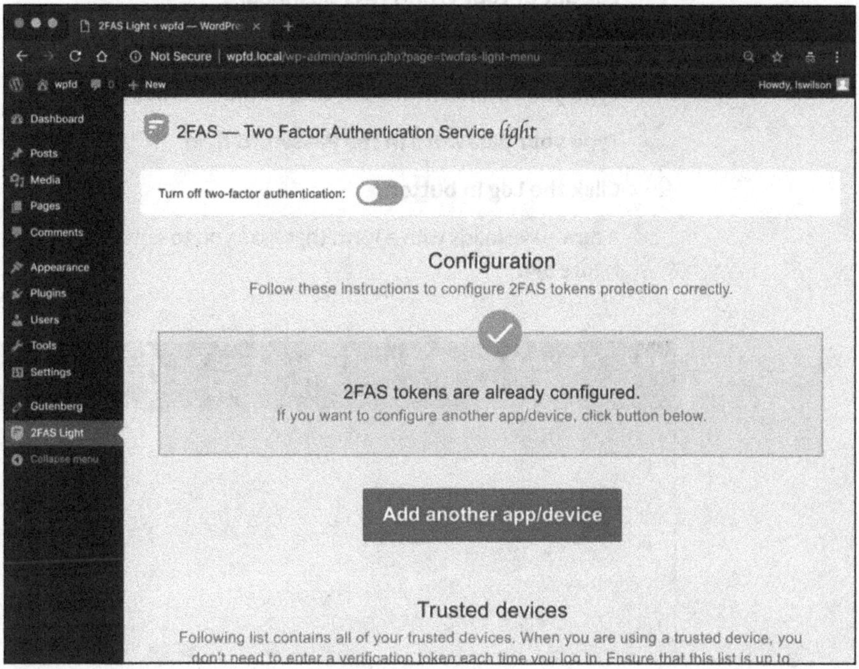

FIGURE 5-3: Two-Factor Authenticator settings.

Now, with the Google Authenticator plugin in place, whenever anyone tries to log in to your WordPress Dashboard, she has to fill in his username and password, as usual, but with multifactor authentication in place, she also needs to enter the authentication code that was sent to her mobile device. Without this unique code, the user can't log in to the WordPress Dashboard.

WARNING

The Google Authenticator application verification code is time-based, which is why it's very important that your mobile phone and your WordPress site are set to the same time zone. If you get the message that the Google Authentication verification code you're using is invalid or expired, you need to delete the plugin and then go to your WordPress Dashboard to make sure that the time zone is set to the same time zone that your mobile or tablet device uses. See Book 3, Chapter 2 for information on time settings for your WordPress site.

Activating multifactor authentication

The following steps show you how the multifactor authentication is implemented on your site:

1. **Log out of your WordPress Dashboard.**

   The WordPress login form displays in your browser window.

2. **Type your username in the Username or Email field.**
3. **Type your password in the Password field.**
4. **Click the Log In button.**

   A new page loads with a form that asks you to enter your token, as shown in Figure 5-4.

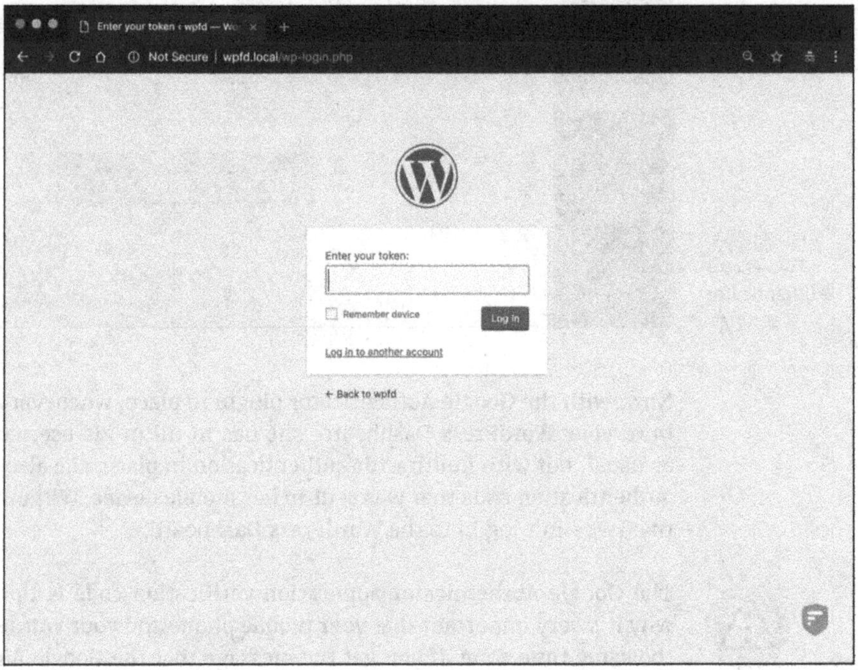

FIGURE 5-4: The WordPress login form with Google Authenticator.

5. **Open the Google Authenticator application on your mobile or tablet device, and locate the six-digit code assigned to your blog.**

   This six-digit code refreshes every 60 seconds. If you have more than one blog that uses the application, find the code that corresponds with your site.

6. **Type the six-digit code in the Token field.**

7. **Click the Log In button.**

   You're successfully logged in to your WordPress Dashboard via a two-factor authentication method.

TIP

If you don't have access to a mobile device, WordPress has a couple of plugins you can use, including these two:

- **NoPassword:** `https://wordpress.org/plugins/nopassword-free-muti-factor-authentication`
- **Loginizer:** `https://wordpress.org/plugins/loginizer`

Limiting login attempts

Limiting the number of times a user can attempt to log in to your WordPress site helps reduce the risk of brute-force attack. A *brute-force attack* happens when an attacker tries to gain access by guessing your username and password through the process of cycling through combinations.

To help protect against brute-force attacks, you want to limit the number of times any user can try to log in to your website. You can accomplish this task in WordPress easily enough by using the Limit Login Attempts plugin. You can find this plugin in the WordPress Plugin list: `https://wordpress.org/plugins/wp-limit-login-attempts/`. See Book 7, Chapters 1 and 2 for information on finding, installing, and activating it.

When you have the Limit Login Attempts plugin installed, follow these steps to configure the settings:

1. **Click the WP Limit Login link on the Settings menu of your Dashboard.**

   The Limit Login Attempts Settings page opens in your Dashboard, as shown in Figure 5-5.

2. **Select a configuration option.**

   You can change the value of any of the following four options if you upgrade to the premium version (at a cost of $19 per year). The defaults should be sufficient for you, however.

   - *Number of Login Attempts:* This setting is the maximum number of times users are allowed to retry failed logins. Default is 5.
   - *Lockdown Time in Minutes:* This setting is the amount of time a user is prevented from retrying a login after she reaches the maximum allowed number. Default is 10.

- *Number of Attempts for Captcha:* This option sets the number of time a user can attempt to enter the captcha. Default is 3.
- *Enable Captcha:* Captcha is enabled by default.

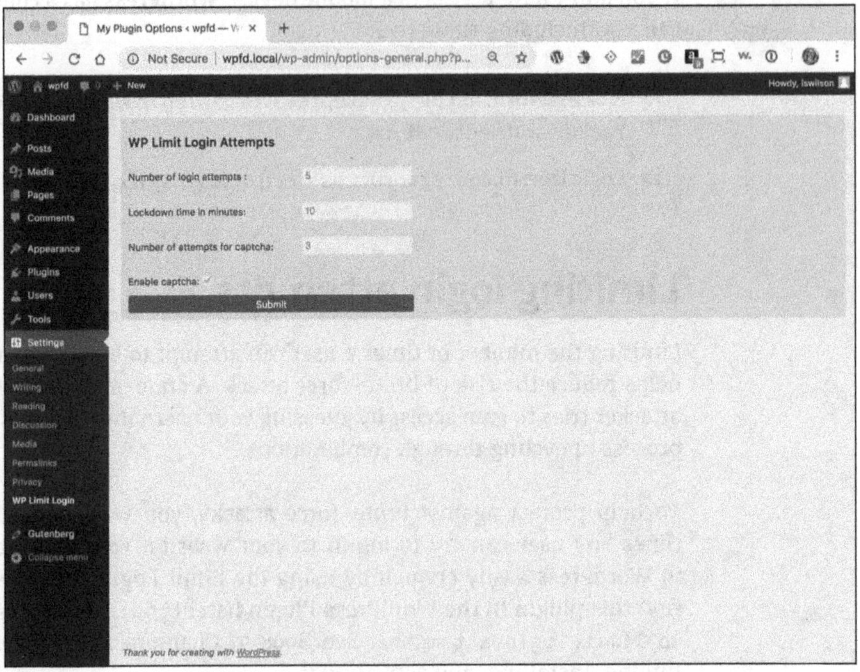

FIGURE 5-5: WP Limit Login Attempts Setting screen.

TIP

If you're managing your own server, monitor your login attempts to see whether a malicious attacker is making repeated attempts to obtain passwords and usernames. Keep track of those IP addresses from your logs, and if an address repeatedly attempts to log in, add it to your server firewall to prevent it from burdening your server access points.

Disabling theme and plugin editors

By default, when you log in to the WordPress Dashboard, you can edit any theme and plugin file by using the Theme Editor (click the Appearance link on the Editor menu) and the Plugin Editor (click the Plugins link on the Editor menu). The idea makes a lot of sense; it gives you the ability to do everything within your Admin panel without having to worry about logging in to your server via SFTP to edit files.

Unfortunately, having the theme and plugin editors available also gives any attacker who gains access to the Dashboard full rights to modify any theme or plugin file, which is very dangerous, because even one line of malware code embedded within any file can grant an attacker remote access to your environment without ever having to touch your Dashboard.

You can prevent this situation by disabling the Theme Editor and Plugin Editor. To do so, add a WordPress constant (or rule) to the WordPress configuration file (wp-config.php), which is in the installation folder on your web server. Download the wp-config.php via SFTP (see Book 2, Chapter 2), and open the file in a text editor, such as Notepad (PC) or TextEdit (Mac). Look for the following line of code:

```
define( 'DB_COLLAT', '' );
```

Add the following constant (rule) on the line directly below the preceding line:

```
define( 'DISALLOW_FILE_EDIT',true );
```

Although adding this constant won't prevent an attack, it helps reduce the impact of a compromise. You can find information about other constants you can add to the wp-config.php file at https://codex.wordpress.org/Editing_wp-config.php.

TIP

You can also disable the automatic updates in WordPress (the feature in place that automatically updates WordPress core and WordPress plugins) to include the administrator. If you do, you'd have to do everything manually, via SFTP. To do disable automatic updates, use the following constant in your wp-config.php file:

```
define( 'DISALLOW_FILE_MODS',true );
```

Filtering by IP address

Another option is to limit access to the Dashboard to specific IP addresses. This method is also referred to as *whitelisting* (allowing) access, which complements *blacklisting* (disallowing) solutions.

Everything that touches the Internet — such as your computer, a website, or a server network — has an IP address. An IP is like your home address; it uniquely identifies you so that the Internet knows where your computer is located. An example of an IP is 12.345.67.89 — a series of numbers that uniquely identifies the physical location of a computer or network.

You can edit the .htaccess file on your web server so that only IPs that you approve can access your Admin Dashboard, thereby blocking everyone else from having Dashboard access.

The lines of code that define the access rules get added to the .htaccess file located on your web server where WordPress is installed, in a folder called /wp-admin. Download that file to your computer via SFTP; open it with a text editor, such as Notepad (PC) or TextEdit (Mac); and add the following lines to it:

```
order allow,deny
deny from all
allow from 12.345.67.89
```

In this example, the order defines what comes first. An IP that follows the allow rules is given access; any IP that doesn't follow the allow rules is denied access. In this example, only the IP 12.345.67.89 can access the Admin Dashboard; all other IPs are denied.

TIP

If the /wp-admin folder in your WordPress installation doesn't contain a file called .htaccess, you can easily create one using your SFTP program. Open the /wp-admin folder, right-click with your mouse in the SFTP program window to open a shortcut menu, and choose New File. Give that new file the name .htaccess, and make sure to add the new rules from "Disabling theme and plugin editors" earlier in this chapter.

Limiting access via IP carries the following potential negatives:

- **This technique works only with static IP addresses.** A dynamic IP changes constantly. You have ways to make this technique work with dynamic IPs, but those methods are beyond the scope of this chapter.
- **The ability to use .htaccess is highly dependent on a web server that's running Apache.** This technique won't do you any good if your web server is Windows-based or IIS, or if you're using the latest NGINX web server.
- **Your Apache web server needs to be configured to allow directives to be defined by .htaccess files.** Ask your web host about configuration.

Killing PHP execution

For most backdoor intrusion attempts to function, a PHP file has to be executed. The term *backdoor* describes ways of obtaining access to a web server through means that bypass regular authentication methods, such as file injections through programming languages such as PHP and JavaScript. Disabling PHP execution prevents an attack or compromise from taking place because PHP can't executed at all.

To disable PHP execution, add four lines of code to the `.htaccess` file on your web server:

```
<Files *.php>
Order allow,deny
Deny from all
</Files>
```

By default, you have an `.htaccess` file in the WordPress directory on your web server. You can also create an `.htaccess` file in other folders — particularly the folders in which you want to disable PHP execution.

To disable PHP execution for maximum security, create an `.htaccess` file with those four lines of code in the following folders in your WordPress installation:

- `/wp-includes`
- `/wp-content/uploads`
- `/wp-content`

This WordPress installation directory (the directory WordPress is installed in) is important because it's the only directory that has to be writeable for WordPress to work. If an image is uploaded with a modified header, or if a PHP file is uploaded and PHP execution is allowed, an attacker could exploit this weakness to create havoc in your environment. When PHP execution is disabled, however, an attacker is unable to create any havoc.

IN THIS CHAPTER

» Finding upgrades notifications

» Backing up your database before upgrading

» Deactivating plugins

» Upgrading from the dashboard

» Upgrading manually

Chapter 6
Updating WordPress

As I discuss in Book 1, Chapter 3, the schedule of WordPress development and release cycles shows you that WordPress releases a new version (upgrade) of its platform roughly once every 120 days (or every 4 months). That chapter also explains why you need to keep your WordPress software up to date by using the most recent version — mostly for security purposes, but also to make sure you're taking advantage of all the latest features the WordPress developers pack within every major new release.

In this chapter, you discover the WordPress upgrade notification system and find out what to do when WordPress notifies you that a new version is available. This chapter also covers the best practices for upgrading the WordPress platform on your site to ensure the best possible outcome (that is, how not to break your website after a WordPress upgrade).

REMEMBER

The upgrade process occurs on a regular basis — at least three or four times per year. For some users, this process is a frustrating reality of using WordPress. This active development environment, however, is part of what makes WordPress the most popular platform available. Because WordPress is always adding great new features and functions to the platform, upgrading always ensures that you're on top of the game and using the latest tools and features.

Getting Notified of an Available Update

After you install WordPress and log in for the first time, you can see the version number on the WordPress Dashboard, as shown in Figure 6-1. (Note that I've scrolled down in the figure — you see the version number in the bottom-right corner.) Therefore, if anyone asks what version you're using, you know exactly where to look to find out.

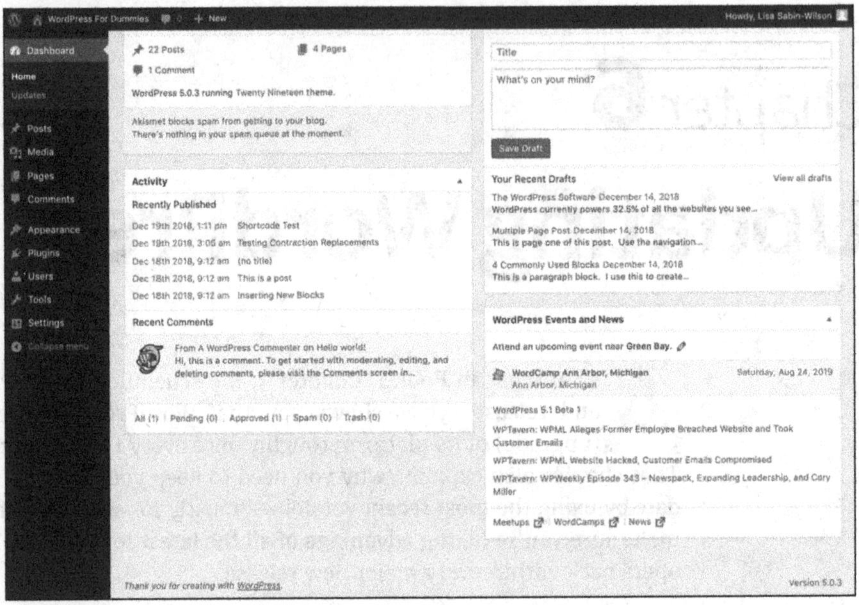

FIGURE 6-1: The WordPress version displayed in the Dashboard.

Suppose that you have WordPress installed, and you've been happily publishing content to your website with it for several weeks, maybe even months. Then one day, you log in to your Dashboard and see a message at the top of your screen you've never seen before: `WordPress X.X.X is available! Please update now.` Figure 6-2 displays the update message on the Dashboard, as well as a small bubble next to the Dashboard Updates links that indicate how many updates are available.

Both the message at the top of the page and the notification bubble on the Dashboard menu are visual indicators that you're using an outdated version of WordPress and that you can (and need to) upgrade the software.

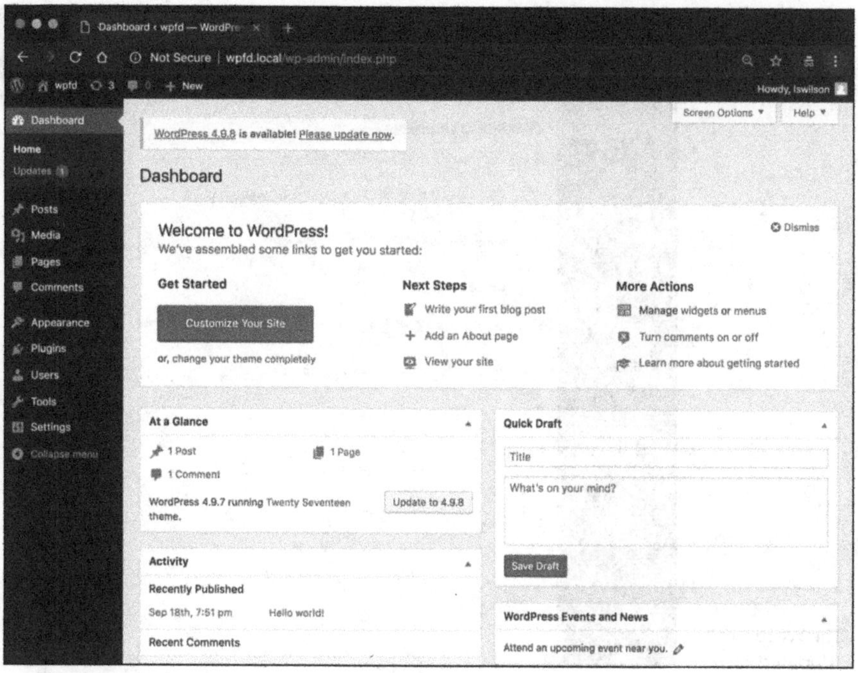

FIGURE 6-2: A Dashboard notification of an available WordPress upgrade.

The message at the top of your Dashboard includes two links that you can click for more information. (Refer to Figure 6-2.) The first is a link called `WordPress 4.9.8`. Clicking this link takes you to the WordPress Codex page titled Version 4.9.8, which is filled with information about the version upgrade, including

- Installation/upgrade information
- Summary of the development cycle for this version
- List of files that have been revised

The second link, `Please update now`, takes you to another page of the WordPress Dashboard: the WordPress Updates page, shown in Figure 6-3.

At the top of the WordPress Updates page is another important message for you:

```
Important: before updating, please back up your database and
files. For help with updates, visit the Updating WordPress Codex
page.
```

Both links in the message take you to pages in the WordPress Codex that contain helpful information on creating backups and updating WordPress.

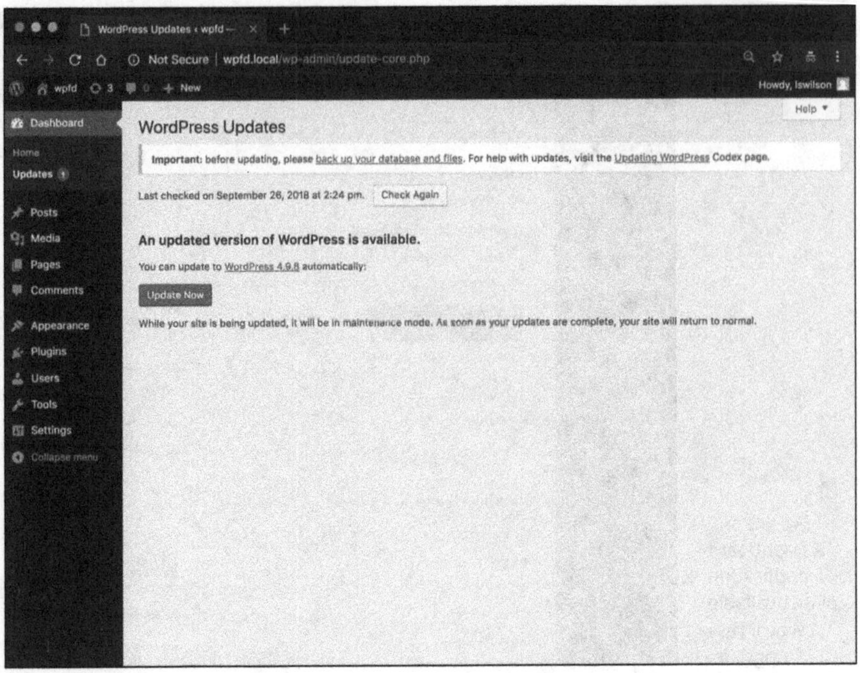

FIGURE 6-3: The WordPress Updates page.

TIP

Book 2, Chapter 7 has extensive information on how to back up your WordPress website, content, and files.

The WordPress Updates page tells you that an updated version of WordPress is available. You can update in two ways:

- Automatically, by using the built-in WordPress updater
- Manually, by downloading the files and installing them on your server

These ways to update are discussed later in the chapter.

Backing Up Your Database

Before upgrading your WordPress software installation, make sure that you back up your database. This step isn't required, of course, but it's a smart step to take to safeguard your website and ensure that you have a complete copy of your website data in the event that your upgrade goes wrong.

The best way to back up your database is to use the MySQL administration interface provided to you by your web hosting provider. (Book 2, Chapter 4 takes you through the steps of creating a new database by using the phpMyAdmin interface.)

TIP

cPanel is a web hosting interface, provided by many web hosts as a web hosting account management tool, that contains phpMyAdmin as the preferred tool for managing and administering databases. Not all web hosts use cPanel or phpMyAdmin, however, so if yours doesn't, you need to consult the user documentation for the tools that your web host provides. The instructions in this chapter use cPanel and phpMyAdmin.

Follow these steps to create a database backup by using the phpMyAdmin interface:

1. **Log in to the cPanel for your hosting account.**

   Typically, you browse to `http://`*`yourdomain.com`*`/cpanel` to bring up the login screen for your cPanel. Enter your specific hosting account username and password in the login fields, and click OK to log in.

2. **Click the phpMyAdmin icon.**

   The phpMyAdmin interface opens and displays your database.

3. **Click the name of the database that you want to back up.**

   If you have more than one database in your account, the left-side menu in phpMyAdmin displays the names of all of them. Click the one you want to back up; the database loads in the main interface window.

4. **Click the Export tab at the top of the screen.**

   The page refreshes and displays the backup utility page.

5. **Choose the SQL option from the Format drop-down menu.**
6. **Click the Go button.**

   A pop-up window appears, allowing you to select a location on your computer to store the database backup file.

7. **Click the Save button to download the backup file and save it to your computer.**

TIP

Book 2, Chapter 7 contains in-depth information on making a complete backup of your website, including all your files, plugins, themes, and images. For the purposes of upgrading, a database backup is sufficient, but be sure to check out that chapter for valuable information on extensive backups, including how to restore a database backup in case you ever need to go through that process.

TIP

Almost all web hosting companies have a built-in backup feature and backup your website on a daily basis, as well as on demand. You don't always have to go into your database to back up your data if your hosting provider has a reliable backup tool that's ready for you to use. Also, a few WordPress plugins help you get the backup job done, including Jetpack by WordPress.com (`https://jetpack.com`) and All-in-One WP Migration (`https://wordpress.org/plugins/all-in-one-wp-migration`).

Updating WordPress Automatically

WordPress provides an easy, quick, and reliable method to update the core software from within your Dashboard. I recommend using this option whenever possible to make sure that you're accurately updating the WordPress software.

To update WordPress automatically, follow these steps:

1. **Back up your WordPress website.**

   REMEMBER

   Backing up your website before updating is an important step in case something goes wrong with the upgrade. Give yourself some peace of mind by knowing that you have a full copy of your website that can be restored, if needed. My advice is not to skip this step under any circumstances. If you're not sure how to back up, back up (pun intended!) to the preceding section.

2. **Deactivate all plugins.**

   This step prevents any plugin conflicts caused by the upgraded version of WordPress from affecting the upgrade process, and it ensures that your website won't break after the upgrade is completed. Find more information on working with and managing plugins in Book 7. For the purposes of this step, you can deactivate plugins by following these steps:

   (a) *On the Dashboard, hover your pointer over Plugins on the navigation menu, and click the Installed Plugins link. The Plugins page appears.*

   (b) *Select all plugins by selecting the check box to the left of the plugin names listed on that page. (See Figure 6-4.)*

   (c) *From the drop-down list at the top, choose Deactivate.*

   (d) *Click the Apply button.*

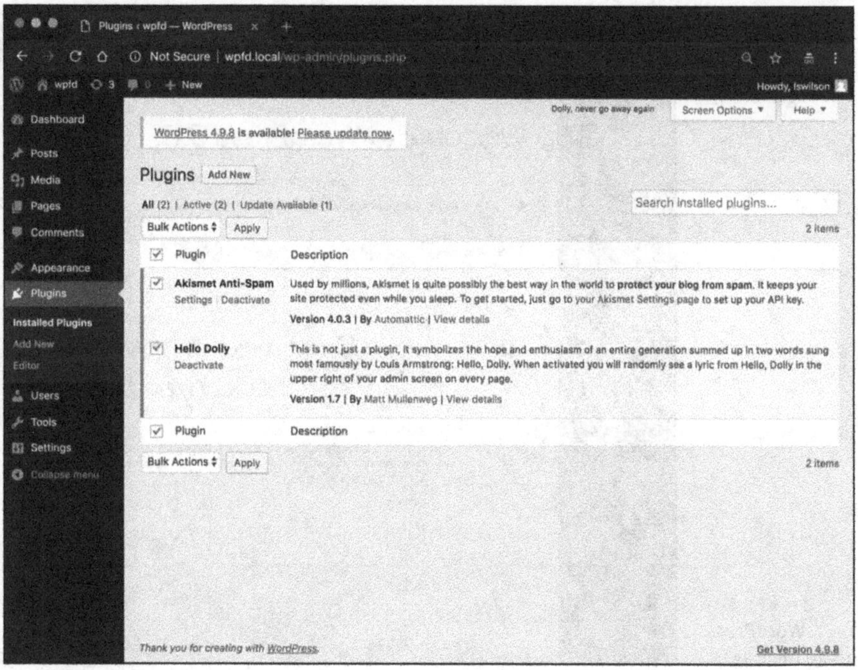

FIGURE 6-4: The Plugins page with all plugins selected, ready to deactivate.

3. **Choose Dashboard ⇨ Updates.**

   The WordPress Updates page appears. (Refer to Figure 6-3.)

4. **Click the Update Automatically button.**

   The Update WordPress page appears with a series of messages (as shown in Figure 6-5).

5. **Wait for the Dashboard to refresh, or click the link in the last update message to visit the main Dashboard screen.**

   The Dashboard page appears in your web browser. Notice that both the update alert message at the top of the site and the notification bubble on the Dashboard menu are no longer visible. Your WordPress installation is using the latest version of WordPress.

After you complete the WordPress software upgrade, you can revisit the Plugins page and reactivate the plugins you deactivated in step 2 of the preceding list. (Refer to Figure 6-4.)

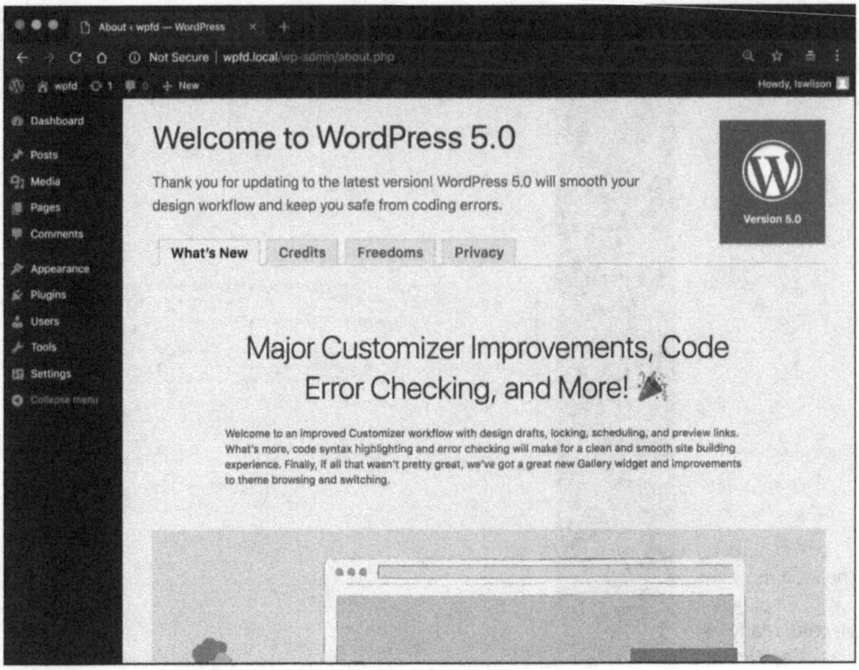

FIGURE 6-5: WordPress update messages.

Updating WordPress Manually

The second, less-used method of upgrading WordPress is the manual method. The method is less used mainly because the automatic method, discussed in the preceding section, is so quick and easy to accomplish. In certain circumstances, however — probably related to the inability of your hosting environment to accommodate the automatic method — you have to upgrade WordPress manually.

To upgrade WordPress manually, follow these steps:

1. **Back up your WordPress website, and deactivate all plugins.**

   Refer to steps 1 and 2 of "Upgrading WordPress Automatically" earlier in this chapter.

2. **Navigate to the Get WordPress page on the WordPress website (`https://wordpress.org/download`).**

3. **Click the Download button.**

   A dialog box opens that allows you to save the `.zip` file of the latest WordPress download package to your computer, as shown in Figure 6-6.

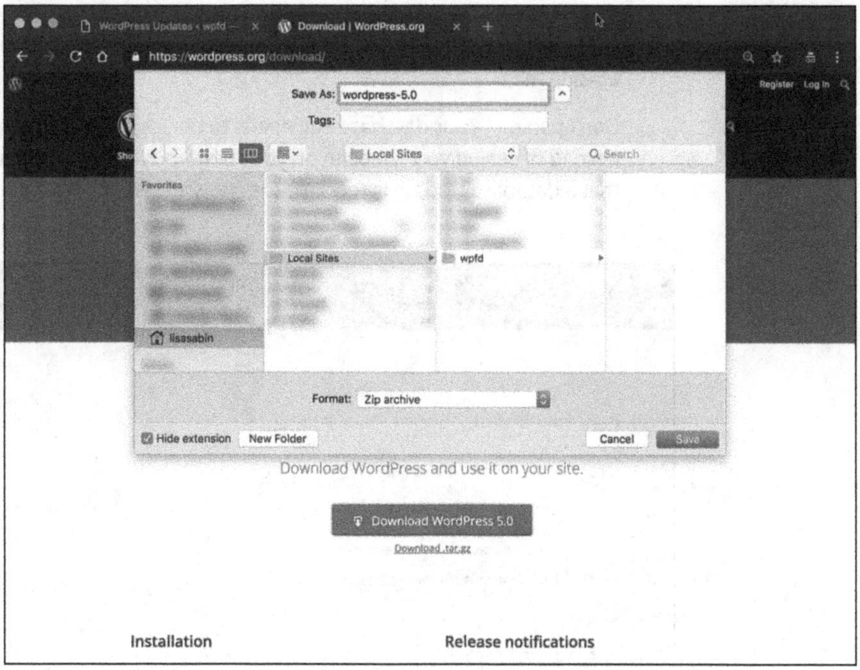

FIGURE 6-6: Downloading the WordPress files to your computer.

4. **Select a location to store the download package, and click Save.**

   The `.zip` file downloads to your selected location on your computer.

5. **Browse to the `.zip` file on your computer.**

6. **Unzip the file.**

   Use a program like WinZip (`https://www.winzip.com/`).

7. **Connect to your web server via SFTP.**

   See Book 2, Chapter 2 for details on using SFTP.

8. **Delete all the files and folders in your existing WordPress installation directory *except* the following:**

   - `/wp-content` folder (contains all your themes, plugins, and media uploads)
   - `.htaccess`
   - `wp-config.php`

9. **Upload the contents of the `/wordpress` folder to your web server — not the folder itself.**

   Most SFTP client software lets you select all the files to drag and drop them to your web server. Other programs have you highlight the files and click a Transfer button.

10. **Navigate to the following URL on your website: `http://`*`yourdomain.com`*`/wp-admin`.**

Don't panic — your database still needs to be upgraded to the latest version, so instead of seeing your website on your domain, you see a message telling you that a database update is required, as shown in Figure 6-7.

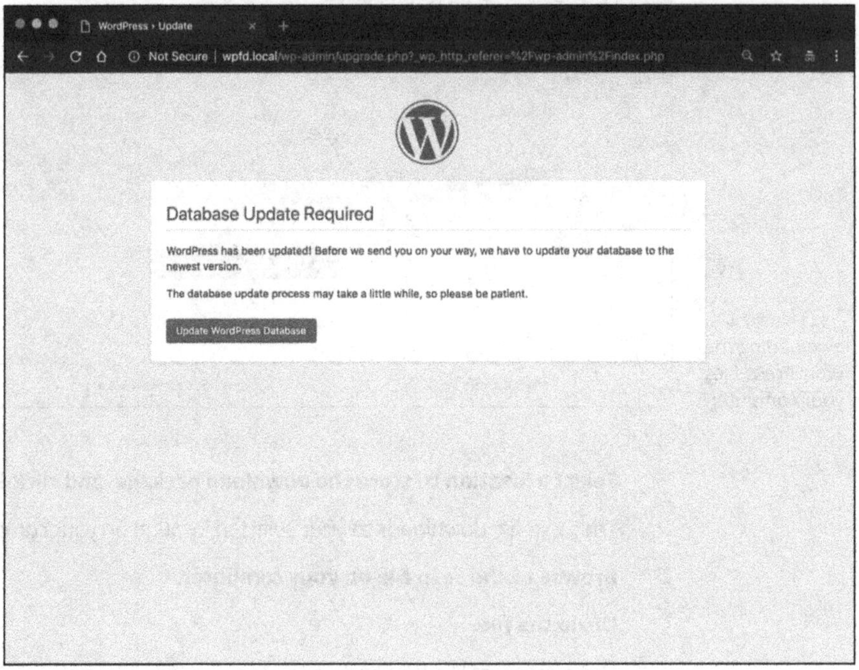

FIGURE 6-7: Click the button to update your WordPress database.

11. **Click the Update WordPress Database button.**

WordPress initiates the upgrade of the MySQL database associated with your website. When the database upgrade is complete, the page refreshes and displays a message that the process has finished.

12. **Click the Continue button.**

Your browser loads the WordPress login page. The upgrade is complete, and you can continue using WordPress with the upgraded features.

TIP

If you're uncomfortable with performing administrative tasks, such as upgrading and creating database backups, you can hire someone to perform these tasks for you — either an employee of your company (if you run a business) or a WordPress consultant who's skilled in the practice of performing these tasks. Book 1, Chapter 4 includes a list of experienced consultants who can lend a hand.

IN THIS CHAPTER

» Moving to WordPress from a different platform

» Handling the database backup management

» Backing up plugins and themes

» Storing images and media files

» Exporting data from WordPress

» Using plugins to make backups and moving easier

Chapter 7
Backing Up, Packing Up, and Moving to a New Host

As a WordPress website owner, you may need to move your site to a different home on the web, either to a new web host or to a different account on your current hosting account. Or maybe you're an owner who needs to move your site right now.

This chapter covers the best way to migrate a site that exists within a different platform (such as Movable Type or TypePad) to WordPress. This chapter also takes you through how to back up your WordPress files, data, and content and then move them to a new hosting provider or a different domain.

Migrating Your Existing Site to WordPress

So you have a site on a different content management system (CMS) and want to move your site to WordPress? This chapter helps you accomplish just that. WordPress makes it relatively easy to pack up your data and archives from one platform and move to a new WordPress site.

By default, WordPress lets you move your site from such platforms as Blogger, TypePad, and Movable Type. It also gives you a nifty way to migrate from any platform via RSS feeds, as long as the platform you're importing from has an RSS feed available. Some platforms, such as Medium (`https://medium.com`), have some limitations on RSS feed availability, so be sure to check with your platform provider. In this chapter, you discover how to prepare your site for migration and how to move from the specific platforms for which WordPress provides importer plugins.

Movin' on up

TECHNICAL STUFF

For each platform, the WordPress.org platform provides a quick and easy way to install plugins so that you can import and use your content right away. The importers are packaged in a plugin format because most people use an importer just once, and some people don't use the importer tools at all. The plugins are there for you to use if you need them. WordPress.com, on the other hand, has the importers built into the software. Note the differences for the version you're using.

Website owners have a variety of reasons to migrate from one system to WordPress:

- **Simple curiosity:** WordPress currently powers more than 32% of all websites on the Internet today, people are naturally curious to check out software that is popular for generating content.
- **More control of your website:** This reason applies particularly to those who have a site on Blogger, TypePad, or any other hosted service. Hosted programs limit what you can do, create, and mess with. When it comes to plugins, add-ons, and theme creation, hosting a WordPress site on your own web server wins hands down. In addition, you have complete control of your data, archives, and backup capability when you host your site on your own server.
- **Ease of use:** Many people find the WordPress interface easier to use, more understandable, and a great deal more user-friendly than many of the other publishing platforms available today.

REMEMBER

In the WordPress software, the importers are added to the installation as plugins. The importer plugins included in this chapter are the plugins packaged within the WordPress software; you can also find them by searching the Plugins page at `https://wordpress.org/plugins/tags/importer`. You can import content from several other platforms by installing other plugins that aren't available from the official WordPress Plugin page, but you may have to do an Internet search to find them.

Preparing for the big move

Depending on the size of your site (that is, how many posts and comments you have), the migration process can take as little as 5 minutes in some cases or more than 30 minutes in others. As with any major change or update you make, no matter where your site is hosted, the very first thing you need to do is create a backup of your site. You should back up the following:

- **Archives:** Posts, comments, and trackbacks
- **Template:** Template and image files
- **Plugins:** Plugin files (do this by transferring the `/wp-content/plugins` folder from your hosting server to your local computer via SFTP)
- **Links:** Any links, banners, badges, and elements you have on your current site
- **Media:** Any media files (images, video, audio, or documents) you use on your site

Table 7-1 gives you a few tips on creating the export data for your site in a few major publishing platforms. *Note:* This table assumes that you're logged in to your site software.

TABLE 7-1 Backing Up Your Website Data on Major Platforms

Publishing Platform	Backup Information
Movable Type	Click the Import/Export button on the menu of your Movable Type Dashboard and then click the Export Entries From link. When the page stops loading, save it on your computer as a `.txt` file.
TypePad	Click the name of the site you want to export and then click the Import/Export link on the Overview menu. Click the Export link at the bottom of the Import/Export page. When the page stops loading, save it on your computer as a `.txt` file.
Blogger	Back up your template by copying the text of your template to a text editor, such as Notepad. Save it on your computer as a `.txt` file.
LiveJournal	Browse to `https://livejournal.com/export.bml`, and enter your information; choose XML as the format. Save this file on your computer.

(continued)

TABLE 7-1 *(continued)*

Publishing Platform	Backup Information
Tumblr	Browse to `https://www.tumblr.com/oauth/apps`, and follow the directions there to create a Tumblr app. When you're done, copy the OAuth Consumer Key and Secret Key, and paste them into a text file on your computer. Use these keys to connect your WordPress site to your Tumblr account.
WordPress	Choose Tools⇨Export in the Dashboard, choose your options on the Export page, and then click the Download Export File button. Save this file on your computer.
RSS feed	Point your browser to the URL of the RSS feed you want to import. Wait until it loads fully. (You may need to set your feed to display all posts.) View the source code of the page, copy and paste that source code into a `.txt` file, and save the file on your computer.

TIP

The WordPress import script allows for a maximum file size of 128MB. If you get an "out of memory" error, try dividing the import file into pieces and uploading them separately. The import script is smart enough to ignore duplicate entries, so if you need to run the script a few times to get it to take everything, you can do so without worrying about duplicating your content. (You could also attempt to temporarily increase your PHP memory limit by making a quick edit of the `wp-config.php` file; for more information on this technique, see Book 2, Chapters 3 and 4.)

Converting templates

Every program has a unique way of delivering content and data to your site. Template tags vary from program to program; no two tags are the same. Also, each template file requires conversion if you want to use *your* template with your new WordPress site. In such a case, you have two options:

- **Convert the template yourself.** To accomplish this task, you need to know WordPress template tags and HTML. If you have a template that you're using on another platform and want to convert it for use with WordPress, you need to swap the original platform tags for WordPress tags. The information provided in Book 6 gives you the rundown on working with themes, as well as basic WordPress template tags; you may find that information useful if you plan to attempt a template conversion yourself.
- **Hire an experienced WordPress consultant to do the conversion for you.** See Book 1, Chapter 4 for a list of WordPress consultants.

To use your own template, make sure that you've saved *all* the template files, the images, and the stylesheet from your previous site setup. You need them to convert the template(s) for use in WordPress.

REMEMBER

Thousands of free themes are available for use with WordPress, so it may be a lot easier to abandon the template you're currently working with and find a free WordPress template that you like. If you paid to have a custom design done for your site, contact the designer of your theme, and hire him or her to perform the template conversion for you. Alternatively, you can hire several WordPress consultants to perform the conversion for you — including yours truly.

Moving your site to WordPress

You've packed all your stuff, and you have your new place prepared. Moving day has arrived!

This section takes you through the steps for moving your site from one platform to WordPress. This section assumes that you already have the WordPress software installed and configured on your own domain.

Find the import function that you need by following these steps:

1. **In the Dashboard, choose Tools⇨Import.**

   The Import page appears, listing blogging platforms such as Blogger and Movable Type from which you can import content. (See Figure 7-1.)

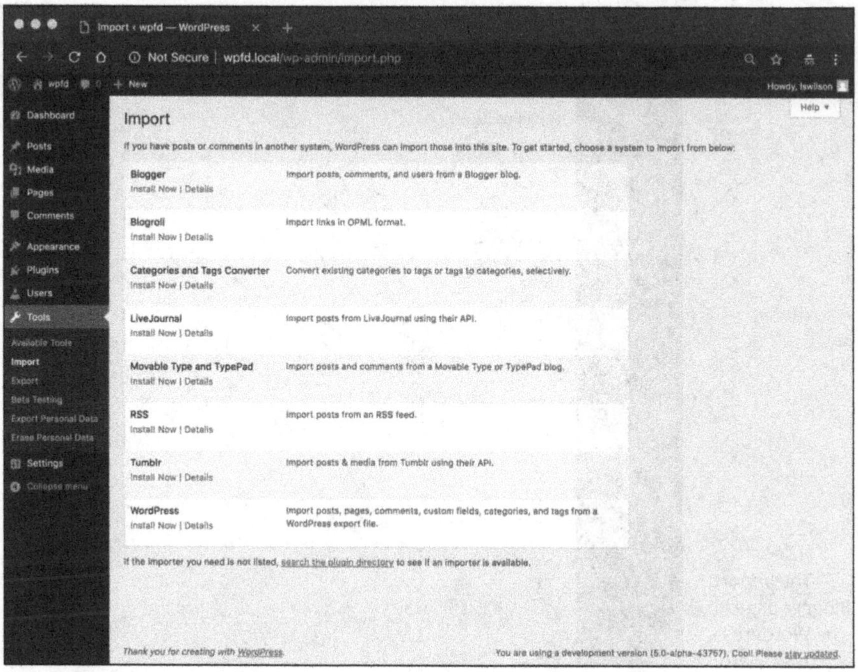

FIGURE 7-1: The Import feature of the (self-hosted) WordPress.org Dashboard.

2. **Find the publishing platform you're working with.**
3. **Click the Install Now link to install the importer plugin and begin using it.**

The following sections provide some import directions for a few of the most popular platforms (other than WordPress, that is). Each platform has its own content export methods, so be sure to check the documentation for the platform you're using.

Importing from Blogger

Blogger is the blogging application owned by Google.

To begin the import process, first complete the steps in "Moving your site to WordPress," earlier in this chapter. Then follow these steps:

1. **Click the Install Now link below the Blogger heading on the Import page, and install the plugin for importing from Blogger.**
2. **Click the Run Importer link.**

   The Import Blogger page loads, with instructions for importing your file, as shown in Figure 7-2.

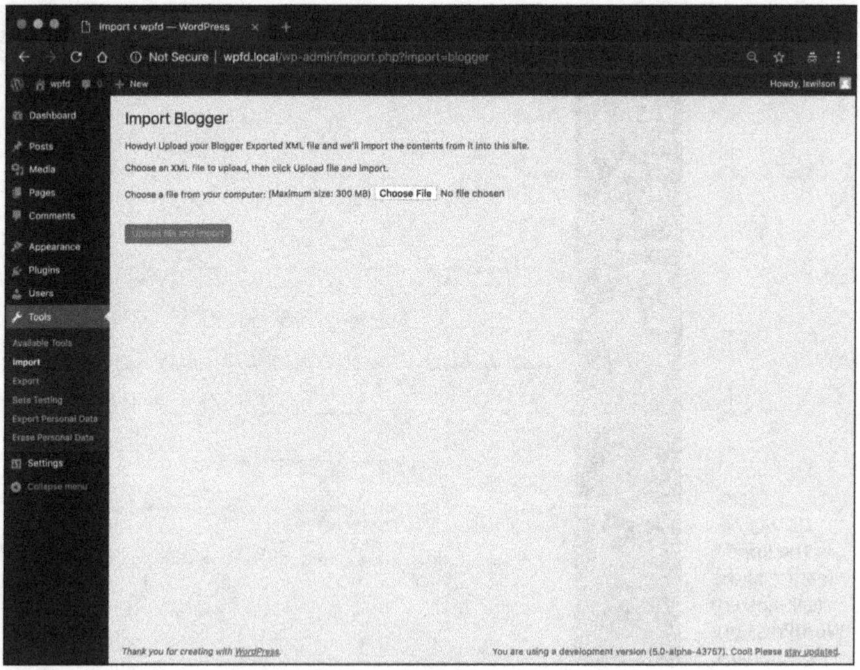

FIGURE 7-2: The Import Blogger page in the WordPress Dashboard.

3. **Log in to your Blogger account.**
4. **In your Blogger account, click the blog you'd like to import.**
5. **In your Blogger account, choose Settings➪Other.**

   This link is on the left menu.
6. **In your Blogger account, choose Back Up Content➪Save to Your Computer.**

   Save the `.xml` file to your computer.
7. **In your WordPress Dashboard, on the Import Blogger page, click the Choose File button to upload the Blogger XML file.**
8. **Click the Upload and Import button.**

   This step uploads the file. The screen refreshes to the Import Blogger → Assign Authors screen.
9. **Click the Set Authors button to assign the authors to the posts.**

   The Blogger username appears on the left side of the page; a drop-down menu on the right side of the page displays the WordPress login name.
10. **Assign authors by choosing them from the drop-down menu.**

    If you have only one author on each blog, the process is especially easy: Use the drop-down menu on the right to assign the WordPress login to your Blogger username. If you have multiple authors on both blogs, each Blogger username is listed on the left side with a drop-down menu to the right of each username. Choose a WordPress login for each Blogger username to make the author assignments.
11. **Click Save Changes.**

    You're done!

Importing from LiveJournal

Both WordPress.com and WordPress.org offer an import script for LiveJournal users, and the process of importing from LiveJournal to WordPress is the same for each platform.

To export your site content from LiveJournal, log in to your LiveJournal site and then type `https://www.livejournal.com/export.bml` in your browser's address bar.

LiveJournal lets you export the XML files by month, so if you have a site with several months' worth of posts, be prepared to be at this process for a while. First, you have to export the entries one month at a time; then you have to import them into WordPress — yep, you guessed it — one month at a time.

TIP

To speed the process a little, you can save all the exported XML LiveJournal files in one text document by copying and pasting each month's XML file into one plain-text file (created in a text editor such as Notepad, for PC, or TextEdit on a Mac), thereby creating one long XML file with all the posts from your LiveJournal blog. Then you can save the file as an XML file to prepare it for import into your WordPress site.

After you export the XML file from LiveJournal, return to the Import page of your WordPress Dashboard, and follow these steps:

1. **Click the Install Now link below the LiveJournal heading, and install the plugin for installing from LiveJournal.**
2. **Click the Run Importer link.**

   The Import LiveJournal page loads, with instructions for importing your file, as shown in Figure 7-3.

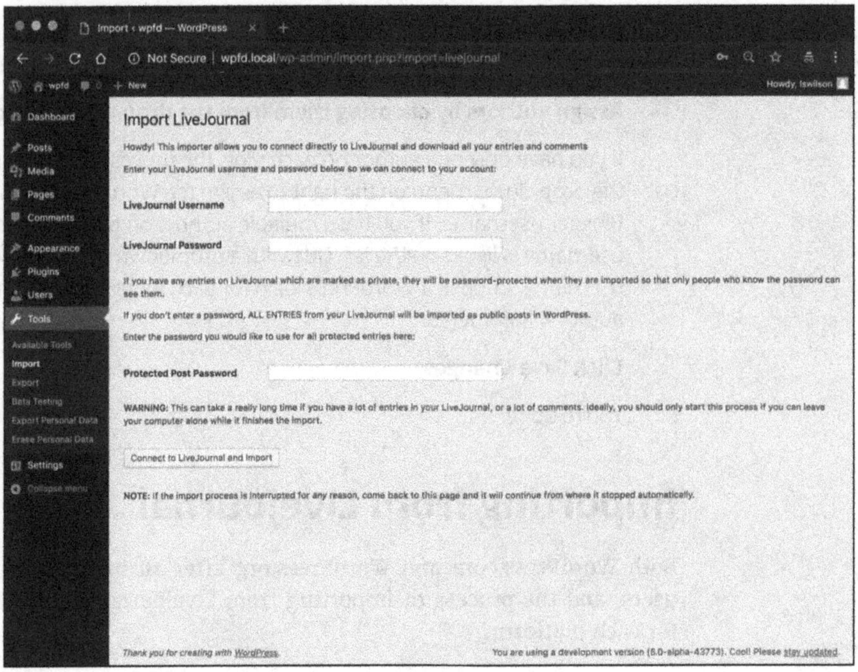

FIGURE 7-3: The Import LiveJournal page in the WordPress Dashboard.

3. **In the LiveJournal Username field, type the username for your LiveJournal account.**
4. **In the LiveJournal Password field, type the password for your LiveJournal account.**

5. **In the Protected Post Password field, enter the password you want to use for all protected entries in your LiveJournal account.**

   WARNING

   If you don't complete this step, every entry you import into WordPress will be viewable by anyone. Be sure to complete this step if any of your entries in your LiveJournal account is password-protected (or private).

6. **Click the Connect to LiveJournal and Import button.**

   This step connects your WordPress site to your LiveJournal account and automatically imports all entries from your LiveJournal into your WordPress installation. If your LiveJournal site has a lot of entries, this process could take a long time, so be patient.

Importing from Movable Type and TypePad

Six Apart created both Movable Type and TypePad. These two platforms run on essentially the same code base, so the import/export procedure is the same for both. Refer to Table 7-1, earlier in this chapter, for details on how to run the export process in both Movable Type and TypePad. This import script moves all your site posts, comments, and trackbacks to your WordPress website.

Go to the Import page of your WordPress Dashboard by following steps 1 and 2 in the "Moving your site to WordPress" section, earlier in this chapter. Then follow these steps:

1. **Click the Install Now link below the Movable Type and TypePad heading, and install the plugin for importing from Movable Type and TypePad.**
2. **Click the Run Importer link.**

   The Import Movable Type or TypePad page loads, with instructions for importing your file, as shown in Figure 7-4.

3. **Click the Choose File button.**

   A window opens, listing your files.

4. **Double-click the name of the export file you saved from your Movable Type or TypePad blog.**
5. **Click the Upload File and Import button.**

   Sit back and let the import script do its magic. When the script finishes, it reloads the page with a message confirming that the process is complete.

6. **When the import script finishes, assign users to the posts, matching the Movable Type or TypePad usernames with WordPress usernames.**

   If you have only one author on each blog, this process is easy; you simply assign your WordPress login to the Movable Type or TypePad username by using the drop-down menu. If you have multiple authors on both blogs, match the Movable Type or TypePad usernames with the correct WordPress login names.

7. **Click Save Changes.**

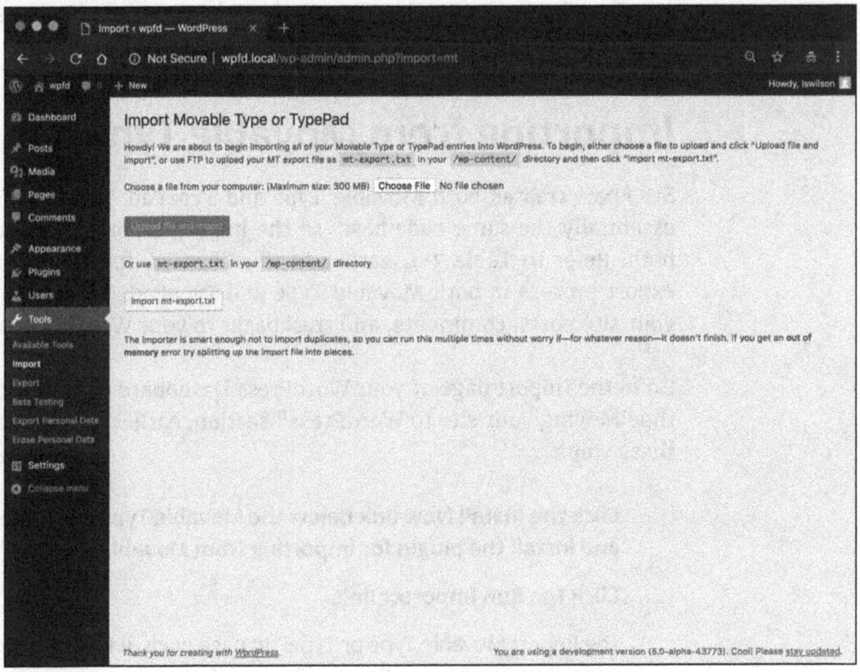

FIGURE 7-4: The Import Movable Type or TypePad page on the WordPress Dashboard.

Importing from Tumblr

With the Tumblr import script for WordPress, it's easy to import the content from your Tumblr account to your WordPress blog. To complete the import, follow these steps:

1. **Go to** `https://www.tumblr.com/oauth/apps`.

   The Tumblr login page appears.

2. **Enter your email address and password to log in to your Tumblr account.**

   The Register Your Application page appears.

3. **Complete the Register Your Application form by filling in the following fields:**

   - *Application Name:* Type the name of your WordPress website in the text box.
   - *Application Website:* Type the URL of your WordPress website in the text box.
   - *Default Callback URL:* Type the URL of your WordPress website in the text box.

   Seven text fields are in this form, but you have to fill in these only these three fields; you can leave the rest blank.

4. **Click the Register button.**

   Make sure to select the check box that says `I'm not a robot` to prove that you're human and not a spammer.

   The Applications page refreshes and displays your registered app information at the top.

5. **Copy the OAuth Consumer Key, and paste it into a text file on your computer.**

6. **Copy the Secret Key, and paste it into the same text file where you placed the OAuth Consumer Key in step 5.**

7. **In your Dashboard, choose Tools⇨Import and then click the Tumblr link.**

   The Import Tumblr page of your Dashboard opens.

8. **Insert the OAuth Consumer Key into the indicated text box.**

   Use the OAuth Consumer Key you saved to a text file in step 5.

9. **Insert the Secret Key in the indicated text box.**

   Use the Secret Key you saved to a text file in step 6.

10. **Click the Connect to Tumblr button.**

    The Import Tumblr page appears, with a message instructing you to authorize Tumblr.

11. **Click the Authorize the Application link.**

    The Authorization page on the Tumblr website asks you to authorize your WordPress site access to your Tumblr account.

12. **Click the Allow button.**

    The Import Tumblr page opens in your WordPress Dashboard and displays a list of your sites from Tumblr.

13. Click the Import This Blog button in the Action/Status section.

The content of your Tumblr account is imported into WordPress. Depending on how much content you have on your Tumblr site, this process may take several minutes to complete. Then the Import Tumblr page refreshes with a message telling you that the import is complete.

Importing from WordPress

With the WordPress import script, you can import one WordPress site into another; this is true for both the hosted and self-hosted versions of WordPress. WordPress imports all your posts, comments, custom fields, and categories into your site. Refer to Table 7-1, earlier in this chapter, to find out how to use the export feature to obtain your site data.

When you complete the export, follow these steps:

1. **Click the Install Now link below the WordPress title on the Import page, and install the plugin to import from WordPress.**
2. **Click the Run Importer link.**

   The Import WordPress page loads, with instructions for importing your file, as shown in Figure 7-5.

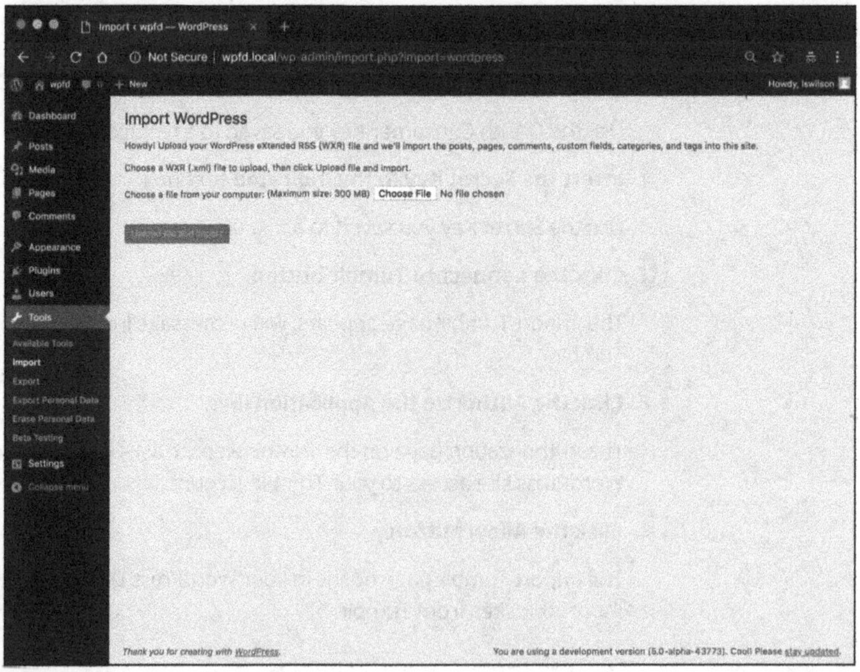

FIGURE 7-5: The Import WordPress page in the WordPress Dashboard.

3. **Click the Choose File button.**

   A window opens, listing the files on your computer.

4. **Double-click the export file you saved earlier from your WordPress blog.**
5. **Click the Upload File and Import button.**

   The import script gets to work, and when it finishes, it reloads the page with a message confirming that the process is complete.

Importing from an RSS feed

If all else fails, or if WordPress doesn't provide an import script that you need for your current site platform, you can import your site data via the RSS feed for the site you want to import. With the RSS import method, you can import posts only; you can't use this method to import comments, trackbacks, categories, or users.

REMEMBER

WordPress.com currently doesn't let you import site data via an RSS feed; this function works only with the self-hosted WordPress.org platform.

Refer to Table 7-1, earlier in this chapter, for the steps to create the file you need to import via RSS. Then follow these steps:

1. **On the Import page of the WordPress Dashboard, click the Install Now link below the RSS heading, and install the plugin to import from an RSS feed.**
2. **Click the Run Importer link.**

   The Import RSS page loads, with instructions for importing your RSS file, as shown in Figure 7-6.

3. **Click the Choose File button on the Import RSS page.**

   A window opens, listing the files on your computer.

4. **Double-click the export file you saved earlier from your RSS feed.**
5. **Click the Upload File and Import button.**

   The import script does its magic and then reloads the page with a message confirming that the process is complete.

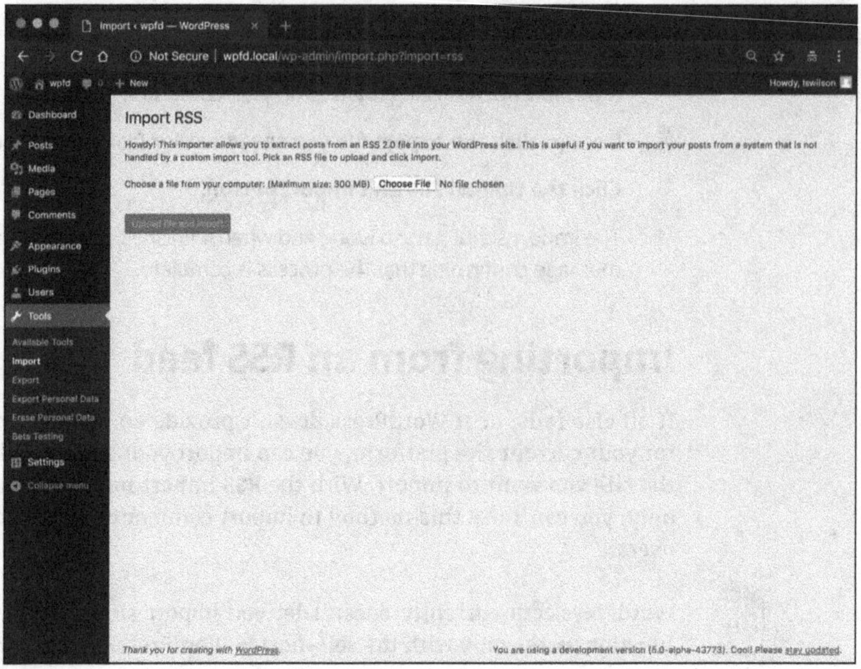

FIGURE 7-6: The Import RSS page of the WordPress Dashboard.

Finding other import resources

The WordPress Codex has a long list of other available scripts, plugins, workarounds, and outright hacks for importing from other platforms. You can find that information at `https://codex.wordpress.org/Importing_Content`.

REMEMBER

Note, however, that volunteers run the WordPress Codex. When you refer to it, be aware that not everything listed in it is necessarily up to date or accurate, including import information (or any other information about running your WordPress site).

Moving Your Website to a Different Host

There may come a time that you decide that you need to switch from your current hosting provider to a new one. There are numerous reasons why you'd have to do this. Perhaps you're unhappy with your current provider and want to move to a new one, or your current provider is going out of business and you're forced to move. Yet transferring an existing website — with all its content, files, and data — from one host to another can seem to be a very daunting task. This section of the chapter should make it easier for you.

You can go about it two ways:

- Backing up your database and downloading essential files manually
- Using a plugin to automate as much of the process as possible

Obviously, using a tool to automate the process for you is the more desirable way to go, but just in case you need to do it manually, in the next section of this chapter, I provide the instructions for both methods.

Creating a backup and moving manually

Book 2, Chapter 6 provides step-by-step instructions for making a backup of your database by using phpMyAdmin. Follow the steps in that chapter, and you'll have a backup of your database with all the recent content you've published to your site — *content* being what you (or someone else) wrote or typed on your site via the WordPress Dashboard, including

- Blog posts, pages, and custom post types
- Categories and tags
- Post and page options, such as excerpts, time and date, custom fields, post categories, post tags, and passwords
- WordPress settings you configured on the Settings menu of the Dashboard
- All widgets that you created and configured
- All plugin options that you configured for the plugins you installed

Other elements of your website aren't stored in the database, so you need to download those elements, via SFTP, from your web server. Following is a list of those elements, with instructions on where to find them and how to download them to your computer:

- **Media files:** Media files are the files you uploaded by using the WordPress media upload feature, including images, videos, audio files, and documents. Media files are located in the `/wp-content/uploads` folder. Connect to your web server via SFTP, and download that folder to your computer.
- **Plugin files:** Although all the plugin settings are stored in the database, the plugin *files* are not. The plugin files are located in the `/wp-content/plugins` folder. Connect to your web server via SFTP, and download that folder to your computer.

» **Theme files:** Widgets and options you've set for your current theme are stored in the database, but the physical theme template files, images, and stylesheets are not. They're stored in the `/wp-content/themes` folder. Connect to your web server via SFTP, and download that folder to your computer.

Moving the database and files to the new host

When you have your database and WordPress files stored safely on your computer, moving them to a new host just involves reversing the process. Follow these steps:

1. **Create a new database in your new hosting account.**

   The steps for creating a database are in Book 2, Chapter 4.

2. **Import your database backup into the new database you just created:**

   (a) Log in to the cPanel for your hosting account.

   (b) Click the phpMyAdmin icon, and click the name of your new database on the left menu.

   (c) Click the Import tab at the top.

   (d) Click the Browse button and select the database backup from your computer.

   (e) Click the Go button. The old database imports into the new.

3. **Install WordPress in your new hosting account.**

   The steps for installing WordPress are in Book 2, Chapter 4.

4. **Edit the `wp-config.php` file to include your new database name, username, password, prefix, and database host.**

   Information on editing the information in the `wp-config.php` file is in Book 2, chapters 3 and 4.

5. **Upload all that you downloaded from the `/wp-content` folder to your new hosting account.**

   Be sure that you upload these files into the `/wp-content` folder in your new hosting account.

6. **Browse to your domain in your web browser.**

   Your website should work, and you can log in to the WordPress Dashboard by using the same username and password as before because that information is stored in the database you imported.

BACKING UP AND MOVING WITH A PLUGIN

A plugin that I use on a regular basis to move a WordPress website from one hosting environment to another is aptly named BackupBuddy. This plugin isn't free or available in the WordPress Plugin Directory; you need to pay for it. But it's worth every single penny because it takes the entire backup and migration process and makes mincemeat out of it. In other words, it's very easy to use, and you can do the job in minutes instead of hours.

You can purchase the BackupBuddy plugin from iThemes at `https://ithemes.com/purchase/backupbuddy`; at this writing, pricing starts at $80 per year. After you've purchased the plugin, you can download and install it (see plugin installation instructions in Book 7). Then follow the instructions given to you in the WordPress Dashboard to make a backup copy of your website and move it to another server.

3

Exploring the WordPress Dashboard

Contents at a Glance

IN THIS CHAPTER

» Logging in to your WordPress Dashboard

» Finding your way around the Dashboard

» Configuring Dashboard modules

» Getting some help

Chapter 1
Logging In and Taking a Look Around

With WordPress successfully installed, you can explore your new publishing software. This chapter guides you through the preliminary setup of your new WordPress website by using the Dashboard. When you publish with WordPress, you spend a lot of time in the Dashboard, which is where you make all the exciting behind-the-scenes stuff happen. In this Dashboard, you can find all the settings and options that enable you to set up your site just the way you want it. (If you still need to install and configure WordPress, check out Book 2, Chapter 4.)

Feeling comfortable with the Dashboard sets you up for successful entrance into the WordPress publishing world. You'll tweak your WordPress settings several times throughout the life of your site. In this chapter, as you go through the various sections, settings, options, and configurations available to you, understand that nothing is set in stone. You can set options today and change them at any time.

Logging In to the Dashboard

I find that the direct approach (also known as *jumping in*) works best when I want to get familiar with a new software tool. To that end, follow these steps to log in to WordPress and take a look at the guts of the Dashboard:

1. **Open your web browser, and type the WordPress login-page address (or URL) in the address box.**

   The login-page address looks something like this:

   `https://www.yourdomain.com/wp-login.php`

   TIP

   If you installed WordPress in its own folder, include that folder name in the login URL. If you installed WordPress in a folder ingeniously named `wordpress`, the login URL becomes

   `https://www.yourdomain.com/wordpress/wp-login.php`

2. **Type your username or email address in the Username or Email Address text box and your password in the Password text box.**

   REMEMBER

   In case you forget your password, WordPress has you covered. Click the Lost Your Password link (located near the bottom of the page), enter your username or email address, and then click the Get New Password button. WordPress resets your password and emails the new password to you.

   After you request a password, you receive two emails from your WordPress site. The first email contains a link that you click to verify that you requested the password. After you verify your intentions, you receive a second email containing your new password.

3. **Select the Remember Me check box if you want WordPress to place a cookie in your browser.**

   The cookie tells WordPress to remember your login credentials the next time you show up. The cookie set by WordPress is harmless and stores your WordPress login on your computer. Because of the cookie, WordPress remembers you the next time you visit. Because this option tells the browser to remember your login, don't select Remember Me when you're using your work computer, other devices (such as a tablet or mobile phone), or a computer at an Internet café.

   Note: Before you set this option, make sure that your browser is configured to allow cookies. (If you aren't sure how, check the help documentation of the Internet browser you're using.)

4. **Click the Log In button.**

After you log in to WordPress, you see the Dashboard page.

Navigating the Dashboard

You can consider the Dashboard to be a control panel of sorts because it offers several quick links and areas that provide information about your site, starting with the actual Dashboard page shown in Figure 1-1. When you view your Dashboard for the very first time, all the modules appear in the expanded (open) position by default.

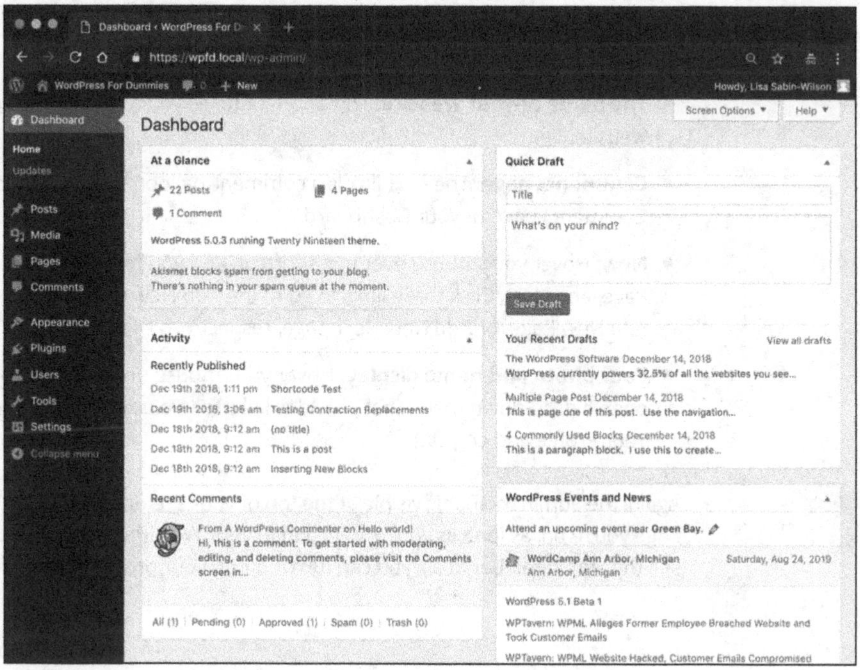

FIGURE 1-1: The WordPress Dashboard.

You can change how the WordPress Dashboard looks by modifying the order in which the modules (such as At a Glance and Activity) appear in it. You can expand (open) and collapse (close) the individual modules by clicking anywhere within the title bar of the module. This feature is really nice because it lets you use the Dashboard for just those modules that you use regularly. The concept is easy: Keep the modules you use all the time open, and close the ones that you use only occasionally; open the latter modules only when you really need them. You save screen space by customizing your Dashboard to suit your needs.

TIP

The navigation menu of the WordPress Dashboard appears on the left side of your browser window. When you need to get back to the main Dashboard page, click the Dashboard link at the top of the navigation menu on any of the screens within your WordPress Dashboard.

DISCOVERING THE ADMIN TOOLBAR

The admin toolbar is the menu you see at the top of the Dashboard (refer to Figure 1-1). The admin toolbar appears at the top of every page on your site by default, and it appears at the top of every page of the Dashboard if you set it to do so in your profile settings (see Book 3, Chapter 3). The nice thing is that the only person who can see the admin toolbar is you, because it displays only for the user who is logged in. The admin toolbar contains shortcuts that take you to the most frequently viewed areas of your WordPress Dashboard, from left to right:

- **WordPress links:** This shortcut provides links to various WordPress.org sites.
- **The name of your website:** This shortcut takes you to the front page of your website.
- **Comments page:** The next link is a comment-balloon icon; click it to visit the Comments page of your Dashboard.
- **New:** Hover your mouse over this shortcut, and you find links titled Post, Media, Page, and User. Click these links to go to the Add New Post, Upload New Media, Add New Page, or Add New User page, respectively.
- **Your photo and name display:** Hover your mouse pointer over this shortcut to open a drop-down menu that provides links to two areas of your Dashboard: Edit Your Profile and Log Out.

Again, the admin toolbar is visible at the top of your site only to you, no matter what page you're on, as long as you're logged in to your WordPress site. If you prefer not to see the admin toolbar at all, you can turn it off on your profile page in the Dashboard.

In the following sections, I cover the Dashboard page as it appears when you log in to your WordPress Dashboard for the first time. Later in this chapter, in "Arranging the Dashboard to Your Tastes," I show you how to configure the appearance of your Dashboard so that it best suits how you use the available modules.

Welcome to WordPress!

This module, shown in Figure 1-2, appears at the top of your Dashboard screen the first time you log in to your new WordPress installation. It can stay there, if you want it to. Also notice a small link on the right side of that module labeled Dismiss. That link allows you to remove this module if you'd rather not have it there.

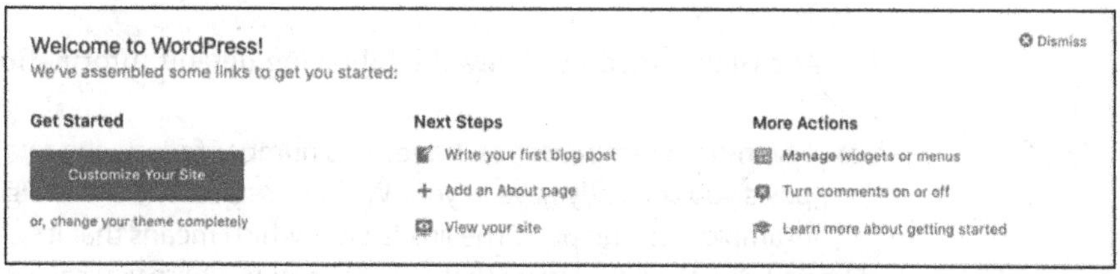

FIGURE 1-2: The Welcome to WordPress! module provides helpful links to get you started.

The makers of the WordPress software have done extensive user testing to discover what items users want to use immediately when they log in to a new WordPress site. The result of that user testing is a group of links presented in the Welcome to WordPress! module, including

- **Get Started:** This section contains a button that, when clicked, opens the Customizer, where you can customize the active theme. Additionally, this section provides a link that takes you to the Themes page, where you can change your theme. Book 6 contains tons of information about choosing a theme, as well as customizing it to look the way you want it to.
- **Next Steps:** This section provides links to various areas within the WordPress Dashboard to get you started publishing content, including writing your first post and adding an About page. (Book 4, Chapter 1 provides information about publishing posts, and Book 4, Chapter 2 gives you information about publishing pages.) Additionally, the View Your Site link in this section opens your site, allowing you to view what it looks like to your visitors.
- **More Actions:** This section contains a few links that help you manage your site, including a link to manage widgets or menus (see Book 6, Chapter 1) and turning comments on or off (see Book 3, Chapter 4). This section also contains a link to the First Steps with WordPress link of the WordPress Codex, where you can read more information about how to start using your new WordPress site.

At a Glance

The At a Glance module of the Dashboard shows what's going on in your website right now — this very second! Figure 1-3 shows the expanded At a Glance module in a brand-spanking-new WordPress site.

FIGURE 1-3: The At a Glance module of the Dashboard, expanded so that you can see the available features.

The At a Glance module shows the following default information:

- **The number of posts you have:** This number reflects the total number of posts you currently have in your WordPress site. The site in Figure 1-3, for example, has one post. The link is blue, which means that it's clickable. When you click the link, you go to the Posts screen, where you can view and manage the posts in your site. (Book 4, Chapter 1 covers managing posts.)
- **The number of pages:** The number of pages in your site, which changes when you add or delete pages. (*Pages,* in this context, refers to the static pages you create in your blog.) Figure 1-3 shows that the site has one page.

  Clicking this link takes you to the Pages screen, where you can view, edit, and delete your current pages. (Find the difference between WordPress posts and pages in Book 4, Chapter 2.)
- **The number of comments:** The number of comments on your site. Figure 1-3 shows that this blog has one comment.

  Clicking the Comments link takes you to the Comments screen, where you can manage the comments on your site. Book 3, Chapter 4 covers comments.

The last section of the Dashboard's At a Glance module shows the following information:

- **Which WordPress theme you're using:** Figure 1-3 shows that the website is using the theme called Twenty Nineteen. The theme name is a link that, when clicked, takes you to the Manage Themes page, where you can view and activate themes on your website.
- **The version of WordPress you're using:** Figure 1-3 shows that this site is using WordPress version 5.0.3. This version announcement changes if you're using an earlier version of WordPress. When WordPress software is upgraded, this statement tells you that you're using an outdated version of WordPress and encourages you to upgrade to the latest version.

Activity

The module below the At a Glance module is Activity, shown in Figure 1-4. Within this module, you find

- **Recently Published:** WordPress displays a maximum of five of the most recently published posts in this area. Each one is clickable and takes you to the Edit Post screen, where you can view and edit the post.

- **Recent Comments:** WordPress displays a maximum of five of the most recent comments on your site.
- **The author of each comment:** The name of the person who left the comment appears below it. This section also displays the author's picture (or avatar), if she has one.
- **A link to the post the comment was left on:** The post title appears to the right of the commenter's name. Click the link to go to that post in the Dashboard.
- **An excerpt of the comment:** This excerpt is a snippet of the comment this person wrote.
- **Comment management links:** When you hover your mouse pointer over the comment, six links appear below it. These links give you the opportunity to manage those comments right from your Dashboard: The first link is Unapprove, which appears only if you have comment moderation turned on. The other five links are Reply, Edit, Spam, Trash, and View. (These links don't appear in Figure 1-4 because they appear only after you've hovered your mouse pointer over the comment).
- **View links:** These links — All, Pending, Approved, Spam, and Trash — appear at the bottom of the Activity module and give you the ability to click and view specific types of comments on your site.

FIGURE 1-4: The Activity module of the Dashboard.

TIP

You can find even more information on managing your comments in Book 3, Chapter 4.

Quick Draft

The Quick Draft module, shown in Figure 1-5, is a handy form that allows you to write and save a post from your WordPress Dashboard. Using this module saves your new post as a draft only; it doesn't publish the post to your live site. When you've typed a title in the Title text field and written the content in the What's On Your Mind? text box, click the Save Draft button to save the post. A link appears; you can click it to go to the Edit Post page to further edit the post and configure the post settings, including publishing. I cover the options for posts in Book 4, Chapter 1.

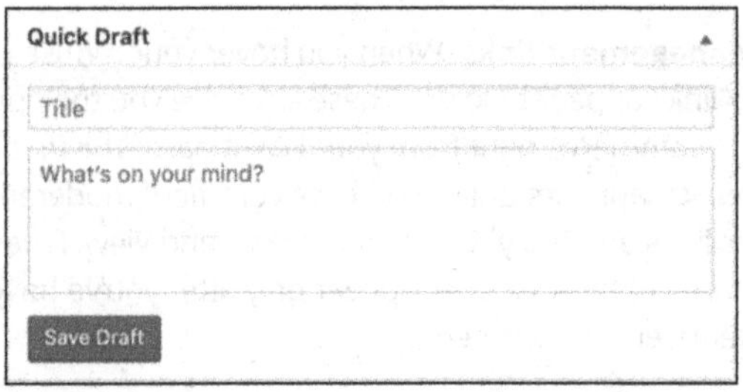

FIGURE 1-5: The Quick Draft module of the Dashboard.

WordPress Events and News

The WordPress Events and News module of the Dashboard (see Figure 1-6) gives you details about WordPress events in your area. (I discuss various WordPress events, such as Meetups and WordCamps, in Book 1, Chapter 4.) In this module, click the small pencil icon next to the Attend an Upcoming Event link to enter your location. Then the WordPress Events and News module displays events that are local to you.

FIGURE 1-6: The WordPress Events and News module.

The WordPress News portion of this module is updated with content that pulls in posts from a site called WordPress Planet (`http://planet.wordpress.org`). By keeping the default setting in this area, you stay in touch with several posts made by folks who are involved in WordPress development, design, and troubleshooting. You can find lots of interesting and useful tidbits if you keep this area intact. Quite often, I find great information about new plugins or themes, problem areas and support, troubleshooting, and new ideas, so I tend to stick with the default setting.

Arranging the Dashboard to Your Tastes

One feature of WordPress that I'm quite fond of allows me to create my own workspace within the Dashboard. In the following sections, you can find out how to customize your WordPress Dashboard to fit your individual needs, including modifying the layout, changing links and RSS feed information, and even rearranging the modules on different pages of the Dashboard. Armed with this information, you can open your Dashboard and create your very own workspace.

Changing the order of modules

You can arrange the order of the modules in your Dashboard to suit your tastes. WordPress places a great deal of emphasis on user experience, and a big part of that effort results in your ability to create a Dashboard that you find most useful. You can very easily change the modules to display and the order in which they display.

Follow these steps to move the At a Glance module so that it appears on the right side of your Dashboard page:

1. **Hover your mouse pointer on the title bar of the At a Glance module.**

   When the mouse is hovering over the title, your pointer changes to the Move pointer (a cross with arrows).

2. **Click and hold your mouse button, and drag the At a Glance module to the right side of the screen.**

   While you drag the module, a light-gray dotted line appears on the right side of your screen (see Figure 1-7). That line is a guide that shows you where you can drop the module.

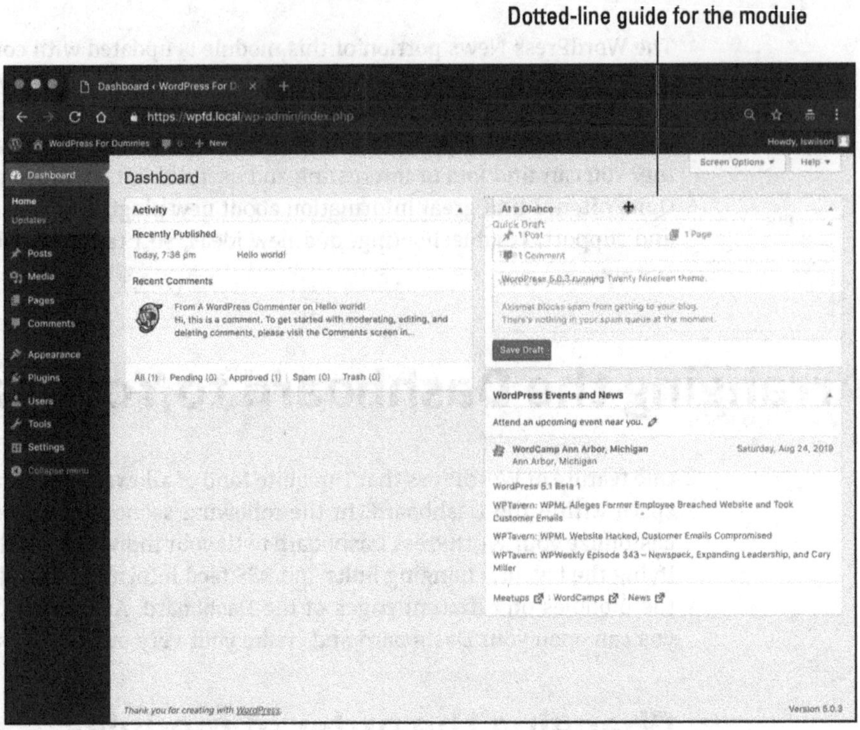

FIGURE 1-7: A light gray box appears as a guide when you drag and drop modules in the WordPress Dashboard.

3. **Release the mouse button when you have the At a Glance module in place.**

   The At a Glance module is positioned on the right side of your Dashboard page.

   The other modules on the right side of the Dashboard have shifted down, and the Activity module is the module in the top-left corner of the Dashboard page.

4. **(Optional) Click the title bar of the At a Glance module.**

   The module collapses. Click the title bar again to expand the module. You can keep that module open or closed, based on your preference.

Repeat these steps with each module that you want to move on the Dashboard by dragging and dropping them so that they appear in the order you prefer.

REMEMBER

When you navigate away from the Dashboard, WordPress remembers the changes you made. When you return, you still see your customized Dashboard, and you don't need to redo these changes in the future. The changes you make in the layout of your Dashboard are unique to you. Even if you have a WordPress site with multiple user accounts, WordPress remembers the changes you make in your Dashboard but doesn't apply those changes to any other users on your site. That feature makes this experience unique to your needs and preferences.

Removing Dashboard modules

If you find that your Dashboard contains a few modules that you never use, you can get rid of them by following these steps:

1. **Click the Screen Options button at the top of the Dashboard.**

   The Screen Options drop-down menu opens, displaying the title of each module with a check box to the left of each title.

2. **Deselect the check box for the module you want to hide.**

   The check mark disappears from the check box, and the module disappears from your Dashboard.

TIP

If you want a module that you hid to reappear, enable that module by selecting the module's check box on the Screen Options drop-down menu.

Finding Inline Documentation and Help

The developers of the WordPress software really put in time and effort to provide tons of inline documentation that gives you several tips and hints right inside the Dashboard. You can generally find inline documentation for nearly every WordPress feature you'll use.

Inline documentation refers to those small sentences or phrases that you see alongside or below a feature in WordPress, providing a short but very helpful explanation of the feature. Figure 1-8 shows the General Settings screen, where a lot of inline documentation and guiding tips corresponds with each feature. These tips can clue you into what the features are, how to use those features, and what recommended settings to use for those features.

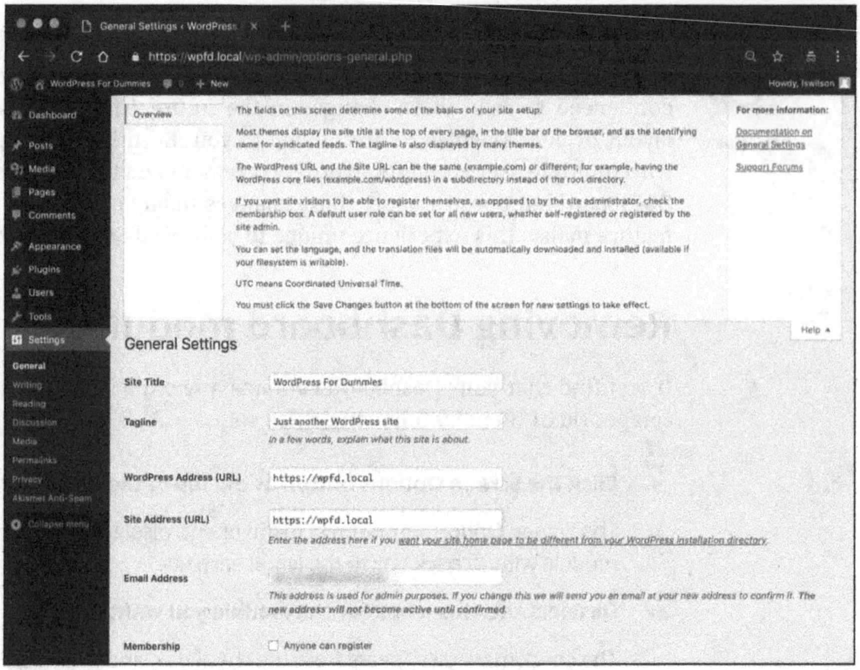

FIGURE 1-8: Inline documentation on the General Settings page in the WordPress Dashboard.

In addition to the inline documentation that you find scattered throughout the Dashboard, a useful Help tab is located in the top-right corner of your Dashboard. Click this tab to open a panel containing help text that's relevant to the screen you're currently viewing in your Dashboard. If you're viewing the General Settings screen, for example, the Help tab displays documentation relevant to the General Settings screen. Likewise, if you're viewing the Add New Post screen, the Help tab displays documentation with topics relevant to the settings and features you find on the Add New Post page of your Dashboard.

TIP

The inline documentation and the topics and text you find in the Help tab exist to assist you while you work with the WordPress platform, making the experience as easy to understand as possible. Another place you can visit to find help and useful support for WordPress is the WordPress Forums support page, at `https://wordpress.org/support`.

IN THIS CHAPTER

» Configuring your WordPress general settings

» Putting together your personal profile

» Formatting your website

Chapter 2 Exploring Tools and Settings

As exciting as it is to dig in and start publishing right away, you should attend to a few housekeeping items first, including adjusting the settings that allow you to personalize your website. I cover these settings first in this chapter because they create your readers' experience with your website.

In this chapter, you explore the Settings menu of the WordPress Dashboard and discover how to configure items such as date and time settings, the title of your website, and email notification settings. This chapter also covers important aspects of your website configuration, such as permalinks, discussion options, and privacy settings.

Some of the menu items, such as those for creating and publishing new posts, are covered in detail in other chapters, but they're well worth a mention here as well.

Configuring the Settings

At the very bottom of the navigation menu, you find the Settings option. Hover over the Settings link. A menu appears that contains the following links, which I discuss in the sections that follow:

- General
- Writing
- Reading
- Discussion
- Media
- Permalinks
- Privacy

General

After you install the WordPress software and log in, you can put a personal stamp on your site by giving it a title and description, setting your contact email address, and identifying yourself as the author of the site. You take care of these and other settings on the General Settings screen.

To begin personalizing your site, start with your general settings by following these steps:

1. **Choose Settings⇨General.**

   The General Settings screen appears, as shown in Figure 2-1.

2. **Enter the name of your site in the Site Title text box.**

   The title you enter here is the one that you give your site to identify it as your own. In Figure 2-1, I gave the new site the title *WordPress All-In-One For Dummies,* which appears on my website, as well as in the title bar of the viewer's web browser.

   TIP

   Give your website an interesting and identifiable name. You can use *Fried Green Tomatoes,* for example, if you're writing about the topic, the book, the movie, or even anything remotely related to the lovely Southern dish.

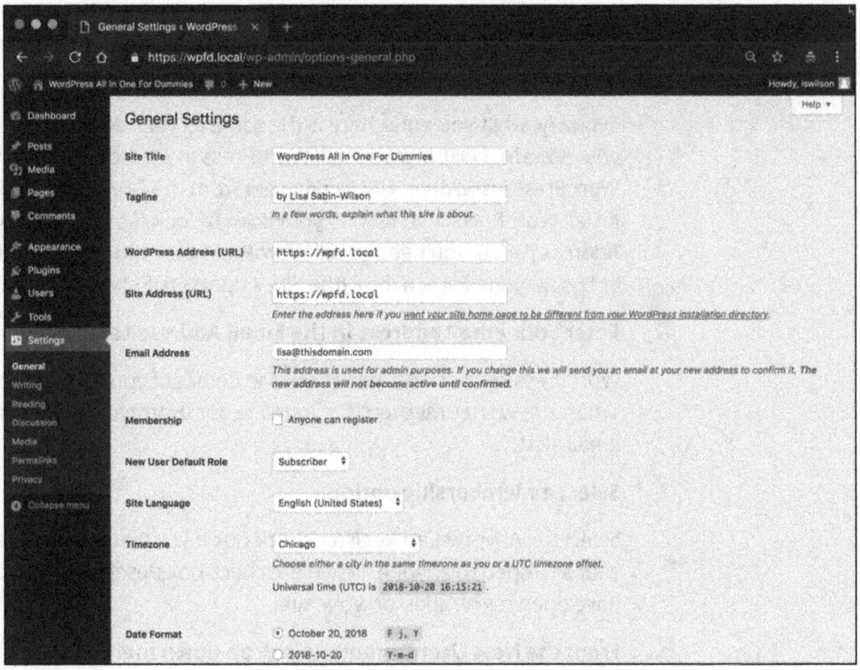

FIGURE 2-1: Personalize the settings of your WordPress site on the General Settings screen.

3. **In the Tagline text box, enter a five- to ten-word phrase that describes your site.**

   Figure 2-1 shows that the tagline is *by Lisa Sabin-Wilson*. Therefore, this site displays the site title, followed by the tagline: *WordPress All-in-One For Dummies by Lisa Sabin-Wilson.*

   REMEMBER

   The general Internet-surfing public can view your site title and tagline, which various search engines (such as Google, Yahoo!, and Bing) grab for indexing, so choose your words with this fact in mind. (You can find more information about search engine optimization, or SEO, in Book 5.)

4. **In the WordPress Address (URL) text box, enter the location where you installed the WordPress software.**

   Be sure to include the `https://` portion of the URL and the entire path to your WordPress installation, such as `https://yourdomain.com`. If you installed WordPress in a folder in your directory — in a folder called `wordpress`, for example — you need to make sure to include it here. If you installed WordPress in a folder called `wordpress`, the WordPress address would be `https://yourdomain.com/wordpress` (where *`yourdomain.com`* is your domain name).

5. **In the Site Address (URL) text box, enter the web address where people can find your site by using their web browsers.**

   Typically, what you enter here is the same as your domain name (`https://yourdomain.com`). If you install WordPress in a subdirectory of your site, the WordPress installation URL is different from the Site Address (URL). If you install WordPress at `https://yourdomain.com/wordpress/` (WordPress Address [URL]), you need to tell WordPress that you want the site to appear at `https://yourdomain.com` (the Site Address [URL]).

6. **Enter your email address in the Email Address text box.**

   WordPress sends messages about the details of your site to this email address. When a new user registers for your site, for example, WordPress sends you an email alert.

7. **Select a Membership option.**

   Select the Anyone Can Register check box if you want to keep registration on your site open to anyone. Leave the check box deselected if you'd rather not have open registration on your site.

8. **From the New User Default Role drop-down menu, choose the role that you want new users to have when they register for user accounts in your site.**

   You need to understand the differences among the user roles because each user role is assigned a different level of access to your site, as follows:

   - *Subscriber:* The default role. You may want to maintain this role as the one assigned to new users, particularly if you don't know who's registering. Subscribers have access to the Dashboard screen, and they can view and change the options in their profiles in the Profile screen. (They don't have access to your account settings, however — only to their own.) Each user can change his username, email address, password, bio, and other descriptors in his user profile. Subscribers' profile information is stored in the WordPress database, and your site remembers them each time they visit, so they don't have to complete the profile information each time they leave comments on your site.
   - *Contributor:* In addition to the access subscribers have, contributors can upload files and write, edit, and manage their own posts. Contributors can write posts, but they can't publish the posts; the administrator reviews all contributor posts and decides whether to publish them. This setting is a nice way to moderate content written by new authors.
   - *Author:* In addition to the access contributors have, authors can publish and edit their own posts.

- *Editor:* In addition to the access authors have, editors can moderate comments, manage categories, manage links, edit pages, and edit other authors' posts.
- *Administrator:* Administrators can edit all the options and settings in the WordPress site.

9. **From the Site Language drop-down menu, choose your preferred language.**

   The default language for WordPress is English.

10. **From the Timezone drop-down menu, choose your UTC time.**

    This setting refers to the number of hours that your local time differs from Coordinated Universal Time (UTC). This setting ensures that all the posts and comments left on your site are time-stamped with the correct time. If you're lucky enough, as I am, to live on the frozen tundra of Wisconsin, which is in the Central Standard Time (CST) zone, you choose **–5** from the drop-down menu because that time zone is 5 hours off UTC.

    TIP

    If you're unsure what your UTC time is, you can find it at the Greenwich Mean Time (`https://greenwichmeantime.com`) website. GMT is essentially the same thing as UTC. WordPress also lists some major cities in the Timezone drop-down menu so that you can more easily choose your time zone if you don't know it. (Figure 2-1 displays Chicago in the drop-down menu because that's the major city closest to where I live.)

    Note: The following options aren't shown in Figure 2-1; you need to scroll down to access them.

    REMEMBER

    If you live in a state in the United States that recognizes Daylight Savings Time (DST), your GMT will change by an hour during different times of the year. In the spring and summer months, my GMT is –5 until early November, when I turn my clocks back an hour; then it's –6. If you choose the city nearest to you from the Timezone drop-down menu, WordPress automatically makes those GMT changes for you, so you don't have to remember to do it when your state is under DST.

11. **For the Date Format option, select the format in which you want the date to appear in your site.**

    This setting determines the style of the date display. The default format displays time like this: April 1, 2019.

    Select a different format by selecting the radio button to the left of the option you want. You can also customize the date display by selecting the Custom option and entering your preferred format in the text box provided. If you're feeling adventurous, you can find out how to customize the date format at `https://codex.wordpress.org/Formatting_Date_and_Time`.

12. **For the Time Format option, select how you want time to display on your site.**

    This setting is the style of the time display. The default format displays time like this: 12:00 a.m.

    Select a different format by selecting the radio button to the left of the option you want. You can also customize the date display by selecting the Custom option and entering your preferred format in the text box provided; find out how at `https://codex.wordpress.org/Formatting_Date_and_Time`.

    TIP: You can format the time and date in several ways. Go to `http://php.net/manual/en/function.date.php` to find potential formats at the PHP website.

13. **From the Week Starts On drop-down menu, choose the day on which the week starts in your calendar.**

    Displaying the calendar in the sidebar of your site is optional. If you choose to display the calendar, you can select the day of the week on which you want your calendar to start.

REMEMBER: Click the Save Changes button at the bottom of any page where you set new options. If you don't click Save Changes, your settings aren't saved, and WordPress reverts to the preceding options. Each time you click the Save Changes button, WordPress reloads the current screen, displaying the new options that you just set.

Writing

Choose Settings⇨Writing, and the Writing Settings screen opens. (See Figure 2-2.)

This screen of the Dashboard lets you set some basic options for writing your content. Table 2-1 gives you some information on choosing how your content looks and how WordPress handles some specific conditions.

REMEMBER: After you set your options, be sure to click the Save Changes button; otherwise, the changes won't take effect.

TIP: Go to `https://codex.wordpress.org/Update_Services` for comprehensive information on update services.

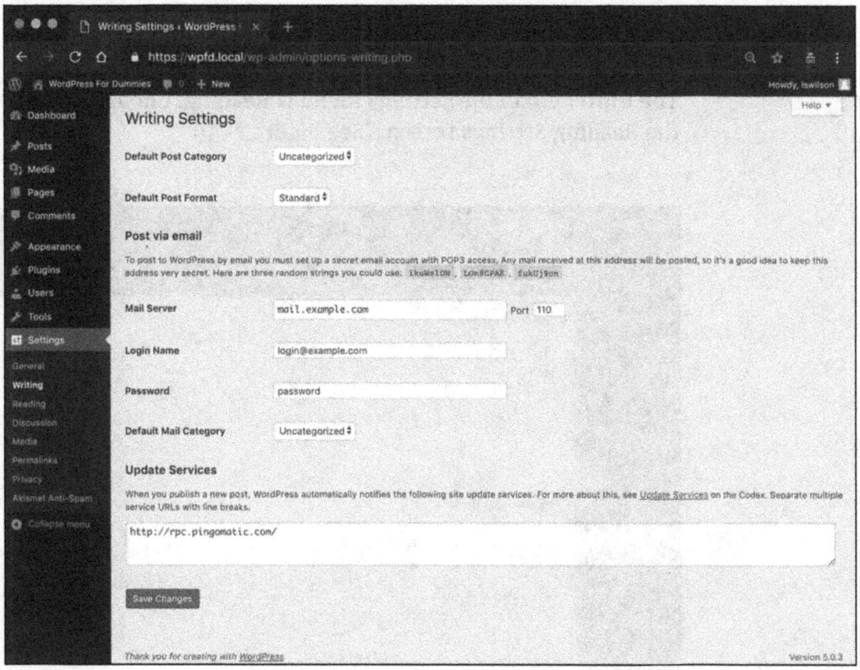

FIGURE 2-2: The Writing Settings screen.

TABLE 2-1 **Writing Settings Options**

Option	Function	Default
Default Post Category	Choose the category that WordPress defaults to any time you forget to choose a category when you publish a post.	Uncategorized
Default Post Format	Choose the format that WordPress defaults to any time you create a post and don't assign a post format. (This option is theme-specific; not all themes support post formats. See Book 6, Chapter 6.)	Standard
Post via Email	Publish content from your email account by entering the mail server, port, login name, and password for the account you'll be using to send posts to your WordPress site.	N/A
Default Mail Category	Set the category that posts made via email are submitted to when these types of posts are published.	Uncategorized
Update Services ***Note:*** This option is available only if you allow your site to be indexed by search engines (covered in the "Reading" settings section).	Indicate which ping service you want to use to notify the world that you've made updates, or new posts. The default, XML-RPC (`http://rpc.pingomatic.com`), updates all the popular services simultaneously.	`http://rpc.pingomatic.com`

Reading

The third item in the Settings menu is Reading. Choose Settings⇨Reading to open the Reading Settings screen. (See Figure 2-3.)

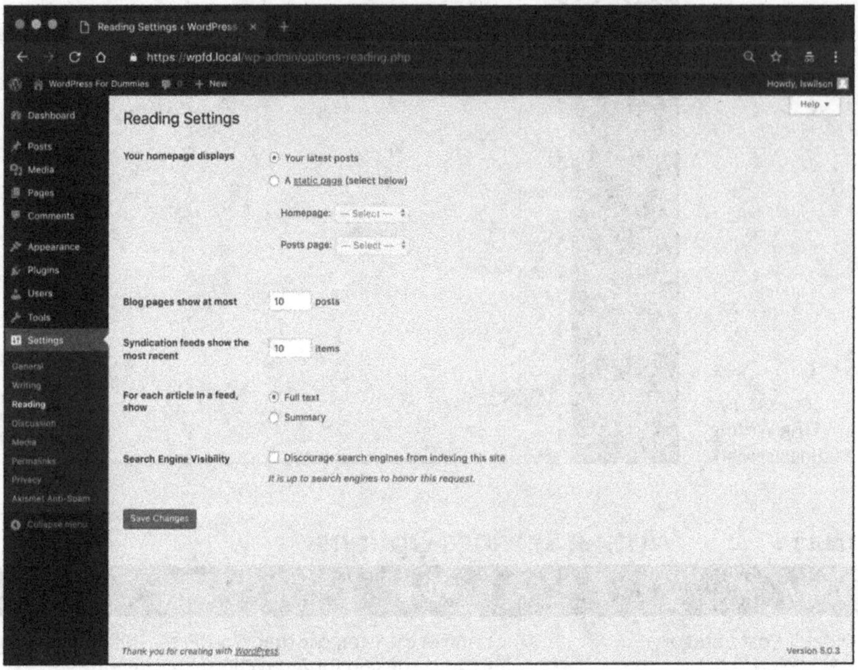

FIGURE 2-3: The Reading Settings screen.

You can set the following options on the Reading Settings screen:

- **Your Home page Displays:** Select the radio button to show a page instead of your latest posts on the front page of your site. You can find detailed information about using a static page for your front page in Book 4, Chapter 2, including information on how to set it up by using the fields in this section that appear after you select the radio button.
- **Blog Pages Show at Most:** In the text box, enter the maximum number of posts you want to appear on each site page (default: 10).
- **Syndication Feeds Show the Most Recent:** In the text box, enter the maximum number of posts that you want to appear in your RSS feed at any time (default: 10).
- **For Each Article in a Feed, Show:** Select the Full Text or Summary radio button. Full Text publishes the entire post to your RSS feed, whereas Summary publishes an excerpt. (Check out Book 1, Chapter 1 for more information on WordPress RSS feeds.)

- **Search Engine Visibility:** By default, your website is visible to all search engines, such as Google and Yahoo! If you don't want your site to be visible to search engines, select the check box labeled Discourage Search Engines from Indexing This Site.

TIP

Generally, you want search engines to be able to find your site. If you have special circumstances, however, you may want to enforce privacy on your site. A friend of mine has a family site, for example, and she blocks search engine access to it because she doesn't want search engines to find it. When you have privacy enabled, search engines and other content bots can't find your website or list it in their search engines.

REMEMBER

Be sure to click the Save Changes button after you set all your options on the Reading Settings screen to make the changes take effect.

Discussion

Discussion is the fourth item on the Settings menu; choose Settings⇨Discussion to open the Discussion Settings screen. (See Figure 2-4.) The sections of this screen let you set options for handling comments and publishing posts to your site.

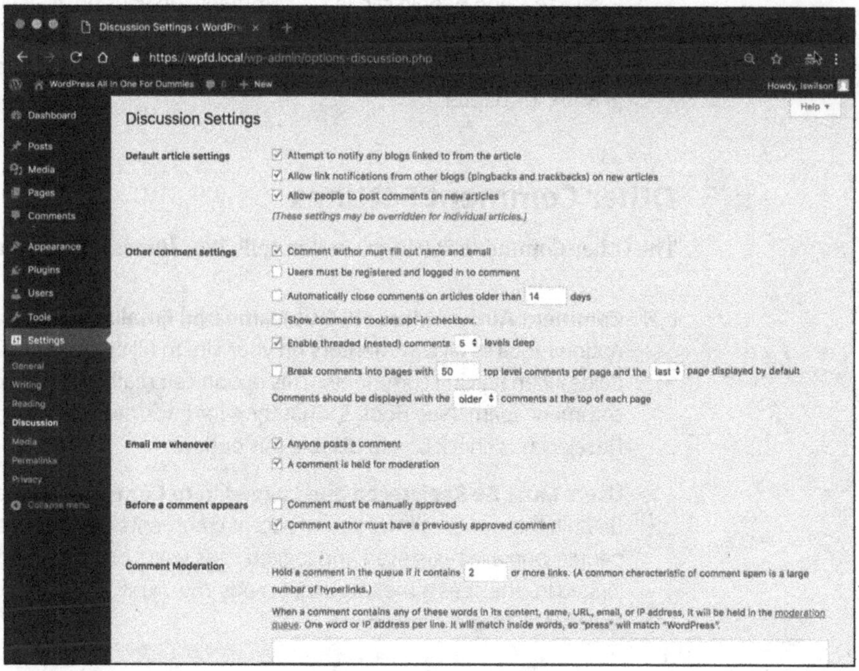

FIGURE 2-4: The Discussion Settings screen.

The following sections cover the options available to you on the Discussion Settings screen, which deals mainly with how comments and trackbacks are handled on your site.

Default Article Settings

With the Default Article Settings options, you can tell WordPress how to handle post notifications. Here are your options:

- **Attempt to Notify Any Blogs Linked to from the Article:** If you select this check box, your site sends a notification (or *ping*) to any site you've linked to in your posts. This notification is also commonly referred to as a *trackback*. (Find out more about trackbacks in Book 3, Chapter 4.) Deselect this check box if you don't want these notifications sent.
- **Allow Link Notifications from Other Blogs (Pingbacks and Trackbacks) on New Articles:** By default, this check box is selected, and your site accepts notifications via pings or trackbacks from other sites that have linked to yours. Any trackbacks or pings sent to your site appear on your site in the Comments section of the post. If you deselect this check box, your site doesn't accept pingbacks or trackbacks from other sites.
- **Allow People to Post Comments on New Articles:** By default, this check box is selected, and people can leave comments on your posts. If you deselect this check box, no one can leave comments on your content. (You can override these settings for individual articles. Find more information about this process in Book 4, Chapter 1.)

Other Comment Settings

The Other Comment Settings section tells WordPress how to handle comments:

- **Comment Author Must Fill Out Name and Email:** Enabled by default, this option requires all commenters on your site to fill in the Name and Email fields when leaving comments. This option can really help you combat comment spam. (See Book 3, Chapter 4 for information on comment spam.) Deselect this check box to disable this option.
- **Users Must Be Registered and Logged in to Comment:** Not enabled by default, this option allows you to accept comments on your site only from people who are registered and logged in as users on your site. If the user isn't logged in, she sees a message that reads `You must be logged in in order to leave a comment.`

- **Automatically Close Comments on Articles Older Than *X* Days:** Select the check box next to this option to tell WordPress you want comments on older articles to be closed automatically. Fill in the text box with the number of days you want to wait before WordPress closes comments on articles (default: 14).

  Many people use this very effective antispam technique to keep comment and trackback spam down on their sites.

REMEMBER

- **Show Comments Cookies Opt-In Checkbox:** If you select the check box next to this option, which is unchecked by default, WordPress places a check box underneath the comments form on your website and a notice that says `Save my name, email, and website in this browser for the next time I comment.` When the user selects this box, WordPress remembers set a cookie in the user's browser that remembers their information the next time they visit your site.
- **Enable Threaded (Nested) Comments *X* Levels Deep:** From the drop-down menu, you can choose the level of threaded comments you want to have on your site. The default is five; you can choose up to ten levels. Instead of displaying all comments on your site in chronological order, nesting them allows you and your readers to reply to comments within a comment.
- **Break Comments into Pages with *X* Top Level Comments per Page and the Last/First Page Displayed by Default:** Fill in the text box with the number of comments you want to appear on one page (default: 50). This setting can really help sites that receive a large number of comments. It allows you to break a long string of comments into several pages, which makes the comments easier to read and helps speed the load time of your site because the page isn't loading such a large number of comments at the same time. If you want the last (most recent) or first page of comments to display, choose Last or First from the drop-down menu.
- **Comments Should Be Displayed with the Older/Newer Comments at the Top of Each Page:** From the drop-down menu, choose Older or Newer. Older displays the comments on your site in the order oldest to newest. Newer does the opposite: It displays the comments on your site from newest to oldest.

Email Me Whenever

The two options in the Email Me Whenever section are enabled by default:

- **Anyone Posts a Comment:** Enabling this option means that you receive an email notification whenever anyone leaves a comment on your site. Deselect the check box if you don't want to be notified by email about every new comment.

- **A Comment Is Held for Moderation:** This option lets you receive an email notification whenever a comment is awaiting your approval in the comment moderation queue. (See Book 3, Chapter 4 for more information about the comment moderation queue.) You need to deselect this option if you don't want to receive this notification.

Before a Comment Appears

The two options in the Before a Comment Appears section tell WordPress how you want WordPress to handle comments before they appear in your site:

- **Comment Must Be Manually Approved:** Disabled by default, this option keeps every single comment left on your site in the moderation queue until you, as the administrator, log in and approve it. Select this check box to enable this option.
- **Comment Author Must Have a Previously Approved Comment:** Enabled by default, this option requires comments posted by all first-time commenters to be sent to the comment moderation queue for approval by the administrator of the site. After comment authors have been approved for the first time, they remain approved for every comment thereafter (and this setting can't be changed). WordPress stores each comment author's email address in the database, and any future comments that match any stored emails are approved automatically. This feature is another measure that WordPress has built in to combat comment spam.

Comment Moderation

In the Comment Moderation section, you can set options to specify what types of comments are held in the moderation queue to await your approval.

To prevent spammers from spamming your site with a *ton* of links, enter a number in the Hold a Comment in the Queue If It Contains *X* or More Links text box. The default number of links allowed is 2. Try that setting, and if you find that you're getting a lot of spam comments that contain links, consider dropping that number to 1, or even 0, to prevent those comments from being published on your site. Sometimes, legitimate commenters include a link or two in the body of their comments; after a commenter is marked as approved, she's no longer affected by this method of spam protection.

The large text box in the Comment Moderation section (not shown in Figure 2-4 because it's at the bottom of the page) lets you type keywords, URLs, email addresses, and IP addresses so that if they appear in comments, you want to hold those comments in the moderation queue for your approval.

WHAT ARE AVATARS, AND HOW DO THEY RELATE TO WordPress?

An *avatar* is an online graphical representation of a person. It's a small icon that people use to represent themselves on the web in areas where they participate in conversations, such as discussion forums and site comments.

Gravatars are globally recognized avatars; they're avatars that you can take with you wherever you go. They appear alongside comments, posts, and discussion forums as long as the site you're interacting with is Gravatar-enabled. In October 2007, Automattic, the core group behind the WordPress platform, purchased the Gravatar service and integrated it into WordPress so that everyone could enjoy and benefit from the service.

Gravatars aren't automatic; you need to sign up for an account with Gravatar so that you can receive an avatar via your email address. Find out more about Gravatar by visiting `https://gravatar.com`.

Comment Blacklist

In this section, type a list of words, URLs, email addresses, and/or IP addresses that you want to flat-out ban from your site. Items placed here don't even make it into your comment moderation queue; the WordPress system filters them as spam. I'd give examples of blacklist words, but the words I have in my blacklist aren't family-friendly and have no place in a nice book like this one.

Avatars

The final section of the Discussion Settings screen is Avatars. (See the nearby sidebar "What are avatars, and how do they relate to WordPress?" for information about avatars.) In this section, you can select different settings for the use and display of avatars on your site, as follows:

1. **For the Avatar Display option (see Figure 2-5), decide how to display avatars on your site.**

   Select the Show Avatars check box to have your site display avatars.

2. **Next to the Maximum Rating option, select the radio button for the maximum avatar rating you want to allow for the avatars that do appear on your site.**

   This feature works much like the American movie-rating system. You can select G, PG, R, and X ratings for the avatars that appear on your site, as shown in Figure 2-5. If your site is family-friendly, you probably don't want it to display R- or X-rated avatars, so select G or PG.

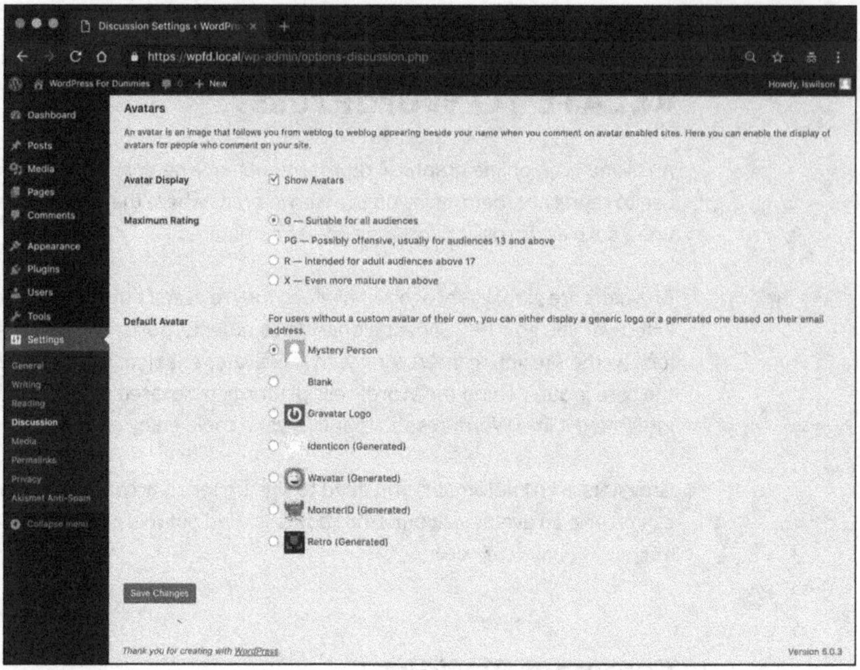

FIGURE 2-5: Default avatars that you can display.

3. **Select the radio button for a default avatar next to the Default Avatar option (refer to Figure 2-5).**

   Avatars appear in a couple of places:

   - *The Comments screen of the Dashboard:* In Figure 2-6, the first two comments display either the commenter's avatar or the default avatar if the commenter hasn't created his or her own.
   - *The comments on individual site posts in your site:* Comments displayed on your website show the users' avatars. If a user doesn't have an avatar assigned from `https://gravatar.com`, the default avatar appears.

   To enable the display of avatars in comments on your site, the Comments template (`comments.php`) in your active theme has to contain the code to display them. Hop on over to Book 6 to find information about themes and templates, including template tags that allow you to display avatars in your comment list.

REMEMBER

Click the Save Changes button after you set all your options on the Discussion Settings screen to make the changes take effect.

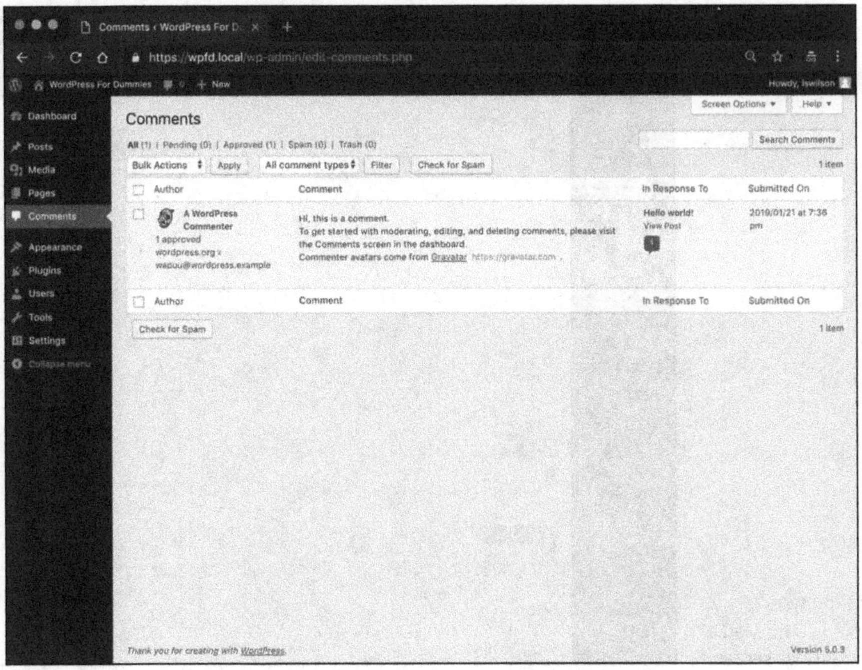

FIGURE 2-6: Comment authors' avatars appear in the Comments screen of the WordPress Dashboard.

Media

The next item on the Settings menu is Media. Choose Settings➪Media to make the Media Settings screen open. (See Figure 2-7.)

On the Media Settings screen, you can configure the options for how your image files (graphics and photos) are resized for use in your site.

The first set of options on the Media Settings page deals with images. WordPress automatically resizes your images for you in three sizes. The dimensions are referenced in pixels first by width and then by height. (The setting 150 x 150, for example, means 150 pixels wide by 150 pixels high.)

- **Thumbnail Size:** The default is 150 x 150; enter the width and height of your choice. Select the Crop Thumbnail to Exact Dimensions check box to resize the thumbnail to the exact width and height you specify. Deselect this check box to make WordPress resize the image proportionally.
- **Medium Size:** The default is 300 x 300; enter the width and height numbers of your choice.
- **Large Size:** The default is 1024 x 1024; enter the width and height numbers of your choice.

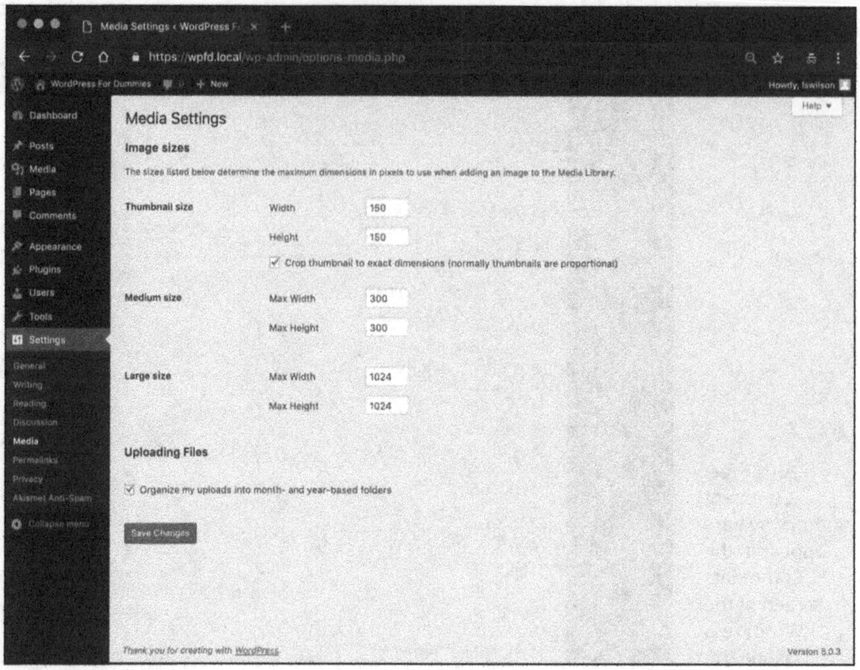

FIGURE 2-7: The Media Settings screen.

TIP

Book 6 goes into detail about WordPress themes and templates, including how you can add image sizes other than these three. You can use these additional image sizes in and around your website. There's also a feature called Featured Image, which you can use in posts and articles that display on archive and search results pages.

The last option on the Media Settings screen is the Uploading Files section. Here, you can tell WordPress where to store your uploaded media files. Select the Organize My Uploads into Month- and Year-Based Folders check box to have WordPress organize your uploaded files in folders by month and by year. Files you upload in April 2019, for example, would be in the following folder: `/wp-content/uploads/2019/04/`. Likewise, files you uploaded in January 2019 would be in `/wp-content/uploads/2019/01/`.

This check box is selected by default; deselect it if you don't want WordPress to organize your files by month and year.

REMEMBER

Be sure to click the Save Changes button to save your configurations.

Book 4, Chapter 3 details how to insert images into your WordPress posts and pages.

Permalinks

The next link on the Settings menu is Permalinks. Choose Settings⇨Permalinks to view the Permalink Settings screen, shown in Figure 2-8.

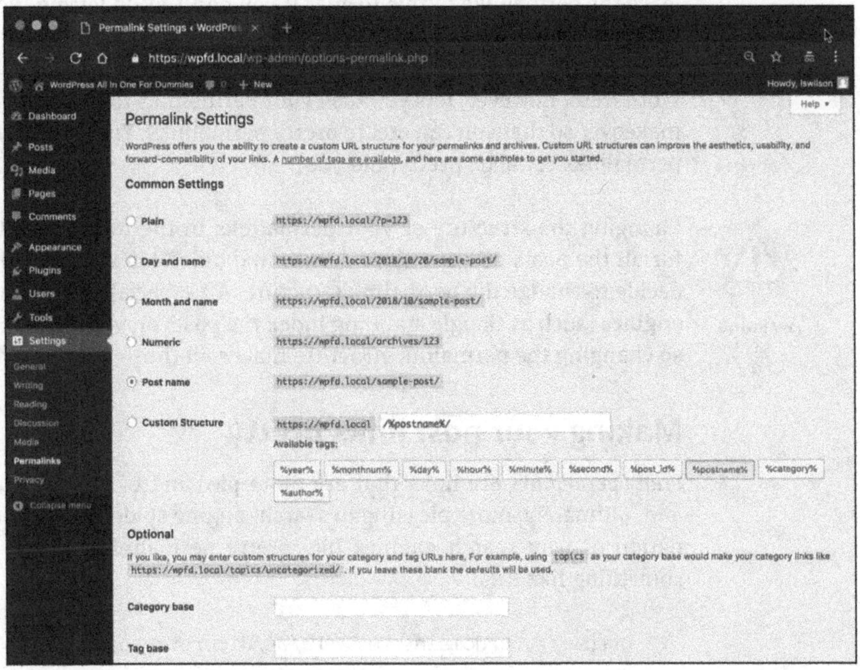

FIGURE 2-8: The Permalink Settings screen.

Each WordPress post is assigned its own web page, and the address (or URL) of that page is called a *permalink.* Posts that you see in WordPress sites usually have the post permalink in four typical areas:

- The title of the post
- The Comments link below the post
- A Permalink link that appears (in most themes) below the post
- The titles of posts appearing in a Recent Posts sidebar

Permalinks are meant to be permanent links to your posts (which is where the *perma* part of that word comes from, in case you're wondering). Ideally, the permalink of a post never changes. WordPress creates the permalink automatically when you publish a new post.

A plain post permalink in WordPress looks like this:

```
https://yourdomain.com/?p=100
```

The `p` stands for *post*, and `100` is the ID assigned to the individual post. You can leave the permalinks in this format if you don't mind letting WordPress associate each post with an ID number.

WordPress, however, lets you take your permalinks to the beauty salon for a bit of makeover so that you can create pretty permalinks. You probably didn't know that permalinks could be pretty, did you?

WARNING

Changing the structure of your permalinks in the future affects the permalinks for all the posts on your site . . . new and old. Keep this fact in mind if you ever decide to change the permalink structure. An especially important reason: Search engines (such as Google and Bing index the posts on your site by their permalinks, so changing the permalink structure makes all those indexed links obsolete.

Making your post links pretty

Pretty permalinks are links that are more pleasing to the eye than standard links and, ultimately, more pleasing to search-engine spiders. (See Book 5 for an explanation of why search engines like pretty permalinks.) Pretty permalinks look something like this:

```
https://yourdomain.com/2019/04/01/pretty-permalinks
```

Break down that URL, and you see the date when the post was made, in year/month/day format. You also see the topic of the post.

To choose how your permalinks look, choose Settings⇨Permalinks in the Dashboard. The Permalink Settings screen opens. (Refer to Figure 2-8.)

On this page, you can find several options for creating permalinks:

- **Plain** (ugly permalinks): WordPress assigns an ID number to each site post and creates the URL in this format: `https://yourdomain.com/?p=100`.
- **Day and Name** (pretty permalinks): For each post, WordPress generates a permalink URL that includes the year, month, day, and post slug/title: `https://yourdomain.com/2018/10/20/sample-post/`.
- **Month and Name** (also pretty permalinks): For each post, WordPress generates a permalink URL that includes the year, month, and post slug/title: `https://yourdomain.com/2018/10/sample-post/`.

- **Numeric** (not so pretty): WordPress assigns a numerical value to the permalink. The URL is created in this format: `https://yourdomain.com/archives/123`.
- **Post Name** (my preferred): WordPress takes the title of your post or page and generates the permalink URL from those words. If I were to create a page that contains my bibliography of books and give it the title *Books,* with the Post Name permalink structure, WordPress would create the permalink URL `https://webdevstudios.com/books`. Likewise, a post titled "WordPress Is Awesome" would get a permalink URL like this `http://webdevstudios.com/wordpress-is-awesome`.
- **Custom Structure:** WordPress creates permalinks in the format you choose. You can create a custom permalink structure by using tags or variables, as I discuss in the next section.

To create the pretty-permalink structure, select the Day and Name radio button; then click the Save Changes button at the bottom of the page.

Exploring Tools and Settings

Customizing your permalinks

A *custom permalink structure* is one that lets you define which variables you want to see in your permalinks by using the tags in Table 2-2.

TABLE 2-2 Custom Permalinks

Permalink Tag	Results
`%year%`	Four-digit year (such as 2019)
`%monthnum%`	Two-digit month (such as 01 for January)
`%day%`	Two-digit day (such as 30)
`%hour%`	Two-digit hour of the day (such as 15 for 3 p.m.)
`%minute%`	Two-digit minute (such as 45)
`%second%`	Two-digit second (such as 10)
`%postname%`	Text — usually, the post name — separated by hyphens (such as `making-pretty-permalinks`)
`%post_id%`	The unique numerical ID of the post (such as 344)
`%category%`	The text of the category name in which you filed the post (such as `books-i-read`)
`%author%`	The text of the post author's name (such as `lisa-sabin-wilson`)

If you want your permalink to show the year, month, day, category, and post name, select the Custom Structure radio button in the Customize Permalink Structure page, and type the following tags in the Custom Structure text box:

```
/%year%/%monthnum%/%day%/%category%/%postname%/
```

If you use this permalink format, a link for a post made on January 1, 2019, called "WordPress All-in-One For Dummies" and filed in the Books I Read category, would look like this:

```
https://yourdomain.com/2019/01/01/books-i-read/wordpress-
all-in-one-for-dummies
```

REMEMBER

Be sure to include the slashes before tags, between tags, and at the end of the string of tags. This format ensures that WordPress creates correct, working permalinks by using the correct rewrite rules located in the `.htaccess` file for your site. (See the following section for more information on rewrite rules and `.htaccess` files.)

REMEMBER

Don't forget to click the Save Changes button at the bottom of the Customize Permalink Structure screen; otherwise, your permalink changes aren't saved.

Making sure that your permalinks work with your server

After you set the format for the permalinks for your site by using any options other than the default, WordPress writes specific rules, or directives, to the `.htaccess` file on your web server. The `.htaccess` file in turn communicates to your web server how it should serve up the permalinks, according to the permalink structure you chose to use.

To use an `.htaccess` file, you need to know the answers to two questions:

- Does your web server configuration use and give you access to the `.htaccess` file?
- Does your web server run Apache with the `mod_rewrite` module?

If you don't know the answers, contact your hosting provider to find out.

If the answer to both questions is yes, proceed to the following section. If the answer is no, check out the sidebar "Working with servers that don't use Apache `mod_rewrite`" later in this chapter.

Creating .htaccess files

You and WordPress work together in glorious harmony to create the `.htaccess` file that lets you use a pretty-permalink structure in your site.

To create the `.htaccess` file, you need to be comfortable uploading files via SFTP and changing permissions. Turn to Book 2, Chapter 2 if you're unfamiliar with either of those tasks.

TIP

If `.htaccess` already exists, you can find it in the root of your directory on your web server — that is, the same directory where you find your `wp-config.php` file. If you don't see it in the root directory, try changing the options of your SFTP client to show hidden files. (Because the `.htaccess` file starts with a period [`.`], it may not be visible until you configure your SFTP client to show hidden files.)

If you don't already have an `.htaccess` file on your web server, follow these steps to create an `.htaccess` file on your web server and create a new permalink structure:

1. **Using a plain-text editor (such as Notepad for Windows or TextEdit for a Mac), create a blank file; name it `htaccess.txt` and upload it to your web server via SFTP.**
2. **After the file is uploaded to your web server, rename the file `.htaccess` (notice the period at the beginning), and make sure that it's writable by the server by changing permissions to 755 or 777.**
3. **Create the permalink structure on the Customize Permalink Structure page of your WordPress Dashboard.**
4. **Click the Save Changes button at the bottom of the Customize Permalink Structure page.**

   WordPress inserts into the `.htaccess` file the specific rules necessary for making the permalink structure functional on your site.

If you follow the preceding steps correctly, you have an `.htaccess` file on your web server with the correct permissions set so that WordPress can write the correct rules to it. Your pretty-permalink structure works flawlessly. Kudos!

If you open the `.htaccess` file and look at it now, you see that it's no longer blank. It should have a set of code in it called *rewrite rules*, which looks something like this:

```
# BEGIN WordPress
<IfModule mod_rewrite.c>
RewriteEngine On
RewriteBase /
RewriteCond %{REQUEST_FILENAME} !-f
RewriteCond %{REQUEST_FILENAME} !-d
RewriteRule . /index.php [L]
</IfModule>

# END WordPress
```

TECHNICAL STUFF

I could delve deeply into `.htaccess` and all the things you can do with this file, but I'm restricting this chapter to how it applies to WordPress permalink structures. If you want to unlock more mysteries about `.htaccess`, check out "Comprehensive Guide to .htaccess" at `www.javascriptkit.com/howto/htaccess.shtml`.

WORKING WITH SERVERS THAT DON'T USE APACHE MOD_REWRITE

Using permalink structures requires your web hosting provider to have a specific Apache module option called mod_rewrite activated on its servers. If your web hosting provider doesn't have this item activated on its servers, or if you're hosting your site on a Windows server, the custom permalinks work only if you type **index.php** in front of any custom permalink tags.

Create the custom permalink tags like this:

/index.php/%year%/%month%/%date%/%postname%/

This format creates a permalink like this:

`https://yourdomain.com/index.php/2019/01/01/wordpress-all-in-one-for-dummies`

You don't need an .htaccess file to use this permalink structure.

Privacy

The next link on the Settings menu is Privacy. Choose Settings⇨Privacy to view the Privacy Settings screen, shown in Figure 2-9.

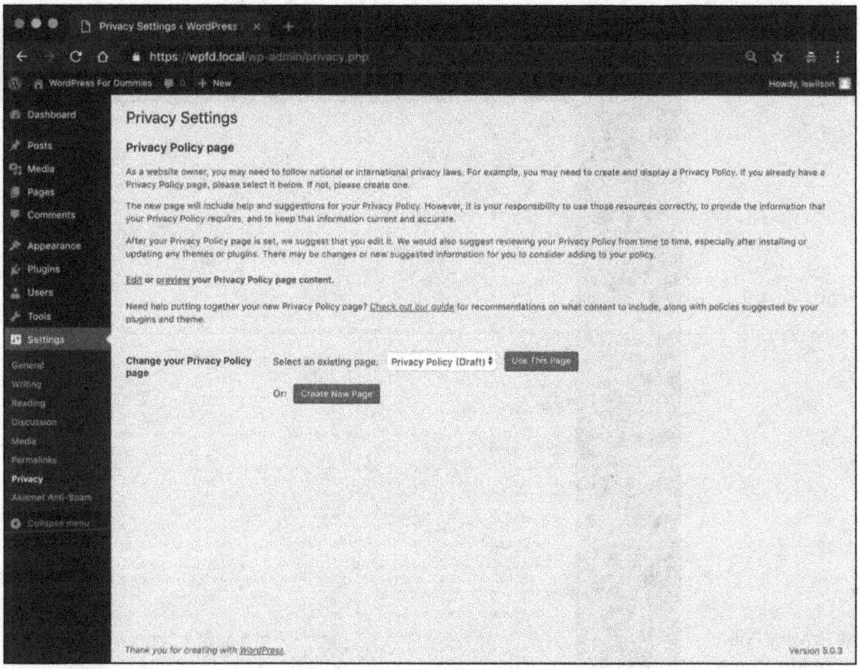

FIGURE 2-9: The Privacy Settings screen.

On May 25, 2018, the European Union (EU) enacted a law called General Data Protection Regulation, or GDPR for short. The GDPR is a set of rules designed to give European citizens more control of their personal data that's stored on websites they browse on the Internet. As an owner of a website, you may be required to follow these laws to protect the privacy of your visitors' and users' data on your website. Part of this law requires you to publish a privacy page on your website that lays out your privacy policy, which helps your website remain in compliance with GDPR rules.

To help you, every new WordPress installation comes with a Privacy Policy page in draft form. The Privacy Settings screen displays this draft page in the Change Your Privacy Policy Page drop-down menu. Click the Use This Page button to use the default page that WordPress provided, or click the Create New Page button to create your own.

This is where I tell you that I'm not a lawyer and am not equipped to give you any legal advice on what your privacy policy page should contain to make your website compliant with the GDPR, but WordPress offers a handy guide. Click the Check Out Our Guide link on the Privacy Settings screen to view the Privacy Policy Guide screen in your Dashboard (see Figure 2-10). In addition to tips, the screen offers a template for a good privacy policy page.

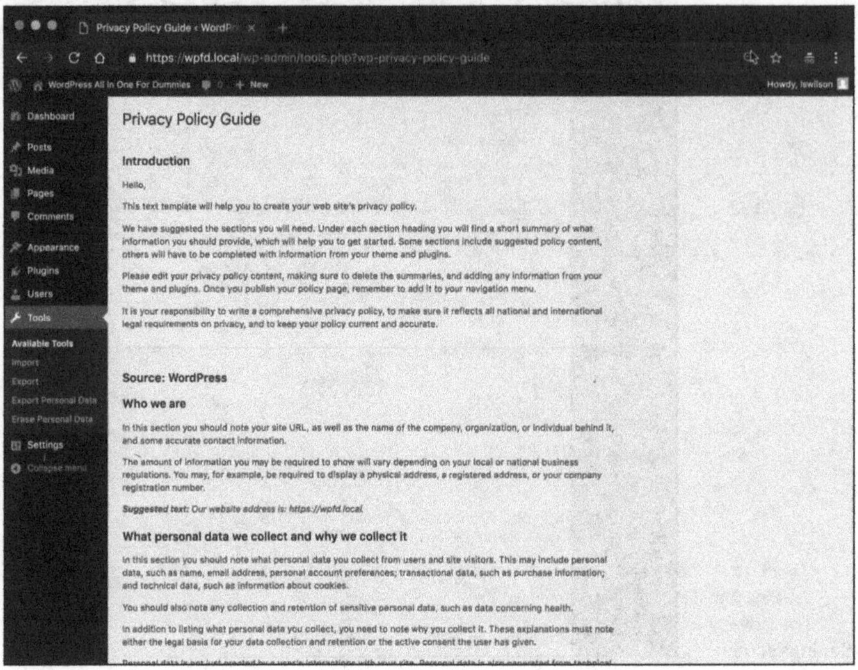

FIGURE 2-10: The Privacy Policy Guide screen.

TIP

Even though the GDPR was written to pertain to citizens of the EU, there are international implications, as well, particularly if visitors to your website are located in the EU. Because you can't know whether an EU citizen is going to visit your site, it's a good rule of thumb for your website to have a basic privacy policy. You can read more about the GDPR at `https://eugdpr.org`.

Creating Your Personal Profile

To personalize your site, visit the Profile screen of your WordPress Dashboard.

To access the Profile screen, hover over the Users link in the Dashboard navigation menu, and click the Your Profile link. The Profile screen appears, as shown in Figure 2-11.

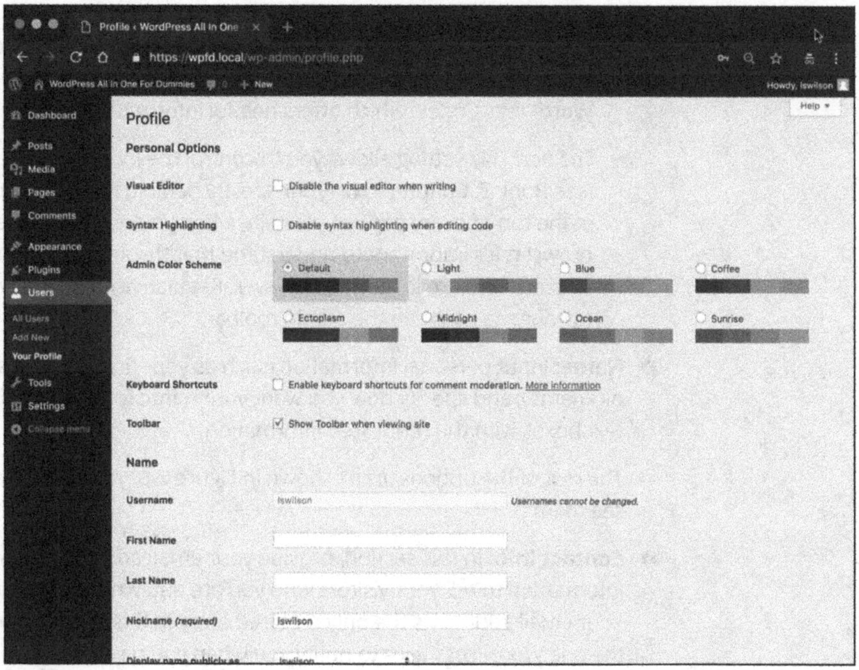

FIGURE 2-11: Establish your profile details on the Profile screen.

Here are the settings on this page:

- **Personal Options:** In the Personal Options section, you can set these preferences for your site:
  - *Visual Editor:* Select this check box to indicate that you want to use the Visual Editor when writing your posts. The Visual Editor refers to the formatting options you find on the Write Post screen (discussed in detail in Book 4, Chapter 1). By default, the check box is deselected, which means that the Visual Editor is off. To turn it on, select the check box.
  - *Syntax Highlighting*: Select this check box to disable syntax highlighting. This option disables the feature in the Dashboard theme and plugin code editors that displays code in different colors and fonts, according to the type of code being used (HTML, PHP, CSS, and so on). I cover theme and plugin code in Books 6 and 7, respectively.
  - *Admin Color Scheme:* These options set the colors for your Dashboard. The Default color scheme is automatically selected for you in a new installation, but you have other color options, including Light, Blue, Coffee, Ectoplasm, Midnight, Ocean, and Sunrise.
  - *Keyboard Shortcuts:* This check box enables you to use keyboard shortcuts for comment moderation. To find out more about keyboard shortcuts,

click the More Information link; you're taken to the Keyboard Shortcuts page (`https://codex.wordpress.org/Keyboard_Shortcuts`) of the WordPress Codex, which offers helpful information.

  - *Toolbar:* This setting allows you to control the location of the admin toolbar (see Book 3, Chapter 1) on your site. By default, the admin toolbar appears at the top of every page of your site when you're viewing the site in your browser. It's important to understand that the admin toolbar appears only to users who are logged in, however. Regular visitors who aren't logged in to your site can't see the admin toolbar.

- **Name:** Input personal information (such as your first name, last name, and nickname), and specify how you want your name to appear publicly. Fill in the text boxes with the requested information.

  The rest of the options aren't shown in Figure 2-9; you have to scroll down to see them.

- **Contact Info:** In this section, provide your email address and other contact information to tell your visitors who you are and where they can contact you. Your email address is the only required entry in this section. This address is the one WordPress uses to notify you when you have new comments or new user registrations on your site. Make sure to use a real email address so that you get these notifications. You can also insert your website URL into the website text field.

- **About Yourself:** Provide a little bio for yourself, and change the password for your site, if you want:

  - *Biographical Info:* Type a short bio in the Biographical Info text box. This information can appear publicly if you're using a theme that displays your bio, so be creative!

    WARNING

    When your profile is published to your website, anyone can view it, and search engines, such as Google and Yahoo!, can pick it up. Always be careful with the information in your profile. Think hard about the information you want to share with the rest of the world!

  - *Profile Picture:* Display the current photo that you've set in your Gravatar account. You can set up a profile picture or change your existing one within your Gravatar account at `https://gravatar.com`.

- **Account Management:** Manage your password and user sessions, as follows:

  - *New Password:* When you want to change the password for your site, click the Generate Password button in the New Password section. You can use the password that WordPress generates for you or type your own password in the text field that appears.

TIP

Directly below the New Password text field is a password helper, where WordPress helps you create a secure password. It alerts you if the password you chose is too short or not secure enough by telling you that it's Weak or Very Weak. When creating a new password, use a combination of letters, numbers, and symbols to make it hard for anyone to guess (such as *b@Fmn2quDtnSLQblhml%jexA*). When you create a password that WordPress thinks is a good one, it lets you know by saying that the password is Strong.

WARNING

Change your password frequently. Some people on the Internet make it their business to attempt to hijack sites for their own malicious purposes. If you change your password monthly, you lower your risk by keeping hackers guessing.

- *Sessions:* If you're logged in to your site on several devices, you can log yourself out of those locations by clicking the Log Out Everywhere Else button. This option keeps you logged in at your current location but logs you out of any other location where you may be logged in. If you're not logged in anywhere else, the button is inactive, and a message appears that says `You are only logged in at this location.`

REMEMBER

When you finish setting all the options on the Profile screen, don't forget to click the Update Profile button to save your changes.

Setting Your Site's Format

In addition to setting your personal settings in the Dashboard, you can manage the day-to-day maintenance of your site. The following sections take you through the links to these pages on the Dashboard navigation menus.

Posts

Hover your mouse over the Posts link on the navigation menu to reveal a submenu with four links: All Posts, Add New, Categories, and Tags. Each link gives you the tools you need to publish content to your site:

- **All Posts:** Opens the Posts screen, where a list of all the saved posts you've written on your site appears. On this screen, you can search for posts by date, category, or keyword. You can view all posts, only posts that have been published, or only posts that you've saved but haven't published (drafts). You can also edit and delete posts from this page. Check out Book 4, Chapter 1 for more information on editing posts on your site.

- **Add New:** Opens the Add New Post screen, where you can compose your posts, set the options for each post (such as assigning a post to a category, or making it a private or public post), and publish the post to your site. You can find more information on posts, post options, and publishing in Book 4, Chapter 1.

  TIP

  You can also get to the Add New Post screen by clicking the Add New button on the Posts screen or by clicking the +New link on the admin toolbar and choosing Post.

- **Categories:** Opens the Categories screen, where you can view, edit, add, and delete categories on your site. Find more information on creating categories in Book 3, Chapter 5.
- **Tags:** Opens the Tags screen in your WordPress Dashboard, where you can view, add, edit, and delete tags on your site. Book 3, Chapter 5 provides more information about tags and using them on your site.

Media

Hover your mouse over the Media link on the navigation menu to reveal a submenu with two links:

- **Library:** Opens the Media Library screen. On this screen, you can view, search, and manage all the media files you've ever uploaded to your WordPress site.
- **Add New:** Opens the Upload New Media screen, where you can use the built-in uploader to transfer media files from your computer to the media directory in WordPress. Book 4, chapters 3 and 4 take you through the details of uploading images, videos, audio, and documents by using the WordPress upload feature.

  TIP

  You can also get to the Upload New Media screen by clicking the Add New button on the Media Library screen or by clicking the +New link on the admin toolbar and choosing Media.

Pages

People use this feature to create pages on their sites such as About Me or Contact Me. Turn to Book 4, Chapter 2 for more information on pages. Hover your mouse over the Pages link on the navigation menu to reveal a submenu list with two links:

- **All Pages:** Opens the Pages screen, where you can search, view, edit, and delete pages on your WordPress site.
- **Add New:** Opens the Add New Page screen, where you can compose, save, and publish a new page on your site. Book 4, Chapter 2 describes the difference between a post and a page. The difference is subtle, but posts and pages are very different!

  You can also get to the Add New Page screen by clicking the Add New button on the Pages screen or by clicking the +New link on the admin toolbar and choosing Page.

Comments

Comments in the navigation menu don't have a submenu of links. You simply click Comments to open the Comments screen, where WordPress gives you the options to view the following:

- **All:** Shows all comments that currently exist on your site, including approved, pending, and spam comments
- **Pending:** Shows comments that you haven't yet approved but are pending in the moderation queue
- **Approved:** Shows all comments that you previously approved
- **Spam:** Shows all the comments that are marked as spam
- **Trash:** Shows comments that you marked as Trash but haven't deleted permanently from your site

Book 3, Chapter 4 gives you details on how to use the Comments section of your WordPress Dashboard.

Appearance

When you hover your mouse over the Appearance link on the Dashboard navigation menu, a submenu appears, displaying the following links:

- **Themes:** Opens the Themes screen, where you can manage the themes available on your site. Check out Book 6, Chapter 2 to find out about using themes on your WordPress site and managing themes on this page.
- **Customize:** Opens the Customizer screen, where you can edit various features available in the active theme on your site.

- **Widgets:** Opens the Widgets screen, where you can add, delete, edit, and manage the widgets that you use on your site.
- **Menus:** Opens the Menus screen, where you can build navigation menus that will appear on your site. Book 6, Chapter 1 provides information on creating menus by using this feature.
- **Header:** Opens the Header Media screen in the Customizer, where you can upload an image to use in the *header* (top) of your WordPress site. This menu item and screen exist only if you're using a theme that has activated the Custom Header feature (covered in Book 6). The Twenty Seventeen theme is activated by default on all new WordPress sites, which is why I include this menu item in this list. Not all WordPress themes use the Header Media feature, so you don't see this menu item if your theme doesn't take advantage of that feature.
- **Editor:** Opens the Edit Themes screen, where you can edit your theme templates. Book 6 has extensive information on themes and templates.

TIP

Uploading header images helps you individualize the visual design of your website. You can find more information on tweaking and customizing your WordPress theme in Book 6, as well as a great deal of information about how to use WordPress themes (including where to find, install, and activate them in your WordPress site) and detailed information about using WordPress widgets to display the content you want.

Book 6 provides information about WordPress themes and templates. You can dig deep into WordPress template tags and tweak an existing WordPress theme by using Cascading Style Sheets (CSS) to customize your theme a bit more to your liking.

Plugins

The next item on the navigation menu is Plugins. Hover your mouse over the Plugins link to view the submenu:

- **Installed Plugins:** Opens the Plugins screen, where you can view all the plugins currently installed on your site. On this page, you also have the ability to activate, deactivate, and delete plugins on your site. (Book 7 is all about plugins.)
- **Add New:** Opens the Add Plugins screen, where you can search for plugins from the official WordPress Plugin Directory by keyword, author, or tag. You can also install plugins directly to your site from the WordPress Plugin page; find out all about this exciting feature in Book 7, Chapter 2.

» **Editor:** Opens the Edit Plugins screen, where you can edit the plugin files in a text editor. Don't plan to edit plugin files unless you know what you're doing (meaning that you're familiar with PHP and WordPress functions). Head over to Book 7, Chapter 4 to read more information on editing plugin files.

Users

The Users submenu has three links:

» **All Users:** Opens the Users screen, where you can view, edit, and delete users of your WordPress site. Each user has a unique login name and password, as well as an email address assigned to his account. You can view and edit a user's information on the Users page.

» **Add New:** Opens the Add New User screen, where you can add new users to your WordPress site. Simply type the user's username, first name, last name, email (required), website, and a password in the fields provided, and click the Add User button. You can also specify whether you want WordPress to send login information to a new user by email. If you want, you can also assign a new role for the new user. Turn to "Configuring the Settings" earlier in this chapter for more info about user roles.

» **Your Profile:** Turn to "Creating Your Personal Profile" earlier in this chapter for more information about creating a profile page.

Tools

The last item on the navigation menu (and subsequently in this chapter!) is Tools. Hover your mouse over the Tools link to view the submenu:

» **Available Tools:** Opens the Tools screen on your Dashboard. WordPress comes packaged with two extra features that you can use on your site, if needed. These features are Press This and Category/Tag Converter.

» **Import:** Opens the Import screen of your Dashboard. WordPress allows you to import from a different publishing platform. This feature is covered in depth in Book 2, Chapter 7.

» **Export:** Opens the Export screen of your Dashboard. WordPress allows you to export your content from WordPress so that you can import it into a different platform or to another WordPress-powered site.

- **Export Personal Data:** Opens the Export Personal Data screen. This screen gives you the opportunity to input the username or email address of a registered user on your site and obtain an authorization from the user to verify and approve the request to download personal data. After verification is complete, the user receives an email with a link to download their personal data in `.zip` format.
- **Erase Personal Data:** Opens the Erase Personal Data screen in the Dashboard. This screen gives you the ability to input the user name or email address of a registered user to obtain verification from that user to erase his personal data from the site. After the user has completed the verification, she receives an email confirming that his personal data has been erased from the site.

IN THIS CHAPTER

» Deciding what roles to assign users

» Allowing new users to register

» Adding a new user

» Making changes to user profiles

» Using tools to manage multiauthor sites

Chapter 3

Managing Users and Multiple Authors

A *multiauthor site* involves inviting others to coauthor, or contribute articles, posts, pages, or other content to your site. You can expand the offerings on your website by using multiauthor publishing because you can have several people writing on different topics or offering different perspectives on the same topic. Many people use this type of site to create a collaborative writing space on the web, and WordPress doesn't limit the number of authors you can add to your site.

Additionally, you can invite other people to register as *subscribers*, who don't contribute content but are registered members of the site, which can have benefits too. (You could make some content available to registered users only, for example.)

This chapter takes you through the process of adding users to your site, takes the mystery out of the different user roles and capabilities, and gives you some tools for managing a multiauthor website.

Understanding User Roles and Capabilities

Before you start adding new users to your site, you need to understand the differences among the user roles, because each user role is assigned a different level of access and grouping of capabilities to your site, as follows:

- **Subscriber:** Subscriber is the default role. Maintain this role as the one assigned to new users, particularly if you don't know who's registering. Subscribers get access to the Dashboard page, and they can view and change the options in their profiles on the Profile screen. (They don't have access to your account settings, however — only to their own.) Each user can change her username, email address, password, bio, and other descriptors in her user profile. The WordPress database stores subscribers' profile information, and your site remembers them each time they visit, so they don't have to complete the profile information each time they leave comments on your site.
- **Contributor:** In addition to the access subscribers have, contributors can upload files and write, edit, and delete their own posts. Contributors can write posts, but they can't publish the posts; the administrator reviews all contributor posts and decides whether to publish them. This setting is a nice way to moderate content written by new authors.
- **Author:** In addition to the access contributors have, authors can publish and edit their own posts.
- **Editor:** In addition to the access authors have, editors can moderate comments, manage categories, manage links, edit pages, and edit other authors' posts.
- **Administrator:** Administrators can edit all the options and settings in the WordPress blog.
- **Super Admin:** This role exists only when you have the multisite feature activated in WordPress. See Book 8 for more about the multisite feature.

Table 3-1 gives you an at-a-glance reference for the basic differences in roles and capabilities for WordPress users.

TIP

Table 3-1 doesn't offer exhaustive information by any means, but it covers the basic user roles and capabilities for WordPress or the most common capabilities for each user role. For a full list of user roles and capabilities, check out the WordPress Codex at `https://codex.wordpress.org/Roles_and_Capabilities`.

TABLE 3-1 WordPress User Roles and Capabilities

	Super Admin	Administrator	Editor	Author	Contributor	Subscriber
Manage multisite features	Yes	No	No	No	No	No
Add/edit users	Yes	Yes	No	No	No	No
Add/edit/ install plugins	Yes	Yes	No	No	No	No
Add/edit/ install themes	Yes	Yes	No	No	No	No
Manage comments	Yes	Yes	Yes	No	No	No
Manage categories, tags, and links	Yes	Yes	Yes	No	No	No
Publish posts	Yes	Yes	Yes	Yes	No (moderated)	No
Edit published posts	Yes	Yes	Yes	No	No	No
Edit others' posts	Yes	Yes	Yes	No	No	No
Edit own posts	Yes	Yes	Yes	Yes	Yes	No
Publish pages	Yes	Yes	Yes	No	No	No
Read	Yes	Yes	Yes	Yes	Yes	Yes

Allowing New User Registration

As you can see in Table 3-1, each user level has a different set of capabilities. Book 3, Chapter 2 discusses the General Settings of the WordPress Dashboard, in which you set the default role for users who register on your website. Keep the default role set to Subscriber because when you open registration to the public, you don't always know who's registering until after they register — and you don't want to arbitrarily hand out higher levels of access to the settings of your website unless you know and trust the user.

When users register on your website, you, as the administrator, get an email notification (sent to the email address you set on the General Settings screen) so you always know when a new user registers; then you can go to your Dashboard and edit the user to set his role any way you see fit.

REMEMBER

New users can register on your site only after you enable the Anyone Can Register option on the General Settings screen within your Dashboard (Book 3, Chapter 2). If you don't have this option enabled, users see a message on the Registration page telling them that registration isn't allowed, as shown in Figure 3-1.

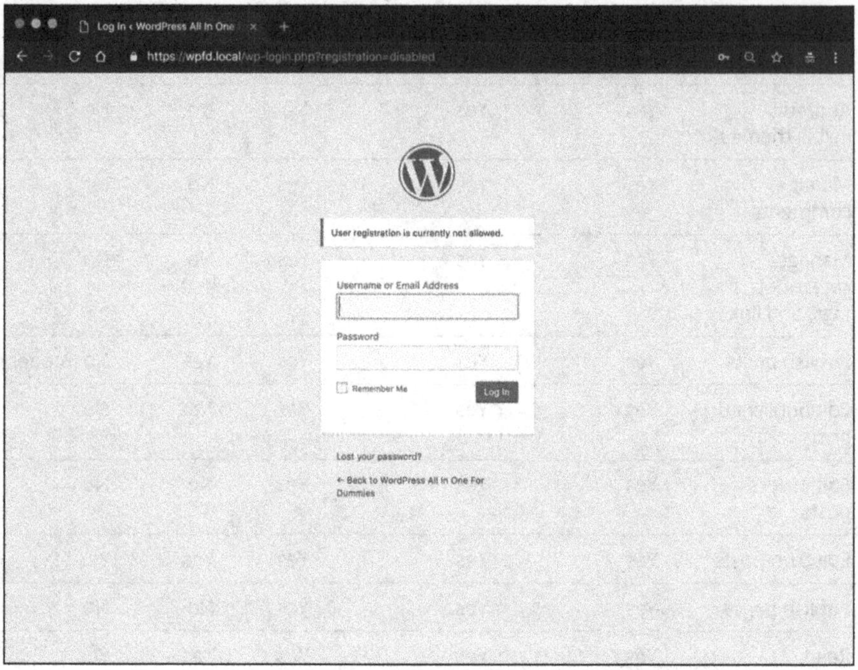

FIGURE 3-1: The message to users that registration isn't allowed.

By the way, the direct URL for registration on a blog that has registration enabled is `https://yourdomain.com/wp-login.php?action=register`. With registration enabled (in General Settings), a user sees a form inviting her to input her desired username and email address. After she does, she gets a confirmation notice in her inbox including an authorization link that she must click to authenticate her registration.

After a user has registered, you, as the site administrator, can manage her user account and assign a user role. (Refer to Table 3-1.)

Adding New Users Manually

Allowing new users to register by using the WordPress registration interface is only one way to add users to your site. As the site administrator, you have the ability to add new users manually by following these steps:

1. **Log in to your WordPress Dashboard by inputting your username and password in the form at** `https://yourdomain.com/wp-login.php`**.**
2. **Click the Add New link in the Users submenu of the Dashboard.**

   The Add New User screen loads, as shown in Figure 3-2.

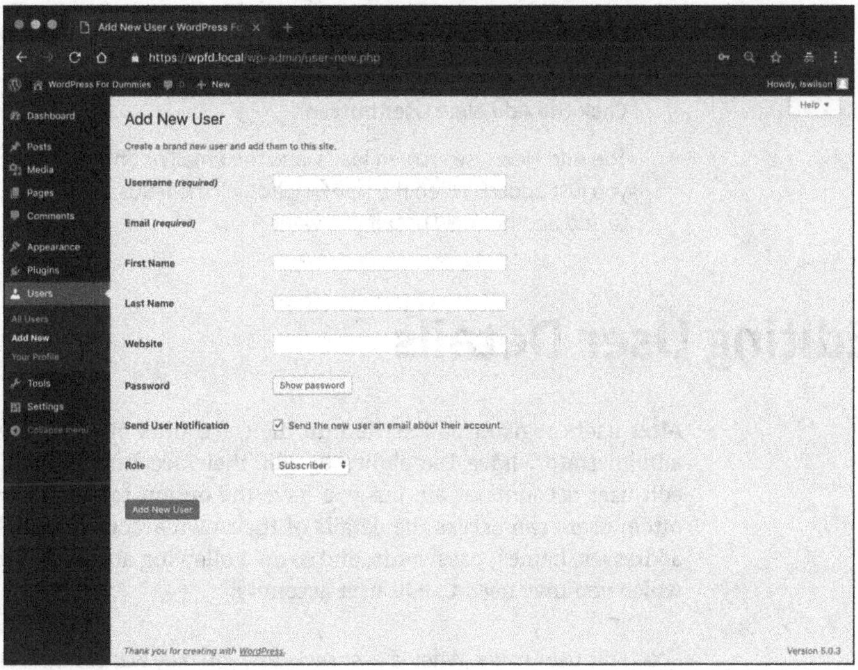

FIGURE 3-2: The Add New User screen of the WordPress Dashboard.

3. **Enter the username in the Username text box.**

   You can't skip this text box. The new user types this username when he's prompted to log in to your site.
4. **Enter the user's email address in the Email text box.**

   You can't skip this text box, either. The user receives notifications from you and your site at this email address.
5. **Enter the user's first name in the First Name text box.**
6. **Enter the user's last name in the Last Name text box.**
7. **Enter the URL of the user's website in the Website text box.**
8. **Click the Show Password button.**

   WordPress provides a random, strong password for you, or you can type your own password in the text field. WordPress provides a strength indicator that

Managing Users and Multiple Authors

gives you an idea of how strong (secure) your chosen password is. You want secure passwords so that no one can easily guess them, so make the password at least seven characters long, and use a combination of letters, numbers, and symbols (such as @, #, $, and ^).

9. **If you want the user to receive his password by email, select the Send the New User an Email about Their Account check box.**
10. **From the Role drop-down menu, choose Subscriber, Contributor, Author, Editor, or Administrator.**
11. **Click the Add New User button.**

    The Add New User screen loads, and the email notification is sent to the user you just added. When the screen loads, all the fields are cleared, allowing you to add another new user if you want.

Editing User Details

After users register and settle into their accounts on your site, you, as the site administrator, have the ability to edit their accounts. You may never have to edit user accounts at all, but you have the option to do so if you need to. Most often, users can access the details of their own accounts and change their email addresses, names, passwords, and so on. Following are some circumstances under which you may need to edit user accounts:

- **Edit user roles.** When a user registers, you may want to increase her role, or level of access, on your site; promote an existing user to administrator; or demote an existing administrator or editor a notch or two.
- **Edit user emails.** If a user loses access to the email account that she registered with, she may ask you to change her account email address so that she can access her account notifications again.
- **Edit user passwords.** If a user loses access to the email account with which she registered, she can't use WordPress's Lost Password feature, which allows users to gain access to their account password through email recovery. In that case, a user may ask you to reset her password for her so that she can log in and access her account again.

In any of these circumstances, you can make the necessary changes by clicking the Users link on the Users menu of your WordPress Dashboard, which loads the Users screen, shown in Figure 3-3.

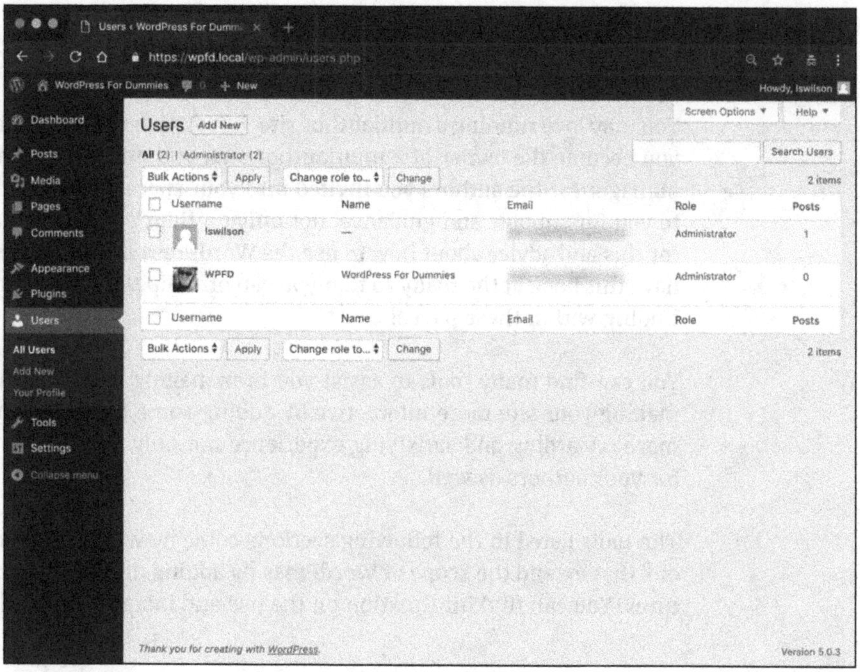

FIGURE 3-3: The Users screen lets you manage all the users on your site.

Figure 3-3 shows the Users screen for a site that has multiple users with different levels of access, or roles. When you hover your mouse over the name of a user, an Edit link appears below the user listing. Click that Edit link to access the Edit User screen, where you can edit different pieces of information for that user, including

- **Personal Options:** These options include Visual Editor, Color Scheme, Keyboard Shortcuts, and Toolbar preferences.
- **Name:** Specify a user's role, first and last names, nickname, and display name.
- **Contact Info:** These options include the user's email address and website.
- **Biographical Info:** This section provides a few lines of biographical info for the user (optional, but some WordPress themes display authors' biographies). This section also displays the user's profile picture.
- **New Password:** Here, you can change the password for the user.

The Edit User screen looks the same, and has the same features, as the Profile screen that you deal with in Book 3, Chapter 2. Feel free to visit that chapter to get the lowdown on the options and settings on this screen.

Managing a Multiauthor Site

You may love running a multiauthor site, but the job has its challenges. The minute you become the owner of a multiauthor site, you immediately assume the role of manager for the authors you invited into your space. At times, those authors look to you for support and guidance, not only on their content management, but also for tips and advice about how to use the WordPress interface. It's a good thing you have this book at the ready so that you can offer up the gems of information you're finding within these pages!

You can find many tools to assist you in managing a multiauthor site, as well as making your site more interactive by adding some features, which can make it a more rewarding and satisfying experience not only for you and your readers, but for your authors as well.

The tools listed in the following sections come by way of plugins, which are add-ons that extend the scope of WordPress by adding different functionality and features. You can find information on the use and installation of plugins in Book 7.

Tools that help authors communicate

When you're running a multiauthor site, communication is crucial for sharing information, giving and receiving inspiration, and making certain that no two authors are writing the same article (or similar articles) on your site. Use the following tools to manage the flow of communication among everyone involved:

- **Post Status Notifications:** In "Understanding User Roles and Capabilities" earlier in this chapter, I mention that the role of contributor can write and save posts to your site, but those posts don't get published to the site until an administrator approves them. This plugin notifies the administrator, via email, when a new post is submitted for review. Additionally, the contributing author gets an email notification when an administrator has published the post to the site.

  `https://wordpress.org/plugins/wpsite-post-status-notifications`

- **Editorial Calendar:** This plugin gives you an overview of scheduled posts, post authors, and the dates when you scheduled the posts to publish to your site. This plugin can help you prevent multiple author posts from publishing too close together or, in some cases, right on top of one another; you simply reschedule posts by using a drag-and-drop interface.

  `https://wordpress.org/plugins/editorial-calendar`

- **Email Users:** This plugin allows you to send emails to all registered users of your site, and users can send emails to one another by using the plugin interface of the Dashboard. This tool enables the authors and users on your multiauthor site to keep in touch and communicate with one another.

`https://wordpress.org/plugins/email-users`

» **User Notes:** When you run a website that has multiple authors, you may find it helpful to leave notes on an user profile that are visible to site administrators only. These notes can be helpful and can serve as a tool for reminders.

`https://wordpress.org/plugins/user-notes`

Tools to promote author profiles

One way to operate a successful multiauthor site involves taking every opportunity to promote your authors and their information. Authors often get involved in posting content on websites in addition to yours, for exposure. The plugins in this list give you tools to promote authors bios, links, social network feeds, and more:

» **Authors Widget:** This plugin gives you a widget you can place on your site that displays a list of authors along with the number of posts they've published, a link to the RSS feeds for their posts, and their names and photos (see Figure 3-4).

`https://wordpress.org/plugins/authors`

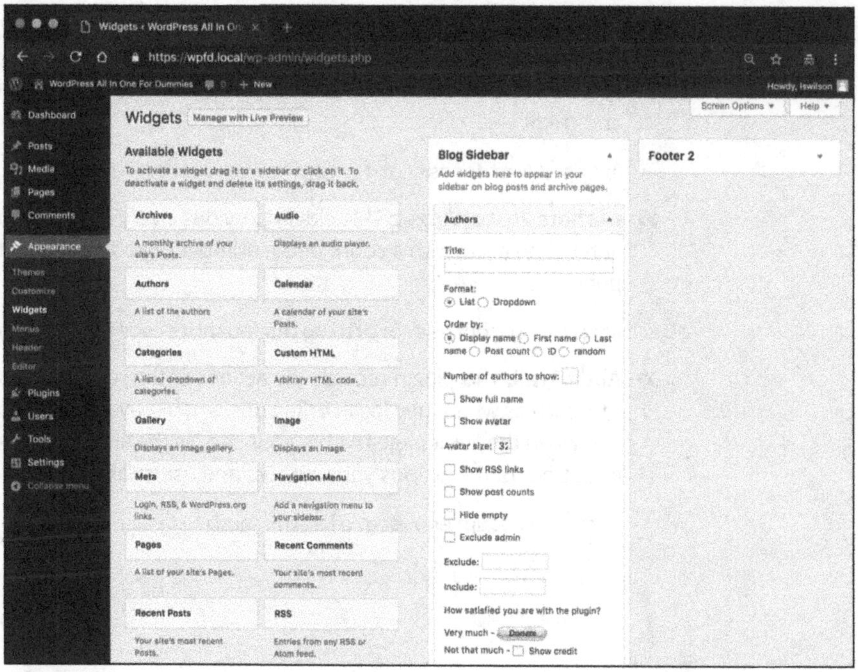

FIGURE 3-4: The Authors Widget options.

- **Author Avatars List:** This plugin gives you a widget to display a list of authors on your website. This plugin enables the display of author avatars, names, and short bios of the author.

  https://wordpress.org/plugins/author-avatars

- **Author Spotlight:** This plugin provides a widget that you can place on your sidebar, displaying the profile of the author of the post being viewed. The author information automatically appears on a single post page and displays the profile of the author of the post.

  https://wordpress.org/plugins/author-profile

- **Author Recent Posts:** This plugin gives you a widget that allows an author to display a listing of her recent posts in the sidebar of posts she's published on your site.

  https://wordpress.org/plugins/author-recent-posts

Tools to manage multiauthor blog posts

The plugins listed in this section can help you, the site administrator, manage your group of authors and registered users by giving you some tools to track users' activity, list their posts, and stay up to date and notified when your authors publish new content:

- **Co-Authors Plus:** This plugin allows you to assign multiple authors to one post, which you may find especially helpful when you have several authors collaborating on one article, allowing those authors to share the byline and credit.

  https://wordpress.org/plugins/co-authors-plus

- **Authors Posts Widget:** This plugin provides a very easy way to show a list of authors on a site with a count of the number of posts each author has published.

  https://wordpress.org/plugins/authors-posts-widget/

- **Audit Trail:** This plugin records the actions of the registered users on your site, such as when they log in or log out, when they publish posts and pages, and when they visit pages within your site. As the site administrator, you can keep track of the actions your authors and users take on your website.

  https://wordpress.org/plugins/audit-trail

IN THIS CHAPTER

» Making the decision to allow comments

» Using comments to interact with readers

» Working with comments and trackbacks

» Using Akismet to help combat spam

Chapter 4

Dealing with Comments and Spam

One of the most exciting aspects of publishing with WordPress is getting feedback from your readers on articles you publish to your site. Feedback, also known as *comments,* is akin to having a guestbook on your site.

People leave notes for you that are published to your site, and through these notes, you can respond to and engage your readers in conversation about the topic. Having this function on your site allows you to expand the thoughts and ideas you present in your posts by giving readers the opportunity to add their two cents' worth.

In this chapter, you can decide whether to allow comments on your site, figure out how to manage those comments, use trackbacks, and discover the negative aspects of allowing comments (such as spam).

Deciding to Allow Comments on Your Site

Some publishers say that a blog without comments isn't a blog at all because the point of having a blog on your website, in some minds, is to foster communication and interaction between the site authors and the readers. This belief is common in the publishing community because experiencing visitor feedback via comments is part of what's made Internet publishing so popular. Allowing comments is a personal choice, however, and you don't have to allow them if you don't want to.

Positive aspects of allowing comments

Allowing comments on your site lets audience members actively involve themselves in your site by creating a discussion and dialogue about your content. Mostly, readers find commenting to be a satisfying experience when they visit sites because comments make them part of the discussion.

Depending on the topic you write about, allowing comments sends the message that you, as the author/owner of the site, are open to the views and opinions of your readers. Having a comment form on your site that readers can use to leave their feedback on your articles (such as the one shown in Figure 4-1) is like having a great big Welcome to My Home sign on your site; it invites users in to share thoughts and participate in discussions.

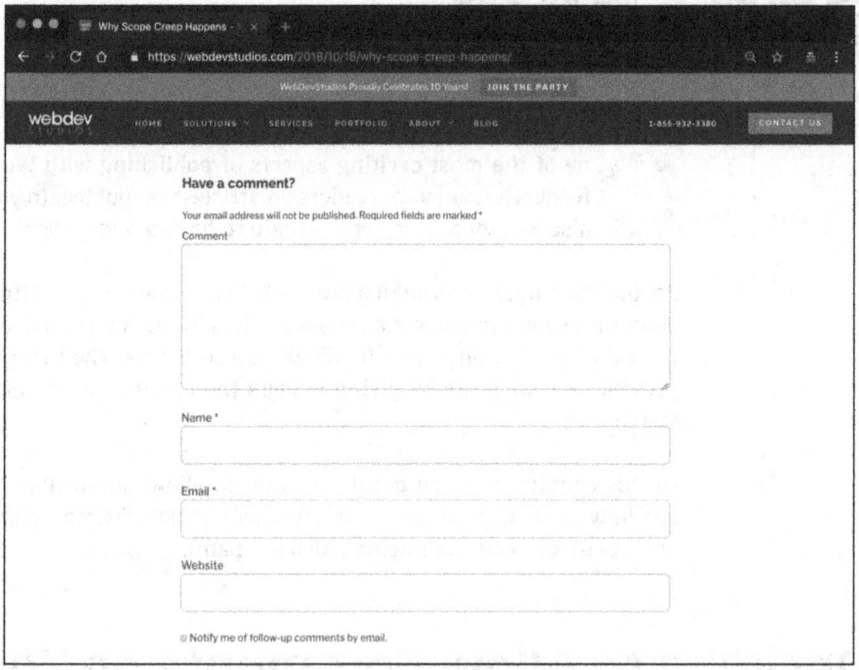

FIGURE 4-1: Readers use the Have a Comment? form to share their comments.

If you want to build a community of people who come back to your site frequently, respond to as many comments that your readers leave on your posts as possible.

When people take the time to leave you a comment on your content, they like to know that you're reading it, and they appreciate hearing your feedback to them. Also, open comments keep discussions lively and active on your site. Figure 4-2 illustrates what comments look like after they're published to your site. (*Note:* The actual design and layout of the comments on sites varies from theme to theme; you can find information on theme design in Book 6.)

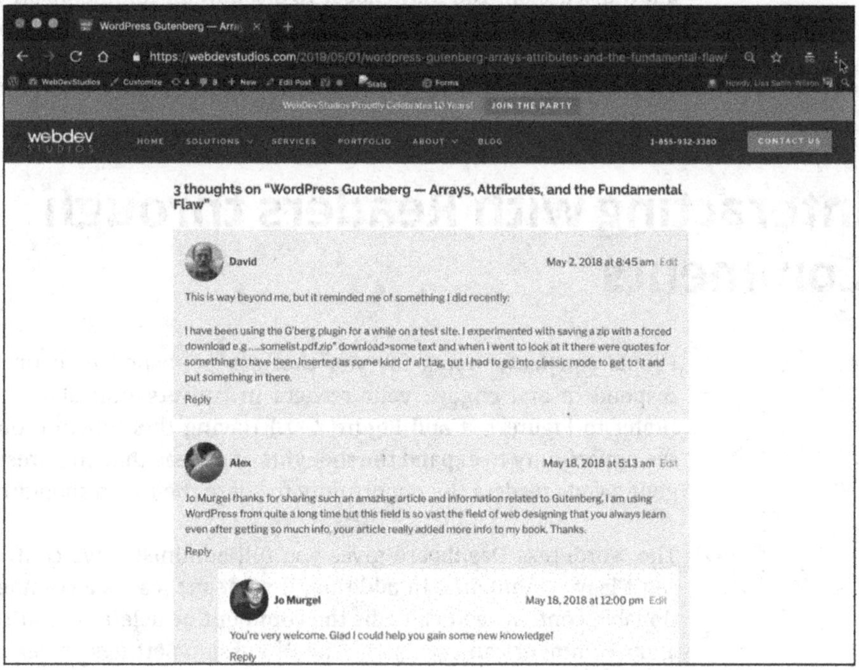

FIGURE 4-2: Visitors comment on a post.

Reasons to disallow comments

Under certain circumstances, you may not want to allow readers to leave comments freely on your site. If you wrote a post on a topic that's considered to be very controversial, for example, you may not want to invite comments, because the topic may incite flame wars or comments that are insulting to you or your readers. If you're not interested in the point of view or feedback of readers on your site, or if your content doesn't really lend itself to reader feedback, you may decide to disallow comments.

REMEMBER

In making the decision to have comments, you have to be prepared for the fact that not everyone is going to agree with what you write — especially if you're writing on a topic that invites a wide array of opinions, such as politics or religion. As a site owner, you make the decision ahead of time about whether you want readers dropping in and leaving their own views, or even disagreeing with you about yours (sometimes vehemently!).

If you're on the fence about whether to allow comments, the WordPress platform allows you to toggle that decision on a per-post basis. Therefore, each time you publish a post or article on your website, you can indicate in Post Options (on the Add New Post screen of your Dashboard) whether this particular post should allow discussion. You may choose to disallow all comments on your site (a setting that you can configure in Discussion Settings) or disallow them for only certain posts (a setting that you can configure on the Edit Post page, which I talk about in Book 4, Chapter 1).

Interacting with Readers through Comments

People can leave notes for you that are published to your site, and you can respond to and engage your readers in conversation about the topic at hand. (Refer to Figure 4-1 and Figure 4-2.) Having this function on your site creates the opportunity to expand the thoughts and ideas that you present in your post by giving your readers the opportunity to share their own thoughts.

The WordPress Dashboard gives you full administrative control of who can and can't leave comments. In addition, if someone leaves a comment that has questionable content, you can edit the comment or delete it. You're also free to disallow comments on your blog. The Discussion Settings screen of your Dashboard contains all the settings for allowing or disallowing comments on your site. See Book 3, Chapter 2 to dig into those settings, what they mean, and how you can use them to configure the exact interactive environment that you want for your site.

Tracking back

The best way to understand trackbacks is to think of them as comments except for one thing: *Trackbacks* are comments left on your blog by other blogs, not by actual people. Although this process may sound mysterious, it's actually perfectly reasonable.

A trackback happens when you make a post on your site and, within that post, you provide a link to a post made by another author on a different site. When you publish that post, your site sends a sort of electronic memo to the site you linked to. That site receives the memo and posts an acknowledgment of receipt in a comment within the post that you linked to on that site. Trackbacks work between most publishing platforms — between WordPress and Blogger, for example, as well as between WordPress and Typepad.

That memo is sent via a *network ping* (a tool used to test, or verify, whether a link is reachable across the Internet) from your site to the site you link to. This process works as long as both sites support trackback protocol. Trackbacks can also come to your site by way of a *pingback* — which really is the same thing as a trackback, but the terminology varies from platform to platform.

Sending a trackback to a site is a nice way of telling the author that you like the information she presented in her post. Every author appreciates the receipt of trackbacks to her posts from other authors.

Enabling comment and trackback display

Almost every single WordPress theme displays comments at the bottom of each post published in WordPress. You can do custom styling of the comments so that they match the design of your site by using several items:

- **WordPress template tags:** Template tags are related to the display of comments and trackbacks. For more on these tags, see Book 6, Chapter 3.
- **Basic HTML:** Using HTML markup helps you provide unique styles to display content. For information about the use of basic HTML, check out Book 6.
- **CSS:** Every WordPress theme has a Cascading Style Sheets (CSS) template called `style.css`. Within this CSS template, you define the styles and CSS markup that creates a custom look and feel for the comment and trackback display on your site. You can find more information about using CSS in Book 6.
- **Graphics:** Using graphics to enhance and define your branding, style, and visual design is an integral part of web design. Because a single chapter isn't sufficient to fully cover graphic design, you may want to check out *WordPress Web Design For Dummies,* 3rd Edition (John Wiley & Sons, Inc.), which I wrote, for great information on graphic and website design with WordPress.
- **WordPress widgets:** WordPress has a built-in widget to display the most recent comments published to your site by your visitors. You also can find several plugins that display comments in different ways, including top comments, most popular posts based on the number of comments, and comments that display the author's photo. For information about widgets and plugins for these purposes, flip to Book 6, Chapter 1 and Book 7, chapters 1 and 2, respectively.

Managing Comments and Trackbacks

When you invite readers to comment on your site, you, as the site administrator, have full access to manage and edit those comments through the Comments page, which you can access in your WordPress Dashboard.

To find your comments, click the Comments link on the Dashboard navigation menu; the Comments screen opens. (See Figure 4-3.)

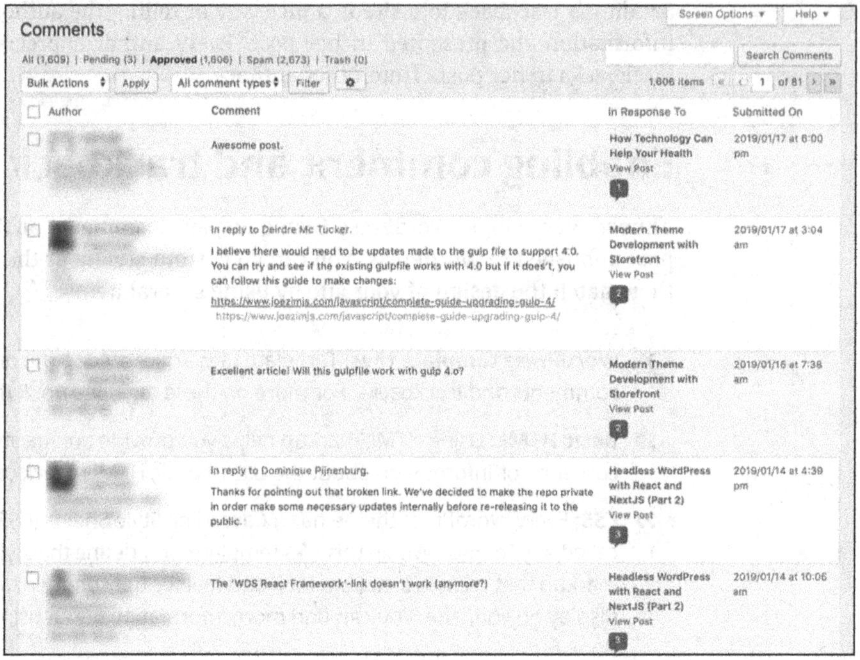

FIGURE 4-3: The Comments screen contains all the comments and trackbacks on your site.

When you hover your mouse pointer over a comment, several links appear that give you the opportunity to manage the comment:

- **Unapprove:** This link appears only if you have comment moderation turned on. Also, it appears only on approved comments. The comment is placed in the moderation queue, which you can get to by clicking the Pending link that appears below the Comments page header. The moderation queue is kind of a holding area for comments that haven't yet been published to your site.
- **Reply:** This link makes a text box visible. In the text box, you can type and submit your reply to this person. This feature eliminates the need to load your live site to reply to a comment.

- **Quick Edit:** This link opens the comment options inline without leaving the Comments page. You can configure options such as name, email address, URL, and comment content. Click the Save button to save your changes.
- **Edit:** This link opens the Edit Comment screen, where you can edit the different fields, such as name, email address, URL, and comment content. (See Figure 4-4.)

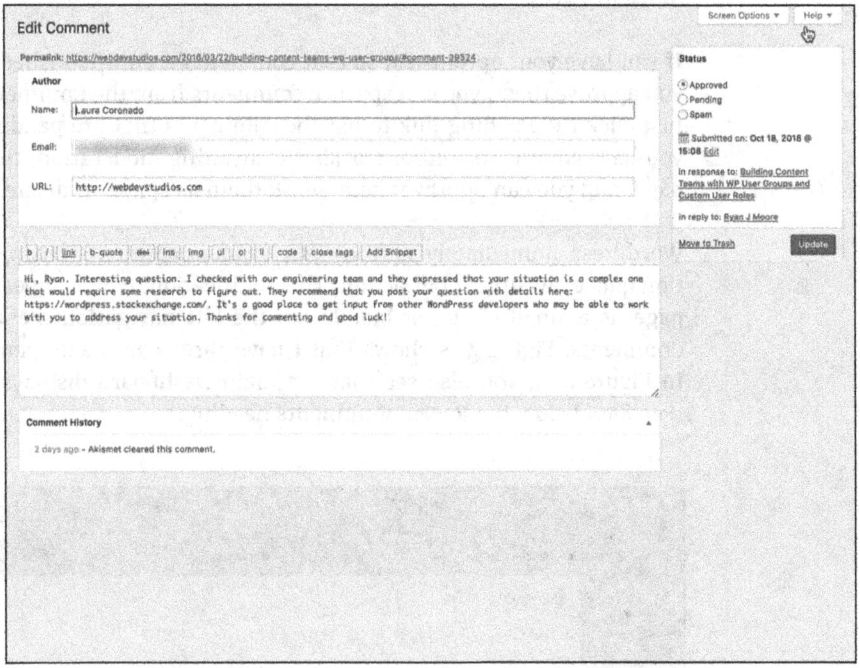
Edit Comment
Screen Options
Help
Permalink: https://webdevstudios.com/2016/03/22/building-content-teams-wp-user-groups/#comment-39524
Author
Name: Laura Coronado
Email:
URL: http://webdevstudios.com
b
i
link
b-quote
del
ins
img
ul
ol
li
code
close tags
Add Snippet
Hi, Ryan. Interesting question. I checked with our engineering team and they expressed that your situation is a complex one that would require some research to figure out. They recommend that you post your question with details here: https://wordpress.stackexchange.com/. It's a good place to get input from other WordPress developers who may be able to work with you to address your situation. Thanks for commenting and good luck!
Comment History
2 days ago - Akismet cleared this comment.
Status
Approved
Pending
Spam
Submitted on: Oct 18, 2018 @ 15:08 Edit
In response to: Building Content Teams with WP User Groups and Custom User Roles
In reply to: Ryan J Moore
Move to Trash
Update

FIGURE 4-4: Edit a user's comment on the Edit Comment screen.

- **History:** This link opens the Edit Comment screen and scrolls down to the Comment History section of that screen, which displays the history of that comment, such as when it was approved and when the Akismet plugin cleared the comment as not spam (if you have the Akismet plugin installed; see "Tackling Spam with Akismet" later in this chapter for information on this antispam plugin.)
- **Spam:** This link marks the comment as spam and marks it as spam in the database, where it will never be heard from again! (Actually, it's stored in the database as spam; you just don't see it in your comments list unless you click the Spam link at the top of the Comments screen.)

- **Trash:** This link does exactly what it says: sends the comment to the trash and deletes it from your blog. You can access comments that have been sent to the trash to permanently delete them from your blog or to restore them.

TIP

If you have a lot of comments listed in the Comments screen and want to edit them in bulk, select the check boxes to the left of all the comments you want to manage. Then choose one of the following from the Bulk Actions drop-down menu in the top-left corner of the page: Unapprove, Approve, Mark As Spam, or Move to Trash.

If you have your options set so that comments aren't published to your site until you approve them, you can approve comments from the Comments screen as well. Just click the Pending link to list the comments that are pending moderation. If you have comments and/or trackbacks awaiting moderation, they appear on this page, and you can approve them, mark them as spam, or delete them.

WordPress immediately notifies you of any comments sitting in the moderation queue, awaiting your action. This notification, which appears on every single page, is a small circle, or bubble, on the left navigation menu, to the right of Comments. Figure 4-5 shows that I have three comments pending moderation. In Figure 4-5, you also see that the main Dashboard displays the comment as *[Pending]* below the Recent Comments heading.

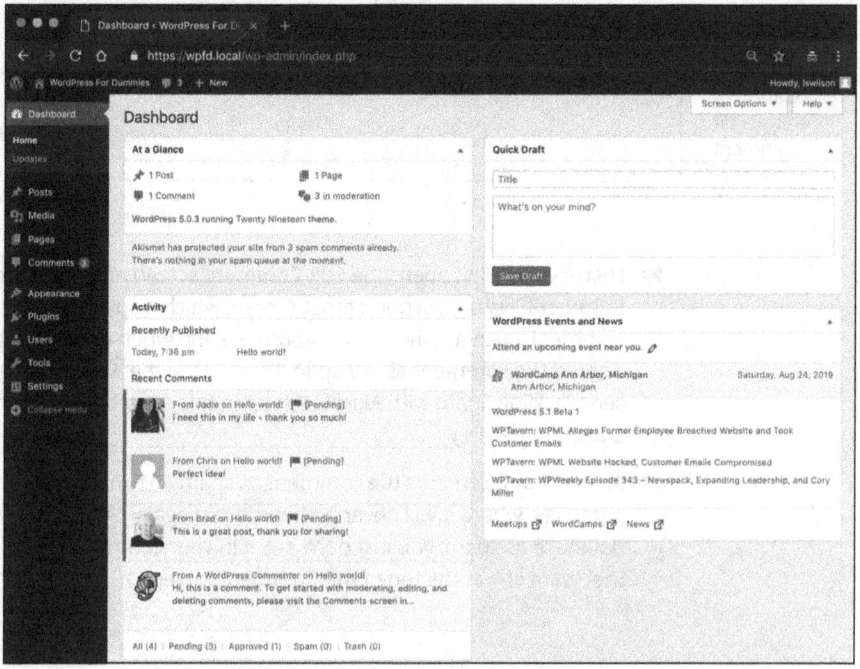

FIGURE 4-5: A small circle tells me that I have three comments pending moderation.

Tackling Spam with Akismet

No one likes spam. In fact, services such as WordPress have spent untold hours in the name of stopping spammers in their tracks, and for the most part, the services have been successful. Occasionally, however, spammers sneak through. Many spammers are offensive, and all of them are frustrating because they don't contribute to the ongoing conversations that occur in blogs. (A spammer's only goal is to generate traffic to his website.)

All WordPress installations have one significant thing in common: Akismet, a WordPress plugin. It's my humble opinion that Akismet is the mother of all plugins and that no WordPress site is complete without a fully activated version of Akismet running on it.

Apparently, WordPress agrees, because the plugin has been packaged in every WordPress software release beginning way back in version 2.0. Akismet was created by the folks at Automattic, the same folks who brought you the WordPress.com hosted version.

Akismet is the answer to combating comment and trackback spam. The Akismet website (`https://akismet.com`) explains this plugin quite well: "Used by millions of websites, Akismet filters out hundreds of millions of spam comments from the Web every day. Add Akismet to your site so you don't have to worry about spam again."

I started blogging in 2002 with the Movable Type platform and moved to WordPress in 2003. As blogging became more and more popular, comment and trackback spam became more and more of a nuisance. One morning in 2004, I found that 2,300 pieces of disgusting comment spam had been published to my blog. Something had to be done!

The folks at Automattic did a fine thing with Akismet. Since the emergence of Akismet, I've barely had to think about comment or trackback spam except for the few times a month I check my Akismet spam queue.

This chapter wouldn't be complete if I didn't show you how to activate and use the Akismet plugin on your site. Book 7 covers the use, installation, and management of other plugins for your WordPress site.

Activating Akismet

Akismet is already included in every WordPress installation; you don't have to worry about downloading and installing it, because it's already there. Follow these steps to activate and begin using Akismet:

1. **Click the Plugins link on the left navigation menu of the Dashboard to load the Plugins screen.**
2. **Click the Activate link below the Akismet plugin name and description.**

   A green box appears at the top of the page, saying `Almost done- configure Akismet and say goodbye to spam.` (See Figure 4-6.)

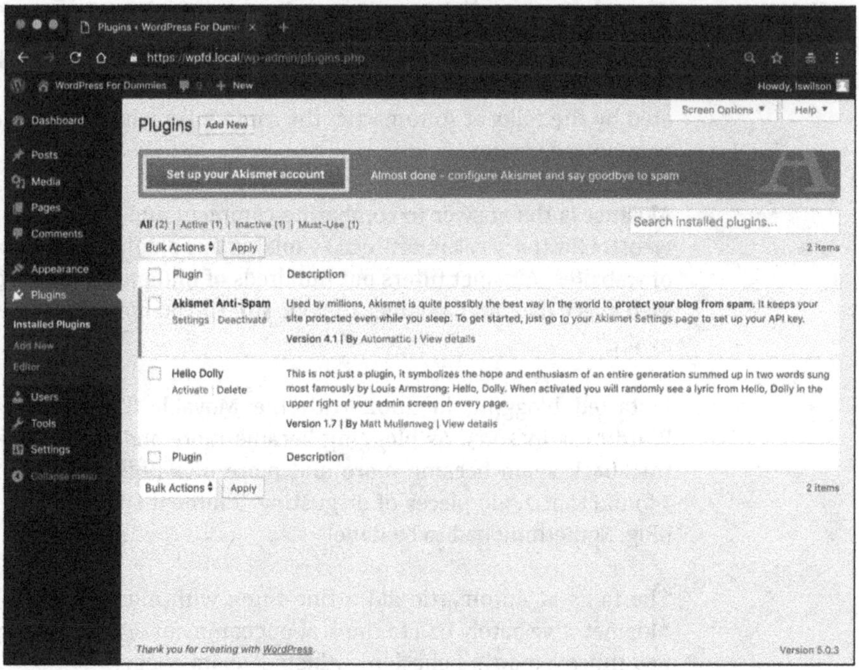

FIGURE 4-6: After you activate Akismet, WordPress tells you that the plugin isn't quite ready to use.

3. **Click the Set up Your Akismet Account button in the green box to navigate to the Akismet screen.**
4. **If you already have an API key, enter it in the Enter an API Key text field; then click the Connect with API Key button to save your changes.**

   You can stop here if you already have a key, but if you don't have an Akismet key, keep following the steps in this section.

An *API key* is a string of numbers and letters that functions like a unique password given to you by Akismet; it's the key that allows your WordPress.org application to communicate with your Akismet account.

5. **Click the Get Your API key button on the Akismet Configuration screen.**

   The WordPress page of the Akismet website opens (`https://akismet.com/wordpress`).

6. **Click the Activate Akismet button.**

   The sign-up page for WordPress.com opens. Because Akismet was created and is owned by Automattic, the company behind WordPress.com, you need to create an account on WordPress.com to use Akismet.

7. **Enter your email address, desired username, and password in the provided text fields; then click the Continue button.**

   The Pick Your Plan page opens.

8. **Choose among these options for obtaining an Akismet key:**

   - *Enterprise:* $550 per year for people who own professional sites, a large network, or multisite installations of WordPress and want additional priority support and an unlimited number of sites.
   - *Plus:* $59 per year for people who own a small commercial or professional site or blog.
   - *Personal:* Name your price. Type the amount you're willing to pay for the Personal plan. This option is for people who own one small, personal WordPress-powered site. You can choose to pay nothing ($0), but if you'd like to contribute a little cash toward the cause of combating spam, you can opt to spend up to $120 per year for your Akismet key subscription.

9. **Select and pay for (if needed) your Akismet key.**

   After you've gone through the sign-up process, Akismet provides you an API key. Copy that key by selecting it with your mouse pointer, right-clicking, and choosing Copy from the shortcut menu.

10. **Go to the Akismet screen by clicking the Akismet Anti-spam link on the Settings menu in your WordPress Dashboard.**

11. **Enter the API key in the Enter an API Key text box, and click the Save Changes button to fully activate the Akismet plugin (as shown in Figure 4-7).**

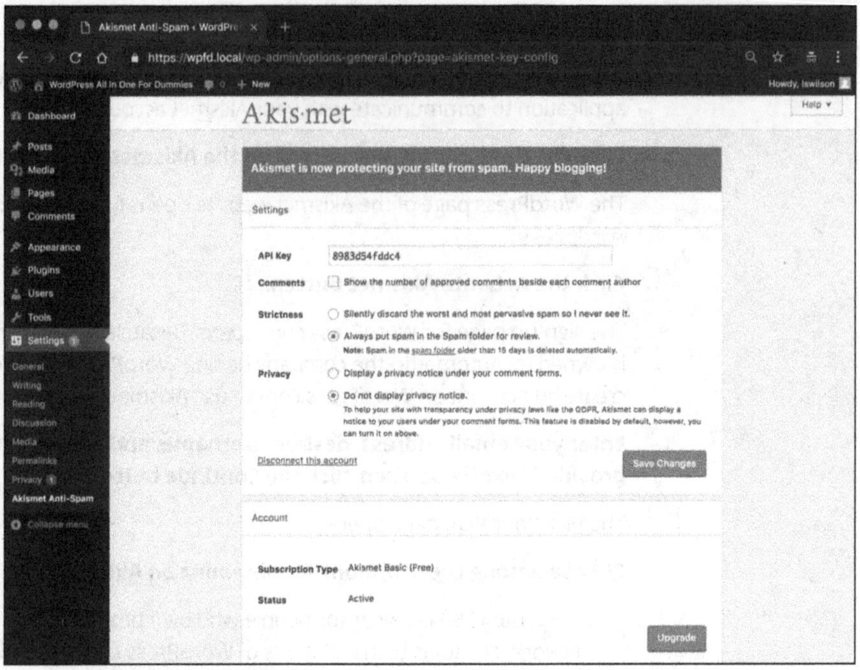

FIGURE 4-7: Akismet verification confirmation message on the Akismet screen.

Configuring Akismet

On the Akismet screen, after you've entered and saved your key, you can configure three options to further configure your spam protection:

- **Comments:** Select this option to display the number of approved comments beside each comment author.
- **Strictness:** By default, Akismet puts spam in the Spam comment folder for you to review at your leisure. If you feel that this setting isn't strict enough, you can select the option to have Akismet silently delete the worst and most pervasive spam so that you never have to see it.
- **Privacy:** Here, you can configure Aksimet to display a privacy notice below the comment form on your posts. Displaying this notice can help you adhere to the GDPR guidelines. (See Book 3, Chapter 2 for information on GDPR.)

Akismet catches spam and throws it into a queue, holding the spam for 15 days and then deleting it from your database. It's probably worth your while to check the Akismet Spam page once a week to make sure that the plugin hasn't captured any legitimate comments or trackbacks.

Rescuing nonspam comments and trackbacks

You can rescue any nonspam captured comments and trackbacks by following these steps (after you log in to your WordPress Dashboard):

1. **Click Comments on the left navigation menu.**

   The Comments screen appears, displaying a list of the most recent comments on your site.

2. **Click the Spam link.**

   The Comments screen displays all spam comments that the plugin caught.

3. **Browse the list of spam comments, looking for any comments or trackbacks that are legitimate.**

4. **If you locate a comment or trackback that's legitimate, click the Approve link directly below the entry.**

   The comment is marked as legitimate. In other words, WordPress recognizes that you don't consider this comment to be spam. Then WordPress approves the comment and publishes it on your site.

REMEMBER

Check your spam filter often. I just found four legitimate comments caught in my spam filter and was able to de-spam them, releasing them from the binds of Akismet and unleashing them upon the world.

IN THIS CHAPTER

» Exploring content archive options in WordPress

» Creating and editing categories

» Creating tags and editing them

Chapter 5 Creating Categories and Tags

WordPress provides you many ways to organize, categorize, and archive content on your website. Packaged within the WordPress software is the capability to automatically maintain chronological, categorized archives of your publishing history, which provides your website visitors different ways to find your content. WordPress uses PHP and MySQL technology to sort and organize everything you publish in an order that you and your readers can access by date and category. This archiving process occurs automatically with every post you publish to your site.

In this chapter, you find out all about WordPress archiving, from categories to tags and more. You also discover how to take advantage of the category description feature to improve your search engine optimization (SEO), how to distinguish between categories and tags, and how to use categories and tags to create topical archives of your site content.

Archiving Content with WordPress

When you create a post on your WordPress site, you can file that post in a category that you specify. This feature makes for a nifty archiving system in which you and your readers can find articles/posts that you've placed within a specific category. Articles you post are also sorted and organized by date (day/month/year) so that you can easily locate articles that you posted at a certain time. A plugin called Archive Page gives you the ability to easily create a nicely formatted site map that displays the archives of a site on a page.

Visit `https://wp-time.com/archives` to see an example of an archive page. The example page contains chronological sections by day, month, and year. It also contains the latest posts and the different categories and tags found within that site. If you click a date, tag or category on that page, you're taken to a page with a full listing of articles from that date, tag, or category, and each article title is linked to that article. (See Figure 5-1.)

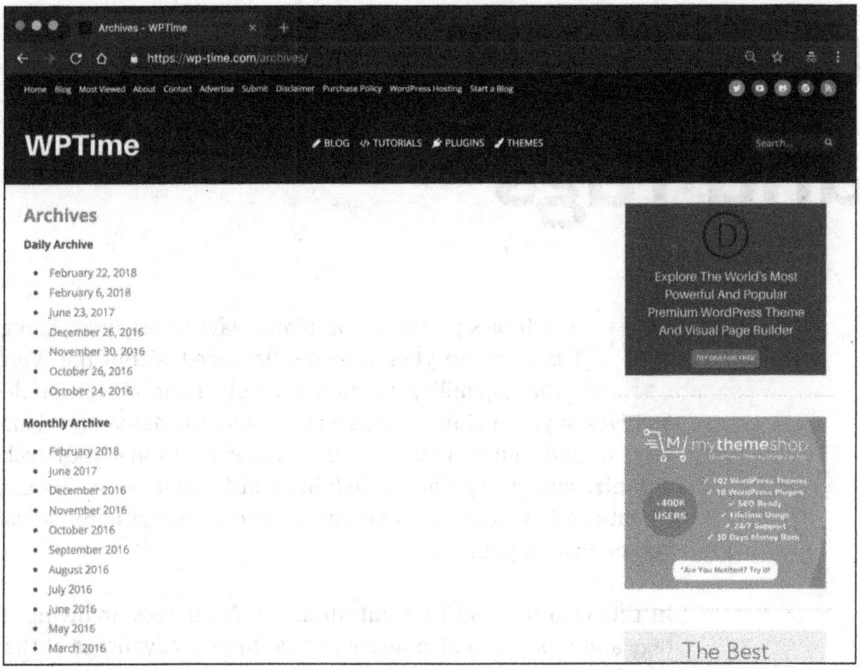

FIGURE 5-1: An archive listing of published posts by date, tag, or category.

TIP

You can easily create an archive listing like the one shown in Figure 5-1 by using a WordPress plugin called Archive Page, which you can find in the WordPress Plugins page at `https://wordpress.org/plugins/archive-page`. This plugin is easy to install and to use. You just need to create a page and add any of the short codes provided by the plugin to automatically build an archives page that links to all the content you've published on your site. Easy archives!

WordPress archives and organizes your content for you in more ways than by date and category. In this section, I give you an overview of the several other ways. The different types of archives and content are the following:

- **Categories:** Create categories of topics in which you can file your articles so that you can easily archive relevant topics. Many websites display content by category; all content is displayed by topic rather than in a simple chronological listing. Figure 5-2 shows an example of a magazine theme that uses this method. You can find out how to create one of your own by customizing your site (see Book 6). Also be sure to check out Book 6, Chapter 6 to discover how to use template tags and category templates to display category-specific content. Exciting stuff!

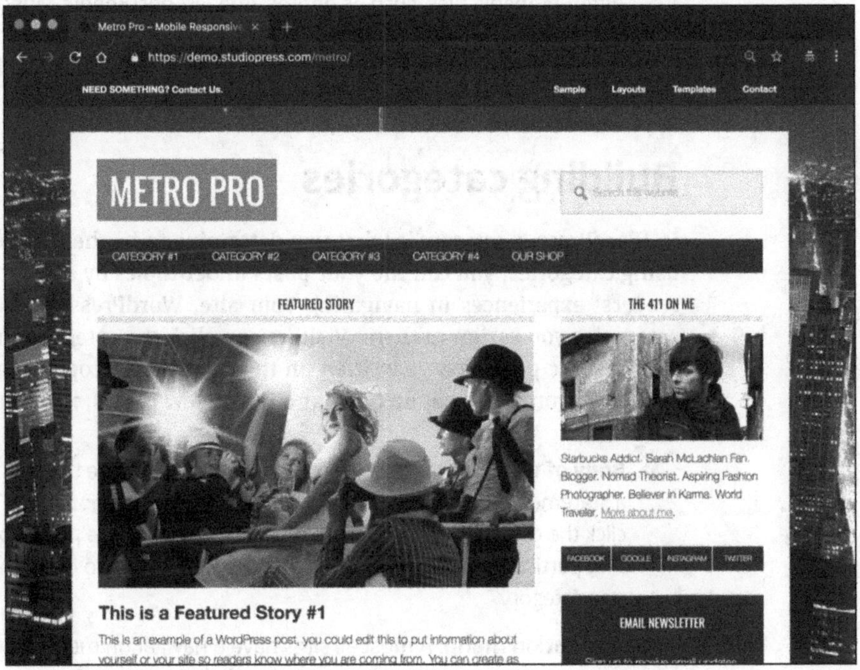

FIGURE 5-2: A magazine theme created with WordPress (Metro Pro by StudioPress).

- **Tags:** Tagging your posts with micro keywords, called *tags,* further defines related content within your site, which can improve your site for SEO purposes by helping the search engines find related and relevant content, as well as provide additional navigation to help your readers find relevant content on your site.

- **Date Based:** Your content is automatically archived by date based on the day, month, year, and time of day you publish it.
- **Author:** Content is automatically archived by author based on the author of the post and/or page. You can create an author archive if your site has multiple content contributors.
- **Keyword (or Search):** WordPress has a built-in search function that allows you and your readers to search for keywords, which presents an archive listing of content that's relevant to your chosen keywords.
- **Custom Post Types:** You can build custom post types based on the kind of content your site offers. You can find detailed information on custom post types and how to create them in Book 6, Chapter 7.
- **Attachments:** WordPress has a built-in media library where you can upload different media files, such as photos, images, documents, videos, and audio files (to name a few). You can build an archive of those files to create things such as photo galleries, eBook archives (PDFs), and video galleries.

Building categories

In WordPress, a *category* is what you determine to be the main topic of a post. By using categories, you can file your posts under topics by subject. To improve your readers' experiences in navigating your site, WordPress organizes posts by the categories you assign to them. Visitors can click the categories they're interested in to see the posts you've written on those particular topics. You can display the list of categories you set up on your site in a few places, including the following:

- **Body of the post:** In most WordPress themes, you see the title followed by a statement such as `Filed In: Category 1, Category 2`. The reader can click the category name to go to a page that lists all the posts you've made in that particular category. You can assign a single post to more than one category.
- **Navigation menu:** Almost all sites have a navigation menu that visitors can use to navigate your site. You can place links to categories on the navigation menu, particularly if you want to draw attention to particular categories.
- **Sidebar of your blog theme:** You can place a full list of category titles in the sidebar by using the Categories widget included in your WordPress installation. A reader can click any category to open a page on your site that lists the posts you made within that particular category.

Subcategories (also known as *category children*) can further refine the main category topic by listing specific topics related to the main (*parent*) category. In your

WordPress Dashboard, on the Manage Categories page, subcategories appear directly below the main category. Here's an example:

Books I Enjoy (main category)

Fiction (subcategory)

Nonfiction (subcategory)

Trashy romance (subcategory)

Biographies (subcategory)

For Dummies (subcategory)

You can create as many levels of categories as you like. Biographies and *For Dummies* could be subcategories of Nonfiction, for example, which is a subcategory of the Books I Enjoy category. You aren't limited to the number of category levels you can create.

Changing the name of a category

When you install WordPress, it gives you one default category called Uncategorized. (See the Categories screen shown in Figure 5-3.) This category name is pretty generic, so you definitely want to change it to one that applies to you and your blog. (On my site, I changed it to Life in General. Although that name's still a bit on the generic side, it doesn't sound quite so . . . well, uncategorized.)

REMEMBER

The default category also serves as kind of a fail-safe. If you publish a post to your site and don't assign that post to a category, the post is assigned to the default category automatically, no matter what you name the category.

So how do you change the name of that default category? When you're logged in to your WordPress Dashboard, just follow these steps:

1. **Click the Categories link on the Posts submenu of the Dashboard navigation menu.**

   The Categories screen opens, containing all the tools you need to set up and edit category titles for your site.

2. **Click the title of the category that you want to edit.**

   If you want to change the Uncategorized category, click the word *Uncategorized* to open the Edit Category screen. (See Figure 5-4.)

3. **Type the new name for the category in the Name text box.**

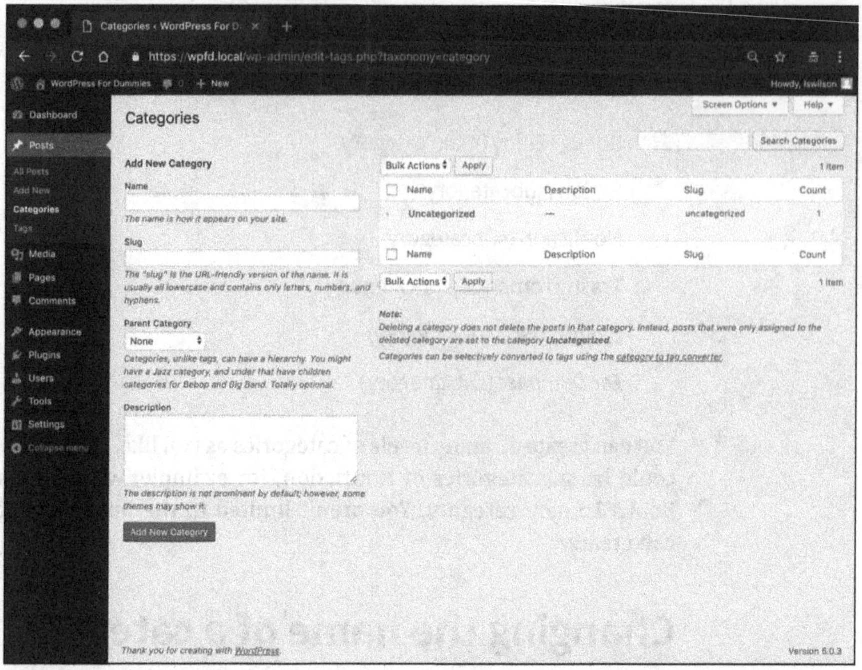

FIGURE 5-3: The Categories screen in the Dashboard of a brand-new WordPress site shows the default Uncategorized category.

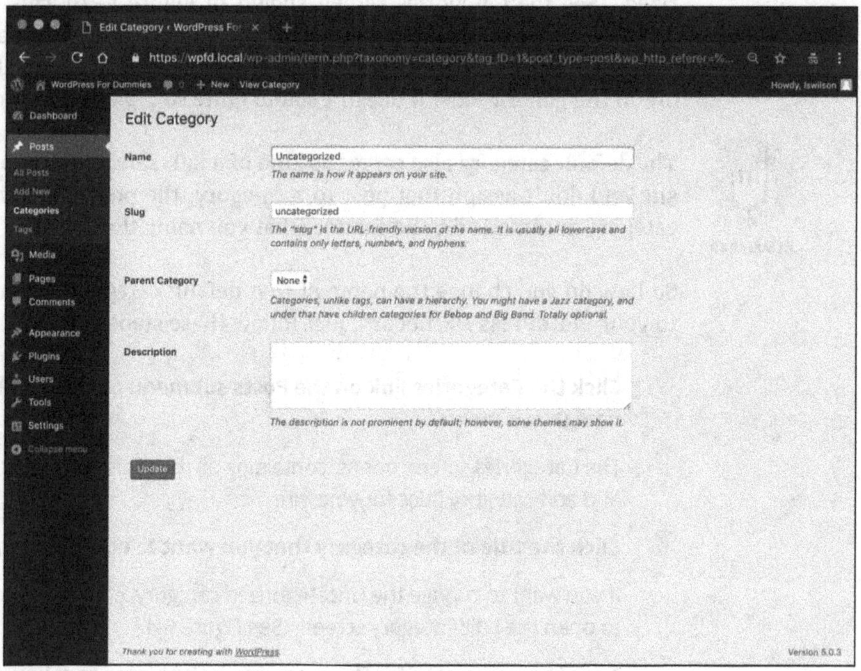

FIGURE 5-4: Editing a category in WordPress on the Edit Category screen.

4. **Type the new slug in the Slug text box.**

   The term *slug* refers to the word(s) used in the web address for the specific category. The category Books, for example, has a web address of `https://yourdomain.com/category/books`; if you change the Category Slug to Books I Like, the web address is `https://yourdomain.com/category/books-i-like`. (WordPress automatically inserts a dash between the slug words in the web address.)

5. **Choose a parent category from the Parent Category drop-down menu.**

   If you want this category to be a main category, not a subcategory, choose None.

6. **(Optional) Type a description of the category in the Description text box.**

   Use this description to remind yourself what your category is about. Some WordPress themes display the category description right on your site, too, which your visitors may find helpful. (See Book 6 for more about themes.) You know that your theme is coded in this way if your site displays the category description on the category page(s).

7. **Click the Update button.**

   The information you just edited is saved, and the Categories screen reloads, showing your new category name.

Creating new categories

Today, tomorrow, next month, next year — while your site grows in size and age, continuing to add new categories further defines and archives the history of your posts. You aren't limited in the number of categories and subcategories you can create for your site.

Creating a new category is as easy as following these steps:

1. **Click the Categories link on the Posts submenu, which is on the Dashboard navigation menu.**

   The Categories screen opens. The left side of the Categories page displays the Add New Category section. (See Figure 5-5.)

2. **Type the name of your new category in the Name text box.**

   Suppose that you want to create a category in which you file all your posts about the books you read. In the Name text box, type something like **Books I Enjoy**.

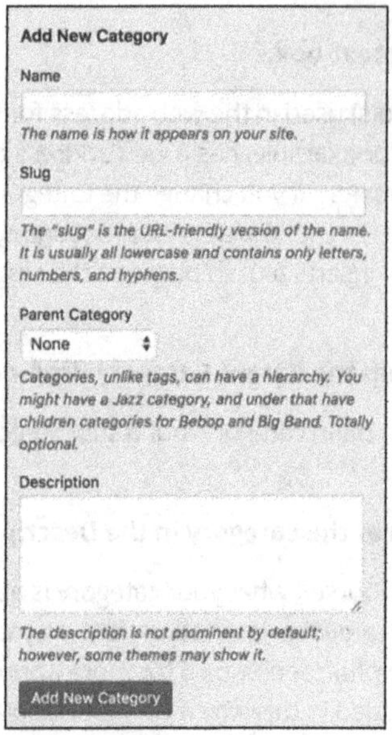

Add New Category
Name
The name is how it appears on your site.
Slug
The "slug" is the URL-friendly version of the name. It is usually all lowercase and contains only letters, numbers, and hyphens.
Parent Category
None
Categories, unlike tags, can have a hierarchy. You might have a Jazz category, and under that have children categories for Bebop and Big Band. Totally optional.
Description
The description is not prominent by default; however, some themes may show it.
Add New Category

FIGURE 5-5: Create a new category on your site.

3. **Type a name in the Slug text box.**

   The slug creates the link to the category page that lists all the posts you made in this category. If you leave this field blank, WordPress automatically creates a slug based on the category name. If the category is Books I Enjoy, WordPress automatically creates a category slug like `http://yourdomain.com/category/books-i-enjoy`. If you want to shorten it, however, you can! Type **books** in the Slug text box, and the link to the category becomes `http://yourdomain.com/category/books`.

4. **Choose the category's parent from the Parent Category drop-down menu.**

   Choose None if you want this new category to be a parent (or top-level) category. If you want to make this category a subcategory of another category, choose the category that you want to be the parent of this one.

5. **(Optional) Type a description of the category in the Description text box.**

   Some WordPress templates are set up to display the category description directly below the category name. (See Book 6.) Providing a description further defines the category intent for your readers. The description can be as short or as long as you want.

6. **Click the Add New Category button.**

   That's it! You've added a new category to your site. Armed with this information, you can add an unlimited number of categories to your new site.

You can delete a category by hovering your mouse pointer on the title of the category you want to delete and then clicking the Delete link that appears below the category title.

REMEMBER

Deleting a category doesn't delete the posts and links in that category. Instead, posts in the deleted category are reassigned to the Uncategorized category (or whatever you named the default category).

TECHNICAL STUFF

If you have an established WordPress site that has categories already created, you can convert some or all of your categories to tags. To do so, look for the Category to Tag Converter link in the bottom-right corner of the Category page of your WordPress Dashboard. Click that link to convert your categories to tags. (See the nearby sidebar "What are tags, and how/why do I use them?" for more information on tags.)

Book 6, Chapter 6 shows you how to take advantage of categories in WordPress to build a dynamic theme that displays your content in a way that highlights the different topics available on your site. Book 6 describes how to use WordPress template tags to manipulate category archives for display and distribution on your website.

WHAT ARE TAGS, AND HOW/WHY DO I USE THEM?

Don't confuse tags with categories (as a lot of people do). *Tags* are clickable, comma-separated keywords that help you microcategorize a post by defining the topics in it. Unlike WordPress categories, tags don't have a hierarchy; you don't assign parent tags and child tags. If you write a post about your dog, for example, you can put that post in the Pets category — but you can also add some specific tags that let you get a whole lot more specific, such as *poodle* or *small dogs*. If someone clicks your *poodle* tag, he finds all the posts you ever made that contain the *poodle* tag.

Besides defining your post topics for easy reference, you have another reason to use tags: Search-engine spiders harvest tags when they crawl your site, so tags help other people find your site when they search for specific words.

You can manage your tags in the WordPress Administration panel by choosing Tags from the Pages drop-down menu. The Tags page opens, allowing you to view, edit, delete, and add tags.

Creating and Editing Tags

In Book 4, Chapter 1, you can find out all about publishing your posts in WordPress and assigning tags to your content. This section takes you through the steps of managing tags, which is similar to the way you manage categories. To create a new tag, follow these steps:

1. **Click the Tags link on the Posts submenu, which is on the Dashboard's navigation menu.**

   The Tags screen opens, as shown in Figure 5-6. The left side of the screen displays the Add New Tag section.

   TIP

   Unlike what it does for categories and links, WordPress doesn't create a default tag for you, so when you visit the Tags page for the first time, no tags are listed on the right side of the page.

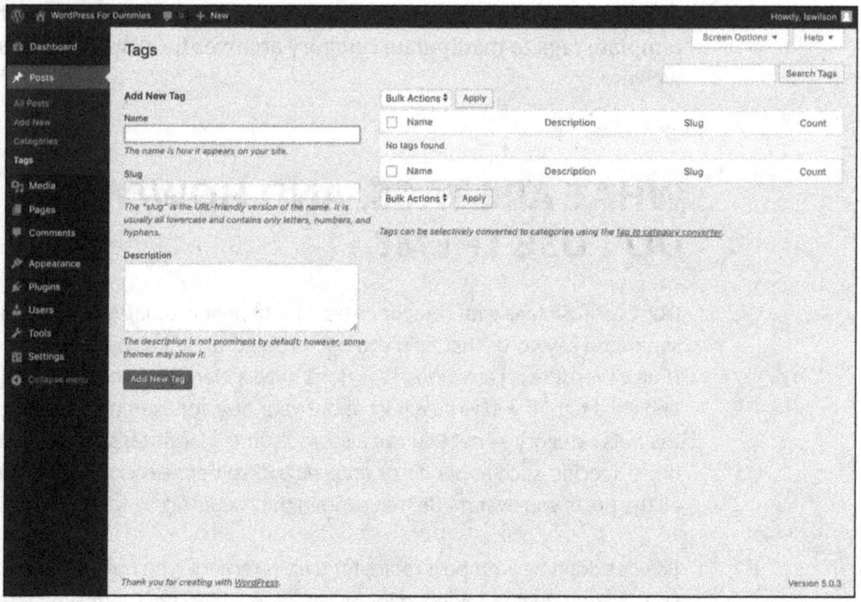

FIGURE 5-6: The Tags screen of the Dashboard.

2. **Type the name of your new tag in the Name text box.**

   Suppose that you want to create a tag in which you file all your posts about the books you read. In the Name text box, type something like **Fiction Books**.

3. **Type a name in the Slug text box.**

   The *slug* is the permalink of the tag and can help identify tag archives on your site by giving them their own URL, such as `https://yourdomain.com/tag/fictional-books`. By default, the tag slug adopts the words from the tag name.

4. **(Optional) Type a description of the tag in the Description text box.**

   Some WordPress templates are set up to display the tag description directly below the tag name. Providing a description further defines the category intent for your readers. The description can be as short or as long as you want.

5. **Click the Add New Tag button.**

   That's it! You've added a new tag to your site. The Add New Tag screen refreshes in your browser window with blank fields, ready for you to add another tag to your site.

6. **Repeat Steps 1 through 5 to add an unlimited number of tags to your blog.**

Once you have several Tags on your website, you can delete them on the Tags screen by clicking the Delete link underneath each tag when you hover over it with your mouse. Alternatively, you can delete multiple tags at once by selecting the check mark to the left of each tag you want to edit, select delete from the Bulk Actions drop-down menu at the top of the Tags screen, and then click the Apply button. The Bulk Actions menu gives you the ability to delete several tags with just one action, rather than having to delete them all individually — most helpful if you have hundreds of tags!

TIP

You use the Tags and Categories pages of your Dashboard to manage, edit, and create new tags and categories to which you assign your posts when you publish them. Book 4, Chapter 1 contains a lot of information about how to go about assigning tags and categories to your posts, as well as a few good tips on how you can create new categories and tags right on the Edit Posts screen.

4 Publishing Your Site with WordPress

Contents at a Glance

IN THIS CHAPTER

» Navigating the Edit Post screen

» Discovering the block editor

» Inserting new and editing existing blocks

» Publishing your post

» Creating a unique work space for writing

Chapter 1

Writing Your First Post

It's time to write your first post on your new WordPress site! I leave it to you to decide on the topic you write about and the writing techniques you use to get your message across; I have my hands full writing this book! I *can* tell you, however, all about the techniques you'll use to write the wonderful passages that can bring you fame. Ready?

This chapter covers everything you need to know about the basics of publishing a post on your site, from writing a post to formatting, categorizing, tagging, and publishing it to your site.

Composing Your Post

Composing a post is a lot like typing an email: You give it a title, you write the message, and you click a button to send your words into the world. By using the different options that WordPress provides — content blocks, discussion options, categories, and tags, for example — you can configure each post however you like. This section, however, covers the minimal steps you take to compose and publish a post on your site.

Follow these steps to write a basic post:

1. **Click the Add New link on the Posts menu of the Dashboard.**

   The Edit Post screen opens, as shown in Figure 1-1.

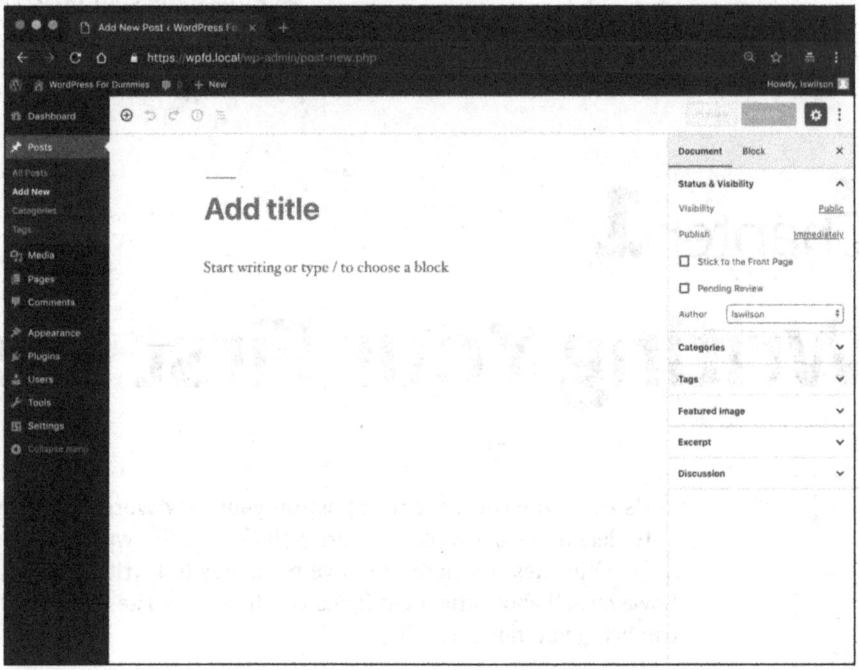

FIGURE 1-1: Give your post a title, and write your post body.

2. **Type the title of your post in the Add Title text field at the top of the Edit Post screen.**

3. **Type the content of your post in the area below the Add Title field.**

   The first time you visit the Edit Post screen, this area displays a message that says `Start writing or type to choose a new block`. I cover blocks in "Using the block editor" later in this chapter. For the purposes of this section, you'll type the text of your new post in this area.

4. **Click the Save Draft link, located in the top-right corner of the Edit Post screen.**

   The Save Draft link changes to a message that says Saved.

   WordPress has a built-in autosave feature to make sure that your content is saved and protected from being lost. Imagine spending an hour writing a long post and then the power goes out due to a storm in your area! You don't need to worry about all your work being lost because WordPress thoughtfully saved it for you. The default interval is 10 seconds, so if you don't click the Save Draft link, WordPress saves your post for you automatically. When the storm is over, you'll find a draft of the post you were working on before lightning struck.

At this point, you can skip to "Publishing Your Post" later in this chapter for information on publishing your post to your site, or you can continue with the following sections to discover how to refine the options for your post.

Using the Block Editor

In 2018, WordPress introduced a brand-new way of writing and editing content with version 5.0 of the software. The purpose of this new editing experience is to put more publishing control and formatting options in the hands of the users in a way that doesn't require any specialized knowledge or training in the technology that makes it happen, such as PHP, JavaScript, HTML, or CSS. Now editors can create and format posts and pages more easily than ever before. You can insert images, change font sizes and color, and create tables and columns in ways that you weren't able to before the 5.0 version of WordPress, released in December 2018.

The idea behind the block editor is to give users a variety of blocks with which to create posts and pages on their WordPress sites. Compare WordPress blocks to the blocks you played with as a child; you were able to take one block and stack it on top of the next block and the next to build a tower of blocks to the moon. Each block within the WordPress editor gets filled with content (text, images, video, and so on) and is stacked atop another block with more content, and so on, until you have a full page of content created with blocks that you can configure with options to control formatting and display and move around on the page to create the experience you want for your readers.

This section of the chapter takes you through the new block editor in WordPress.

TIP

WordPress named the new block editor Gutenberg after Johannes Gutenberg, the inventor of the printing press. Generically, everyone refers to it as the block editor, but if you hear or see the term *Gutenberg* tossed around in the WordPress support forums or at a WordPress meetup or WordCamp, you'll know that people are talking about the editor in WordPress.

Discovering available blocks

By default, when you first load the Edit Post screen in your Dashboard (refer to Figure 1-1), the area where you type the text of your post consists of standard paragraph blocks. Hover over this area with your mouse, and you see that the block is outlined, as shown in Figure 1-2.

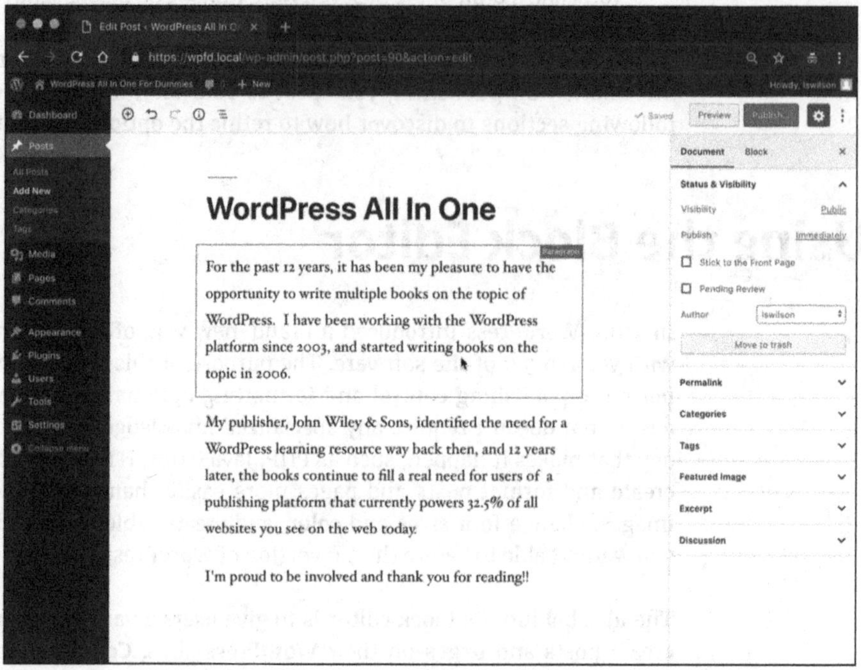

FIGURE 1-2: Default paragraph block in the WordPress block editor.

You can use the standard paragraph blocks to write your posts and leave it at that. But the block editor has many features that give you a variety of options for formatting your content by using a variety of blocks.

You can discover the different types of blocks available by clicking the small plus sign in the top-left corner of the Edit Post (or Edit Post) screen. Clicking that icon displays a drop-down menu of blocks, as shown in Figure 1-3.

Each block you find in the block editor has settings that give you display options such as color settings, font size and color, and width. In this section, you discover what blocks are available for you to use. In "Configuring block settings" later in this chapter, you see how to configure the block settings.

In a new installation of WordPress, the following blocks are available for you to use:

- **Most Used:** When you first install WordPress, the blocks listed in the Most Used section are the same as the ones listed in the Common Blocks section (see the next bullet point). As you use WordPress more and more, the software learns your habits and lists the blocks that you use most when writing and editing posts. Click the Most Used heading to display a drop-down list of available blocks in this section.

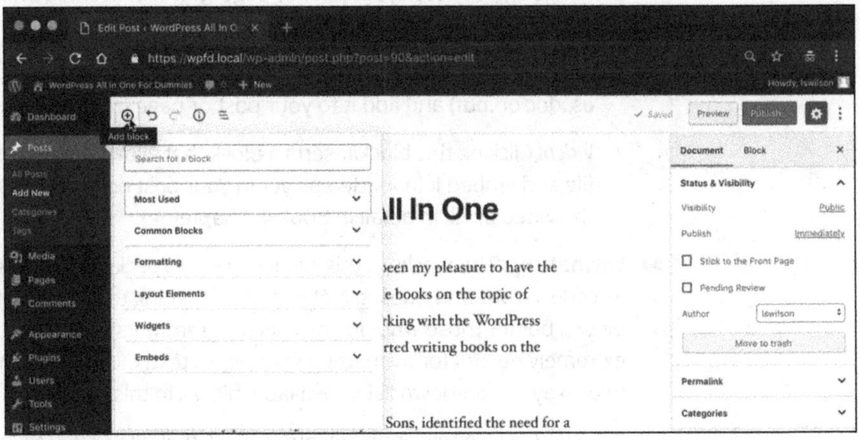

FIGURE 1-3: Menu of available blocks in the WordPress block editor.

» **Common Blocks:** The blocks included in this section are common, which means that most users use these blocks when writing and editing posts. Click the Common Blocks heading to display a drop-down list of available blocks in this section:

- *Paragraph:* Clicking this option inserts a block that allows you to create a standard paragraph of text.
- *Image:* Clicking this option inserts a block that allows you to insert an image into your post or page.
- *Heading:* Clicking this option inserts a block that allows you to insert header text with H1, H2, H3, H4, H5, and H6 tags to help your visitors (and search engines) understand the structure of your content. (See Book 5, Chapter 4 for search engine optimization tips.)
- *Gallery:* Clicking this option inserts a block that allows you to upload and display multiple images in your post or page. (I discuss the use of the Gallery block in detail in Book 4, Chapter 3.)
- *List:* Clicking this option inserts a block that allows you to create a bulleted or numbered list.
- *Quote:* Clicking this option inserts a block that allows you to enter a quote with a citation that's stylized for visual emphasis.

- *Audio:* Clicking this option inserts a block that allows you to upload an audio file and embed it in an audio player in your post or page. (I discuss the use of the Audio block in detail in Book 4, Chapter 4.)
- *Cover:* Clicking this option inserts a block that allows you to upload an image and add it to your post or page with text overlaid on it. (I discuss the use of the Cover block in detail in Book 4, Chapter 3.)
- *File:* Clicking this option inserts a block that allows you to upload a file (such as .doc or .pdf) and add it to your post or page for your visitors to download.
- *Video:* Clicking this block inserts a block that allows you to upload a video file and embed it in a video player in your post or page. (I discuss the use of the Video block in detail in Book 4, Chapter 4.)

» **Formatting:** The blocks in this section are for special formatting needs such as code, HTML, and quotes. Not everyone is going to use these formatting blocks, but for those who do (such as programmers), these blocks are extremely helpful for formatting specialized text. Click the Formatting heading to display a drop-down list of available blocks in this section:

- *Code:* Clicking this option inserts a block that allows you to insert and display code snippets that respect standard code-formatting rules and prevents the application from executing the code you've written.
- *Classic:* Clicking this option inserts a block that users of earlier WordPress versions are used to and may be more comfortable with.
- *Custom HTML:* Clicking this option inserts a block with an HTML editor that allows you to write HTML code and preview it as you type and edit.
- *Preformatted:* Clicking this option inserts a block that allows you to add text that gets displayed exactly as is intended in code or HTML format. The text is typically displayed in a monospace font (such as Courier), and the Preformatted editor respects your spacing and tabs, keeping them in place. (Preformatted text is helpful for people who include code samples within their posts or pages. Also, this option prevents the application from executing the code.)
- *Pullquote:* Clicking this option inserts a block that allows you to enter a quote, with citation, that gives special visual emphasis to the text. The `Code is Poetry. – WordPress` example in Figure 1-4 is a Pullquote.
- *Table:* Clicking this option inserts a table editor that allows you to include a table of rows and columns, much as you'd do in a standard word processing program such as Microsoft Word.
- *Verse:* Clicking this option inserts a verse editor that allows you to enter a verse of poetry or song lyrics or to quote a small number of lyrics or lines of poetry. The text gets special formatting and spacing to give it visual emphasis. Figure 1-5 shows example song lyrics from a popular sports song.

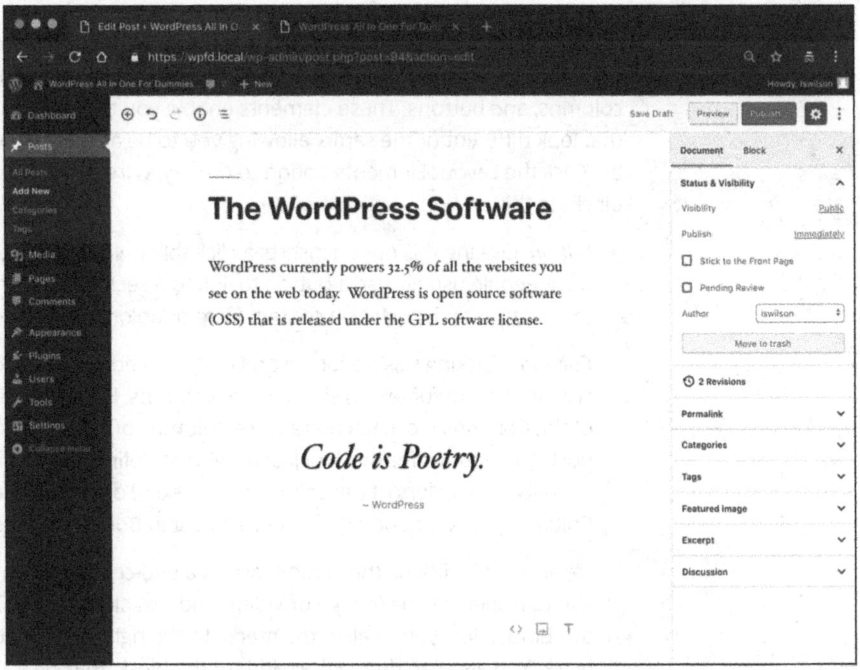

FIGURE 1-4: A Pullquote block in the WordPress block editor.

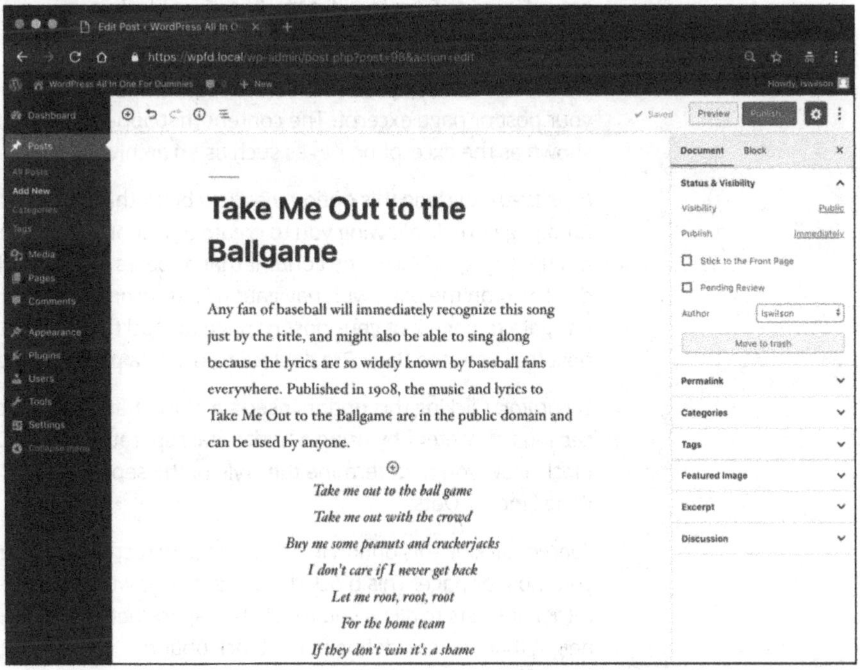

FIGURE 1-5: An example of the Verse block in the WordPress block editor.

- **Layout Elements:** The blocks in this section allow you to create different layouts for your content on every post or page. The layouts include tables, columns, and buttons. These elements enable you to create pages and posts that look different or the same, allowing you to be as creative as you want to be. Click the Layout Elements option to display a drop-down menu of available blocks in this section:
  - *Button:* Clicking this option inserts a clickable button within your page or post. People usually use a button to link to a section of their site that they feel is important, such as a contact form or an online shop.
  - *Columns:* Clicking this option inserts a column editor that allows you to create a section of text in side-by-side columns. Figure 1-6 shows the use of the Columns block to create three columns of text with headers in a post. The options for this block allow you to define the number of columns as well as the colors of the columns and text. (I discuss the use of the Columns block for adding images in a post in Book 4, Chapter 3.)
  - *Media & Text:* Clicking this option inserts a two-column block that allows you to display media (image or video) and text side by side. The options for this block allow you to align the media to the right or the left of the text block. You also can define the width of the block, making it the width of the reader's computer screen or the width of the rest of the content on your page. Figure 1-7 displays the Media & Text block in use on a web page on which the media is displayed to the left of the text.
  - *More:* Clicking this option inserts a block that serves as a marker point for your post or page excerpt. The content that appears above this block is shown as the excerpt on pages such as an archive or search results page.
  - *Page Break:* Clicking this option inserts a block that serves as a marker point for a page break, allowing you to create a post or a page that has a multipage experience. The content that appears above this block is displayed on the page with navigation links, prompting the reader to navigate to page 2 of your post or page to read the rest. Figure 1-7 shows a post that uses the Page Break block to create a post that spans two pages.
  - *Separator:* Clicking this option inserts a block that creates a break between sections of content by using a horizontal separator or line. Options for this block allow you to determine the style of the separator line: Short Line, Wide Line, or Dots.
  - *Spacer:* Clicking this option inserts a block that creates white space within your post or page. This block doesn't get filled with any kind of content; rather, it exists to allow you to create a space between content blocks at a height that you can define in the block options.

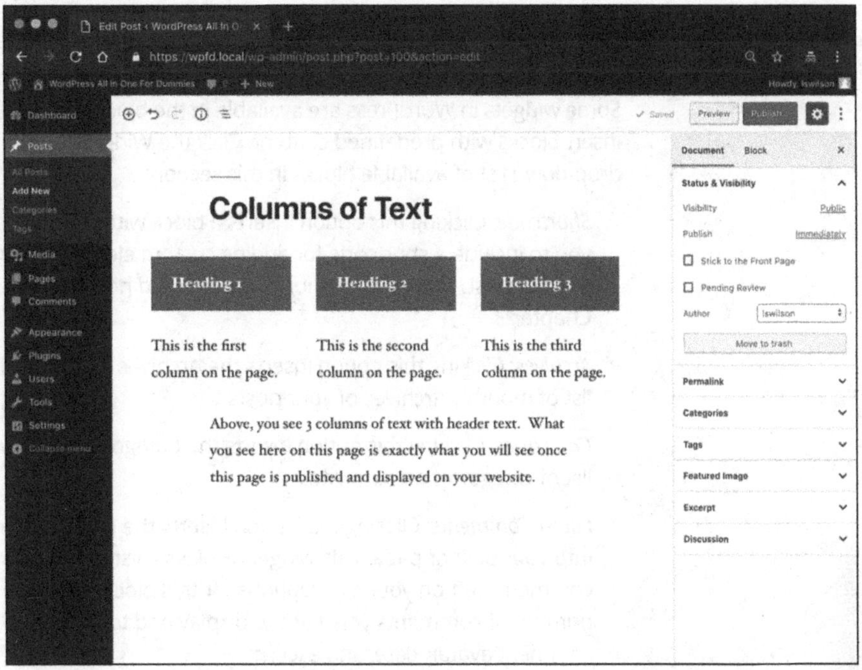

FIGURE 1-6: An example of the Columns block in the WordPress block editor.

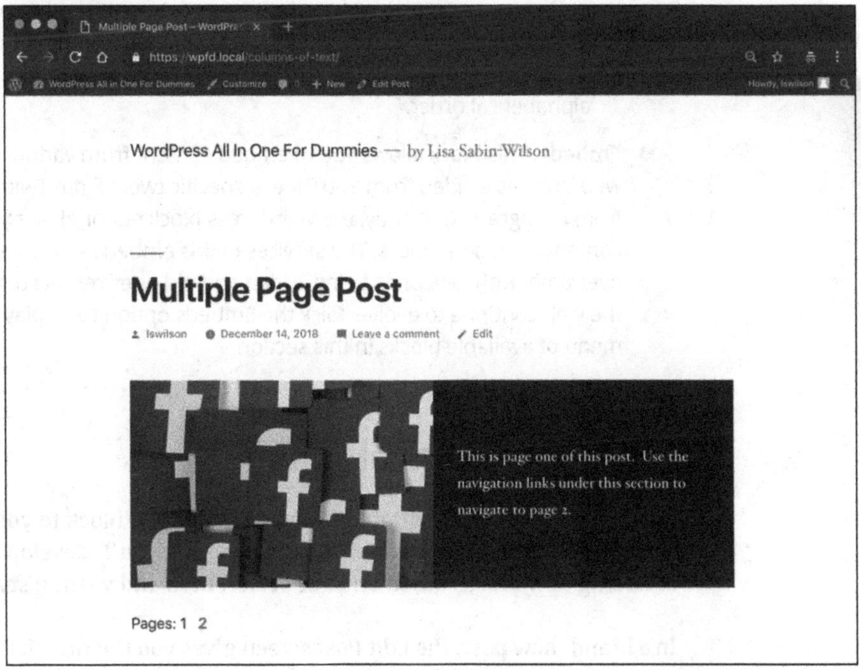

FIGURE 1-7: An example of the Media & Text and Page Break blocks on a website.

- **Widgets:** I cover the use of WordPress widgets on your website in Book 6, Chapter 1, so see that chapter to find out what widgets are and what they do. Some widgets in WordPress are available in the block editor to allow you to insert blocks with predefined content. Click the Widgets option to display a drop-down list of available blocks in this section:
  - *Shortcode:* Clicking this option inserts a block with a text field that allows you to include a shortcode for adding custom elements to your WordPress page or post. I cover what shortcodes are and how they're used in Book 7, Chapter 3.
  - *Archives:* Clicking this option inserts the Archives widget, which displays a list of monthly archives of your posts.
  - *Categories:* Clicking this option inserts the Category widget, which displays a list of categories on your site.
  - *Latest Comments:* Clicking this option inserts the Latest Comments widget into your post or page. This widget displays a list of the most recent comments left on your site. Options for this block allow you to define the number of comments you want to display and to toggle the display of the comment avatar, date, and excerpt.
  - *Latest Posts:* Clicking this option inserts the Recent Posts widget into your post or page. This widget displays a list of the most recent posts you've published to your site. Options for this block allow you to sort the post list by newest to oldest, oldest to newest, and ascending or descending in alphabetical order.
- **Embeds:** This block allows you to embed content from various services on the web, such as a video from YouTube, a specific tweet from Twitter, or a photo from Instagram. Currently, the WordPress block editor allows you to embed content from 34 services. The services in this embed list are likely to change over time, with new ones being added and old ones removed, as services on the web continue to evolve. Click the Embeds option to display a drop-down menu of available blocks in this section.

Inserting new blocks

WordPress gives you a variety of ways to add a new block to your post or page. As you work with the block editor more and more, you'll develop a favorite method of adding new blocks based on your preferences and writing style.

In a brand-new post, the Edit Post screen gives you the title field to type your page title in and a Paragraph block to write the content of your page. From there, you can add new blocks to add different types of content to your page. You can insert a new block into your page by using any of the following methods:

- **Use the Top Block Inserter.** This method is covered in "Discovering available blocks" earlier in this chapter and illustrated in Figure 1-3.
- **Use the Editor Block Inserter.** When you've added a block, put content in it, and are ready to add a new block, hover your mouse over the existing block. You see an icon that looks like a plus sign. Click that icon to display a list of available blocks that you can add to your page (refer to Figure 1-8). Choosing a block from that list inserts the block directly below the existing one.

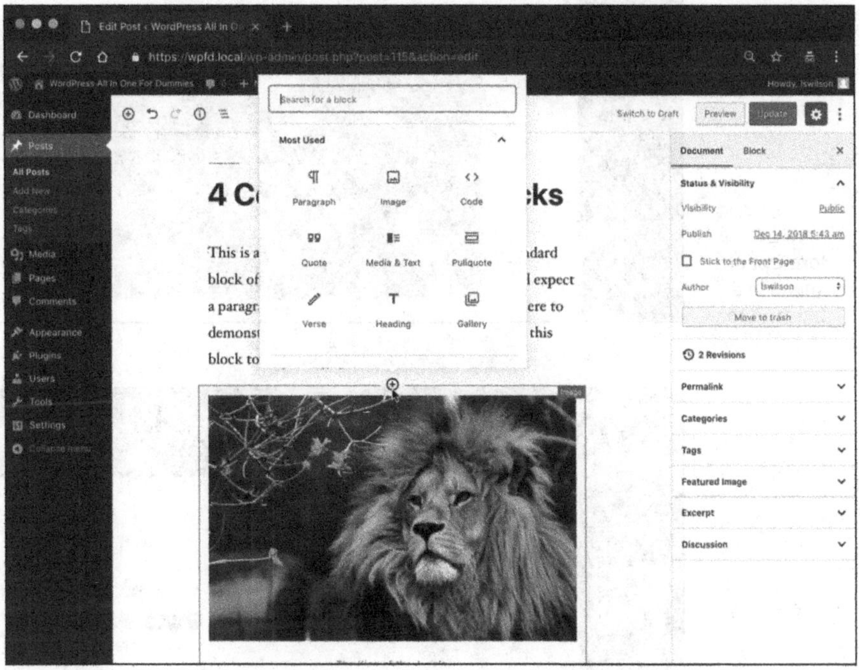

FIGURE 1-8: Add a new block to your page by using the Top Block Inserter.

- **Use More Options.** Every block has a small toolbar of styling options for that block (discussed in "Configuring block settings" later in this chapter). The item on the right side of the toolbar menu is labeled More Options; click that item to display a drop-down list of additional settings (see Figure 1-9). Two of those options are labeled Insert Before and Insert After. Click either option to insert a standard Paragraph block above or below the block you're currently working in. Then you can configure the block type by using the Editor Block Inserter (refer to Figure 1-8).
- **Use shortcut icons.** On the Edit Post screen, three icons allow you to add three commonly used blocks: Image, Code, and Quote (see Figure 1-10). Click one of those icons to add the corresponding block to your page.

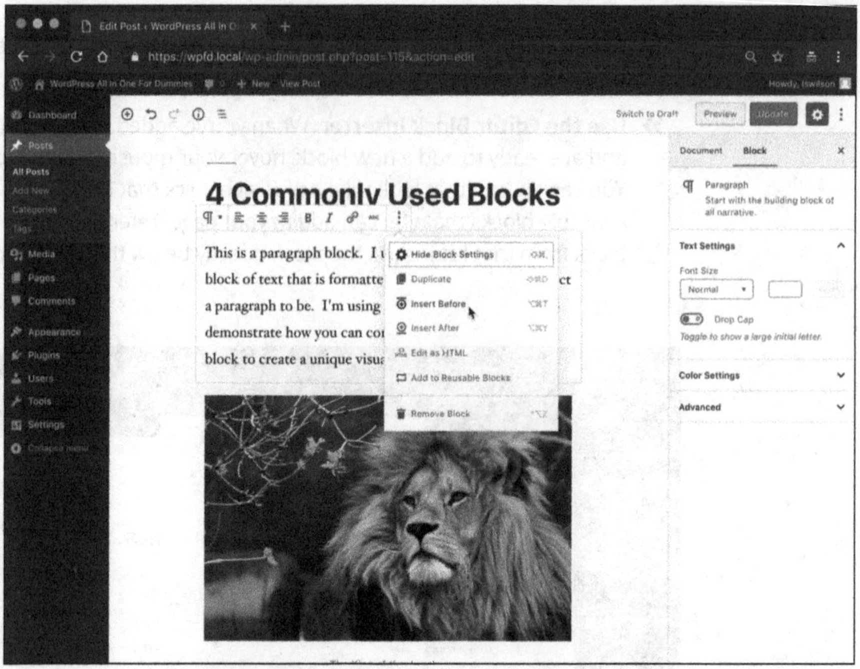

FIGURE 1-9: More Options menu in the block editor.

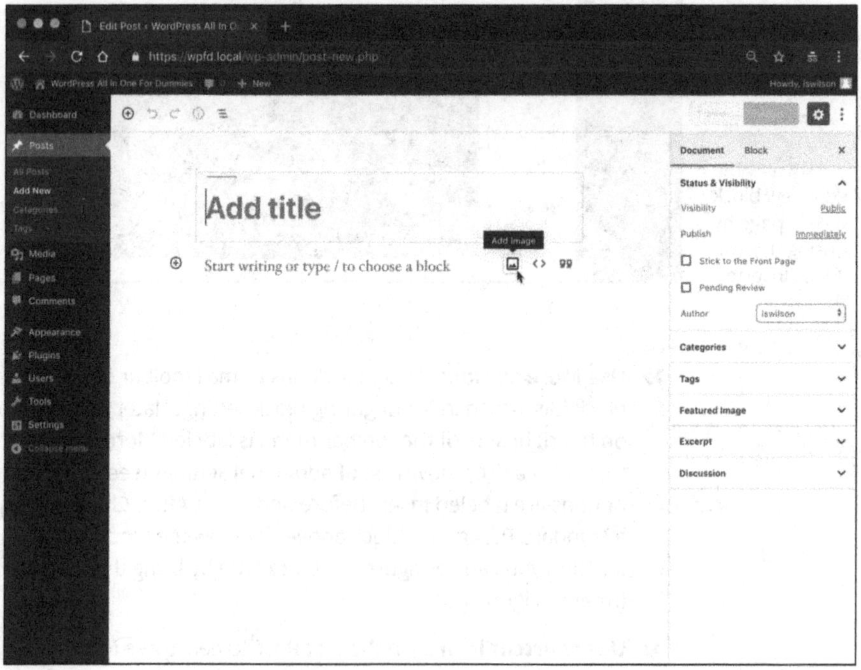

FIGURE 1-10: The block editor has three shortcuts for adding Image, Code, and Quote blocks.

- **Press Enter (or Return on a Mac).** Press the Enter key on your keyboard when you're in a standard Paragraph block to insert a new Paragraph block into your page. Then you can continue using the Paragraph block or use the Editor Block Inserter (refer to Figure 1-8) to change the block type.
- **Use slash commands.** When you click inside a standard Paragraph block and press the slash (/) key on your keyboard, a list of blocks appears. This list enables you to add a block without moving your hands away from the keyboard.

  Figure 1-11 shows the blocks that are available when you press the slash key. You can navigate to the block you need by pressing the down-arrow key and then pressing Enter to select it, or you can finish typing the name of the block and then press the Enter key to insert it into your page. This editing experience is intended to be mouseless; you can keep typing away and adding blocks from your keyboard.

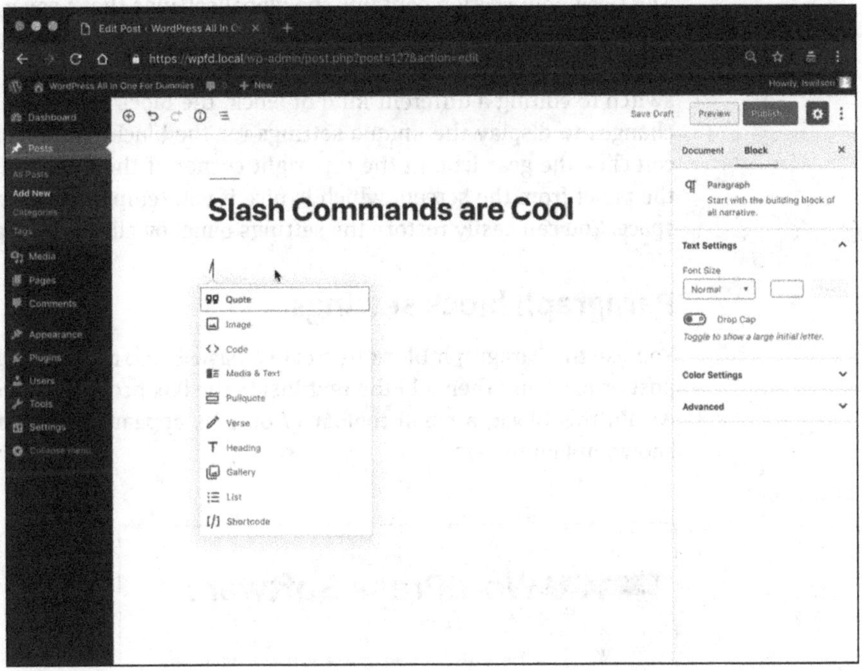

FIGURE 1-11: Slash commands give you a mouseless experience when adding blocks.

Configuring block settings

Each block on the block editor menus has options so you can configure display settings for your content, such as font size, font color, background color, and block width and/or height. Each block has its own set of options.

In this section, you discover how to configure the settings and options for four of the most commonly used blocks:

- Paragraph
- Image
- Media & Text
- Pullquote

You configure options for the block you're using in two areas of the Edit Post screen: the block itself and the settings panel on the right side of the screen.

TIP

The settings panel does not appear as an official label in the Dashboard, but it is the terminology being used currently by the WordPress dev team and refers to the panel that appears on the right side of the Add Post page, as seen in most of the figures in this chapter. The settings panel has two sections: Document and Block. The Document section contains the global settings that I cover in "Refining Your Post Options" later in this chapter. The Block section of the settings panel contains additional settings that you can configure for each block. Notice that as you switch to editing a different kind of block, the Block section of the settings panel changes to display the unique settings for the block you're currently using. You can click the gear icon in the top-right corner of the Edit Post screen to remove the panel from the screen, which is nice if you temporarily want a larger writing space. You can easily restore the settings panel by clicking the gear icon again.

Paragraph block settings

You use the Paragraph Block to create a basic block of text. Add the block to your post or page and then add the text inside the box provided. When you're working within this block, a small toolbar of options appears at the top of the block, as shown in Figure 1-12.

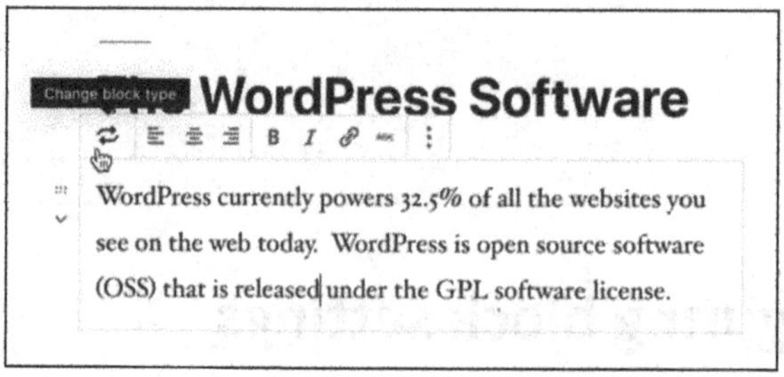

FIGURE 1-12: Options toolbar in a Paragraph block.

This toolbar provides a variety of options, including the following (from left to right):

» **Change Block Type:** Clicking this option allows you to change the type of block you're using. If you want to change from a Paragraph to a Quote block, for example, click the Change Block Type icon and then choose the Quote block to swap it. The block types you can change to from a Paragraph block include Quote, Verse, Heading, List, and Preformatted.

» **Align Text Left:** This block-formatting option positions the text within a Paragraph block to the left side of the page.

» **Align Text Center:** This block-formatting option positions the text within a Paragraph block to the center of the page.

» **Align Text Right:** This block-formatting option positions the text within a Paragraph block to the right side of the page.

» **Bold:** This text-formatting option changes the selected text within a Paragraph block to a bold (darker) font. Select the text you want to format and then click the Bold icon. Example: **bold text.**

» **Italic:** This text-formatting option changes the selected text within a Paragraph block to an italic (slanted) font. Select the text you want to format and then click the Italic icon. Example: *italic text.*

» **Link:** This text-formatting option changes the selected text within a Paragraph block to a hyperlink (text that readers can click to visit a new web pages or website, in their browser). Select the text you want to format and then click the Link icon.

» **Strikethrough:** This text-formatting option changes the selected text within a Paragraph block to display with a line through it. Select the text you want to format and then click the Strikethrough icon. Example: ~~strikethrough text~~.

» **More Options:** Clicking this icon reveals a drop-down menu of options for the entire block, not just the content within the block. (This option exists on every block toolbar, so I'll cover it here and you can refer to this list for other blocks later in this section.) Click the More Options icon on the block toolbar to reveal a drop-down list of options:

- *Hide Block Settings:* Clicking this option removes the settings panel on the right side of the Edit Post screen, giving you a larger space in which to create your content.
- *Duplicate:* Clicking this option duplicates the block you're currently using and inserts it below the current block.
- *Insert Before:* Clicking this option inserts a blank default block directly above the block you're currently using.
- *Insert After:* Clicking this option inserts a blank default block directly below the block you're currently using.

Writing Your First Post

USING KEYBOARD SHORTCUTS

Some people appreciate the ability to use keyboard shortcuts to accomplish things that normally take a mouse click to do. Keyboard shortcuts can make quick work of common editing actions by reducing dependence on the computer mouse, which can also benefit those who have carpal tunnel syndrome or other ailments associated with joint or muscle pain and strain. WordPress provides a variety of keyboard shortcuts to accomplish things like making text bold or italic, saving a post, and undoing changes. In the top-right corner of the Edit Post screen is an icon that looks like three dots stacked on top of one another. Hover your mouse over this icon, and you see the label Show More Tools & Options. Click this icon to open a menu of options. Choose Keyboard Shortcuts to open a small window that shows you the shortcuts you can use when editing and creating posts and pages in WordPress.

- *Edit As HTML:* Clicking this option changes the block editor to an HTML editor so you can view and create content in HTML code.
- *Add to Reusable Blocks:* Click this option to save the block you're currently using to a library of blocks that you can reuse in other places on your site. This feature is helpful when you create blocks on one page and want to use the same blocks on other pages. Saving a block as a Reusable block makes it available for use on other pages, exactly as it appeared when you saved it. Editing the block applies those changes everywhere the block is used on your site.

  TIP: When you create a Reusable block, it's stored on the Blocks menu (refer to Figure 1-3) in a new section labeled Reusable.
- *Remove Block:* Clicking this option removes the block from the Edit Post screen. Use this feature carefully, because when you remove a block, it's gone (unless you've saved it as a Reusable block).

Additional options for the Paragraph block are available in the settings panel on the right side of the Edit Post screen, as shown in Figure 1-13.

Those options include

» **Font Size:** You have two ways to define the size of the font you're using in the block that you're editing. In the Text Settings section of the settings panel, you can choose Small, Normal, Large, or Huge from the Font Size drop-down menu to adjust the text sizes that are predefined by WordPress. Alternatively, you can enter a specific number in the text box to the right of the Font Size menu if you want to use a specific-size font. When you adjust the Text Settings in the settings panel, the changes immediately occur in the block you're editing.

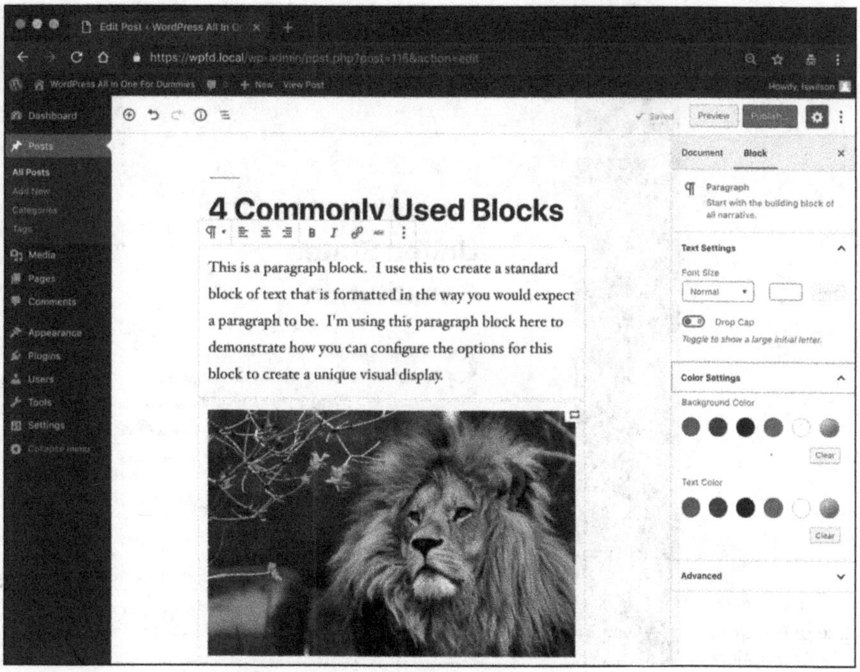

FIGURE 1-13: Options in the settings panel for the Paragraph block.

- **Drop Cap:** A drop cap can be applied to a paragraph of text to make the first letter of the paragraph much larger and bolder than the rest of the text within the block. You often see this method used in magazine and newspaper articles; it can have a dramatic effect on articles that appear on the web. Figure 1-14 shows an example of several paragraphs that use the Drop Cap method. To enable it, click the Drop Cap toggle button.
- **Background Color:** Within the Color Settings section of the settings panel, you can select a background color for the Paragraph block you're currently using. Choose one of five preselected colors or click the custom color picker icon to select another color (see Figure 1-15).
- **Text Color:** In the Color Settings section of the block settings panel, you can change the color of the text used in the Paragraph block you're currently using. Choose one of five preselected colors or click the custom color picker icon to select another color. Figure 1-16 shows a Paragraph block with a blue background and white text.

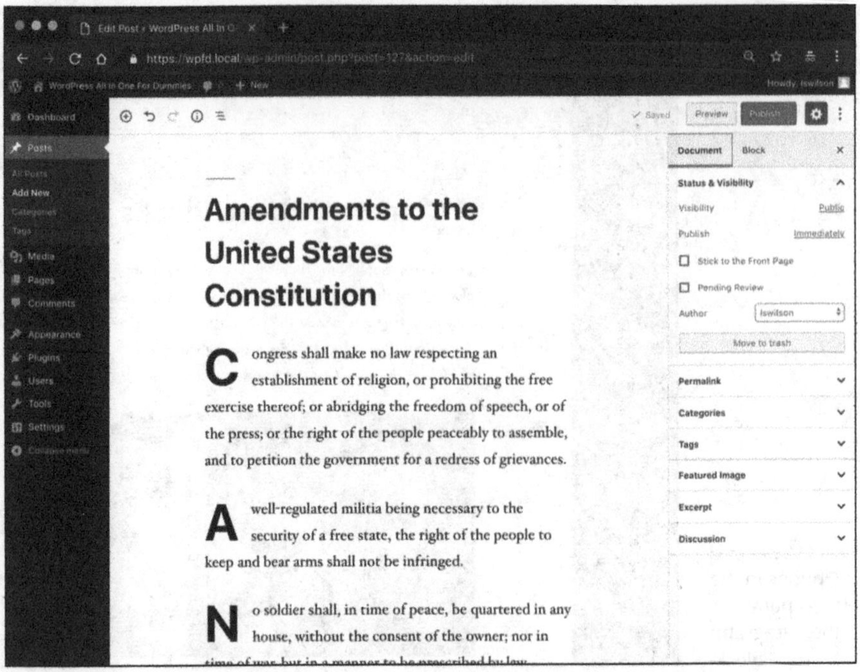

FIGURE 1-14: Use of the Drop Cap option.

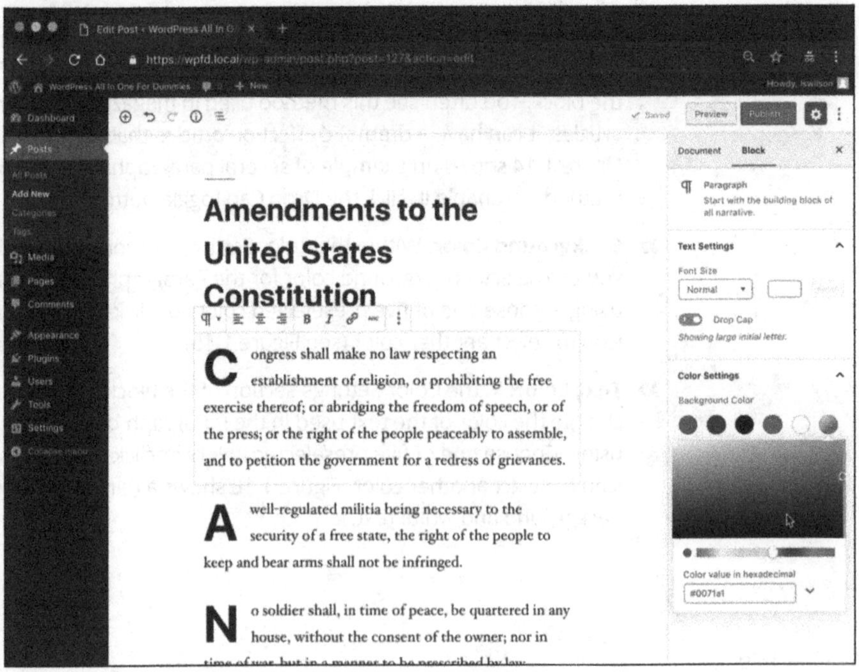

FIGURE 1-15: The custom color picker tool in the settings panel.

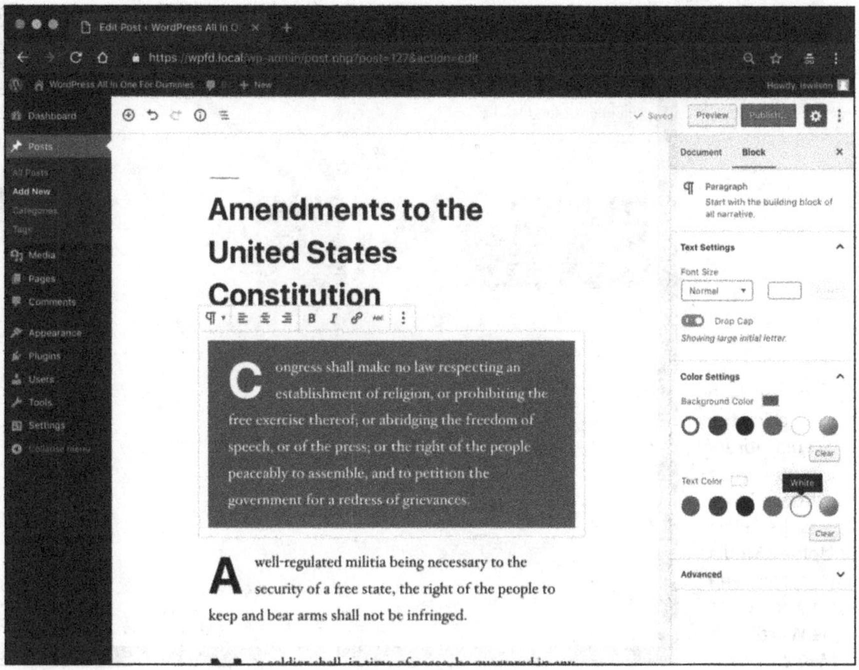

FIGURE 1-16: A Paragraph block with a blue background and white text.

Image block settings

You use the Image block to add a single image to your post. Add the block to your post or page and then use one of these options:

- **Upload:** Click the Upload button to select an image from your computer. This action uploads the image from your computer to your website and inserts the image into your post via an Image block. WordPress also adds this image to your Media Library so you can reuse this image in the future.
- **Media Library:** Click the Media Library button to choose an image from the WordPress Media Library (see Figure 1-17). When the Select or Upload Media screen opens, select an image in the Media Library section and then click the Select button to add the image to your post.
- **Insert from URL:** Click the Insert from URL button to display a small text box where you can paste or type the URL (or link) for the image you want to use. Press the Enter key on your keyboard or click the Apply button to insert the image into the Image block you're using.
- **Drag an Image:** This cool option allows you to select an image from your computer and drag it into the WordPress block editor to add it to a block. The dragged image also gets added to the Media Library for future use. In Figure 1-18, I clicked an image titled `lion.jpg` and dragged it from my computer to the WordPress block editor to add it to the Image block I was using.

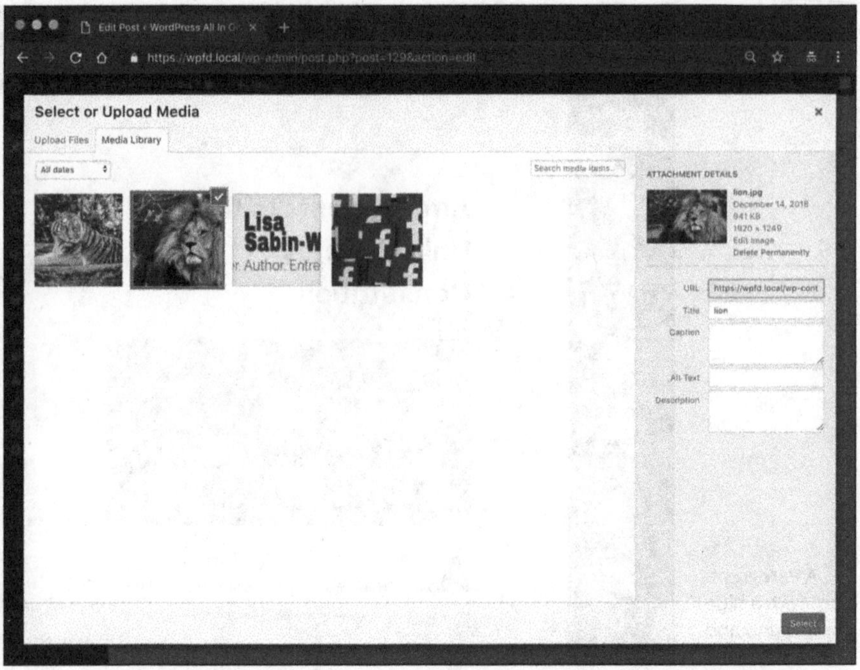

FIGURE 1-17: Clicking the Media Library button in an Image block opens the Select or Upload Media screen and displays images in the WordPress Media Library.

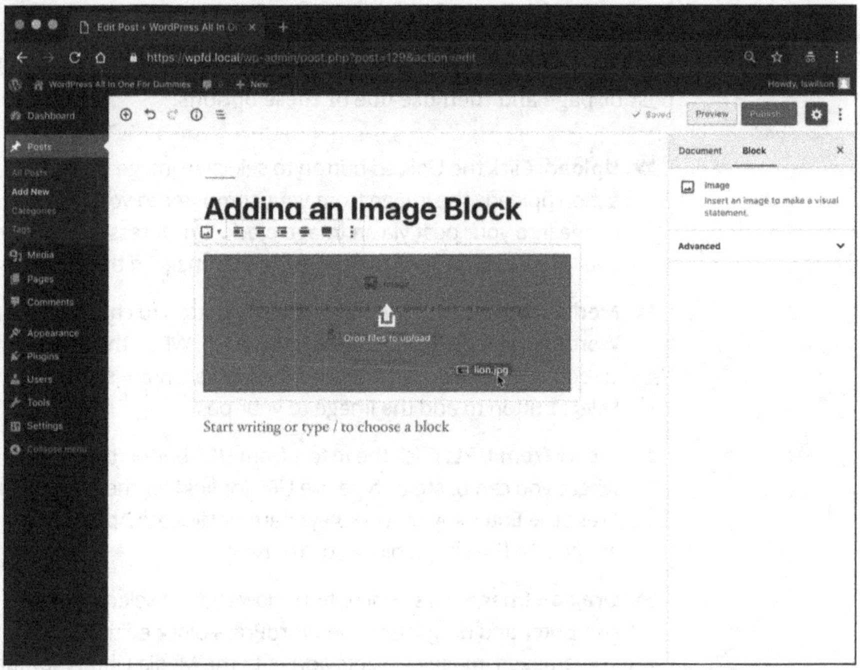

FIGURE 1-18: Dragging an image from your computer to the Image block adds the image to the block and to the WordPress Media Library.

» **Write Caption:** When you've have added an image to an Image block, you see an optional field directly below it labeled Write Caption. This field is optional; if you do nothing with it, nothing displays on your site. If you type words in this field, however, those words appear below the image as a caption.

When you're working within this block, notice the small toolbar of options that appears at the top of the block, as shown in Figure 1-19. This toolbar provides a variety of options for the Image block, including the following (from left to right):

FIGURE 1-19: Options toolbar in the Image block.

» **Change Block Type:** Click this option to change the type of block you're using. If you want to change from an Image block to a Cover block, for example, click the Change Block Type icon and then select the Cover block to swap it. The block types you can change from an Image block include Media & Text, Gallery, Cover, and File.

» **Align Left:** This block-formatting option positions the image within the Image block against the left margin of the page.

» **Align Center:** This block-formatting option positions the image within the Image block in the center of the page.

» **Align Right:** This block-formatting option positions the image within the Image block against the right margin of the page.

» **Wide Width:** Click this option to set the width of the image to the width of the content on the page.

- **Full Width:** Click this option to increase the width of the image to the width of the screen you're viewing the content on. In Figure 1-20, you see a post that I created with a full-width image. Notice that the left and right edges of the image extend all the way to the left and right sides of the viewing screen.

FIGURE 1-20: Example of an Image block with the Full Width setting.

TIP

If you don't select Wide Width or Full Width on the Image block toolbar, you can set the desired width of the image in the Image block settings panel, as covered in the next section.

- **Edit Image:** Click this option to open the Select or Upload Media screen (refer to Figure 1-17) and change the image you're currently using in the Image block.
- **More Options:** The settings here are the same as the ones discussed in "Paragraph block settings" earlier in this chapter.

Additional options are available for the Image block in the settings panel on the right side of the Edit Post screen, as shown in Figure 1-21.

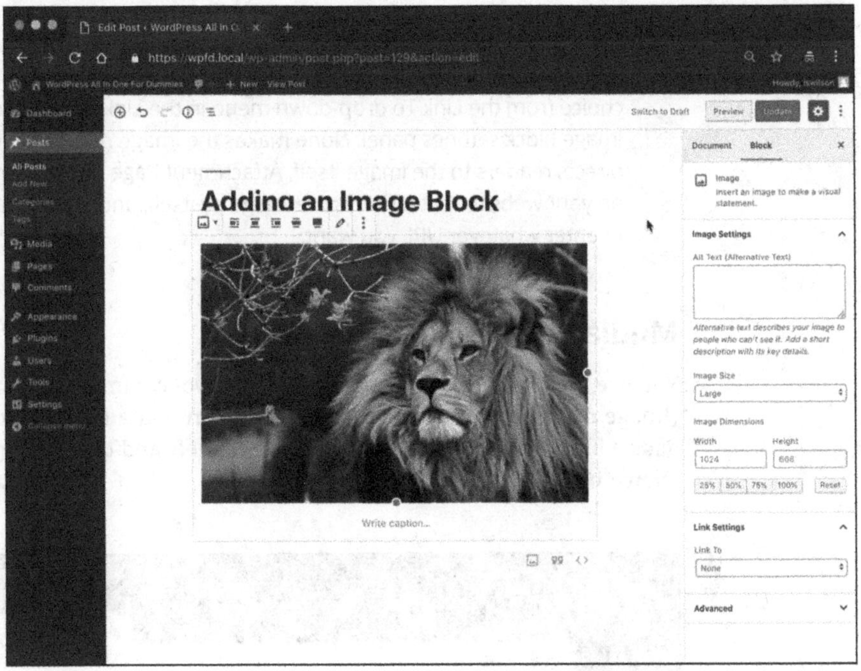

FIGURE 1-21: Options in the settings panel for the Image block.

The options include

- **Alt Text:** Enter descriptive text in the Alt Text field to describe the image you're using in the Image block. Also referred to as Alternative Text, this description helps people who can't see the image on your site; when the image doesn't load on your site, the Alt Text is displayed, providing context for the missing image. This option is also an accessibility feature that helps those who use screen readers to browse the web. (Screen readers allow visually impaired users to understand the text that's displayed on the website with a speech synthesizer or Braille display.) Additionally, Alt Text descriptions assist in search engine optimization (SEO), which I cover in Book 4, Chapter 3, and Book 5, Chapter 4.
- **Image Size:** To set the size of the image used in the Image block, choose a predefined size from the Image Size drop-down menu in the Image block settings panel. The available options are Thumbnail, Medium, Large, and Full Size. The dimensions for these options are defined in the WordPress settings on your Dashboard (see Book 3, Chapter 2); to see them, choose Settings ➪ Media.
- **Image Dimensions:** To set a specific width and height for the image used in the Image block, enter numbers in the Width and Height fields in the Image Dimensions section of the Image block settings panel.

» **Link To:** Attach a hyperlink to an image so that when a visitor to your website clicks the image, he visits a new page in his browser. To define the link, make a choice from the Link To drop-down menu in the Link Settings section of the Image block settings panel. None makes the image nonclickable, Media File directs readers to the image itself, Attachment Page directs readers to a page on your website that displays the image by itself, and Custom URL allows you to enter whatever URL you want.

Media & Text block settings

You use the Media & Text block to insert a two-column block that displays media (image or video) and text side by side. When you add the block to your post, it adds a block with the image settings on the left and text settings on the right, as shown in Figure 1-22.

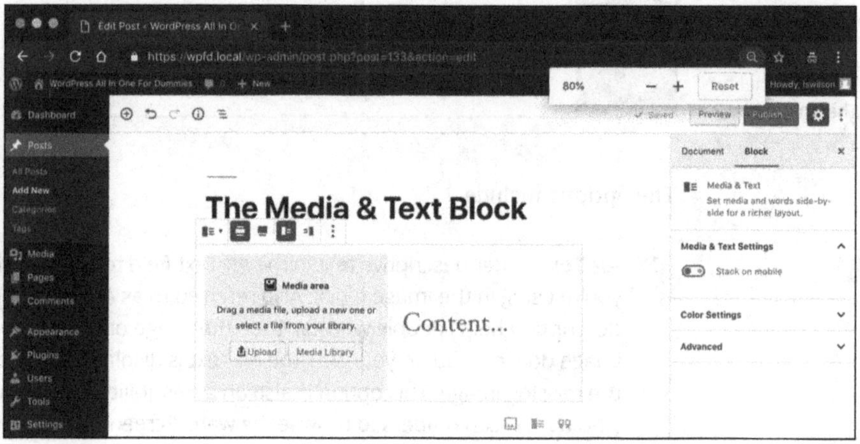

FIGURE 1-22: The Media & Text block.

In this block, you add the media in the Media Area section on the left, using the method covered in "Image block settings" earlier in this chapter and adding your text in the Content section on the right, as shown in Figure 1-23.

TIP

When you enter text in the Content section on the right side, a toolbar of text-formatting options appears. This toolbar has the same options that I cover in "Paragraph block settings" earlier in this chapter.

» **Wide Width:** Click this option to set the width of the Media & Text block to the width of the content on the page.

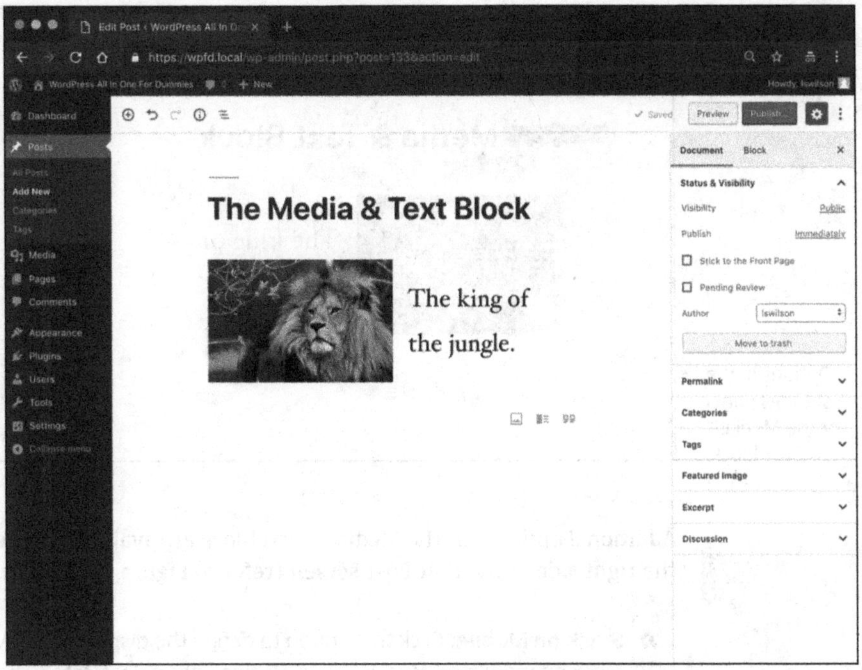

FIGURE 1-23: Media on the left with text on the right, using the Media & Text block.

- **Full Width:** Click this option to increase the width of the image to the width of the screen you're viewing the content on. The left and right edges of the block extend all the way to the left and right sides of the viewing screen.
- **Show Media on Left:** Click this option to set the media on the left and the text on the right (refer to Figure 1-23). This option is the default setting.
- **Show Media on Right:** Click this option to set the text on the left and the media on the right.
- **Edit Image:** Click this option to open the Select or Upload Media screen (refer to Figure 1-17) and change the image you're currently using in the Image block.
- **More Options:** The settings here are the same as the ones I discuss in "Paragraph block settings" earlier in this chapter.

When you're working within this block, a small toolbar of options appears at the top of the block, as shown in Figure 1-24. This toolbar provides a variety of options for the paragraph block, including the following (from left to right):

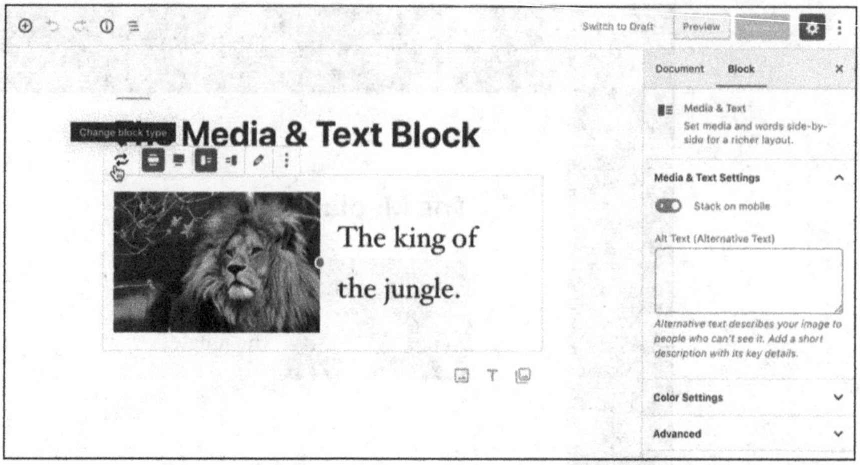

FIGURE 1-24: Options in the settings panel for the Media & Text block.

Additional options for the Media & Text block are available in the settings panel on the right side of the Edit Post screen (refer to Figure 1-24). Those options include

- **Stack on Mobile:** Click this option to define the display of the Media & Text block on mobile devices. If you leave this option deselected, the block spans the width of the mobile screen, and depending on the image and text you've included in the block, the block could be difficult to read. Select the Stack on Mobile option to display the content within Media & Text blocks stacked on top of one another. If you have the media set to display on the left with the text on the right, for example, on mobile devices, the media displays above the text. Compare Figure 1-23 (desktop view) with Figure 1-25 (mobile phone view) to see what I'm describing.
- **Alt Text:** Enter descriptive text in the Alt Text field to describe the image you're using in the Image block. Also referred to as Alternative Text, this description helps people who can't see the image on your site; when the image doesn't load on your site, the Alt Text is displayed, providing context for the missing image. This option is also an accessibility feature that helps those who use screen readers to browse the web. (Screen readers allow visually impaired users to understand the text that's displayed on the website with a speech synthesizer or Braille display.) Additionally, Alt Text descriptions assist in SEO, which I cover in Book 4, Chapter 3, and Book 5, Chapter 4.
- **Background Color:** Within the Color Settings section of the settings panel, you can select a background color for the Media & Text block you're currently using. Choose one of five preselected colors or click the custom color picker icon to select another color.

FIGURE 1-25: The Media & Text block displayed on a mobile device with the option to Stack on Mobile set to On.

TIP When you're creating content inside of any block on a page, and you find that you've made a mistake, the Undo button at the top of the Edit Post screen undoes the last action you took on the screen. Alternatively, a Redo button allows you to redo the last undone action.

Pullquote block settings

You use the Pullquote block to insert a quotation with a citation and give it special design emphasis to set it apart from the rest of the text on your site. Figure 1-4 earlier in this chapter shows what a Pullquote block looks like.

When you're working within this block, a small toolbar of options appears at the top of the Pullquote block, as shown in Figure 1-26. This toolbar provides a variety of options for the block, including the following (from left to right):

- **Change Block Type:** Clicking this option allows you to change the style or type of block you're currently using. You can change the style by choosing Regular or Solid Color from the drop-down menu. By default, Pullquote style is Regular.

  You also can change the block type. If you want to change from a Pullquote block to a Quote block, for example, click the Change Block Type icon and then select the Quote block to swap it. The only block type you can switch to from a Pullquote block is a Quote block.

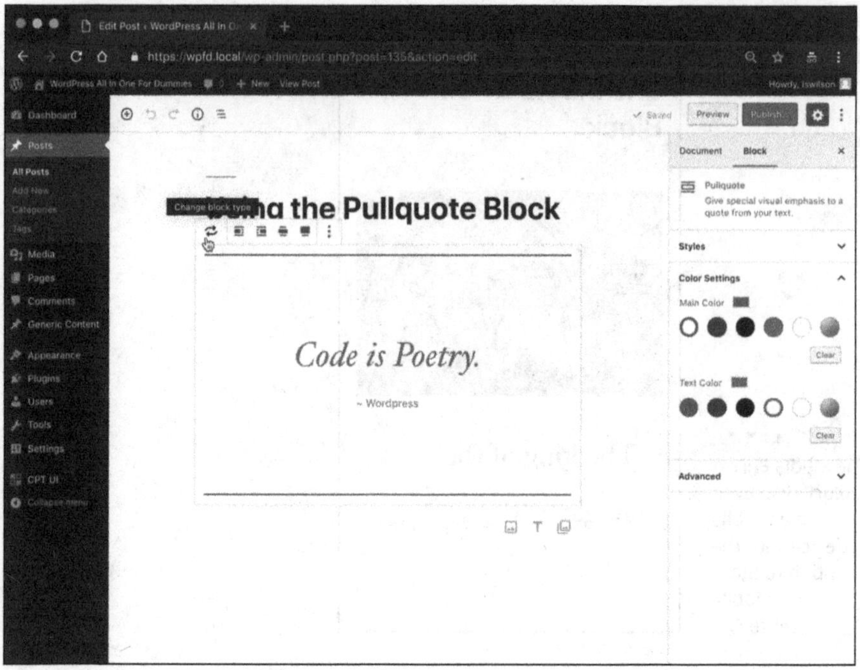

FIGURE 1-26: Options in the settings panel for the Pullquote block.

- **Align Left:** This block-formatting option positions the text within the Pullquote block against the left margin of the page.
- **Align Right:** This block-formatting option positions the text within the Pullquote block against the right margin of the page.
- **Wide Width:** This block-formatting option positions the image within the Image block against the left margin of the page.
- **Full Width:** This block-formatting option positions the image within the Image block in the center of the page.
- **Bold:** This text-formatting option changes the selected text within the Pullquote block to a bold (darker) font. Select the text you want to format and then click the Bold icon. Example: **bold text.**
- **Italic:** This text-formatting option changes the selected text within the Pullquote block to an italic (slanted) font. Select the text you want to format and then click the Italic icon. Example: *italic text.*
- **Link:** This text-formatting option changes the selected text within the Pullquote block to a hyperlink (text that your readers can click to visit a new web page or websites in their browser). Select the text you want to format and then click the Link icon.

- **Strikethrough:** This text-formatting option changes the selected text within the Pullquote block to display with a line through it. Select the text you want to format and then click the Strikethrough icon. Example: ~~strikethrough text.~~
- **More Options:** The settings here are the same as the ones discussed in "Paragraph block settings" earlier in this chapter.

Additional options are available for the Pullquote block in the settings panel on the right side of the Edit Post screen, as shown in Figure 1-27.

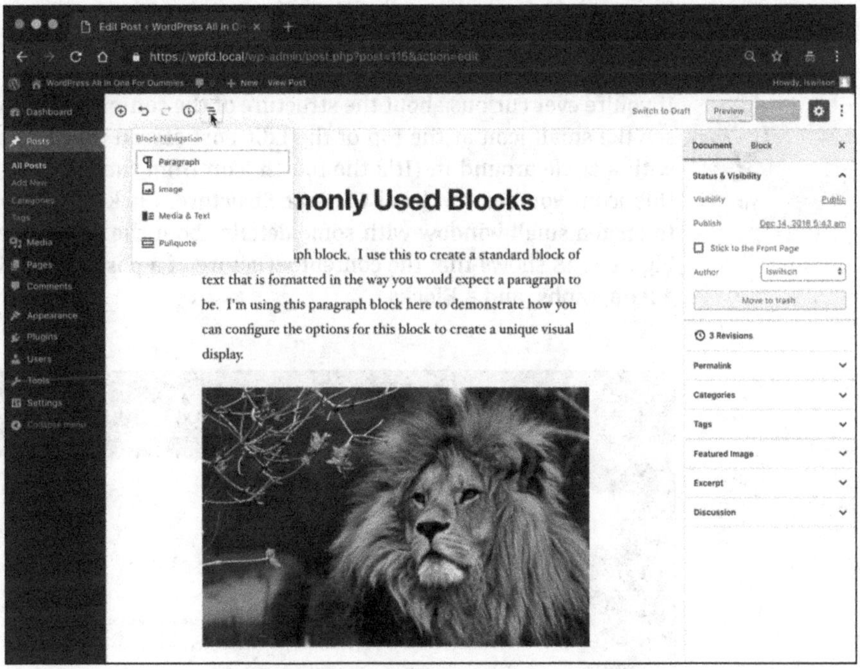

FIGURE 1-27: The Block Navigation menu makes it easy to navigate to a specific block to edit it.

The options include

- **Regular:** This setting is the default option for the Pullquote block, displaying the block as black text on a white background.
- **Solid Color:** Select this option to change the style to white text on a blue background.
- **Main Color:** Within the Color Settings section of the settings panel, you can choose one of five predefined colors or click the custom color picker icon to select another color. When you're using Regular style, the Main Color setting changes the color of the border. When you're using the Solid Color style, the Main Color setting changes the color of the background of the block.

- **Text Color:** Within the Color Settings section of the settings panel, you can choose one of five predefined colors to change the color of the text within the Pullquote block. You also can click the rainbow-colored icon to select a custom color of your choice.

TIP

When you're working on a post or page that has several blocks in use, scrolling up and down the page to find the block you want to edit can be cumbersome. At the top of the Edit Post screen is a row of icons, and the last icon on the right is labeled Block Navigation. Click that icon to open the Block Navigation drop-down menu, which displays all the blocks in use in the post you're editing (refer to Figure 1-27). You can use the Block Navigation menu to navigate to the block you want to edit.

TIP

If you're ever curious about the structure of the content on a page you're creating, see the small icon at the top of the Edit Post screen that looks like a lowercase *i* with a circle around it. (It's the fourth icon from the left.) When you hover over this icon, you see the label Content Structure. Click the Content Structure icon to open a small window with some details about the post or page you're editing. Figure 1-28 shows that the content structure of a post has 72 Words, 0 Headings, 2 Paragraphs, and 5 Blocks.

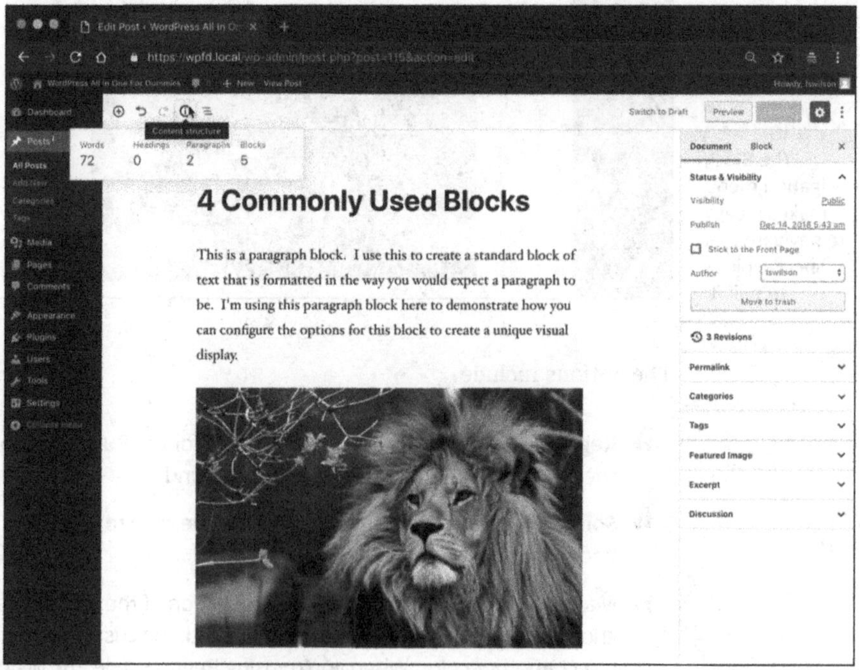

FIGURE 1-28: The Content Structure window gives you some details about the page you're creating.

If you're a total geek like me and like to work with code, or if you're curious to see the underlying HTML code for the blocks you're creating, WordPress provides a way to do that. In the top-right corner of the Edit Post screen is an icon that looks like three dots stacked on top of one another. Hover your mouse over this icon, and you see the label Show More Tools & Options. Click the icon to open a menu of options. To view the code versions of the blocks you've created on your site, choose the Code Editor option on the Editor section of the menu. This action changes the display of your post content to code rather than the default visual editor. Figure 1-29 shows a post in code.

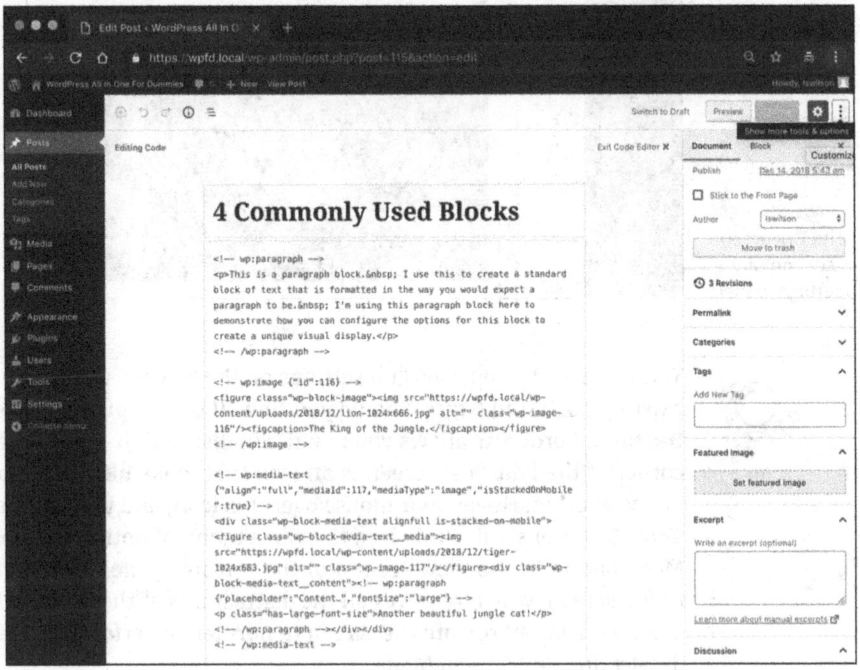

FIGURE 1-29: Using the Code Editor on a post.

Refining Your Post Options

After you write the post, you can choose a few extra options before you publish it for the entire world to see. On the right side of the Edit Post screen is the settings panel, which you should be familiar with from earlier sections of this chapter. Click the Document link at the top to view the options you can set for the post globally (See Figure 1-30.). Unlike settings for individual blocks, the Document settings pertain to the entire post.

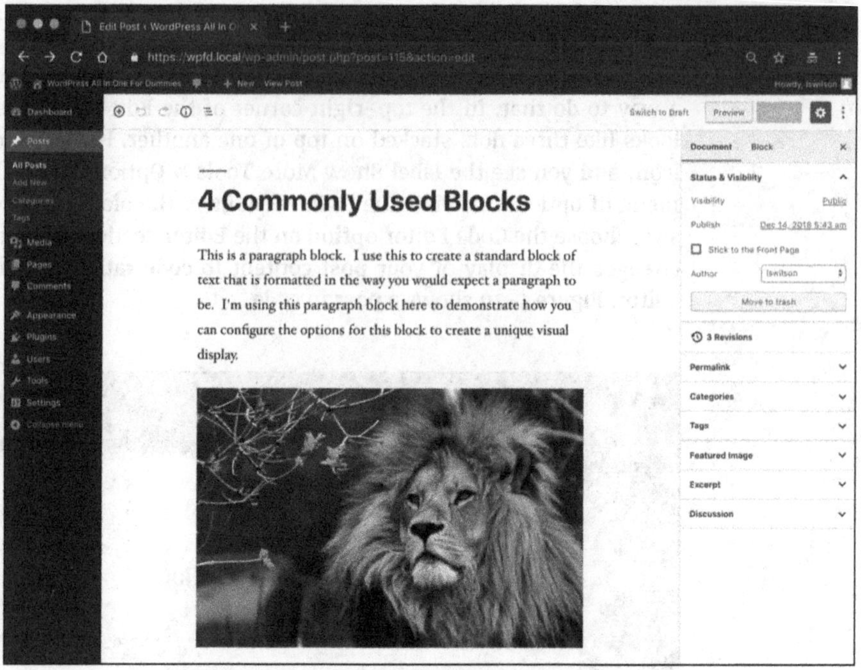

FIGURE 1-30: The Document section of the settings panel.

TIP

You'll see a lot of options and settings on the screens where you add new and edit existing posts and pages. Should you find all those options, links, and menus distracting, WordPress allows you to write in distraction-free mode. In the top-right corner of the Edit Post screen is an icon that looks like three dots stacked on top of one another. Hover your mouse over this icon, and you see the label Show More Tools & Options. Click this icon to open a menu of options. Choose the Full Screen Mode option in the View section of the settings panel to change the screen view to full screen, which removes all the distractions of those pesky links, menus, and settings. You can restore the screen to normal by performing the same action and deselecting Full Screen Mode.

The Document settings include the following:

- **Status and Visibility:** By default, the visibility status of your post is set to Public. You can select three status options by clicking the Public link in the Status and Visibility panel:
  - *Public:* Select this option to make the post viewable by everyone who visits your site.
  - *Private:* Select this option to make the post viewable only by site administrators and editors. Saving a post with this status prevents anyone else from viewing the post on your site.

- *Password Protected:* Select this option to create a password for your post. By assigning a password to a post, you can publish a post that only you can see. You also can share the post password with a friend who can see the content of the post after she enters the password. But why would anyone want to password-protect a post? Suppose that you just ate dinner at your mother-in-law's house, and she made the *worst* pot roast you've ever eaten. You can write all about it! Protect it with a password and give the password to your trusted friends so that they can read about it without offending your mother-in-law.
- *Publish:* By default, WordPress assigns the publish date and time as the exact date and time when you originally published the post to your site. If you want to future-publish this post, you can set the time and date for any time in the future. If you have a vacation planned and don't want your site to go without updates while you're gone, for example, you can write a few posts and set the date for a time in the future. Those posts are published to your site while you're somewhere tropical, diving with the fish. Click the date and time displayed, and a date and time picker appears. Use this picker to set the date and time when you'd like this post to publish to your site.
- *Stick to the Front Page:* Select this check box to have WordPress publish the post to your site and keep it at the top of all posts until you change this setting; this type of post is known as a *sticky post*. Typically, posts are displayed in chronological order on your site, with the most recent post at the top. If you make a post sticky, it remains at the top no matter how many other posts you make after it. When you want to unstick the post, deselect the Front Page check box.
- *Pending Review:* Select this check box to save the post as a draft with the status of Pending Review. This option alerts the administrator of the site that a contributor created a post that's waiting for administrator review and approval. (This feature is helpful for sites that have multiple authors.) Generally, only contributors use the Pending Review option. Note that this option is available only for new posts. You won't see it in the settings panel of posts that have already been published.
- *Author:* If you're running a multiauthor blog, you can choose the name of the author you want to assign to the post you're editing. By default, your own author name is selected in the Author drop-down list.
- *Move to Trash:* Click this button to delete the post you've been working on. This action doesn't permanently delete the post, however. You can find and restore that post by visiting the Posts screen in your Dashboard (choose Posts ⇨ All Posts) and clicking the Trash link.

- **Revisions:** In "Composing Your Post" earlier in this chapter, I talk about the autosave feature. Its function is to automatically save the work you've done on posts you're creating so that you don't lose any of it. Each time you edit a post, WordPress automatically saves the old version of your post and stores it as a revision, making it available for you to access later. This section gives you an indication of how many revisions a post has. When you click the Revisions link, you see the Compare Revisions screen, where you can review and restore revisions of your post.
- **Permalink:** A permalink is the direct link, or URL, to the post you're about to publish (see Book 5, Chapter 4). Although you can't change the domain portion of this URL (`https://domain.com`), you can adjust the part of the URL that appears in the link after the final slash at the end of your domain. For a post titled "WordPress Tips," WordPress automatically creates a URL from that title like `http://domain.com/wordpress-tips`. Use the URL field in the Permalink section of the settings panel to set different words for your post (or page) from the ones that WordPress automatically creates for you. You could shorten the slug for the post title WordPress Tips to wordpress so that the URL for the post is `http://domain.com/wordpress`.
- **Categories:** You can file your posts in different categories to organize them by subject. (See more about organizing your posts by category in Book 3, Chapter 5.) Select the check box to the left of the category you want to use.

  TIP

  Don't see the category you need in the Category section? Click the Add New Category link and add a new category right there on the page you're using to create or edit your post.
- **Tags:** Type your desired tags in the Add New Tag text box. Be sure to separate tags with commas so that WordPress knows where each tag begins and ends. Cats, Kittens, Feline represents three different tags, for example, but without the commas, WordPress would consider those three words to be one tag. See Book 3, Chapter 5 for more information on tags and how to use them.
- **Featured Image:** Some WordPress themes are configured to use an image (photo) to represent each post on your site. The image can appear on the home/front page, blog page, archives page, search results page, or anywhere within the content displayed on your website. If you're using a theme that has this option, you can easily define it by clicking Set Featured Image in the Featured Image section of the settings panel. This action opens a window that allows you to upload a new image or select an existing image from the Media Library. You can find more information about using featured images in Book 6, Chapter 6.
- **Excerpt:** Excerpts are short summaries of your posts. Many authors use snippets to show teasers of their posts on their website, thereby encouraging readers to click the Read More links to read the posts in their entirety. By default, WordPress automatically creates an excerpt based on the text

contained in the first paragraph of your post. But if you want to control what text is displayed for the excerpt of your post, type your desired text in the Write an Excerpt box, which is displayed when you click the Excerpt section in the setting panel. Excerpts can be any length in terms of words, but the point is to keep them short and sweet to tease your readers into clicking the Read More link.

- **Discussion:** Decide whether to let readers submit comments through the comment system by selecting Allow Comments in the Discussion section of the settings panel. Additionally, you can enable pingbacks and trackbacks by clicking the check box in the Discussion section labeled Allow Pingbacks & Trackbacks. By default, both options are selected for posts you create on your site. For more on trackbacks, see Book 3, Chapter 4.

Publishing Your Post

You've given your new post a title and written the content of the post by assembling all the content blocks you need to create the post you desire. Maybe you've even added an image or other type of media file to the post (see Book 4, chapters 3 and 4), and you've configured the tags, categories, and other options in the settings panel. Now the question is this: To publish or not to publish (yet)?

WordPress gives you three options for saving or publishing your post when you're done writing it. These options are located in the top-right corner of the Add New (or Edit) Post screen. Figure 1-31 shows the available options: Save Draft, Preview, and Publish.

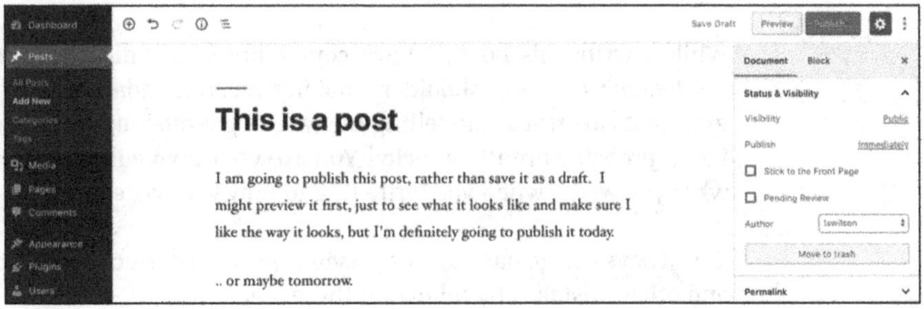

FIGURE 1-31: The publish options for your posts and pages.

The options for saving or publishing your post include

- **Save Draft:** Click this link to save your post as a draft. The Save Draft link refreshes with a message that says Saved, indicating that your post has been successfully saved as a draft. The action of saving as a draft also saves all the post options you've set for the post, including blocks, categories, tags, and featured images. You can continue editing now, tomorrow, the next day, or next year; the post is saved as a draft until you decide to publish it or delete it. Posts saved as drafts can't be seen by visitors to your site. To access your draft posts in your Dashboard, visit the Posts screen (choose Posts ⇨ All Posts), and click the Drafts link on the top menu.
- **Preview:** Click the Preview button to view your post in a new window, as it would appear on your live site if you'd published it. Previewing the post doesn't publish it to your site yet. Previewing simply gives you the opportunity to view the post on your site and check it for any formatting or content changes you want to make.
- **Publish:** Click the Publish button when you're ready to publish your post or page to your website and allow your visitors to view it when they visit. WordPress puts a small fail-safe feature in place to make sure that you want to publish the post live; when you click the Publish button, the settings panel changes to a panel with the heading `Do you really want to publish?` This panel even provides the option to double-check some of your settings, such as visibility and date. Click the Publish button at the top a second time to publish the post to your website.

Being Your Own Editor

While I write this book, I have copy editors, technical editors, and proofreaders looking over my shoulder, making recommendations, correcting typos and grammatical errors, and telling me when I get too long-winded. You, on the other hand, probably aren't so lucky! You are your own editor and have full control of what you write, when you write it, and how you write it.

You always can go back to edit previous posts to correct typos, grammatical errors, and other mistakes by following these steps:

1. **Find the post that you want to edit by clicking the All Posts link on the Posts menu of the Dashboard.**

   The Posts screen opens, listing the 20 most recent posts you've created.

TIP

To filter that listing of posts by date, choose a date from the All Dates drop-down menu at the top of the Posts screen (choose Dashboard ⇨ Posts). If you choose January 2019, the Posts page reloads, displaying only those posts that were published in January 2019.

You also can filter the post listing by category. Choose your desired category from the All Categories drop-down list.

2. **When you find the post you need, click its title.**

   Alternatively, you can click the Edit link that appears below the post title when you hover your mouse over it.

   The Edit Post screen opens. In this screen, you can edit the post and/or any of its options.

TIP

If you need to edit only the post options, click the Quick Edit link that appears below the post title when you hover your mouse over it. A Quick Edit menu appears, displaying the post options that you can configure, such as title, status, password, categories, tags, comments, and time stamp. Click the Update button to save your changes.

3. **Edit your post; then click the Update Post button.**

   The Edit Post screen displays a message that the post has been updated.

Congratulations on publishing your first post on your site! This chapter took you through the mechanics of working with the WordPress block editor, creating content, and setting your post options to get you familiar with the tools WordPress provides for publishing content. The next chapters in this book help you discover specific content management options such as categories, tags, and image galleries.

IN THIS CHAPTER

» Differentiating posts and pages

» Creating a new static page on your website

» Adding a blog to your site

Chapter 2
Creating a Static Page

In Book 3, Chapter 5, I discuss the different ways that content gets archived by WordPress, and in Book 3, Chapter 1, I give you a very brief introduction to the concept of pages and where to find them on the WordPress Dashboard.

This chapter takes you through the full concept of pages in WordPress, including how to write and publish them. This chapter also fully explains the difference between posts and pages in WordPress so that you know which to publish for different situations.

Understanding the Difference between Posts and Pages

Pages, in WordPress, are different from posts because they don't get archived the way your posts do. They aren't categorized or tagged, don't appear in your listing of recent posts or date archives, and aren't syndicated in the RSS feeds available on your site — because content within pages generally doesn't change. (Book 3, Chapter 5 gives you all the details on how the WordPress archives work.)

REMEMBER

Use pages for static or stand-alone content that exists separately from the archived post content on your site, such as an About or Contact page.

With the page feature, you can create an unlimited number of static pages separate from your posts. People commonly use this feature to create About Me or Contact Me pages, among other things. Table 2-1 illustrates the differences between posts and pages by showing you the different ways the WordPress platform handles them.

TABLE 2-1 Differences between a Post and a Page

WordPress Options	Page	Post
Appears in blog post listings	No	Yes
Appears as a static page	Yes	No
Appears in category archives	No	Yes
Appears in monthly archives	No	Yes
Appears in Recent Posts listings	No	Yes
Appears in site RSS feed	No	Yes
Appears in search results	Yes	Yes
Uses tags and/or categories	No	Yes

Creating the Front Page of Your Website

For the most part, when you visit a site powered by WordPress, the blog can appear on the main page or as a separate page of the site. My business partner, Brad Williams, keeps a personal blog at `https://strangework.com`, powered by WordPress (of course). His personal website shows his latest blog posts on the front page, along with links to the post archives (by month or by category) in the sidebar. This setup is typical of a site run by WordPress. (See Figure 2-1.)

On the other hand, the front page of our business site at `https://webdevstudios.com`, also powered by WordPress, doesn't display any blog posts, but the website does contain a blog section. (See Figure 2-2.) Instead, it displays the contents of a static page that we created in WordPress. This static page serves as a portal that displays pieces of content from other sections of the site. The site includes a blog but also serves as a full business website with all the sections we need to provide our clients the information they need.

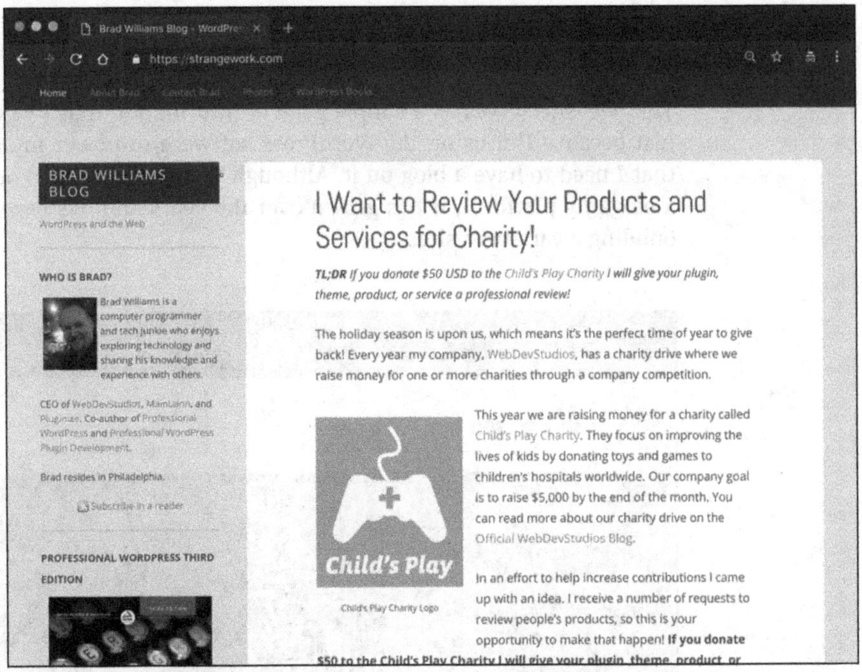

FIGURE 2-1: A personal blog.

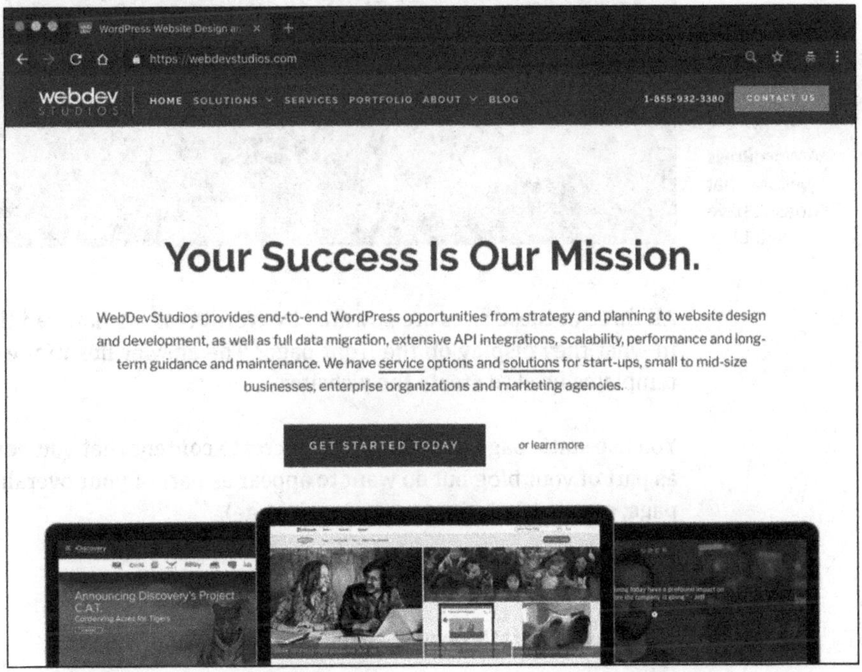

FIGURE 2-2: My business site, set up as a business website that has a blog.

My personal website at `https://lisasabin-wilson.com` is also built with WordPress, but that site doesn't contain a blog anywhere. (See Figure 2-3.) That website serves as a simple page of information that I've chosen to publish. Just because I'm using the WordPress software to power my site doesn't mean that I need to have a blog on it. Although WordPress started out being known as a blogging platform, it has grown over the years and has become a platform for building a variety of sites.

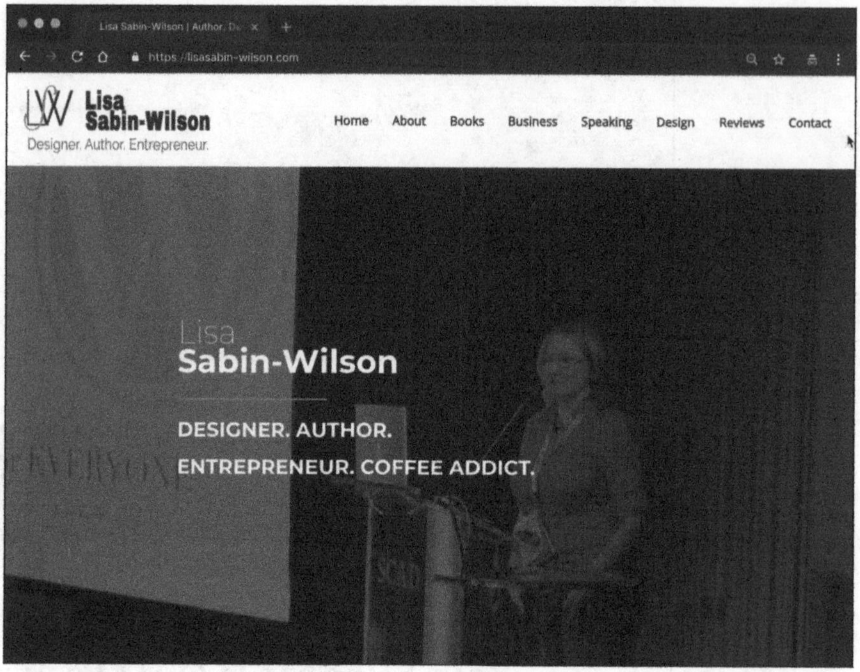

FIGURE 2-3: A WordPress website that doesn't have a blog.

All three of these sites are powered by WordPress, so how can they differ so much in what they display on the front page? The answer lies in the content types and templates used to create the websites.

You use static pages in WordPress to create content that you don't want to appear as part of your blog but do want to appear as part of your overall site (such as a bio page, a page of services, and a home page).

Creating a front page is a three-step process:

1. **Create a static page.**
2. **Set that static page to be used as the home page of your site.**
3. **Tweak the page to look however you like.**

REMEMBER

By using this method, you can create unlimited numbers of static pages to build an entire website. You don't even need to have a blog on your site unless you want one.

Creating the static page

To have a static page appear on the home page of your site, first you need to create that page in the WordPress Dashboard. Follow these steps:

1. **In the Dashboard, click the Add New link on the Pages menu.**

   The Edit Page screen opens, allowing you to create a new page for your WordPress site, as shown in Figure 2-4.

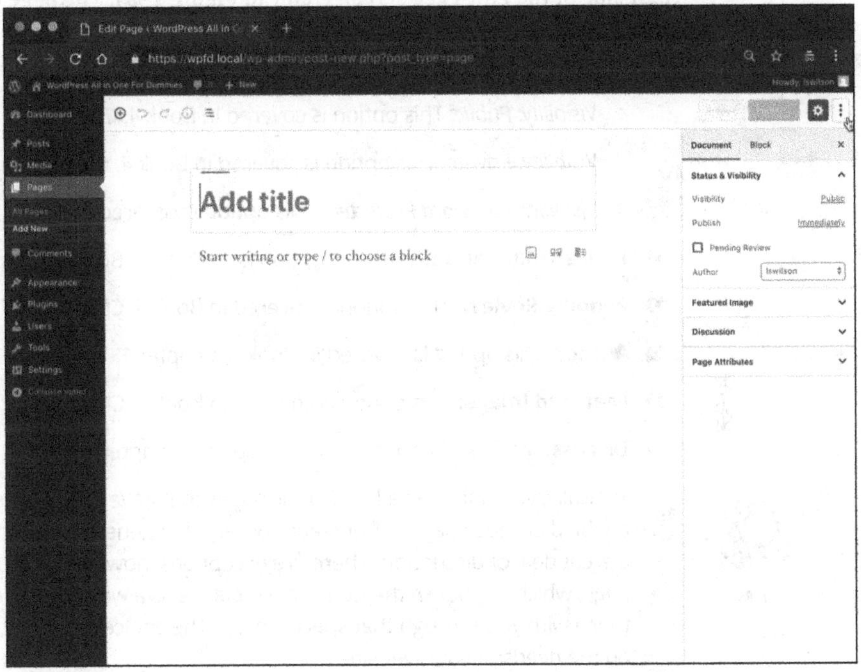

FIGURE 2-4: Create the static page that you want to use as your home page.

2. **Type a title for your page in the Add Title text box at the top.**
3. **Create content for this page, using the Block Editor (Book 4, Chapter 1).**
4. **Set the options for this page.**

   I explain the options on this page in the following section.

5. **Click the Publish button.**

   The page is saved to your database and published to your WordPress site with its individual URL (or *permalink*). The URL for the static page consists of your blog URL and the title of the page. If you titled your page About Me, for example, the URL of the page is `http://`*`yourdomain`*`.com/about-me`. (See Book 3, Chapter 2 for more information about permalinks.)

Setting page options

Before you publish a new page to your site, you can change options to use different features in WordPress. These features are similar to the ones available for publishing posts, which you can read about in Book 4, Chapter 1. For a static page, however, you don't find as many options. Those options appear in the settings panel on the right side of the Edit Page screen (refer to Figure 2-4). The page options include

- **Status and Visibility**
  - *Visibility: Public:* This option is covered in Book 4, Chapter 1.
  - *Visibility: Private:* This option is covered in Book 4, Chapter 1.
  - *Visibility: Password Protected:* This option is covered in Book 4, Chapter 1.
- **Publish (date and time):** This option is covered in Book 4, Chapter 1.
- **Pending Review:** This option is covered in Book 4, Chapter 1.
- **Author:** This option is covered in Book 4, Chapter 1.
- **Featured Image:** This option is covered in Book 4, Chapter 1.
- **Discussion:** This option is covered in Book 4, Chapter 1.

  TIP

  Typically, you don't see a lot of static pages that have the Comments feature enabled because pages offer static content that generally doesn't lend itself to a great deal of discussion. There are exceptions, however, such as a Contact page, which might use the Comments feature as a way for readers to get in touch with you through that specific page. The choice is yours to make based on the needs of your website.
- **Page Attributes**
  - *Parent Page:* Select a parent for the page you're publishing. Book 3, Chapter 5 covers the archiving options, including the ability to have a hierarchical structure for pages that create a navigation of main pages and subpages (called parent and child pages).
  - *Order:* By default, this option is set to 0 (zero). You can enter a number, however, if you want this page to appear in a certain spot on the page menu of your site.

If you're using the built-in menu feature in WordPress, you can use this option. A page with the page order of 1 appears first on your navigation menu, a page with the page order of 2 appears second, and so on. Book 6, Chapter 1 covers the Menu feature in greater detail. You don't have to use the Order option, however, because you can define the order of pages and how they appear on your menu by using the WordPress menu builder (Book 6, Chapter 1).

Assigning a static page as the home page

After you create the page that you want to use for the home page of your website, you need to let WordPress know your intentions. Follow these steps to set a static page as the home page:

1. **In the Dashboard, click the Reading link on the Settings menu.**

   The Reading Settings screen displays.

2. **In the Your Home page Displays section, select the option labeled A Static Page.**
3. **From the Home page drop-down list, choose the page you want to use as the home page (see Figure 2-5).**

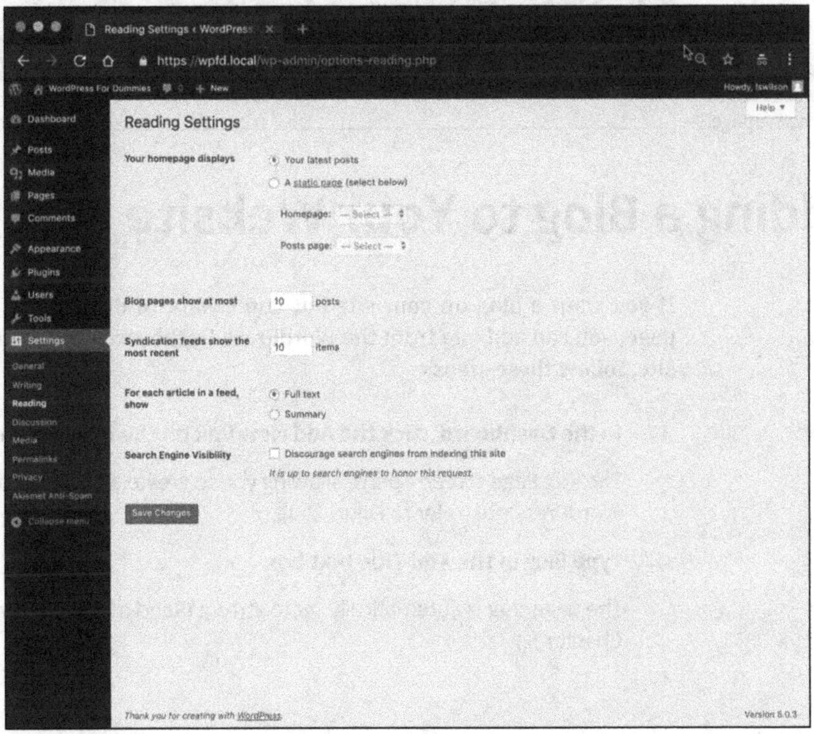

FIGURE 2-5: Choosing which page to display as the home page.

4. **Click the Save Changes button at the bottom of the Reading Settings screen.**

   WordPress displays the page you selected in step 3 as the front page of your site. Figure 2-6 shows my site displaying a static page as the home page.

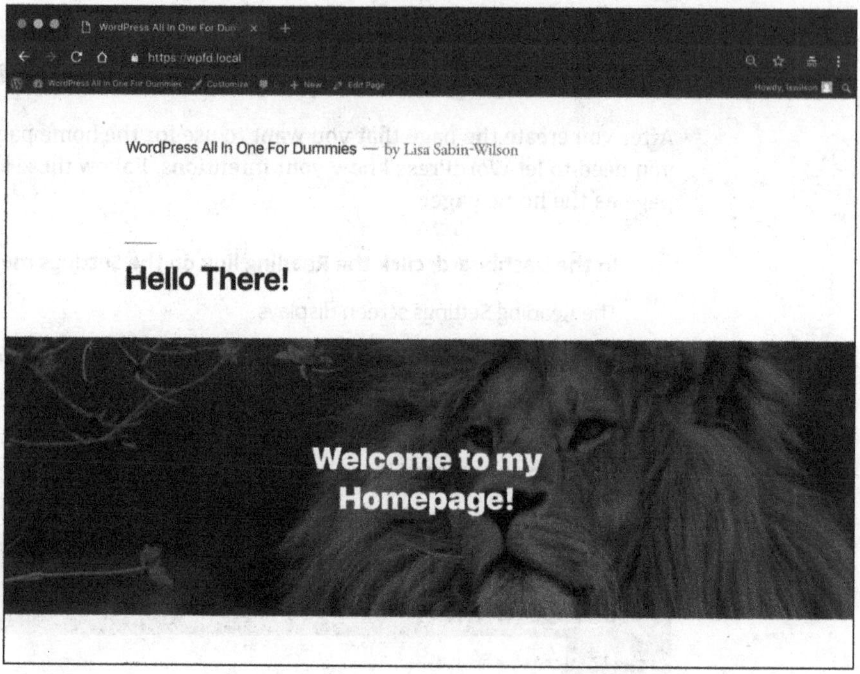

FIGURE 2-6: WordPress displays the page you selected as your home page.

Adding a Blog to Your Website

If you want a blog on your site but don't want to display the blog on the home page, you can add one from the WordPress Dashboard. To create the blog for your site, follow these steps:

1. **In the Dashboard, click the Add New link on the Pages menu.**

   The Edit Page screen opens, allowing you to create a new page for your WordPress site (refer to Figure 2-4).

2. **Type** Blog **in the Add Title text box.**

   The page slug is automatically set to `/blog`. (Read more about slugs in Book 3, Chapter 5.)

3. **Leave the rest of the page blank.**

   Don't add any text content or use any blocks from the Block Editor on this page.

4. **Click the Publish button.**

   WordPress asks you whether you're sure you want to publish this page. Click the Publish button a second time and the Blog page you created is saved to your database and published to your WordPress site. Now you have a blank page that redirects to `http://`*`yourdomain`*`.com/blog`.

   Next, you need to assign the page you created as your blog page.

5. **In the Dashboard, click the Reading link on the Settings menu.**

   The Reading Settings screen displays.

6. **Choose the Blog page from the drop-down menu labeled Posts Page.**

7. **Click the Save Changes button.**

   The options you set are saved, and your blog is at `http://`*`yourdomain.com`*`/blog` (where *`yourdomain.com`* is the actual domain name of your site). When you navigate to `http://`*`yourdomain.com`*`/blog`, your blog appears.

REMEMBER

This method of using the `/blog` page slug works only if you're using custom permalinks with your WordPress installation. (See Book 3, Chapter 2 if you want more information about permalinks.) If you're using the default permalinks, the URL for your blog page is different; it looks something like `http://`*`yourdomain.com`*`/?p=4` (where 4 is the ID of the page you created for your blog).

IN THIS CHAPTER

» Using the built-in image-upload feature

» Inserting a photo into your post

» Add multiple images displayed side by side

» Add a cover photo to your post

» Creating photo galleries in WordPress

Chapter 3

Uploading and Displaying Photos and Galleries

Adding images and photos to your posts can really dress up the content. By using images and photos, you give your content a dimension that you can't express in plain text. Through visual imagery, you can call attention to your post and add depth to it. With WordPress, you can insert single images or photographs, or you can use a few nifty plugins to turn some of the pages in your site into a full-fledged photo gallery.

In this chapter, you discover how to add some special touches to your site posts by adding images and photo galleries, all by using the built-in image-upload feature and image editor in WordPress.

Inserting a Single Image into a Post

Adding an image to a post is easy with the WordPress image uploader. Jump right in and give it a go. From the Dashboard, click the Add New link on the Posts menu, and the Edit Post screen loads in your browser. On the Edit Post screen, you see three icons that are shortcuts allowing you to add one of three commonly used blocks in the WordPress Block Editor (see Book 4, Chapter 1). Click the Image icon to add and open an Image block, shown in Figure 3-1.

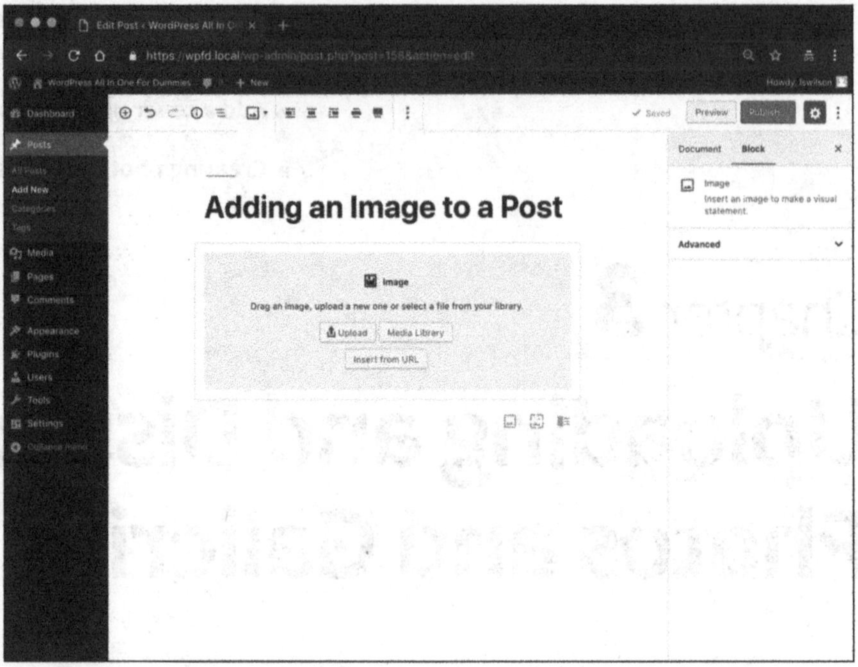

FIGURE 3-1: An Image block in the WordPress block Editor.

The Image block gives you four ways to add an image to your post, all described in detail in the following sections of this chapter.

- **Upload:** Select an image from your computer, and upload it to your site.
- **Media Library:** Select an image from the WordPress Media Library.
- **Insert from URL:** Use an image from a different source by adding an image URL.
- **Drag an Image:** Drag an image from your computer to your WordPress site.

Uploading an image from your computer

After you've added the Image block to your post, you can add an image from your computer's hard drive by following these steps:

1. **Click the Upload button in the Image block.**

   A dialog box opens, allowing you to select an image (or multiple images) from your computer's hard drive. (See Figure 3-2.)

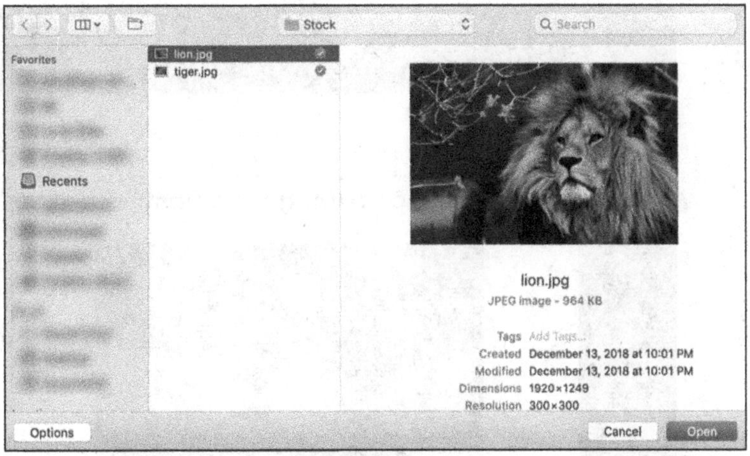

FIGURE 3-2: Uploading an image from your computer.

2. **Select your image(s) from your hard drive and then click the Open button.**

   The image is uploaded from your computer to your website, and the Edit Post screen displays your uploaded image ready for editing, if needed.

3. **Edit the details for the image in the Image Settings section of the settings panel on the right side of the Edit Post screen (see Figure 3-3).**

   The Image Settings section provides several image options, all covered in Book 4, Chapter 1:

   - *Alt Text*
   - *Image Size*
   - *Image Dimensions*
   - *Link To*

   TIP

   WordPress automatically creates small and medium-size versions of the original images you upload through the built-in image uploader. A thumbnail is a smaller version of the original file. You can edit the size of the thumbnail by clicking the Settings link and then clicking the Media menu link. In the Image Sizes section of the Media Settings page, designate the desired height and width of the small and medium thumbnail images generated by WordPress.

4. **Use the Image block toolbar to set the display options for the image.**

   Figure 3-4 shows the toolbar for the Image block. Book 4, Chapter 1 covers how to work with the toolbar options for the Image block at length. If you want to edit the image you've uploaded, continue to the next step in this list for image-editing steps; if you don't need to edit your image, skip to step 12.

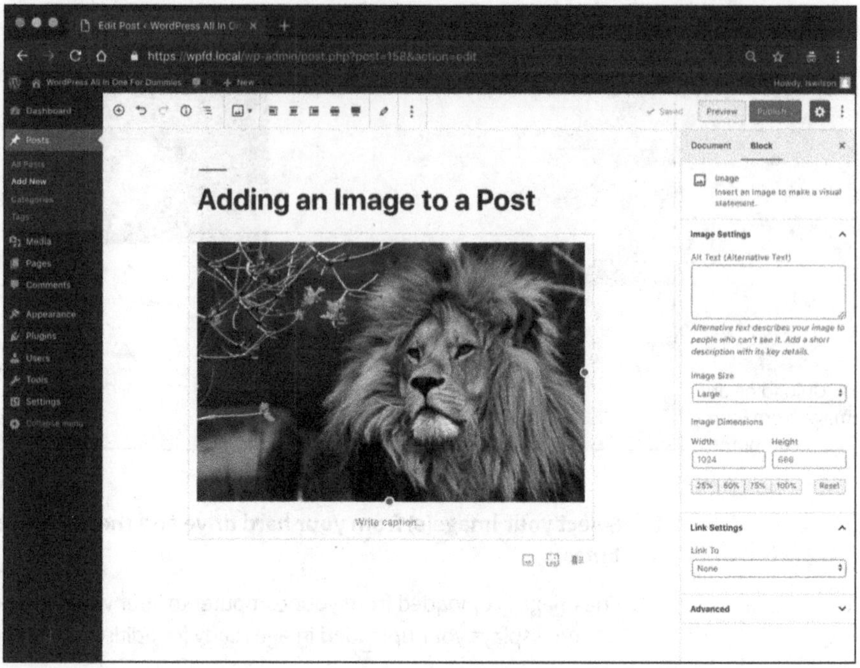

FIGURE 3-3: You can set several options for your image after you add it to your post.

FIGURE 3-4: When you click the Image block, the toolbar appears at the top of the Edit Post screen.

5. **Click the Edit Image icon in the Image block toolbar to edit the appearance of the image or change the image.**

   The Select or Upload Media screen opens with the image selected (see Figure 3-5). You can select a different image to use in this screen or proceed to steps 6–11 to edit the image you've chosen.

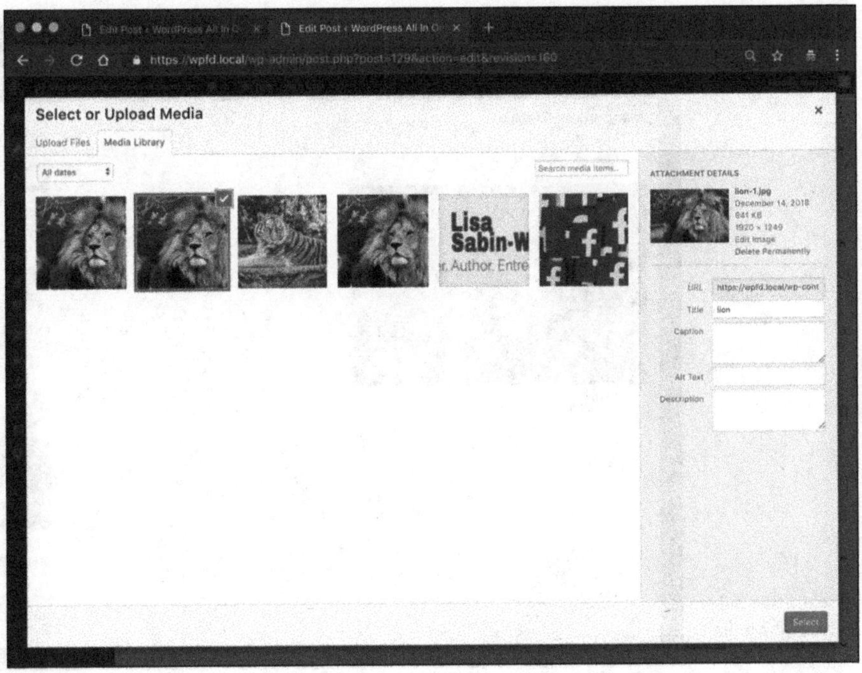

FIGURE 3-5: The Select or Upload Media screen.

6. **Click the Edit Image link in the Attachment Details section of the Select or Upload Media screen.**

   The Edit Media screen opens, as shown in Figure 3-6.

7. **Use the Image Edit toolbar above the image you uploaded (refer to Figure 3-6) to make changes to the image.**

   Click the icons in the menu to edit your image, and be sure to click the Save button underneath the image to save your changes. From left to right, the icons are

   - *Crop:* Cut the image to a smaller size. Click inside the image, drag your mouse to make your crop selection (see Figure 3-7), and then click the Crop icon to apply your selection.
   - *Rotate Counterclockwise:* Rotate the image to the left.
   - *Rotate Clockwise:* Rotate the image to the right.
   - *Flip Vertically:* Flip the image upside down and back again.
   - *Flip Horizontally:* Flip the image from right to left and back again.
   - *Undo:* Undo any changes you've made.
   - *Redo:* Redo image edits that you've undone.

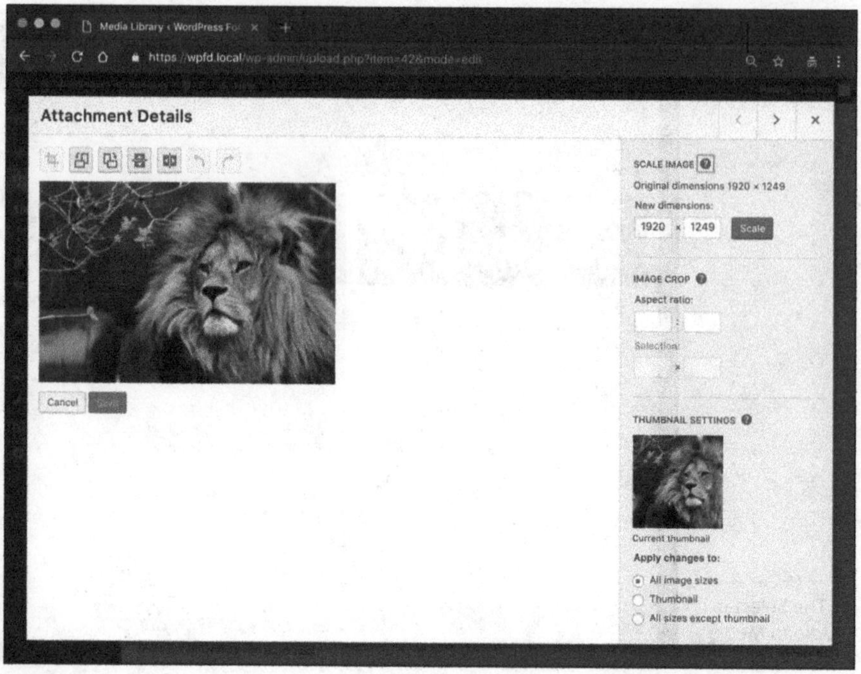

FIGURE 3-6: The Edit Media screen.

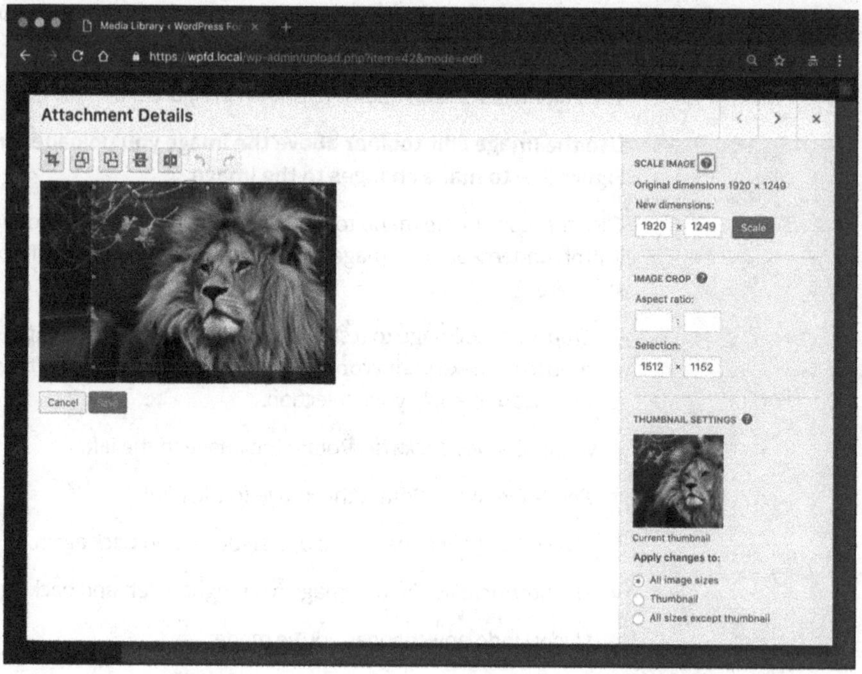

FIGURE 3-7: The Edit Media Screen displaying the crop selection for an image.

8. **Set image dimensions in the Scale Image section on the right side of the Edit Media screen.**

   The Scale Image section displays the actual dimensions of your image. Change the width and height by typing numbers in the corresponding text boxes to define new dimensions for your image; then click the Scale button to save your settings.

9. **Crop your image in the Image Crop section on the right side of the Edit Media screen by defining the Aspect Ratio and Crop Selection.**

   The *aspect ratio* is the relationship between the width and height of the image. Use the two text boxes to specify the aspect ratio, such as 1:1 (square), 4:3, or 16:9. After you've made your crop selection (step 7), you can refine and adjust it by entering the size in pixels. The minimum selection size is the thumbnail size set in the Media settings (choose Dashboard ⇨ Settings ⇨ Media).

10. **Select options to apply the image-edit changes to all image sizes, only the Thumbnail size, or all image sizes except Thumbnail.**

    These options are in the Thumbnail Settings section on the right side of the Edit Media screen.

11. **Click the Update button when you're done editing the image.**

    The Edit Media screen reloads and displays the message `Media file updated`.

12. **Continue adding content to your post, or publish it.**

Inserting an image from the Media Library

The WordPress Media Library (see Book 3, Chapter 2) contains all the images you've ever uploaded to your website, making those images available for use in any post or page you create on your site. After you've added an Image block to your post, you can add an image from the Media Library by following these steps:

1. **Click the Media Library button in the Image block (refer to Figure 3-1).**

   The Select or Upload Media screen opens with the Media Library section displayed (refer to Figure 3-5).

2. **Select the image you want to use by clicking it.**
3. **Click the Select button.**

   The Select or Upload Media screen closes, and the Edit Post screen reappears. WordPress inserts the image you've chosen into the post you're creating.

4. **Set the options for the image.**

   Complete steps 3 and 4 of "Uploading an image from your computer" earlier in this chapter.

5. **Continue adding content to your post, or publish it.**

TIP

You can insert an image into your post by using a URL or by dragging an image from your computer to your WordPress website, as well. These techniques are covered in Book 4, Chapter 1.

Using the Columns block to Insert Multiple Images in a Row

The Layout Elements section of the WordPress Block Editor has a block called Columns. You can use this block to add a row of columns to your post and then insert images into those columns to create a row of multiple images for display in your post. Figure 3-8 displays a post with a grid of images created by using a variety of columns and images. I used the standard Image block for the first image you see; then I used a Columns block to create the two side-by-side images on the page.

FIGURE 3-8: A grid of images in a blog post using the Columns and Image blocks.

To add and configure a Columns block with images in your post, follow these steps:

1. **Add the Columns block in your post on the Edit Post screen.**

   You can find the methods for adding blocks to your post in Book 4, Chapter 1. Figure 3-9 shows the Cover Image block inserted into a post. By default, adding the Columns block to your post adds two columns side by side.

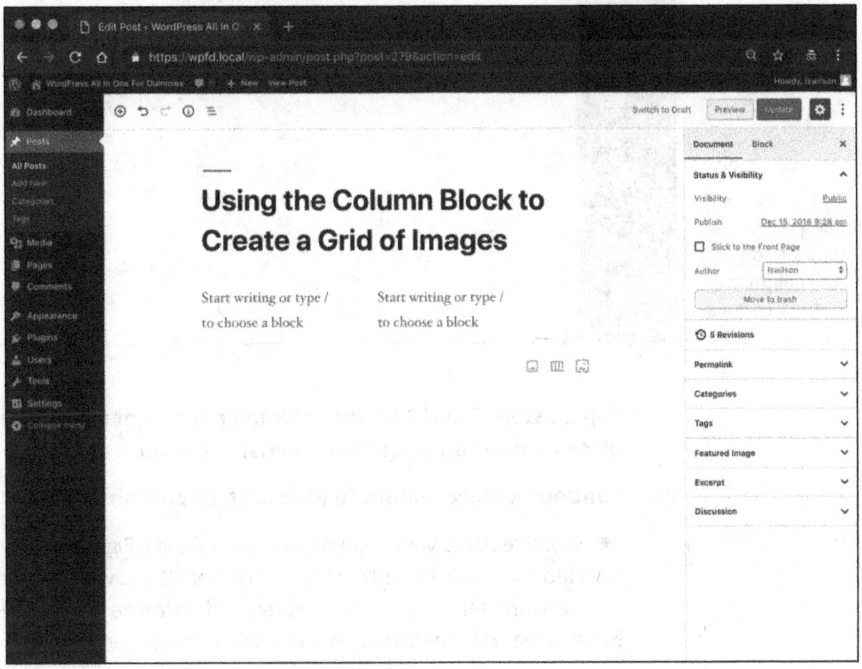

FIGURE 3-9: The Columns block in the WordPress Block Editor.

2. **Click the Add Block icon to add an Image block in the left column.**

   When you hover your mouse in the first (left) column, a small plus icon appears. When you click that icon, the WordPress block-selector window appears, and you can select the Image block, as shown in Figure 3-10.

3. **Add your image to the left column, using the Image block options.**

   Follow the steps in "Inserting a Single Image into a Post" earlier in this chapter.

Uploading and Displaying Photos and Galleries

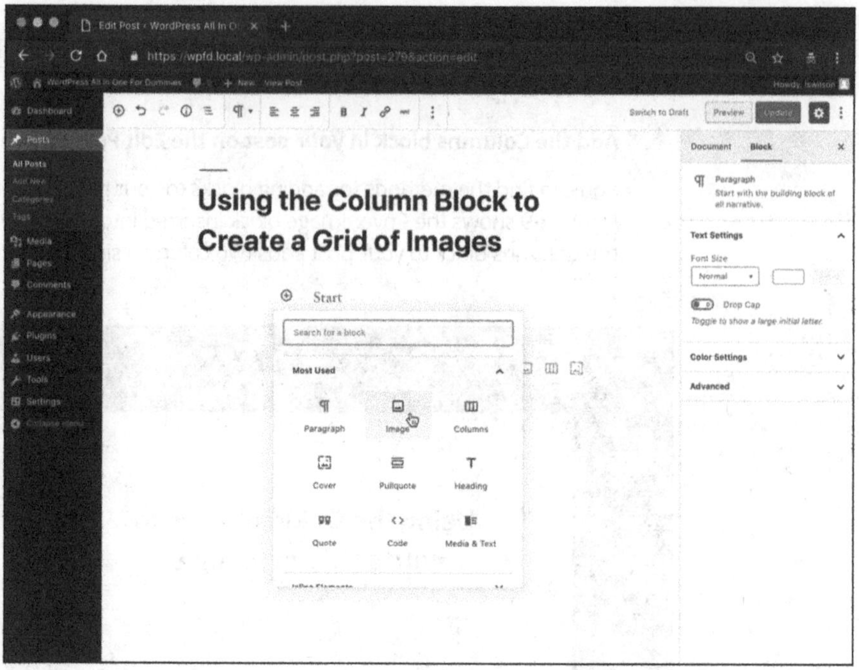

FIGURE 3-10: Adding the Image block to one of the columns in the Columns block.

4. **Repeat steps 2 and 3 for the column on the right side of the Columns block to insert an image into the right column.**

5. **Continue adding content to your post, or publish it.**

   When you're done, your Edit Post screen looks like Figure 3-11, with your two selected images displayed next to each other. (If you want to create a grid like the one in Figure 3-8 earlier in this chapter, add an Image block above the Columns block in the Edit Post screen to add a single image, for a grid of three images.)

TIP

You can add more than two columns by using the Columns block. In the settings panel for the Columns block (on the right side of the Edit Post screen), you can define how many columns you want the Columns block to have. You could can have three or four images displayed in a row, for example. You could get creative, creating grids of images by stacking multiple Columns blocks on top of one another, each with differing numbers of columns. You might have four rows of images in which the first row has two columns, the second row has four columns, the third row has two columns, and the fourth row has one column. That arrangement would create an interesting image grid.

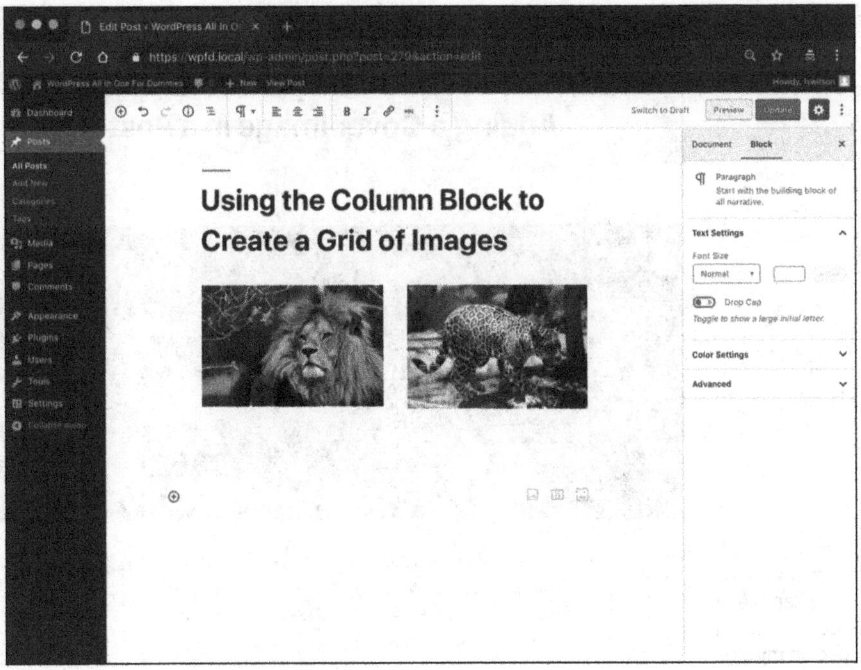

FIGURE 3-11: The Columns block on the Edit Post screen.

Inserting a Cover Image into a Post

The WordPress Block Editor has a Cover block, which you can use in place of a heading to add additional emphasis to a section of your site. The Cover block allows you to display a short line of text on top of an image of your choice. Figure 3-12 displays a post I created on my site about tigers. You can see the cover image displayed below the title of the post (Beautiful Jungle Cat).

Using the Cover block is a nice way to separate different sections of your post content. You can use it in place of a regular heading to add more visual emphasis and appeal to your content, for example.

To add and configure a Cover block in your post, follow these steps:

1. **Add the Cover block in your post on the Edit Post screen.**

   You can find the methods for adding blocks to your post in Book 4, Chapter 1. Figure 3-13 shows the Cover block inserted into a post.

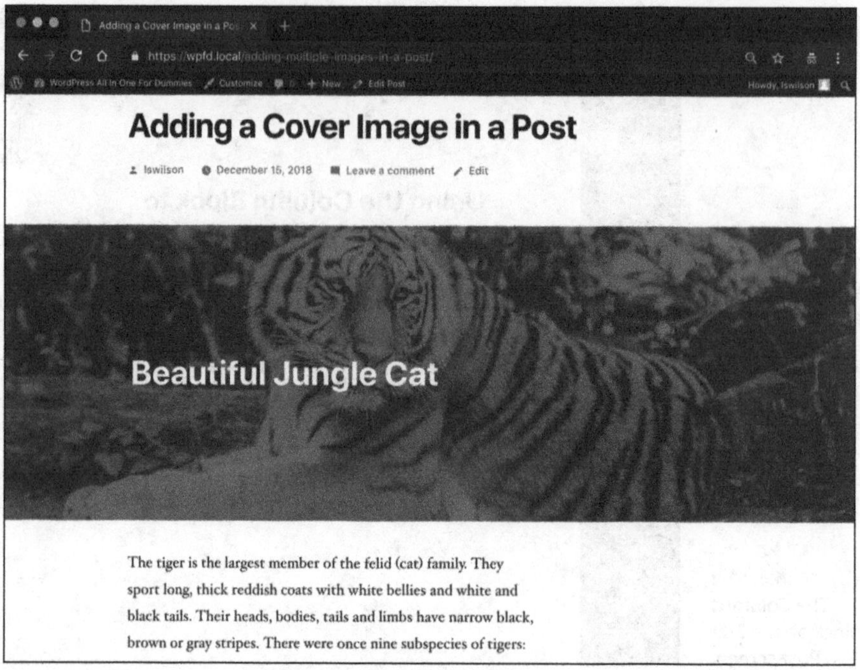

FIGURE 3-12: An example of the Cover block in use on my site.

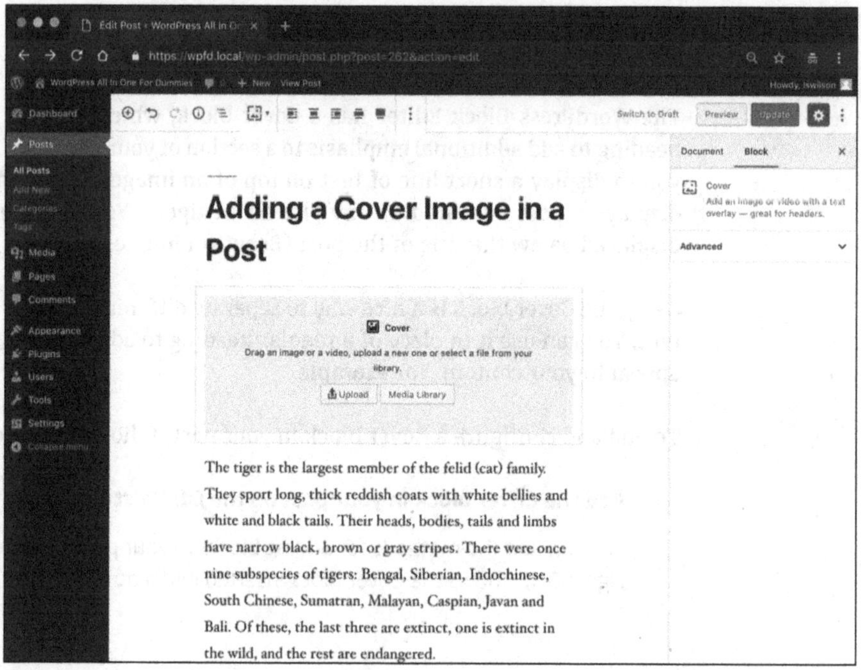

FIGURE 3-13: The Cover block in the WordPress Block Editor.

2. **Click the Upload button to select an image from your computer or the Media Library button to select an image from the Media Library.**

   The steps for these two methods are listed in "Uploading an image from your computer" and "Inserting an image from the Media Library," earlier in this chapter. When you're done, the image appears in your content on the Edit Post screen.

3. **Add your desired text in the Cover block.**

   Click the text `Write title` in the Cover block and type your own text over it. In Figure 3-14, I added text that displays on top of the image I added in the Cover block.

4. **(Optional) Edit the display of the text you added in step 3.**

   Figure 3-14 shows the text added to the Cover block. You also see a small toolbar above the text with four icons you can use to adjust the format of the text added to the image:

   - *Bold:* Click this icon to make the text bold (darker). Example: **bold text.**
   - *Italic:* Click this icon to make the text italic (slanted). Example: *italic text.*
   - *Link:* Click this icon to create a hyperlink by adding a URL to the text.
   - *Strikethrough:* Click this icon to apply a line through the text. Example: ~~strikethrough text~~.

5. **(Optional) Adjust text alignment by using the Cover block toolbar.**

   Click one of these three icons to align the text in the Cover block: Align Text Left, Align Text Center, or Align Text Right. By default, text is center-aligned.

6. **Use the Cover block toolbar to set the display options for the image.**

   Figure 3-15 shows the toolbar for the Cover block. The options include (from left to right)

   - *Change Block Type:* Click this option to change the type of block you're currently using. If you want to change from a Cover block to a Heading block, for example, click the Change Block Type icon and then select the Heading block to swap it. The only block types you can change to from a Cover block are Image and Heading.
   - *Align Left:* This block-formatting option positions the image within the Cover block against the left margin of the page.
   - *Align Center:* This block-formatting option positions the image within the Cover block in the center of the page.

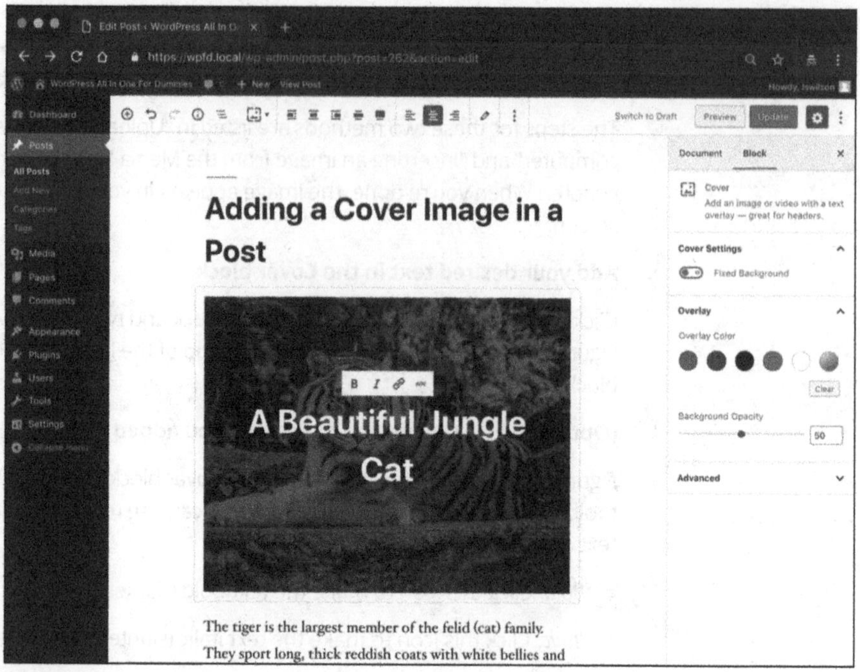

FIGURE 3-14: Adding text in the Cover block.

FIGURE 3-15: The Cover block toolbar.

- *Align Right:* This block-formatting option positions the image within the Cover block against the right margin of the page.
- *Wide Width:* Click this option to set the width of the image to the width of the content on the page.

- *Full Width:* Click this option to increase the width of the image to the width of the screen you're viewing the content on. In Figure 3-7 earlier in this chapter, you see a post I created with a Full Width cover image. Notice that the left and right edges of the image extend all the way to the left and right sides of the viewing screen.
- *Edit Image:* Click this option if you want to edit the image. Follow step 7 of "Uploading an image from your computer" earlier in this chapter.
- *More Options:* The settings here are the same as the ones discussed in Book 4, Chapter 1.

7. **(Optional) Set the Cover block settings to a fixed background.**

   In the settings panel on the right of the Edit Post screen, you see settings for the Cover block. In the Cover Settings section is a toggle setting called Fixed Background. By default, this setting is set to off. Click the toggle button to set the background image to fixed. A fixed background means that the image is locked in place and doesn't move as your visitors scroll down the page of your website. It's a neat effect; give it a try! If you don't like the effect, you set the Fixed Background option to off.

8. **(Optional) Set a color overlay for the image in the Cover block.**

   In the settings panel, you see a section called Overlay, with these options:

   - *Overlay Color:* You can set the color for the background of the image as one of the five predefined colors in the settings panel, or click the custom color picker icon to set a specific image. The color you choose is overlaid on the image.
   - *Background Opacity:* When you've set the overlay color, you can set the opacity of that color as well. *Opacity* refers to the transparency of the color. Suppose that the image you're using is hanging on a wall in your house, and you want to hang a curtain in front of it. If that curtain is solid black, you could say that the curtain has 100 percent opacity (or zero transparency) because you can't see the image on the wall through the curtain.

     The same concept applies to the background opacity on the image in the Cover block. Set the opacity to 0 to achieve full transparency; set it to 50 to achieve half transparency or 100 to no transparency. You can use the slider in the settings panel to set the opacity to any point between 0 and 100. Figure 3-16 shows a Cover block on my website with the overlay color set to light gray and 80 percent opacity.

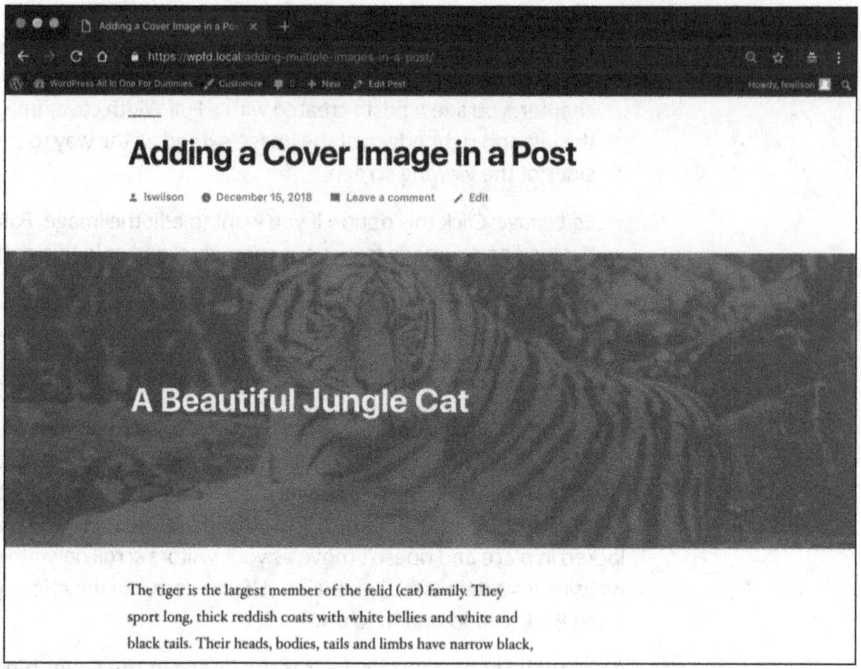

FIGURE 3-16: The Cover block used on a site with an image that has a light gray overlay color set to 80 percent opacity.

Inserting a Photo Gallery

You can also use the WordPress Block Editor to insert a full photo gallery into your posts. Upload all your images; then, instead adding an Image block, use the Gallery block.

Follow these steps to insert a photo gallery into a blog post:

1. **Add the Gallery block to your post on the Edit Post screen.**

   You can find the methods for adding blocks to your post in Book 4, Chapter 1. Figure 3-17 shows the Gallery block inserted into a post.

2. **Click the Upload button to select an image from your computer or the Media Library button to select an image from the Media Library.**

   The Create Gallery screen opens. The steps for these two methods appear in "Uploading an image from your computer" and "Inserting an image from the Media Library" earlier in this chapter. The only difference is that you can select multiple images to include in the Gallery block; when selected, the selected images appear at the bottom of the Create Gallery screen.

3. **Click the Create a New Gallery button.**

   The Edit Gallery screen opens, displaying all the images you selected in step 2.

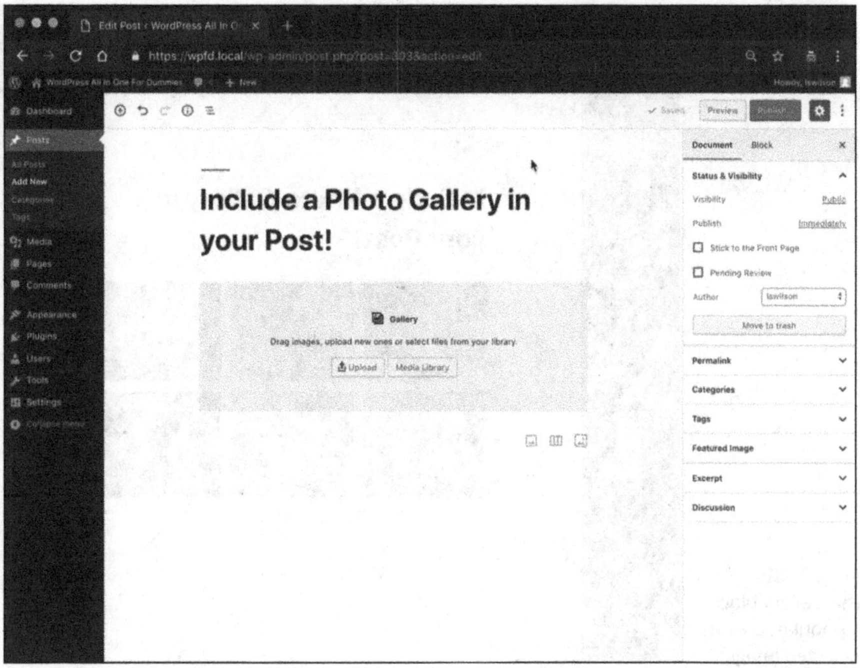

FIGURE 3-17: The Gallery block in the WordPress Block Editor.

4. **(Optional) Add a caption for each image by clicking the Caption This Image area and typing a caption or short description for the image.**

5. **(Optional) Set the order in which the images appear in the gallery by using the drag-and-drop option on the Edit Gallery page.**

   Drag and drop images to change their order.

6. **Click the Insert Gallery button.**

   WordPress inserts the selected images into your post in the Gallery block (see Figure 3-18).

7. **Use the Gallery block toolbar to set the display options for the gallery.**

   Figure 3-19 shows the toolbar for the Gallery block. The options include (from left to right)

   - *Change Block Type:* Click this option to change the type of block you're currently using. If you want to change from a Gallery block to an Image block, for example, click the Change Block Type icon and then select the Image block to swap it. The only block type you can change to from a Gallery block is an Image block.
   - *Align Left:* This block-formatting option positions the image within the Gallery block against the left margin of the page.
   - *Align Center:* This block-formatting option positions the image within the Gallery block in the center of the page.

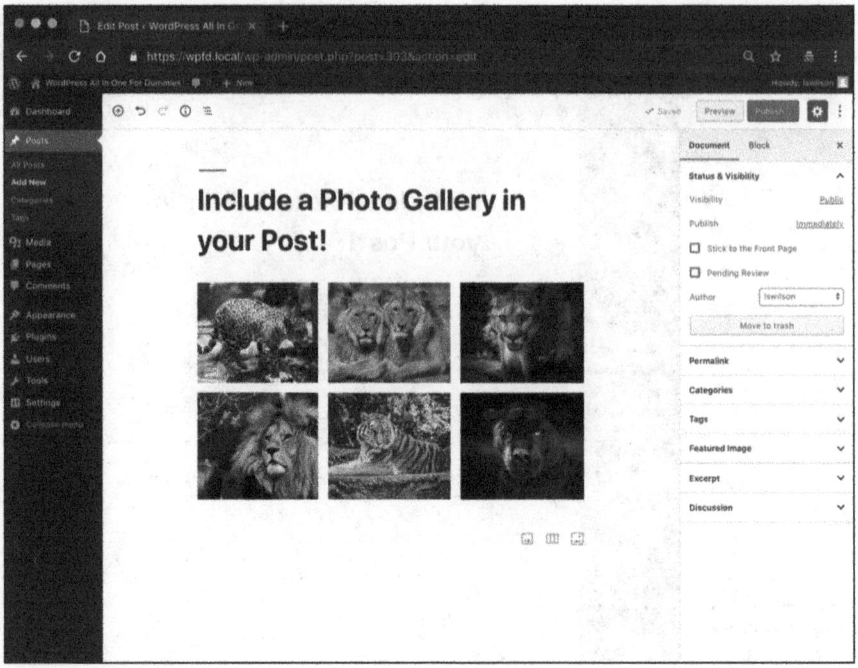

FIGURE 3-18: The Gallery block populated with selected images.

FIGURE 3-19: The Gallery block toolbar.

- *Align Right:* This block-formatting option positions the image within the Gallery block against the right margin of the page.
- *Wide Width:* Click this option to set the width of the image to the width of the content on the page.
- *Full Width:* Click this option to increase the width of the Gallery to the full width of the screen you're viewing the content on. In Figure 3-20, you see a post I created with a full-width gallery. Notice that the left and right edges of the image extend all the way to the left and right sides of the viewing screen.

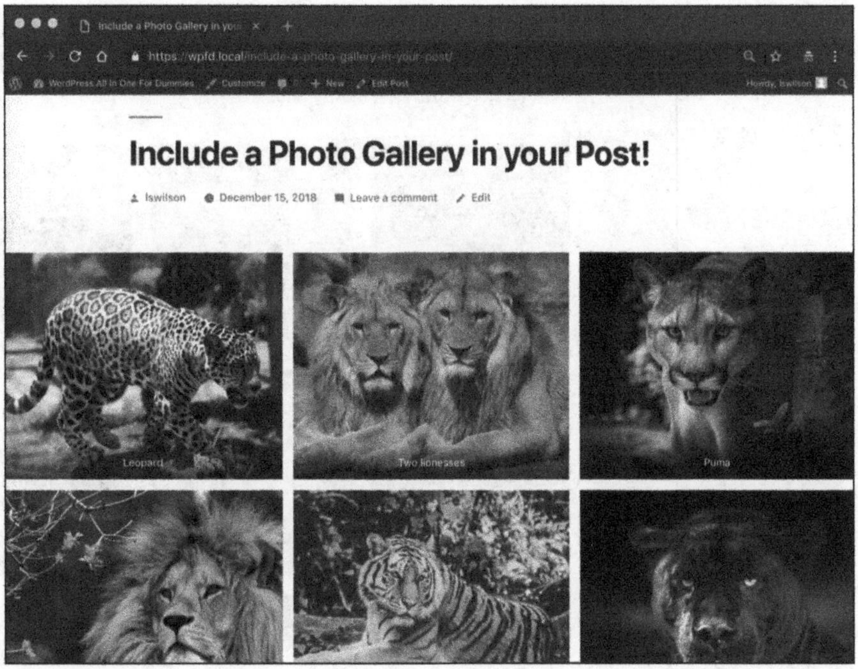

FIGURE 3-20: A photo gallery on my website using the Gallery block.

- *Edit Gallery:* Click this option if you want to edit the gallery to choose different images or arrange the order in which the images in appear.
- *More Options:* These settings are the same ones discussed in Book 4, Chapter 1.

8. **Use the Gallery block options in the setting panel on the right side of the Edit Post page to configure options for your gallery.**
   - *Columns:* Select how many columns of images you want to appear in your gallery.
   - *Crop Images:* By default, this option creates image thumbnails that are cropped to the same size so that they align evenly. You can turn this setting off if you prefer different-size thumbnails in your gallery.
   - *Link To:* Select Attachment Page, Media File, or None to tell WordPress what you'd like the images in the gallery to link to.

Check out the "WordPress image and gallery plugins" sidebar for a few interesting and helpful plugins that can help you create beautiful image galleries and photo albums on your website.

TIP

Matt Mullenweg, co-founder of the WordPress software, created a blog on his site that uses only photos and images in a grid format that creates an interesting photo blog. Check out his photo blog (`https://matt.blog`) in Figure 3-21.

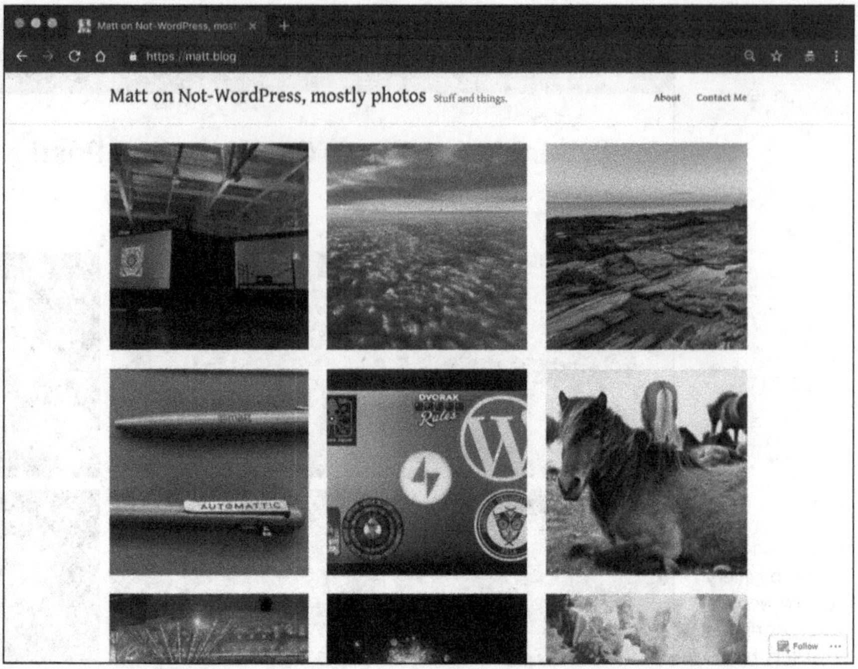

FIGURE 3-21: Matt Mullenweg's photo blog.

WordPress IMAGE AND GALLERY PLUGINS

You can find some great WordPress plugins for handling images and galleries. Check out Book 7 for information on installing and using WordPress plugins.

Here are a few great plugins for images and galleries:

- **NextGen Gallery Plugin** (`https://wordpress.org/plugins/nextgen-gallery`): Gives you a complete WordPress gallery management system with options for batch-uploading photos, importing photo metadata, and sorting photos, group galleries, and photo albums.
- **Smart Slider 3** (`https://wordpress.org/plugins/smart-slider-3`): Gives you options to create beautiful image sliders that are responsive on mobile and search-engine optimized, and a slide library with several premade slides to get you started.
- **FooGallery** (`https://wordpress.org/plugins/foogallery`): Quick and easy-to-use image gallery creator with multiple options for photo galleries and photo albums.

IN THIS CHAPTER

» Uploading and embedding videos in posts

» Adding audio files to posts

» Exploring podcasting and vlogging

» Using the Media Library

Chapter 4

Exploring Podcasting and Video Blogging

Many website owners want to go beyond offering written content for the consumption of their visitors by offering different types of media, including audio and video files. WordPress makes it easy to include these different types of media files in your posts and pages by using the built-in file-upload feature.

The audio files you add to your site can include music or voice in formats such as `.mp3`, `.midi`, or `.wav` (to name a few). Some website owners produce their audio files in regular episodes, called *podcasts,* to create Internet radio shows. Often, you can find these audio files available for syndication on a variety of streaming services, such as iTunes and Spotify.

You can include videos in posts or pages by embedding code offered by popular third-party video providers such as YouTube (`https://www.youtube.com`) and Vimeo (`https://vimeo.com`). Website owners also can produce and upload video shows they've created — an activity known as *vlogging* (video blogging).

This chapter takes you through the steps required to upload and embed audio and video files within your content. It also provides some tools that can help you embed those files without having to use elaborate coding techniques.

WARNING

When dealing with video and audio files on your site, remember to upload and use only media that you own or have permission to use. Copyright violation is a very serious offense, especially on the Internet, and using media that you don't have permission to use can have serious consequences, such as having your website taken down, facing heavy fines, and even going to jail. I'd really hate to see that happen to you. So play it safe, and use only those media files that you have permission to use.

Inserting Video Files into Your Content

Whether you're producing your own videos for publication or embedding other people's videos, placing a video file in a post or page has never been easier with WordPress.

Several video services on the web allow you to add videos to your website by embedding them in your posts and pages. Google's YouTube service (`https://www.youtube.com`) is a good example of a third-party video service that allows you to share its videos.

Adding a link to a video on the web

Adding a video from the web adds a hyperlink to the video. Follow these steps if all you want to do is provide a text link to a page that has the video on it, rather than embed the video in your post or page (covered in "Adding video with the Embed block" later in this chapter).

To add a link to a video from the web, follow these steps:

1. **Add a Paragraph block to your post, and type your content in it.**
2. **Select the text you want to link.**
3. **Click the Link icon on the Paragraph block toolbar.**

   A small text box opens.
4. **Type the URL (Internet address) of the video in the text box.**

   Type the full URL, including the `http://` and `www.` portions of the address. Video providers such as YouTube usually list the direct links for the video files on their sites; you can copy and paste one of those links in the text box, as shown in Figure 4-1
5. **Press Enter.**

   A link to the video is inserted into your post, as shown in Figure 4-2. WordPress doesn't embed the actual video in the post; it inserts only a link to the video. Your site visitors click the link to load another page on which the video plays.

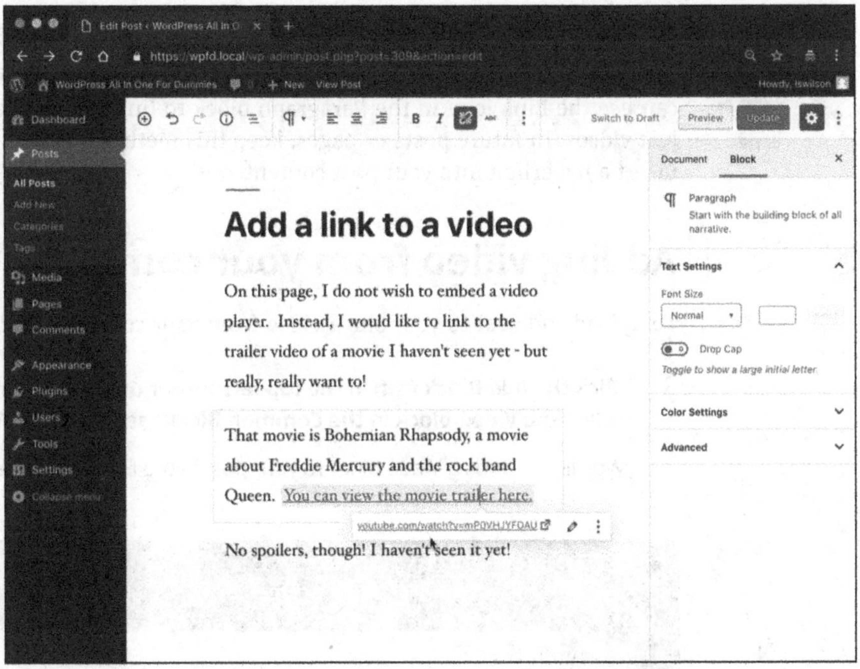

FIGURE 4-1: Add a video by linking to a URL.

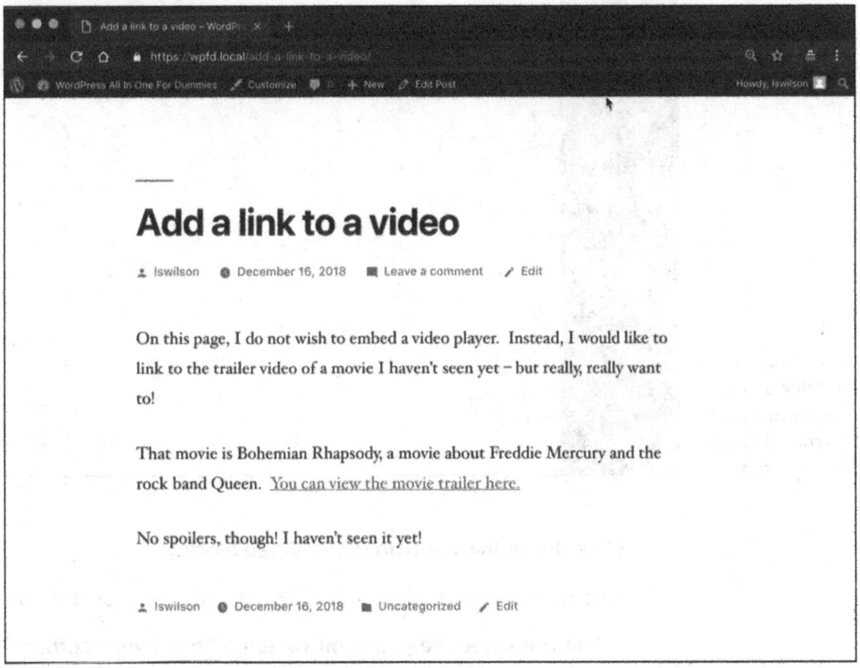

FIGURE 4-2: A link to a video in my blog post.

TIP

I'm using the Link icon in the Paragraph block to illustrate how you can link to a web page or service that contains a video for the purposes of this chapter. But you can use the Link icon in the Paragraph block to link to any URL on the web, not just videos. In future posts or pages, keep this method in mind when you want to insert a hyperlink into your post content.

Adding video from your computer

To upload and post to your site a video from your computer, follow these steps:

1. **Click the Add Block icon in the top-left corner of the Edit Post screen, and select the Video block in the Common Blocks section. (See Figure 4-3.)**

   WordPress adds a Video block to your post in the Edit Post screen.

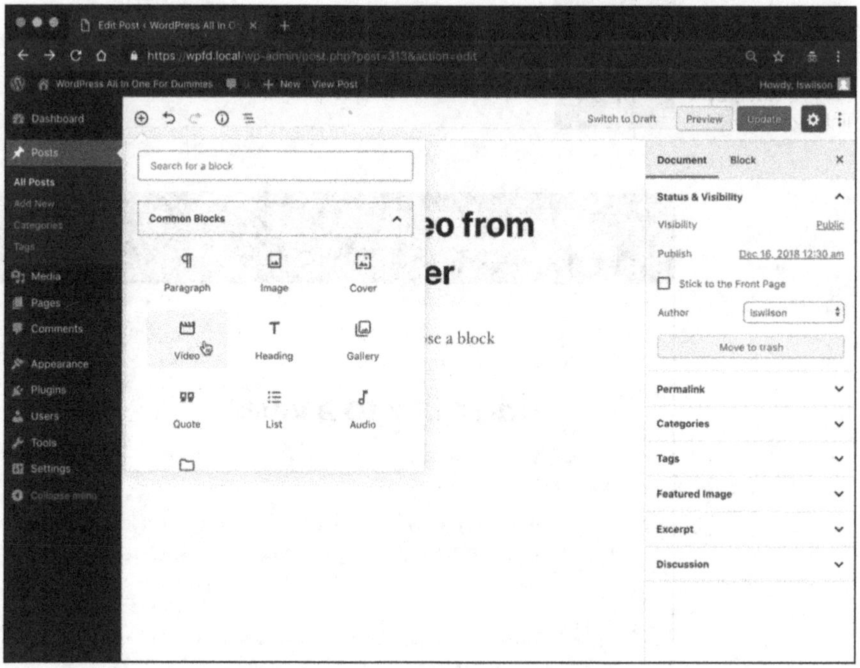

FIGURE 4-3: Adding a Video block to a post on the Edit Post screen.

2. **Click the Upload button in the Video block.**

   A window opens, displaying the files that exist on your computer.

3. **Select the video file you want to upload from your computer and then click Open.**

   The video is uploaded from your computer to your web server and gets inserted into the Video block on the Edit Post screen.

4. **(Optional) Add a caption in the text field below the video player.**

5. **Use the Video block toolbar to set display options for the video.**

   At the top of the block, you see the toolbar for the Video block with the following options:

   - *Change Block Type:* Clicking this option allows you to change the type of block you're currently using. If you want to change from a Video block to a Cover block, for example, click the Change Block Type icon and then select the Cover block to swap it. The block types you can change to from a Video block are Cover, Media & Text, and File.
   - *Align Text Left:* This block-formatting option positions the video within the Video block to the left side of the page.
   - *Align Text Center:* This block-formatting option positions the video within the Video block to the center of the page.
   - *Align Text Right:* This block-formatting option positions the video within the Video block to the right side of the page.
   - *Wide Width:* Click this option to set the width of the video to the width of the content on the page.
   - *Full Width:* Click this option to increase the width of the video to the full width of the screen you're viewing the content on. The left and right edges of the video extend all the way to the left and right sides of the viewing screen.
   - *Edit Video:* Click this option if you want to change the video by uploading a new one or selecting a different video from the Media Library.
   - *More Options:* The settings here are exactly the same as the ones discussed in Book 4, Chapter 1.

6. **In the settings panel on the right side of the Edit Post screen, configure the options for the video you uploaded in step 3:**

   - *Autoplay:* By default, this option is set to off. Turn it on to set the video to start playing automatically when your visitors load this post in their browsers.
   - *Loop:* By default, this option is set to off. Turn it on to set the video to play, on repeat, when your visitors load this post in their browsers.
   - *Muted:* By default, this option is set to off. Turn it on to automatically mute the sound of the video when it plays, requiring your visitors to toggle the sound on when they play your video.
   - *Playback Controls:* This option is set to on by default. Toggle it off to remove playback controls (Play button, Pause button, and so on) from your video. This option seems like an odd thing to enable; after all, why put a video on your page if no one can click the Play button to view it? Well, if you use this

option in conjunction with the Autoplay option, you can set a video to play automatically for your visitors without giving them a way to pause or mute the video. Please don't do this; it's a horrible experience for visitors to your site. Always give visitors the ability to pause, play, and mute the videos you offer on your website. The people of the internet will thank you.

- *Preload:* Preload is an HTML5 attribute that tells the web browser how much of the video data it should fetch and cache (or store) when a web page with a video is visited. Preload can reduce the amount of lag time it could take to load a video, especially if the video file is large. This attribute is used when a video is being served from the same web server as the website it's on, meaning that it's not an attribute used to embed third-party videos from YouTube, for example. The options are Auto (fetches the entire video), Metadata (fetches only the metadata, such as video dimensions and length), and None (fetches none of the video data). The default attribute is Metadata; you can change it by making a different choice from the Preload drop-down menu.
- *Poster Image:* When you embed a video in a post, by default, the first thing your visitor sees is the first frame of that video. Figure 4-4 shows a video of a lion that I uploaded to my post. The video displays the first frame of that video as the first thing my visitors see before they click the Play button. Using the Poster Image option, I uploaded an image of a lion that replaces the first frame and makes for a nicer appearance of the video when the visitor first sees it. Figure 4-5 shows the video on my site after I applied the Poster Image to the video. Click the Select Poster Image button to upload an image, or select an image from the Media Library, to use as the video poster image on your site.

TIP

The default format for web video is `.mp4` or `.webm`. Trying to load a different format like `.mov` or `.avi` is not going to work on your website.

7. **Save and publish your post, or continue to add more content and publish it later.**

TIP

I don't recommend uploading your own videos directly to your WordPress site, if you can help it. Many video service providers, such as YouTube and Vimeo, give you free storage for your videos. Embedding videos in a WordPress page or post from one of those services is easy, and by using those services, you're not using your own storage space or dealing with bandwidth limitations to provide these videos on your site. Additionally, if you have a lot of people visiting your site viewing your video(s) at the same time, loading it from a third-party site like YouTube will make the experience much faster for all of them.

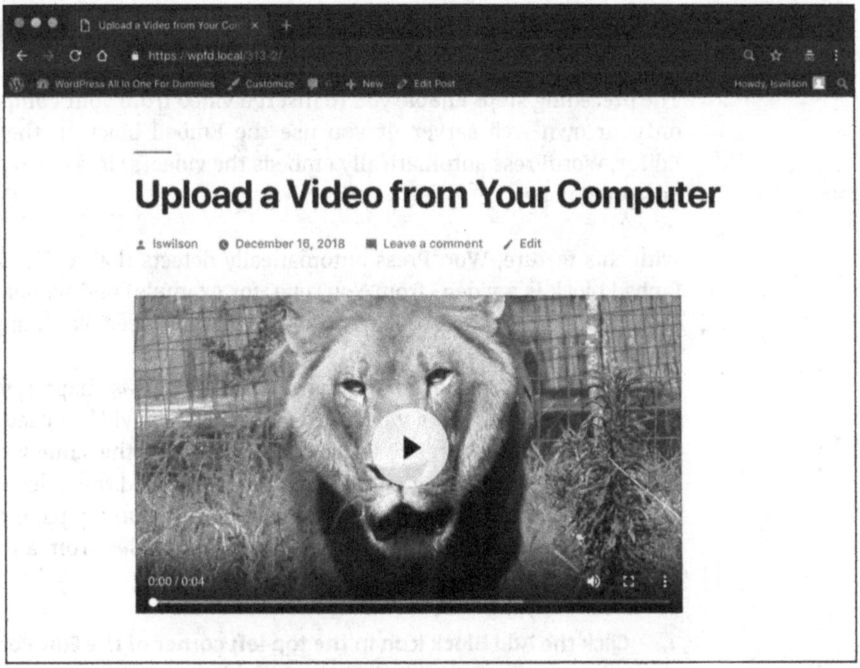

FIGURE 4-4: A video displayed without a poster image defined.

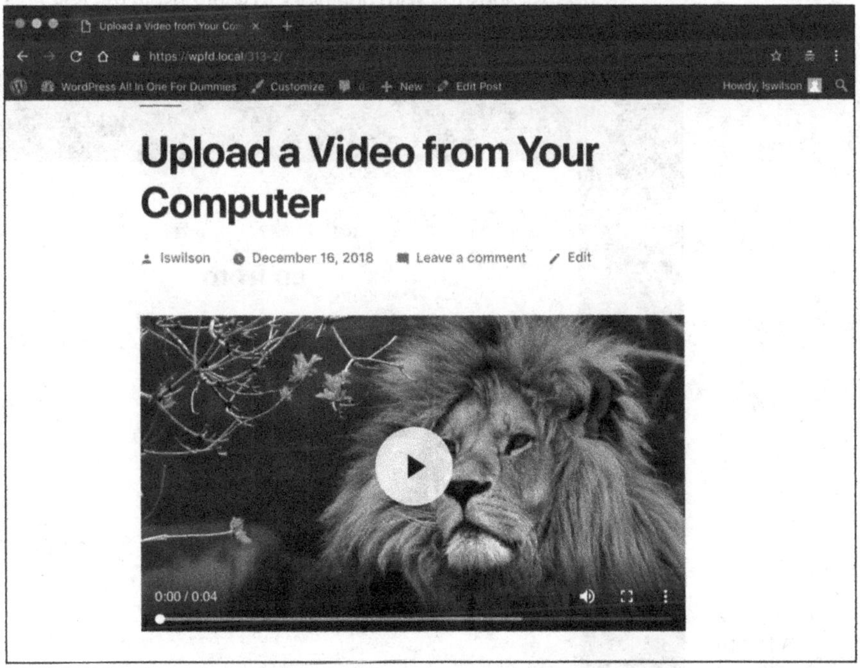

FIGURE 4-5: A video displayed with a poster image defined.

Adding video with the Embed block

The preceding steps enable you to insert a video from your computer that's hosted on your own web server. If you use the Embed block in the WordPress Block Editor, WordPress automatically embeds the video(s) in a video player within your posts and pages.

With this feature, WordPress automatically detects that a URL you include in the Embed block is a video (from YouTube, for example) and wraps the correct HTML embed code around that URL to make sure that the video player appears in your post.

In "Adding a link to a video on the web" earlier in this chapter, you discovered the steps to insert a link to a video into your post. The video I used in my post was a trailer from a movie I really want to see. I'm using the same video as an example here, but instead of using a link, I'm going to embed the video in my post so that readers can click the Play button to view the video on my page rather than on the YouTube website. Follow these steps to embed a video from a third-party service with the Embed block:

1. **Click the Add Block icon in the top-left corner of the Edit Post screen, and select the YouTube block in the Embed section. (See Figure 4-6.)**

   WordPress adds the YouTube block to your post in the Edit Post screen.

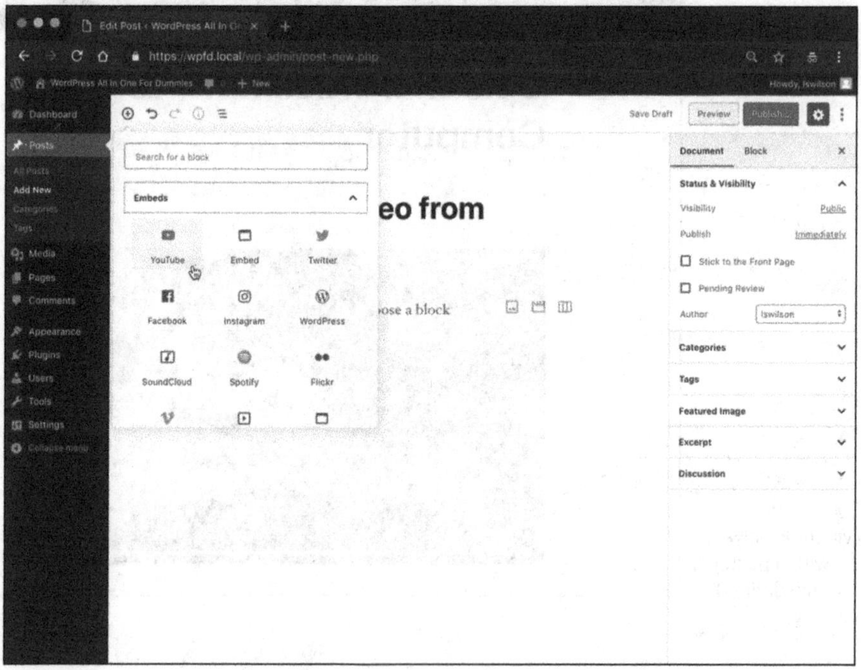

FIGURE 4-6: Adding a YouTube block to your post on the Edit Post screen.

2. **Enter the desired YouTube URL in the text field labeled Enter URL to Embed Here; then press Enter to embed the video (see Figure 4-7).**

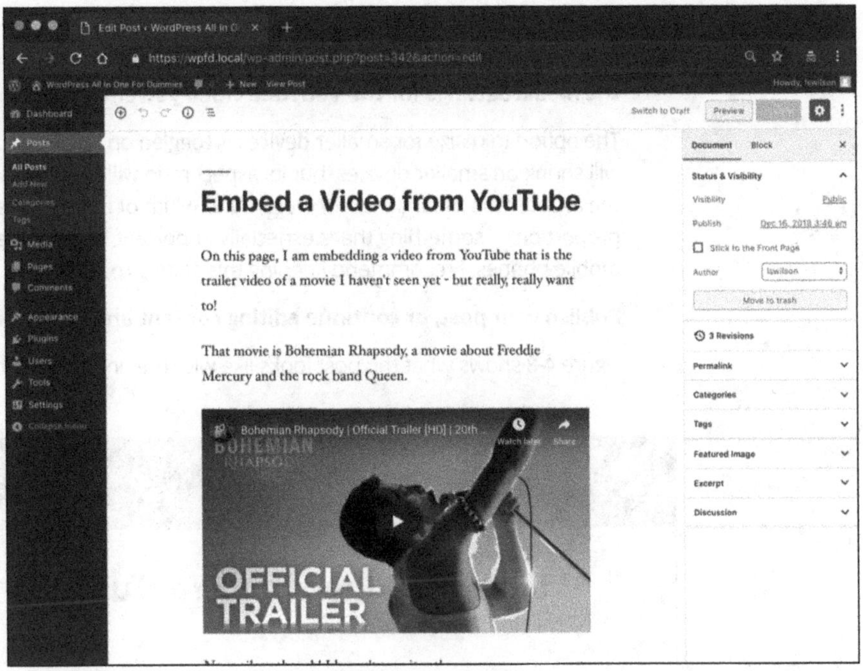

FIGURE 4-7: A YouTube video embedded in a post on the Edit Post screen.

3. **Add a caption in the text field below the video player, if desired.**
4. **Use the YouTube block toolbar to set display options for the video.**

   At the top of the block, you see the toolbar for the YouTube block with the following options:

   - *Align Left:* This block-formatting option positions the video within the YouTube block to the left side of the page.
   - *Align Center:* This block-formatting option positions the video within the YouTube block to the center of the page.
   - *Align Right:* This block-formatting option positions the video within the YouTube block to the right side of the page.
   - *Wide Width:* Click this option to set the width of the video to the width of the content on the page.
   - *Full Width:* Click this option to increase the width of the video to the full width of the screen you're viewing the content on. The left and right edges of the video extend all the way to the left and right sides of the viewing screen.

- *Edit Video:* Click this option if you want to change the YouTube URL you're using.
- *More Options:* The settings here are the same ones discussed in Book 4, Chapter 1.

5. **In the settings panel on the right side of the Edit Post screen, configure the Media Settings for the YouTube video you embedded in step 3.**

   The option to resize for smaller devices is toggled on by default. The video will shrink on smaller devices, but its aspect ratio will be preserved. Preserving the aspect ratio means that the height and width of the video remain in proportion — something that's especially important on small devices like mobile phones. I recommend keeping this setting toggled on.

6. **Publish your post, or continue editing content and publish it later.**

   Figure 4-8 shows what the post looks like with the embedded YouTube video.

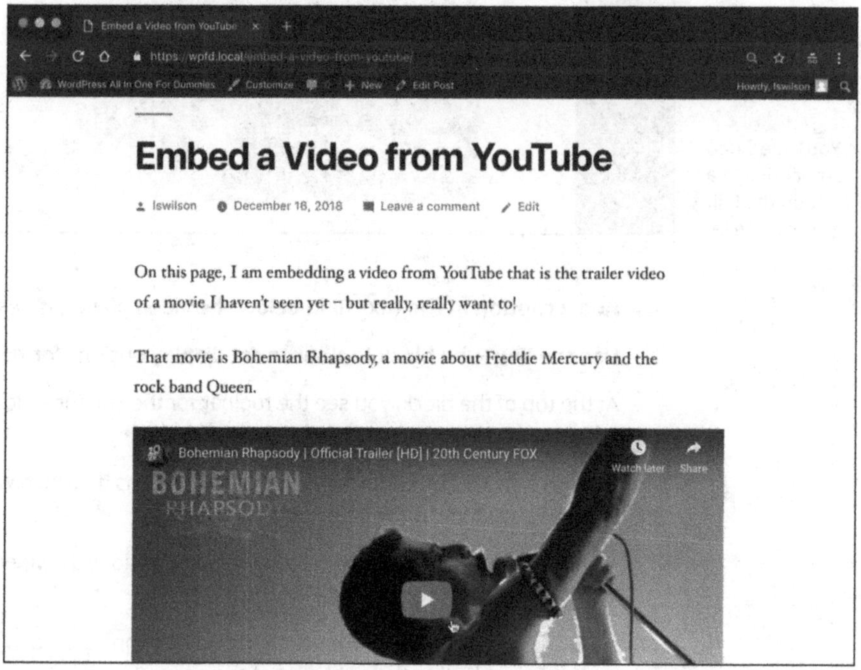

FIGURE 4-8: A YouTube video embedded in a post on my website.

TECHNICAL STUFF

I'm using the Embed block in this example to illustrate how you can embed a video from YouTube. Several Embed blocks are available to embed all kinds of date from different services on the web. Book 4, Chapter 1 covers the Embed block in greater detail.

Inserting Audio Files into Your Blog Posts

Audio files can be music files or voice recordings, such as recordings of you speaking to your readers. These files add a nice personal touch to your site. You can easily share audio files on your blog by using the Audio block in the WordPress Block Editor. After you insert an audio file into a post, your readers can listen to it on their computers or download it to an MP3 player and listen to it while driving to work, if they want.

To insert an audio file into your site, follow these steps:

1. **Click the Add Block icon in the top-left corner of the Edit Post screen, and select the Audio block in the Common Blocks section. (See Figure 4-9.)**

   WordPress adds the Audio block to your post in the Edit Post screen.

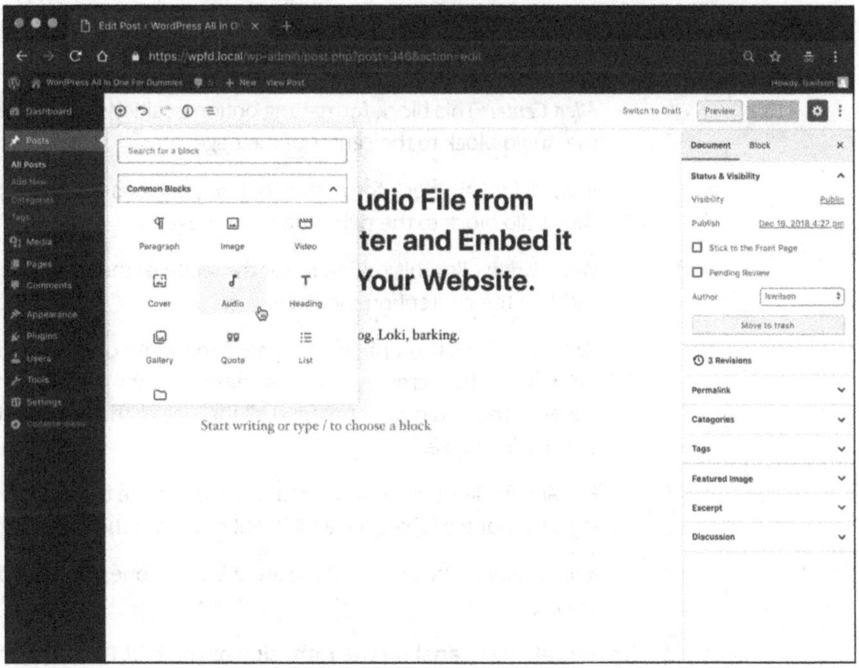

FIGURE 4-9: Adding an Audio block to a post in the Edit Post screen.

2. **Click the Upload button in the Audio block.**

   A window opens, displaying the audio files that exist on your computer.

3. **Select the audio file you want to upload from your computer and then click Open.**

   The audio is uploaded from your computer to your web server and gets inserted into the Audio block on the Edit Post screen. Note that the standard format for audio on the web are `.mp3` or `.wav` audio file types.

4. **Add a caption in the text field below the audio player, if desired.**
5. **Use the Audio block toolbar to set display options for the audio file.**

   At the top of the block, you see the toolbar for the Video block with the following options:

   - *Change Block Type:* Clicking this option allows you to change the type of block you're currently using. If you want to change from an Audio block to a File block, for example, click the Change Block Type icon and then select the File block to swap it. The only block type you can change to from an Audio block is File.
   - *Align Left:* This block-formatting option positions the audio player within the Audio block to the left side of the page.
   - *Align Center:* This block-formatting option positions the audio player within the Audio block to the center of the page.
   - *Align Right:* This block-formatting option positions the audio player within the Audio block to the right side of the page.
   - *Wide Width:* Click this option to set the width of the audio player to the width of the content on the page.
   - *Full Width:* Click this option to increase the width of the audio player to the full width of the screen you're viewing the content on. The left and right edges of the audio player extend all the way to the left and right sides of the viewing screen.
   - *Edit Audio:* Click this option if you want to change the audio file by uploading a new one or selecting a different one from the Media Library.
   - *More Options:* The settings here are the same ones discussed in Book 4, Chapter 1.

6. **In the settings panel on the right side of the Edit Post screen, configure the options for the audio file you uploaded in step 3:**

   - *Autoplay:* By default, this option is set to off. Turn it on to set the audio to start playing automatically when your visitors load this post in their browsers.
   - *Loop:* By default, this option is set to off. Turn it on to set the audio to play, on repeat, when your visitors load this post in their browsers.

- *Preload:* Set this option to Auto (fetches the entire video), Metadata (fetches only the metadata, such as video dimensions and length), or None (fetches none of the video data). The default attribute is to None; you can change it by making a different choice from the Preload drop-down menu. I describe the Preload attribute in detail in "Adding video from your computer" earlier in this chapter.

7. **Save and publish your post, or continue to add more content and publish it later.**

   Figure 4-10 shows a post with an embedded audio player and an uploaded audio file.

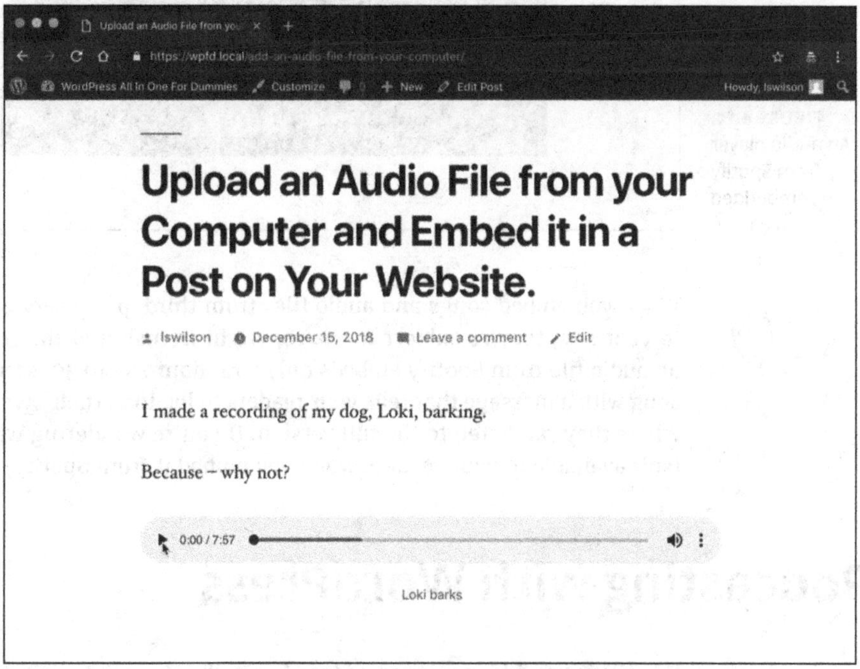

FIGURE 4-10: An audio player embedded in a post.

Inserting Audio with the Embed Block

In this chapter, and in Book 4, Chapter 1, I mention various services that you can embed by using the Embed block in the WordPress Block Editor. Some of those services allow you to embed audio files from sources such as Spotify, Soundcloud, Mixcloud, and ReverbNation, to name a few. To embed audio from any of these sources, follow the steps in the previous section for embedding video. All you need is the direct URL from the service for the audio you want to embed. Figure 4-11 shows a post with an embedded audio file from Spotify.

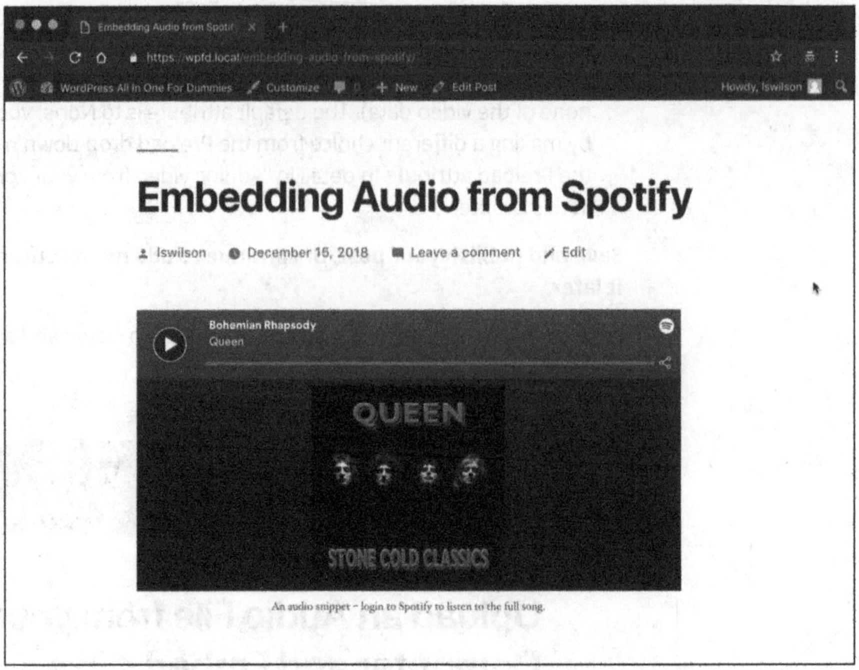

FIGURE 4-11: An audio player from Spotify embedded in a post.

TIP

When you embed songs and audio files from third-party services such as Spotify in your site, they're subject to the copyright licensing of the service. Embedding an audio file from Spotify embeds only a random 25- to 30-second sample of the song with a message that tells your readers to log in to their own Spotify accounts, where they can listen to the full version. If you're wondering why the entire song isn't available to your readers when you embed it from Spotify, now you know!

Podcasting with WordPress

When you provide regular episodes of an audio show that visitors can download to a computer and listen to on an audio player, you're *podcasting*. Think of a podcast as a weekly radio show that you tune in to, except that it's hosted on the Internet rather than on a radio station.

In this chapter, you find a few plugins that allow you to easily insert audio files in your WordPress posts and pages. The plugins that are dedicated to podcasting provide features that go beyond embedding audio files in a website. Some of the most important of these features include

- **Archives:** You can create an archive of your audio podcast files so that your listeners can catch up on your show by listening to past episodes.

- **RSS Feed:** An RSS feed of your podcast show gives visitors the opportunity to subscribe to your syndicated content so that they can be notified when you publish future episodes.
- **Promotion:** A podcast isn't successful without listeners, right? You can upload your podcast to services like Apple Podcasts (`https://www.apple.com/itunes/podcasts`) so that when people search iTunes for podcasts by subject, they find your podcast.

These plugins go beyond audio-file management. They're dedicated to podcasting and all the features you need:

- **Simple Podcasting** (`https://wordpress.org/plugins/simple-podcasting`): Simple Podcasting includes full Apple Podcasts support and allows you to upload audio files by using the usual WordPress methods (Audio blocks. It also includes a specific Podcast block in the new WordPress Block Editor for easy publishing of podcasts on your website.
- **Seriously Simple Podcasting** (`https://wordpress.org/plugins/seriously-simple-podcasting`): This plugin uses the native WordPress interface with minimal settings to make it as easy as possible to podcast with WordPress. You can run multiple podcasts; obtain stats on who's listening; do both audio- and video-casting; and publish to popular services such as iTunes, Google Play, and Stitcher.

TIP

I discuss web hosting requirements in Book 2. If you're a podcaster who intends to store audio files in your web hosting account, you may need to increase the storage and bandwidth for your account so that you don't run out of space or incur higher fees from your web hosting provider. Discuss these issues with your web hosting provider to find out up front what you have to pay for increased disk space and bandwidth needs.

Keeping Media Files Organized

If you've been running your website for any length of time, you can easily forget what files you've uploaded by to your WordPress site over time. The WordPress Media Library allows you to conveniently and easily discover which files are in your Uploads folder.

To find an image, a video, or an audio file you've already uploaded, follow these steps:

1. **Click the Library link on the Media menu in the Dashboard.**

   The Media Library screen opens and displays all the files you've ever uploaded to your site (see Figure 4-12).

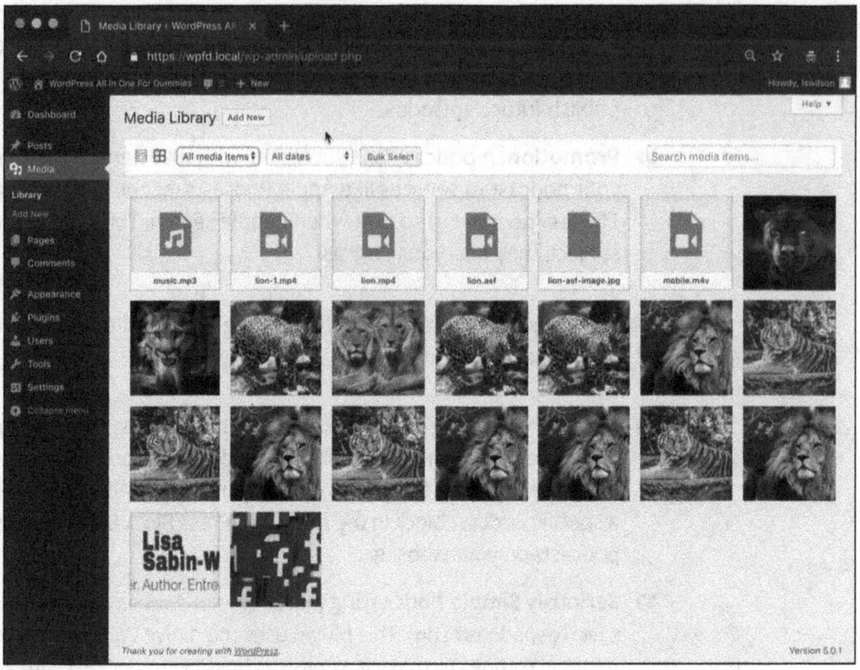

FIGURE 4-12: The Media Library shows all the files you've ever uploaded to your site.

2. Filter your file search by using the drop-down menus at the top of the Media Library screen.

You can filter files on the Media Library screen by using several methods:

- *Filter media files by date.* If you want to view all media files that were uploaded in January 2019, click the drop-down menu labeled All Dates (refer to Figure 4-12) and choose January 2019. All the files you uploaded in January 2019 appear on the Media Library screen, making it easier for you to find a specific file.
- *Filter media files by keyword.* If you want to search your Media Library for all files that reference kittens, type the word *kittens* in the Search box in the top-right corner of the Media Library screen (refer to Figure 4-12). As you type, the Media Library screen displays any files associated with the keyword you entered.
- *Filter media files by type.* If you want to view only audio files that you've uploaded to your site, click the drop-down menu labeled All Media Items (refer to Figure 4-12), and choose Audio. The Media Library screen displays all audio files you've uploaded. The same concept applies if you want to view only videos or images.

IN THIS CHAPTER

» Understanding what Custom Fields can do for you

» Working with the Custom Fields interface

» Adding custom field codes to your templates

» Using custom fields in a variety of ways

Chapter 5
Working with Custom Fields

In Book 4, Chapter 1, I discuss all the elements you can add to your blog posts and pages when you publish them. By default, WordPress allows you to give your posts and pages titles and content, to categorize and tag posts, to select a date and time for publishing, and to control the discussion options on a per-post or per-page basis.

Sometimes, however, you may want to add extra items to your posts — items you may not want to add to every post, necessarily, but that you add often enough to make manually adding them each time you publish a nuisance. These items can include a multitude of things, from telling your readers your current mood to what you're currently listening to or reading — pretty much anything you can think of.

WordPress gives you the ability to create and add *metadata* (additional data that can be added to define you and your post) to your posts by using a feature called Custom Fields. In this chapter, I go through Custom Fields in depth by explaining what they are and how to implement them, as well as offering some cool ideas for using Custom Fields on your site.

Understanding Custom Fields

A WordPress template can contain static pieces of data that you can count on to appear on your site. These static items include elements such as the post title, the content, the date, and so on. But what if you want more? Suppose that you write a weekly book review on your site and want to include a listing of recent reviews and accompanying thumbnails of the books. Through the use of Custom Fields, you can do all that without having to retype the list each time you do a review.

REMEMBER

You can add thousands of autoformatted pieces of data (such as book reviews or movie reviews) by adding Custom Fields to your WordPress site. Okay, thousands of Custom Fields would be pretty difficult, if not impossible, to manage; my point here is that the Custom Fields feature doesn't limit the number of fields you can add to your site.

You create Custom Fields on a per-post or per-page basis, which means that you can create an unlimited amount of them and add them only to certain posts. They help you create extra data for your posts and pages by using the Custom Fields interface, which is covered in the following section.

So what can you do with Custom Fields? Really, the only right answer is this: anything you want. Your imagination is your only limit when it comes to the different types of data you can add to your posts by using Custom Fields. Custom Fields allow you the flexibility of defining certain pieces of data for each post.

To use Custom Fields, you do need a bit of knowledge about how to navigate WordPress theme templates because you have to insert a WordPress function tag, with specific parameters, into the body of the template file. Book 6 takes you through all the information you need to understand WordPress themes, templates, and template tags, so you may want to hit that minibook before you attempt to apply what I discuss in the rest of this chapter. If you're already comfortable and familiar with WordPress templates and tags, you probably won't have any trouble with this chapter at all.

Exploring the Custom Fields Interface

The Custom Fields interface isn't enabled by default on the Edit Post or Edit Page screens in your Dashboard; you have to enable it first by clicking the Show More Tools & Options icon in the top-right corner of the Edit Post screen. Clicking that icon displays a drop-down menu. Click the Options link to open a small window labeled Options (see Figure 5-1). Click the check box to the left of the Custom Fields label and then close the Options window by clicking the small X in the top-right corner.

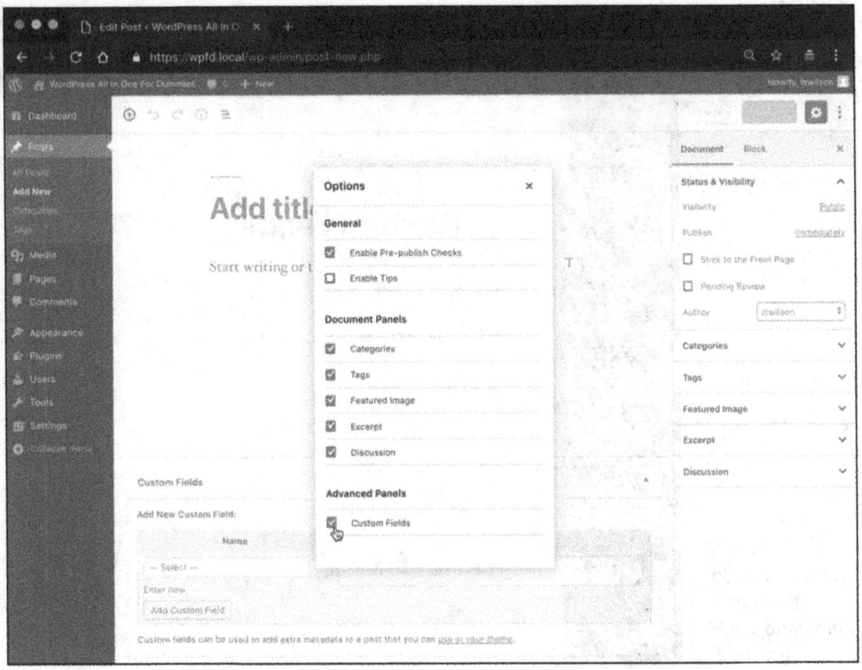

FIGURE 5-1: Add the Custom Fields interface to the Edit Post screen.

With the Custom Fields interface displayed on the Edit Post screen, you see that it contains two text boxes:

- **Name** (also known as the Key): You assign a name to the Custom Field you're planning to use. The name needs to be unique because it's used in the template tag that you can read about in "Adding Custom Fields to Your Template File" later in this chapter. Figure 5-2 shows a Custom Field with the name `mood`.
- **Value:** You assign a value to the Custom Field name and displayed in your blog post on your site if you use the template tag (see "Adding Custom Fields to Your Template File" later in this chapter). In Figure 5-2, the value assigned to the `mood` (the Custom Field name) is `Happy`.

Simply fill out the Name and Value text boxes and then click the Add Custom Field button to add the data to your post or page. Figure 5-2 shows a Custom Field that I added to my post with the Name of `mood` and with the assigned value `Happy`. In "Adding Custom Fields to Your Template File" later in this chapter, I show you the template tag you need to add to your WordPress theme template to display this Custom Field, which appears in my post like this: `My Current Mood is: Happy`. In Figure 5-3, the Custom Field appears at the beginning of my post.

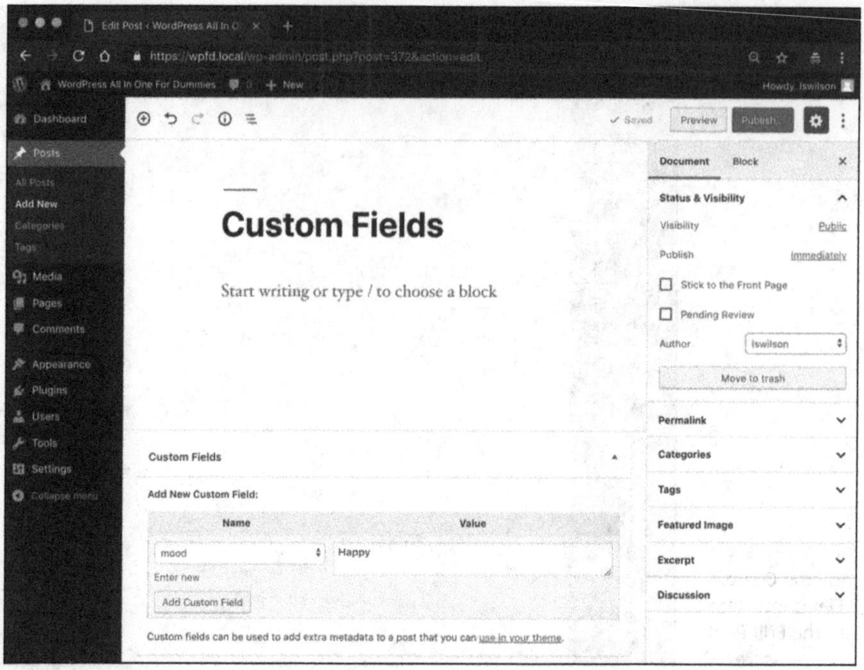

FIGURE 5-2: A Custom Field that has a name and value assigned.

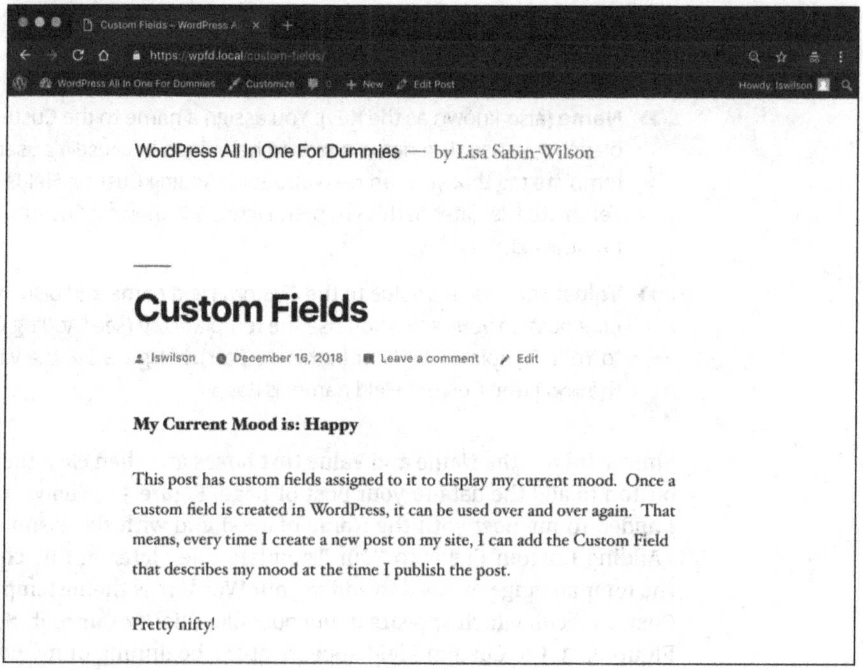

FIGURE 5-3: Custom Field output in a published post.

You can add multiple Custom Fields to one post. To do so, simply add the name and the value of the Custom Field in the appropriate text boxes on the Edit Post screen; then click the Add Custom Field button to assign the data to your post. Do this for each Custom Field you want to add to your post.

TIP

After you add a particular Custom Field (such as the `mood` Custom Field in Figure 5-2), you can always add it to future posts, so you can make a post tomorrow and use the `mood` Custom Field to assign a different value to it. If tomorrow you assign the value `Sad`, your post displays `My Current Mood is: Sad`. You can easily use just that one Custom Field on subsequent posts and have each post display a different value.

You can access your Custom Fields from the drop-down menu below the Name field. You can easily select a Custom Field again and assign a new value to it for future posts because WordPress saves that Custom Field Key, assuming that you may want to use it again sometime in the future.

TECHNICAL STUFF

Custom Fields are considered to be extra data, separate from the post content itself, for your posts. WordPress refers to Custom Fields as *metadata*. The Custom Field name and value get stored in the database in the `wp_postmeta` table, which keeps track of which names and values are assigned to each post. See Book 2, Chapter 4 for more information about the WordPress database structure and organization of data.

REMEMBER

You can find a Custom Fields module on the Edit Post screen of the Dashboard as well, so you can add Custom Fields to your posts or pages as needed.

Adding Custom Fields to Your Template File

If you followed along in the preceding sections and added the `mood` Custom Field to your site, notice that the data didn't appear on your site the way it did on mine. To get the data to display properly, you must open the template files and dig into the code a little bit. If the idea of digging into the code of your template files intimidates you, you can put this section aside and read up on WordPress themes, template files, and template tags in Book 6.

You can add Custom Fields to your templates in several ways to display the output of the fields you've set. The easiest way involves using the `get_post_meta();` template tag function, which looks like this:

```
<?php

$key="NAME";

echo get_post_meta( $post->ID, $key, true );

?>
```

Here's how that function breaks down:

- `<?php`: Starts the PHP function. Every template tag or function needs to start PHP with `<?php`. You can read more about basic PHP in Book 2, Chapter 3.
- `$key="NAME";`: Defines the name of the key that you want to appear. You define the name when you add the Custom Field to your post.
- `echo get_post_meta`: Grabs the Custom Field value from the database and displays it on your site.
- `$post->ID,`: A parameter of the `get_post_meta` function that dynamically defines the specific ID of the post being displayed so that WordPress knows which metadata to display.
- `$key,`: A parameter of the `get_post_meta` function that gets the value of the Custom Field based on the name, as defined in the `$key="NAME";` setting earlier in the code string.
- `true);`: A parameter of the `get_post_meta` function that tells WordPress to return a single result rather than multiple results. (By default, this parameter is set to `true`; typically, you don't change it unless you're using multiple definitions in the Value setting of your Custom Field.)
- `?>`: Ends the PHP function.

Based on the preceding code, to make the `mood` Custom Field example, you define the `key` name as `mood` (replace the *NAME* in the preceding code with the word `mood`). It looks like this:

```
<?php

$key="mood";

echo get_post_meta( $post->ID, $key, true );

?>
```

The part of the function that says `$key="mood";` tells WordPress to return the value for the Custom Field with the Name field of `mood`.

Entering the code in the template file

So that you can see how to enter the code in your template file, I use the default WordPress theme called Twenty Nineteen in this section. If you're using a different theme (thousands of WordPress themes are available), you need to adapt these instructions to your particular theme.

For the purposes of this chapter, I'm using the Twenty Nineteen theme, which is the default theme and is included in every new installation of WordPress. You should have installed WordPress by now, so chances are good that you already have the Twenty Nineteen theme.

WARNING

Normally, when I practice coding on a website, I use a code repository with version control so that I can keep automatic backups of my template files; this practice allows me to easily and quickly reverse any changes I've made in the files if I've made a mistake or want to undo something I've done. The use of a code repository with version control is a topic for a whole other book. (You could try *Professional Git* by Brent Laster from Wrox Publishing.) For the purposes of the coding exercises in the book, you'll be downloading, editing and re-uploading the files via Secure FTP (SFTP), so I strongly recommend that you keep a copy of the files on your computer in a different folder, safe from any alterations. That way, you can restore the original files to your web server if needed.

Follow these steps to add the template tag to your theme, along with a little HTML code to make it look nice. (These steps assume that you've already added the `mood` Custom Field to your blog post and assigned a value to it.)

1. **Log in to your web server via SFTP.**

   For details on connecting to your website via SFTP, refer to Book 2, Chapter 2.

2. **Navigate to the Twenty Nineteen theme folder.**

   On your web server, that folder is `/wp-content/themes/twentynineteen/`.

3. **Locate the `content-single.php` file.**

   This file is located on your web server at `wp-content/themes/twentynineteen/template-parts/content/`.

4. **Download the `content-single.php` file, and open it in a text editor.**

   You may use any text editor you prefer, such as Notepad (PC) or TextEdit (Mac).

5. **Scroll down to locate the HTML tag that looks like this: `<div class="entry-content">`.**

   This HTML tag appears on line 21 of the `content-single.php` file.

6. **On the new line directly below the line in step 5, type this:**

   ```
   <p>My Current Mood is:
   ```

   `<p>` open the HTML tag for a paragraph, followed by the words to display in your template (`My Current Mood is:`). When you're done typing, press Enter to start a new line.

7. **On the newly created line, type the PHP that makes the Custom Field work:**

   ```
   <php
     $key="mood";
     echo get_post_meta( $post->ID, $key, true );
   ?>
   ```

8. **Press Enter to create a new line, and type the `</p>` HTML tag.**

   This code closes the HTML paragraph tag you opened in step 6. Figure 5-4 displays the template in an editor with the new code highlighted.

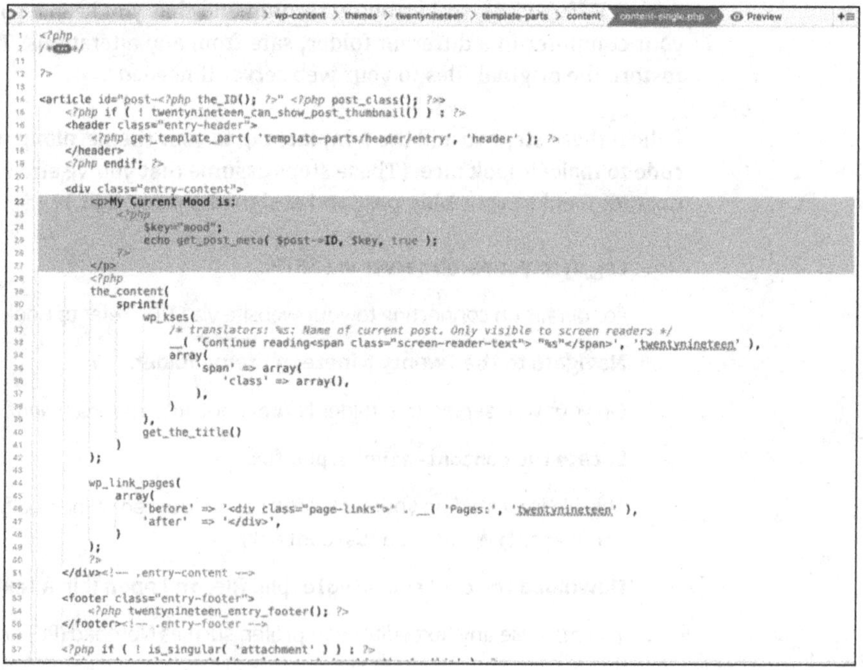

```
> wp-content > themes > twentynineteen > template-parts > content   content-single.php   Preview
1  <?php
2  /*...*/
11
12 ?>
13
14 <article id="post-<?php the_ID(); ?>" <?php post_class(); ?>>
15     <?php if ( ! twentynineteen_can_show_post_thumbnail() ) : ?>
16     <header class="entry-header">
17         <?php get_template_part( 'template-parts/header/entry', 'header' ); ?>
18     </header>
19     <?php endif; ?>
20
21     <div class="entry-content">
22         <p>My Current Mood is:
23             <?php
24                 $key="mood";
25                 echo get_post_meta( $post->ID, $key, true );
26             ?>
27         </p>
28         <?php
29         the_content(
30             sprintf(
31                 wp_kses(
32                     /* translators: %s: Name of current post. Only visible to screen readers */
33                     __( 'Continue reading<span class="screen-reader-text"> "%s"</span>', 'twentynineteen' ),
34                     array(
35                         'span' => array(
36                             'class' => array(),
37                         ),
38                     )
39                 ),
40                 get_the_title()
41             )
42         );
43
44         wp_link_pages(
45             array(
46                 'before' => '<div class="page-links">' . __( 'Pages:', 'twentynineteen' ),
47                 'after'  => '</div>',
48             )
49         );
50         ?>
51     </div><!-- .entry-content -->
52
53     <footer class="entry-footer">
54         <?php twentynineteen_entry_footer(); ?>
55     </footer><!-- .entry-footer -->
56
57     <?php if ( ! is_singular( 'attachment' ) ) : ?>
```

FIGURE 5-4: The content-single.php file with the new Custom Fields code in a code editor.

9. **Save the `content-single.php` file in your editor, and upload it to your web server.**

   Be sure that you upload the `content-single.php` file, with the new changes, to the same location where you downloaded it from your web server: `/wp-content/themes/twentynineteen/template-parts/content/`.

10. **Refresh your post on your site to see your Custom Field data displayed.**

    The data should look like the `My Current Mood is: Happy` message shown in Figure 5-3 earlier in this chapter.

WordPress now displays your current mood at the beginning of the posts to which you've added the `mood` Custom Field.

The entire code, put together, should look like this in your template:

```
<p>
  My Current Mood is:
  <?php
    $key="mood";
    echo get_post_meta( $post->ID, $key, true );
  ?>
</p>
```

WARNING

The code is case-sensitive, which means that the words you enter for the key in your Custom Field need to match the case of the `$key` in the code. If you enter `mood` in the Key field, for example, the code needs to be lowercase as well: `$key="mood"`. If you attempt to change the case to `$key="Mood"`, the code won't work.

You have to add this code for the `mood` Custom Field only one time. After you add the template function code to your template for the `mood` Custom Field, you can define your current mood in every post you publish to your site by using the Custom Fields interface.

REMEMBER

This example is just one type of Custom Field that you can add to your posts.

Getting WordPress to check for your Custom Field

The previous sections show you how to add the necessary code to your template file to display your Custom Field. But what if you want to publish a post in which you *don't* want the `mood` Custom Field to appear? If you leave your template file as you set it up by following the steps in the preceding sections, even if you don't add the mood Custom Field, your post will still display My Current Mood is: without a mood because you didn't define one.

You can easily make WordPress check first to see whether the Custom Field is added. If it finds the Custom Field, WordPress displays your mood; if it doesn't find the Custom Field, WordPress doesn't display the Custom Field.

If you followed along in the preceding sections, the code in your template currently looks like this:

```
<p>
  My Current Mood is:
  <?php
    $key="mood";
    echo get_post_meta( $post->ID, $key, true );
  ?>
</p>
```

To make WordPress check whether the mood Custom Field exists, add this code to the line above your existing code:

```
<?php if ( get_post_meta( $post->ID, 'mood', true ) ) : {
```

Then add this line of code to the line below your existing code:

```
 }
 endif;
?>
```

Put together, the lines of code in your template look like this:

```
<?php
 if ( get_post_meta( $post->ID, 'mood', true ) ) :
  echo '<p>My Current Mood is: ';
  $key="mood";
  echo get_post_meta( $post->ID, $key, true );
  echo '</p>
';
 endif;
?>
```

IF, ELSE

In your daily life, you probably deal with IF, ELSE situations every day, as in these examples:

- **IF** I have a dollar, I'll buy coffee, or **ELSE** I won't.
- **IF** it's warm outside, I'll take a walk, or **ELSE** I won't.
- **IF** I understand this code, I'll be happy, or **ELSE** I won't.

The first line is an IF statement that asks, "Does the mood key exist for this post?" If it does, the value gets displayed. If it doesn't, WordPress skips the code, ignoring it so that nothing gets displayed for the mood Custom Field. The final line of code simply puts an end to the IF question. See the nearby "IF, ELSE" sidebar to find out about some everyday situations that explain the IF question. Apply this statement to the code you just added to your template, and you get this: IF the mood Custom Field exists, WordPress will display it, or ELSE it won't.

REMEMBER

You can find extensive information on working with WordPress template files within your theme in Book 6.

Exploring Different Uses for Custom Fields

In this chapter, I use the example of adding your current mood to your site posts by using Custom Fields. But you can use Custom Fields to define all sorts of data on your posts and pages; you're limited only by your imagination when it comes to what kind of data you want to include.

Obviously, I can't cover every possible use for Custom Fields, but I can give you some ideas that you may want to try on your own site. At the very least, you can implement some of these ideas to get yourself into the flow of using Custom Fields, and they may spark your imagination on what types of data you want to include on your site:

» **Music:** Display the music you're currently listening to. Use the same method I describe in this chapter for your current mood, except create a Custom Field named music. Use the same code template, but define the key as `$key="music";` and alter the wording from *My Current Mood is* to *I am Currently Listening to.*

- **Books:** Display what you're currently reading by creating a Custom Field named book, defining the key in the code as $key="book";, and then altering the wording from *My Current Mood is* to *I Am Currently Reading.*
- **Weather:** Let your readers know what the weather is like in your little corner of the world by adding your current weather conditions to your published blog posts. Create a Custom Field named `weather`, and use the same code for the template. Just define the key as `$key="weather";` and alter the wording from *My Current Mood is* to *Current Weather Conditions.*

IN THIS CHAPTER

» Defining a content management system

» Creating a template for each static page, post category, and sidebar

» Working with custom styles for sticky posts, categories, and tags

» Using Custom Post Types

» Optimizing for search engine success

Chapter 6
Using WordPress as a Content Management System

If you've avoided using WordPress as a solution for building your own website because you think that it's only a blogging platform and you don't want to have a blog (not every website owner does, after all), it's time to rethink your position. WordPress is a powerful content management system that's flexible and extensible enough to run an entire website — with no blog at all, if you prefer.

A *content management system* (CMS) is a system used to create and maintain your entire site. It includes tools for publishing and editing, as well as for searching and retrieving information and content. A CMS lets you maintain your website with little or no knowledge of HTML. You can create, modify, retrieve, and update your content without ever having to touch the code required to perform those tasks.

This chapter shows you a few ways that you can use the WordPress platform to power your entire website, with or without a blog. It covers different template configurations that you can use to create separate sections of your site. This chapter also dips into a feature in WordPress called Custom Post Types, which lets you control how content is displayed on your website.

TIP

This chapter touches on working with WordPress templates and themes, a concept that's covered in depth in Book 6. If you find templates and themes intimidating, check out Book 6 first.

You can do multiple things with WordPress to extend it beyond the blog. I use the Twenty Nineteen theme to show you how to use WordPress to create a fully functional website that has a CMS platform — anything from the smallest personal site to a large business site.

Creating Different Page Views Using WordPress Templates

As I explain in Book 4, Chapter 2, a *static page* contains content that doesn't appear on the blog page or in blog archives but as a separate page within your site. You can have numerous static pages on your site, and each page can have a different design, based on the template you create. (Flip to Book 6 to find out all about choosing and using templates on your site.) You can create several static-page templates and assign them to specific pages within your site by adding code to the top of the static-page templates.

Here's the code that appears at the top of the static-page template used for an About page:

```
<?php
     /*
     Template Name: About
     */
?>
```

Using a template on a static page is a two-step process: Upload the template and then tell WordPress to use the template by tweaking the page's code.

TIP

In Book 6, you can discover information about Custom Menus, including how to create different navigation menus for your website. You can create a menu of links that includes all the pages you created on your WordPress Dashboard. You can display that menu on your website by using the WordPress Menus feature.

Uploading the template

To use a page template, you have to create one. You can create this file in a text-editor program, such as Notepad or TextEdit. (To see how to create a template, turn to Book 6, which gives you extensive information on WordPress templates and themes.) To create an About page, for example, you can save the template with the name `about.php`.

TIP

For beginners, the best way to get through this step is to make a copy of your theme's `page.php` file, rename the file `about.php`, and then make your edits (outlined in this section) in the new `about.php` file. As you gain more confidence and experience with WordPress themes and template files, you'll be able to create these files from scratch without having to copy other files to make them — or you can keep copying from other files. Why re-create the wheel?

When you have your template created, follow these steps to make it part of your WordPress theme:

For the purposes of this chapter, I'm using the Twenty Nineteen theme, which is the default theme and is included in every new installation of WordPress. You should have installed WordPress by now, so chances are good that you already have the Twenty Nineteen theme.

WARNING

Normally, when I practice coding on a website, I use a code repository with version control so that I can keep automatic backups of my template files; this practice allows me to easily and quickly reverse any changes I've made in the files if I've made a mistake or want to undo something I've done. The use of a code repository with version control is a topic for a whole other book. (You could try *Professional Git* by Brent Laster from Wrox Publishing.) For the purposes of the coding exercises in the book, you'll be downloading, editing and re-uploading the files via Secure FTP (SFTP), so I strongly recommend that you keep a copy of the files on your computer in a different folder, safe from any alterations. That way, you can restore the original files to your web server if needed.

Follow these steps to add the template tag to your theme, along with a little HTML code to make it look nice. (These steps assume that you've already added the `mood` Custom Field to your blog post and assigned a value to it.)

1. **Log in to your web server via SFTP.**

   For details on how to connect to your website via SFTP, refer to Book 2, Chapter 2.

2. **Navigate to the Twenty Nineteen theme folder**

   On your web server, that folder is /wp-content/themes/twentynineteen/.

3. **Locate the page.php template file.**
4. **Download the page.php template file to your computer.**
5. **Open the page.php file in a text editor.**

   Use Notepad if you're on a PC or TextEdit if you're using a Mac.

6. **In lines 1–13 in the page.php file, locate the following lines of code:**

```
<?php
/**
 * The template for displaying all single posts
 *
 * @link https://developer.wordpress.org/themes/basics/template-
   hierarchy/#single-post
 *
 * @package WordPress
 * @subpackage Twenty_Nineteen
 * @since 1.0.0
 */

get_header();
?>
```

7. **Click line 2 after /**, and press Enter.**

   This step creates a new blank line in the template on line 3.

8. **Type the Template Name tag on the new blank line you created in step 7.**

   To create an About Page template, the code to create the Template name looks like this:

```
Template Name: About
```

9. **Double-check the code in the template.**

   The Template Name tag is on line 3, and the full block of code at the top of the template in lines 1–14 now looks like this:

```
<?php
/**
 * Template Name: About
 * The template for displaying all single posts
 *
```

```
 * @link https://developer.wordpress.org/themes/basics/template-
   hierarchy/#single-post
 *
 * @package WordPress
 * @subpackage Twenty_Nineteen
 * @since 1.0.0
 */

get_header();
?>
```

10. **Save the file on your computer with the filename `about.php`.**

11. **Upload the new `about.php` template to the Twenty Nineteen theme folder on your web server via SFTP.**

    The correct path is `/wp-content/themes/twentynineteen/`.

12. **Verify that you uploaded the template file in the correct place.**

    In your Dashboard, click the Editor link on the Appearance menu to load the Theme Editor screen. If you see the `about.php` template listed on the list of templates on the right side of the page, you've uploaded the `about.php` file to the correct place!

Figure 6-1 shows the About Page template on the Edit Themes screen in the WordPress Dashboard, displaying the code needed to define a specific name for the template.

Assigning the template to a static page

After you create the template and name it the way you want, assign that template to a page by following these steps:

1. **Click the Add New link on the Pages menu of the Dashboard.**

   The Edit Page screen opens, allowing you to write a new page for your WordPress site.

2. **Type the title in the Title text box, and add content blocks to create the content for your page.**

   See Book 4, Chapter 1 for detailed information about content blocks.

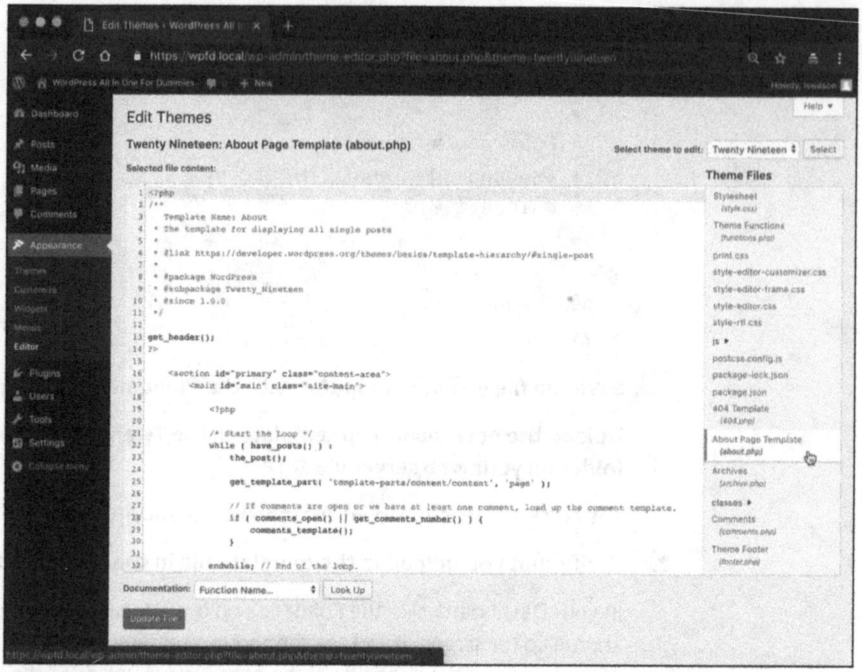

FIGURE 6-1: New About Page template displayed on the Edit Themes screen of the Dashboard.

3. **Choose the page template from the Template drop-down list.**

   The Template drop-down list is in the Page Attributes section of the settings panel on the right side of the page, as shown in Figure 6-2.

4. **Click the Publish button to save and publish the page to your site.**

As an example of how different pages on a website in WordPress can look completely different through the use of unique page templates, Figure 6-3 shows the layout of the home page on my business site at `https://webdevstudios.com` and the information it contains, whereas Figure 6-4 shows the layout and information provided on the Team page at `https://webdevstudios.com/about/team`. Both pages are on the same site, in the same WordPress installation, with different page templates to provide different looks, layouts, and sets of information.

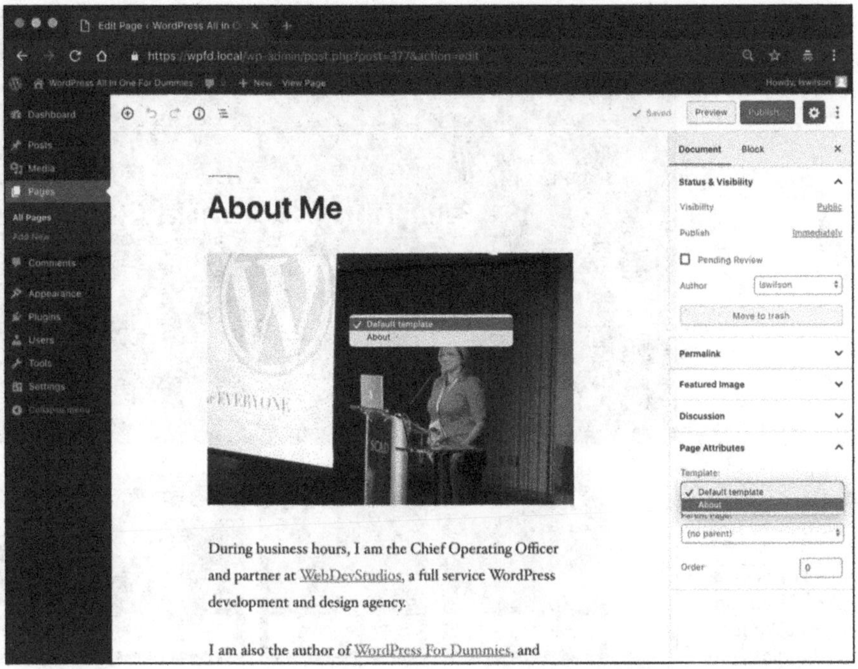

FIGURE 6-2: The Template drop-down menu on the Edit Page screen.

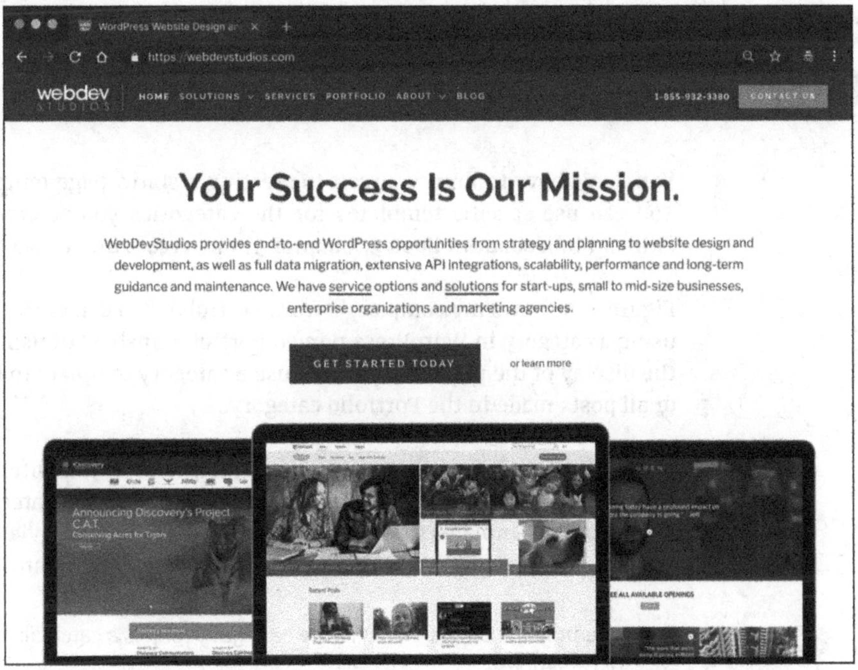

FIGURE 6-3: The home page at WebDevStudios.com.

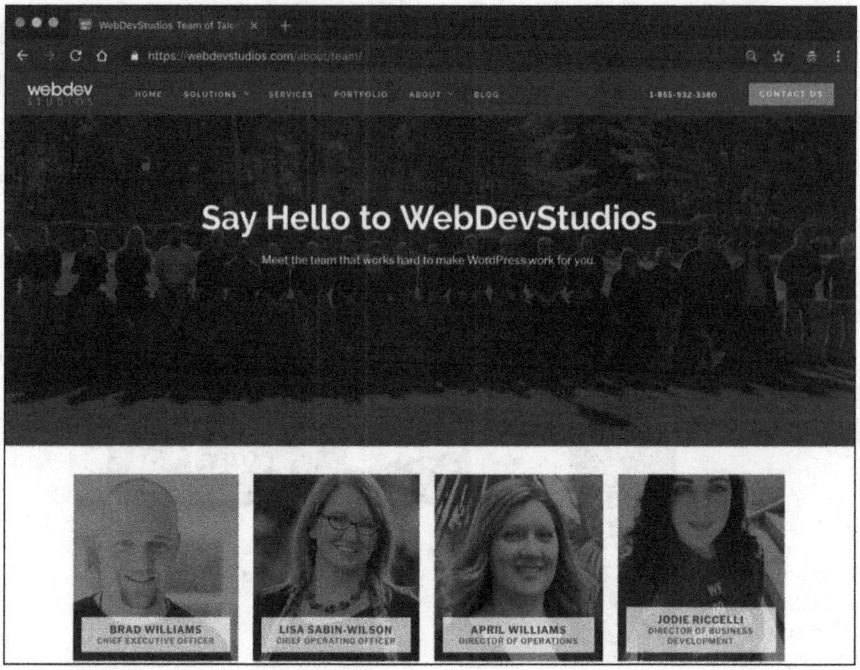

FIGURE 6-4: The Team page at WebDev Studios.com

Creating a Template for Each Post Category

You don't have to limit yourself to creating a static-page template for your site. You can use specific templates for the categories you've created on your blog (which I talk about in Book 3, Chapter 5) and create unique sections for your site.

Figure 6-5 shows my company's work portfolio. You can create a page like this by using a category in WordPress named Portfolio. Instead of using a static page for the display of the portfolio, you can use a category template to handle the display of all posts made in the Portfolio category.

You can create category templates for all categories in your site simply by creating template files that have filenames that correspond to the category slug and then upload those templates to your WordPress `themes` directory via SFTP. (See Book 2, Chapter 2.) Here's the logic behind creating category templates:

- A template that has the filename `category.php` is a catch-all for the display of categories.

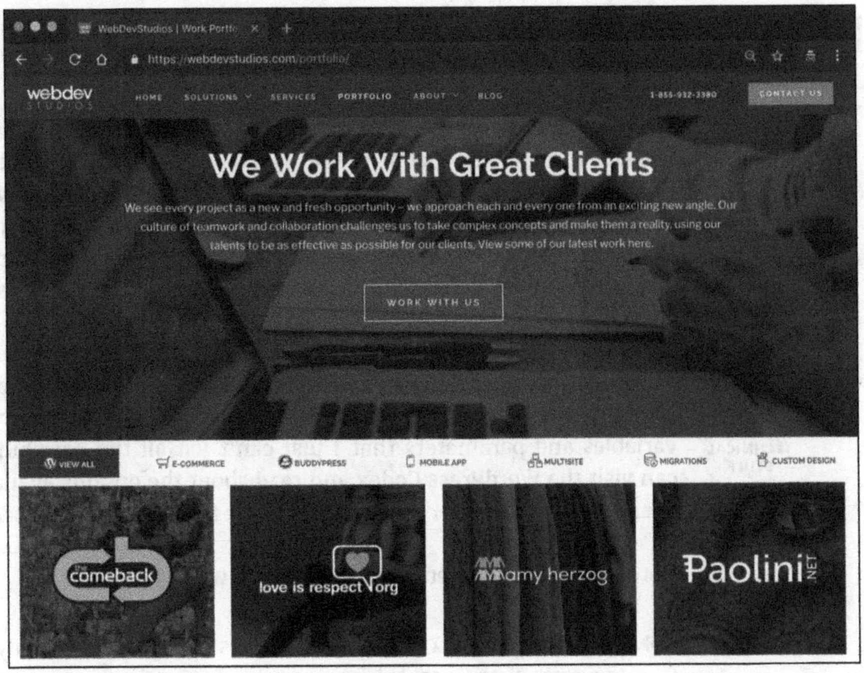

FIGURE 6-5: A Portfolio page on a WordPress website.

- Add a dash and the category name (also referred to as a *slug*) to the end of the filename (shown in Table 6-1) to specify a template for an individual category.
- If you don't have a `category.php` or `category-slug.php` file, the category display gets defined from the Main Index template (`index.php`).

Table 6-1 shows three examples of the category template naming requirements.

TABLE 6-1

WordPress Category Template Naming Conventions

If the Category Slug Is	The Category Template Filename Is
portfolio	`category-portfolio.php`
books	`category-books.php`
music-i-like	`category-music-i-like.php`

Pulling In Content from a Single Category

WordPress makes it possible to pull in very specific types of content on your website through the use of the `WP_Query` class. If you include `WP_Query` before The Loop (see Book 6, Chapter 3), WordPress lets you specify which category you want to pull information from. If you have a category called WordPress and want to display the last three posts from that category — on your front page, on your sidebar, or somewhere else on your site — you can use this class.

TECHNICAL STUFF

The `WP_Query` class accepts several parameters that let you display different types of content, such as posts in specific categories and content from specific pages/posts or dates in your blog archives. The `WP_Query` class lets you pass so many variables and parameters that I just can't list all the possibilities. Instead, you can visit the WordPress Codex and read about the options available with this tag: `https://codex.wordpress.org/Class_Reference/WP_Query%23Parameters`.

Here are two parameters that you can use with `WP_Query`:

- `posts_per_page=`*X*: This parameter tells WordPress how many posts you want to display. If you want to display only three posts, enter **posts_per_page=3**.
- `category_name=`*`slug`*: This parameter tells WordPress that you want to pull posts from the category with a specific slug. If you want to display posts from the WordPress category, enter `category_name=wordpress`.

Following is a code snippet that you can use in any theme template to display posts from a single category anywhere on your site. This snippet of code uses the `WP_Query` class to construct a query that pulls content from posts in a category named `wordpress`. With the snippet in place, your site displays the title of the post, hyperlinked to the URL of the post, surrounded by HTML `<p> .. </p>` tags for some formatting. Using techniques covered in Book 6, Chapter 4 on using CSS to customize the style of HTML tags on your site, you can create a unique look for these posts. You may need to change the `wordpress` portion of this snippet to pull content from a category that you use on your own site.

```
<?php
 $args = array( 'category_name' => 'wordpress' );
 $query = new WP_Query( $args );
   if( $query->have_posts() ) :
   while( $query->have_posts() ) :
     $query->the_post(); {
       echo '<p><a href="';
       echo the_permalink();
```

```
.        echo '">';
.        echo the_title();
.        echo '</a></p>';
.     }
.   endwhile; endif;
?>
```

TECHNICAL STUFF

In past versions of WordPress, people used the `query_posts();` function to pull content from a specific category, but the `WP_Query` class is more efficient. Although the `query_posts();` function provides the same result, it increases the number of calls to the database and also increases page load and server resources, so please don't use `query_posts();` (no matter what you see written on the Internet!).

Using Sidebar Templates

You can create separate sidebar templates for different pages of your site by using a simple `include` statement. When you write an `include` statement, you're telling WordPress that you want it to include a specific file on a specific page.

The code that pulls the usual Sidebar template (`sidebar.php`) into all the other templates, such as the Main Index template (`index.php`), looks like this:

```
<?php get_sidebar(); ?>
```

What if you create a page and want to use a sidebar that has different content from what you already have in the Sidebar template (`sidebar.php`)? You can accomplish that by following these steps to create a new Sidebar template and include it in any template file you need to:

1. **Create a new sidebar template in a text editor such as Notepad.**

   See Book 6 for information on template tags and themes.

2. **Save the file as `sidebar2.php`.**

   In Notepad, choose File ⇨ Save. When you're asked to name the file, type **sidebar2.php** and then click Save.

3. **Upload `sidebar2.php` to your Themes folder on your web server.**

   See Book 2, Chapter 2 for SFTP information, and review Book 6, Chapter 2 for information on how to locate the Themes folder.

The template is now in your list of theme files on the Edit Themes screen. (Log in to your WordPress Dashboard and click the Editor link on the Appearance drop-down menu.)

4. **To include the `sidebar2.php` template in one of your page templates, replace `<?php get_sidebar(); />` with this code:**

```
<?php get_template_part( 'sidebar2' ); ?>
```

This code calls in a template you've created within your theme.

TIP

By using that `get_template_part` function, you can include virtually any file in any of your WordPress templates. You can use this method to create footer templates for pages on your site, for example. First, create a new template that has the filename `footer2.php`. Then locate the following code in your template

```
<?php get_footer(); ?>
```

and replace it with this code:

```
<?php get_template_part( 'footer2' ); ?>
```

TECHNICAL STUFF

Every single WordPress theme is different, so you'll find that one theme may have a Sidebar template (`sidebar.php`) in the main directory of its theme folder. Likewise, you may find that another theme puts its Sidebar template in a folder called `/includes` or a folder called `/content`. The default Twenty Nineteen theme, for example, doesn't use a Sidebar template at all, where the default theme used before the latest version of WordPress, called Twenty Seventeen, does have a Sidebar template in the main directory of the theme folder. Each theme you encounter is different, with a different method of structuring the file directory of the theme, so you may have to dig around a little to discover the mysteries of the theme you are working with. Or you can visit Book 6, Chapter 3 to discover how to create your own theme from scratch!

Creating Custom Styles for Sticky, Category, and Tag Posts

In Book 6, you can find the method for putting together a basic WordPress theme, which includes a Main Index template that uses the WordPress Loop. You can use a custom tag to display custom styles for sticky posts, categories, and tags on your blog. That special tag looks like this:

```
<article id="post-<?php the_ID(); ?>" <?php post_
  class(); ?> >
```

The `post_class()` section is the coolest part of the template. This template tag tells WordPress to insert specific HTML markup into your template that allows you to use CSS to make custom styles for sticky posts, categories, and tags.

REMEMBER

In Book 4, Chapter 1, I tell you all about how to publish new posts to your site, including the different options you can set for your blog posts, such as categories, tags, and publishing settings. One of the settings is the Stick This Post to the Front Page. In this chapter, I show you how to custom-style those sticky posts. It's not as messy as it sounds!

Suppose that you publish a post with the following options set:

- Stick this post to the front page.
- File it in a category called WordPress.
- Tag it News.

When the `post_class()` tag is in the template, WordPress inserts HTML markup that allows you to use CSS to style *sticky posts* (posts assigned top priority for display) with different styling from the rest of your posts. WordPress inserts the following HTML markup for your post:

```
<article class="post sticky category-wordpress tag-news">
```

In Book 6, you can discover CSS selectors and HTML markup, and see how they work together to create style and format for your WordPress theme. With the `post_class()` tag in place, you can go to the CSS file (`style.css`) in your theme and define styles for the following CSS selectors:

- `.post`: Use this tag as the generic style for all posts on your site. The CSS for this tag is

  ```
  .post {
  background: #ffffff;
  border: 1px solid silver;
  padding: 10px;
  }
  ```

  A style is created for all posts to have a white background with a thin silver border and 10 pixels of padding space between the post text and the border of the post.

- `.sticky`: You stick a post to your front page to call attention to that post, so you may want to use different CSS styling to make it stand out from the rest of the posts on your site:

```
.sticky {
 background: #ffffff;
 border: 4px solid red;
 padding: 10px;
}
```

  This CSS style creates a style for all posts that have been designated as sticky in the settings panel on the Edit Post page to appear on your site with a white background, a thick red border, and 10 pixels of padding space between the post text and border of the post.

- `.category-wordpress`: Because I blog a lot about WordPress, my readers may appreciate it if I give them a visual cue as to which posts on my blog are about that topic. I can do that through CSS by telling WordPress to display a small WordPress icon in the top-right corner of all my posts in the WordPress category:

```
.category-wordpress {
 background: url(wordpress-icon.jpg) top right no-repeat;
 height: 100px;
 width: 100px;
}
```

  This CSS style inserts a graphic — `wordpress-icon.jpg` — that's 100 pixels in height and 100 pixels in width in the top-right corner of every post I assign to the WordPress category on my site.

- `.tag-news`: I can style all posts tagged with News the same way I style the WordPress category:

```
.tag-news {
 background: #f2f2f2;
 border: 1px solid black;
 padding: 10px;
}
```

  This CSS styles all posts tagged with News with a light gray background and a thin black border with 10 pixels of padding between the post text and border of the post.

You can easily use the `post-class()` tag, combined with CSS, to create dynamic styles for the posts on your site!

Working with Custom Post Types

A nice feature of WordPress is Custom Post Types. This feature allows you, the site owner, to create content types for your WordPress site that give you more creative control of how different types of content are entered, published, and displayed on your WordPress website.

REMEMBER

I wish that WordPress had called this feature Custom Content Types so that people didn't incorrectly think that Custom Post Types pertain to posts only. Custom Post Types aren't really the posts that you know as blog posts. Custom Post Types are a way of managing your blog content by defining what type of content it is, how it's displayed on your site, and how it operates — but Custom Post Types aren't necessarily posts.

By default, WordPress already has post types built into the software, ready for you to use. These default post types include

- Blog posts
- Pages
- Navigation menus (see Book 6, Chapter 1)
- Attachments
- Revisions

Custom Post Types give you the ability to create new and useful types of content on your website, including a smart, easy way to publish those content types to your site.

You have endless possibilities for using Custom Post Types, but here are a few ideas that can kick-start your imagination (some of the most popular and useful ideas that people have implemented on their sites):

- Photo gallery
- Podcast or video
- Book reviews
- Coupons and special offers
- Events calendar

Book 6, Chapter 6 takes you through the mechanics of creating Custom Post Types on your site. If you're ready to dig into a little theme development work to make that happen, flip over to that chapter to get started!

Optimizing Your WordPress Site

Search engine optimization (SEO) is the practice of preparing your site to make it as easy as possible for the major search engines to crawl and cache your data in their systems so that your site appears as high as possible in the search returns. Book 5 contains more information on search engine optimization, as well as information about marketing your site and tracking its presence in search engines and social media by using analytics. This section gives you a brief introduction to SEO practices with WordPress. From here, you can move on to Book 5 to take a hard look at some of the things you can do to improve and increase traffic to your website.

If you search for the keywords *WordPress website design and development* in Google, my business site at WebDevStudios is in the top-ten search results for those keywords (at least, it is while I'm writing this chapter). Those results can change from day to day, so by the time you read this book, someone else may very well have taken over that coveted first position. The reality of chasing those high-ranking search engine positions is that they're here today, gone tomorrow. The goal of SEO is to make sure that your site ranks as high as possible for the keywords that you think people will use to find your site. After you attain those high-ranking positions, the next goal is to keep them.

WordPress is equipped to create an environment that's friendly to search engines, giving them easy navigation through your archives, categories, and pages. WordPress provides this environment with a clean code base, content that's easily updated through the WordPress interface, and a solid navigation structure.

To extend SEO even further, you can tweak five elements of your WordPress posts, pages, and templates:

- **Custom permalinks:** Use custom permalinks, rather than the default WordPress permalinks, to fill your post and page URLs with valuable keywords. Check out Book 3, Chapter 2 for information on WordPress permalinks.
- **Posts and page titles:** Create descriptive titles for your posts and pages to provide rich keywords in your site.
- **Text:** Fill your posts and pages with keywords for search engines to find and index. Keeping your site updated with descriptive text and phrases helps the search engines find keywords to associate with your site.
- **Category names:** Use descriptive names for the categories you create in WordPress to place great keywords right in the URL for those category pages, if you use custom permalinks.

» **Images and <ALT> tags:** Place <ALT> tags in your images to further define and describe the images on your site. You can accomplish this task easily by using the description field in the WordPress image uploader.

Planting keywords in your website

If you're interested in a higher ranking for your site, use custom permalinks. By using custom permalinks, you're automatically inserting keywords into the URLs of your posts and pages, letting search engines include those posts and pages in their databases of information on those topics. If a provider that has the Apache `mod_rewrite` module enabled hosts your site, you can use the custom permalink structure for your WordPress-powered site.

Keywords are the first step on your journey toward great search engine results. Search engines depend on keywords, and people use keywords to look for content.

The default permalink structure in WordPress is pretty ugly. When you're looking at the default permalink for any post, you see a URL something like this:

```
http://yourdomain.com/p?=105
```

This URL contains no keywords of worth. If you change to a custom permalink structure, your post URLs automatically include the titles of your posts to provide keywords, which search engines absolutely love. A custom permalink may appear in this format:

```
http://yourdomain.com/2019/01/01/your-post-title
```

I explain setting up and using custom permalinks in full detail in Book 3, Chapter 2.

Optimizing your post titles for search engine success

Search engine optimization doesn't completely depend on how you set up your site. It also depends on you, the site owner, and how you present your content.

You can present your content in a way that lets search engines catalog your site easily by giving your blog posts and pages titles that make sense and coordinate with the actual content being presented. If you're doing a post on a certain topic, make sure that the title of the post contains at least one or two keywords about that particular topic. This practice gives the search engines even more ammunition to list your site in searches relevant to the topic of your post.

REMEMBER

As your site's presence in the search engines grows, more people will find your site, and your readership will increase as a result.

A post with the title A Book I'm Reading doesn't tell anyone *what* book you're reading, making it difficult for people who are searching for information on that particular book to find the post. If you give the post the title *WordPress All-in-One For Dummies: My Review*, however, you provide keywords in the title, and (if you're using custom permalinks) WordPress automatically inserts those keywords into the URL, giving the search engines a triple keyword play:

- Keywords exist in your blog post title.
- Keywords exist in your blog post URL.
- Keywords exist in the content of your post.

Writing content with readers in mind

When you write your posts and pages and want to make sure that your content appears in the first page of search results so that people will find your site, you need to keep those people in mind when you're composing the content.

When search engines visit your site to crawl through your content, they don't see how nicely you've designed your site. They're looking for words to include in their databases. You, the site owner, want to make sure that your posts and pages use the words and phrases that you want to include in search engines.

If your post is about a recipe for fried green tomatoes, for example, you need to add a keyword or phrase that you think people will use when they search for the topic. If you think people would use the phrase *recipe for fried green tomatoes* as a search term, you may want to include that phrase in the content and title of your post.

A title such as A Recipe I Like isn't as effective as a title such as A Recipe for Fried Green Tomatoes. Including a clear, specific title in your post or page content gives the search engines a double-keyword whammy.

Creating categories that attract search engines

One little-known SEO tip for WordPress users: The names you give the categories you create for your site provide rich keywords that attract search engines like honey attracts bees. Search engines also see your categories as keywords that are relevant to the content on your site. So make sure that you're giving your categories names that are relevant to the content you're providing.

If you sometimes write about your favorite recipes, you can make it easier for search engines to find your recipes if you create categories specific to the recipes you're blogging about. Instead of having one Favorite Recipes category, you can create multiple category names that correspond to the types of recipes you blog about: Casserole Recipes, Dessert Recipes, Beef Recipes, and Chicken Recipes, for example.

REMEMBER

Creating specific category titles not only helps search engines, but also helps your readers discover content that's related to topics they're interested in.

You also can consider having one category called Favorite Recipes and creating subcategories (also known as *child categories*) that give a few more details on the types of recipes you've written about. (See Book 3, Chapter 5 for information on creating categories and child categories.)

Categories use the custom permalink structure, just like posts do. So links to your WordPress categories also become keyword tools within your site to help the search engines — and, ultimately, search engine users — find the content. Using custom permalinks creates category page URLs that look something like this:

```
http://yourdomain.com/category/category_name
```

The `category_name` portion of that URL puts the keywords right in the hands of search engines.

Using the <ALT> tag for images

When you use the WordPress Media Library to upload and edit images, an ALT Text field appears; in it, you can enter a description of the image. (I cover uploading and inserting images into your posts and pages in great detail in Book 4, Chapter 3.) This text automatically becomes what's referred to as the `<ALT>` tag, otherwise known as alternative text.

The `<ALT>` tag's real purpose is to provide a description of the image for people who, for some reason or another, can't see the image. In a text-based browser that doesn't display images, for example, visitors see the description, or `<ALT>` text, telling them what image would be there if they could see it. Also, the tag helps people who have impaired vision and rely on screen-reading technology because the screen reader reads the `<ALT>` text from the image. You can read more about website accessibility for people with disabilities at `https://www.w3.org/WAI/people-use-web`.

An extra benefit of <ALT> tags is that search engines gather data from them to further classify the content of your site. The following code inserts an image with the <ALT> tag of the code in bold to demonstrate what I'm talking about:

```
<img src="http://yourdomain.com/image.jpg" alt="This is an ALT
  tag"/>
```

Search engines harvest those <ALT> tags as keywords. The WordPress image uploader gives you an easy way to include those <ALT> tags without having to worry about inserting them into the image code yourself. Just fill out the Description text box before you upload and add the image to your post. Book 4, Chapter 3 provides in-depth information on adding images to your site content, including how to add descriptive text for the <ALT> tag and keywords.

5

Examining SEO and Social Media

Contents at a Glance

IN THIS CHAPTER

- » Making your content easy for readers to share
- » Figuring out when to interact with readers
- » Using Twitter through WordPress
- » Connecting Facebook to your WordPress website

Chapter 1
Exposing Your Content

After you launch your website, getting your content in front of an interested audience is one of the most important strategic decisions you make, and this chapter focuses on how to get your content in front of potential new readers. The idea that people will eventually find any content you write is a pretty big falsehood. You may have the best rock band in the world, but if you don't leave your garage and get your music in front of potential fans, you can't ever sell out arenas.

By creating good content, making it easily shareable, and then participating within groups of interested people, you can establish expertise and build a community around your content. A community is much more powerful than a bunch of silent visitors; people in a community often become advocates and cheerleaders for your site.

REMEMBER

You want to gain readers, not random visitors. There's a big difference between readers and visitors. *Readers* visit your site on a consistent basis. *Visitors* check out your site and then move on to the next page that grabs their attention.

Understanding the Three Cs of the Social Web

Before I dive into the technical how-to stuff, I should talk about general social media philosophy. Technical tips without philosophy are meaningless. If you don't have the general philosophy down, your results are going to be poor because your interactions are going to be very one-sided affairs.

You can concentrate your daily actions on the web on the three Cs: content, communication, and consistency. The next few sections go into detail about each topic. By applying the three Cs, you can avoid a lot of mistakes and have success with your website and blog.

Content

The first pillar of the social web is content. Although the web has seen a growing shift from content to community, content is still king. Communities based on common interests fall flat unless they have the content for people to gravitate to. Facebook groups, for example, dominate because of the wealth of content they offer: the posts, links, videos, and other media that people create within that group. Without the content, the group wouldn't exist.

Content for the sake of content isn't necessarily in your best interest, however. To ensure that you provide the best content possible, make sure that you do these things:

- **Focus your content.** People expect tailored content. If you write about just anything, people won't know what to expect and will visit less often or stop coming to your site altogether. People will come back to your site for certain reasons, and they want content tailored to what they expect. The most successful publishers have a narrow focus, and they write for a niche.

CONSIDERING SOCIAL-VOTING TOOLS

A lot of online vendors recommend that you drive as many eyeballs as possible to your site by using social-voting tools (such as Facebook's Like button and Twitter's Tweet button) and other methods. Although this strategy increases your traffic numbers and may temporarily boost your confidence, it's a short-term solution. Most of your new visitors won't have a lot of interest in your content and therefore won't return to your site.

When Problogger.net author Darren Rowse (`https://problogger.com`), an authority on professional online publishing, began blogging, he tried a wide-ranging approach but discovered it didn't work. Rowse said:

> "My blog had four main themes and different readers resonated differently with each one. A few readers shared my diverse interests in all four areas, but most came to my blog to read about one of the (or at most a couple of) topics. A number of regular loyal readers became disillusioned with my eclectic approach to blogging and gave up coming."

Stick to two or three related topics (such as WordPress and related technology topics); you can still cover and talk about a wide variety of subjects that you excel in. People will know what they're coming to your site for and what to expect from you.

- **Have a voice that people want to hear.** Some people don't necessarily care about the mechanics of your writing as much as they care about your voice. Publishers, especially ones that post large amounts of content, often have typos and errors in their posts. Tucker Max (`http://tuckermax.com`), one of the most popular comedy bloggers, switches between past and present tense often — a grammar no-no. He's aware of this problem and doesn't care, and neither do his readers.

  Max knows that he's developing his own style:

  > "I know, I know. The whole concept of tense in speech has always given me problems. In undergrad and law school, I never really took any creative writing or English courses; it was pretty much all econ, law, history, etc., so some of the basic things that most writers get right, I fail. Of course I could learn tenses, but I have never really made an effort to get it right for a reason: I want to write in my own voice, regardless of whether or not it is 'correct' grammar or not. By switching tenses, I write the way I speak, and by alternating between past and present I put the reader into the story, instead of just recounting it."

  Max says that the only time people complain about his grammar mistakes is when they want to argue about the content of his site. They use the grammar mistakes as a plank in their attack. This attempt to belittle him hasn't slowed his growth or success, however. His voice, after all, is what has made him successful.

REMEMBER

Your grammar and spelling don't always have to be perfect, but you should always ensure that your posts are readable. Just don't let perfect grammar get in the way of your individual voice.

» **Present your content well.** The actual look of your presentation matters greatly. Adding images, for example, enhances your posts in several ways, including

- Giving posts a visual point of interest
- Grabbing attention (making casual readers stop and read)
- Drawing people's eyes down beyond the first few lines of a post
- Illustrating examples
- Giving your site a personal touch
- Engaging the emotions and senses of readers
- Giving posts a professional feel, which can lead to an air of authority

REMEMBER

Be sure that the only images you use on your website are those images you have permission to use. The best-case scenario is that you use images that you, yourself, own the copyright to. Otherwise, be sure that you've obtained permission from the owner of the image before using it on your website. Alternatively, you can purchase images for use through reputable, commercial stock-photography sites such as iStock (`https://www.istockphoto.com`) and Getty Images (`https://www.gettyimages.com`) or free-image sources such as FreeImages (`https://www.freeimages.com`) and Pixabay (`https://pixabay.com`).

If you write long, poorly formatted articles, people most likely won't comment or interact with your content — not because of the length of those postings per se, but because of the way that you displayed them, as long paragraphs of endless text. Pictures, highlighted words, bullet points, and other such tricks give the reader's eye a break and can make your published content more attractive and more professional-looking.

» **Write often.** The more you write, the more people will spread the word about your writing, and you can grow your audience. Successful publishers tend to publish content multiple times per week.

All these publishing elements are extremely important on the social web. People want to read and view information that they find interesting, content that's well presented, and content that's specific to their needs. Make sure that you consider all these facets of a website when you create content for your site.

Communication

Communication is the second pillar of the social web. The more you write, the more comments you'll get, assuming that you have comments enabled on your site. Use these tips to manage communication with commenters:

- **Respond to those comments!** The whole point of the social web is communication, and people expect to engage you in a conversation. Successful publishers engage readers in the comment section and create conversations; they use articles as jumping-off points for larger discussions.

  WordPress guru Lorelle VanFossen (`https://lorelle.wordpress.com`) expresses the true value of comments and how they changed how she uses the web:

  > "Comments change how you write and what you write. I suddenly wasn't writing static information. People could question what I said. They could make me think and reconsider my point of view. They could offer more information to add value to my words. And most of all, they could inspire me to write more. Comments made writing come alive."

- **Develop a community.** When you participate in the conversation, you'll retain more readers, who times will revisit your page many during the day to see the new comments and replies in the discussion. The evolution into community discussion can result in a drastic increase in traffic and comments on your site. VanFossen writes of her site:

  > "My site isn't about 'me' or 'my opinion' any more. It's about what I have to say and you say back and I say, and then she says, and he says, and he says to her, and she reconsiders, and I jump in with my two shekels, and then he responds with another view . . . and it keeps going on. Some of these conversations never end. I'm still having discussions on topics I wrote 11 months ago."

- **Don't ignore a person's comments on multiple posts.** You can offend a commenter and lose him. Reply to most comments that your site receives, even if it's only to say thanks for the comments.

REMEMBER

Having the approach that you only want to take from the social web ultimately leaves you unsuccessful. No matter how great your content is, you need to participate and make people feel that you're communicating with them, not just speaking at them.

COMMENTING ON OTHER SITES

In addition to responding to comments on your site, you should go to different sites and take part in the discussions there. Choose sites that are similar to yours; you can be part of the larger publishing community beyond your own. (Visitors of those sites will see your witty comments and most likely follow you to your site, thereby building your audience.)

Understanding the social aspect of the social web is vital to your success. People use the social web as a major mode of communication. The communication aspects of your site and others play into the overall online conversation that's going on — a conversation that can get started by an article, which a writer covers in a post on her site about that topic, which a reader comments on, which prompts another person to compose a response to those comments or that article, which gets its own set of comments. Having a grasp of this concept and seeing how it operates not only brings you better success on the social web, but also makes you a better participant.

Consistency

The final pillar of the social web is consistency. When you produce and offer any type of content multiple times a week or on a daily basis, people begin to expect consistency. Many online publishers don't post consistently, and as a result, they frustrate their readers.

TIP

Although consistency applies to online publishing in general, it really matters on social networks such as Twitter, Instagram, and Facebook, where interconnectivity between the author and the audience reaches new heights. If you have large followings on Facebook, Instagram, and/or Twitter and use those services as your main point of contact with your readers, be sure to post on a regular basis as well.

Build good habits by following these consistency guidelines:

- **Set a schedule, and stick to it.** As a site owner, you have to give people a pattern to expect so that eventually, they know when to look for your posts. This idea is like knowing when a favorite TV program is on; you come to expect it and maybe even plan around it. If you miss a day on which you usually post, you just might hear from readers wondering where your post is for that day.

If you plan to write five days a week, actually write five days a week, and try not to deviate from that schedule. If you plan to post only two to three times a week, stick to the days that you usually post (unless you want to cover some important breaking news).

- **Don't let the increasing number of readers and comments affect your posting schedule.** The last thing you want to do is overpost. Although some people would argue that you should keep momentum on a particularly popular post, you run the risk of overexposing yourself and burning yourself out. Also, your content can quickly become watered down. The quality of the content — what the people are there for — quickly begins to erode, and you can lose the audience you've built.

  WARNING

  By sticking with a routine and establishing consistency in your posting, you let readers know what to expect, and your site becomes a part of their routine. If you ingrain yourself in someone's life, he or she is going to return to your site frequently and become an advocate for what you're doing.

- **Plan.** You also need to account for long breaks in your posting schedule. You can prewrite posts when you have a lot to say and save them as drafts so that you can post them at times when you aren't inspired to write.

  WARNING

  Some online publishers take a month off from writing or post very sporadically. But if you really want to build an audience, you can't suddenly decide to take a month off because you're tired of it. Taking a long stretch of time off can kill your site's momentum and audience.

  You can explore other options instead of leaving your site dormant. If you've built an audience, you can easily find a guest author to step in for a bit to publish content on your site.

- **Keep the quality consistent.** Take pains to ensure that the quality content you produce doesn't suffer for any reason. Sites often capitalize on a popular post, gain an audience, and then become inconsistent with the quality of their content. They either shift away from their original niche or begin to post poorly thought-out or poorly put-together articles. When their content quality suffers, those sites begin to lose their audience, and sometimes, they never recover.

- **Expect some ups and downs.** You can't easily judge which articles are going to be successful and which aren't. You might write articles in five minutes that get more views and have a better reception than articles you take hours to craft. But readers can really tell when you're posting for the sake of posting. If you repeatedly have to force yourself to post, and if that goes on for too long, the quality of your content and your consistency can go out the window.

Making It Easy for Users to Share Your Content

When I was a child, I loved to go to a country store on a lake near where I lived. One time, my mother and I went to the store to pick up a few things, but my mother didn't have any cash (this was before ATMs were everywhere) and wanted to pay by check or credit card. The store owner told her that they accepted cash only. We put the items back on the shelves and headed to a large supermarket.

When we got into the car, my mother said to me, "I wanted to give them money, but they made it too hard for me to do it." That sentiment has stuck with me my entire life: Never put up barriers to actions that will ultimately benefit you. I'm sure that the store had reasons for not taking checks or credit cards, but it ultimately lost a sale and probably a customer.

Think of your site as the store and your content as the products. When people want to take your content and give it to someone, you put up a barrier if you make it hard for them to pass that content along. Make it as easy as possible for people to share your content with their friends, family members, and co-workers.

One of the best things about the social web is that you can share what you find with other people. Sharing is a basic concept — an easy, thoughtful, and fun thing to do. You find content that you like and share it with your friends on the web, who might find what you shared helpful or interesting and pass it on to their friends. But a lot of sites do a very poor job of allowing users to share content. While you set up your WordPress site, think about how you want readers to share your content.

REMEMBER

Test, test, and test some more. How to best lay out your sharing options on your site takes continual testing. You can't get it right the first time — or the first five times. Sometimes, it takes months to find the right mix.

The following sections give you some simple tips that make sharing content from your website easy.

Enable the user to share content

Enabling sharing is the first thing you want to do. If people don't have the ability to share your content, that content isn't going to go anywhere.

TIP

Sharing content doesn't mean just social media sharing; your content can get spread through other methods. Allow readers to email or print your posts. Although you may feel that email and printing are outdated features, your users may not.

AddToAny VERSUS SHARETHIS

WordPress offers a multitude of plugins (see Book 7) that blend social sharing with more traditional options, such as individual share icons, printing, and emailing. The AddToAny Share Buttonsplugin (`https://wordpress.org/plugins/add-to-any`) provides share buttons for almost all the popular social networks (Facebook, Twitter, Pinterest, WhatsApp, and more than 100 other sites), as well as universal email sharing and Google Analytics integration that allows you to track your content-sharing analytics.

Other popular plugins offer similar options, with some drawbacks. The ShareThis plugin (`https://www.sharethis.com`), for example, provides a green button that, when clicked, expands so that users can select the networks on which they want to share your content, or print or email that content. Making users click an additional button to see their sharing options adds an extra step to the process.

The AddToAny plugin puts individual icons on your posts, getting rid of the extra step that users must take to share your content through ShareThis.

Just remember that when you use the ShareThis button, a reader can easily overlook it. The individual buttons are more visible and not as easily overlooked. Test these plugins to see which method gets more shares.

Don't overwhelm the user with choices

Sites can include too many sharing options. The reader becomes overwhelmed and probably also has trouble finding the network that he or she uses.

Pick a few sharing sites to which you want to link, test them, and cycle in new ones that people may use. Offer a low number of sharing options at a time so that people can share your content easily. Determine which of these networks your content applies to. If you write celebrity gossip, your content may do better being distributed on sites where people can share quickly with their friends, such as Facebook (`https://www.facebook.com`) and Twitter (`https://twitter.com`). If you write in-depth technical resources, a social bookmarking site such as Reddit (`https://www.reddit.com`) may be a better place to share your content and bring your blog additional traffic. If you write about fashion and beauty, perhaps providing a sharing button to Pinterest (`https://www.pinterest.com`) can get you traffic from people who are interested in those topics.

Make sure that the sharing options you give visitors apply to sites where your content makes sense. Don't be afraid to try different sites. Study your statistics to see where readers are discovering your content. Many of these sites allow you to search by domain, so you can check to see how often people are sharing your website and what specific content they're sharing.

Put sharing buttons in the right place

Where you present the sharing buttons really depends on the type of content you're posting and the audience reading it. If you post a picture and include a comment below it, the content could push your sharing buttons below the fold, so make sure that your major sharing options appear next to or above the content. Some of the most popular places to display sharing buttons are the top of the post, the bottom of the post, and the left and right margins of the website.

TECHNICAL STUFF

Below the fold refers to what doesn't appear in a user's web browser unless the user scrolls down to view it. The term is taken from newspaper printing, in which some items appear below the fold on the front page.

TIP

To get some ideas about how best to deploy your sharing buttons, check out sites that are similar to yours, and see where some of the most successful site publishers place their buttons.

Think about the user, not yourself

Take this major lesson away from this section. Too many times, people get excited about the latest gadget or tool for their sites. They get eager to try it out and excited to deploy it, but in the end, they aren't thinking about whether it can help the user and whether the user is going to enjoy it.

REMEMBER

How you use the web and how you navigate a site can be completely different from how most other people use it. Review button use and where people are sharing your posts. Also use tools such as Google Analytics to see how people interact with your page.

TIP

By using its site-overlay feature, Google Analytics (see Book 5, Chapter 3) allows you to see how often someone clicks various items on your website. You can sign up for Google Analytics for free and deploy it very easily. (You just need to paste the tracking code in

The site-overlay feature currently works in the Google Chrome browser on either a Mac or PC. To access the site-overlay feature from your Google Analytics Dashboard, follow these steps:

1. **Go to the Page Analytics (by Google) page in the Chrome Webstore.**

   This page is at `https://chrome.google.com/webstore/detail/page-analytics-by-google/fnbdnhhicmebfgdgglcdacdapkcihcoh`.

2. **Click the Add to Chrome button.**

   This step installs and adds the extension to your Chrome browser by adding a Page Analytics icon to the browser toolbar.

3. **Visit your website in your browser window.**
4. **Click the Page Analytics button on your browser toolbar.**

   The page analytics tool, using the Site Overlay feature, is shown in Figure 1-1. The \tool displays information such as the frequency of clicks on links on your site and statistics for visitors and pageviews.

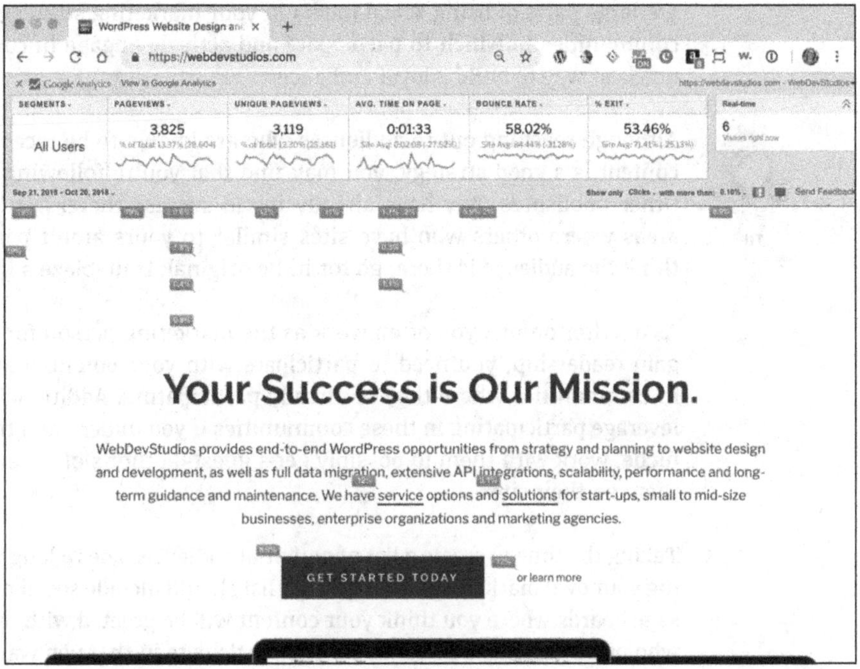

FIGURE 1-1: The Site Overlay feature in Google Analytics.

Now, on the home page of your site, little text boxes for the various links on your home page appear, displaying percentages. (Refer to Figure 1-1.) The percentages within these text boxes reflect how popular the various links are within your site. If you navigate your site while using the Site Overlay feature, you can see, page by page, how people are interacting with your navigation, content, sharing features, and other content.

Determining Where You Need to Participate

Communication is an important part of social media, and communication is a two-way street. In social media, communication isn't a bullhorn; you need to interact with people. If you want the rewards of participation, you need to listen as well as talk. This idea often gets lost when people start using social media to promote their content.

Determining whom you want to interact with and where to interact with them are large parts of using social media in your marketing strategy. Finding the best communities in which to participate and actively engage in conversations is the quickest way to build a loyal audience.

TIP

Although reaching out to audiences who are known to be receptive to your site's content is a good strategy, you may find that you're following a well-trod path. Other publishers may have already found success there. Don't be afraid to try areas where others who have sites similar to yours aren't participating. If you think the audience is there, go for it. Be original; trail-blaze a little.

As a writer online, you often work as the marketing person for your own site. To gain readership, you need to participate with your potential audience members in communities where they're already participating. Additionally, you can really leverage participating in these communities if you understand the authors in your niche, work with them to possibly get a guest-author slot, or even get links from them on their sites.

Taking the time to create a list of potential audiences goes a long way toward creating your own marketing strategy. Your list should include social networks and message boards where you think your content will be greeted with open arms, authors who publish content in the niche you participate in that you want to monitor, and users who have influence on other social networks (such as someone who has a large Twitter following in your niche or your particular area of interest/expertise).

The most important thing you can do while constructing a list is understand the niche in which you're building a readership. Here are some items of interest to look for when finding out about a niche:

- **Who's in the niche?** Check out the links in a post. Start with a major site in your niche, and see where the links lead, including the links to commenters' sites and the sites they mention in their content, to get a wide view of the niche. Knowing who associates with whom and what circles people run in can help you discover a lot about a niche. You can determine who the power players are, as well as whether the niche is competitive or has a collegial atmosphere. This information helps you determine how you want to approach your outreach.

- **Does a niche social media site or group act as a connecting point for the community?** Often in various groups, you can find one or more niche social media sites that connect websites. These sites can be great resources for discovering some of the top sites, and they may help you flesh out your list of writers quickly. Additionally, see whether you can get your site listed on these sites. Most of these kinds of sites allow free submittals and offer forms to fill out or email addresses to which you can submit your content.

  This kind of online community might be a directory with social features, a Facebook community, or a group on a large social network. Whatever the case may be, you can often find large groups that have discussions within a niche. These niche sites can tell you what people in the niche you are targeting find important, what the hot topics are, and what other people are doing in this niche, such as pitches people have made to other site owners. TastyKitchen.com (`https://tastykitchen.com`) is a great example of a niche community — in this case, a community of people who like to cook and share recipes.

  TIP

  Additionally, these sites feature the type of content that people in your niche may find interesting. Keep a Microsoft Word document open to write down content ideas based on the conversations on these sites.

- **Are common discussions occurring throughout the community?** You can often discover opportunities to get your site in front of new people or for topics to cover by looking for common threads within a niche. Maybe the community is talking about how public-relations people are pitching them, a charity cause that they all support, or an event that they regard as being important. A common theme may give you information, opportunity, or direction on how you should approach this niche.

- **Do they use other media to have discussions?** Find out what other social media sites people in this niche use. Maybe they use Twitter a lot, or maybe you see high use of Facebook, LinkedIn, Pinterest, Reddit, or YouTube. You may find secondary ways to reach this niche where you can build a following for your site.

  It pays to determine the social media sites your niche prefers. Certain niches (such as wine sites) have taken to Twitter; others have strong ties to Facebook or other social networking sites. Make the most of these sites when you pitch your blog to people. They may prefer that method of connection.

You may think you can simply buy a list, slam a bunch of search results into a spreadsheet, and then mass-email everyone whom you want to contact. Without studying how your niche operates, however, you can't create mutually beneficial relationships, you can't become a voice in the community, and you probably won't see a lot of success. Instead, you come off as an outsider trying to push your message down the throats of these publishers, and your campaign will have very poor results.

Finding Influencers

After you compile lists of sites you want to target, you can begin to break the list down and determine who are the influencers in your niche, including the hidden influencers. *Hidden influencers* are people who have a large social imprint that doesn't necessarily show up on their sites. Some people don't have a lot of commenters on their articles, for example, but their Twitter feeds are followed by tens of thousands of people. Here are some ways to determine whether a blogger is an influencer:

- **Subscriber count:** A lot of sites that have large audiences display their subscriber numbers on their websites. (See Figure 1-2.)

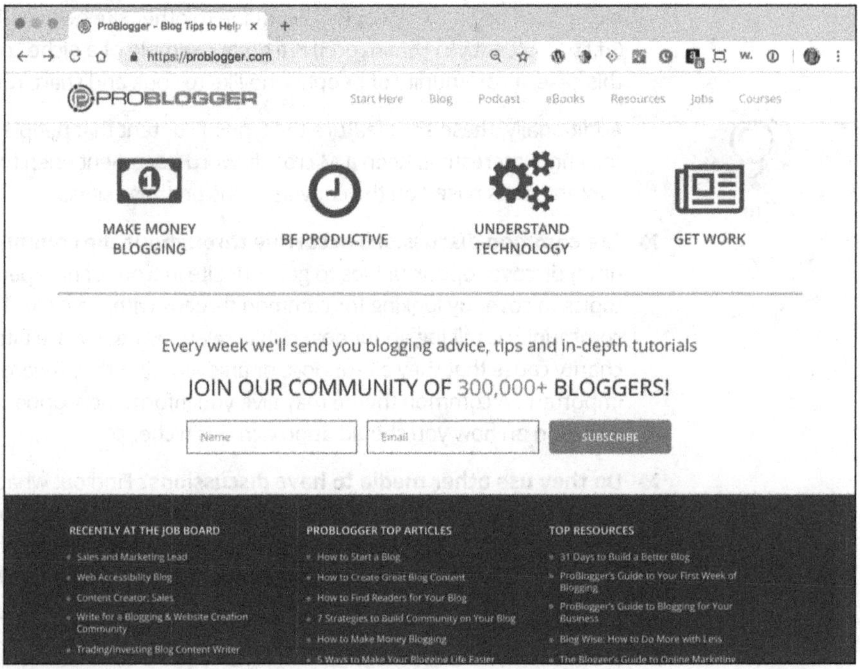

FIGURE 1-2: Subscriber count on Problogger.net – a community of more than 300,000 bloggers.

- **Comment count:** An active community and commentary group on a blog usually shows that the blog has a large readership. Be wary of a site whose author interacts with only two or three people. When an author pays attention to only a couple of commenters, she usually has a pretty narrow vision. You want to target authors who participate with more people in their audience.

- **Amazon Alexa score:** Alexa (`https://www.alexa.com/siteinfo`) measures traffic to a site. It isn't 100 percent accurate, but it does a decent job of giving you a picture of the amount of traffic a site gets. Add a column to your list of sites where you can record the Alexa score, and see how the scores compare with yours.

After you identify the influencers, you want to attract them to your site. If influencers read your site, they may offer you guest-author spots, share your content, recommend your site to their readers, and form a mutually beneficial relationship with you.

To turn these influencers into readers, you can try multiple tactics, including the following:

- **Comment on their content.** Reading and commenting on a popular site can help you start to build your name in your niche — if you leave quality, well-thought-out comments, of course. Most sites allow your username to link back to a website; make sure that you use this link as a way for people to find your site.

  You can get the attention of a popular writer by engaging in conversation on his or her site, and also get the attention of that author's reader. If the readers and commentators like your contribution, you can get additional traffic, new readers, and even potentially high-ranking backlinks into your website, all because you left a comment on the site.
- **Email them.** Depending on the niche, top influencers may get slammed with email, so this approach may not be the best way to reach out to them. But it doesn't hurt to write a personal note that lets the author know about you and your site, and perhaps offer to guest-write if he or she ever accepts posts from other people. Make sure that the email isn't all about you, which is the quickest way to turn someone off. Talk about the person's site, and show that you have knowledge about what he's writing about. Show that you've actually read his site, and demonstrate genuine interest in what he's doing.
- **Interact with them on their platforms of choice.** Sometimes, influencers and popular writers participate in areas other than their sites. They might use message boards, forums, Twitter, Facebook, or other types of social media sites. Interacting with an author on his or her platform of choice can help you differentiate yourself from other sites.
- **Link to them.** Linking to sites in the content you create — especially if you're posting rebuttals to their posts — can really get influencers' attention.

REMEMBER

When you use any of the tactics in the preceding list, the three Cs (see "Understanding the Three Cs of the Social Web" earlier in this chapter) come into effect. When you communicate with other site authors, you need to make sure that you have consistent content on your own site. Trying to reach out to another author when you have only three posts total doesn't present the most credibility. After you've worked at it for a few months, doing outreach can provide a good way to grow your audience.

Leveraging Twitter for Social Media Success

Twitter has become one of the most effective ways for site owners to build an audience. You can use Twitter to find people who have the same interests that you do, communicate with them, and steer a ton of traffic to your site.

Building a Twitter profile into a successful tool to generate traffic is pretty straightforward. Just follow these steps in your account at `https://twitter.com`:

1. **Make sure that your profile is completely filled out, including your picture.**
2. **Follow the three Cs — content, communication, and consistency — when you post to Twitter.**

   By posting quality content consistently on Twitter, you *will* build an audience. Period. When you mix in the communication aspect and retweet the quality content of others, answer questions, and interact with other Twitter users, your profile will grow that much more.
3. **Find people who are interested in what you're writing about, and interact with them.**
4. **Use a tool such as Twitter Search (`https://twitter.com/search-home`) to search for specific keywords related to content that you're writing about, and then discover the people who follow that content as well.**

   You may want to follow and interact with these people.

Building your Twitter account by using automated tools

I hesitate to include this section, because using automated tools is a fast way to get your account deleted by Twitter. Automated tools allow you to do mass additions or removals to your account. You can remove people who aren't active or who aren't following you, as well as target the friends list of other users to add them to your account. Using these mass adding-and-removal tools goes against the spirit of Twitter, where you're supposed to be discovering cool content and not just mass-promoting. So I'm warning you right now: If you go down this path, you need to see losing your account as an acceptable risk. If you use the Twitter tool that I discuss in a logical and nonaggressive way, it can help you target and build an audience quickly.

I include automated tools in my discussion of building your social media accounts because a lot of people use this technique, including people who shun them. (A lot of social media experts who deride these tools have used them to get where they are.) I don't believe in giving you half the information; you need to make this choice on your own.

WARNING

If you hyperaggressively add people and then unfollow them, Twitter probably will quickly ban you.

To target users on Twitter, here are the steps you can take:

1. **Go to Refollow (**`https://www.re-follow.com`**).**

   Refollow.com is a great service, but it isn't free. You can sign up for a free six-day trial; then, if you want to pay for the service, click the Upgrade button at the top of the site to upgrade. Prices range from $20 to $150 per month.

2. **Log in to Refollow by using your Twitter account login information.**

   This step loads the Refollow dashboard page, shown in Figure 1-3.

3. **Click the link labeled Create New Campaign.**
4. **From the Find Users Who drop-down menu, choose Follow.**
5. **Type** WordPress **in the next text field.**
6. **Select the search options of your choice, such as**
   - Language Preferences
   - People Who Have Actively Tweeted within the Past Week
   - People Who Already Follow You
   - People Who Have a Photo
7. **Click the Save Settings button.**

   The page refreshes and displays the Twitter users who follow the account you specified in step 4. On this page, you can follow these users on Twitter or remove them from your dashboard.

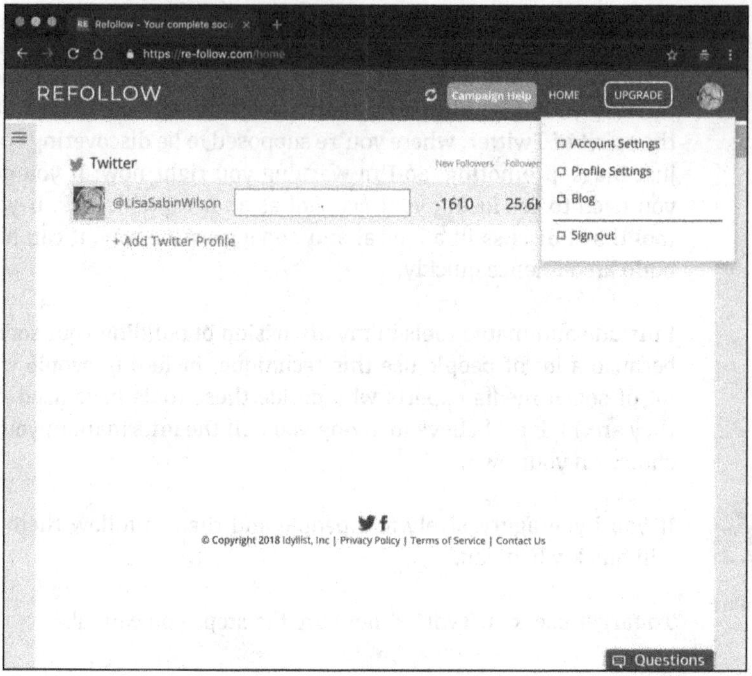

FIGURE 1-3: The Refollow dashboard.

WARNING

Don't follow more than 100 to 200 people a day. This tool allows you to follow up to 500, but if you follow that many people each day, Twitter probably will ban you after a few days.

You can use Refollow to find people who are following people within your niche and add them to your Twitter account so that they may notice your content. I advise adding people in bulk only once in a 24-hour period so you don't look like you're gaming the system. Once a week, unfollow everyone who isn't following you back to balance your following ratio. You shouldn't be following more people than are following you.

Updating Twitter from your WordPress blog

Getting back to WordPress (that's why you bought the book, right?), you can find tons of plugins to integrate Twitter into your WordPress site. From how the tweets show up on your sidebar to how tweets are integrated into your comments, the WordPress community has tons of solutions to help you show off your Twitter account on your site.

These plugins change often, so try different ones, depending on how you want to integrate Twitter into your site. But if you want to turn your WordPress Dashboard into more of a social media command center, you can tweet right from your WordPress Dashboard.

Although tools such as TweetDeck (`https://tweetdeck.twitter.com`), Buffer (`https://buffer.com`), and Hootsuite (`https://hootsuite.com`) are designed for an active and strategic Twitter presence, having the ability to tweet from your WordPress Dashboard allows you to update all your social media from one spot. If you're getting started in social media, this integration makes your social media use efficient and continually reminds you to participate.

TIP

One of the best WordPress integration plugins for this purpose is the Jetpack for WordPress plugin by Automattic (`https://jetpack.com`). This plugin can update your Twitter feed whenever you publish a new post. You can update Twitter about new posts by using Hootsuite, Buffer, and other free tools, but going with the Jetpack plugin allows you to automatically post your new content to Twitter.

Engaging with Facebook

Facebook integration is another key strategy to consider when you're setting up your website. First, integrate the Facebook-sharing feature within your website, which you can do with the WordPress Social Sharing Plugin (`https://wordpress.org/plugins/sassy-social-share`) or AddThis plugin (`https://wordpress.org/plugins/addthis`). With more than 1.86 billion users, Facebook is a must-have sharing option for any website.

Next, decide how you want your website to interact with Facebook. Are you running a personal site? If so, you may want to use a Facebook profile as your connecting place on Facebook. Some WordPress plugins (such as the Facebook Dashboard Widget) integrate a Facebook profile so that you can update your status right from the WordPress Dashboard.

If you don't want your personal Facebook account attached to your website, you may want to consider creating a Facebook page. A Facebook page allows you to leverage your social media presence. By setting up a Facebook page, you can deeply integrate the Facebook Like option, which allows users to like your site and become followers of your page with a couple of clicks. Integrating this feature allows you to get exposure for your website through each of your followers' friends on Facebook.

When you have a Facebook page, you can display a community widget on the side of your WordPress site, letting everyone know who your followers are on Facebook. If a Facebook user clicks the Like button on your page, he can show up in this widget. Facebook offers a lot of badges and Like-button integration features in its Developers section at `https://developers.facebook.com/docs/plugins/like-button`.

In this Developers section, you can dig deep into integrating Facebook into your site. You can display the friends of a visitor who likes your site, recommendations based on what the visitor's friends have liked, and numerous other combinations.

IN THIS CHAPTER

» Understanding why you need to monitor your brand

» Finding out which monitoring tools are right for you

» Cleaning and aggregating your monitoring data

» Turning your WordPress Dashboard into a listening post

Chapter 2 Creating a Social Media Listening Hub

This chapter focuses on the importance of listening to social media, using the free monitoring services available to you, and integrating these sources into your WordPress installation so that you can turn your run-of-the-mill WordPress installation into a social media listening hub.

A *social media listening hub* is a collection of information from several sources, including mentions of your site, keywords, or topics that you write about, and even information about competitors. You can sign up for services that monitor these topics, such as Salesforce Marketing Cloud (`https://www.salesforce.com/products/marketing-cloud/overview`) and Gigya (`https://www.gigya.com`). But most of these services cost money and give you another place to log in to, and you may not use these kinds of services to their full capacity. For a small business or an independent site owner, the investment (both time and financial) doesn't always make sense. By leveraging the power of the WordPress platform, you can easily cut down on both the time and financial commitment of monitoring platforms.

In this chapter, I walk you through determining what sources you should pull your data from, determining and searching for the keywords you deem important, and integrating your search results into your WordPress Dashboard. Additionally, I look at some other tools that can help you expand your monitoring practices.

Exploring Reasons for a Social Media Listening Hub

When you begin to engage in the world of social media, one of the most important things you can do is monitor what Internet users are saying about your company, your site, you, or your products. By investigating what Internet users are saying, you can find and participate in discussions about your site or company and come to an understanding about the way your community views your site (or brand). With this information, you can participate by responding to comments on other sites, like Twitter, or Facebook Groups or by creating targeted content on your own site.

The conversations happening about your area of interest or niche amount to really great intelligence. For a business, regardless of whether you participate in social media, social media users are talking about your company, so you need to be aware of what they're saying. If you're blogging about a particular topic, you can evolve your content by tracking what members of your niche are saying about it.

Eavesdropping on yourself

By monitoring your niche, you can eavesdrop on thousands of conversations daily and then choose the ones in which you want to participate. The social media listening hub you create allows you to follow various conversations going on through microblogging services such as Twitter, Facebook, blogs, news sites, Reddit, and even comments on YouTube. If someone says something negative about you, you can respond quickly to fix the situation. You can attempt to step in and make sure that people are informed about what you're doing.

Keeping tabs on your brand

Think about what keywords or phrases you want to monitor. You want to monitor your name and your blog/company name, of course, as well as other keywords that are directly associated with you.

TIP

Monitor common misspellings and permutations of the name of your brand. The Bing Ads Intelligence tool (`https://advertise.bingads.microsoft.com/en-us/solutions/tools/bing-ads-intelligence`) can help you determine all the common spellings and uses of the keywords you're monitoring. You can also find common misspellings for your brand by examining some of the terms people used to find your page with Google Analytics (`https://marketingplatform.google.com/about/analytics`) or a paid tool such as Trellian Keyword Discovery Tool (`https://www.keyworddiscovery.com/search.html`).

If Green Bay Packers quarterback Aaron Rodgers wanted to set up a monitoring service, for example, he might use the keywords *Aaron Rodgers, Arron Rodgers, Aaron Rogers, Green Bay Packers Quarterback,* and perhaps even the phrase associated with his touchdown celebration: *discount double check.* If he wanted to expand this service past direct mentions of him or his team, he could also include more general terms such as *NFL Football* or even *NFC Teams.* The general term *NFL Football* may be *too* general, though, producing too many results to monitor.

Additionally, you may want to view your site or company through the lens of your customers. What terms do they associate with your company? Looking at your site from other points of view can provide good ideas for keywords, but not always. Although you don't always want your company to be known for these terms and may not see yourself that way, getting the perspective of other people can open your eyes to how users view your website.

Don't think of this process as just pulling in keywords, either. You can pull in multiple feeds, just as you do with an RSS reader, which allows you to monitor specific sites. So if you concentrate on an industry, and a website deals specifically with your industry and has an active news flow pushed through an RSS feed, you may want to consider adding specific websites to the mix of feeds you run through WordPress.

The setup in WordPress that I describe in this chapter gives you the convenience of having everything in one place and can help you monitor your brand, company, or website. If you own a restaurant, hotel, or bar and want to pick up review sites such as Yelp and TripAdvisor, these tools can't do the job. Most social media monitoring tools don't count review sites as social media. Tools such as Reputation Ranger (`http://reputationranger.com`) can monitor ratings sites for a nominal monthly fee if you want to pay attention to those types of sites.

REMEMBER

When your content changes, change what you're monitoring to match the evolution of what you're writing about.

Exploring Different Listening Tools

You can find tons of monitoring and listening tools that oversee the social media space. If you work for a large company, you can use large, paid tools such as Salesforce Marketing Cloud (`https://www.salesforce.com/products/marketing-cloud/overview`), Gigya (`https://www.gigya.com`), Alterian (`https://www.alterian.com`), and Lithium (`https://www.lithium.com`). Pricing for these tools runs from a few hundred dollars to tens of thousands per month. Most individuals and small businesses can't make that investment. If you're one of the smaller guys, you can create your own monitoring service right in WordPress by importing free monitoring tools into your Dashboard to create a social media listening hub.

Some monitoring tools pick up site coverage, Twitter remarks, and message-board comments. Other tools pick up content created with video and pictures. Try the monitoring services mentioned in the following sections, and determine which give you the best results and which make you feel the most comfortable. Then choose the best tools to create a good monitoring mix. One solution probably can't cover everything, so experiment with different combinations of tools.

TIP

Most, but not all, of these tools use Boolean search methods, so you need to understand how to narrow your searches. If you want to combine terms, put AND between two items (*cake AND pie*). If you use OR, you can broaden your search, such as to track common misspellings *(MacDonalds OR McDonalds)*. Finally, if you want to exclude terms, you can use the NOT operator to exclude items from your search. Use NOT if you want to search for a term that could have an alternative meaning that's irrelevant to what you're actually looking for (*Afghan NOT blanket*, for example, if you're writing about Afghanistan).

Although some of the monitoring tools in the following sections don't apply to every type of website, I'd include them in most monitoring setups.

For each search that you do on a monitoring service, you need to log the feed address. To make recording these addresses easy, open a spreadsheet or a document into which you can paste the various feeds. You can collect them in one place before you begin to splice them together (which you do in "Creating Your Own Personal Monitoring Mix" later in this chapter). Think of this document as a holding area.

Monitoring with Google Alerts

Most social media experts consider Google Alerts (`https://www.google.com/alerts`) to be a must-use monitoring source for anyone dabbling in social media. Google Alerts allows you to set up monitoring on news sites, blogs, pictures, videos, and groups. You can toggle the amount of results you see, from 20 to 50, and you can choose how often they come in (in real time, daily, or weekly). You can also have Google deliver your alerts to your email or via RSS.

Google Alerts isn't perfect, but it doesn't have many drawbacks. Some of the specialized searches (such as Boardreader, which targets message boards; see "Searching communities with Boardreader" later in this chapter) pick up more in their areas of expertise than Google Alerts does, but in general and compared with other tools, Google Alerts covers the widest range of content.

You can easily set up Google Alerts by following these steps:

1. **Navigate to `https://www.google.com/alerts` in your web browser.**

   The Alerts page loads, welcoming you to the Google Alerts website.

2. **In the search text box, type the keyword or phrase that you want to monitor.**

   If you enter a phrase in which the words have to go in that particular order, put the phrase in quotation marks.

3. **From the Show Options drop-down menu, choose the type of monitoring that you want to use.**

   The options send you different kinds of alerts:

   - *How Often:* Determine how often you'll receive these notices. Because you'll receive the updates via RSS and not email (which you set up in step 4), you want the highest frequency possible, so choose the As-It-Happens option. Other options include a daily, weekly, and monthly digest.
   - *Sources:* Select the type of sources you want Google Alerts to search in (news, blogs, video, and so on).
   - *Language:* Select the language you want Google Alerts to search.
   - *Region*: Select the region you want Google Alerts to search.
   - *How Many:* Select how many results you want to receive. If you choose As-It-Happens for How Often, for example, you receive items in real time, so you don't need to specify the number of items; choose Only the Best Results or All Results.

4. **Choose your delivery type from the Deliver To drop-down menu.**

   To make the delivery source an RSS feed, as opposed to an email, choose RSS Feed.

5. **Click the Create Alert button.**

   You see your Google Alert Management screen, where you can get the RSS feeds for all your Google Alerts.

6. **To get the URL of the RSS feed, right-click the RSS Feed icon shown to the right of the alrt you created, and choose Copy Link Address from the shortcut menu that appears.**
7. **Paste the copied link location into a document in which you list all the feeds that you plan to aggregate later.**
8. **Repeat steps 2 through 7 for all the alerts you want to monitor.**

TIP

Before you start importing the feed into your WordPress Dashboard, you may want to receive the update via email for a few days to test the quality of the results you're getting. If your results aren't quite right, you can always narrow your search criteria. Doing this saves you the time of parsing all your RSS feeds, blending them, and then having to go back and edit everything because your RSS feeds are set up wrong. Using email as a test is a massive time saver.

Tracking conversations on Twitter with RSS

Tracking mentions on Twitter via RSS is relatively simple. You just need to know what you're looking for and how to build the RSS links so you can monitor them. You can look for several items to monitor your brand and reputation via the Twitter social network, including the following:

- **Username:** Monitor when your Twitter name is mentioned and by whom.
- **Hashtags:** Monitor specific Twitter hashtags (such as #wordpress).
- **Keywords:** Monitor Twitter for a specific word.

The Twitter service itself doesn't make RSS feeds available for public consumption on the web, but a service called TwitRSS will turn your Twitter searches into RSS feeds. You can find this service by visiting `https://twitrss.me`. TwittRSS, which currently is free, allows you to create RSS feeds for a specifc user or search term on Twitter. When you're on the site, type a specific search term in the Twitter Search text box. (See Figure 2-1.)

Following are examples of Twitter RSS links that I created:

- Twitter RSS URL for my Twitter username: `https://twitrss.me/twitter_search_to_rss/?term=Lisa+Sabin-Wilson`
- Twitter RSS URL for the keywords *WordPress For Dummies*: `https://twitrss.me/twitter_search_to_rss/?term=WordPress+For+Dummies`
- Twitter RSS URL for the hashtag #WordPress: `https://twitrss.me/twitter_search_to_rss/?term=%23WordPress`

Build the Twitter RSS URLs that you want to monitor by copying the link provided by TwitRSS (displayed in your browser's address bar) and including it in the document where you're listing all the RSS feeds you want to aggregate later.

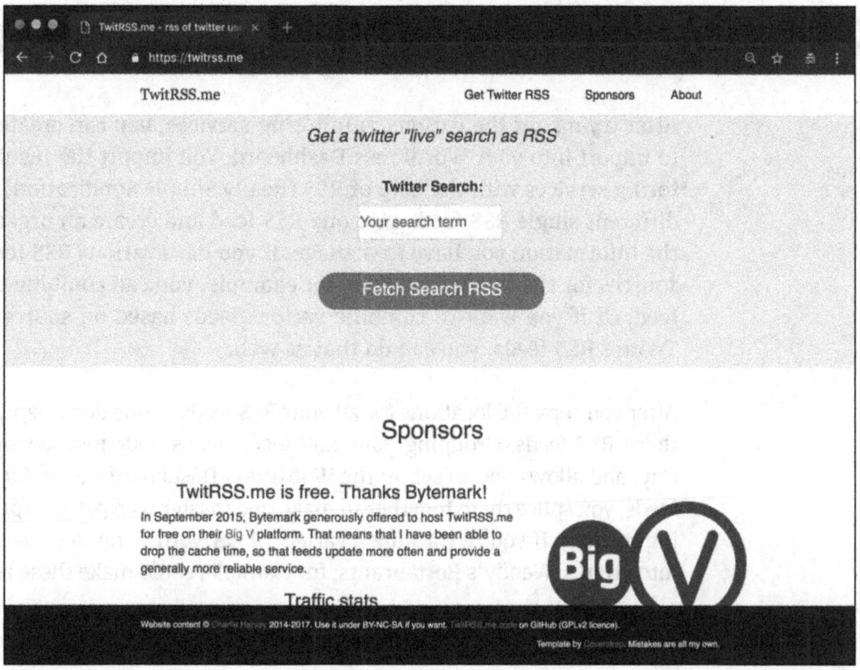

FIGURE 2-1: TwitRSS search service.

Searching communities with Boardreader

Boardreader (`http://boardreader.com`) is a must-add tool because it focuses on groups and message boards, where conversations have been happening much longer than on Facebook and Twitter. Many other monitoring tools overlook these areas when talking about monitoring the web, but you can find many vibrant communities that are worth being part of, in addition to monitoring what's being said about your blog or company.

To set up your Boardreader tracking, follow these steps:

1. **Navigate to `http://boardreader.com`.**
2. **In the text box, type the search term that you want to monitor; then click the Search button.**
3. **Copy the URL from your browser's address bar.**
4. **Paste this URL into a document in which you list all the feeds that you plan to aggregate later.**
5. **Repeat steps 2 through 4 to search for and monitor as many search terms as you want.**

Creating Your Own Personal Monitoring Mix

After trying out the various monitoring services, you can create a mix of services to import into your WordPress Dashboard. You import the results of these monitoring services with the help of RSS (Really Simple Syndication). You can combine different single RSS feeds into one RSS feed and create an organized setup for all the information you have to manage. If you have various RSS feeds from different sources for the keyword *cookies*, for example, you can combine them into one RSS feed. Or if you want to combine various feeds based on sources such as all your Twitter RSS feeds, you can do that as well.

After you copy the locations for all your RSS feeds in one document, you need to group those RSS feeds. Grouping your RSS feeds keeps your monitoring system nice and tidy, and allows you to set up the WordPress Dashboard easily. After you group these feeds, you splice them together to make one master feed per grouping (see the following section). If you're tracking a variety of keywords, you may want to put your feeds into groups. Wendy's Restaurants, for example, could make these keyword groupings:

- **Grouping 1:** Your brand, products, and other information about your company
  - Wendy's (the company name)
  - Frosty (a prominent product name)
  - Wendy Thomas (a prominent person in the company)
- **Grouping 2:** Competitors
  - McDonald's
  - Burger King
  - In-N-Out
- **Grouping 3:** Keyword-based searches (Burgers)
  - Hamburgers
  - Cheeseburgers
- **Grouping 4:** Keyword-based searches (Fast Food)
  - Fast food
  - Drive-through
- **Grouping 5:** Keyword-based searches (Chicken)
  - Chicken sandwiches
  - Chicken salad
  - Chicken nuggets

In each of these groups, you place your Google Alerts feed, Twingly feed, and whatever other feeds you feel will provide information about that subject area. You can blend each group of feeds into one master feed for that group and bring them into WordPress.

REMEMBER

WordPress limits you to five groups. Any more than five groups slows the Dashboard and is more than WordPress can handle.

Grouping all your various feeds gives you the most complete monitoring solution by covering multiple monitoring tools and blending them. You get more coverage of your brand or blog than you would by using Google Alerts alone. On the down side, you may see some duplicates because of overlaps between the services.

If you feel overwhelmed by duplicate search results, you can blend one feed that covers only your brand, or you can simplify setting up your monitoring even more by keeping one feed for each item, as follows:

- **General overview:** Google Alerts or social mention
- **Message boards:** Boardreader
- **Microblogging:** Twitter search

Editing the Dashboard to Create a Listening Post

After you choose your data sources, clean up your feeds, and put them all in individual RSS feeds, you can finally bring them into WordPress and set up your social media listening hub.

You can bring these RSS feeds into your Dashboard through a plugin called Dashboard Widgets Suite, which you can find in the WordPress Plugins page at `https://wordpress.org/plugins/dashboard-widgets-suite`.

Follow these steps to set up the Dashboard Widgets Suite plugin and configure it to create a social-listening Dashboard in WordPress:

1. **From the Plugins menu on the left side of your WordPress installation, choose Add New.**

   This step takes you to the form where you can search for new plugins.

2. **In the Search text box, type** Dashboard Widgets Suite; **then click the Search Plugins button.**

   The search results page appears.

3. **Search for the Dashboard Widgets Suite plugin, and click the Install Now link, which installs the plugin on your site.**
4. **When the installation is complete, activate the plugin by clicking the Activate button on the Add Plugins screen that appears to the right of the Dashboard Widgets Suite plugin name.**
5. **Choose Dashboard Widgets from the Dashboard Settings menu.**

   The Dashboard Widgets screen appears.

6. **Ensure that the Enable the Control Panel Widget check box is selected (as it should be by default).**
7. **Leave all the rest of the default settings in place, and click the Save Changes button.**
8. **Click the Widgets link on the Appearance menu.**

   The Widget Settings page appears.

9. **Add the RSS widget to the Dashboard Widgets Suite widget area.**

   Drag the RSS widget into the Dashboard Widgets Suite widget.

10. **Configure the RSS widget to display information from your selected RSS feed (see Figure 2-2):**
    - Enter the RSS feed's URL.
    - Optionally, give the RSS feed a title by typing a title in the text field.
11. **Repeat steps 8 through 10 for the other widgets on your Dashboard by using your other selected feeds.**

    After you have your feeds set up, you can configure the appearance of your WordPress Dashboard.

12. **Drag and drop the new widget boxes where you want them on your Dashboard.**

Figure 2-3 displays my Dashboard with the RSS feed from the search I found on TwitRSS for the term *WordPress For Dummies*, shown in the top-right corner. Now, whenever I log in to my WordPress site, I can see what's being said on Twitter about my book in real time.

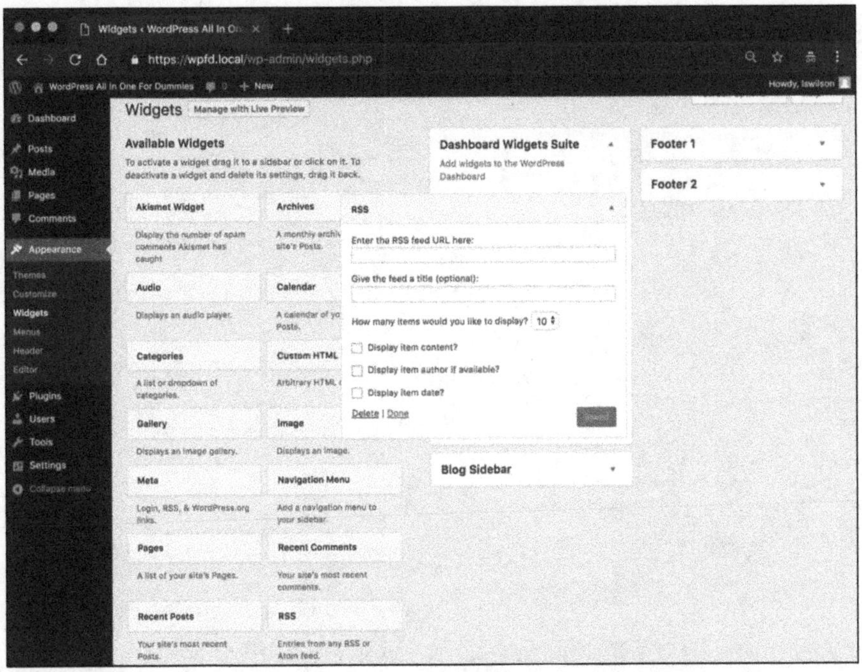

FIGURE 2-2: Configuring the Feed Box widget.

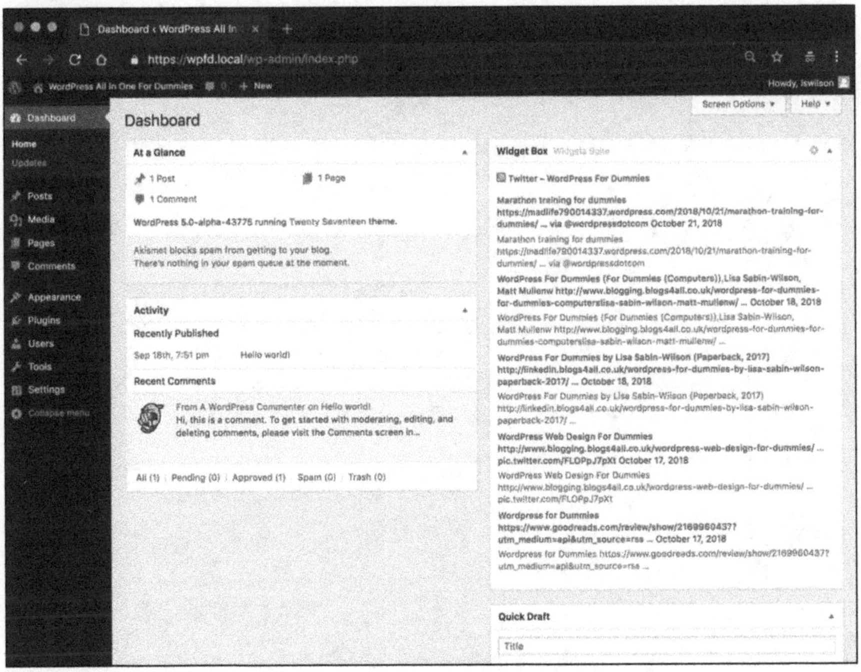

FIGURE 2-3: *WordPress For Dummies* search term displayed in the WordPress Dashboard.

IN THIS CHAPTER

» Understanding what analytics can tell you about your site

» Choosing an analytics-tracking option

» Deciphering analytics terminology

» Working with Google Analytics

Chapter 3 Understanding Analytics

Every business on the face of the Earth needs to figure out what works and what doesn't if it wants to succeed. Site owners often know basic statistics about their sites, such as the current number on their hit counters or how many people visit their site daily or weekly. These stats may give you the big picture, but they don't really address why something is or isn't working.

You need to get at least a basic understanding of analytics if you want to make the most of your site. The data provided by free programs such as Google Analytics can really help you grow as a content publisher. In this chapter, you discover how to incorporate various data-measuring tools into your WordPress installation, decipher what the data is telling you, and determine how to act on it.

Google Analytics provides you a tremendous amount of information about your content. The goal of this chapter is to help you interpret the data, understand where your traffic is coming from, understand which of your content is the most popular among your visitors, know how to draw correlations between various data sets, and use this information to shape the content you write. This process may sound very geeky and accountantlike, but in reality, it gives you a road map that helps you improve your business.

Understanding the Importance of Analytics

Personally, I avoid math like my nephew avoids vegetables. Most people's eyes glaze over when they hear the word *analytics* followed by *stats*, any type of *percentages*, and anything that sounds like accountant-speak.

You should view analytics not as a bunch of numbers, however, but as a tool set that tells a story. It can tell you how people are finding your content, what content is most popular, and where users are sharing that content. Knowing what type of content is popular, where your site is popular (in which time zones, countries, and states, for example), and even what time of day your posts get more readers is all valuable information. Understanding your audience's interest in your content, as well as their preferences on when and how they read your content, is important.

At one point in my life, I had a pretty popular political blog. Through studying analytics and reactions to my content, I figured out that if I posted my blog between 9:30 a.m. and 10 a.m. EST, my posts garnered the most comments and got the most traffic throughout the day. When I posted after noon, my articles got about half as many comments and half as much traffic over a 24-hour period. Additionally, I saw that my site was getting shared and voted for on the social news site Reddit (`https://www.reddit.com`) more often than on Facebook (`https://www.facebook.com`), so I prioritized the Reddit share button over the Facebook share button. This change increased the amount of traffic I received from Reddit because people had the visual reminder to share the post with their friends and vote for posts as favorites.

I was able to continue to drill down from there. Not only did I have the information on where my content was being shared, but also, I was able to garner more information for analytics. Posts that had a picture mixed in with the first three paragraphs often had a lower *bounce rate* (the interval of time it takes for a visitor to visit a site and then bounce away to a different site) than posts that had no picture at all. If I wrote the post while elevating my left leg and wearing a tinfoil helmet, I saw a 25 percent bump in traffic. (Okay, maybe that last one isn't true.)

Exploring the Options for Tracking Data

You have a lot of options when it comes to tracking data on your site. Google Analytics is the most popular tool, but several options are available. Analytics is popular because of its widespread use, the amount of content written on how to maximize it, and the fact that it's free.

Here are three popular tools:

» **StatCounter** (`https://statcounter.com`)**:** StatCounter has both a free and a paid service. The paid service doesn't kick in until you get to 250K Pageviews a month.

StatCounter (shown in Figure 3-1) uses the log generated by your server and gives you the ability to configure the reports to fit your needs. If you want to use a log file, you need to have a self-hosted blog and to know where your log file is stored. StatCounter requires a little more technical knowledge than your average analytics app because you have to deal with your log file instead of cutting and pasting a line of code into your site. The main advantage of StatCounter is that it reports in real time, whereas Google Analytics always has a little bit of lag in its reporting.

FIGURE 3-1: StatCounter offers real-time stats.

» **Jetpack** (`https://wordpress.org/plugins/jetpack`)**:** The Jetpack plugin provides a pretty good stat package for its hosted-blog users. Shortly after launching, WordPress.com provided a WordPress Stats plugin that self-hosted users can use. (See Figure 3-2.) If you use this package, your stats appear on the WordPress Dashboard, but to drill down deeper into them, you need to access the stats on WordPress.com. The advantages of WordPress stats are that they're pretty easy to install and present a very simplified overview of your data. On the down side, they don't drill as deep as Google Analytics, and the reporting isn't as in-depth. Neither can you customize reports.

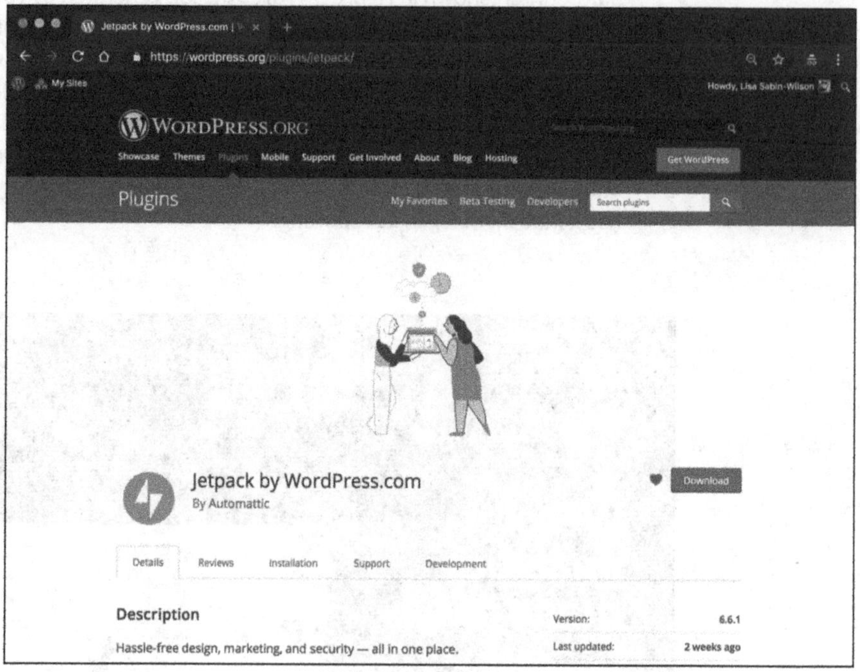

FIGURE 3-2: Try the Jetpack plugin.

- **Google Analytics** (`https://marketingplatform.google.com/about/analytics`)**:** Google Analytics can seem overwhelming when you sit in front of it for the first time, but it has the most robust stats features this side of Omniture. (Omniture is an enterprise-level stats package, which is overkill if you're a personal or small-business site owner.)

  WordPress plugins (covered in "Adding Google Analytics to Your WordPress Site" later in this chapter) bring a simplified version of Google Analytics (see Figure 3-3) to your WordPress Dashboard, much like the WordPress.com Stats plugin. If you feel overwhelmed by Google Analytics and prefer to have your stats broken down in a much more digestible fashion, this plugin is for you: It provides a good overview of analytics information, including goals that you can set up. Although the plugin doesn't offer everything that Google Analytics brings to the table, it provides more than enough so that you can see the overall health of your website and monitor where your traffic is coming from, what posts are popular, and how people are finding your website. Besides the Dashboard Stats Overview, this plugin gives you a breakdown of traffic to each post, which is a nice bonus.

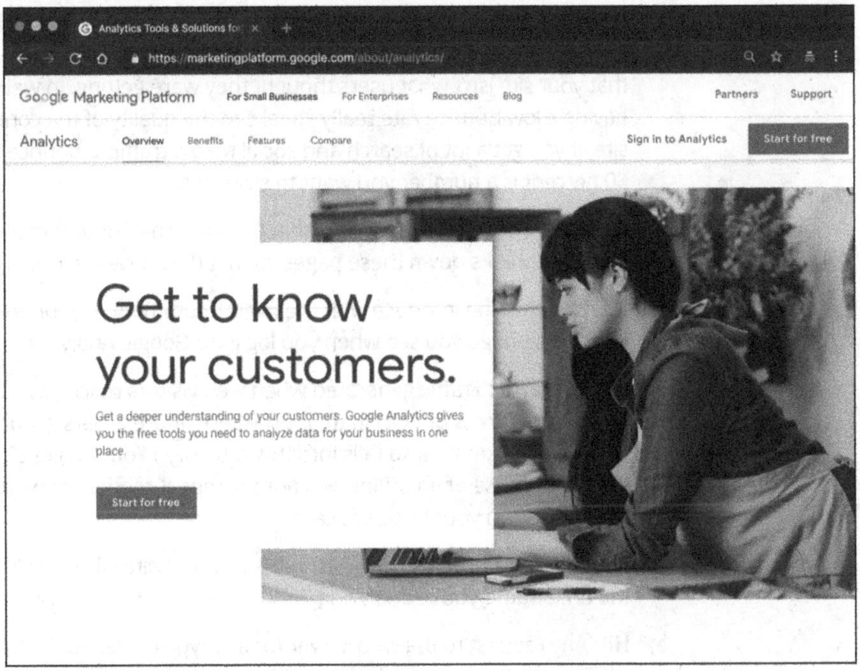

FIGURE 3-3: Google Analytics is a powerful tool.

Understanding Key Analytics Terminology

One of the reasons why people find analytics programs so overwhelming is that they use obscure terminology and jargon. Here, I've taken the time to define some of the most popular terms. (I even spent the time to put them in alphabetical order for you; you can thank me later.)

- **Bounce rate:** The percentage of single-page visits or visits in which the person leaves your site from the entrance page. This metric measures visit quality. A high bounce rate generally indicates that visitors don't find your site entrance pages relevant to them.

  The more compelling your landing pages are, the more visitors stay on your site and convert to purchasers or subscribers, or complete whatever action you want them to complete. You can minimize bounce rates by tailoring landing pages to each ad that you run (in the case of businesses) or to the audience based on the referring site (a special bio page for your Twitter profile, for example). Landing pages should provide the information and services that the ad promises.

When it comes to site content, a high bounce rate from a social media source (such as a social news site like Reddit) can tell you that users didn't find the content interesting, and a high bounce rate from search engines can mean that your site isn't what users thought they were getting. In web publishing, having a low bounce rate really speaks to the quality of the content on your site. If you get a lot of search and social media traffic, a bounce rate below 50 percent is a number you want to strive for.

- **Content:** The different pages within the site. (The Content menu of Google Analytics breaks down these pages so that they have their own statistics.)
- **Dashboard:** The interface with the overall summary of your analytics data. It's the first page you see when you log in to Google Analytics.
- **Direct traffic:** Traffic generated when web visitors reach your site by typing your web address directly in their browsers' address bars. (Launching a site by clicking a bookmark also falls into this category.) You can get direct-traffic visitors because of an offline promotion, repeat readers or word of mouth, or simply from your business card.
- **First-time unique visitor:** A visitor to your website who hasn't visited before the time frame you're analyzing.
- **Hit:** Any request to the web server for any type of file, not just a post on your site, including a page, an image (JPEG, GIF, PNG, and so on), a sound clip, or any of several other file types. An HTML page can account for several hits: the page itself, each image on the page, and any embedded sound or video clips. Therefore, the number of hits a website receives doesn't give you a valid popularity gauge, but indicates server use and how many files have been loaded.
- **Keyword:** A database index entry that identifies a specific record or document. (That definition sounds way fancier than a keyword actually is.) Keyword searching is the most common form of text search on the web. Most search engines do text query and retrieval by using keywords. Unless the author of the web document specifies the keywords for his or her document (which you can do by using meta tags), the search engine has to determine them. (So you can't guarantee how Google indexes the page.) Essentially, search engines pull out and index words that it determines are significant. A search engine is more likely to deem words important if those words appear toward the beginning of a document and are repeated several times throughout the document.

- **Meta tag:** A special HTML tag that provides information about a web page. Unlike normal HTML tags, meta tags don't affect how the page appears in a user's browser. Instead, meta tags provide information such as who created the page, how often it's updated, the title of the page, a description of the page's content, and keywords that represent the page's content. Many search engines use this information when they build their indexes, although most major search engines rarely index the `keywords` meta tag anymore because it has been abused by people trying to fool search results.
- **Pageview:** Refers to the number of unique views a web page has received. A *page* is defined as any file or content delivered by a web server that generally would be considered to be a web document, which includes HTML pages (`.html`, `.htm`, `.shtml`), posts or pages within a WordPress installation, script-generated pages (`.cgi`, `.asp`, `.cfm`), and plain-text pages. It also includes sound files (`.wav`, `.aiff`, and so on), video files (`.mov`, `.mpeg`, and so on), and other nondocument files. Only image files (`.jpeg`, `.gif`, `.png`), JavaScript (`.js`), and Cascading Style Sheets (`.css`) are excluded from this definition. Each time a file defined as a page is served or viewed in a visitor's web browser, a *pageview* is registered by Google Analytics. The pageview statistic is more important and accurate than a hit statistic because it doesn't include images or other items that may register hits on your site.
- **Path:** A series of clicks that results in distinct pageviews. A path can't contain nonpages, such as image files.
- **Referral:** Event that occurs when a user clicks any hyperlink that takes him or her to a page or file in another website, which could be text, an image, or any other type of link. When a user arrives at your site from another site, the server records the referral information in the hit log for every file requested by that user. If the user found the link by using a search engine, the server records the search engine's name and any keywords used as well. Referrals give you an indication of what social-media sites, as well as links from other websites, are directing traffic to your site.
- **Referrer:** The URL of an HTML page that refers visitors to a site.
- **Traffic sources:** A metric that tells you how visitors found your website, such as via direct traffic, referring sites, or search engines.
- **Unique visitors:** The number of unduplicated (counted only once) visitors to your website over the course of a specified time period. The server determines a unique visitor by using *cookies,* which are small tracking files stored in your visitors' browsers that keep track of the number of times they visit your site.

» **Visitor:** A stat designed to come as close as possible to defining the number of distinct people who visit a website. The website, of course, can't really determine whether any one "visitor" is really two people sharing a computer, but a good visitor-tracking system can come close to the actual number. The most accurate visitor-tracking systems generally employ cookies to maintain tallies of distinct visitors.

Adding Google Analytics to Your WordPress Site

In the following sections, you sign up for Google Analytics, install it on your blog, and add the WordPress plugin to your site.

Signing up for Google Analytics

To sign up for Google Analytics, follow these steps:

1. **Go to** `https://marketingplatform.google.com/about/analytics`**, and click the Start For Free button, which is located in the top-right corner of the page.**

   A page where you can sign up for a Google account or sign in via an existing Google account appears. If you don't have a Google account, follow the link to sign up for one.

2. **Sign in via your Google account by entering your email address and password in the text boxes and then clicking Sign In.**

   The first of a series of walk-through pages appears.

3. **Click the Sign Up button.**
4. **On the page that appears (see Figure 3-4), fill in this information:**
   - *Account Name:* A name to identify your account (which doesn't matter; you can put your own name here)
   - *Website Name:* The name of the website you want to track.
   - *Website URL:* The URL of your website
   - *Industry Category:* The industry category of your website
   - *Reporting Time Zone:* The country and time zone you're in

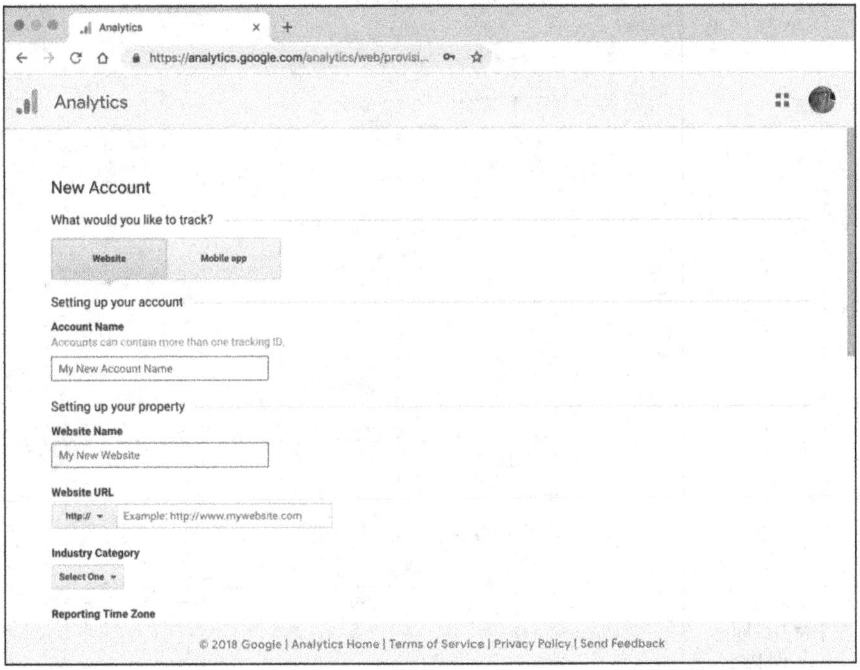

FIGURE 3-4: New Account page in Google Analytics.

5. **Scroll down to see and click the Get Tracking ID button.**

   The Tracking ID page appears. (See Figure 3-5.)

6. **Copy the tracking ID by selecting it and pressing Ctrl+C on a PC or ⌘+C on a Mac.**

7. **Paste the Google tracking code into your WordPress site.**

   If you're not sure how to complete this step, see "Installing the tracking code" later in this chapter.

8. **Click the Save and Finish button.**

Installing the tracking code

After you set up your Google Analytics account and obtain the tracking ID to install in your WordPress site, you're ready for the installation. The easiest way to accomplish this task is to use the Google Analytics plugin for WordPress (`https://wordpress.org/plugins/googleanalytics`) by following these steps:

1. **Log in to your WordPress Dashboard.**

2. **Click the Add New link on the Plugins menu.**

   The Add Plugins screen appears.

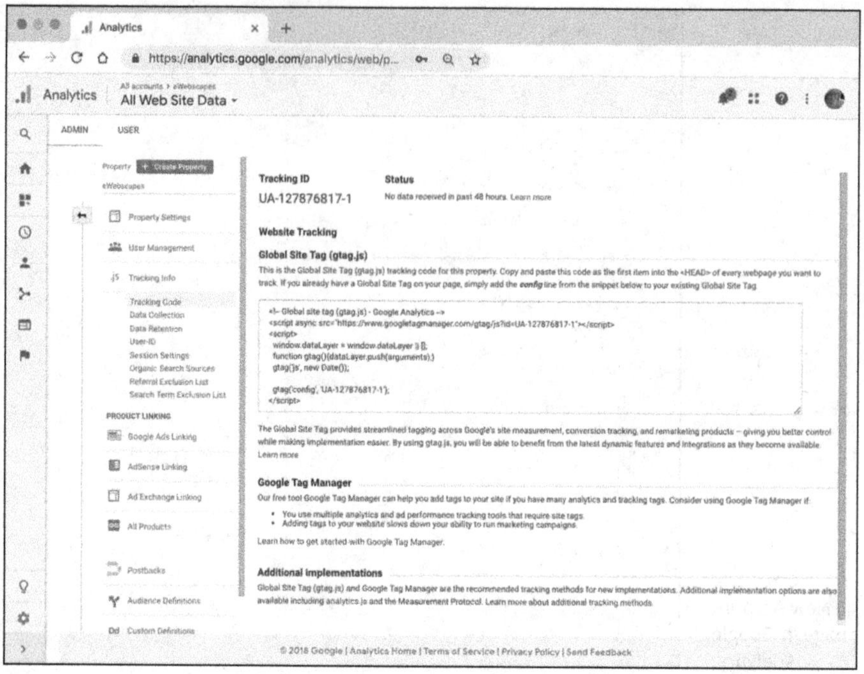

FIGURE 3-5: The Tracking ID page.

3. **Search for the Google Analytics plugin, and install and activate it.**
4. **Click the Settings link in the Google Analytics menu.**

   The Google Analytics Setting screen appears.
5. **Authenticate with your Google account by clicking the link on this page.**

   When you've authenticated with your Google account, Google gives you an access code that you need to copy and paste into the Access Code text field in the resulting window. (See Figure 3-6.)
6. **Click the Save Changes button.**

   This step saves your access code and reloads the Settings screen.
7. **Choose the website property you want to add from the Google Analytics Account drop-down menu.**

   If you have more than one Google Analytics property in your account, all these properties appear in this drop-down menu. Choose the one that you want to associate with the site you're currently on.
8. **Click the Save Changes button at the bottom of the Settings screen.**

   This action saves the configuration settings you made, and also inserts the correct JavaScript code into your website so that Google Analytics can start tracking your website stats.

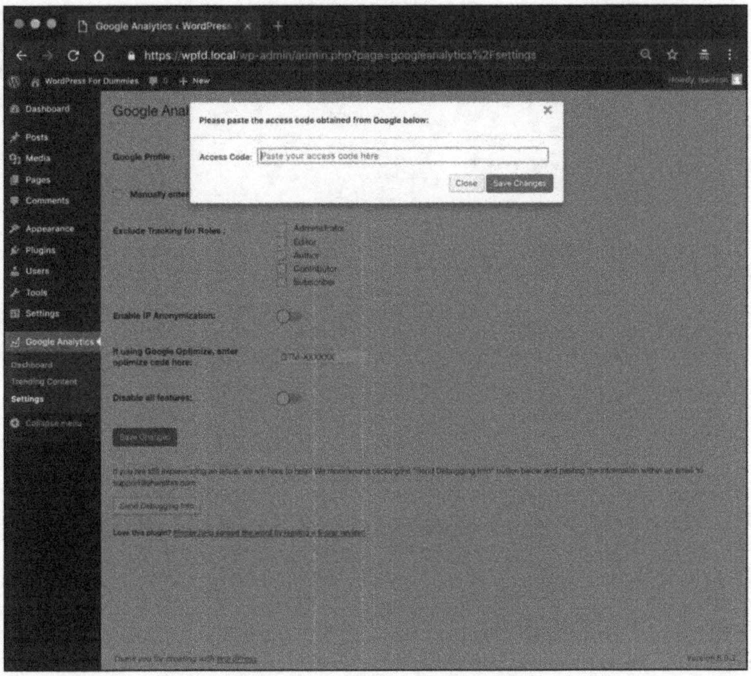

FIGURE 3-6: Adding the Google Analytics access code on the Settings screen.

Verifying that you installed the code properly

After you install your code, check whether you installed it correctly. When you log back in to Google Analytics, your Dashboard appears. (See Figure 3-8.) The Dashboard shows that Google is receiving data from your website, which means that the installation of your tracking ID was a success. (See Figure 3-7.)

Installing and configuring the Analytics Dashboard plugin

Another plugin that I like to use is the Google Analytics Dashboard plugin, which not only installs the Google Analytics Tracking code on your website, but also generates a handy analytics report right in the WordPress Dashboard. To install this plugin, follow these steps:

1. **Log in to your WordPress Dashboard.**
2. **On the Plugins menu, click the Add New link.**

   A search box appears.

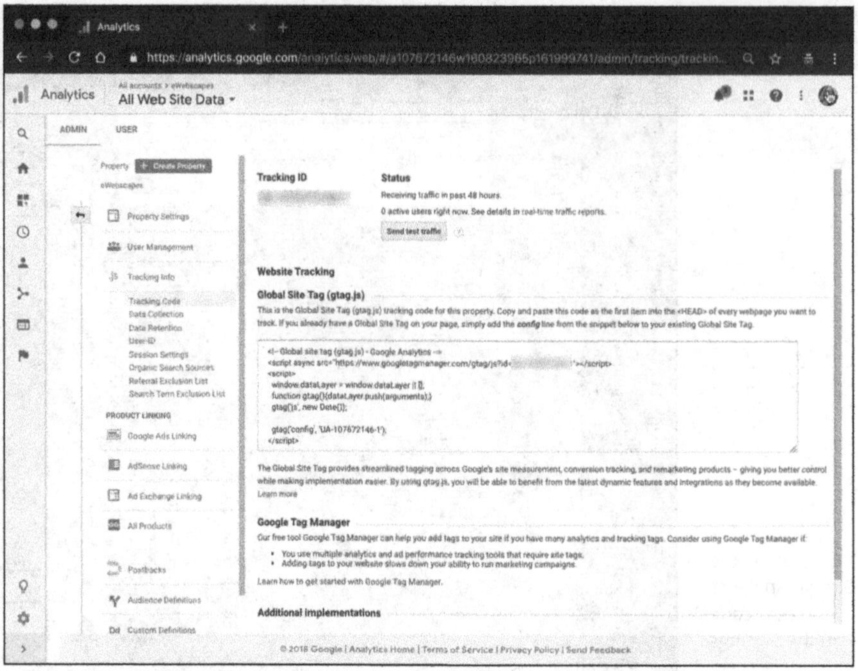

FIGURE 3-7: Tracking code in place and collecting data.

3. **In the Search text box, type** google analytics dashboard **and then click the Install Now link.**

   This step takes you to the Installing Plugin page.

4. **Activate the plugin by clicking the Activate button.**
5. **Click the Google Analytics link on the WordPress Dashboard menu.**

   You see the Google Analytics Settings – Plugin Authorization screen.

6. **Click the Authorize Plugin button.**

   You see a page where you log in to your Google account; then the Google Analytics Settings screen reloads.

7. **Click the Get Access Code link.**

   You see a page where Google gives you an access code; copy that code.

8. **Enter the access code from step 7 in the Access Code text box on the Google Analytics screen in your Dashboard.**
9. **Click the Save Access Code button.**

   The Google Analytics Settings screen appears. (See Figure 3-8.)

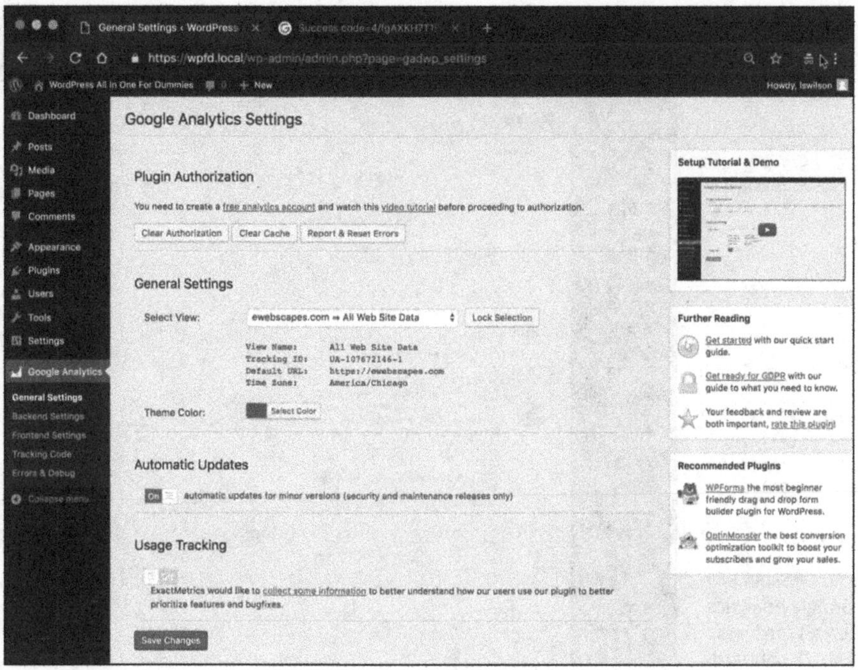

FIGURE 3-8: The Google Analytics Settings screen.

10. From the Select View drop-down menu, choose the analytics account from which you want to pull your stats.

11. Click the Save Changes button.

The plugin appears on your Dashboard.

12. Drag and drop the plugin to the position you prefer.

Figure 3-9 shows a WordPress Dashboard with the Google Analytics plugin displayed in the top-right corner.

Using the data from the plugin

After you install Google Analytics on your WordPress Dashboard, you can examine the data that it provides. Your Dashboard displays analytics stats, such as Sessions, Users, Pageviews, Bounce Rate, Organic Search, Pages/Session, Time on Page, Page Load Time, and Session Duration. These stats can be filtered by options such as Real-Time, Today, Yesterday, Last 7 Days, Last 14 Days, Last 30 Days, Last 90 Days, One Year, and Three Years.

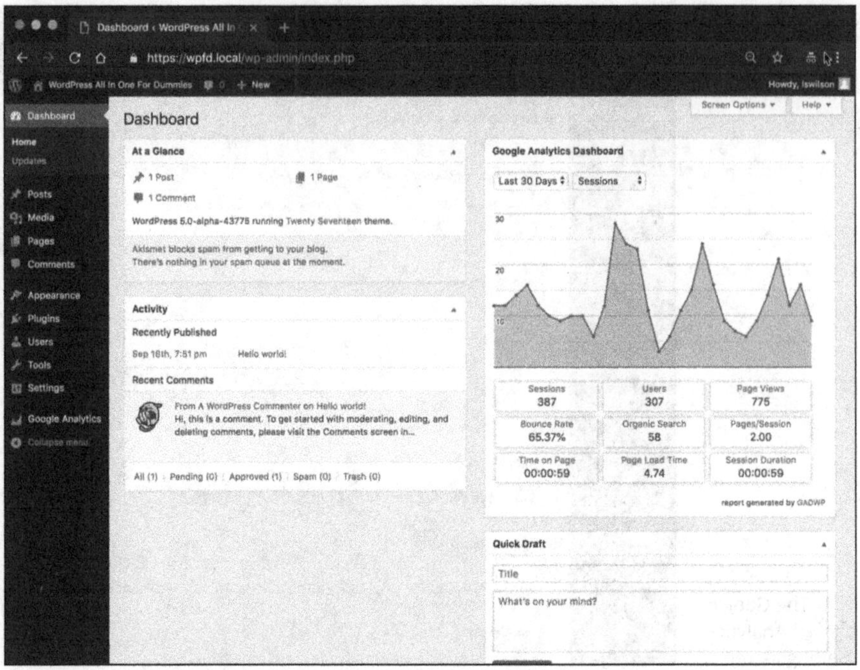

FIGURE 3-9: Google Analytics on a WordPress Dashboard.

These stats show you the most popular content on your site, the ways people are finding your site, and the sources of your traffic. If you want even more detailed information on high-performing individual pages, you can configure the Dashboard widget to display the number of views on Pages (see Figure 3-10) by choosing Pages from the second drop-down menu; this setting displays per-page stats for your site.

By examining the two data sets, you can get a handle on the traffic that's coming to your blog. Pay attention to the data, and use it to answer the following questions:

- What posts are popular?
- Do the popular posts have a unique theme or type?
- Do long posts or short posts help increase traffic?
- Do videos, lists, or any other specific types of posts give you more traffic than the rest?

The answers to these questions can help you draw various conclusions and adapt your publishing schedule, content type, and writing style to optimize the popularity of your website.

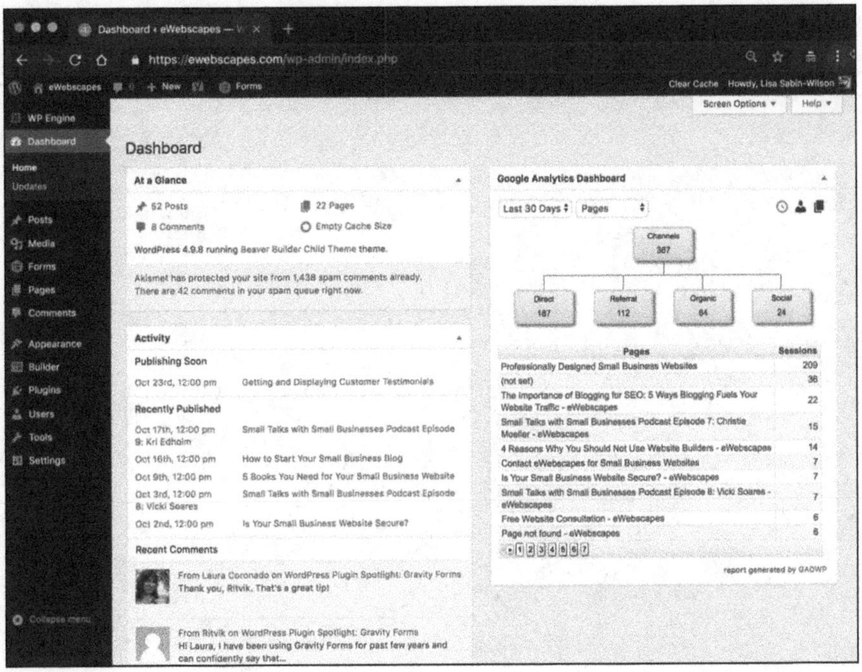

FIGURE 3-10: A per-page breakdown by Google Analytics for WordPress.

IN THIS CHAPTER

» Appreciating SEO benefits

» Improving your SEO with WordPress

» Getting your blog into good SEO shape

» Finding information about your niche

» Creating SEO-improvement strategies

Chapter 4
Search Engine Optimization

Google, Yahoo!, Bing, and other search engines have a massive impact on a website. Search engines can easily refer the largest amount of traffic to your site and, if dealt with properly, can help you grow a large audience over time. Often, bloggers don't discover the importance of search engine optimization (SEO) until their sites have been around for a while. By taking the time to make sure that you're following SEO best practices from the get-go, you can reap the rewards of a consistent flow of search engine traffic.

If you've been publishing content on the web for a while and haven't been following the practices in this chapter, roll up your sleeves and dive back into your site to fix some of the SEO practices that you may have overlooked (or just didn't know about) over the history of your website. If you've been publishing content on your website for only a few months, this process doesn't take long. If you have a large backlog of content . . . well, pull up a chair; this fix is going to take a while. But don't worry; you're in safe hands. This chapter helps you through the difficult task of optimizing your site for search engines.

Understanding the Importance of Search Engine Optimization

Talk about SEO usually puts most people to sleep. I'm not going to lie: Hardcore SEO is a time-consuming job that requires a strong analytical mind. Casual bloggers and even most small-business owners don't need to understand all the minute details that go into SEO. Everyone with a website who desires traffic, however, needs to get familiar with some of the basic concepts and best practices. Why, you ask?

One thousand pageviews. That's why.

You're not going to get 1,000 Pageviews right off the bat by changing your SEO, of course. SEO deals with following best practices when it comes to writing content on the web. By following these simple guidelines and by using WordPress, you can increase search engine traffic to your site. Period. To be honest, you probably won't rank number one in really tough categories just by following SEO best practices. But you definitely can increase your traffic significantly and improve your rank for some long-tail keywords. *Long-tail keywords* are keywords that aren't searched for often, but when you amass ranking for a lot of them over a period of time, the traffic adds up.

REMEMBER

You want as many search results as possible on the first two pages of Google and other search engines to be from your site(s). (Most search-engine visitors don't go past the first two pages of Google.) This search-results aim is a more reasonable goal than trying to rank number one for a highly competitive keyword.

TIP

If you really do want to rank number one in a competitive space, check out sites such as SEOBook (`www.seobook.com`) and Moz (`https://moz.com`), which can help you achieve that difficult goal.

Outlining the Advantages That WordPress Presents for SEO

Using WordPress as your content management system comes with some advantages, including the fact that WordPress is designed to function well with search engines. Search engines can crawl the source code of a WordPress site pretty easily, which eliminates issues that a lot of web programmers face when optimizing a site. The following list outlines some of WordPress's SEO advantages:

» **Permalinks:** URLs where your content is permanently housed. As your site grows and you add more content, the items on your front page get pushed and replaced by recent content. Visitors can easily bookmark and share permalinks so that they can return to that specific post on your site, so these old articles can live on. One of the technical benefits of WordPress is that it uses the Apache `mod_rewrite` module to establish the permalink system, which allows you to create and customize your permalink structure. (See Book 3, Chapter 2 for more information on custom permalinks.)

» **Pinging:** When you post new content, WordPress has a built-in pinging system that notifies major indexes automatically so that they can come crawl your site again. This system helps speed the indexing process and keeps your search results current and relevant.

» **Plugins:** The fact that WordPress is so developer-friendly allows you to use the latest SEO plugins. Do you want to submit a site map to Google? There's a plugin for that. Do you want to edit the metadata of a post? There's a plugin for that. More than 56,000 plugins were available in the WordPress Plugins repository at press time, which means that you can use an advanced plugin ecosystem to help power your website. Book 5, Chapter 5 covers a few key plugins that can help you with SEO.

» **Theme construction:** SEO, social media, and design go hand in hand. You can push a ton of people to your web page by using proper SEO and robust social media profiles, but if your site has a confusing or poorly done design, visitors aren't going to stay. Likewise, a poorly designed site prevents a lot of search engines from reading your content.

  In this situation, *poorly designed* doesn't refer to aesthetics — how your site looks to the eye. Search engines ignore the style of your site and your CSS, for the most part. But the structure — the coding — of your site can affect search engines that are attempting to crawl your site. WordPress is designed to accommodate search engines: It doesn't overload pages with code so that search engines can easily access the site. Most WordPress themes have valid code, which is code that's up to standards based on the recommendations of the World Wide Web Consortium (`https://www.w3.org`). Right from the start, having valid code allows search engines to access your site much more easily.

REMEMBER

When you start changing your code or adding a lot of plugins to your site, check to see whether your code validates. *Validated* code means that the code on your website fits a minimum standard for browsers. Otherwise, you could be preventing search engines from easily crawling your sites.

TIP

If you want to check out whether your site validates, use the free validator tool at `http://validator.w3.org`. (See Figure 4-1.)

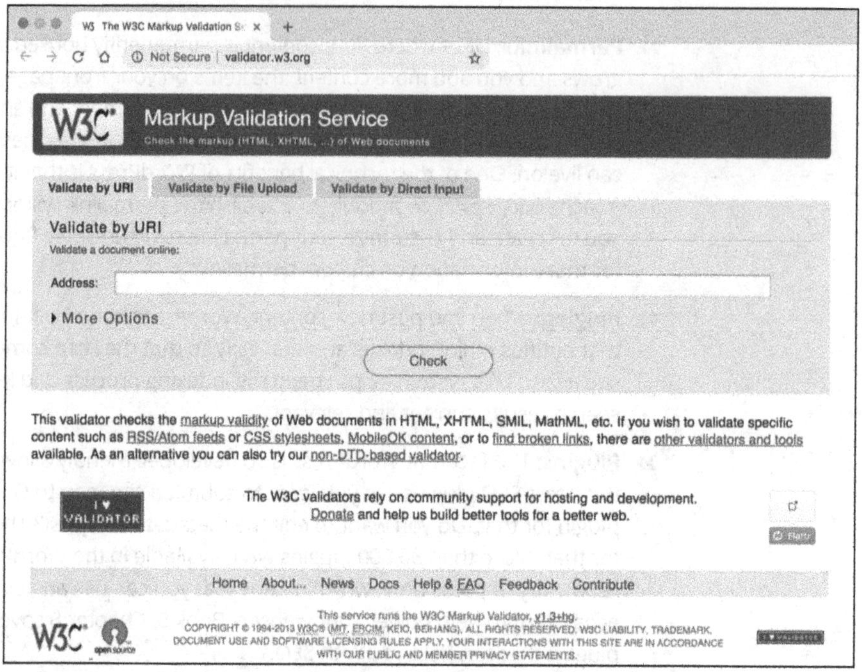

FIGURE 4-1: The W3C Markup Validation Service.

Understanding How Search Engines See Your Content

Search engines don't care what your site looks like because they can't see what your site looks like; their crawlers care only about the content. The crawlers care about the material on your site, the way it's titled, the words you use, and the way you structure those words.

You need to keep this focus in mind when you create the content of your site. Your URL structure and the keywords, post titles, and images you use in posts all have an effect on how your website ranks. Having a basic understanding of how search engines view your content can help you write content that's more attractive to search engines. Here are a few key areas to think about when you craft your content:

- **Keywords in content:** Search engines take an intense look at the keywords or combination of keywords you use. Keywords are often compared with the words within links that guide people to the post and in the title of the post itself to see whether they match. The better these keywords align, the better ranking you get from the search engine.

- **Post title:** Search engines analyze the title of your post or page for keyword content. If you're targeting a specific keyword in your content, and that keyword is mentioned throughout the post, mention it in the post title as well. Also, both people and search engines place a lot of value on the early words of a title.
- **URL structure:** One of the coolest things about WordPress is the way it allows you to edit permalinks for a post or page. (See Figure 4-2.) You can always edit the URL to be slightly different from the automated post title so that it contains relevant keywords for search terms, especially if you write a cute title for the post.

  Suppose that you write a post about reviewing Facebook applications and title it "So Many Facebook Applications, So Little Time." You can change the URL structure to something much more keyword-based — perhaps something like `facebook-applications-review`. This reworking removes a lot of the fluff words from the URL and goes right after keywords you want to target.

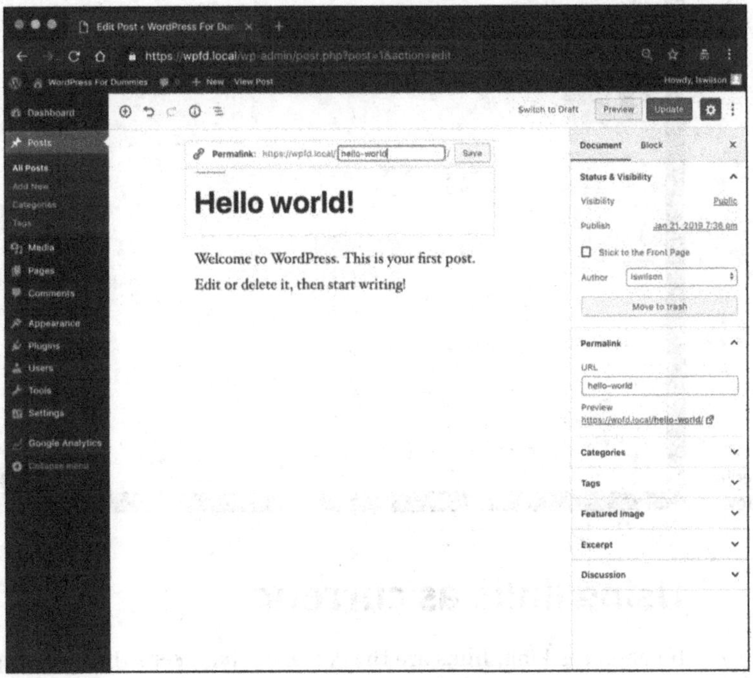

FIGURE 4-2: Editing a permalink.

- **Image titles and other image information:** This item is probably the most-missed item when it comes to SEO. You need to fill out the image information for your posts in the Select or Upload Media window (see Figure 4-3) because this information is a powerful way for people to discover your content and an additional piece of content that can tie keywords to your posts. This information includes the filename of your image. Saving an image file to your site as `DS-039.jpg`, for example, offers nothing for readers or search engines and thus has no value to search engines or for you because it doesn't contain a real keyword. Name a picture of a Facebook application, for example, `Facebook-application.jpg`. Leverage the keyword title and alt tags (alternative text added to the image within the HTML markup that tells search engines what the picture is) because they provide extra content for the search engines to see, and using them can help you get a little more keyword saturation within your posts.

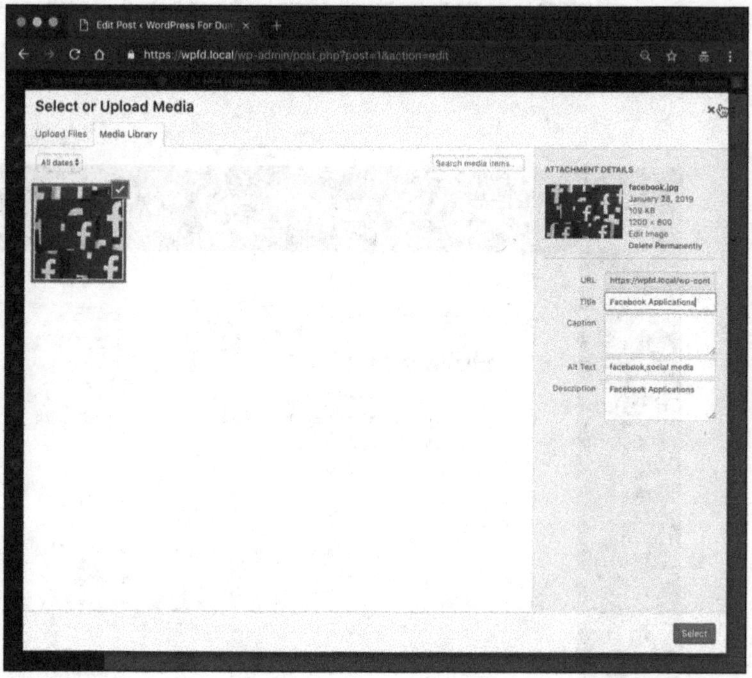

FIGURE 4-3: The Add Media window.

Using links as currency

If content is king, links are the currency that keeps the king in power. No matter how good a site you have, how great your content is, and how well you optimize that content, you need links. Search engines assess the links flowing into your site for number and quality, and they evaluate your website accordingly.

If a high-quality site that has high Google search rankings features a link to your page, search engines take notice and assume that you have some authority on a subject. Search engines consider these high-quality links to be more important than low-quality links. Having a good amount of mid-quality links, however, can help as well. (This tactic, like many well-known approaches to improving site rank, is based only on trial and error. Google keeps its algorithm a secret, so no one knows for sure.)

Being included in a listing of links on a site, having a pingback or trackback when other authors mention your content in their articles, or even leaving a comment on someone's site can provide links back to your site. If you want to check out how many links you currently have coming to your site, go to Google, type **link:** `www.`*`yoursite`*`.com` in the search text box, and click Google Search. You can also search for competitors' sites to see where they're listed and to what sites they're linked.

Although you do need to try to get other sites to link to your site (called outside links) because outside links factor into search engine algorithms, you can help your own ranking by adding internal links. If you have an authoritative post or page on a particular subject, you should link internally to it within your site. Take ESPN.com (`http://www.espn.com`), for example. The first time this site mentions an athlete in an article, it links to the profile of that athlete on the site. It essentially tells the search engines each time they visit ESPN.com that the player profile has relevancy, and the search engine indexes it. If you repeatedly link some of your internal pages that are gaining page rank to a profile page over a period of time, that profile page is going to garner a higher search engine ranking (especially if external sites are linking to it too).

This internal and external linking strategy uses the concept of pillar posts (authoritative or popular), in which you have a few pages of content that you consider to have high value and try to build external and internal links to them so that you can get these posts ranked highly in search results.

Submitting to search engines and directories

After you get some content on your website (ten posts or so), submit your website to some search engines. Plenty of sites out there charge you to submit your site to search engines, but honestly, you can submit your site easily yourself. Also, with the help of some plugins (described in Book 5, Chapter 5), you can get your information to search engines even more easily than you may think.

After you submit your website or site map, a search engine reviews it for search engine crawling errors; if everything checks out, you're on your way to having your site crawled and indexed. This process — from the submission of your site through its first appearance in search engine results — can easily take four to six weeks, so be patient. Don't resubmit, and don't freak out that search engines are never going to list your site. Give the process time.

Not to be confused with search engines are website and blog directories. Directories can lead to a small amount of traffic, and some directories, such as Online Society (`www.onlinesociety.org`), actually supply information to search engines and other directories. The main benefit of getting listed in directories isn't really traffic but the amount of backlinks (links to your site from other websites) that you can build into your site.

TIP

Although submitting your site to directories may not be as important as submitting to search engines, you may still want to do it. Because filling out 40 or more forms is pretty monotonous, create a single document in which you prewrite all the necessary information: site title, URL, description, contact information, and your registration information. This template helps speed the submission process to these sites.

Optimizing Your Site under the Hood

Some optimization concepts happen under the hood. You can't readily see these adjustments on your page, but they have an effect on how search engines deal with your content.

Metadata

The metadata on a website contains the information that describes to search engines what your site is about. Additionally, the information often contained in the metadata shows up as the actual search engine results in Google. The search engine pulls the page title and page description that appear in search results from the header of your site. If you do nothing to control this information, Google and other search engines often pull their description from the page title and the first few sentences of a post or page.

Although the title and the first few sentences sound good in principle, they probably don't represent what your site is actually about. You probably don't sum up your topic in the first two sentences of a post or page. Those first few lines likely aren't the best ad copy or the most enticing information. Fortunately, some plugins (such as the Yoast SEO plugin, which is on the WordPress Plugins page at `https://wordpress.org/plugins/wordpress-seo`) allow you to control these details on a post and page level. Additionally, some theme frameworks (see Book 6, Chapter 7) such as Genesis offer you more control of your SEO information.

Include descriptive page titles, descriptions, and targeted keywords for each post via these plugins or frameworks. This information has an effect on your results and often helps people decide to click the link to your website.

The robots.txt file

When a search engine goes to your website, it first looks at your `robots.txt` file to get the information about what it should and shouldn't be looking for and where to look.

You can alter your `robots.txt` file to direct search engines to the information that they should crawl and to give specific content priority over other content. Several plugins allow you to configure your `robots.txt` file.

Researching Your Niche

When you're working to improve your SEO, you can use a lot of publicly available data. This data can help you determine where you should try to get links and what type of content you may want to target. These two sites can help you get a general picture of the niche you're working in:

- **Google** (`https://www.google.com`): You can find what types of links are flowing into a website by typing **link:** `www.`*`yoursite`*`.com` in the Google search text box and clicking Google Search. (Replace *yoursite.com* with the domain you want to target.) Google gives you a list of the sites linking to your site. By doing this search for other websites in your niche, you can find out the sources of their links — industry-specific directories you may not know about, places where they've guest-authored, and other resource sites that you may be able to get listed on.

  This data gives you information about what to target for a link-building campaign.
- **SEMrush** (`https://www.semrush.com`): SEMrush (see Figure 4-4) offers both paid and free versions, and spending a few dollars for a month's access to the light version of the product can be a good investment. (The free version lets you look up only ten results at a time.) SEMrush allows you to see the terms for which other websites rank. Use this information to judge the health of the

competitor's domain, the number of terms for which it ranks in Google's top 20, and the terms themselves.

You can use this information in a lot of ways. You can see what terms you may want to work into your content, for example. SEMrush provides not only information about what terms search engines use to rank these sites, but also information about how competitive your site's keywords are with the same keywords on other websites.

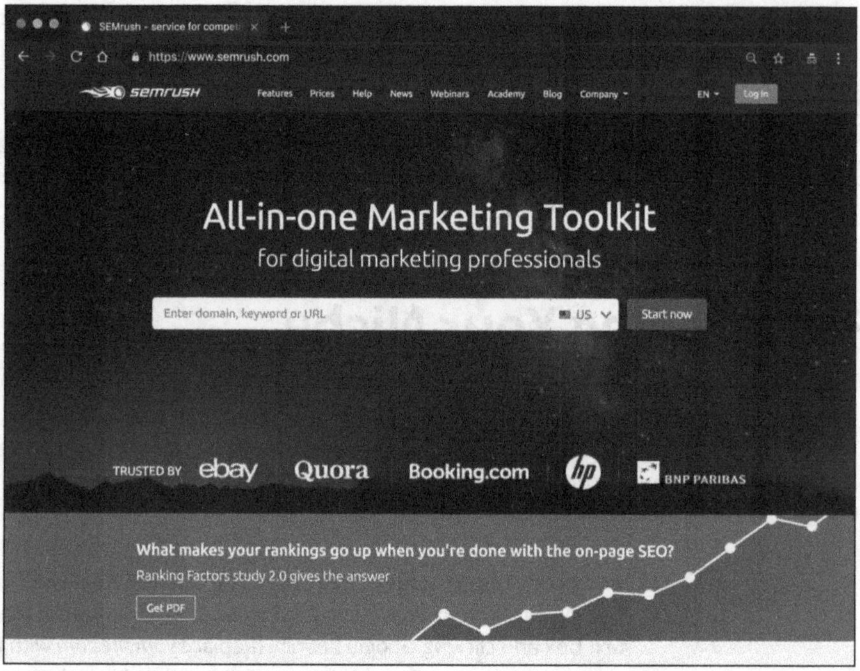

FIGURE 4-4: SEMrush helps you evaluate your competition.

Creating Search Engine Strategies

You can use the techniques discussed in previous sections of this chapter when you set up your site, write strategic content, and begin to build links into your website. The next section deals with setting up your website so that it's optimized for search engines.

Setting up your site

When setting up your site, you're going to want to follow some best practices to make sure that your site is optimized for search engines. Following are some of these best practices:

» **Permalinks:** First, set up your permalink structure. Log in to your WordPress account, and on the sidebar, select Permalinks in the Settings section. The Permalink Settings page appears. (See Figure 4-5.) Select the Post Name radio button.

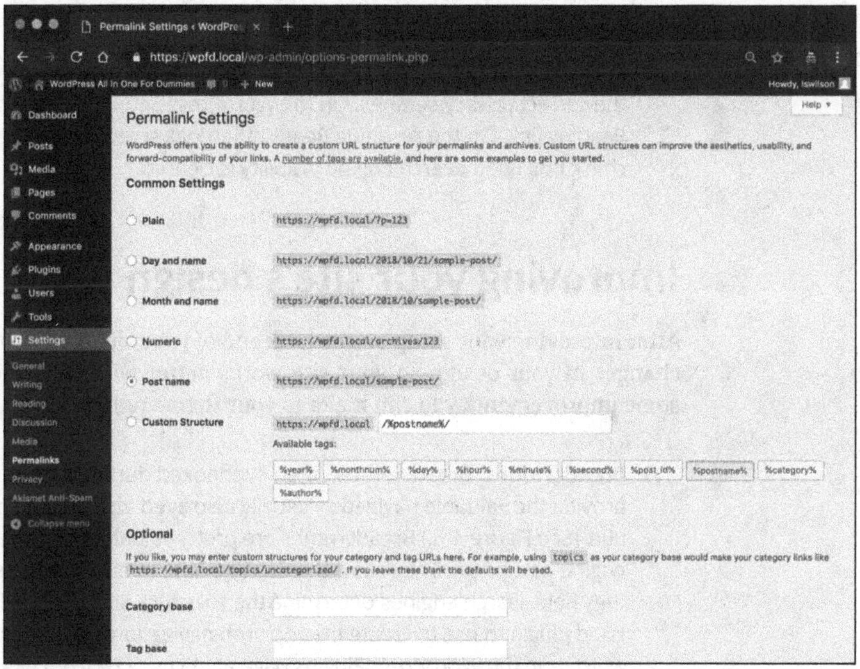

FIGURE 4-5: The WordPress Permalinks Settings page.

Making this change gives you a URL that contains just your domain and the title of your post. If you use a focused category structure in which you've carefully picked out keywords, you may want to add the category to the URL. In that case, you enter ***/%category%/%postname%/*** in the text box.

Avoid using the default URL structure, which includes just the number of your post, and don't use dates in the URL. These numbers have no real value when doing SEO. WordPress by default numbers all your posts and pages with specific ID numbers. If you haven't set up a custom permalink structure in

WordPress, permalinks for your posts end up looking something like this: `http://yourdomain.com/?p=12` (where 12 is the specific post ID number). Although these numbers are used for many WordPress features, including exclusions of data and customized RSS feeds, you don't want these numbers in your URLs because they don't contain any keywords that describe the post.

Also, if you already have an established site and are just now setting up these permalinks, you must take the time to install a redirection plugin. You can find several of these plugins available in the Plugin Directory on WordPress.org. You must establish redirection for your older content so that you don't lose the links that search engines, such as Google and Yahoo!, have already indexed for your site. One good redirection plugin to use is simply called Redirection; you can find it at `https://wordpress.org/plugins/redirection`.

- **Privacy:** You don't want your site to fail to be indexed because you didn't set the correct privacy settings. On the WordPress Settings menu, click the Reading link. On the resulting Reading Settings screen, make sure that the check box titled Search Engine Visibility is cleared.

Improving your site's design

After improving your setup on the back end of your site, you'll want to make some changes in your design so your site works better with search engines. Here are some improvements you can make to your theme templates:

- **Breadcrumbs:** Breadcrumbs, often overlooked during website creation, provide the valuable navigation usually displayed above on a page above the title. (See Figure 4-6.) Breadcrumbs are pretty valuable for usability and search engine navigation. They allow the average user to navigate the site easily, and they help search engines determine the structure and layout of your site. A good plugin to use to create breadcrumb navigation is Breadcrumb NavXT, which is in the WordPress Plugins page at `https://wordpress.org/plugins/breadcrumb-navxt`.
- **Validated code and speed:** If you're not a professional web designer, you probably don't do a lot of coding on your site. But if you make some small edits to your WordPress installation or add a lot of code through widgets, do it properly by putting it directly in your CSS rather than coding into your site. Coding these features properly helps improve the speed of your site and the way search engines crawl it. Book 6 contains a great deal of information about coding the templates in your theme; check out that minibook for more information about correct coding.

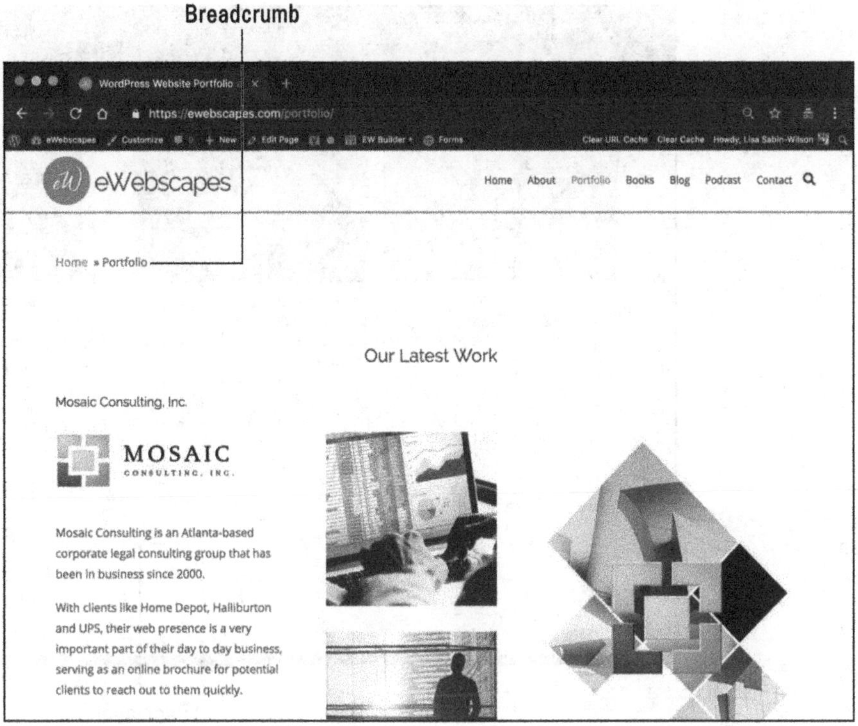

FIGURE 4-6: Users and search engines can follow the breadcrumbs.

When it comes to improving site speed, proper code has a lot to do with performance. You can take other steps to help improve the speed of your site, such as installing caching plugins, including the W3 Total Cache plugin (`https://wordpress.org/plugins/w3-total-cache`). The quality of your hosting (Book 2, Chapter 1), the size of your image files (make sure that you set image-file quality to web standards), the number of images you're using, and third-party widgets or scripts (such as installing a widget provided by Twitter or Facebook) can all affect the speed and performance of your site.

- **Pagination:** Another basic design feature that's often overlooked during site setup, *pagination* creates bottom navigation that allows people and search engines to navigate to other pages. (See Figure 4-7.) Pagination can really help both people and search engines navigate your category pages.

  Some themes don't have built-in pagination, so you may need to add a plugin to accomplish this effect. A few of these kinds of plugins are on the market; check out Book 5, Chapter 5.

REMEMBER

Links pass on authority. When you link to a site or a site links to you, the link is saying that your site has value for the keyword in the link. So evaluate the links that you have, and think about whether you really want to link to those websites.

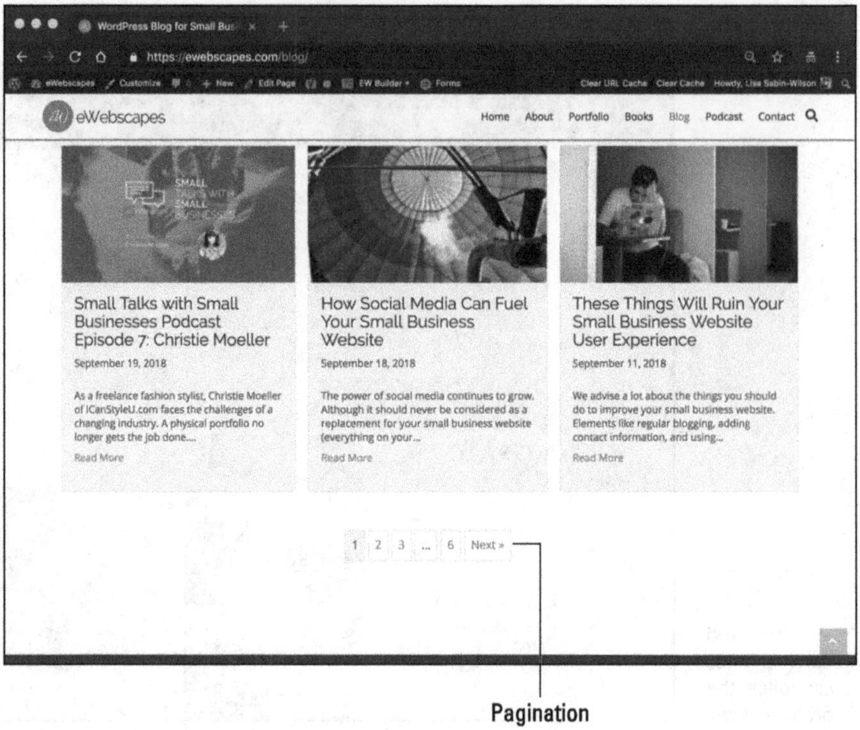

FIGURE 4-7: Pagination in action.

Dealing with duplicate content

WordPress does have one major problem when it comes to SEO: It creates so many places for your content to live that duplicate content can confuse search engines. Fortunately, plugins and some basic editing easily take care of these issues. Here's what to do:

- **Take care of your archive page on your site.** This page displays archives such as category, date-based archives, and so on. You don't want your archive page to present full posts — only truncated versions (short excerpts) of your posts. Check your theme to see how your archive is presented. If your archive shows complete posts, see whether your theme has instructions about how to change your archive presentation. (Each theme is unique, but check out the information in Book 6; it's full of great information about tweaking and altering theme template files.)
- **Make sure that search engines aren't indexing all your archives by using a robots plugin.** You want robots going through only your category archive, not the author index and other archives.

Creating an editorial SEO list/calendar

Planning your posts from now until the end of time can take some of the fun out of publishing. Still, it doesn't hurt to create a list of keywords that your competitors rank for and some of the content they've discussed. Take that list and apply it to new posts, or write *evergreen content* (topics that aren't time-sensitive) centered on what you want to say. Planning your content can really help in figuring out what keywords you want to target when you want to write content to improve for ranking for targeted keywords.

TIP

If you feel that your site content is more news- or current-events-oriented, create a reference list of keywords to incorporate into your newer posts so that you can rank for these targeted terms.

Establishing a routine for publishing on your site

Although you can't really call this high strategy, getting into the habit of posting content regularly on your site helps you get the basics down. Here are some things to keep in mind:

- **Properly title your post.** Make sure that your post includes the keyword or phrase for which you're trying to rank.
- **Fix your URL.** Get rid of stop words or useless words from your URL, and make sure that the keywords you want to target appear in the URL of your post. *Stop words* are filler words such as *a*, *so*, *in*, *an*, and so on. For a comprehensive list of stop words, check out `https://www.link-assistant.com/seo-stop-words.html`.
- **Choose a category.** Make sure that you have your categories set up and that you place your posts in the proper categories. Whatever you do, don't use the uncategorized category; it brings no SEO value to the table.
- **Fill out metadata.** If you're using a theme framework, the form for metadata often appears right below the post box. If you aren't using a theme framework, you can use the Yoast SEO plugin (`https://wordpress.org/plugins/wordpress-seo`) (see Figure 4-8). When activated, this plugin usually appears toward the bottom of your posting page. Make sure that you completely fill out the title, description, keywords, and other information that the plugin or theme framework asks for.
- **Tag posts properly.** You may want to get into the habit of taking the keywords from the Yoast SEO plugin and pasting them into the tags section of the post.

Search Engine Optimization

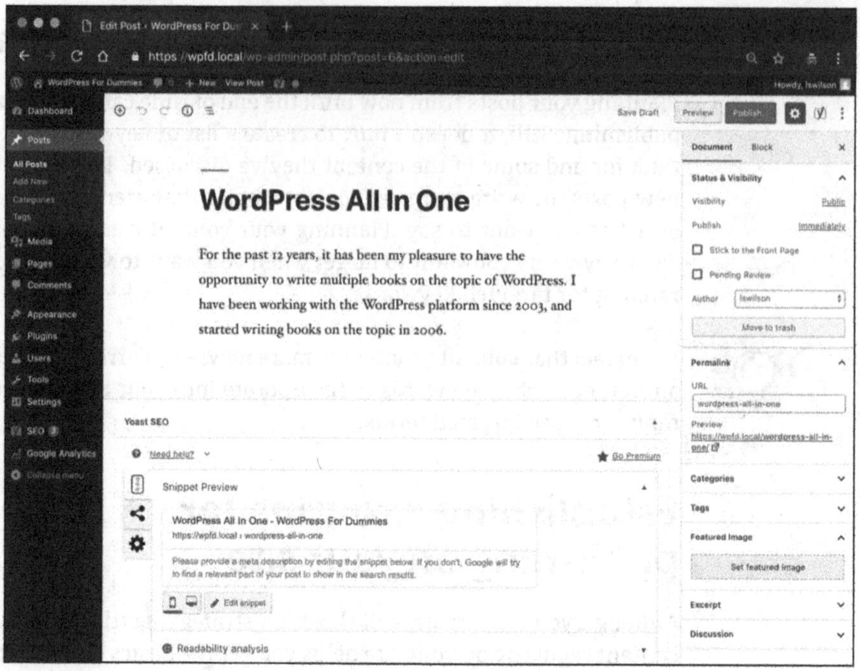

FIGURE 4-8: The Yoast SEO metadata form.

- **Fill out image info.** Take the time to completely fill out your image info whenever you upload pictures to your posts. Every time you upload an image to WordPress, you see a screen in which you can fill in the URL slug, description, and alt text for the image you've uploaded.

Creating a link-building strategy

In previous sections of this chapter, I tackle most of the onsite SEO strategy and concepts. In this section, I explain how you can start working on your off-page strategy. Here are some things to keep in mind:

- **Fill out your social media profiles.** As I discuss in Book 5, Chapter 1, a lot of social media sites pass on page rank through their profiles. Take the time to fill out your social media profile properly, and list your site in these profiles.

  Social media sites allow you to link to your site with a descriptive word. Industry professionals say that this link has value to search engines, which is debatable, but adding it can never hurt.

- **Use forum signatures.** If you participate in forums, you can easily generate traffic and earn some links to your website from other websites by including your site URL in your forum signature.
- **Examine your competitor's links.** See where your competitors or other people in your niche are getting links — such as directories, lists, guest blogs, and friends' sites — and then try to get links on those sites. Try to determine the relationships, and figure out whether you can establish a relationship with those sites as well.
- **Guest-author.** Find some of the top sites in your niche and then ask them whether you can guest-author. Guest-authoring gives you a link from a respected source and builds a relationship with other content creators. Also, guest-authoring can't hurt your subscriber numbers; often, you see a bump after you guest-author on a large site.
- **Use website directory registration.** Directory registration, albeit a time-consuming affair, can often provide a large number of backlinks to your site from respected sources.
- **Comment on other sites.** A lot of sites pass on page rank because the links in their comment section are live. Make sure that when you engage other people, you properly fill out your information before you post, including the URL to your site. Don't start posting inane comments on random sites to get links. Doing so is considered to be rude and can lead to your site's being marked as spam in various commenting systems.
- **Participate in social sharing.** Getting involved in Reddit, Facebook, Twitter, and other social communities allows you to participate in social media with people who have similar interests, and you can build links to your site by submitting content to social news and community sites.

IN THIS CHAPTER

» Using plugins for SEO best practices

» Breaking down your SEO configuration options

» Generating site maps

» Using redirect plugins

» Adding pagination

Chapter 5
Exploring Popular SEO Plugins

When you have the concepts of search engine optimization (SEO) down and the beginnings of your strategy properly mapped out, you can install the tools you need. In this chapter, I go through some of the most popular SEO-related plugins. All these plugins have good developers behind them and good track records.

Several plugins in the WordPress Plugins page assist with SEO, so it's hard to decide which ones to use. In Book 7, I cover plugins in detail, but in this chapter, I discuss the most common plugins, as well as the ones that I use myself, because they're solid, reliable plugins that deliver good SEO results.

Exploring Must-Use Plugins for SEO Best Practices

Here are the plugins that this chapter covers:

- **Yoast SEO:** Gives you complete control of the search-engine optimization of your site.

- **Google XML Sitemaps:** Generates an XML site map that's sent to Google, Yahoo!, Bing, and Ask.com. When your site has a site map, site crawlers can more efficiently crawl your site. One of the bonuses of the site map is that it notifies search engines every time you post.
- **Redirection:** Helps when you move from an old site to WordPress or when you want to change the URL structure of an established site. It allows you to manage 301 redirections (when the web address of a page has changed, a 301 redirect tells search engines where they can find the new web address of the page), track any 404 errors (errors that are displayed when you try to load a page that doesn't exist) that occur on the site, and manage any possible incorrect web address (URL) issues with your website.
- **WP-PageNavi:** Helps you achieve pagination for your WordPress site by allowing you to display page links at the bottom of each archive and/or category page.

TIP

Check out Book 7, Chapter 2 for information on plugin installation.

Yoast SEO

The Yoast SEO plugin (`https://wordpress.org/plugins/wordpress-seo`) makes your life much easier because it automates many SEO tasks for you. Of all the plugins I cover, this one is an absolute must for your site. It gives you a lot of control of your SEO, and it's very flexible.

This plugin breaks down each option on the configuration page, which allows you to preselect options right off the bat or make some changes to the plugin.

After you install this plugin, click the SEO link on the Dashboard to open the Yoast SEO Dashboard page, shown in Figure 5-1.

Then click the General tab and follow these steps:

1. **Click the Open the Configuration Wizard button.**

   This step opens the welcome page (refer to Figure 5-1) and starts the configuration process.

2. **Click the Configure Yoast SEO button.**

   This step takes you to the next page of the Yoast SEO for WordPress installation wizard and opens the Environment screen.

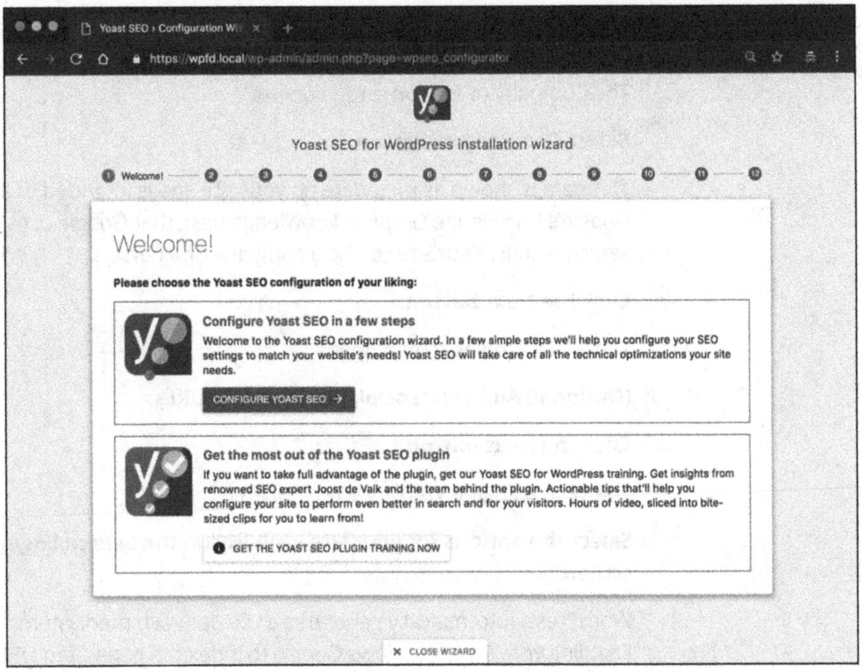

FIGURE 5-1: The Yoast SEO Welcome page.

3. **Select Production on the Environment screen.**

   The options on this page include

   - *Option A:* My site is live and ready to be indexed.
   - *Option B*: My site is under construction and should not be indexed.

4. **Click the Next button.**

   The Site Type screen opens.

5. **Select the type of site you're building.**

   Available options on this page include

   - Blog
   - Online shop
   - News channel
   - Small offline business
   - Corporation
   - Portfolio
   - Something else

6. **Click the Next button.**

   The Company or Person screen opens.

7. **Select Company or Person.**

   This data is shown as metadata on your site and is intended to appear in Google's Knowledge Graph, a knowledge base that Google uses to enhance its search results. Your site can be a company or a person.

8. **Click the Next button.**

   The Social Profiles screen opens.

9. **(Optional) Add your social media profile URLs.**

10. **Click the Next button.**

    The Search Engine Visibility screen opens.

11. **Select the options for your site visibility on the Search Engine Visibility screen.**

    WordPress automatically generates a URL for each media item in the library. Enabling visibility here allows Google to index the generated URL. Select Visible or Hidden options for the following post types:

    - Posts
    - Pages
    - Media

12. **Click the Next button.**

    The Multiple Authors screen opens.

13. **Select the desired option (multiple authors or no multiple authors), and click the Next button.**

    The Google Search Console screen opens.

14. **(Optional) Enter your authentication code.**

    This step allows Yoast SEO to fetch your Google Search Console information. You can skip this section if you don't use Google Search Console.

15. **Click the Next button.**

    The Title Settings screen opens.

16. **Enter your website name, and in the Title Separator section, select the character you want to use to separate your site title and content title.**

    Type the title of your website in the Website Name text box. (This title is the same one that you entered in the General Settings page, as I discuss in Book 3, Chapter 2.)

The title separator appears, for example, between your post title and site name. Symbols such as a dash and an arrow are shown at the size in which they'll appear in the search results.

17. **Click the Next button.**

    The Newsletter screen opens.

18. **(Optional) Enter your email address in the Email text box.**

    This step subscribes you to the Yoast SEO newsletter.

19. **Click the Next button.**

    The You Might Like screen opens, displaying information about other Yoast products you may like.

20. **Click the Next button.**

    The Success screen opens.

21. **Click the Close button.**

    The General – Yoast SEO screen opens in your Dashboard.

If you find that you need to change any of the settings in the configuration wizard, click any of the links on the SEO menu in your WordPress Dashboard to change the title tags, meta tags, and social media profile URLs.

Most of the remaining options that are selected by default should work fine for your site. Make sure, however, that Noindex is selected for the Archives pages (to find this setting, choose SEO⇨Titles & Metas⇨Archives) to make sure that the search engines aren't indexing your archive pages. Indexing archive pages would provide the search engines duplicate content — one of the top ways of getting penalized by Google, which means that you run the risk of having your site removed from Google's search engine results.

After you make your selections, click the Save Changes button at the bottom of any of the Yoast SEO settings pages where you made any changes.

TIP

You can use the Yoast SEO plugin without changing any of the default options. If you aren't confident about fine-tuning it, you don't have to. But don't forget to put in the proper information for your home page, including title, description, and keywords.

The Yoast SEO plugin also gives you full control of SEO settings for each individual page and post on your site by allowing you to configure the following:

- Facebook and Twitter share title, description, and image
- Title

- Slug (or permalink)
- Meta description (the short snippet of text that appears in search engine listings)
- Preferred focus keywords

Another nice feature of the Yoast SEO plugin is that it gives you real-time analysis of your content by rating its readability and keyword analysis. It also makes recommendations for improving both before you publish your content.

Yoast SEO creates Google XML site maps for you, which you can configure by choosing Dashboard⇨SEO⇨XML Sitemaps. Don't worry, though — if you decide not to use the Yoast SEO plugin, the next section has you covered with a plugin that creates XML site maps for you as well.

Google XML Sitemaps for WordPress

You can use Google XML Sitemaps (`https://wordpress.org/plugins/google-sitemap-generator`) right out of the box with very little configuration. If you use the Yoast SEO plugin mentioned in the previous section, you don't need this plugin because Yoast SEO generates sitemaps the same way this plugin does. After you install it, you need to tell the plugin to create your site map for the first time. You can accomplish this easy task by following these steps:

1. **Click the XML-Site map link on the Settings menu on your Dashboard.**

   The XML Sitemap Generator for WordPress options page appears in your browser window. (See Figure 5-2.)

2. **In the top module, titled Search Engines Haven't Been Notified Yet, click the Your Sitemap link in the option that begins with the words *Notify Search Engines*.**

   The XML Sitemap Generator for WordPress page refreshes, and the Search Engines Haven't Been Notified Yet module is replaced by the Result of the Last Ping module, showing the date when your site map was last generated.

3. **(Optional) View your site map in your browser.**

   Click the first site-map link in the top module or visit `http://`*`yourdomain`*`.com/sitemap.xml` (where *yourdomain*.com is your actual domain).

You never need to visit your site map or maintain it. The XML Sitemap Generator maintains the file for you. Every time you publish a new post or page on your website, the plugin automatically updates your site map with the information and notifies major search engines — such as Google, Bing, and Ask.com — that you've updated your site with new content. Basically, the plugin sends an invitation to the search engines to come to your site and index your new content in their search engines.

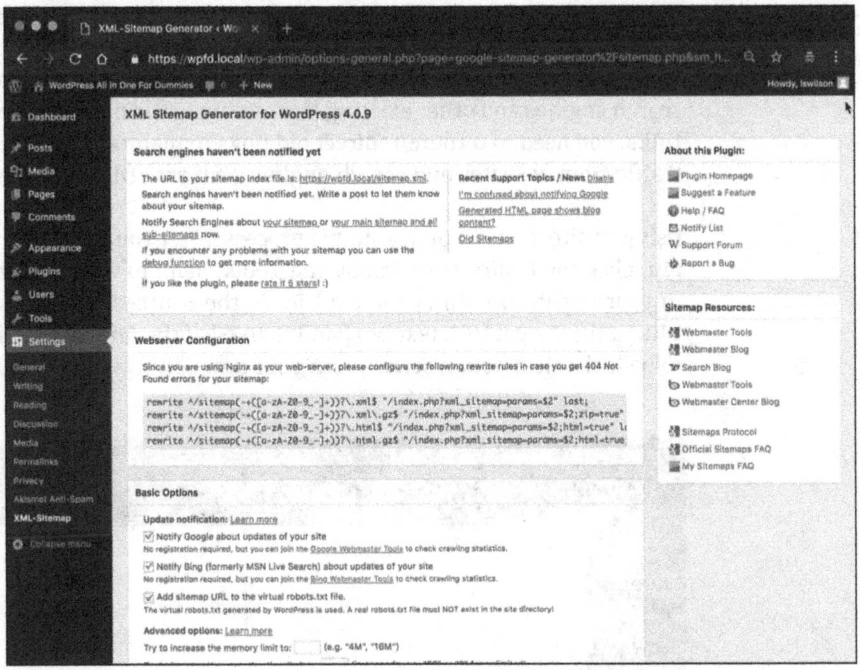

FIGURE 5-2: XML Sitemap Generator for WordPress settings.

TIP Having a Google Search Console account can help Google find and index new content on your site. If you don't already have one of these accounts, visit `https://search.google.com/search-console/about`, click the Start Now button on that page, log in with your existing Google account, and follow the onscreen steps to create a new Google account. After you sign in to the account, you can set up the Google Webmaster tools and add your site map to Google.

In the Basic Options section of the XML Sitemap Generator for WordPress plugin page (refer to Figure 5-2), select every check box you see.

All the other default settings are fine for you to use, so leave those as they are. In the Sitemap Content section, which is in the middle of the XML Sitemap Generator for WordPress page, select the following check boxes: Include Home page, Include Posts, Include Static Pages, Include Categories, and Include the Last Modification Time. Making these selections allows search engines to crawl your site in the most efficient way.

Redirection

If you're redoing the URL (permalink) structure of your site or moving a site to WordPress from another blogging platform, such as Blogger or Tumblr, you really need to use the Redirection plugin (`https://wordpress.org/plugins/redirection`). Redirection allows you to maintain the links that are currently coming into your site by rerouting (or redirecting) people coming in through search engines and other existing links going to the new permalink. If you change URLs, you need to reroute/redirect old links to maintain the integrity of incoming traffic from websites and search engines that are still using the old URL.

Using Redirection is a pretty simple process. After you install the Redirections plugin, click the Redirection link on the Tools menu to view the Redirections screen in your Dashboard. Enter the old URL in the Source URL text box, enter the new URL in the Target URL text box, and then click the Add Redirection button, which reloads the Redirection screen with your new settings displayed. (See Figure 5-3.)

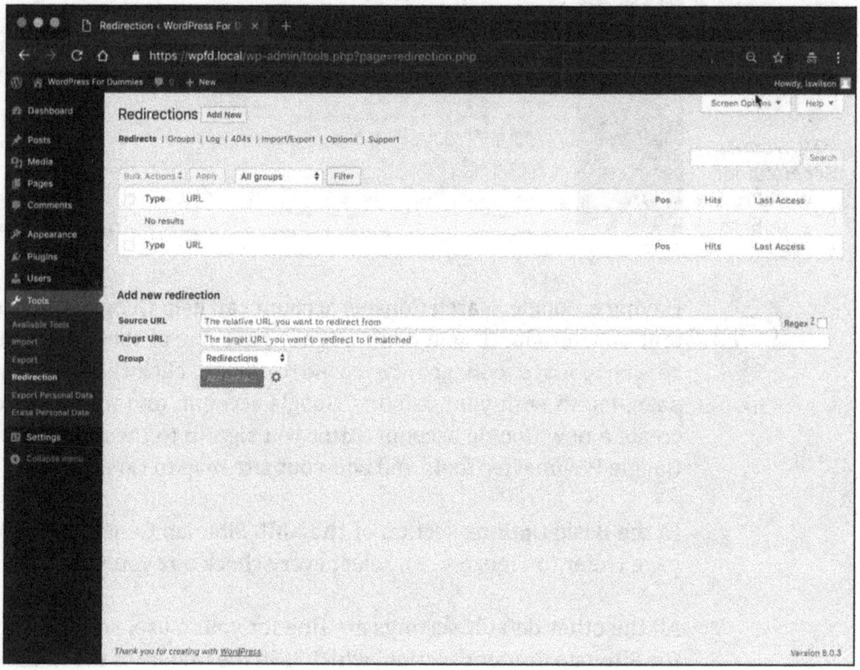

FIGURE 5-3: The Redirection plugin allows you to redirect traffic from your old URL.

WP-PageNavi

To create page navigation links below your site posts and archive listings for sites that have numbered pages, you need to install the WP-PageNavi plugin (`https://wordpress.org/plugins/wp-pagenavi`). Adjust the WP-PageNavi plugin settings to your liking. The default settings are shown in Figure 5-4.

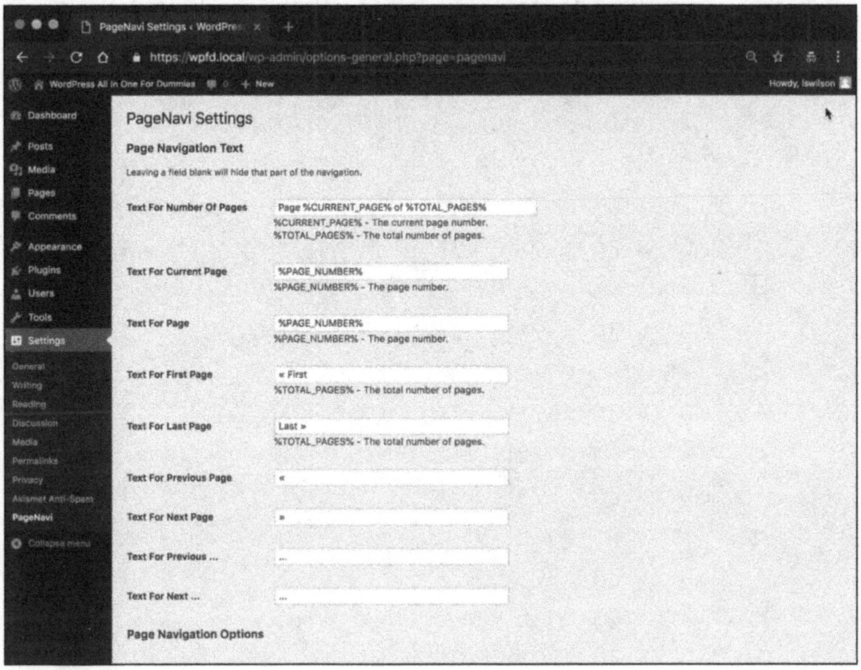

FIGURE 5-4: Adjust the WP-PageNavi settings.

This plugin provides a better user experience for your readers by making it easier for them to navigate your content; it also allows search engines to go through your web page easily to index your pages and posts. After you install and activate the plugin, you need to insert the following code into your Main Index template (`index.php`) or any template your theme uses to display archives (such as a blog page, category page, or search page):

```
<?php wp_pagenavi( );?>
```

TECHNICAL STUFF

The wp_pagenavi(); template tag needs to be added on a line directly after The Loop. See Book 6, Chapter 3 for extensive discussion of The Loop in the Main Index template file to find out where to add this line of code.

You can experiment with where you place the wp_pagenavi() code in your template file to produce the look and feel you want. Additionally, you can control the look of the plugin by providing styling in your CSS (style.css) theme file for the WP-PageNavi plugin display, or you can have the plugin insert its default CSS into your regular CSS by deselecting the Use Pagenavi.css? option.

6 Customizing the Look of Your Site

Contents at a Glance

IN THIS CHAPTER

» Discovering Twenty Nineteen's layout features

» Tweaking your logo and colors

» Installing custom navigation menus

» Exploring widgets on your website

Chapter 1

Examining the Default Theme: Twenty Nineteen

Bundled with the release of WordPress 5.0 in December 2018 is the new default theme, Twenty Nineteen. The goal of the core development team for WordPress is to release a new default theme every year, which is why, with every new installation of WordPress, you find themes called Twenty Fifteen, Twenty Sixteen, and Twenty Seventeen (named to correspond with the year when they were created). Version 5.0 of WordPress was a pretty big release that took more than a year to complete; therefore, WordPress ended up skipping a Twenty Eighteen theme and ended up naming the new default theme Twenty Nineteen because it was released at the end of 2018.

Twenty Nineteen is a powerful theme with built-in support for the new block editor, custom menus, footer widgets, custom colors, social icon colors, and more. These features make Twenty Nineteen an excellent base for your site needs.

This chapter shows you how to manage all the features of the default Twenty Nineteen theme, such as handling layouts; editing the logo, social icons, and background colors; installing and using custom navigation menus; and using widgets on your site to add some great features.

Exploring the Layout and Structure

If you want a simple look for your site, look no further than Twenty Nineteen. This theme offers a clean design style that's highly customizable through the use of the WordPress Block Editor, covered in Book 4, Chapter 1. As such, the font treatments are sharp and easy to read. Many of the new built-in theme features enable you to make simple yet elegant tweaks to the theme, including uploading your logo and adjusting the color scheme. Figure 1-1 shows the Twenty Nineteen WordPress default theme as it looks out of the box, meaning that it's a brand-new installation, and I haven't made any modifications to it yet.

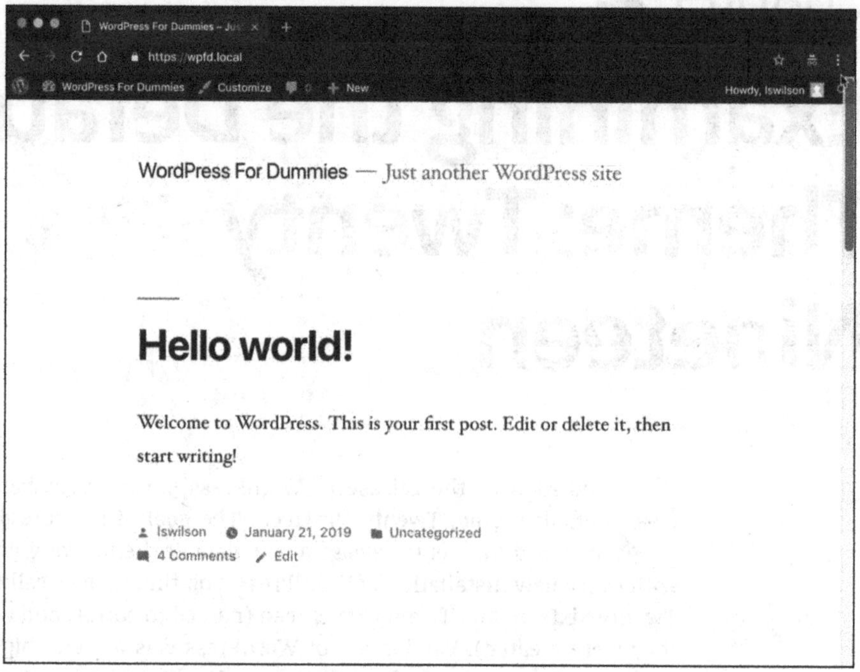

FIGURE 1-1: The default theme for WordPress, Twenty Nineteen.

The Twenty Nineteen theme's distinctive layout features include

- **One-column, no-sidebar default layout:** A one-column, full-width layout that lacks a sidebar of any kind is a trend you see on many blogs these days. It's the default display in Twenty Nineteen, providing a clean look and feel that lacks clutter.
- **Site Logo:** Twenty Nineteen allows you to upload and display a logo of your choosing by using the theme customizer, covered in "Adding a Logo to Your Website" later in this chapter.

- **Footer widget area:** Twenty Nineteen's one-column, full-width layout doesn't lend itself to having a sidebar on full display, making the content of your post or page the focal point of the site when your readers first view it. But a full widget area in the footer of Twenty Nineteen can be populated with WordPress Widgets, enabling you to include a search bar or a listing of recent post and categories, for example. Discover how to use widgets in WordPress in "Enhancing Your Website with Widgets" later in this chapter. Figure 1-2 shows the footer widget area of Twenty Nineteen with the default widgets on display.

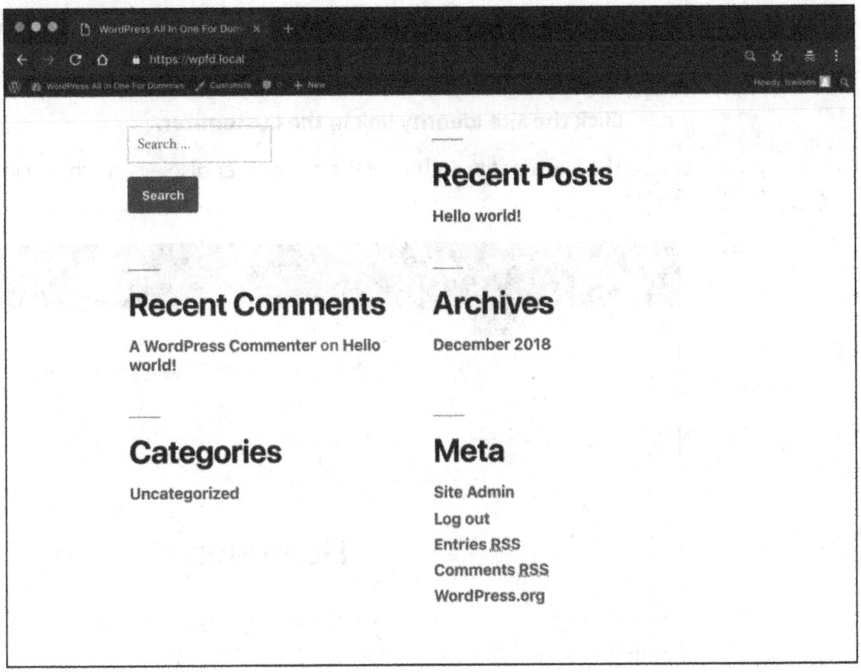

FIGURE 1-2: Twenty Nineteen's footer widget area.

- **Primary color:** By default, design elements such as links, buttons, and labels in the Twenty Nineteen theme are blue, and the background color is white. You can change the colors of the design elements by using the theme customizer (see "Customizing Colors in Twenty Nineteen" later in this chapter).

Adding a Logo to Your Website

Another feature in Twenty Nineteen is the logo uploader, which allows you to upload a unique logo graphic or photo for display in the header area of your WordPress site.

The logo area in the Twenty Nineteen header is pretty small and doesn't lend itself well to large logos or graphics that have a lot of detail or text. Follow these steps to upload a logo to the Twenty Nineteen theme, and you'll see what I'm talking about with regard to the logo size in the header area:

1. **Click the Customize link on the Appearance menu in the Dashboard.**

   The Customizer panel opens on the left side of the screen.

2. **Click the Site Identity link in the Customizer.**

   The Site Identity section of the customizer displays, as shown in Figure 1-3.

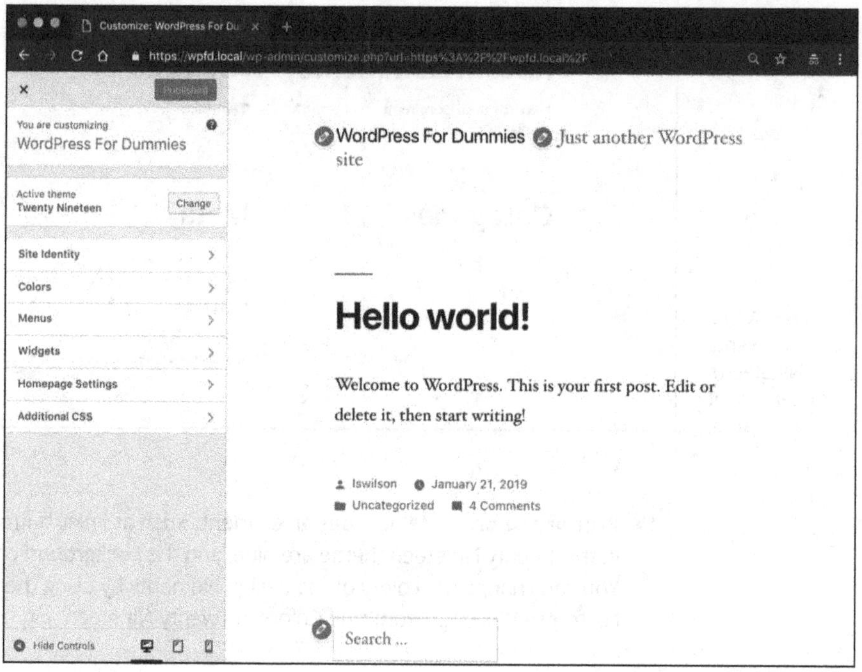

FIGURE 1-3: The Customizer screen for the default Twenty Nineteen theme.

3. **Click the Select Logo button to add your logo to your website.**

   The Select Logo screen opens.

4. **Upload an image from your computer's hard drive or select an existing image from the WordPress Media Library.**

5. **(Optional) Crop the image to your liking.**

   To resize and crop your image, drag one of the eight boxes located at the corners and sides of the image. You also can click within the image and move the entire cropping field up or down to get the optimal placement and cropping effect that you want. (See Figure 1-4.)

FIGURE 1-4: Using the crop tool.

TIP

The aspect ratio for the logo uploader in the Twenty Nineteen theme makes sure that your logo image remains perfectly square. You'll notice as you crop your logo image that all four sides of the cropping field remain equal in size; you can't create a nonsquare rectangular image.

6. **Click the Crop button.**

   The Crop Logo image goes away, and you see the Customizer panel with your new logo image displayed in the Site Identity section. You also see your new logo displayed on your site to the right of the Customizer panel. Your logo hasn't yet been published to your site; the area to the right of the Customizer panel shows you only a preview of your site and how it would look with the changes you've just made.

7. **Click the Publish button at the top of the Customizer panel to save and publish your logo to your site.**

   Figure 1-5 displays my site with an image in the logo area.

FIGURE 1-5: The Twenty Nineteen theme with new header image.

TIP

You can see in Figure 1-5 that the logo image is a small circle, which is how the Twenty Nineteen theme crops and displays your logo. As you can imagine, if you have a logo that's rectangular or some other shape, it won't work very well in this area. The Twenty Nineteen theme wasn't developed to be used as theme for a business website, really. Most businesses have a larger logo that has more detail or text on it, whereas the logo area in the Twenty Nineteen theme is meant for an avatar-like photos rather than logos. When you're selecting a theme for your business website, you may want to use a different theme unless your logo is a small circle.

Customizing Colors in Twenty Nineteen

After you explore the header logo settings, you may want to pick a color of that corresponds with your logo. The default color in the Twenty Nineteen theme is blue, but with the Color options in the Twenty Nineteen theme, you can change the default color to something different. Here's how:

1. **Click the Customize link on the Appearance menu in the Dashboard.**

   The Customizer panel opens on the left side of the screen.

2. **Click the Colors link in the Customizer.**

   The Customizing Colors section appears.

3. **Select the Custom option below the Primary Color heading.**

   The custom color bar displays, allowing you to click and drag the slider along the color spectrum to select the color you'd like to use, as shown in Figure 1-6.

TIP

It's hard to illustrate the color changes in Figure 1-6 because the figures in this book are black and white, but when you drag the slider in the color bar in step 3, you notice color changes in certain design elements on your site preview, displayed on the right side of your screen. The elements that change color include hyperlinks, buttons, and forms.

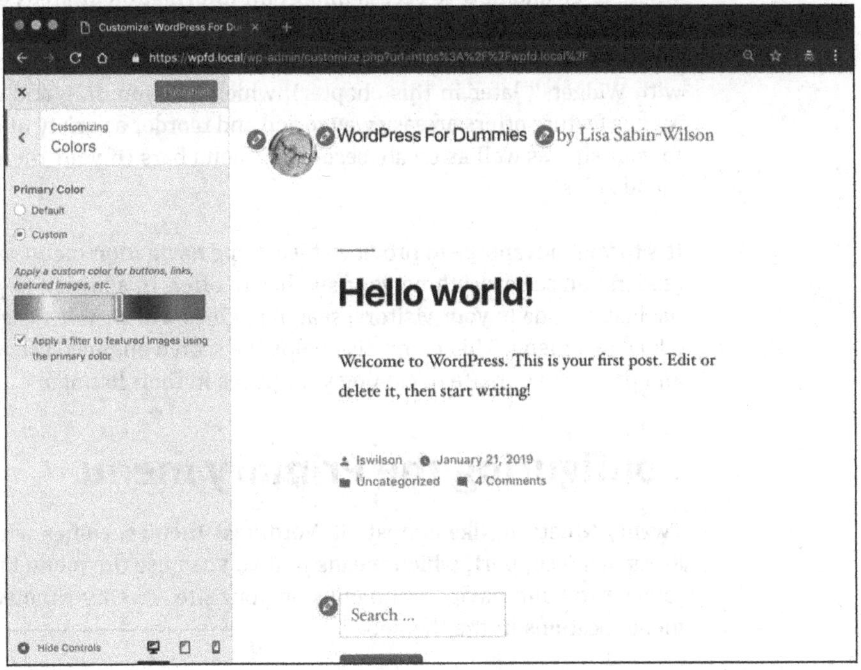

FIGURE 1-6: The Twenty Nineteen theme's color options.

4. **Select or clear the check box below the color picker, based on your preference.**

   The option is labeled Apply a Filter to Featured Images Using the Primary Color. By default, this option is selected; it tells WordPress to apply the color you chose in step 2 as an overlay color for your feature's images throughout your site. See Book 4, Chapter 3 for information about color overlay and opacity.

5. **Click the Publish button at the top of the Customizer panel to save and publish your color preferences to your site.**

Including Custom Navigation Menus

A *navigation menu* is a list of links displayed on your site. These links can be to pages, posts, or categories within your site, or they can be links to other sites. You can define navigation menus on your site by using the built-in Custom Menu feature of WordPress.

Navigational menus are vital parts of your site's design. They tell your site visitors where to go and how to access important information or areas of your site.

Similar to the WordPress Widgets feature (covered in "Enhancing Your Website with Widgets" later in this chapter), which lets you drag and drop widgets, the Menus feature offers an easy way to add and reorder a variety of navigational links to your site, as well as create secondary menu bars (if your theme offers multiple menu areas).

It's to your advantage to provide at least one navigation menu on your site so that readers can see everything your site has to offer. In addition to providing a visual navigation aide to your visitors, search engines will be able to see the links you've added to a menu. This menu also helps the search engines discover other sections and pages of your site to catalog your pages in their listings.

Configuring the Primary menu

Twenty Nineteen, like almost all WordPress themes, comes with built-in WordPress menu support, which means that you can use the menu builder in the Customizer to build navigation menus on your site. Twenty Nineteen provides three menu locations in the theme:

- **Primary:** A navigation menu that displays directly below the site title and tagline
- **Footer:** A navigation menu that displays at the bottom of your website
- **Social Links:** A navigation menu of social media icons that displays directly below the Primary navigation menu

To create a Primary menu in the Twenty Nineteen theme, follow these steps:

1. **Click the Customize link on the Appearance menu in the Dashboard.**

   The Customizer panel opens on the left side of the screen.

2. **Click the Menus link in the Customizer.**

   The Menus section appears, with a message telling you to create a menu because currently there aren't any menus (see Figure 1-7),

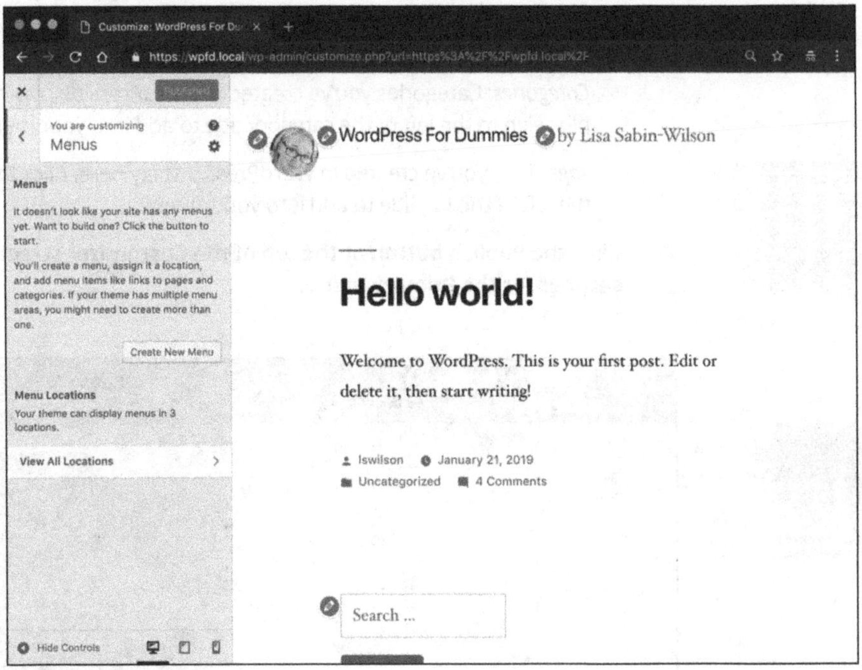

FIGURE 1-7: The Menu section of the Customizer panel for the Twenty Nineteen theme.

3. **Click the Create New Menu button.**

   The New Menu screen opens in the Customizer panel.

4. **Enter a name in the Menu Name field.**

   You can use any name you want for the menu.

5. **Select the check box to the left of the Primary label.**

   This step assigns the new menu to the Primary location.

6. **Click the Next button at the bottom of the Customizer.**

   The Customizer panel reloads and displays the menu screen with the name of your new menu at the top.

7. **Click the Add Items button.**

   A new panel opens, with options for adding new links to the menu you're creating. (See Figure 1-8.) Those options include

   - *Custom Links:* You can add a link to any web page on the internet by using the Custom Links module. Type the URL in the Link text box and then type the title of the link in the Link Text field.
   - *Pages:* Pages you've created in WordPress appear here. Click the plus sign to the left of the page title to add it to your menu.
   - *Posts:* Posts you've created in WordPress display here. Click the plus sign to the left of the post title to add it to your menu.
   - *Categories:* Categories you've created in WordPress display here. Click the plus sign to the left of the category title to add it to your menu.
   - *Tags:* Tags you've created in WordPress display here. Click the plus sign to the left of the tag title to add it to your menu.

8. **Click the Publish button at the top of the Customizer screen to save the settings for the Primary menu.**

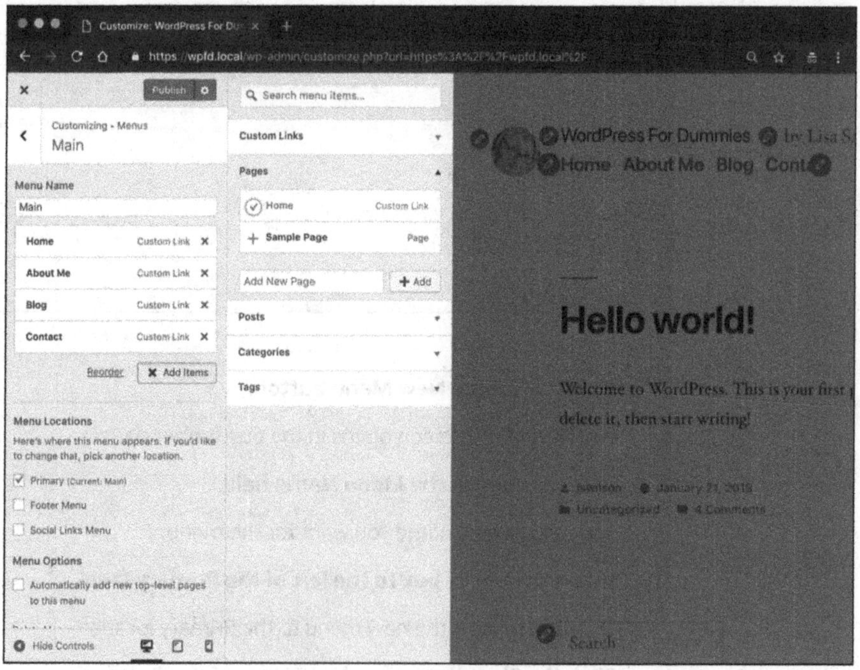

FIGURE 1-8: The Menu section of the Customizer panel for the Twenty Nineteen theme.

After you save your navigation menu, you can use the drag-and-drop interface in the Customizer to reorder and rearrange your menu items. In Figure 1-9, I'm dragging the Blog menu item above the About Me menu item. You can accomplish this task by clicking a menu item and, without releasing the button on your mouse, dragging it to the position where you want it. When you release the mouse button, the menu item drops into place. Additionally, you can create submenus below top-level menu items by moving menu items slightly to the right below the top-level items.

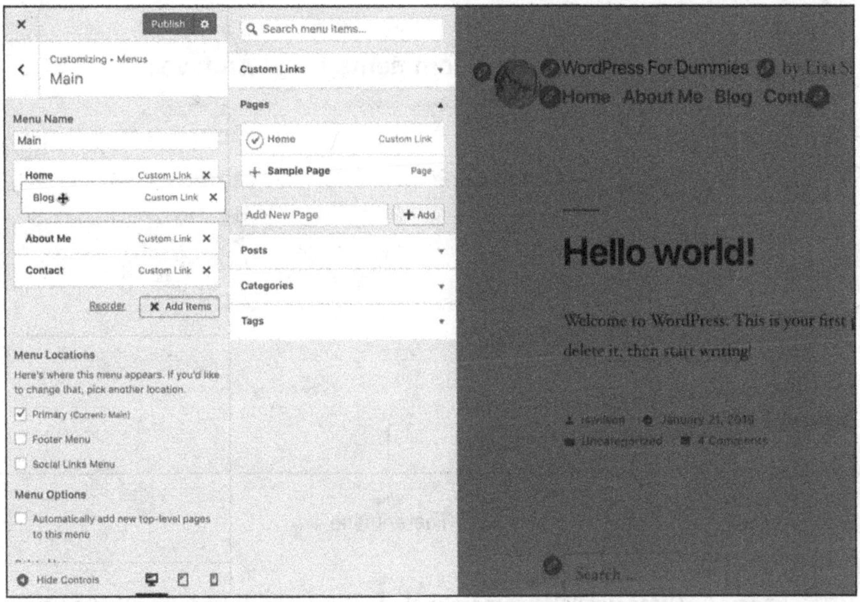

FIGURE 1-9: The drag-and-drop interface of the WordPress Menus feature.

TIP

Use the submenus feature to avoid cluttering the navigation bar if you have a large quantity of items that you want to include in the navigation menu. By organizing content logically, you can help readers find what they want faster even if you have lots of content for them to look through.

Configuring the Footer menu

To set up the Footer menu, follow the same steps as for the Primary menu. The only difference is in step 5 where you select the Footer menu location in the Customizer to tell WordPress that the menu you're building is one that you want to display in the footer (at the bottom) of your website.

When you're done building the Footer menu and publishing it to your site, it appears as shown in Figure 1-10.

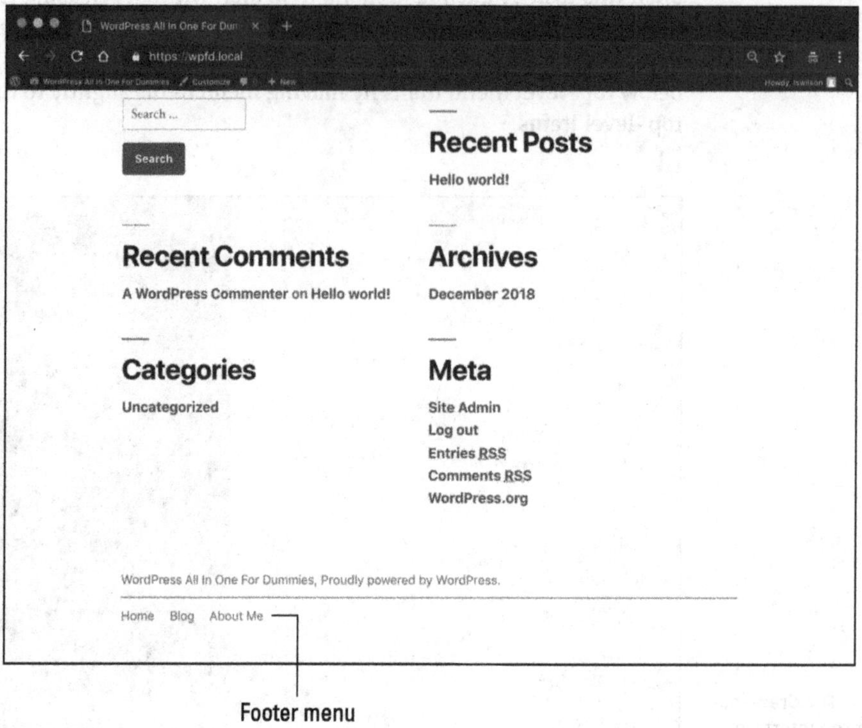

FIGURE 1-10: Footer menu displayed on a website with the Twenty Nineteen theme.

TIP

Often, website owners include the same links in the Footer menu as they do in the Primary menu. That way, the navigation links at the top of the site when visitors come to your site also are available at the bottom of your site when they finish scrolling through your content. Providing the same menu at the bottom of your site is a nice feature; visitors don't have to scroll all the way back to the top of your site to click another link on your navigation menu.

Configuring the Social Links menu

The Social Links menu in the Twenty Nineteen theme is unique because instead of inserting text links into the menu, it inserts social media icons. This is a nice little feature; on most websites, when people link to their Twitter or Facebook profiles, you see the icons from those sites instead of a text link. The Social menu in the Twenty Nineteen theme makes it easy to do that without having to get your hands dirty inside the code of the theme.

The Twenty Nineteen theme accomplishes the addition of social media icons through the automatic recognition of various social media URLs. The social links menu configured in the Twenty Nineteen theme knows, for example, when you've typed in a URL that points to the Twitter website by recognizing the twitter.com domain and inserting the Twitter icon instead of a text link. Add links to Twitter, Facebook, and Instagram by following these steps:

1. **Click the Customize link on the Appearance menu in the Dashboard.**

   The Customizer panel opens on the left side of the screen.

2. **Click the Menus link in the Customizer.**
3. **Click the Create New Menu button.**

   The New Menu screen opens in the Customizer panel.

4. **Enter a name in the Menu Name field.**

   You can use any name you want for the menu.

5. **Select the check box to the left of the Social Links Menu label.**

   This step assigns the new menu to the Social Links Menu location, which appears directly below the Primary navigation menu on your website.

6. **Click the Next button at the bottom of the Customizer.**

   The Customizer panel reloads and displays the menu screen with the name of your new menu at the top.

7. **Click the Add Items button.**
8. **Click the Custom Links section.**

   The Custom Links section drops down, revealing two text fields.

9. **Type the URL of your Twitter profile in the URL field.**

   My Twitter profile URL, for example, is `https://twitter.com/lisasabinwilson`.

10. **Type the word** Twitter **in the Link Text field.**
11. **Click the Add to Menu button.**

    WordPress adds the link to the Social Links menu.

12. **Repeat steps 9–11 for your Facebook and Instagram profiles.**
13. **Click the Publish button at the top of the Customizer panel.**
14. **Load your website in your browser to see your social media icons displayed below the Primary navigation menu (see Figure 1-11).**

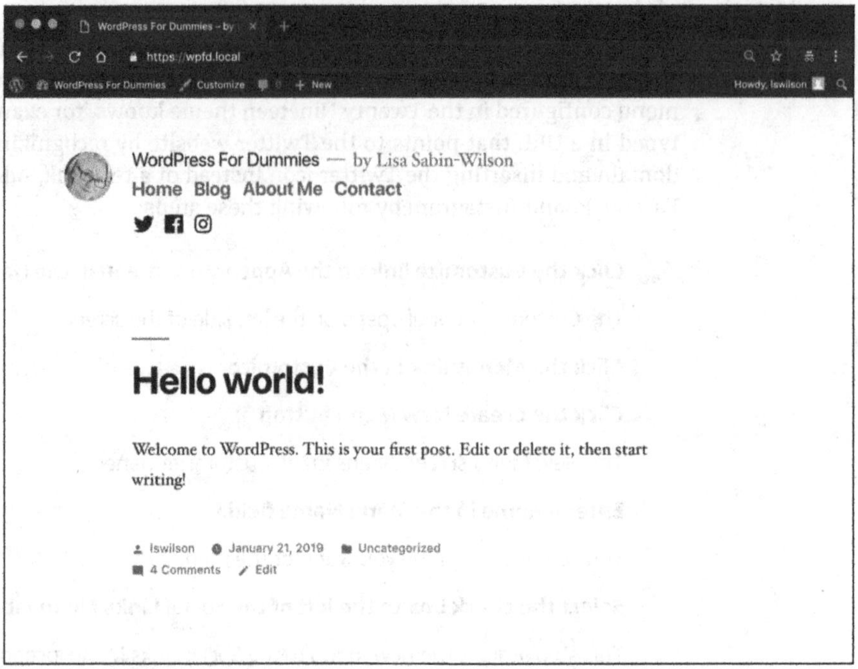

FIGURE 1-11: The Social Links menu appears below the Primary navigation menu.

TIP

For the Social Links menu, you're not limited to the Twitter, Facebook, and Instagram links that you added in this section. The Twenty Nineteen theme recognizes links from several other popular social media platforms, including YouTube, LinkedIn, and Pinterest. You can find a full listing of services supported by the Twenty Nineteen theme in the WordPress Codex at `https://codex.wordpress.org/Twenty_Nineteen#Add_Social_Icons`.

Enhancing Your Website with Widgets

WordPress widgets are helpful tools that are built into the WordPress application. They allow you to arrange the display of content in your site sidebar, such as recent posts, and monthly and category archive lists. With widgets, arrange and display the content in the sidebar of your blog without having to know a single bit of PHP or HTML.

Widget areas are the regions of your theme where you can insert and arrange content (such as a list of your recent blog posts or links to your favorite sites) or custom menus by dragging and dropping (and editing) available widgets (shown on the Dashboard's Widget page) into those corresponding areas.

Many widgets offered by WordPress (and those added by some WordPress themes and plugins) provide drag-and-drop installation of more advanced functions that normally are available only if you write code directly in your theme files.

Click the Widgets link on the Appearance menu of the Dashboard to see the available widgets on the Widgets screen. This feature is a big draw because it lets you control what features you use and where you place them without having to know a lick of code.

The Twenty Nineteen theme has one widget area called Footer. Figure 1-10 earlier in this chapter shows the footer area of a website that uses the Twenty Nineteen theme. Figure 1-12 shows the Widgets screen of the Dashboard, where you find widgets to add to the Footer widget area in the Twenty Nineteen theme.

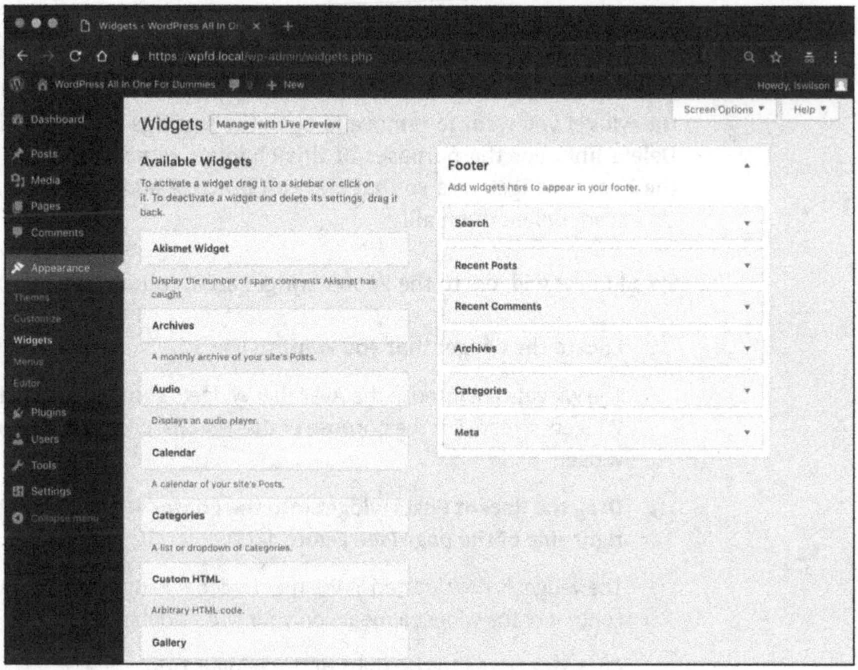

FIGURE 1-12: The Widgets screen of the Dashboard.

Adding widgets to the footer in Twenty Nineteen

The Widgets screen lists all the widgets that are available for your WordPress site. On the right side of the Widgets page is the Footer widget area designated in the

Twenty Nineteen theme. You see that the Footer widget area is already populated with a few widgets to get you started:

- **Search:** Contains a search form for your website
- **Recent Posts:** Provides a list of the most recent posts you've published to your site
- **Recent Comments:** Provides a list of the most recent comments left on posts published to your site
- **Archives:** Provides a list to the monthly archives of the posts published to your site
- **Categories:** Provides a list of the category archives on your site
- **Meta:** Provides a list of a few helpful links, such as the login and register links for your website

If you want to remove any of the existing widgets in the Footer widget area, click the widget you want to remove to open the settings for that widget; then click the Delete link. For the purposes of this chapter, remove all the existing widgets in the Footer widget area so that you can practice adding them in the next section. Go ahead; delete them all!

To add new widgets to the Footer widget area, follow these steps:

1. **Locate the widget that you want to use.**

   The widgets are listed in the Available Widgets section on the left side of the Widgets screen. For the purpose of these steps, choose the Recent Posts widget.

2. **Drag the Recent Posts widget into the Footer widget area section on the right side of the page (see Figure 1-13).**

   The widget is now located in the main sidebar widget area section, and the content of the widget appears on your site's sidebar.

3. **Click the arrow to the right of the widget title.**

   Options for the widget appear. Each widget has different options that you can configure. The Recent Posts widget, for example, lets you configure the title, the number of recent posts you want to display (the default is 5; the maximum is 15), and the date. (See Figure 1-14.)

4. **Select your options, and click the Save button.**

   The options you've set are saved.

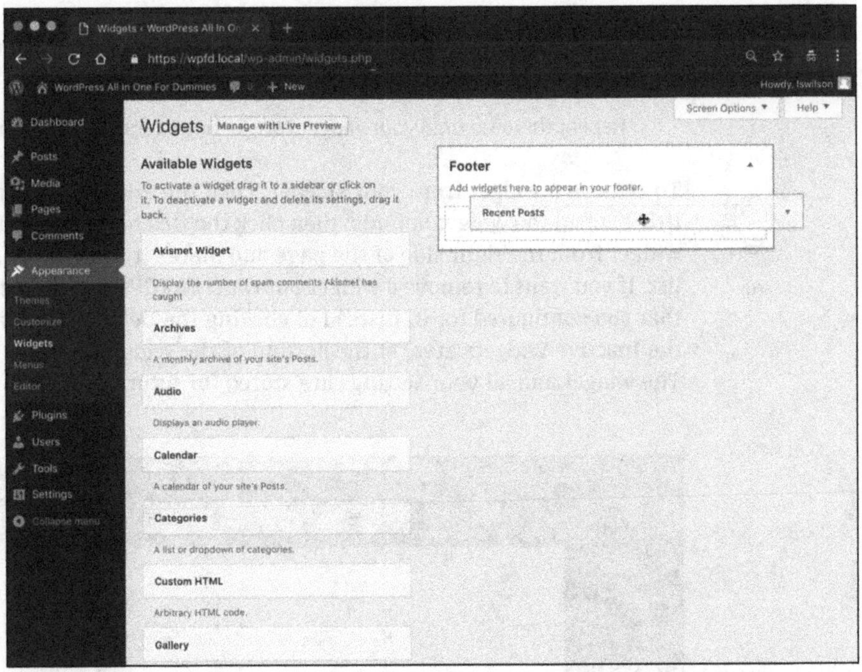

FIGURE 1-13: Adding the Recent Posts widget by dragging it into place.

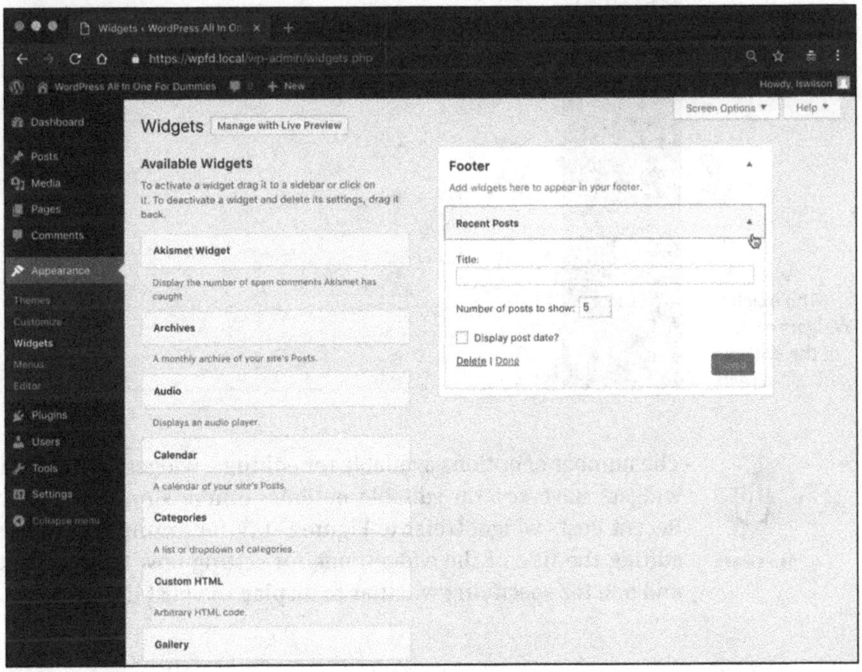

FIGURE 1-14: Editing the Recent Posts widget.

5. **Arrange your widgets in the order in which you want them to appear on your site by dragging and dropping them in the list.**

   Repeat this step until your widgets are arranged the way you want them.

TIP

To remove a widget from your sidebar, click the arrow to the right of the widget title to open the widget options; then click the Delete link. WordPress removes the widget from the right side of the page and places it back in the Available Widgets list. If you want to remove a widget but want WordPress to remember the settings that you configured for it, instead of clicking the Delete link, drag the widget into the Inactive Widgets area, at the bottom of the Widgets screen. (See Figure 1-15.) The widget and all your settings are stored for future use.

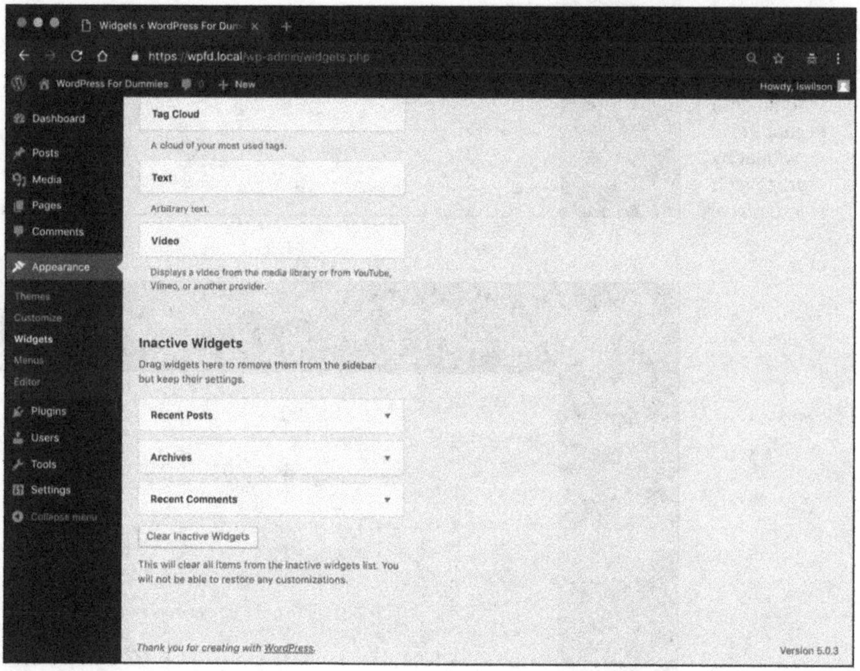

FIGURE 1-15: The Inactive Widgets section of the Widgets screen.

REMEMBER

The number of options available for editing a widget depends on the widget. Some widgets have several editable options; others simply let you write a title. The Recent Posts widget (refer to Figure 1-14), for example, has three options: one for editing the title of the widget, one for setting how many recent posts to display, and one for specifying whether to display the post date.

Using the Text widget

The Text widget is one of the most popular and useful WordPress widgets because it enables you to add a simple block of text and even HTML code to widget areas without editing the theme's template files. Therefore, you can designate several types of information on your site by including your desired text within it.

TIP

I mentioned that you can add HTML code to the Text Widget, however there is the Custom HTML widget included in WordPress is specifically for HTML. Try out the Custom HTML widget, as well!

Here are some examples of how you can use the Text widget:

- **Add an email newsletter subscription form.** Add a form that allows site visitors to sign up for your email newsletter. Because adding an email newsletter subscription form often involves HTML, the Text widget is especially helpful.
- **Display business hours of operation.** Display the days and hours of your business operation where everyone can easily see them.
- **Post your updates from social networks.** Many social networking sites, such as Twitter and Facebook, offer embed codes that let you display your updates on those sites directly on your website. Social networking embed codes often include JavaScript, HTML, and CSS, which you can easily embed with the Text widget.
- **Announce special events and notices.** If your organization has a special sale, an announcement about a staff member or an important notice about weather closings, for example, you can use the Text widget to post this information to your site in a few seconds.

WARNING

The WordPress Text widget doesn't allow you to include PHP code of any kind. Because of the nature of this widget, it doesn't execute PHP code, such as special WordPress template tags or functions (like the ones you find in Book 6, Chapter 3). There is, however, a plugin called the Advanced Text Widget that does allow you to insert and execute PHP code within it. You can download the Advanced Text Widget from the WordPress site at `https://wordpress.org/plugins/advanced-text-widget`. (You can find more information about using and installing WordPress plugins in Book 7.)

To add the Text widget, follow these steps:

1. **On the WordPress Dashboard, click the Widgets link on the Appearance menu.**
2. **Find the Text widget in the Available Widgets section.**

3. Drag the Text widget to the desired widget area.

The Text widget opens, as shown in Figure 1-16.

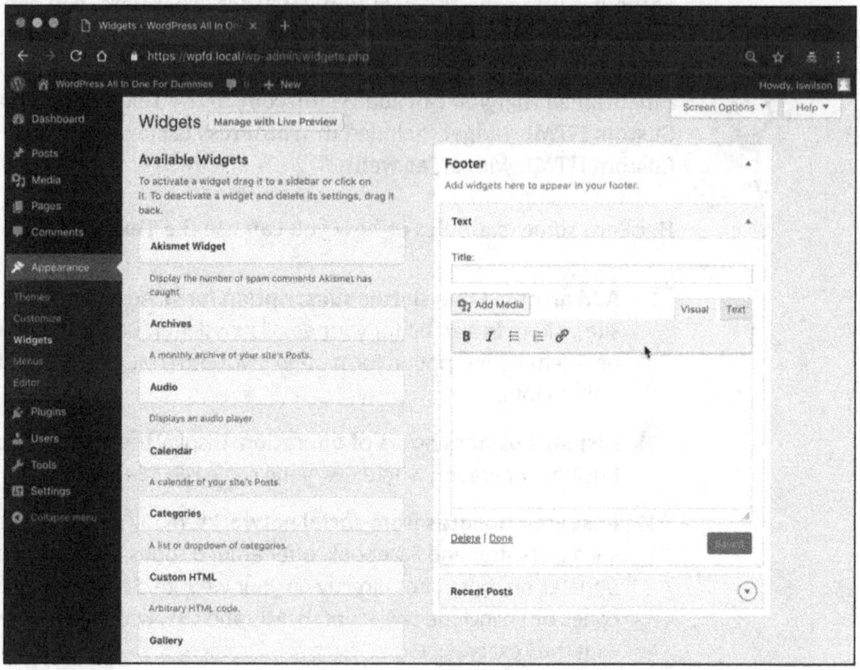

FIGURE 1-16: The Text widget.

4. Type a title in the Title field and any desired text in the content text box.

You can use the WYSIWYG (What You See Is What You Get) editor above the content text box to format your content with options such as including bold or italic text or adding links, a bulleted or numbered list, or an image.

5. Click the Save button.

6. Click the Close link at the bottom of the Text widget box.

Using the RSS widget

The RSS widget allows you to pull headlines from almost any RSS feed, including recent headlines from your other WordPress sites. You also can use it to pull in headlines from news sites or other sources that offer RSS feeds. This practice is commonly referred to as *aggregation*, which means that you're gathering information from a syndicated RSS feed source to display on your site.

After you drag the RSS widget to the appropriate widget area, the widget opens, and you can enter the RSS Feed URL you want to display. Additionally, you can easily tweak other settings, as shown in Figure 1-17, to add information to the widget area for your readers.

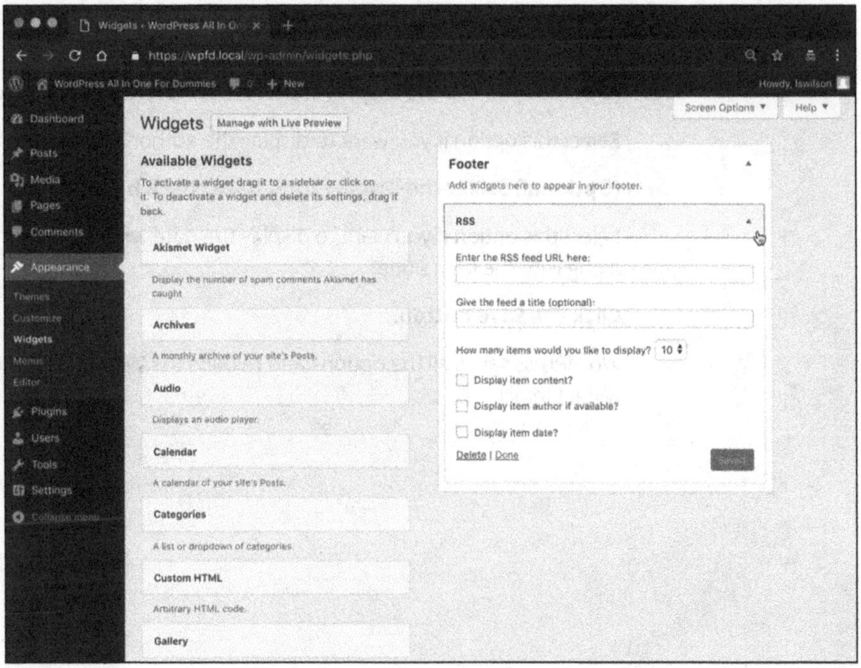

FIGURE 1-17: The RSS widget.

Follow these steps to add the RSS widget to your site:

1. **Add the RSS widget to your sidebar on the Widgets screen.**

   Follow the steps in "Adding widgets to the footer in Twenty Nineteen" earlier in this chapter to add the widget.

2. **Click the arrow to the right of the RSS widget's name.**

   The widget opens, displaying options you can configure.

3. **In the Enter the RSS Feed URL Here text box, type the RSS URL of the site you want to add.**

   You can usually find the RSS Feed URL of a site listed on the sidebar.

4. **Type the title of the RSS widget.**

   This title appears in your site above the links from this site. If I wanted to add the RSS feed from my business site, for example, I'd type **WebDevStudios Feed**.

5. **Choose the number of items from the RSS feed to display on your site.**

   The drop-down menu gives you a choice of 1–20.

6. **(Optional) Select the Display the Item Content check box.**

   Selecting this check box tells WordPress that you also want to display the content of the feed (usually, the content of the post from the feed URL). If you want to display only the title, leave the check box deselected.

7. **(Optional) Select the Display Item Author If Available check box.**

   Select this option if you want to display the author's name with the item's title.

8. **(Optional) Select the Display Item Date check box.**

   Select this option if you want to display the date when the item was published along with the item's title.

9. **Click the Save button.**

   WordPress saves all the options and reloads the Widgets page with your RSS widget intact.

IN THIS CHAPTER

» Understanding free theme options

» Exploring things to avoid with free themes

» Installing, previewing, and activating your new theme

» Discovering premium theme options

Chapter 2

Finding and Installing WordPress Themes

WordPress themes are groups of files, called *templates*, bundled together. When activated in WordPress, themes determine the look and basic function of your site. (See Book 6, Chapter 3 for more about template files.)

Because themes set the design style of your site, including how content displays on it, they're the first and most basic way of customizing your site to fit your unique needs. Some of the most amazing things about the WordPress community are the thousands of free themes that are available — and the new ones that are released each week.

Although finding one WordPress theme among thousands of options can be challenging, it's a fun adventure, and you can explore the various designs and features to ultimately find the right theme for you and your site. In this chapter, you discover the options for finding and installing free themes on your WordPress site. I also discuss premium theme options and tell you a few things to avoid.

Getting Started with Free Themes

WordPress comes packaged with one very useful default theme called Twenty Nineteen (named after the year 2019 and released in version 5.0 of WordPress). Most bloggers who use WordPress usually don't waste any time at all in finding a theme that they like better than the default theme. The Twenty Nineteen theme is meant to get you started. Although you're not limited to the default theme, it's a very functional theme for a basic website. Feel free to use it to get started.

Free WordPress themes are popular because of their appealing designs and their ease of installation and use. They're great tools to use when you launch your new site, and if you dabble a bit in graphic design and CSS (Cascading Style Sheets), you can customize one of the free WordPress themes to fit your needs. (See Book 6, chapters 4 and 5 for some resources and tools for templates and template tags, as well as a few great HTML and CSS references.)

With thousands of free WordPress themes available and new ones appearing all the time, your challenge is to find the right one for your site. Here are a few things to remember while you explore. (Also see the nearby sidebar "Are all WordPress themes free?" for information about free versus commercial themes.)

- **Free themes are excellent starting places.** Find a couple of free themes, and use them as starting points for understanding how themes work and what you can do with them. Testing free themes, their layouts, and their options helps you identify what you want in a theme.
- **You'll switch themes frequently.** Typically, you'll find a WordPress theme that you adore and then, a week or two later, find another theme that fits you or your site better. Don't expect to stay with your initial choice. Something new will pop up on your radar screen. Eventually, you'll want to stick with a theme that fits your needs best and doesn't aggravate visitors because of continual changes.
- **You get what you pay for.** Although a plethora of free WordPress themes exists, largely, you receive limited or no support for them. Free themes are often a labor of love. The designers have full-time jobs and responsibilities; they often release these free projects for fun, passion, and a desire to contribute to the WordPress community. Therefore, you shouldn't expect (or demand) support for these themes. Some designers maintain very active and helpful forums to help users, but those forums are rare. Just be aware that with most free themes, you're on your own.
- **Download themes from reputable sources.** Themes are essentially pieces of software. Therefore, they can contain things that could be scammy, spammy, or potentially harmful to your site or computer. It's vital that you do your homework by reading online reviews and downloading themes from credible, trusted sources. The best place to find free WordPress themes is the Themes Directory of the WordPress website (see Figure 2-1) at `https://wordpress.org/themes`.

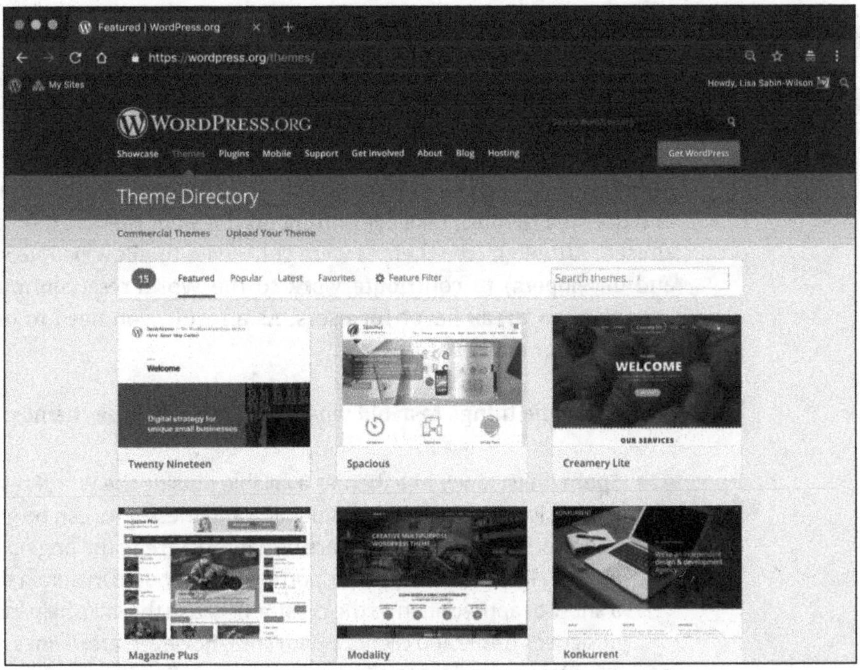

FIGURE 2-1: The most trusted resource for free themes.

ARE ALL WordPress THEMES FREE?

Not all WordPress themes are created equal, and it's important for you, the user, to know the difference between free and premium themes:

- **Free:** These themes are free, period. You can download and use them on your website at absolutely no cost. It's a courtesy to include a link to the designer in the footer of your site, but you can remove that link if you want to.
- **Commercial:** These themes cost money. You usually find commercial themes available for download only after you've paid anywhere from $10 to $500. The designer feels that these themes are a cut above the rest and, therefore, are worth the money you spend for them. Commercial themes also come with a mechanism to obtain support for the use of the theme. Generally, you aren't allowed to remove any designer credits that appear in these themes, and you aren't allowed to redistribute the themes. See "Exploring Premium Theme Options" later in this chapter for information about where to find premium themes.

Understanding What to Avoid with Free Themes

Although free themes are great, you want to avoid some things when you find and use free themes. Like everything on the web, themes have the potential to be abused. Although free themes were conceived to allow people (namely, designers and developers) to contribute work to the WordPress community, they've also been used to wreak havoc for users. As a result, you need to understand what to watch out for and what to avoid.

Here are some things to avoid when searching for free themes:

- **Spam links:** Many free themes available outside the WordPress website include links in the footer or sidebars, and these links can be good or bad. The good uses of these links are designed to credit the original designer and possibly link to her website or portfolio. You should maintain these links as a show of appreciation to the creator because the links help increase the designer's traffic and clients. Spam links, however, aren't links to the designer's site; they're links to sites you may not ordinarily associate with or endorse on your site. The best example is a link in the footer that links to odd, off-topic, and uncharacteristic keywords or phrases, such as *weight loss supplement* or *best flower deals.* Mostly, this spam technique is used to increase the advertised site's search engine ranking for that particular keyword by adding another link from your site or, worse, to take the site visitor who clicks it to a site unrelated to the linked phrase.
- **Hidden malicious code:** Unfortunately, the WordPress community has received reports of hidden, malicious code within a theme. This hidden code can produce spam links, security exploits, and abuses on your WordPress site. Hackers install code in various places that run this type of malware. Unscrupulous theme designers can, and do, place code in theme files that inserts hidden malware, virus links, and spam. Sometimes, you see a line or two of encrypted code that looks like it's just part of the theme code. Unless you have a great deal of knowledge of PHP or JavaScript, you may not know that the theme is infected with dangerous code.
- **Themes that lack continued development:** WordPress software continues to improve with each new update. Two or three times a year, WordPress releases new software versions, adding new features, security patches,

and numerous other updates. Sometimes, a code function is superseded or replaced, causing a theme to break because it hasn't been updated for the new WordPress version. Additionally, to use new features added to WordPress (because the software updates add features), the theme needs to be updated accordingly. Because free themes typically come without any warranty or support, one thing you should look for — especially if a theme has many advanced back-end options — is whether the developer is actively maintaining the theme for current versions of WordPress. This issue typically occurs more with plugins than with themes, but it's worth noting.

- **Endless searches for free themes:** Avoid searching endlessly for the perfect theme. Trust me — you won't find it. You may find a great theme and then see another with a feature or design style you wish that the other theme had, but the new theme may lack certain other features. Infinite options can hinder you from making a final decision. Peruse the most popular themes on the WordPress website; to save time, choose five that fit your criteria; and then move on. You always have the option to change a theme later, especially if you find the vast amount of choices in the directory to be overwhelming.

The results of unsafe theme elements can range from simply annoying to downright dangerous, affecting the integrity and security of your computer and/or hosting account. For this reason, the WordPress website is considered to be a safe place from which to download free themes. WordPress designers develop these themes and upload them to the Theme Directory, and the folks behind the WordPress platform vet each theme. On the official WordPress website, themes that contain unsafe elements simply aren't allowed.

REMEMBER

The WordPress website isn't the only place to find free WordPress themes, but it's the place to find the most functional and *safest* themes available. Safe themes contain clean code and basic WordPress functions that are considered to be fundamental requirements in a theme to ensure that your WordPress site functions with the minimum requirements. The WordPress.org website lists the basic requirements that designers have to meet before their themes are accepted into the Theme Directory; you can find that listing of requirements at `https://wordpress.org/themes/getting-started`. I highly recommend that you stick to the WordPress website for free themes to use on your site; you can be certain that those themes don't contain any unsafe elements or malicious code.

TIP

If you suspect or worry that you have malicious code on your site — either through a theme you're using or a plugin you've activated — the absolutely best place to get your site checked is the Sucuri website (`https://sitecheck.sucuri.net`), which offers a free website malware scanner. Sucuri provides expertise in the field of web security for WordPress users in particular, and it even has a free plugin you can install to check your WordPress site for malware and/or malicious code. You can find that plugin at `https://wordpress.org/plugins/sucuri-scanner`.

Previewing themes on the WordPress website

While you're visiting the WordPress Theme Directory, you can easily browse the various themes by using the following features:

- **Search:** Type a keyword in the search box near the top of the page (refer to Figure 2-1), and press the Enter (or Return on a Mac) key. A new page opens, displaying themes related to the keyword you searched for.
- **Featured:** Click the Featured link to view the themes that WordPress has chosen to feature in the directory. WordPress changes the featured themes listing regularly.
- **Popular:** Click the Popular link to view the themes that have been downloaded most often.
- **Latest:** Click the Latest link to view themes recently added to the directory.
- **Feature Filter:** Click the Feature Filter to view choices available to filter your theme search by, such as layout, features and subject.

When you find a theme in the directory that you want to examine more closely, click the More Info button that appears when you hover your mouse over the theme, and do one of the following:

- **Download:** Click this button (see Figure 2-2) to download the theme to your computer.
- **Preview:** Click the Preview button on the theme page to open a preview window, which gives you a preview of how the theme looks on a website.

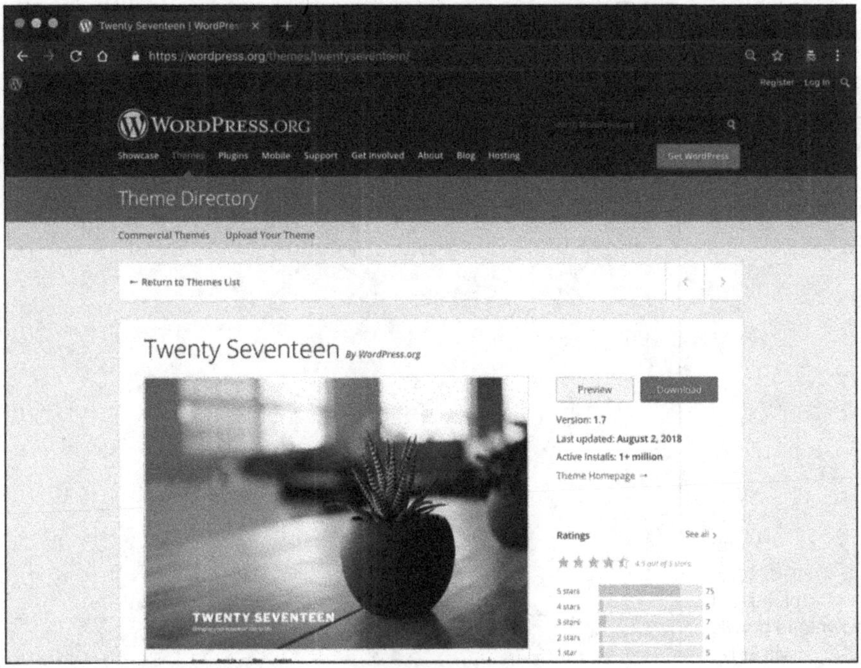

FIGURE 2-2: Download or preview a particular theme from the WordPress website.

Installing a Theme

After you find a WordPress theme, you can install the theme on your WordPress site via SFTP or the WordPress Dashboard.

To install a theme via SFTP, follow these steps:

1. **Download the theme file from the Theme Directory.**

   Typically, theme files are provided in compressed format (`.zip` file).

   (I discuss how you can peruse the WordPress website from your WordPress Dashboard in the next section, "Browsing the free themes.")

2. **Unzip or extract the theme's `.zip` file.**

   You see a new folder on your desktop, typically labeled with the corresponding theme name. (Refer Book 2, Chapter 2 for information on using SFTP.)

3. **Upload the theme folder to your web server.**

   Connect to your hosting server via SFTP, and upload the extracted theme folder to the `/wp-content/themes` folder on your server (see Figure 2-3).

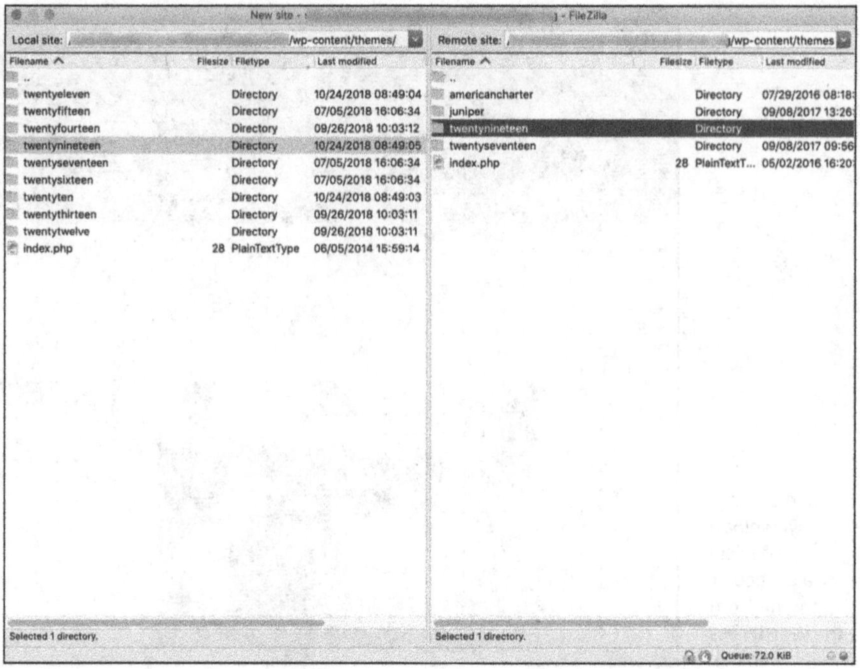

FIGURE 2-3: Upload and download panels via SFTP.

To install a theme via the Dashboard's theme installer, follow these steps:

1. **Download the theme file from the WordPress website to your local computer.**

   Typically, theme files are provided in compressed format (`.zip` file). When you use this method, you don't extract the `.zip` file, because the theme installer does that for you.

2. **Log in to your WordPress Dashboard.**
3. **Click the Themes link on the Appearance menu.**

   The Themes screen appears.

4. **Click the Add New button.**

   The Add Themes screen appears, displaying a submenu of links.

5. **Click the Upload Theme button.**

   The panel displays a utility to upload a theme in `.zip` format.

6. **Upload the `.zip` file you downloaded in step 1.**

   Click the Choose File button and then locate and select the `.zip` file you stored on your computer.

7. **Click the Install Now button.**

   WordPress unpacks and installs the theme in the appropriate directory for you. Figure 2-4 shows the result of installing a theme via this method.

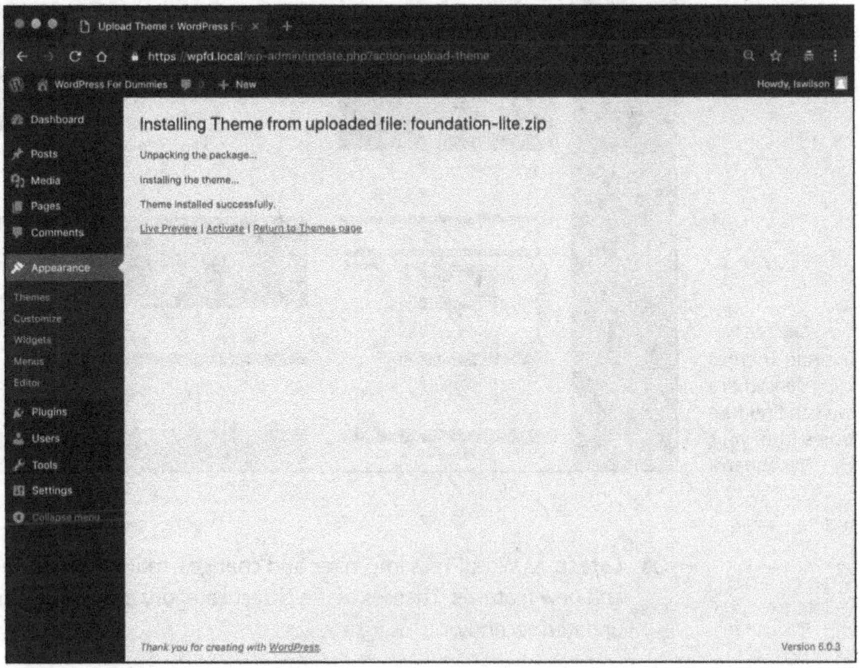

FIGURE 2-4: Installing a theme via the Dashboard's theme installer.

Browsing the free themes

Finding free themes via the Add Themes screen is extremely convenient because it lets you search the WordPress themes on the WordPress website from your own site, in the Dashboard. Start by clicking the Themes link on the Appearance menu of the WordPress Dashboard and then click the Add New button to open the Add Themes screen (see Figure 2-5).

After you navigate to the Add Themes screen, you see the following items:

- **Featured:** The Featured link takes you to themes that WordPress.org has selected. The themes in this section are favorites of the members of the Themes team.
- **Popular:** If you don't have a theme in mind, the themes in this section are some of the most popular. I recommend that you install and test-drive one of them for your site's first theme.

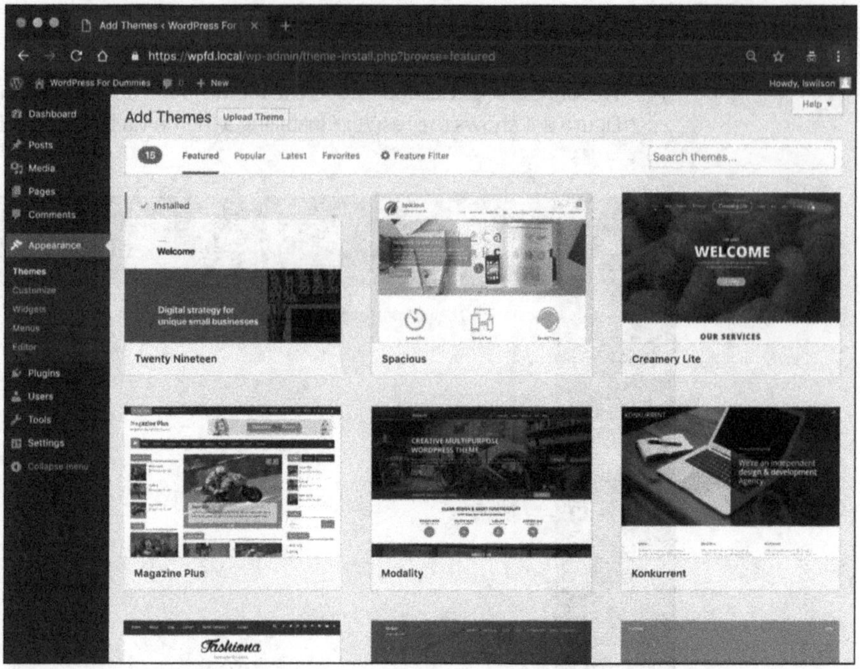

FIGURE 2-5: The Add Themes screen, where you can find free themes from your Dashboard.

- **Latest:** As WordPress improves and changes, many themes need updating to add new features. Themes in the Latest category are themes that have been updated recently.
- **Favorites:** If you marked themes as favorites on the WordPress website, you can find them on the Add Themes screen. After you click the Favorites link, fill in your WordPress.org username in the text field, and click the Get Favorites button. This feature only works if you're logged into your WordPress.org user account.
- **Feature Filter:** This link gives you a variety of filters to choose among to find a theme you're looking for. You can filter by Layout, Features, and Subject. After you select your desired filters, click the Apply Filters button to view the themes that match your set filters.
- **Search:** If you know the name of a free theme, you can easily search for it by keyword, author, or tag. You also can refine your search based on specific features of the theme, including color, layout, and subject (such as Holiday).

After you find the theme that you want, click the Install button that appears when you hover your mouse over the theme's thumbnail.

Previewing and activating a theme

After you upload a theme via SFTP or install it via the theme installer, you can preview and activate your desired theme.

TIP

The WordPress Theme Preview option allows you to see how the theme would look on your site without actually activating it. If you have a site that's receiving traffic, it's best to preview any new theme before activating it to ensure that you'll be happy with its look and functionality. If you're trying to decide among several new theme options, you can preview them all before changing your live site.

To preview your new theme, follow these steps:

1. **Log in to your WordPress Dashboard.**
2. **Click the Themes link on the Appearance menu.**

   The Themes screen appears, displaying your current (activated) theme and any themes that are installed in the `/wp-content/themes` directory on your web server.
3. **Preview the theme you want to use.**

   Click the Live Preview button that appears when you hover your mouse over the theme thumbnail. A preview of your site with the theme appears in your browser, as shown in Figure 2-6.

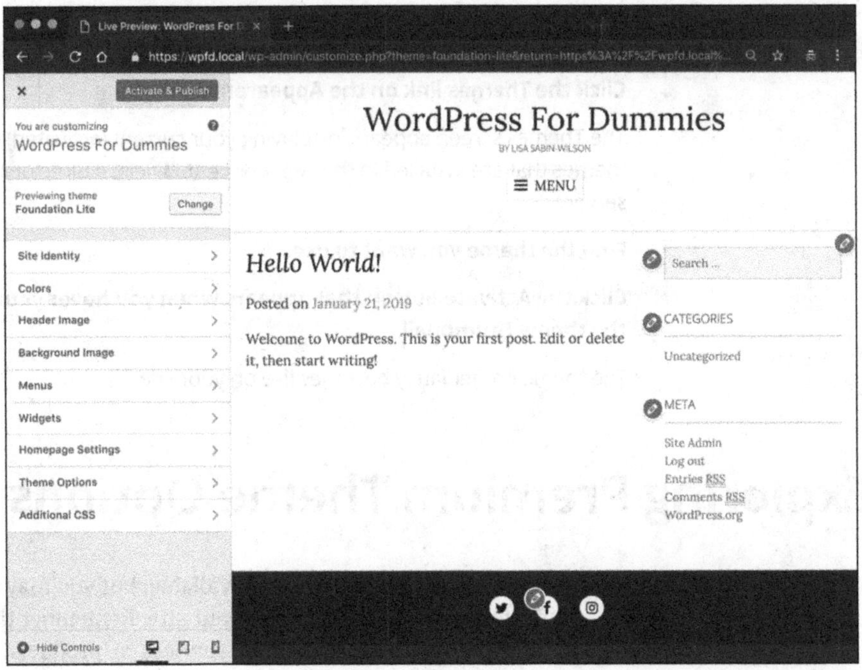

FIGURE 2-6: A WordPress theme preview.

4. **(Optional) Configure theme features.**

   Some, but not all, themes provide customization features. Figure 2-6 shows the customization options for the Twenty Nineteen theme:

   - Site Identity
   - Colors
   - Header Image
   - Background Image
   - Menus
   - Widgets
   - Home page Settings
   - Theme Options
   - Additional CSS

5. **Choose whether to activate the theme.**

   Click the Activate & Publish button in the top-right corner of the configuration panel to activate your new theme with the options you set in step 4, or close the preview by clicking the Cancel (X) button in the top-left corner of the panel.

To activate a new theme without previewing it, follow these steps:

1. **Log in to your WordPress Dashboard.**
2. **Click the Themes link on the Appearance menu.**

   The Themes screen appears, displaying your current (activated) theme and any themes that are installed in the `/wp-content/themes` directory on your web server.

3. **Find the theme you want to use.**
4. **Click the Activate button that appears when you hover your mouse over the theme thumbnail.**

   The theme immediately becomes live on your site.

Exploring Premium Theme Options

Thousands of free WordPress themes are available, but you may also want to consider premium (for purchase) themes for your site. Remember the adage "You get what you pay for" when considering free services or products, including WordPress and free themes.

Typically, when you download and use something that's free, you get no assistance with the product or service. Requests for help generally go unanswered. Therefore, your expectations should be low because you aren't paying anything. When you pay for something, you usually assume that you have support or service for your purchase and that the product is of high (or acceptable) quality.

WordPress, for example, is available free. Except for the active WordPress support forum, however, you have no guarantee of support while using the software. Moreover, you have no right to demand service.

Here are some things to consider when contemplating a premium theme. (I selected the commercial companies listed later in this chapter based on these criteria.)

- **Selection:** Many theme developers offer a rich, diverse selection of themes, including themes designed for specific industries, topics, or uses (such as video, blogging, real estate, or magazines). Generally, you can find a good, solid theme to use for your site from one source.
- **Innovation:** To differentiate them from their free counterparts, premium themes include innovative features such as theme settings or advanced options that extend WordPress to help you do more.
- **Great design with solid code:** Although many beautiful themes are free, premium themes are professionally coded and nicely designed, cost thousands of dollars, and require dozens of hours to build, which simply isn't feasible for many free-theme developers.
- **Support:** Most commercial companies have full-time support staff to answer questions, troubleshoot issues, and point you to resources beyond their support. Often, premium-theme developers spend more time helping customers troubleshoot issues outside the theme products. Therefore, purchasing a premium theme often gives you access to a dedicated support community, which you can ask about advanced issues and upcoming WordPress features; otherwise, you're on your own.
- **Stability:** No doubt you've purchased a product or service from a company only to find later that the company has gone out of business. If you choose to use a premium theme, purchase a theme from an established company with a solid business model, a record of accomplishment, and a dedicated team devoted to building and supporting quality products.

REMEMBER

Although some free themes have some or all of the features in the preceding list, for the most part, they don't. Keep in mind that just because a designer calls a theme *premium* doesn't mean that the theme has passed through any kind of quality review. The view of what constitutes a premium theme can, and will, differ from one designer to the next.

TIP

Fully investigate any theme before you spend your money on it. Here are some things to check out before you pay:

- Email the designer who's selling the premium theme, and ask about a support policy.
- Find people who've purchased the theme, and contact them to ask about their experiences with the theme and the designer.
- Carefully read any terms that the designer has published on his site to find any licensing restrictions that exist.
- If the premium theme designer has a support forum, ask whether you can browse the forum to find out how actively the designer answers questions and provides support. Are users waiting weeks to get their questions answered, for example, or does the designer seem to be on top of support requests?
- Search online for the theme and the designer. Often, users of premium themes post about their experiences with the theme and the designer. You can find both positive and negative information about the theme and the designer before you buy.

The developers in the following list are doing some amazingly innovative things with WordPress themes, and I highly recommend that you explore their offerings:

- **Elegant Themes (`https://www.elegantthemes.com`):** Shown in Figure 2-7, Elegant Themes emphasizes business WordPress themes that use WordPress as a full-fledged and powerful content management system. The site's pride and joy is the Divi theme, which includes a visual drag-and-drop page builder.
- **StudioPress (`https://www.studiopress.com`):** Shown in Figure 2-8, StudioPress has a great team, paid support moderators, and WordPress themes that are as much high-quality (from a code standpoint) as they are beautiful. You can get access to all StudioPress themes if you're a customer of the WP Engine WordPress Hosting service (`https://wpengine.com/more/studiopress-sites`), or you can purchase individual StudioPress themes from the company's website.

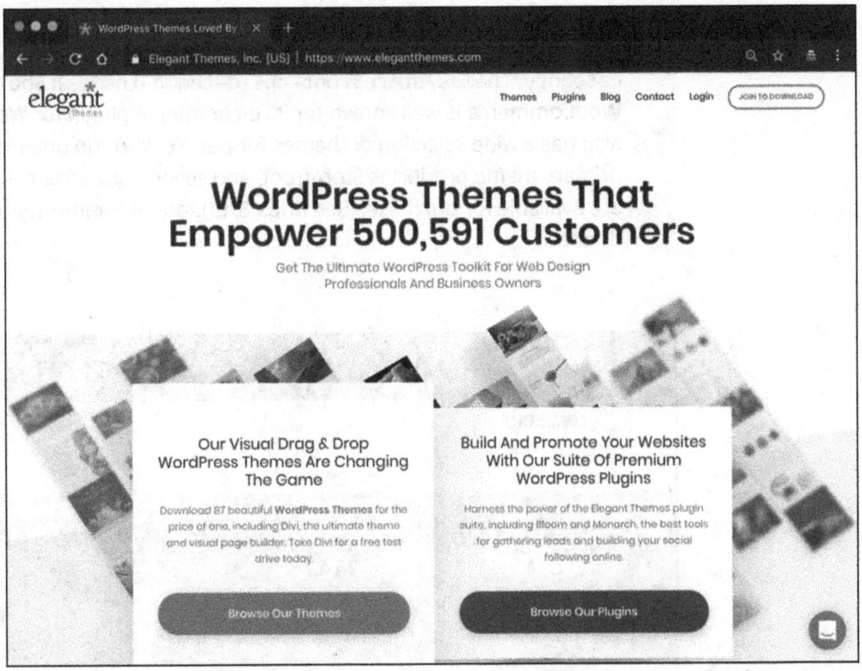

FIGURE 2-7: Elegant Themes, provider of commercial WordPress themes.

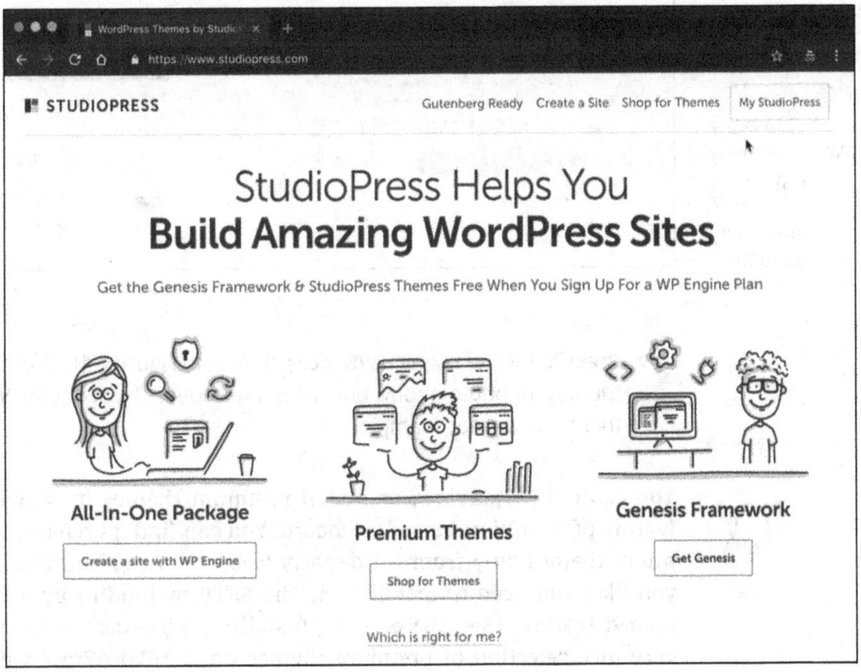

FIGURE 2-8: StudioPress, another provider of commercial WordPress themes.

- **WooCommerce Storefront Themes** (`https://woocommerce.com/product-category/themes/storefront-child-theme-themes`)**:** Shown in Figure 2-9, WooCommerce is well known for its e-commerce plugin for WordPress, but it also has a wide selection of themes for people who run online stores. The primary theme product is Storefront, and several Storefront child themes are available for purchase. (See Book 6, Chapter 5 for information on child themes.)

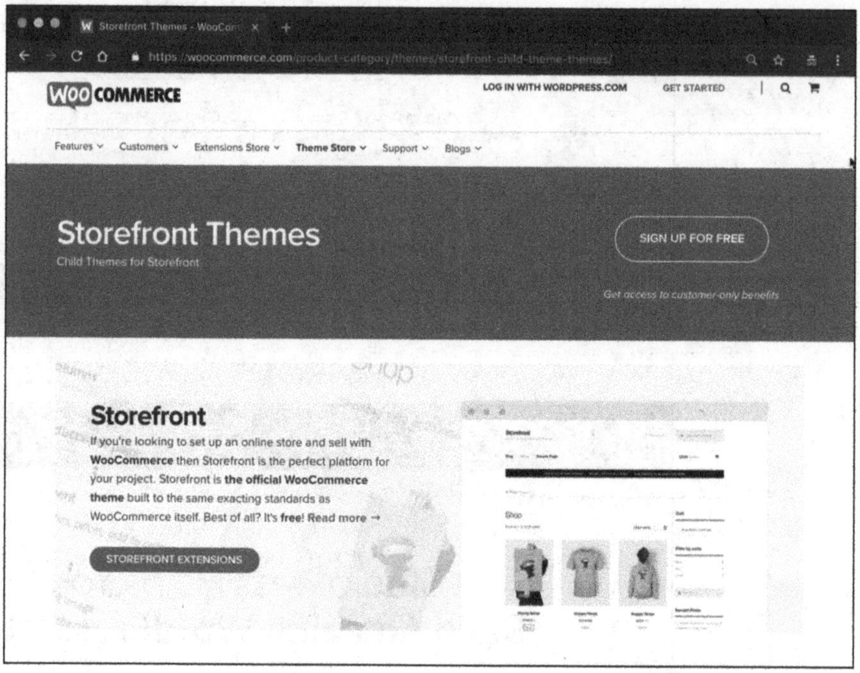

FIGURE 2-9: WooCommerce has premium themes, community, and support.

- **Press75** (`https://press75.com`)**:** Shown in Figure 2-10, Press75 offers niche themes for photography, portfolios, and video. Check out the Video Elements theme for a great example.

TIP

You can't find, preview, or install premium themes by using the Add Themes feature of your WordPress Dashboard. You can find, purchase, and download premium themes only from third-party websites. After you find a premium theme you like, you need to install it via the SFTP method or by using the Dashboard upload feature. (See the earlier "Installing a Theme" section.) You can find a very nice selection of premium themes on the WordPress website at `https://wordpress.org/themes/commercial`.

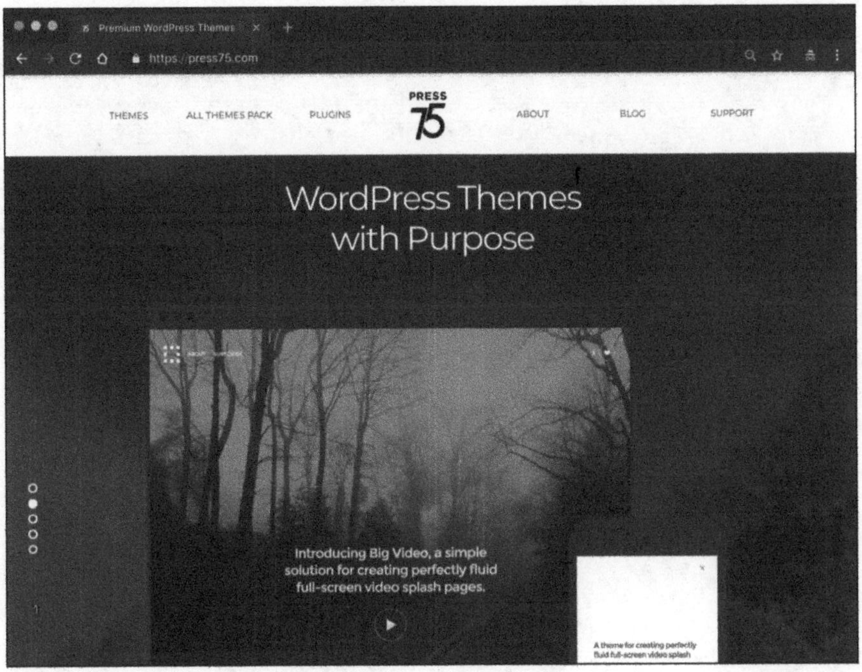

FIGURE 2-10: Press75 offers premium themes, demos, and theme packages.

IN THIS CHAPTER

- **Examining the theme's stylesheet**
- **Exploring template tags**
- **Making widget areas**
- **Understanding the main template files**

Chapter 3

Exploring the Anatomy of a Theme

This chapter breaks down the parts that make up your WordPress theme. Understanding your theme allows you greater flexibility when you customize it. Many of the problems people encounter with themes, such as not knowing which files edit certain functions of a site, comes from lack of understanding all the pieces.

If, like me, you like to get your hands dirty, you need to read this chapter. WordPress users who create their own themes do so in the interest of

- **Individuality:** Having a theme that no one else has. (If you use one of the free themes, you can pretty much count on the fact that at *least* a dozen other WordPress blogs have the same look as yours.)
- **Creativity:** Displaying your personal flair and style.
- **Control:** Having full control of how the blog looks, acts, and delivers your content.

Many of you aren't at all interested in creating your own theme for your WordPress website, however. Sometimes, it's easier to leave matters to the professionals and hire an experienced WordPress theme developer to create a custom look for your WordPress website or to use one of the thousands of free themes provided by WordPress designers. (See Book 6, Chapter 2.)

Creating themes requires you to step into the code of the templates, which can be a scary place sometimes, especially if you don't know what you're looking at. A good place to start is by understanding the structure of a WordPress website. Separately, the parts won't do you any good. But when you put them together, the real magic begins! This chapter covers the basics of doing just that, and near the end of the chapter, you find specific steps for putting your own theme together.

TIP

You don't need to know HTML to use WordPress. If you plan to create and design WordPress themes, however, you need some basic knowledge of HTML and Cascading Style Sheets (CSS). For assistance with HTML, check out *HTML5 and CSS3 All-in-One For Dummies*, 3rd Edition, by Andy Harris (John Wiley & Sons, Inc.).

Starting with the Basics

A WordPress *theme* is a collection of WordPress templates made up of WordPress template tags. When I refer to a WordPress theme, I'm talking about the group of templates that makes up the theme. When I talk about a WordPress *template*, I'm referring to only one of the template files that contain WordPress template tags and functions. WordPress template tags make all the templates work together as a theme. (I cover this topic in the *Exploring Template Tags, Values, and Parameters* section later in this chapter) These files include

- **The theme's stylesheet (`style.css`):** The stylesheet provides the theme's name, as well as the CSS rules that apply to the theme. (Later in this chapter, I go into detail about how stylesheets work.)
- **The main index template (`index.php`):** The index file is the first file that will be loaded when a visitor comes to your site. It contains the HTML as well as any WordPress functions and template tags needed on your home page.
- **An optional functions file (`functions.php`):** This optional file is a place where you can add additional functionality to your site via PHP and/or WordPress-specific functions.

Template and functions files end with the `.php` extension. *PHP* is the scripting language used in WordPress, which your web server recognizes and interprets as such. (Book 2, Chapter 3 covers additional details on the PHP language that you'll find helpful.) These files contain more than just scripts, though. The PHP files also contain HTML markup, which is the basic markup language of web pages.

Within this set of PHP files is all the information your browser and web server need to make your website. Everything from the color of the background to the layout of the content is contained in this set of files.

REMEMBER

The difference between a template and a theme can cause confusion. *Templates* are individual files. Each template file provides the structure in which your content will display. A *theme* is a set of templates. The theme uses the templates to make the whole site.

Understanding where the WordPress theme files are located on your web server gives you the ability to find and edit them, as needed. You can use two different methods to view and edit WordPress theme files by following these steps:

1. **Connect to your web server via Secure FTP (SFTP), and have a look at the existing WordPress themes on your server.**

   The correct location is `/wp-content/themes/`. When you open this folder, you find the `/twentynineteen` theme folder, which is the default theme for WordPress.

   REMEMBER

   If a theme is uploaded to any folder other than `/wp-content/themes`, it won't work.

2. **Open the folder for the Twenty Nineteen theme (`/wp-content/themes/twentynineteen`), and look at the template files inside.**

   When you open the Twenty Nineteen theme folder (see Figure 3-1), you see several files. At minimum, you find these five templates in the default theme:

   - *Stylesheet* (`style.css`)
   - *Functions file* (`functions.php`)
   - *Header template* (`header.php`)
   - *Main index* (`index.php`)
   - *Footer template* (`footer.php`)

   These files are the main WordPress template files, and I discuss them in more detail in this chapter. There are several template files, however, and you should try to explore all of them if you can. Take a peek inside to see the different template functions they contain. Every WordPress theme is different and contains a different number and type of files, but the five files I mention here usually exist in all WordPress themes.

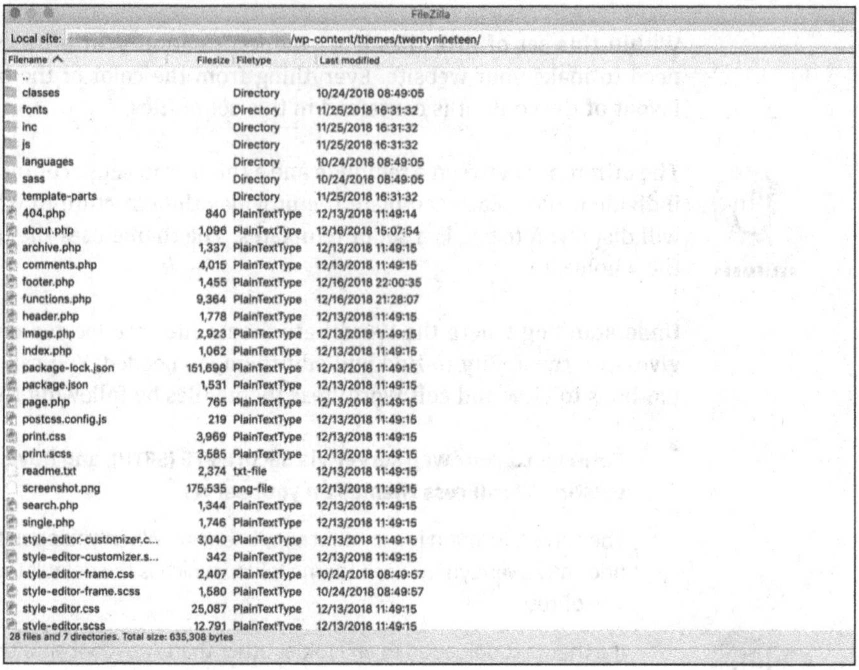

FileZilla
Local site: /wp-content/themes/twentynineteen/
Filename Filesize Filetype Last modified
..
classes Directory 10/24/2018 08:49:05
fonts Directory 11/25/2018 16:31:32
inc Directory 11/25/2018 16:31:32
js Directory 11/25/2018 16:31:32
languages Directory 10/24/2018 08:49:05
sass Directory 10/24/2018 08:49:05
template-parts Directory 11/25/2018 16:31:32
404.php 840 PlainTextType 12/13/2018 11:49:14
about.php 1,096 PlainTextType 12/16/2018 15:07:54
archive.php 1,337 PlainTextType 12/13/2018 11:49:15
comments.php 4,015 PlainTextType 12/13/2018 11:49:15
footer.php 1,455 PlainTextType 12/16/2018 22:00:35
functions.php 9,364 PlainTextType 12/16/2018 21:28:07
header.php 1,778 PlainTextType 12/13/2018 11:49:15
image.php 2,923 PlainTextType 12/13/2018 11:49:15
index.php 1,062 PlainTextType 12/13/2018 11:49:15
package-lock.json 151,698 PlainTextType 12/13/2018 11:49:15
package.json 1,531 PlainTextType 12/13/2018 11:49:15
page.php 765 PlainTextType 12/13/2018 11:49:15
postcss.config.js 219 PlainTextType 12/13/2018 11:49:15
print.css 3,969 PlainTextType 12/13/2018 11:49:15
print.scss 3,586 PlainTextType 12/13/2018 11:49:15
readme.txt 2,374 txt-file 12/13/2018 11:49:15
screenshot.png 175,535 png-file 12/13/2018 11:49:15
search.php 1,344 PlainTextType 12/13/2018 11:49:15
single.php 1,746 PlainTextType 12/13/2018 11:49:15
style-editor-customizer.c... 3,040 PlainTextType 12/13/2018 11:49:15
style-editor-customizer.s... 342 PlainTextType 12/13/2018 11:49:15
style-editor-frame.css 2,407 PlainTextType 10/24/2018 08:49:57
style-editor-frame.scss 1,580 PlainTextType 10/24/2018 08:49:57
style-editor.css 25,087 PlainTextType 12/13/2018 11:49:15
style-editor.scss 12,791 PlainTextType 12/13/2018 11:49:15
28 files and 7 directories. Total size: 635,308 bytes

FIGURE 3-1: Template files contained within the Twenty Nineteen theme folder.

3. **Click the Editor link on the Appearance menu to look at the template files within a theme.**

   This Edit Themes page lists the various templates available within the active theme. (Figure 3-2 shows the templates in the default Twenty Nineteen theme.) A text box in the middle of the screen displays the contents of each template, and this box is also where you can edit the template file(s). To view and edit a template file, click the template's name in the list on the right side of the page.

The Edit Themes page also shows the HTML markup and template tags within the template file. These tags make all the magic happen on your website; they connect all the templates to form a theme. "Connecting the templates" later in this chapter discusses these template tags in detail, showing you what they mean and how they function. "Putting a Theme Together" later in this chapter provides steps for putting the tags together to create your own theme or edit an existing theme.

TIP

Click the Documentation drop-down menu on the Themes screen (as shown in Figure 3-3) to see all the template tags used in the template you're currently viewing. This list is helpful when you edit templates, and it gives you insight into the template tags used to create functions and features in the template you're viewing. (*Note:* The Documentation drop-down menu on the Themes screen doesn't appear when you view the stylesheet because no template tags, or functions, are used in the `style.css` template — only CSS.)

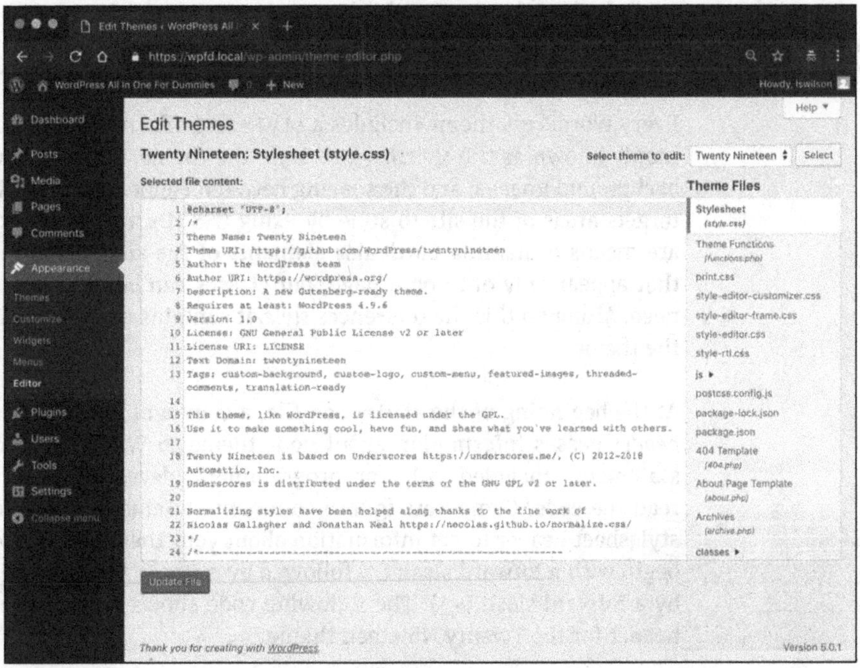

FIGURE 3-2: A list of templates available in the default Twenty Nineteen theme.

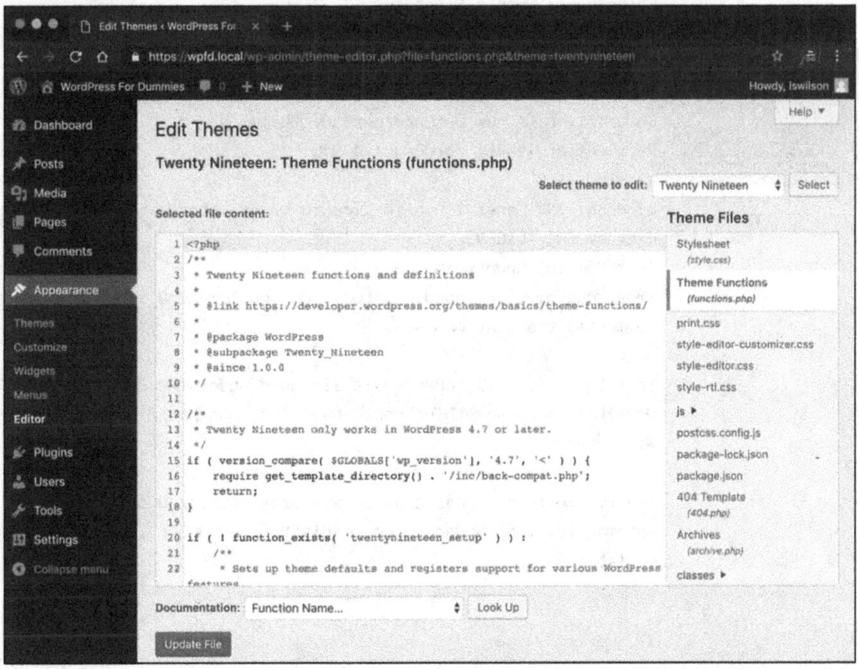

FIGURE 3-3 The Documentation drop down menu on the Edit Themes screen.

Understanding the Stylesheet

Every WordPress theme includes a `style.css` file. A browser uses this file, commonly known as the *stylesheet*, to style the theme. Style can include text colors, background images, and the spacing between elements on the site. The stylesheet targets areas of the site to style by using CSS IDs and classes. *CSS IDs* and *classes* are means of naming particular elements of the site. IDs are used for elements that appear only once on a page, but classes can be used as many times as you need. Although this file references *style*, it contains much more information about the theme.

At the beginning of the `style.css` file, a comment block known as the *stylesheet header* passes information about your theme to WordPress. *Comments* are code statements included only for programmers, developers, and any others who read the code. Computers ignore comment statements, but WordPress uses the stylesheet header to get information about your theme. In CSS, comments always begin with a forward slash (/) followed by a star (*) and end with a star followed by a forward slash (*/). The following code shows an example of the stylesheet header for the Twenty Nineteen theme:

```
/*
Theme Name: Twenty Nineteen
Theme URI: https://github.com/WordPress/twentynineteen
Author: the WordPress team
Author URI: https://wordpress.org/
Description: A new Gutenberg-ready theme.
Requires at least: WordPress 4.9.6
Version: 1.0
License: GNU General Public License v2 or later
License URI: LICENSE
Text Domain: twentynineteen
Tags: custom-background, custom-logo, custom-menu, featured-images, threaded
comments, translation-ready

This theme, like WordPress, is licensed under the GPL.
Use it to make something cool, have fun, and share what you've learned
With others.

Twenty Nineteen is based on Underscores https://underscores.me/, (C) 2012-2018
Automattic, Inc. Underscores is distributed under the terms of the GNU GPL v2
or later.
```

```
Normalizing styles have been helped along thanks to the fine work of
Nicolas Gallagher and Jonathan Neal https://necolas.github.io/normalize.css/
*/
/*--------------------------------------------------------------
>>> TABLE OF CONTENTS:
----------------------------------------------------------------
# Variables
# Normalize
# Typography
    ## Headings
.   ## Copy
# Elements
.   ## Lists
.   ## Tables
# Forms
.   ## Buttons
.   ## Fields
# Navigation
.   ## Links
.   ## Menus
.   ## Next & Previous
# Accessibility
# Alignments
# Clearings
# Layout
# Widgets
# Content
.   ## Archives
.   ## Posts and pages
.   ## Comments
# Blocks
# Media
.   ## Captions
.   ## Galleries
--------------------------------------------------------------*/
/*
 * Chrome renders extra-wide   characters for the Hoefler Text font.
 * This results in a jumping cursor when typing in both the Classic and block
 * editors. The following font-face override fixes the issue by manually
* inserting a custom font that includes just a Hoefler Text space replacement
* for that character instead.
*/
```

Exploring the Anatomy of a Theme

Figure 3-4 shows how the Twenty Nineteen theme information looks on the Themes screen in the Dashboard. Notice that the Title, Author, Description, Version, and Tags information is pulled directly from the `style.css` header.

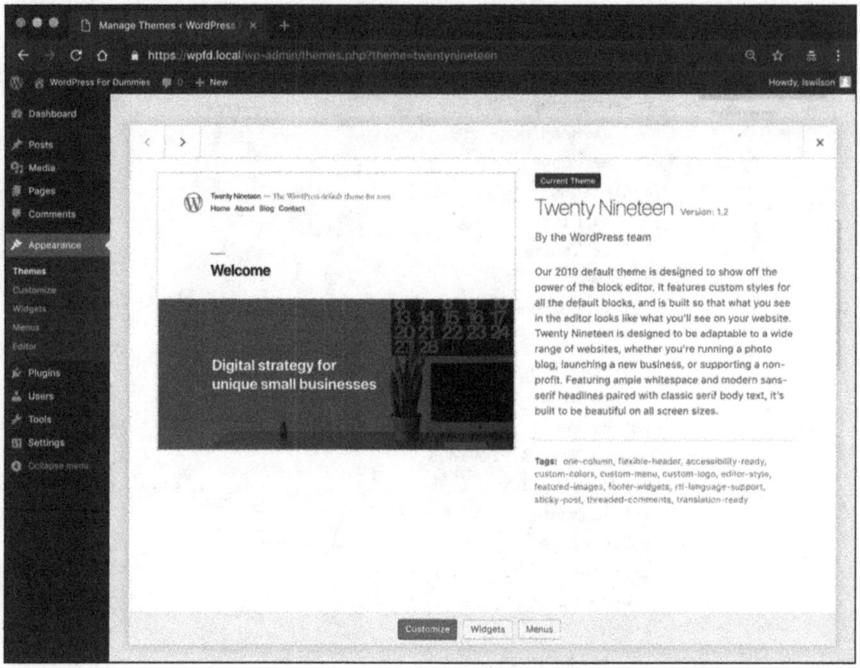

FIGURE 3-4: Twenty Nineteen information on the Themes screen of the Dashboard.

If you make modifications to the stylesheet header, the changes reflect in the WordPress Dashboard on the Themes screen, found by clicking the Theme link in the Appearance menu.

WARNING

Themes must provide this information in the stylesheet header, and no two themes can have the same information. Two themes with the same name and details would cause a conflict in the theme-selection page. If you create your own theme based on another theme, make sure that you change this information first.

Below the stylesheet header are the CSS styles that drive the formatting and styling of your theme.

TIP

Book 6, Chapter 4 goes into detail about CSS, including some examples that you can use to tweak the style of your existing WordPress theme. Check it out!

Exploring Template Tags, Values, and Parameters

Some people are intimidated when they look at template tags. Really, they're just simple bits of PHP code that you can use inside a template file to display information dynamically. Before starting to play around with template tags in your WordPress templates, however, it's important to understand what makes up a template tag and why.

WordPress is based in PHP (a scripting language for creating web pages) and uses PHP commands to pull information from the MySQL database. Every tag begins with a function to start PHP and ends with a function to stop PHP. In the middle of those two commands lives the request to the database that tells WordPress to grab the data and display it.

A typical template tag looks like this:

```
<?php bloginfo();?>
```

This example tells WordPress to do three things:

- » Start PHP (`<?php`).
- » Use PHP to get information from the MySQL database and deliver it to your blog (`bloginfo();`).
- » Stop PHP (`?>`).

In this case, `bloginfo` is the actual tag, which grabs information from the database to deliver it to your site. What information is retrieved depends on what tag appears between the two PHP commands. As you may notice, there's a lot of starting and stopping of PHP throughout the WordPress templates. The process seems as though it would be resource-intensive, if not exhaustive, but it really isn't.

REMEMBER

For every PHP command you start, you need a stop command. Every time a command begins with `<?php`, somewhere later in the code is the closing `?>` command. PHP commands that aren't structured properly cause really ugly errors on your site, and they've been known to send programmers, developers, and hosting providers into loud screaming fits.

Understanding the basics

If every piece of content on your site were *hard-coded* (manually added to the template files), it wouldn't be easy to use and modify. Template tags allow you to add content dynamically to your site. One example of adding information by using a template tag is the `the_category` tag. Instead of typing all the categories and links that each post belongs in, you can use the `the_category()` tag in your template to automatically display all the categories as links.

Using template tags prevents duplication of effort by automating the process of adding content to your website.

When you use a template tag, you're really telling WordPress to do something or retrieve some information. Often, template tags are used to fetch data from the server and even display it on the front end. More than 100 template tags are built into WordPress, and the tags vary greatly in what they can accomplish. You can find a complete list of template tags in the WordPress Codex (documentation for WordPress) at `https://codex.wordpress.org/Template_Tags`.

You can use template tags only inside PHP blocks. The PHP blocks can be opened and closed as many times as needed in a template file. When a PHP block is opened, the server knows that anything contained in the block is to be translated as PHP and then executed. The opening tag (`<?php`) must be followed at some point by the closing tag (`?>`). All blocks must contain these tags. A template tag is used in the same way that PHP functions are. The tag is always text (maybe separated with underscores or dashes), opening and closing brackets, and a semicolon. The following line of code (not a real template tag) shows you how everything looks:

```
<?php template_tag_name();?>
```

PHP is a fairly advanced coding language and has many built-in functions for you to use. If you aren't a PHP developer, keep it simple when you're attempting to add custom PHP. All code must be semantically perfect; otherwise, it won't work. Always read your code to make sure that you entered it correctly.

REMEMBER

You can use some template tags only inside The Loop, so check the Codex for details. You can find out more about The Loop in "Examining the Main Index and The Loop" later in this chapter.

Using parameters

Because a template tag is a PHP function, you can pass parameters to the tag. A *parameter* is a variable that allows you to change or filter the output of a template tag. WordPress has three types of template tags:

- **Tags without parameters:** Some template tags don't require any options, so they don't need any parameters passed to them. The `is_user_logged_in()` tag, for example, doesn't accept any parameters because it returns only `true` or `false`.
- **Tags with PHP function-style parameters:** Template tags with PHP function-style parameters accept parameters that are passed to them by placing one or more values inside the function's parentheses. If you're using the `bloginfo()` tag, for example, you can filter the output to the description by using

  ```
  <?php bloginfo('description');?>
  ```

  REMEMBER

  If multiple parameters are involved, the order in which you list them is very important. Each function sets the necessary order of its variables, so double-check the order of your parameters.

  REMEMBER

  Always place the value in single quotes, and separate multiple parameters with commas.

- **Tags with query-string-style parameters:** Template tags' query-string parameters allow you to change the values of only the parameters you need to change. This feature is useful for template tags that have a large number of options. The `wp_list_authors();` tag, for example, has six parameters. Instead of using the PHP function-style parameters, you can get to the source of what you need and give it a value. If you want to see the full names of your authors in a list, for example, use

  ```
  <?php wp_list_authors('show_fullname=1');?>
  ```

  Query-string-style parameters can be the most difficult kinds to work with because they generally deal with the template tags that have the most possible parameters.

Table 3-1 helps you understand the three variations of parameters used by WordPress.

You need to know these three types of parameters:

- **String:** A line of text that can be anything from a single letter to a long list of words. A string is placed between single quotation marks and sets an option for the parameter or is displayed as text.
- **Integer:** A positive or negative number. Integers are placed within the parentheses and either inside or outside single quotation marks. Either way, WordPress processes them correctly.

TABLE 3-1 **Three Variations of Template Parameters**

Variation	Description	Example
Tags without parameters	These tags have no additional options available. Tags without parameters have nothing within the parentheses.	*the_tag*();
Tags with PHP function-style parameters	These tags have a comma-separated list of values placed within the tag parentheses.	*the_tag*(‘1,2,3’);
Tags with query-string-style parameters	These types of tags have several available parameters. This tag style enables you to change the value for each parameter without being required to provide values for all available parameters for the tag.	*the_tag*(‘parameter= true’);

- **Boolean:** A parameter that sets the options to `true` or `false`. This parameter can be numeric (`0=false` and `1=true`) or textual. Boolean values aren't placed within quotation marks.

REMEMBER

The WordPress Codex, located at `https://codex.wordpress.org`, has every conceivable template tag and possible parameter known to the WordPress software. The tags and parameters that I share with you in this chapter are the ones used most often.

Customizing common tags

Because template tags must be used inside the PHP template files, they can easily be customized with HTML. If you're using the PHP tag `wp_list_authors()`, for example, you could display it in an HTML unordered list so that the pages are easily accessible to the users, like this:

```
<ul>
. <?php wp_list_authors('show_fullname=1');?>
</ul>
```

This code displays all the authors on your WordPress site as an unordered list like this:

- John Doe
- Jane Doe
- Xavier Doe

Another example is titles. You can wrap the titles of your posts or pages in H1 HTML tags, like this:

```
<h1 class="pagetitle">
. <?php the_title();?>
</h1>
```

Creating New Widget Areas

Most themes are *widget-ready*, meaning that you can insert widgets into them easily. Widgets allow you to add functionality to your sidebar without having to use code. Some common widget functionalities include displaying recent posts, displaying recent comments, adding a search box for searching content on a site, and adding static text. Even widget-ready themes have their limitations, however. You may find that the theme you chose doesn't have widget-ready areas in all the places you want them. You can make your own, however.

Registering your widget

To add a widget-ready area to the WordPress Dashboard Widget interface, first you must register the widget in your theme's Functions file (`functions.php`) file by following these steps:

```
function my_widgets_init() {
  register_sidebar(array (
  'name'          => __('My Widget Area'),
  'id'            => 'my-widget-area',
  'description'   => __('A new widget area I created!'),
  'before_widget' => '<li id="%1$s" class="widget-container %2$s">',
  'after_widget'  => "</li>",
  'before_title'  => '<h3 class="widget-title">',
  'after_title'   => '</h3>',
  ));
  }
add_action('widgets_init', 'my_widgets_init');
```

You can insert this code at the very bottom of the Functions file. It's sometimes helpful to add a few extra lines when you're adding code. The extra empty lines are ignored by the browser but greatly increase the readability of the code.

Within that code, you see an *array* with seven key pair values that tell WordPress how you want your widgets to be handled and displayed:

- **name:** This name is unique to the widget and appears on the Widgets screen of the Dashboard. It's helpful to register several widget areas on your site.
- **id:** This array is the unique ID given to the widget.
- **description (optional):** This array is a text description of the widget. The text placed here displays on the Widgets screen of the Dashboard.
- **before_widget:** This array is the HTML markup that gets inserted directly before the widget and is helpful for CSS styling purposes.
- **after_widget:** This array is the HTML markup that gets inserted directly after the widget.
- **before_title:** This array is the HTML markup that gets inserted directly before the widget title.
- **after_title:** This array is the HTML markup that gets inserted directly after the widget title.

REMEMBER

Even though you use `register_sidebar` to register a widget, widgets don't have to appear on a sidebar; they can appear anywhere you want them to. The example code snippet earlier in this section registers a widget named Widget Name on the WordPress Dashboard. Additionally, it places the widget's content in an element that has the CSS class `widget` and puts <h3> tags around the widget's title.

Widgets that have been registered on the WordPress Dashboard are ready to be populated with content. On the Appearance menu of your site's Dashboard, you see a link titled Widgets. When you click the Widgets link, you see the new widget area you registered.

Displaying new widgets on your site

When a widget area is registered with WordPress, you can display the area somewhere on your site. Common places for widget areas are the sidebar and (in the default Twenty Nineteen theme) the footer.

To add a widget area to a template file in your WordPress theme, pick a location within the file and then locate that area in the HTML. (This area can vary from theme to theme.) Many times, theme authors will create their own `sidebar.php` or `footer.php` file, and you can add this code there. After you find the area in the HTML, add the following code to the template:

```
<?php dynamic_sidebar('My Widget Area');?>
```

This code displays the contents of the widget that you previously registered in the admin area.

Simplifying customization with functions

You may find that the simple Widget Area code doesn't accomplish all the functionality that you need. You may want to display a message on the website if a widget area is empty and doesn't yet have any widgets added to it as a visual cue and reminder to add some widgets. A solution is to create a custom PHP function that gives you a few more options. Open `functions.php`, and insert the following code on a new blank line at the end of the file:

```
function add_new_widget_location($name) {
if (!function_exists('dynamic_sidebar') || ! dynamic_sidebar($name)) :?>
  <div class="widget">
    <h4><?php echo $name;?></h4>
    <div class="widget">
    <p>This section is widgetized. If you would like to
add content to this section, you may do so by using the Widgets
panel from within your WordPress Admin Dashboard. This Widget
Section is called "<strong><?php echo $name;?></strong>"</p>
    </div>
  </div>
<?php endif;?>
<?php
}
```

In this function, the first part checks whether a widget is assigned to this area. If so, the widget displays. If not, a message with the name of the widget area displays, which allows users to distinguish the widget area to which they need to add widgets in the Dashboard Widgets screen. Now if you want to display a widget by using this method, you go to the desired template file and insert the following code where you want the widget to appear in the `sidebar.php` or `footer.php`, as in this example:

```
<?php add_new_widget_location('Widget-Name');?>
```

Examining the Main Index and The Loop

At a bare minimum, a theme is required to have only two files. The first is `style.css`. The other is a main index file, known in WordPress as `index.php`. The `index.php` file is the first file WordPress tries to load when someone visits your site.

Extremely flexible, `index.php` can be used as a stand-alone file, or it can include other templates. The Main Index template drags your content (posts, pages, categories, menus, and so on) out of the MySQL database and inserts them into your website for the whole world to see and read. This template is to your site what the dance floor is to a nightclub: It's where all the action happens.

The filename of the Main Index template is `index.php`. You can find it in the `/wp-content/themes/twentynineteen/` folder.

The first template tag in the Main Index template calls in the Header template, meaning that it pulls the information from the Header template (`header.php`) into the Main Index template, as follows:

```
<?php get_header();?>
```

Your theme can work without calling in the Header template, but it will be missing several essential pieces: the CSS and the site name and tagline, for starters.

The Main Index template in the Twenty Nineteen theme connects with three other files in a similar fashion:

- **`get_template_part('template-parts/content/content');`**: This function calls in the template file named `content.php`, located in the `/twentynineteen/template-parts/content/` folder.
- **`get_template_part('template-parts/content/content', 'none');`**: This function calls in the template file named `content-none.php`, located in the `/twentynineteen/template-parts/content/` folder.
- **`get_footer();`**: This function calls in the template file named `footer.php`.

I cover each of these three functions and template files in upcoming sections of this chapter.

REMEMBER

The concept of *connecting with* a template file by using a function or template tag is exactly what the Main Index template does with the four functions for the header, loop, sidebar, and footer templates, explained later in this section.

When I talk about The Loop, I'm not talking about America's second-largest downtown business district, originating at the corner of State and Madison streets in Chicago. I could write about some interesting experiences I've had there . . . but that would be a different book.

The Loop, in this case, is a function that WordPress uses to display content on your site, such as blog posts and page content. The Loop has a starting point and an ending point; anything placed between those points is used to display each post, including any HTML, PHP, or CSS tags and codes.

Here's a look at what the WordPress Codex calls the world's simplest index page:

```
<?php
get_header();
if (have_posts()) :
  while (have_posts()) :
    the_post();
    the_content();
  endwhile;
endif;
get_sidebar();
get_footer();
?>
```

Here's how the code works:

1. The template opens the php tag.
2. The Loop includes the header, meaning that it retrieves anything contained in the header.php file and displays it.
3. The Loop begins with the `while (have_posts()) :` bit.
4. Anything between the `while` and the `endwhile` repeats for each post that displays.

   The number of posts that displays is determined in the General Settings screen of the WordPress Dashboard.
5. If your site has posts (and most do, even when you first install it), WordPress proceeds with The Loop, starting with the piece of code that looks like this:

   ```
   if (have_posts()) :
     while (have_posts()) :
   ```

   This code tells WordPress to grab the posts from the MySQL database and display them on your page.
6. The Loop closes with these tags:

   ```
     endwhile;
   endif;
   ```

Exploring the Anatomy of a Theme

Near the beginning of The Loop template is a template tag that looks like this:

```
if (have_posts()) :
```

In plain English, that tag says `If [this blog] has posts.`

7. If your site meets that condition (that is, if it has posts), WordPress proceeds with The Loop and displays your posts. If it doesn't meet that condition (that is, doesn't have posts), WordPress displays a message that no posts exist.
8. When The Loop ends (at the `endwhile`), the index template goes on to execute the files for sidebar and footer.

Although it's simple, The Loop is one of the core functions of WordPress.

WARNING

Misplacement of the `while` or `endwhile` statements causes The Loop to break. If you're having trouble with The Loop in an existing template, check your version against the original to see whether the `while` statements are misplaced.

REMEMBER

In your travels as a WordPress user, you may run across plugins or scripts with instructions that say something like this: "This must be placed within The Loop." That's The Loop that I discuss in this section, so pay particular attention. Understanding The Loop arms you with the knowledge you need to tackle and understand your WordPress themes.

The Loop is no different from any other template tag; it must begin with a function to start PHP, and it must end with a function to stop PHP. The Loop begins with PHP and then makes a request: "While there are posts in my site, display them on this page." This PHP function tells WordPress to grab the post information from the database and return it to the page. The end of The Loop is like a traffic cop with a big red stop sign telling WordPress to stop the function.

REMEMBER

You can set the number of posts displayed per page in the Reading Settings screen of the WordPress Dashboard (choose Settings⇨Reading). The Loop abides by this rule and displays only the number of posts per page that you've set.

WordPress uses other template files besides the main index, such as the header, sidebar, and footer templates. The next sections give you a closer look at a few of them.

Header template

The Header template for your WordPress themes is the starting point for every WordPress theme because it tells web browsers the following:

» The title of your site
» The location of the CSS
» The RSS feed URL
» The site URL
» The tagline (or description) of the website

In many themes, the first elements in the header are a main image and the navigation. These two elements are usually in the `header.php` file because they load on every page and rarely change. The following statement is the built-in WordPress function to call the header template:

```
<?php get_header();?>
```

TIP

Every page on the web has to start with a few pieces of code. In every `header.php` file in any WordPress theme, you can find these bits of code at the top:

» The DOCTYPE (which stands for *document type declaration*) tells the browser which type of XHTML standards you're using. The Twenty Nineteen theme uses `<!DOCTYPE html>`, which is a declaration for W3C standards compliance mode and covers all major browsers.
» The `<html>` tag (*HTML* stands for *Hypertext Markup Language*) tells the browser which language you're using to write your web pages.
» The `<head>` tag tells the browser that the information contained within the tag shouldn't be displayed on the site; rather, it's information about the document.

In the Header template of the Twenty Nineteen theme, these bits of code look like the following example, and you should leave them intact:

```
<!DOCTYPE html>
<html <?php language_attributes();?>>
<head>
```

TIP

On the Edit Themes screen of the Dashboard (choose Appearance⇨Editor), click the Header template link to display the template code in the text box. Look closely, and you see that the `<!DOCTYPE html>` declaration, `<html>` tag, and `<head>` tag show up in the template.

The `<head>` tag needs to be closed at the end of the Header template, which looks like this: `</head>`. You also need to include a fourth tag, the `<body>` tag, which tells the browser where the information you want to display begins. Both the

<body> and <html> tags need to be closed at the end of the template, like this: </body></html>.

Using bloginfo parameters

The Header template makes much use of one WordPress template tag in particular: `bloginfo();`. It's commonly used in WordPress themes.

What differentiates the type of information that a tag pulls in is a *parameter*. Parameters are placed inside the parentheses of the tag, enclosed in single quotes. For the most part, these parameters pull information from the settings in your WordPress Dashboard. The template tag to get your site title, for example, looks like this:

```
<?php bloginfo('name');?>
```

Table 3-2 lists the various parameters you need for the `bloginfo();` tag and shows you what the template tag looks like. The parameters in Table 3-2 are listed in the order of their appearance in the Twenty Nineteen `header.php` template file and in the `/template-parts/header/site-branding.php` file, and they pertain only to the `bloginfo();` template tag.

REMEMBER

Although the Twenty Nineteen theme breaks the header information into two template files, most WordPress themes have this `bloginfo();` information only in the `header.php` file. The placement of the `bloginfo();` tag varies from theme to theme.

TABLE 3-2 Tag Values for bloginfo();

Parameter	Information	Tag
charset	Character settings, set in the General Settings screen	`<?php bloginfo('charset');?>`
name	Site title, set by choosing Settings⇨General	`<?php bloginfo('name');?>`
description	Tagline for your site, set by choosing Settings⇨General	`<?php bloginfo('description');?>`
url	Your site's web address, set by choosing Settings⇨General	`<?php bloginfo('url');?>`
stylesheet_url	URL of primary CSS file	`<?php bloginfo('stylesheet_url');?>`
pingback_url	Displays the trackback URL for your site on single post pages	`<?php bloginfo('pingback_url');?>`

Creating <title> tags

Here's a useful tip about your site's `<title>` tag: Search engines pick up the words used in the `<title>` tag as keywords to categorize your site in their directories. The `<title>...</title>` tags are HTML tags that tell the browser to display the title of your website on the title bar of a visitor's browser.

REMEMBER

Search engines love the title bar. The more you can tweak that title to provide detailed descriptions of your site (otherwise known as *search engine optimization*, or SEO), the more the search engines love your web site. Browsers show that love by giving your site higher rankings in their results.

The site `<title>` tag is the code that lives in the Header template between these two tag markers: `<title></title>`. In the default Twenty Nineteen theme, that bit of code (located in the theme's `functions.php` template file) looks like this:

```
add_theme_support('title-tag');
```

The `add_theme_support('title-tag');` in the `functions.php` template tells WordPress to place the title tag in the `<head>` section of the website. By adding theme support for the title tag, you're saying that this theme doesn't use a hard-coded `<title>` tag in the document head and that you expect WordPress to provide it.

The way that the `add_theme_support('title-tag');` function displays the title is based on the type of page that's being displayed, and it shrewdly uses SEO to help you with the browser powers that be.

Within some of the WordPress template tags, such as the `<title>` tag example at the beginning of this section, you may notice some weird characters that look like a foreign language. You may wonder what `»` is, for example. It isn't part of any PHP function or CSS style. Rather, it's a *character entity* — a kind of code that enables you to display a special character in your blog. The `»` character entity displays a double right-angle quotation mark.

Displaying your blog name and tagline

Most WordPress themes show your site name and tagline in the header of the site, which means that those items are displayed in easy, readable text for all visitors (not just search engines) to see. My site name and tagline, for example, are

- **Site name:** Lisa Sabin-Wilson
- **Site tagline:** Author of *WordPress For Dummies* and owner of WebDevStudios

You can use the bloginfo(); tag plus a little HTML code to display your site name and tagline. Most sites have a clickable title, which is a site title that takes you back to the main page when it's clicked. No matter where your visitors are on your site, they can always go back home by clicking the title of your site on the header.

To create a clickable title, use the following HTML markup and WordPress template tags:

```
<a href="<?php bloginfo('url');?>"><?php bloginfo('name');?></a>
```

The bloginfo('url'); tag is your main site Internet address, and the bloginfo('name'); tag is the name of your site (refer to Table 3-1). So the code creates a link that looks something like this:

```
<a href="http://yourdomain.com">Your Site Name</a>
```

The tagline generally isn't linked back home. You can display it by using the following tag:

```
<?php bloginfo('description');?>
```

This tag pulls the tagline directly from the one that you've set up on the General Settings screen of your WordPress Dashboard.

This example shows that WordPress is intuitive and user-friendly; you can do things such as change the site name and tagline with a few keystrokes on the Dashboard. Changing your options in the Dashboard creates the change on every page of your site; no coding experience is required. Beautiful, isn't it?

In the Twenty Nineteen templates, these tags are surrounded by tags that look like these: <h1></h1> or <p></p>. These tags are Header and Paragraph tags, which define the look and layout of the site name and tagline in the CSS of your theme. Book 6, Chapter 4 covers CSS.

Sidebar template

The Sidebar template in WordPress has the filename sidebar.php. The sidebar usually appears on the left or right side of the main content area of your WordPress theme. (The default Twenty Nineteen theme doesn't have a sidebar by design.) It's a good place to put useful information about your site, such as a site summary, advertisements, or testimonials.

Many themes use widget areas in the sidebar template to display content on WordPress pages and posts. The following line of code is the built-in WordPress function that calls the Sidebar template:

```
<?php get_sidebar();?>
```

This code calls the Sidebar template and all the information it contains into your page.

Footer template

The Footer template in WordPress has the filename `footer.php`. The footer is generally at the bottom of the page and contains brief reference information about the site, usually including copyright information, template design credits, and a mention of WordPress. Similar to the Header and Sidebar templates, the Footer template gets called into the Main Index template through this bit of code:

```
<?php get_footer();?>
```

TIP

You can write calls for the Sidebar and Footer templates that are written as part of a larger call:

```
<?php
  get_sidebar();
  get_footer();
?>
```

It's possible, and common, to wrap two template tags in one PHP function that way if they appear directly after one another. The examples I give in this chapter separate them into single functions to make sure that you're clear about what the actual function is.

This code calls the Footer and all the information it contains into your website page.

Examining Other Template Files

To make your website work properly, WordPress uses all the theme files together. Some, such as the header and footer, are used on every page. Others, such as the Comments template (`comments.php`), are used only at specific times, to pull in specific functions.

When someone visits your site, WordPress uses a series of queries to determine which templates to use.

You can include many more theme templates in your theme. Here are some of the other template files you may want to use:

- **Comments template (`comments.php`):** The Comments template is required if you plan to host comments on your site; it provides all the template tags you need to display those comments. The template tag used to call the comments into the template is `<?php comments_template();?>`.
- **Single Post template (`single.php`):** When your visitors click the title or permalink of a post you published to your site, they're taken to that post's individual page. There, they can read the entire post, and if you have comments enabled, they see the comments form and can leave comments.
- **Page template (`page.php`):** You can use a Page template for static pages of your WordPress site.
- **Search Results (`search.php`):** You can use this template to create a custom display of search results on your blog. When someone uses the search feature to search your site for specific keywords, this template formats the return of those results.
- **404 template (`404.php`):** Use this template to create a custom 404 page, which is the page visitors get when the browser can't find the page requested and returns that ugly `404 Page Cannot Be Found` error.

REMEMBER

The templates in the preceding list are optional. If these templates don't exist in your WordPress `themes` folder, nothing breaks. The Main Index template handles the display of these items (the single post page, the search results page, and so on). The only exception is the Comments template. If you want to display comments on your site, you must include that template in your theme.

Customizing Your Posts with Template Tags

This section covers the template tags that you use to display the body of each post you publish. The body of a post includes information such as the post date and time, title, author name, category, and content.

Table 3-3 lists the common template tags you can use for posts, available for you to use in any WordPress theme template. The tags in Table 3-3 work only if you place them within The Loop (covered in "Examining the Main Index and The Loop" earlier in this chapter).

TABLE 3-3 Template Tags for Posts

Tag	Function
`get_the_date();`	Displays the date of the post.
`get_the_time();`	Displays the time of the post.
`the_title();`	Displays the title of the post.
`the_permalink();`	Displays the permalink (URL) of the post.
`get_the_author();`	Displays the post author's name.
`the_author_link();`	Displays the URL of the post author's site.
`the_content('Read More...');`	Displays the content of the post. (If you use an excerpt [following], the words *Read More* appear and are linked to the individual post page.)
`the_excerpt();`	Displays an excerpt (snippet) of the post.
`the_category();`	Displays the category (or categories) assigned to the post. If the post is assigned to multiple categories, commas separate them.
`comments_popup_link('No Comments', 'Comment (1)', 'Comments(%)');`	Displays a link to the comments, along with the comment count for the post in parentheses. (If no comments exist, it displays a *No Comments* message.)
`next_posts_link('« Previous Entries')`	Displays the words *Previous Entries* linked to the previous page of blog entries.
`previous_posts_link('Next Entries »')`	Displays the words *Next Entries* linked to the next page of blog entries.

The last two tags in Table 3-3 aren't like the others. You don't place these tags in The Loop; instead, you insert them after The Loop but before the `if` statement ends. Here's an example:

```
<?php endwhile;?>
<?php next_posts_link('&laquo; Previous Entries');?>
<?php previous_posts_link('Next Entries &raquo;');?>
<?php endif;?>
```

Putting a Theme Together

The template files don't work alone; for the theme to function, the files need one another. To tie these files together as one working entity, you use template tags to pull the information from each template — Header, Sidebar, and Footer — into the Main Index. I refer to this procedure as *calling* one template into another.

Connecting the templates

WordPress has built-in functions to include the main template files, such as header.php, sidebar.php, and footer.php, in other templates. An include function is a custom PHP function that is built into WordPress, allowing you to retrieve the content of another template file and display it along with the content of another template file. Table 3-4 shows the templates and the function that include them.

TABLE 3-4 Template Files and Include Functions

Template Name	Include Function
header.php	<?php get_header();?>
sidebar.php	<?php get_sidebar();?>
footer.php	<?php get_footer();?>
search.php	<?php get_search_form();?>
comments.php	<?php comments_template();?>

If you want to include a file that doesn't have a built-in include function, you need a different piece of code. To add a unique sidebar (different from the default sidebar.php file within your existing theme) to a certain page template, name the sidebar file sidebar-page.php. To include it in another template, use the following code:

```
<?php get_template_part('sidebar', 'page');?>
```

In this statement, the get_template_part('sidebar', 'page'); function looks through the main theme folder for the sidebar-page.php file and displays the sidebar. The beautiful part about the get template part() template tag is that WordPress looks for the sidebar-page.php template first, but if it doesn't find that template, it defaults to using the sidebar.php template.

In this section, you put together the guts of a basic Main Index template by using the information on templates and tags from this chapter. There seem to be endless lines of code when you view the template files in the Twenty Nineteen theme, so I've simplified the file for you in a list of steps. These steps should give you a basic understanding of the WordPress Loop and common template tags and functions that you can use to create your own.

WARNING

The theme you're creating in this chapter won't win you any awards. In fact, it's pretty ugly, as you'll see when you activate it on your website. It doesn't have many of the features that you expect from a WordPress theme, it's not responsive on mobile devices, and so on. The intention for the creation of the theme in this chapter is to get you comfortable with the basic concepts and mechanics of themes, including using the template tags that make themes work and understanding how to put different templates together. I didn't want to complicate this theme for beginners. Take the concepts you learn here and apply them as you move forward with more advanced theme development — and please don't use this theme anywhere on the web.

You create a new WordPress theme by using some of the basic WordPress templates. The first steps in pulling everything together are as follows:

1. **Connect to your web server via SFTP, click the `wp-content` folder, and then click the `themes` folder.**

   This folder contains the themes that are currently installed in your WordPress site. (See Book 2, Chapter 2 for more information on SFTP.)

2. **Create a new folder, and call it `my-theme`.**

   In most SFTP programs, you can right-click in the window and choose New Folder from the shortcut menu. (If you aren't sure how to create a folder, refer to your SFTP program's help files.)

3. **In your favored text editor (such as Notepad for the PC or TextEdit for the Mac), create and save the following files with the lines of code I've provided for each:**

   - *Header template:* Create the file with the following lines of code and then save it with the filename `header.php`:

```
<!DOCTYPE html>
<html <?php language_attributes();?>>
  <head>
    <meta charset="<?php bloginfo('charset');?>">
    <link rel="stylesheet" type="text/css" media="all" href="<?php
    bloginfo('stylesheet_url');?>"/>
```

```
    <?php wp_head();?>
  </head>
  <body <?php body_class()?>>
    <header class="masthead">
      <h1><a href="<?php bloginfo('url');?>"><?php bloginfo('name');?>
    </a></h1>
      <h2><?php bloginfo('description');?></h2>
    </header>
  <div id="main">
```

- *Theme Functions:* Create the file with the following lines of code and then save it, using the filename `functions.php`:

```
<?php

add_theme_support('title-tag');

function my_widgets_init() {
  register_sidebar(array (
  'name'          => __('My Widget Area'),
  'id'            => 'my-widget-area',
  'description'   => __('A new widget area I created!'),
  'before_widget' => '<li id="%1$s" class="widget-container %2$s">',
  'after_widget'  => "</li>",
  'before_title'  => '<h3 class="widget-title">',
  'after_title'   => '</h3>',
  ));
  }
add_action('widgets_init', 'my_widgets_init');
```

  The Theme Functions file registers the widget area for your site so that you can add widgets to your sidebar by using the WordPress widgets available on the Widget page of the Dashboard.

- *Sidebar template:* Create the file with the following lines of code and then save it, using the filename `sidebar.php`:

```
<aside class="sidebar">
  <ul>
    <?php dynamic_sidebar('My Widget Area');?>
  </ul>
</aside>
```

The code here tells WordPress where you want the WordPress widgets to display in your theme; in this case, widgets are displayed on the sidebar of your site.

- *Footer template:* Create the file with the following lines of code and then save it with the filename `footer.php`:

```
<footer>
<p>&copy; Copyright <a href="<?php bloginfo('url');?>"><?php
   bloginfo('name');?></a>. All Rights Reserved</p>
</footer>
<?php wp_footer();?>
</body>
</html>
```

- *Stylesheet:* Create the file with the following lines of code and then save it with the filename `style.css`:

```
/*
 Theme Name: My Theme
 Description: Basic Theme from WordPress For Dummies example
 Author: Lisa Sabin-Wilson
 Author URI: http://lisasabin-wilson.com
 */

body {
  color: #333333;
  font-family: verdana, arial, helvetica, sans-serif;
  font-size: 18px;
}

header.masthead {
  background: black;
  color: white;
  margin: 0 auto;
  padding: 15px;
  text-align:center;
  width: 960px;
}

header.masthead h1 a {
  color: white;
  font-family: Georgia;
  font-size: 28px;
  text-decoration: none;
}
```

```
header.masthead h2 {
  color: #eee;
  font-family: Georgia;
  font-size: 16px;
}

#main {
  margin: 0 auto;
  padding: 20px ;
  width: 960px;
}

#main section {
  float:left;
  width: 500px;
}

#main .hentry {
  margin: 10px 0;
}

aside.sidebar {
  float:right;
  margin: 0 15px;
  width: 290px;
}

aside.sidebar ul {
  list-style:none;
}

footer {
  background: black;
  clear:both;
  color: white;
  height: 50px;
  margin: 0 auto;
  width: 960px;
}

footer p {
  padding: 15px 0;
  text-align:center;
}
```

```
footer a {
  color:white;
}
```

Using the tags provided in Table 3-3, along with the information on The Loop and the calls to the Header, Sidebar, and Footer templates provided in earlier sections, you can follow the next steps for a bare-bones example of what the Main Index template looks like when you put the tags together.

WARNING

When typing templates, be sure to use a text editor such as Notepad or TextEdit. Using a word processing program such as Microsoft Word opens a whole slew of problems in your code. Word processing programs insert hidden characters and format quotation marks in a way that WordPress can't read.

Now that you have the basic theme foundation, the last template file you need to create is the Main Index template. To create a Main Index template to work with the other templates in your WordPress theme, open a new window in a text-editor program and then follow these steps. (Type the text in each of these steps on its own line. Press the Enter key after typing each line so that each tag starts on a new line.)

1. **Type** `<?php get_header();?>`.

   This template tag pulls the information in the Header template of your WordPress theme.

2. **Type** `<section>`.

   This HTML5 markup tells the browser that this tag is a grouping of content (in this case, blog posts).

3. **Type** `<?php if (have_posts()) :?>`.

   This tag is an `if` statement that asks, "Does this blog have posts?" If the answer is yes, the tag grabs the post content information from your MySQL database and displays the posts in your blog.

4. **Type** `<?php while (have_posts()) : the_post();?>`.

   This template tag starts The Loop.

5. **Type** `<article <?php post_class()?> id="post-<?php the_ID();?>">`.

   This tag is HTML5 markup that tells the browser that the tag, `<article>`, is the start of a new single article, including the `post_class` CSS designation.

6. **Type** `<h1><a href="<?php the_permalink();?>"><?php the_title();?></a></h1>`.

Exploring the Anatomy of a Theme

This tag tells your blog to display the title of a post that's clickable (linked) to the URL of the post, surrounded by HTML Header tags.

7. **Type** `Posted on <?php the_date();?> at <?php the_time();?>`.

   This template tag displays the date and time when the post was made. With these template tags, the date and time format are determined by the format you set on the Dashboard.

8. **Type** `Posted in <?php the_category( ',' );?>`.

   This template tag displays a comma-separated list of the categories to which you've assigned the post, such as `Posted in: category 1, category 2`, for example.

9. **Type** `<?php the_content('Read More..');?>`.

   This template tag displays the actual content of the blog post. The `'Read More..'` portion of this tag tells WordPress to display the words `Read More`, which are hyperlinked to the post's permalink and take the reader to the page where he or she can read the rest of the post. This tag applies when you're displaying a post excerpt, as determined by the actual post configuration on the Dashboard.

10. **Type** `Posted by: <?php the_author();?>`.

    This template tag displays the author of the post in this manner: `Posted by: Lisa Sabin-Wilson`.

11. **Type** `</article>`.

    This tag is HTML5 markup that tells the browser that the article has ended.

12. **Type** `<?php endwhile;?>`.

    This template tag ends The Loop and tells WordPress to stop displaying blog posts here. WordPress knows exactly how many times The Loop needs to work, based on the setting on the WordPress Dashboard. That setting is exactly how many times WordPress executes The Loop.

13. **Type** `<?php next_posts_link('« Previous Entries');?>`.

    This template tag displays a clickable link that goes to the preceding page of entries, if any.

14. **Type** `<?php previous posts link('» Next Entries');?>`.

    This template tag displays a clickable link that goes to the next page of blog entries, if any.

15. **Type** `<?php else :?>`.

    This template tag refers to the `if` statement in step 3. If the answer is no, this step provides the `else` statement: IF this blog has posts, THEN list them here (steps 3 and 4), or ELSE display the following message.

16. **Type** Not Found. Sorry, but you are looking for something that isn't here.

    This tag is the message followed by the template tag displayed after the `else` statement from step 15. You can reword this statement to say whatever you want.

17. **Type** `<?php endif;?>`.

    This template tag ends the `if` statement from step 3.

18. **Type** `</section>`.

    This HTML5 markup closes the `<section>` tag that was opened in step 2 and tells the browser that this grouping of content has ended.

19. **Type** `<?php get_sidebar();?>`.

    This template tag calls in the Sidebar template and pulls that information into the Main Index template.

20. **Type** `</div>`.

    This HTML5 markup closes the `<div id="main">` that was opened in the `header.php` file.

21. **Type** `<?php get_footer();?>`.

    This template tag calls in the Footer template and pulls that information into the Main Index template. ***Note:*** The code in the `footer.php` template ends the `<body>` and `<html>` tags that were started in the Header template (`header.php`).

    When you're done, the display of the Main Index template code looks like this:

```
<?php get_header();?>
<section>
<?php if (have_posts()) :?>

<?php while (have_posts()) : the_post();?>
 <article <?php post_class()?> id="post-<?php the_ID();?>">
   <h1><a href="<?php the_permalink();?>"><?php the_title();?></a></h1>
   Posted on: <?php the_date();?> at <?php the_time();?>
   Posted in: <?php the_category( ',' );?>
   <?php the_content('Read More..');?>
   Posted by: <?php the_author();?>
 </article>

<?php endwhile;?>
<?php next_posts_link('&laquo; Previous Entries');?>
<?php previous_posts_link('Next Entries &raquo;');?>
<?php else :?>
```

Exploring the Anatomy of a Theme

```
<p>Not Found
Sorry, but you are looking for something that isn't here.</p>
<?php endif;?>
</section>
<?php get_sidebar();?>
</div>
<?php get_footer();?>
```

22. **Save this file as `index.php`, and upload it to the `mythemes` folder.**

    In Notepad or TextEdit, you can save the PHP file by choosing File⇨Save As. Type the name of the file in the File Name text box, and click Save.

23. **Activate the theme on the WordPress Dashboard, and view your site to see your handiwork in action!**

TIP

This Main Index template code has one template tag that's explained in Book 6, Chapter 6: `<div <?php post_class()?> id="post-<?php the_ID();?>">`. This tag helps you create some interesting styles in your template by using CSS, so check out Chapter 6 to find out all about it!

This simple, basic Main Index template doesn't have the standard HTML markup in it, so you'll find that the visual display of your site differs from the default Twenty Nineteen theme. I use this example to give you bare-bones basics on the Main Index template and The Loop in action. Book 6, Chapter 4 goes into detail about using HTML and CSS to create nice styling and formatting for your posts and pages.

TIP

If you're having a hard time typing the code provided in this section, I've made this sample theme available for download on my website. The `.zip` file contains the files discussed in this chapter so that you can compare your efforts with mine, electronically. You can download the file here: `http://lisasabin-wilson.com/wpfd/my-theme.zip`.

Now that you have all your template files ready, follow these steps to upload your files to your web server:

1. **Connect to your web server via SFTP, click the `wp-content` folder, and then click the `themes` folder.**

   This folder contains the themes that are currently installed in your WordPress blog. (Go to Book 2, Chapter 2 if you need more information on SFTP.)

2. **Create a new folder, and call it `my-theme`.**

   In most SFTP programs, you can right-click and choose New Folder from the shortcut menu. (If you aren't sure how to create a folder, refer to your SFTP program's help files.)

3. **Upload your `index.php` file to the `my-theme` folder.**
4. **Activate the theme in the WordPress Dashboard, and view your site to see your handiwork in action.**

Using additional stylesheets

Often, a theme uses multiple stylesheets for browser compatibility or consistent organization. If you use multiple stylesheets, the process of including them in the template is the same as for any other stylesheet.

To add a new stylesheet, create a directory in the root theme folder called `css`. Next, create a new file called `mystyle.css` within the `css` folder. To include the file, you must edit the `header.php` file. The following example shows the code you need to include in the new CSS file:

```
<link rel="stylesheet" href="<?php bloginfo('stylesheet_directory');
?>/css/mystyle.css" type="text/css" media="screen"/>
```

Additional stylesheets come in handy when you're working with a concept called parent and child themes, which is the practice of creating a child theme that depends on a separate parent theme for features and functions. I write more about parent and child themes, as well as provide additional information about HTML and CSS, in Book 6, Chapter 5.

IN THIS CHAPTER

» Personalizing your header and background graphics

» Customizing your site with CSS

» Modifying your theme with CSS and HTML

» Customizing basic elements for uniqueness

» Exploring additional resources

Chapter 4
Customizing Your Theme

Customizing your WordPress theme's overall look with unique graphics and colors is one of the most fun, exciting aspects of using WordPress themes. You can take one of your favorite easily customizable themes and personalize it with some simple changes to make it unique. (For more information on finding an existing theme, read Book 6, Chapter 2.)

After you find an existing free (or premium) WordPress theme that suits your needs, the next step is personalizing the theme through some of the following techniques:

- **Plugging in your own graphics:** The easiest way to make a theme your own is to add a graphical header that includes your logo and matching background graphics.
- **Adjusting colors:** You might like the structure and design of your theme but want to adjust the colors to match your own tastes or brand look. You can do this in the CSS, too.
- **Adding/changing fonts:** You may want to change the font, or *typography,* on your site by using different font types, sizes, or colors. You can edit these display properties in the CSS.

Often, the customization process is one of trial and error. You have to mix and match different elements, tweaking and tinkering with graphics and CSS until you achieve design perfection. In this chapter, you explore the easiest ways to customize your WordPress theme through graphics and CSS.

Changing Your Background Graphic

Using background graphics is an easy way to set your site apart from others that use the same theme. Finding a background graphic for your site is much like finding just the right desktop background for your computer. You can choose among a variety of background graphics for your site, such as photography, abstract art, and repeatable patterns.

You can find ideas for new, different background graphics by checking out some of the CSS galleries on the web, such as CSS Drive (`www.cssdrive.com`).

REMEMBER

Sites like these should be used only for inspiration, not theft. Be careful when using images from outside sources.

WARNING

You want to use only graphics and images that you've been given the right (through express permission or reuse licenses) to use on your site. For this reason, always purchase graphics from reputable sources, such as these three online-graphics sites:

- **iStock (`https://www.istockphoto.com`):** iStockphoto offers an extensive library of stock photography, vector illustrations, video and audio clips, and Adobe Flash media. You can sign up for an account and search libraries of image files to find the one that suits you or your client best. The files that you use from iStockphoto aren't free; you do have to pay for them, and be sure that you read the license for each image you use. The site has several licenses. The cheapest one is the Standard license, which has some limitations. You can use an illustration from iStockphoto in one website design, for example, but you can't use that same illustration in a theme design that you intend to sell multiple times (say, in a premium theme marketplace). Be sure to read the fine print!
- **Dreamstime (`https://www.dreamstime.com`):** Dreamstime is a major supplier of stock photography and digital images. Sign up for an account, and search the huge library of digital image offerings. Dreamstime does offer free images at times, so keep your eyes out for those. Also, Dreamstime has different licenses for its image files, and you need to pay close attention to them.

One nice feature is the royalty-free licensing option, which allows you to pay for the image one time and then use the image as many times as you like. You can't redistribute the image in the same website theme repeatedly, however, such as in a template that you sell to the public.

- **GraphicRiver (`https://graphicriver.net`):** GraphicRiver offers stock graphic files such as Adobe Photoshop images, design templates, textures, vector graphics, and icons, to name just a few. The selection is vast, and the cost to download and use the graphic files is minimal.

  As with all graphic and image libraries, be sure to read the terms of use or any licensing attached to each of the files to make sure that you're abiding by the legal terms.

- **Unsplash (`https://unsplash.com`):** Unsplash offers stock imagery that is licensed both for personal and commercial use. Best of all, the images are all free.

To best use background graphics, you must answer a few simple questions:

- **What type of background graphic do you want to use?** You may want a repeatable pattern or texture, for example, or a black-and-white photograph of something in your business.
- **How do you want the background graphic to display in your browser?** You may want to tile or repeat your background image in the browser window, or pin it to a certain position no matter what size your guest's browser is.

The answers to those questions determine how you install a background graphic in your theme design.

REMEMBER

When working with graphics on the web, use GIF, JPG, or PNG image formats. For images with a small number of colors (charts, line art, logos, and so on), GIF format works best. For other image types (screenshots with text and images, blended transparency, and so on), use JPG or PNG.

For web design, the characteristics of each image file format can help you decide which file format you need to use for your site. The most common image file formats and characteristics include

- **JPG:** Suited for use with photographs and smaller images used in your web design projects. Although the JPG format compresses with lossy compression, you can adjust compression when you save a file in JPG format. That is, you can choose the degree, or amount, of compression that occurs, from 1 to 100. Usually, you won't see a great deal of image quality loss with compression levels 1 through 20.

- **PNG:** Suited for larger graphics used in web design, such as the logo or main header graphic that helps brand the overall look of the website. A .png file uses lossless image compression; therefore, no data loss occurs during compression, so you get a cleaner, sharper image. You also can create and save a .png file on a transparent canvas. .jpg files must have a white canvas or some other color that you designate.
- **GIF:** Suited for displaying simple images with only a few colors. Compression of a .gif file is lossless; therefore, the image renders exactly the way you design it, without loss of quality. These files compress with lossless quality when the image uses 256 colors or fewer, however. For images that use more colors (higher quality), GIF isn't the greatest format to use. For images with a lot of colors, go with PNG format instead.

Uploading an image for background use

If you want to change the background graphic in your theme, follow these steps:

1. **Upload your new background graphic via SFTP to the images folder in your theme directory.**

   Typically, the images folder is at wp-content/themes/themename/images.

2. **On the WordPress Dashboard, click the Editor link on the Appearance menu.**

   The Edit Themes screen displays.

3. **Click the Stylesheet (style.css) link on the right side of the page.**

   The style.css template opens in the text-editor box on the left side of the Edit Themes screen.

4. **Scroll down to find the body CSS selector.**

   I discuss CSS selectors later in this chapter. The following code segment is a sample CSS snippet you can use to define the background color of your site (light gray in this example):

```
body {
  background: #f1f1f1;
}
```

5. **(Optional) Modify the background property values from the code in step 4.**

   Change

   ```
   background: #f1f1f1;
   ```

   to

   ```
   background #FFFFFF url('images/newbackground.gif');
   ```

   With this example, you add a new background image (`newbackground.gif`) to the existing code and change the color code to white (#FFFFFF).

6. **Click the Update File button to save the stylesheet changes you made.**

   Your changes are saved and applied to your theme.

Positioning, repeating, and attaching images

After you upload a background graphic, you can use CSS background properties to position it how you want it. The main CSS properties — `background-position`, `background-repeat`, and `background-attachment` — help you achieve the desired effect.

Table 4-1 describes the CSS background properties and the available values for changing them in your theme stylesheet. If you're a visual person, you'll enjoy testing and tweaking values to see the effects on your site.

Suppose that your goal is to *tile* (repeat) the background image so that it scales with the width of the browser on any computer. To achieve this goal, open the stylesheet again and change

```
background: #f1f1f1;
```

to

```
background: #FFFFFF;
background-image: url(images/newbackground.gif);
background-repeat: repeat;
```

TABLE 4-1 CSS Background Properties

Property	Description	Values	Example

`background-position`	Determines the starting point of your background image on your web page	`bottom center`
		`bottom right`
		`left center`
		`right center`
		`center center`
			`background-position: bottom center;`

`background-repeat`	Determines whether your background image will repeat or tile	`repeat` (repeats infinitely) `repeat-y` (repeats vertically) `repeat-x` (repeats horizontally) `no-repeat` (does not repeat)	`background-repeat: repeat-y;`
`background-attachment`	Determines whether your background image is fixed or scrolls with the browser window	`fixed` `scroll`	`background-attachment: scroll;`

`background-origin`	Specifies the positioning area of the background images	`padding-box`
		`border-box`
		`content-box`
		`initial`
		`inherit`
			`background-origin: content-box;`

`background-clip`	Specifies the painting area of the background images	`border-box`
		`padding-box`
		`content-box`
		`initial`
		`inherit`
			`background-clip: padding-box;`

If your goal is to display a fixed image that doesn't scroll or move when your site visitor moves the browser, you can use the `background-position`, `background-repeat`, and `background-attachment` properties to display it exactly as you want it to appear.

To achieve this look, add `background-attachment: fixed`, and change the `background-repeat` to `no-repeat` in your stylesheet to

```
background: #FFFFFF;
background-image: url(images/newbackground.gif);
background-repeat: no-repeat;
background-attachment: fixed;
```

TIP

As you become more comfortable with CSS properties, you can start using shortening methods to make your CSS coding practice more efficient. The preceding block of code, for example, looks like this with shortened CSS practice:

```
background: #fff url(images/newbackground.gif) repeat top left;
```

As you can see from these examples, changing the background graphic by using CSS involves setting options that depend on your creativity and design style more than anything else. When you use these options properly, CSS can take your design to the next level.

Changing Your Header Graphic

Creating unique header graphics is one of the fastest ways to personalize a site and make it unique. The header graphic is typically the strongest graphic design element. Positioned at the top of your theme, a header graphic often includes a logo or other information about your site or business.

Here are some elements you might include in your header graphic:

- **Business name or logo:** This sounds obvious, but the header graphic is the primary way to identify the site. If you don't have a logo, you can stylize your business name for your header graphic, but your brand identity needs to be prominent and polished in the header graphic.
- **Profile photos:** If it's for a site or an independent professional's site (say, for a real estate agent), you may want to include a studio-quality profile photo of the person to help your site guests know who they're dealing with and to add a touch of warmth.
- **Taglines, important slogans, and keywords:** Use the header area to tell your visitors something about your site or business.
- **Contact information:** If you're doing a small-business website, including phone and address information is vital.

- **Background images:** Be creative with the header image behind all this information. Use a pattern or graphic that matches your brand colors and doesn't distract attention from the vital information you want to communicate.

REMEMBER

Most new WordPress themes, particularly premium themes, allow you to upload new header graphics over existing ones easily from the WordPress Dashboard, using a feature called a Custom Header Uploader script or feature. This feature allows you to turn off HTML overlay text and use only graphics for your header, too.

You can personalize your header graphic in the following ways:

- Replace or overwrite the theme's existing header image with an appropriate image of your choice.
- Use a repeating graphic pattern.

Using a repeating graphic pattern is similar to using a repeating background image, which I discuss in "Positioning, repeating, and attaching images" earlier in this chapter. In the following sections, you replace your existing header image (in the free Quick-Vid theme from iThemes) by using the Custom Header feature of many WordPress themes. Figure 4-1 shows the Twenty Seventeen theme's default header image. (*Note:* I'm using the Twenty Seventeen theme here instead of Twenty Nineteen because the former has a Custom Header feature and the latter doesn't.)

FIGURE 4-1: The default header of the Twenty Seventeen theme.

Considering the image dimensions

Generally, you want to replace the existing header image with an image that has exactly the same dimensions (width and height). To determine the dimensions of the existing image, open the default header graphic in an image-editing program such as Adobe Photoshop. Create (or crop) your new header graphic to the same dimensions (in pixels) to minimize problems when adding the image to your theme.

TIP

Adobe Photoshop Elements is a handy design software tool for basic image editing. It has significantly fewer features than its bigger and older brother, Photoshop, but for most image-editing tasks, it does a great job for a fraction of the price.

Customizing the header media

Depending on your theme, replacing an existing header image is a fast and efficient way of making changes; you simply upload the graphic and refresh your site.

Twenty Seventeen's Header Media options allow you to upload custom header graphics or a header video for your WordPress site. The options are called Header Media because you can configure an image or a video (or both) for the design of your site.

The recommended dimensions for your customized header media are 2000 pixels wide by 1200 high. If your photo or video is larger, you can crop it after you've uploaded it to WordPress, although cropping with a graphics program (such as Photoshop) is the best way to get exact results.

Twenty Seventeen comes preloaded with one default header image, but WordPress allows you to upload one of your own. To install a custom header image, follow these steps with the Twenty Seventeen theme activated:

1. **On the WordPress Dashboard, click the Header link on the Appearance menu.**

   The Custom Header page appears, with the Customizing Header Media panel displayed on the left side of the screen, as shown in Figure 4-2.

2. **In the Header Image section, click the Add New Image button.**

   The Choose Image screen opens (see Figure 4-3).

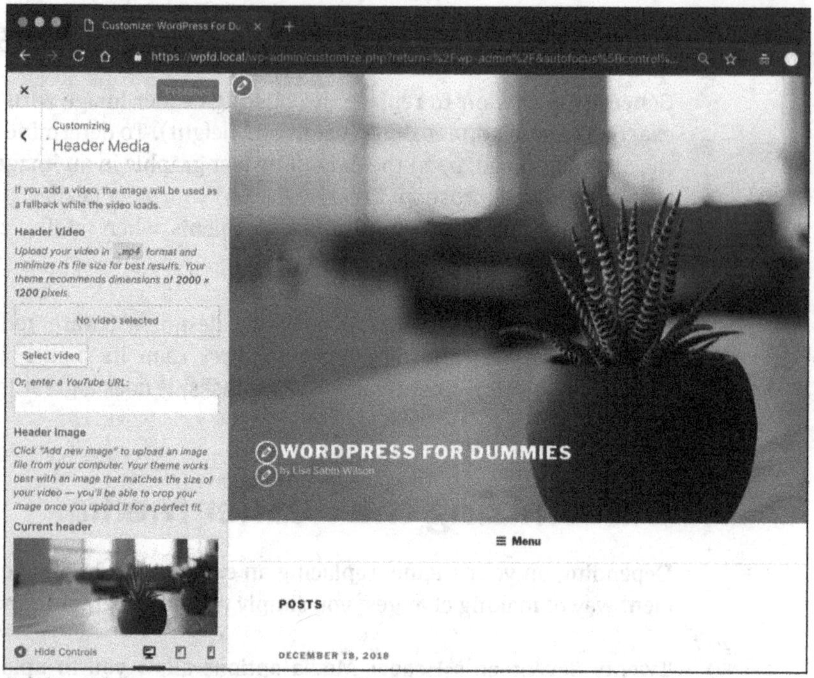

FIGURE 4-2: The Customizing Header Media feature in the Twenty Seventeen theme.

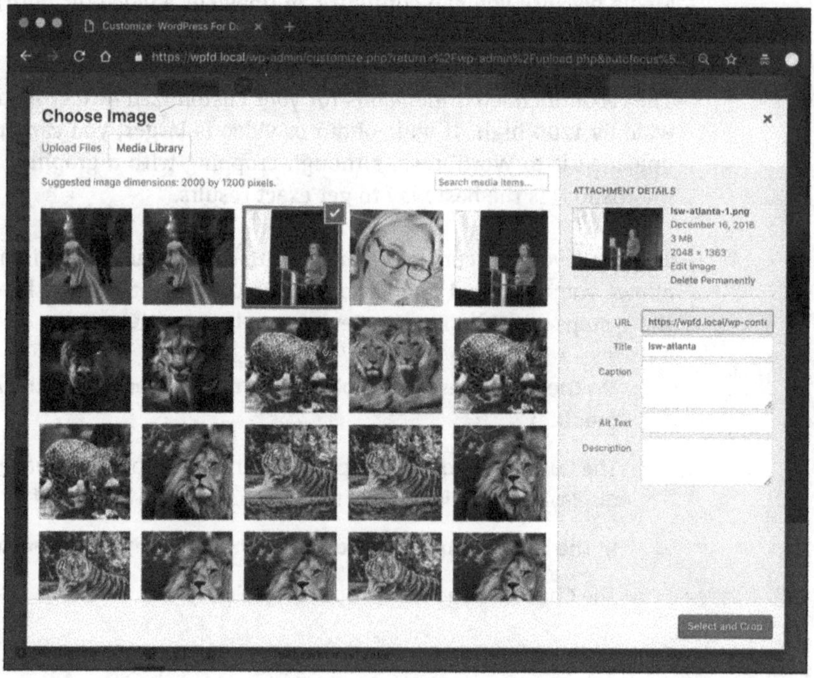

FIGURE 4-3: Selecting an image to use as a header image.

3. **Select the image you want to use.**

   You can select an existing image from the Media Library or upload a new one from your computer.

4. **Click the Select and Crop button.**

   This step opens the Crop Image screen, shown in Figure 4-4.

FIGURE 4-4: Using the crop tool.

5. **(Optional) Crop the image to your liking.**

   To resize and crop your image, drag one of the eight tiny boxes located at the corners and center top and bottom of the image (refer to Figure 4-4). You can also click within the image and move the entire image up or down to get the placement and cropping effect that you want.

6. **Click the Crop Image button to crop your header image.**
7. **Click the Save & Publish button in the top-right corner of the Customizing Header Media screen to save your changes.**

Figure 4-5 shows the Twenty Seventeen theme with a custom header image.

FIGURE 4-5: The Twenty Seventeen theme with a new header image.

TIP

You can upload multiple images to use in the header-image area and click the Randomize Uploaded Headers button in the Customizing Header Media panel to tell the Twenty Seventeen theme that you'd like to see a different header on each new page load. This option adds a little variety to your site!

Including a header video

The Twenty Seventeen theme comes with a default header image but not with a video for you to use as a header. One small text field, however, allows you to include a video from YouTube (`https://www.youtube.com`) so that visitors to your site see a video in the background of your header.

Follow these steps to configure a header video:

1. **On the WordPress Dashboard, click the Header link on the Appearance menu.**

   The Custom Header page appears, with the Customizing Header Media panel displayed on the left side of your screen.

2. **To upload your video file, click the Select Video button in the Header Video section.**

   The Select Video screen open.

3. **Select a video from the WordPress Media Library or upload a video file from your computer's hard drive.**

   The Header video supports the MP4 file format for videos.

   If you'd rather use a video from a service such as YouTube, skip this step and proceed to step 4.

4. **To use a video from YouTube, copy and then paste the link to that video in the Enter a YouTube video URL text field.**

5. **Click the Save & Publish button in the top-right corner of the Customizing Header Media panel.**

   This action saves and publishes any changes you made in the header media.

Personalizing Your Theme with CSS

Cascading Style Sheets (CSS) are part of every WordPress theme. Another way of personalizing your theme with CSS is through your theme's default stylesheet (`style.css`). Through a comment block (shown in Figure 4-6), your theme's `style.css` file tells WordPress the theme name, the version number, and the author, along with other information.

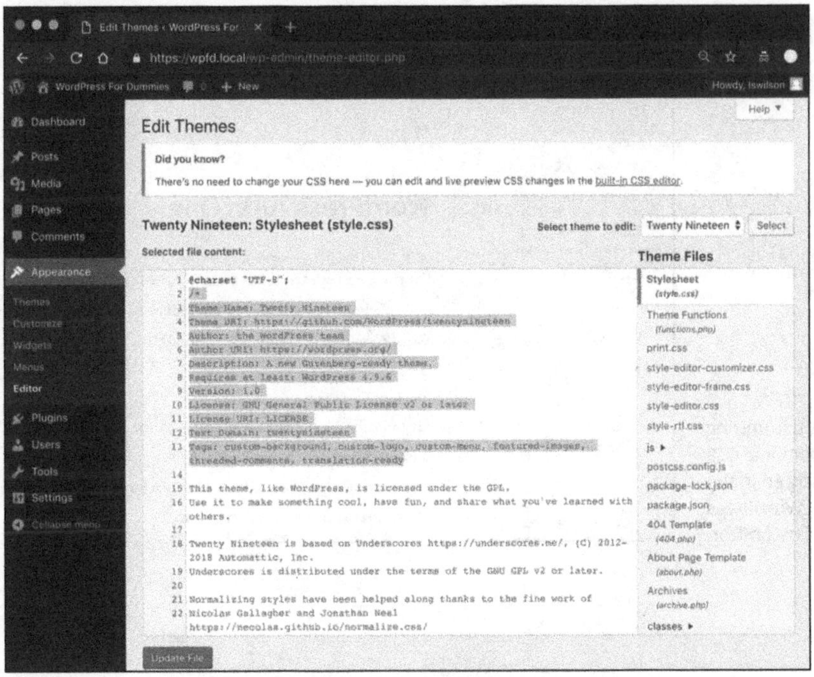

FIGURE 4-6: The comment block of a typical WordPress stylesheet.

With CSS changes to your theme's stylesheet, you can apply unique styling (such as different fonts, sizes, and colors) to headlines, text, links, and borders, and adjust the spacing between them too. With all the CSS options available, you can fine-tune the look and feel of different elements with simple tweaks.

To explore your theme's stylesheet, click the Editor link on the Appearance menu of the WordPress Dashboard. By default, your theme's main stylesheet (`style.css`) should appear (refer to Figure 4-6). You can scroll through the stylesheet to familiarize yourself with the CSS that's used for the theme.

WARNING

Making changes directly in the stylesheet or any other theme file isn't recommended because it can cause your site to load the theme improperly. Don't make any changes or edits in the stylesheet directly; rather, use the WordPress Customizer to add any new CSS styles you want without affecting or changing the default CSS file. At the top of the Edit Themes page (refer to Figure 4-6) is the message `Did you know? There's no need to change your CSS here — you can edit and live preview CSS changes in the built-in CSS editor`. Click the `built-in CSS editor` link, and the Customizer opens with the Customizing Additional CSS screen available to you, as shown in Figure 4-7.

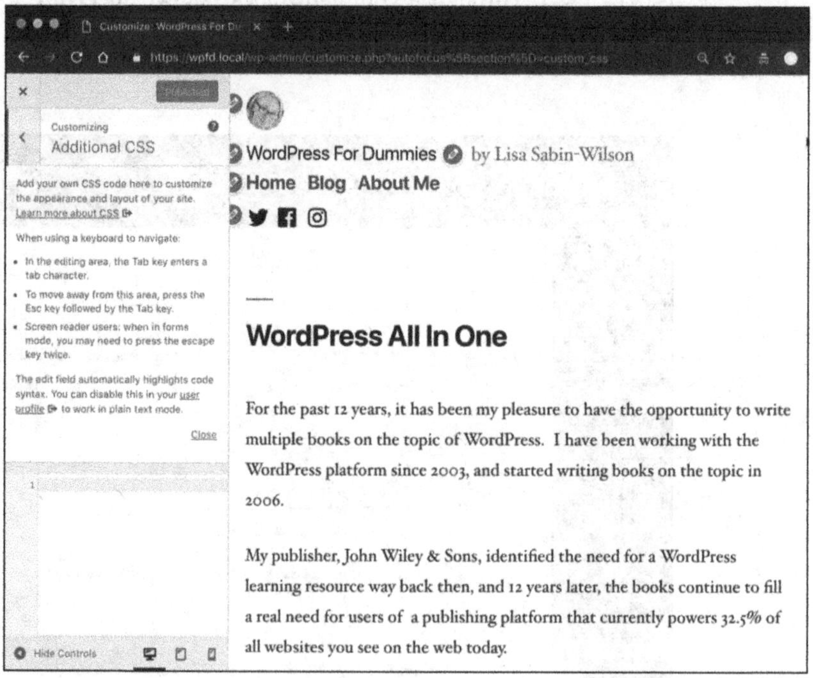

FIGURE 4-7: Customizing Additional CSS screen in the WordPress Customizer.

You can preview the effects of your CSS additions in the Customizer on the right side of the screen, so you're able to confirm that the style changes you're making will look good, and correct, on your site before you click the Publish button in the top-right corner. After you click Publish, the CSS styles you've added in the Customizer take effect on your site.

Knowing some key CSS concepts can help you personalize your theme's CSS. Customizing the stylesheet involves a set of commands that customize the look and feel of your HTML markup. Common commands and tools include selectors, IDs, classes, properties, and values. You use these commands to customize HTML to display your design customizations.

CSS selectors

Typically, CSS *selectors* are named for the corresponding HTML elements, IDs, and classes that you want to style with CSS properties and values. Selectors are very important in CSS because they're used to "select" elements on an HTML/PHP page so that they can be styled appropriately.

With CSS, you can provide style (such as size, color, and placement) to the display of elements on your website (such as text links, header images, font size and colors, paragraph margins, and line spacing). *CSS selectors* contain names, properties, and values to define which HTML elements in the templates you'll style with CSS. You use CSS selectors to declare (or select) which part of the markup the style applies to. Table 4-2 provides some examples of CSS selectors and their uses.

If you were to assign a style to the `h1` selector, that style would affect all `<h1>` tags in your HTML. Sometimes you want to do this; at other times you want to affect only a subset of elements.

CSS IDs and classes

With CSS IDs and classes, you can define more elements to style. Generally, IDs are used to style one broad specific element (such as your header section) on your page. Classes style, define, and categorize more specifically grouped items (such as images and text alignment, widgets, or links to posts).

- **CSS IDs** are identified with the hash mark (#). `#header` indicates the header ID, for example.
- **CSS classes** are identified with a period (.). `alignleft` indicates aligning an element to the left, for example.

Customizing Your Theme

TABLE 4-2 Basic Global CSS Selectors

CSS Selector	Description	HTML	CSS Example
body	Sets the style for the overall body of the site, such as background color and default fonts	<body>	body {background-color: white;} The background color on all pages is white.
a	Defines how text links display on your site	<a href="https://wordpress.org">WordPress</a>	a {color: red;} All text links appear in red.
h1, h2, h3, h4, h5, h6	Provides bold headers for different sections of your site	<h1>This is a site title</h1>	h1 {font-weight: bold;} A font surrounded by the <h1>..</h1> HTML tags is bold.
blockquote	Defines how indented text is styled	<blockquote> "A journey of a thousand miles begins with a single step."</blockquote>	blockquote {font-style: italic} The text appears in italic font.
p	Defines how paragraphs are formatted	<p>This is a paragraph</p>	p {color:black;} The color of the fonts used in all paragraphs is black.

IDs and classes define styling properties for different sections of your WordPress theme. Table 4-3 shows examples of IDs and classes from the `header.php` template in the Twenty Nineteen WordPress theme. Armed with this information, you'll know where to look in the stylesheet when you want to change the styling for a particular area of your theme.

REMEMBER

If you find an element in the template code that says `id` (such as `div id=` or `p id=`), look for the hash symbol in the stylesheet. If you find an element in the template code that says `class` (such as `div class=` or `p class=`), look for the period in the stylesheet followed by the selector name.

CSS properties and values

CSS properties are assigned to the CSS selector name. You also need to provide values for the CSS properties to define the style elements for the particular CSS selector you're working with.

TABLE 4-3 **CSS IDs and Classes Examples**

CSS IDs and Classes	Description	HTML	CSS Example
#page	Targets the layout of your site	<div id="page">	#page { width: 100%;}

#fmasthead	Targets the header section of your site	<header id="masthead">	#masthead {
			background: #ccc;
			}

. site-branding-container	Targets the header container of your site	<div class="site-branding-container">	.site-branding-container {
			margin-bottom: auto;
			}

.site-header	Targets the header area of your site	<div class="site-header">	.site-header {
			padding: 1em;
			}

The body selector that follows defines the overall look of your web page. background is a property, and #DDDDDD (a light gray) is the value; color is a property, and #222222 (very dark gray, almost black) is the value.

```
body {
background: #DDDDDD;
color: #222222;
}
```

REMEMBER

Every CSS property needs to be followed by a colon (:), and each CSS value needs to be followed by a semicolon (;).

The fact that properties are assigned to selectors, as well as your options for the values, makes CSS a fun playground for personalizing your site. You can experiment with colors, fonts, font sizes, and more to tweak the look of your theme.

Understanding Basic HTML Techniques

HTML can help you customize and organize your theme. To understand how HTML and CSS work together, think of it this way: If a website were a building, HTML would be the structure (the studs and foundation), and CSS would be the paint.

HTML contains the elements that CSS provides the styles for. All you have to do to apply a CSS style is use the right HTML element. Here's a very basic block of HTML:

```
<body>
  <div id="content">
    <h1>Headline Goes Here</h1>
      <p>This is a sample sentence of body text. <blockquote>The journey
of a thousand miles starts with the first step.</blockquote> I'm
going to continue on this sentence and end it here. </p>

      <p>Click <a href="http://lisasabin-wilson.com">here</a> to visit my
website.
      </p>
    </div>
</body>
```

All HTML elements must have opening and closing tags. Opening tags are contained in less-than (<) and greater-than (>) symbols. Closing tags are the same except that they're preceded by a forward slash (/).

Here's an example:

```
<h1>Headline Goes Here</h1>
```

The HTML elements must be nested properly. In the fourth line of the preceding example, a paragraph tag is opened (<p>). Later in that line, a block quote is opened (<blockquote>) and is nesting inside the paragraph tag. When editing this line, you can't end the paragraph (</p>) before you end the block quote (</blockquote>). Nested elements must close before the elements within which they're nested close.

REMEMBER

Finally, proper *tabbing*, or indenting, is important when writing HTML, mainly for readability so that you can scan code to find what you're looking for quickly. A good rule to follow is that if you didn't close a tag in the line above, indent one tab over. This practice allows you to see where each element begins and ends. It can also be very helpful for diagnosing problems.

You'll use several basic HTML markup practices over and over in designing and building websites. In "Personalizing Your Theme with CSS" earlier in this chapter, I discuss how to combine CSS styling with HTML markup to create different display styles (borders, fonts, and so on).

For more in-depth tutorials on HTML, see the HTML section of w3schools.com at https://www.w3schools.com/html/default.asp.

Changing Basic Elements for a Unique Look

When you understand the basic concepts of personalizing your site with graphics and CSS, you begin to see how easy it is to change the look and feel of your site with these tools. The next few sections explore some ways to accomplish an interesting design presentation or a unique, creative look.

Background colors and images

Changing the background image can change the feel of your site, but you also can use background colors and images for other elements of your theme.

Background techniques include using solid colors and repeating gradients or patterns to achieve a subtle yet polished effect. (*Note:* Use colors that accent the colors of your logo and don't hamper text readability.)

You can add CSS background colors and image effects to the following areas of your theme:

- Post and page content sections
- Sidebar widgets
- Comment blocks
- Footer area

Font family, color, and size

You can change the fonts in your theme for style or readability. I've seen typographic (or font) design experts use simple font variations to achieve amazing design results. You can use fonts to separate headlines from body text (or widget headlines and text from the main content) to be less distracting. Table 4-4 lists some examples of often-used font properties.

The web is kind of picky about how it displays fonts, as well as what kind of fonts you can use in the `font-family` property. Not all fonts display correctly. To be safe, here are some commonly used font families that display correctly in most browsers:

- **Serif fonts:** Times New Roman, Georgia, Garamond, Bookman Old Style
- **Sans-serif fonts:** Verdana, Arial, Tahoma, Trebuchet MS

TABLE 4-4 Fonts

Font Properties	Common Values	CSS Examples

`font-family`	Georgia, Times, serif	`body {`
		`font-family: Georgia; serif;`
		`}`

`font-size`	px, %, em	`body {`
		`font-size: 14px;`
		`}`

`font-style`	Italic, underline	`body {`
		`font-style: italic;`
		`}`

`font-weight`	bold, bolder, normal	`body {`
		`font-weight: normal;`
		`}`

REMEMBER

Serif fonts have little tails, or curlicues, at the edges of letters. (This book's body text is in a serif font.) *Sans-serif* fonts have straight edges and no fancy styling. (The heading in Table 4-4 uses a sans-serif font. Look, Ma, no tails!)

Font color

With more than 16 million HTML color combinations available, you can find just the right shade of color for your project. After some time, you'll memorize your favorite color codes, also referred to as hex codes. Knowing codes for different shades of gray can help you quickly add an extra design touch. You can use the shades of gray listed in Table 4-5 for backgrounds, borders on design elements, and widget headers, for example.

You can easily change the color of your font by changing the `color` property of the CSS selector you want to tweak. You can use hexadecimal codes to define the colors. Some CSS color values have a shortcut you can use if the all six letters or numbers in the hex code are all the same. In Table 4-5, for example, for the color white, you can use `#FFF` as a shortcut in place of the `#FFFFFF` hex code. Either way you write it, the result is the same: white.

TABLE 4-5 My Favorite CSS Colors

Color	Hex Code
White	#FFFFFF or #FFF
Black	#000000 or #000
Gray	#CCCCCC or #CCC
	#DDDDDD or #DDD
	#333333 or #333
	#E0E0E0

You can define the overall font color in your site by defining it in the body CSS selector, like this:

```
body {
  color: #333;
}
```

Font size

To tweak the size of your font, change the `font-size` property of the CSS selector you want to tweak. Generally, the following units of measurement determine font sizes:

- **px (pixel):** Increasing or decreasing the number of pixels increases or decreases the font size. `12px` is larger than `10px`.
- **pt (point):** As with pixels, increasing or decreasing the number of points affects the font size. `12pt` is larger than `10pt`.
- **`em`:** An *em* is a width measurement, a scalable unit of measurement that's equal to the current font size. (Originally, an em space was equal to the width of the capital letter *M,* hence the name.) If the font size of the body of the site is defined as `12px`, `1em` is equal to `12px`; likewise, `2em` is equal to `24px`, and so on.
- **% (percentage):** Increasing or decreasing the percentage number affects the font size. (If the body of the website uses `14px` as the default, `50%` is the equivalent of 7 pixels, and `100%` is the equivalent of 14 pixels.)

Customizing Your Theme

In the default template CSS, the font size is defined in the <body> tag in pixels, like this:

```
font-size: 12px;
```

Putting all three elements (`font-family`, `color`, and `font-size`) together in the <body> tag styles the font for the entire body of your site. Here's how the elements work together in the <body> tag of the template CSS:

```
body {
  color: #666;
  font-family: Georgia, serif;
  font-size: 18px;
}
```

When you want to change a font family in your CSS, open the stylesheet (`style.css`), search for the property: `font-family`, change the values for that property, and then save your changes.

Borders

CSS borders can add an interesting, unique flair to elements of your theme design. Table 4-6 lists common properties and CSS examples for borders in your theme design.

TABLE 4-6 Common Border Properties

Border Properties	Common Values	CSS Examples

`border-size`	px, em	`body {`
		`border-size: 1px;`
		`}`

`border-style`	solid, dotted, dashed	`body {`
		`border-style: solid;`
		`}`

`border-color`	Hexadecimal values	`body {`
		`border-color: #CCCCCC;`
		`}`

Finding Additional Resources

There may come a time when you want to explore customizing your theme further. Here are some recommended resources:

- **WordPress Codex (`https://codex.wordpress.org`):** Official WordPress documentation
- **W3Schools (`https://www.w3schools.com`):** A free and comprehensive online HTML and CSS reference
- **WP Beginner (`https://www.wpbeginner.com/category/wp-themes`):** Numerous tips and tricks for customizing WordPress themes

IN THIS CHAPTER

» Defining the relationship between parent and child themes

» Tweaking child themes with styles

» Customizing child themes with images

» Modifying child themes with template files

Chapter 5

Understanding Parent and Child Themes

Using a theme exactly as a theme author released it is great. If a new version is released that fixes a browser compatibility issue or adds features offered by a new version of WordPress, a quick theme upgrade is very easy to do.

But there's a good chance you'll want to tinker with the design, add new features, or modify the theme structure. If you modify the theme, you won't be able to upgrade to a newly released version without modifying the theme again. If only you could upgrade customized versions of themes with new features when they're released! Fortunately, child themes give you this best-of-both-worlds theme solution.

This chapter explores what child themes are, how to create a child theme–ready parent theme, and how to get the most out of using child themes.

Customizing Theme Style with Child Themes

A WordPress *theme* consists of a collection of template files, stylesheets, images, and JavaScript files. The theme controls the layout and design that your visitors see on the site. When such a theme is properly set up as a parent theme, it allows a *child theme*, or a subset of instructions, to override its files, ensuring that a child theme can selectively modify the layout, styling, and functionality of the parent theme.

The quickest way to understand child themes is by example. In this section, you create a simple child theme that modifies the style of the parent theme.

Currently, the default WordPress theme is Twenty Nineteen. Figure 5-1 shows how the Twenty Nineteen theme appears on a sample site.

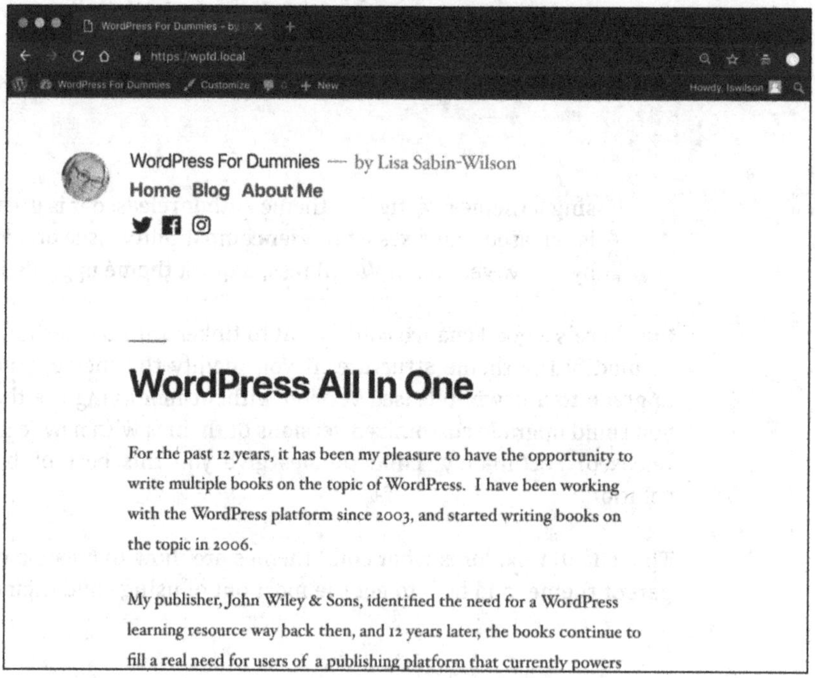

FIGURE 5-1: The Twenty Nineteen theme.

You likely have Twenty Nineteen on your WordPress site, and Twenty Nineteen is child theme–ready; therefore, it's a great candidate for creating a child theme.

Creating a child theme

Like regular themes, a child theme needs to reside in a directory inside the /wp-content/themes directory. The first step in creating a child theme is adding the directory that will hold it. For this example, connect to your hosting account via Secure File Transfer Protocol (SFTP), and create a new directory called twentynineteen-child inside the /wp-content/themes directory.

To register the twentynineteen-child directory as a theme and to make it a child of the Twenty Nineteen theme, create a style.css file, and add the appropriate theme headers. To do this, type the following code in your favorite code or plain-text editor (such as Notepad for the PC or TextEdit for the Mac) and save the file as style.css:

```
/*
Theme Name: Twenty Nineteen Child
Description: My 2019 child theme
Author: Lisa Sabin-Wilson
Version: 1.0
Template: twentynineteen
*/
```

Typically, you can find the following headers in a WordPress theme:

- Theme Name: The theme user sees this name in the back end of WordPress.
- Description: This header provides the user any additional information about the theme. Currently, it appears only on the Manage Themes screen (which you access by clicking the Themes link on the Appearance menu).
- Author: This header lists one or more theme authors. Currently, it's shown only on the Manage Themes screen (which you access by clicking the Themes link on the Appearance menu).
- Version: The version number is useful for keeping track of outdated versions of the theme. It's always a good idea to update the version number when modifying a theme.
- Template: This header changes a theme into a child theme. The value of this header tells WordPress the directory name of the parent theme. Because your child theme uses Twenty Nineteen as the parent, your style.css needs to have a Template header with a value of twentynineteen (the directory name of the Twenty Nineteen theme).

Now activate the new Twenty Nineteen Child theme as your active theme. (For information on how to activate a theme on your site, check out Book 6, Chapter 2.) You should see a site layout similar to the one shown in Figure 5-2.

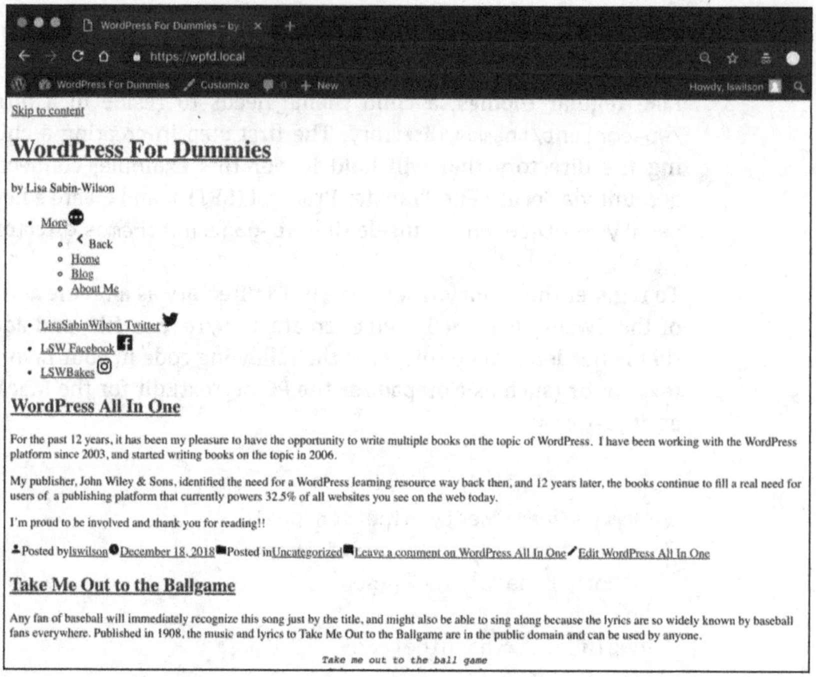

FIGURE 5-2: The Twenty Nineteen Child theme.

The theme shown in Figure 5-2 doesn't look quite right, does it? The problem is that the stylesheet (`style.css`) for the child theme is blank, and it's overriding the stylesheet in the parent theme.

You could just copy and paste the contents of the parent theme's `style.css` file into the child theme stylesheet, but that method would waste some of the potential of child themes.

Loading a parent theme's style

REMEMBER

One great thing about CSS is that rules can override one another. If you list the same rule twice in your CSS, the rule that comes last takes precedence.

Here's an example:

```
a {
color: blue;
}

a {
color: red;
}
```

This example is overly simple, but it nicely shows what I'm talking about. The first rule says that all links (a tags) should be blue, whereas the second rule says that links should be red. With CSS, the last instruction takes precedence, so the links will be red.

Using this feature of CSS, you can inherit all the styling of the parent theme and selectively modify it by overriding the rules of the parent theme. But how can you load the parent theme's `style.css` file so that it inherits the parent theme's styling?

Fortunately, CSS has another great feature that helps you do this with ease. Just add one line to the Twenty Nineteen Child theme's `style.css` file:

```
/*
Theme Name: Twenty Nineteen Child
Description: My 2019 child theme
Author: Lisa Sabin-Wilson
Version: 1.0
Template: twentynineteen
*/
@import url('../twentynineteen/style.css');
```

Several things are going on here, so let me break the code down piece by piece:

- `@import`: This piece of the code tells the browser to load another stylesheet and allows you to pull in the parent stylesheet quickly and easily.
- `url('...')`: This piece of the code indicates that the value is a location, not a normal value.
- `('../twentynineteen/style.css');`: This piece of code is the location of the parent stylesheet. Notice the `/twentynineteen` directory name, which needs to be changed to match the `Template` value in the header so that the appropriate stylesheet is loaded.

Figure 5-3 shows how the site appears after the child theme's `style.css` file is updated to match the listing. It looks the same as Figure 5-1 except for the logo area in the header — an option that gets set in the Customizer and that hasn't yet been set for this Twenty Nineteen child theme.

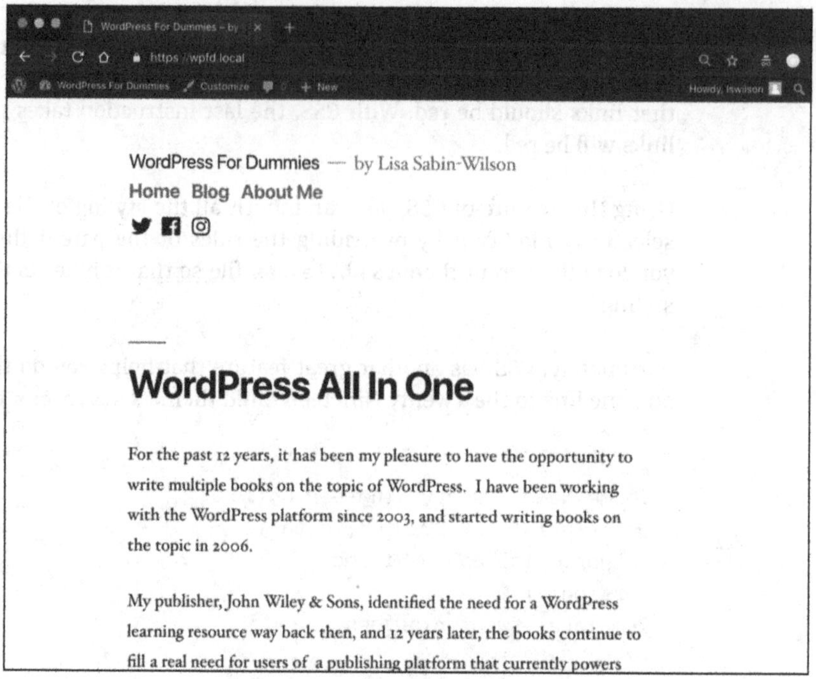

FIGURE 5-3: The updated child theme.

Customizing the parent theme's styling

Your Twenty Nineteen child theme is set up to match the parent Twenty Nineteen theme. Now you can add new styling to the Twenty Nineteen Child theme's `style.css` file. A simple example of how customizing works is to add a style that converts all h1, h2, and h3 headings to uppercase, like so:

```
/*
Theme Name: Twenty Nineteen Child
Description: My 2019 child theme
Author: Lisa Sabin-Wilson
Version: 1.0
Template: twentynineteen
*/

@import url('../twentynineteen/style.css');

h1, h2, h3 {
  text-transform: uppercase;
}
```

Figure 5-4 shows how the child theme looks with the code additions applied. In the preceding code snippet, you targeted the H1, H2, and H3 heading tags for the site and inserted the value `text-transform: uppercase`, which made all of those heading tags appear in uppercase font (or all capital letters) Now the site title and post titles are now all uppercase, which differs from Figure 5-3.

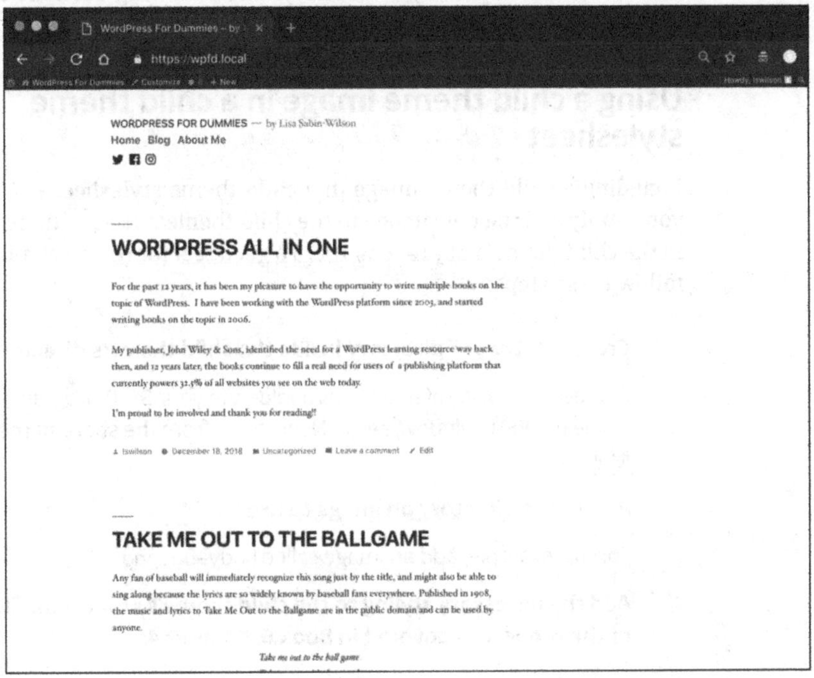

FIGURE 5-4: The updated child theme with uppercase headings.

As you can see, with just a few lines in a `style.css` file, you can create a new child theme that adds specific customizations to an existing theme. The change is quick and easy to make, and you don't have to modify anything in the parent theme to make it work.

TIP

When upgrades to the parent theme are available, you can upgrade the parent to get the additional features, but you don't have to make your modifications again because you made your modifications in the child theme, not the parent theme.

Customizations that are more complex work the same way. Simply add the new rules after the import rule that adds the parent stylesheet.

Using images in child theme designs

Many themes use images to add nice touches to the design. Typically, these images are added to a directory named `images` inside the theme.

Just as a parent theme may refer to images in its `style.css` file, your child themes can have their own `images` directory. The following sections show examples of how you can use these images.

Using a child theme image in a child theme stylesheet

Including a child theme image in a child theme stylesheet is common. To do so, you simply add the new image to the child theme's `images` directory and refer to it in the child theme's `style.css` file. To get a feel for the mechanics of this process, follow these steps:

1. **Create an `images` directory inside the child theme's directory.**

   A directory is also referred to as a folder. In your SFTP program, right-click inside the SFTP window, select New Folder from the shortcut menu, and name it `images`.

2. **Add to the directory an image to use.**

   For this example, add an image called body-bg.png.

3. **Add the necessary styling to the child theme's `style.css` file, using a few of the properties covered in Book 6, Chapter 4:**

```
/*
Theme Name: Twenty Nineteen Child
Description: My 2019 child theme
Author: Lisa Sabin-Wilson
Version: 1.0
Template: twentynineteen
*/

@import url('../twentynineteen/style.css');

body {
  background: url( 'images/body-bg.png' );
  background-attachment: fixed;
  background-position: top right;
  background-repeat: no-repeat;
}
```

With a quick refresh of the site, you see that the site now has a new background. Figure 5-5 shows the WordPress logo displayed as the background image in the top-right corner. If you followed these steps, as you scroll down the site, you see that the image stays in place because you used the `background-attachment: fixed;` CSS rule, which fixes the background image in one spot.

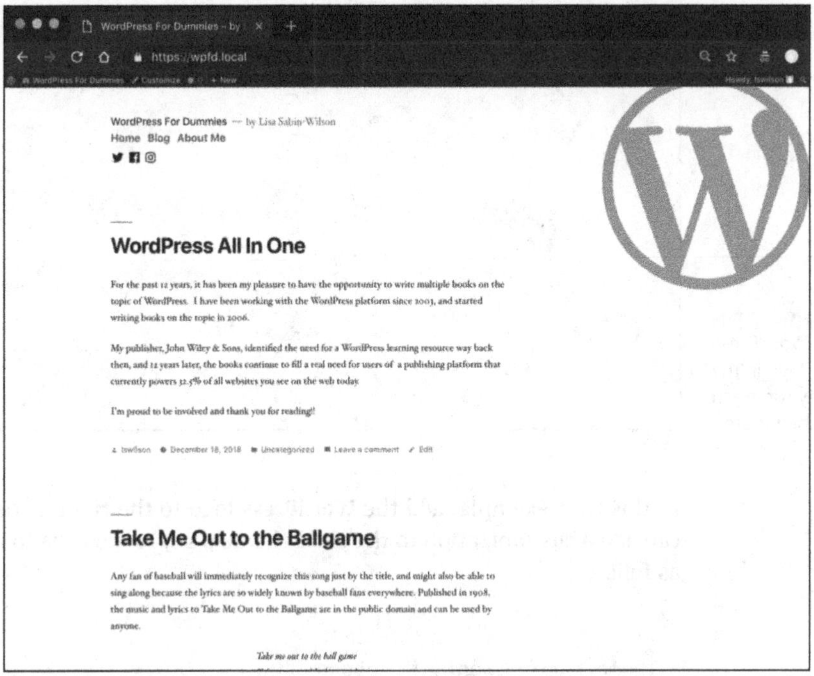

FIGURE 5-5: The Twenty Nineteen child theme after you edited the background image.

Using images in a child theme

Child theme images are acceptable for most purposes. You can add your own images to the child theme even if the image doesn't exist in the parent theme folder, and you can accomplish that task without changing the parent theme.

In the footer of the Twenty Nineteen theme, I added a WordPress logo to the right of the phrase `Proudly powered by WordPress`, as shown in Figure 5-6. By default, the logo doesn't appear in the footer of the Twenty Nineteen theme.

Create a folder in your child theme called `/images`, add your selected images to that folder, and then call those images into your child theme by using the stylesheet (`style.css`) file in your child theme folder.

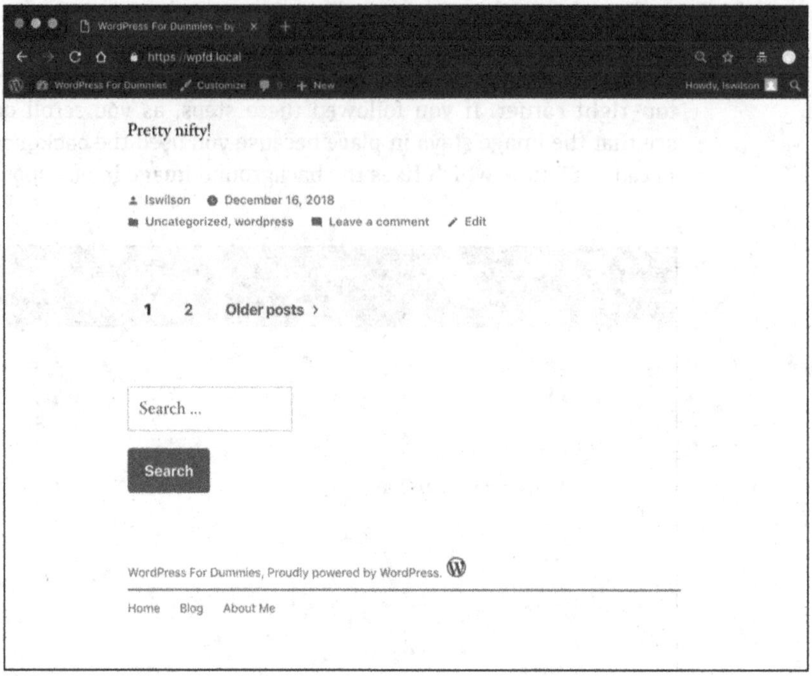

FIGURE 5-6: The WordPress logo in the Twenty Nineteen child footer.

In this next example, add the WordPress logo to the right of the footer text. You can add a customization to the child theme's `style.css` file to make this change, as follows:

```
/*
Theme Name: Twenty Nineteen Child
Description: My 2019 child theme
Author: Lisa Sabin-Wilson
Version: 1.0
Template: twentynineteen
*/

@import url('../twentynineteen/style.css');

#colophon .site-info .imprint {
  background: url( 'images/wordpress.png' );
  background-position: top right;
  background-repeat: no-repeat;
  padding-right: 30px;
  padding-top: 10px;
}
```

The CSS selectors (`#colophon .site-info .imprint`) in the code are from the Twenty Nineteen theme source code. (I wanted to target that footer text to add the logo to, so I looked at the HTML markup for the Twenty Nineteen parent theme to discover which selectors I needed to target.) Save the file, and refresh the site. Now you're showing WordPress pride.

TIP

A zip file of the example Twenty Nineteen child theme, and associated code samples, found in this chapter can be downloaded here: `https://lisasabin-wilson.com/wpfd/twentynineteen-child.zip`.

Modifying Theme Structure with Child Themes

The preceding section shows how to use a child theme to modify the stylesheet of an existing theme. This technique is tremendously powerful. A talented CSS developer can use this technique to create an amazing variety of layouts and designs by using the features and functionality that exist in a parent theme. Creating a child theme removes, or at least reduces, the need to reinvent the wheel by re-creating all the templates in a theme.

This feature is just the beginning of the power of child themes, however. Although every child theme overrides the parent theme's `style.css` file, the child theme can override the parent theme's template (PHP) files, too.

Child themes aren't limited to overriding template files; when needed, child themes also can supply their own template files.

Template files are `.php` files that WordPress runs to render different views of your site. A *site view* is the type of content being looked at. Examples of views are home, category archive, individual post, and page content.

Examples of common template files are `index.php`, `archive.php`, `single.php`, `page.php`, `attachment.php`, and `search.php`. (You can read more about available template files, including how to use them, in Book 6, Chapter 3.)

You may wonder what purpose modifying template files of a parent theme serves. Although modifying the stylesheet of a parent theme can give you powerful control of the design, it can't add new content, modify the underlying site structure, or change how the theme functions. To get that level of control, you need to modify the template files.

Overriding parent template files

When the child theme and parent theme supply the same template file, WordPress uses the child theme file and ignores the parent theme file. This process of replacing the original parent template file is referred to as *overriding.*

REMEMBER

Although overriding each of the theme's template files can defeat the purpose of using a child theme (updates of those template files won't enhance the child theme), sometimes you must do so to produce a needed result.

The easiest way to customize a specific template file in a child theme is to copy the template file from the parent theme folder to the child theme folder. After copying the file, you can customize it, and the child theme reflects the changes.

A good example of a template file that can be overridden is the `footer.php` file. Customizing the footer allows for adding site-specific branding.

Adding new template files

A child theme can override existing parent template files, but it can supply template files that don't exist in the parent, too. Although you may never need your child themes to do this, this option can open possibilities for your designs.

In Book 4, Chapter 6, I cover different page templates you can add to your WordPress theme to achieve a different look and display different types of content on your site. In that chapter, you create an About Page template (`about.php`) that differs from the standard Page (`page.php`) template that already exists in the Twenty Nineteen theme. Applying the information, as you discover in Book 4, Chapter 6, you can create an `about.php` template; upload it to your Twenty Nineteen child theme; and then edit or adjust that file to suit your purposes.

The Twenty Nineteen parent theme doesn't have an `about.php` template, but because your child theme for Twenty Nineteen does, WordPress uses this template to display your About page on your website. WordPress is smart enough to recognize templates in a child theme, even if they don't exist in the parent theme.

Removing template files

You may be asking why you'd want to remove a parent's template file. That's a good question. Unfortunately, the Twenty Nineteen theme doesn't provide a good example, so you must use your imagination a bit.

Suppose that you're creating a child theme from a parent theme called Example Parent. Example Parent is well designed, and you built a great child theme from it quickly. The child theme looks and works exactly the way you want it to, but there's a problem: The Example Parent theme has a home.php template file that provides a highly customized nonblog home page. What you want, however, is a standard blog home page. If the home.php file didn't exist in Example Parent, everything would work perfectly.

You can't remove the home.php file from Example Parent without modifying the theme, so you have to use a trick. Instead of removing the file, override the home.php file, and have it emulate index.php.

You may think that simply copying and pasting the Example Parent index.php code into the child theme's home.php file is a good approach. Although this technique works, there's a better way: You can tell WordPress to run the index.php file so that the intended index.php file is respected. This single line of code inside the child theme's home.php is all you need to add to replace home.php with index.php:

```
<?php locate_template( array( 'index.php' ), true ); ?>
```

The locate_template function does a bit of magic. If the child theme supplies an index.php file, that file is used; if not, the parent index.php file is used.

This technique produces the same result as removing the parent theme's home.php file. WordPress ignores the home.php code and respects the changes in index.php.

Modifying the functions.php file

Like template files, child themes can provide a Theme Functions template, or functions.php file. Unlike in template files, the functions.php file of a child theme doesn't override the file of the parent theme.

When a parent theme and a child theme each have a functions.php file, both the parent and child functions.php files run. The child theme's functions.php file runs first; then the parent theme's functions.php file runs. This setup is intentional because it allows the child theme to replace functions defined in the parent theme. Having two functions.php files works only if the functions are set up to allow having both, however.

The Twenty Nineteen `functions.php` file defines a function called `twentynineteen_setup`. This function handles the configuration of many theme options and activates some additional features. Child themes can replace this function to change the default configuration and features of the theme, too.

The following lines of code summarize how the `functions.php` file allows this to happen:

```
if ( ! function_exists( 'twentynineteen_setup' ) ) :
  /**
  * Sets up theme defaults and registers support for various
  * WordPress features.
  * Note that this function is hooked into the
  * after_setup_theme hook, which
  * runs before the init hook. The init hook is too late for
  * some features, such
  * as indicating support for post thumbnails.
   */

function twentynineteen_setup() {
endif;
```

REMEMBER

Wrapping the function declaration in the `if` statement protects the site from breaking in the event of a code conflict and allows a child theme to define its own version of the function.

In the Twenty Nineteen child theme, you can see how modifying this function affects the theme. Add a new `twentynineteen_setup` function that adds Post Thumbnails support to the Twenty Nineteen child theme's `functions.php` file.

```
<?php
function twentynineteen_setup() {
  add_theme_support( 'post-thumbnails' );
}
```

As a result of this change, the child theme no longer supports other special WordPress features, such as custom editor styling, automatic feed link generation, internationalization and location, and any of the other features that the parent Twenty Nineteen theme supports.

The takeaway from this example is that a child theme can provide its own custom version of the function because the parent theme wraps the function declaration in an `if` block that checks for the function first.

Preparing a Parent Theme

WordPress makes it very easy for you to make parent themes. WordPress does most of the hard work, but you must follow some rules for a parent theme to function properly.

I've used the words *stylesheet* and *template* numerous times in this book in many contexts. Typically, *stylesheet* refers to a CSS file in a theme, and *template* refers to a template file in the theme. But these words also have specific meaning in the context of parent and child themes. You must understand the difference between a stylesheet and a template when working with parent and child themes.

REMEMBER

In WordPress, the active theme is the stylesheet, and the active theme's parent is the template. If the theme doesn't have a parent, the active theme is both the stylesheet and the template.

TECHNICAL STUFF

Originally, child themes could replace only the `style.css` file of a theme. The parent provided all the template files and `functions.php` code. Thus, the child theme provided style, and the parent theme provided the template files. The capabilities of child themes expanded in subsequent versions of WordPress, making the use of these terms for parent and child themes somewhat confusing.

Imagine two themes: parent and child. The following code is in the parent theme's `header.php` file and loads an additional stylesheet provided by the theme:

```
<link type="text/css" rel="stylesheet" media="all" href="<?php
      bloginfo( 'stylesheet_directory' ) ?>/reset.css" />
```

The `bloginfo` function prints information about the site configuration or settings. This example uses the function to print the URL location of the stylesheet directory. The site is hosted at `http://example.com`, and the Parent is the active theme. It produces the following output:

```
<link type="text/css" rel="stylesheet" media="all"
href="http://example.com/wp-content/themes/Parent/reset.css" />
```

If the child theme is activated, the output would be

```
<link type="text/css" rel="stylesheet" media="all"
href="http://example.com/wp-content/themes/Child/reset.css" />
```

Now the location refers to the `reset.css` file in the Child theme. This code could work if every child theme copies the `reset.css` file of the Parent theme, but requiring child themes to add files to function isn't good design. The solution is simple, however. Instead of using the `stylesheet_directory` in the `bloginfo` call, use `template_directory`. The code looks like this:

```
<link type="text/css" rel="stylesheet" media="all" href="<?php
bloginfo( 'template_directory' ) ?>/reset.css" />
```

Now all child themes properly load the parent `reset.css` file.

When you're developing, use `template_directory` in stand-alone parent themes and `stylesheet_directory` in child themes.

IN THIS CHAPTER

» Customizing themes

» Creating new templates

» Activating custom menus

» Exploring Custom Post Types

» Using Post Thumbnails for feature images

» Building a theme options page

Chapter 6
Digging into Advanced Theme Development

The previous chapters of this minibook describe WordPress themes and using their structure to build your site. Delving into deeper topics can help you create flexible themes that offer users options to control the theme.

Whether you're building a theme for a client, the WordPress.org theme directory, or yourself, adding advanced theme features can make theme development easier and faster with a high-quality result. With these advanced theme concepts and tools, you can build robust, dynamic themes that allow for easier design customization and offer a variety of layout options.

Beyond tools and methods of advanced theme development, this chapter provides some development practices that help projects succeed.

Getting Started with Advanced Theming

Before themes were added to WordPress, customizing the design of the site meant modifying the main WordPress `index.php` file and the default `print.css` file.

Way back in 2005, Version 1.5 added the first theme support and rudimentary child theme support. Over time, WordPress began to support other features, such as custom headers, custom backgrounds, and featured images.

Additionally, the capabilities of themes have grown steadily. Incremental improvement — beginning with a small, simple starting point and improving it over time — works very well in theme development. By developing incrementally, you can build a theme from start to completion from an existing, well-tested theme (most themes are part of a larger incremental improvement process) and maximize your development time. I can't think of a single theme I've developed that wasn't built on another theme.

TIP

You don't need to develop each theme from scratch. Choosing a good starting point makes a big difference in how quickly you can get your project off the ground.

Finding a good starting point

Choosing a solid starting point to build your latest and greatest theme design on can be time-consuming. Although exploring all the available themes in detail is tempting, I find that exhaustive searches waste more time than they save.

Begin with the most current theme unless a more suitable one is available. Because the design and capabilities of the theme were recently implemented, modifying it to meet your current project's needs is faster than rediscovering all the nuances of an older, unfamiliar theme.

You may wonder whether I ever build themes from other designers' themes. I have. These days, if a new theme comes out that shows how to integrate some new feature, I play around with the theme to understand the concept but always go back to one of my themes to implement the modification. The reason is simple: If I can implement the feature into my own design, I have a much better appreciation of how it works. Allowing someone else's code or design to do the heavy lifting can limit how I use that feature.

TIP

If you're new to theme development and haven't produced a theme of your own, start with the WordPress default theme, Twenty Nineteen. (See Book 6, Chapter 1 for a full analysis of the Twenty Nineteen theme.) The WordPress development team includes a default theme in every installation of the platform to give new site owners a theme to use right away but also to give new theme developers the ability to discover how themes work.

All the examples in this chapter are built off the WordPress default Twenty Nineteen theme unless noted otherwise.

Customizing the theme to your needs

After you select a theme for your project, you should create a copy of the theme. This way, you can look at the unmodified version in case you accidentally remove something that causes the theme or design to break.

When you find code and styling that you don't need anymore, comment it out rather than delete it. This action removes the functionality but still allows you to add it back if you change your mind.

You comment out a line of PHP code by adding // in front of it, as in this example:

```
// add_editor_style();
```

Comment out CSS by wrapping a section in /* and */, as follows:

```
/* CSS Comment
#content {
. margin: 0 280px 0 20px;
}
*/
```

Comment out HTML by using brackets starting with <!-- and ending with --> surrounding the code, as in this example:

```
<!--<div id="content">this is a content area</div>-->
```

TIP

When you start finalizing the theme, go through the files to remove any blocks of commented styling and code to clean up your files.

Adding New Template Files

Book 6, Chapter 3 introduces the concept of template files and gives you an overview of the template files available to you. Book 6, Chapter 5 explains the idea of overriding template files with child themes. The following sections explore some advanced uses of template files.

Although you rarely need to use all these techniques, being fluent in your options gives you the flexibility to address specific needs quickly when they come up.

Creating named templates

WordPress recognizes three special areas of a theme: header, footer, and sidebar. The `get_header`, `get_footer`, and `get_sidebar` functions default to loading `header.php`, `footer.php`, and `sidebar.php`, respectively. Each of these functions also supports a name argument to allow you to load an alternative version of the file. Running `get_header('main')`, for example, causes WordPress to load `header-main.php`.

You may wonder why you'd use a name argument when you could create a template file named whatever you like and load it directly. The reasons for using the `get_header`, `get_footer`, or `get_sidebar` functions with a name argument are

- Holding to a standard naming convention that other WordPress developers can easily understand
- Automatically providing support for child themes to override the parent theme's template file
- Offering a fallback that loads the unnamed template file if the named one doesn't exist

REMEMBER

In short, use the name-argument feature if you have multiple, specialized header, footer, or sidebar template files.

You can use this named template feature along with the Theme Options (discussed in "Exploring Theme Options in the Customizer" later in this chapter) to allow users to easily switch among header, footer, and sidebar styles. On the Theme Options page, you can enable the user to choose the specific header, footer, or sidebar template file he or she wants, providing an easy way to change the layout or design of the site. For a good example of content you can add to a different sidebar file, see the nearby sidebar "WP_Query posts for category content," which discusses displaying a list of recent posts and filing them in a specific category on the sidebar of your site.

Creating and using template parts

A template part is similar to the header, footer, and sidebar templates except it isn't limited to the header, footer, and sidebar.

The `get_header`, `get_footer`, and `get_sidebar` functions allow code that's duplicated in many of the template files to be placed in a single file and loaded by using a standard process. The purpose of template parts is to offer a standardized function that can be used to load sections of code specific to an individual theme. Sections of code that add a specialized section of header widgets or display a block of ads can be placed in individual files and easily loaded as a template part.

WP_QUERY POSTS FOR CATEGORY CONTENT

WordPress makes it possible to pull in very specific types of content on your website through the `WP_Query();` template class. You place this class before The Loop (see Book 6, Chapter 3), and it lets you specify which category you want to pull information from. If you have a category called WordPress and want to display the last three posts from that category on your front page, in your sidebar, or somewhere else on your site, you can use this template tag.

The `WP_Query();` class has several parameters that let you display different types of content, such as posts in specific categories, content from specific pages/posts, or dates in your blog archives. The `WP_Query();` class lets you pass many variables and parameters. It's not limited to categories, either; you can use it for pages, posts, tags, and more. Visit the WordPress Codex at `https://codex.wordpress.org/Class_Reference/WP_Query` to read about this feature.

To query the posts on your site to pull out posts from one specific category, you can use the following tag with the associated arguments for the available parameters. This example tells WordPress to query all posts that exist on your site and to list the last five posts in the Books category:

```
<?php $the_query = new WP_Query( 'posts_per_page=5&category_name=books' ); ?>
```

Simply place this code on a line above the start of The Loop; you can use it in a sidebar to display clickable titles of the last five posts in the Books category. (When the reader clicks a title, he's taken to the individual post page to read the full post.)

```
<?php $the_query = WP_Query( 'posts_per_page=5&category_name=books' ); ?>
<?php while ($the_query->have_posts()) : $the_query->the_post(); ?>
<strong><a href="<?php the_permalink() ?>" rel="bookmark" title="Permanent
   Link to
<?php the_title_attribute(); ?>"><?php the_title(); ?></a>
   </strong>
<?php the_excerpt(); endwhile; ?>
```

Digging into Advanced Theme Development

You load template parts by using the `get_template_part` function. The `get_template_part` function accepts two arguments: slug and name. The slug argument is required and describes the generic type of template part to be loaded, such as `loop`. The name argument is optional and selects a specialized template part, such as `post`.

A call to `get_template_part` with just the slug argument tries to load a template file with a filename of *slug*`.php`. Thus, a call to `get_template_part('loop')` tries to load `loop.php`, and a call to `get_template_part('header-widgets')` tries to load `header-widgets.php`. See a pattern here? *Slug* refers to the name of the template file, minus the `.php` extension, because WordPress already assumes that it's a PHP file.

A call to `get_template_part` with both the slug and name arguments tries to load a template file with a filename of *slug-name*`.php`. If a template file with a filename of *slug-name*`.php` doesn't exist, WordPress tries to load a template file with a filename of *slug*`.php`. Thus, a call to `get_template_part('loop', 'post ')` first tries to load `loop-post.php` followed by `loop.php` if `loop-post.php` doesn't exist; a call to `get_template_part('header-widgets', 'post')` first tries to load `header-widgets-post.php` followed by `header-widgets.php` if `header-widgets-post.php` doesn't exist.

The Twenty Nineteen theme offers a good example of the template part feature in use. Look in the `theme` folder, and you see a folder called `/template-parts`. Inside that folder are different folders. Opening the `/content` folder reveals multiple templates that use the slug and name convention and can be called into any template file by using `get_template_part();`, as in `content-excerpt.php`, `content-page.php`, and `content-single.php`.

REMEMBER

The Loop is the section of code in most theme template files that uses a PHP `while` loop to loop through post, page, and archive content (to name a few types) and display it. The presence of The Loop in a template file is crucial for a theme to function properly. Book 6, Chapter 3 examines The Loop in detail.

Twenty Nineteen's `index.php` template file shows a template part for the `content` template part in action:

```
<?php
  if (have_posts() ) {

    // Load posts loop.
    while ( have_posts() ) {
      the_post();
      get_template_part( 'template-parts/content/content' );
  }
```

Loading the content by using a template part, Twenty Nineteen cleans up the `index.php` code considerably compared with other themes. This cleanup of the template file code is the icing on the cake. The true benefits are the improvements in theme development.

A child theme (child themes are discussed at length in Book 6, Chapter 5) could supply a `content.php` file to customize only The Loop for `index.php`. A child theme can do this without having to supply a customized `index.php` file because Twenty Nineteen uses template parts and uses both arguments of the `get_template_part` function.

When a theme's code for the header, The Loop, the sidebar, and the footer are placed in separate files, the template files become much easier to customize for specific uses. You can see the difference by comparing the following two blocks of code. The first block includes a sidebar through the use of the `get_sidebar();` function; the second block doesn't.

This page template includes a sidebar:

```
<?php get_header(); ?>
. <div id="primary" class="site-content">
.   <div id="content" role="main">
.     <?php while ( have_posts() ) : the_post(); ?>
        <?php get_template_part( 'content', 'page' ); ?>
        <?php comments_template( '', true); ?>
.     <?php endwhile; // end of the loop. ?>
.   </div><!-- #content -->
. </div><!-- #primary -->
<?php
  get_sidebar();
  get_footer();
?>
```

This page template doesn't include a sidebar:

```
<?php get_header(); ?>
. <div id="primary" class="site-content">
.   <div id="content" role="main">
.     <?php while (have_posts() ) : the_post(); ?>
        <?php get_template_part( 'content', 'page'); ?>
        <?php comments_template( '', true); ?>
.     <?php endwhile; // end of the loop.?>
.   </div><!-- #content -->
. </div><!-- #primary -->
<?php get_footer();?>
```

The only difference between these two blocks of code is that the first block contains the get_sidebar function call and the second one doesn't. With just this modification and a few styling rules added to the CSS, your theme now has a page template that doesn't have a sidebar.

You may wonder how the preceding example shows the value of template parts if it's really about the get_sidebar function. Although the get_sidebar function is the feature of the previous example, the unsung hero is the get_template_part function.

Using a template part means that a modification to a template that displays the same data needs to be made only one time. Both example blocks of code use the get_template_part call, which allows you to create as many customized page templates as you need without having to duplicate The Loop code. Without the duplicate code, the code for The Loop can be easily modified in one place.

TIP

When you start duplicating sections of code in numerous template files, place the code in a separate file, and use the get_template_part function to load it where needed.

Exploring content-specific standard templates

The template files I've discussed so far span a wide scope of site views specific to the view, not the content. The category.php template file, for example, applies to all category archive views but not to a specific category, and the page.php template file applies to all page views but not to a specific page. You can create template files for specific content and not the view, however.

Four content-specific template types are available: author, category, page, and tag. Each one allows you to refer to specific content by the term's ID (an individual author's ID, for example) or by the slug.

REMEMBER

The slug discussed in this section differs from the slug argument of the get_template_part function described earlier in this chapter. In this section, *slug* refers to a post, page, or category slug (to name a few), such as a Press Releases category with a slug of press-releases or a post titled "Hello World" with a slug of hello-world.

Suppose that you have an About Us page with an id of 138 and a slug of about-us. You can create a template for this page by creating a file named page-138.php or page-about-us.php. In the same way, if you want to create a template specific to an awesome author named Lisa with an id of 7 and a slug of lisa, you can create a file named author-7.php or author-lisa.php.

Creating a template by using the slug can be extremely helpful for making templates for sites that you don't manage. If you want to share a theme that you created, you could create a category-featured.php template, and this template would automatically apply to any category view that has a slug of featured. This practice is better than using the category ID, for example, because the ID number of a particular category is going to vary from site to site.

Using categories as the example, the file-naming convention is as follows:

- » A template with the filename category.php is a catch-all (default) for the display for all categories. (Alternatively, a template with the filename of archives.php displays categories if a category.php doesn't exist.)
- » Add a dash and the category ID number to the end of the filename (as shown in Table 6-1) to specify a template for an individual category.
- » Alternatively, you can add a dash and the category slug to the end of the filename (as shown in Table 6-1) to define it as a template for that particular category. If you have a category called Books, the category slug is books; the individual category template file would be named category-books.php.
- » If you don't have a category.php, an archives.php, or category-#.php file, the category display pulls from the Main Index template (index.php).

Table 6-1 gives you some examples of file-naming conventions for category templates.

TABLE 6-1 Category Template File-Naming Conventions

If the Category ID or Slug Is . . .	The Category Template Filename Is . . .
1	category-1.php
2	category-2.php
3	category-3.php
books	category-books.php
Movies	category-movies.php
music	category-music.php

REMEMBER

Because creating a template by using slugs is so useful (and because an ID is relevant only to a specific site), you may wonder why the `id` option exists. The short answer is that the `id` option is legacy support for a time in WordPress before the slug option existed, but it's still valuable in specific instances. You can use the `id` option for a content-specific template without worrying about the customization breaking if the slug changes, for example. This technique is especially helpful if you set up the site for someone and can't trust that he won't edit category slugs (such as changing a category with a slug of `news` to `press-releases`). He can change the slug of a category all day long, but doing so will still maintain the same ID for that category, even when the slug is modified, so using the ID in a template, such as `category-1.php`, will not disrupt the global theme.

Using page templates

Although the page-*slug*.php feature is very helpful, requiring the theme's user to use the name you choose for a specific feature sometimes is too difficult or unnecessary. Page templates allow you to create a stand-alone template (like page.php or `single.php`) that the user can selectively use on any page he or she chooses. As opposed to the page-*slug*.php feature, a page template can be used on more than one page. The combined features of user selection and multiple uses make page templates much more powerful theme tools than page-*slug*.php templates.

For more on page templates, see Book 6, chapters 1, 3, and 5.

To make a template a page template, add `Template Name:` *`Descriptive Name`* to a comment section at the top of the template file. The following code would be at the beginning of a page template that removes a sidebar:

```
<?php
/**
 * Template Name: Full-width Page Template, No Sidebar
 *
 * Description: Use this page template to remove the sidebar from any page.
 *
 */
```

This code registers the template file as a page template and adds Full-width Page Template, No Sidebar to the Page Attributes module's Template drop-down menu, as shown in Figure 6-1. (Check out Book 4, chapters 1 and 2 for information on publishing pages.) Using a template on a static page is a two-step process: Upload the template, and tell WordPress to use the template by tweaking the page's code.

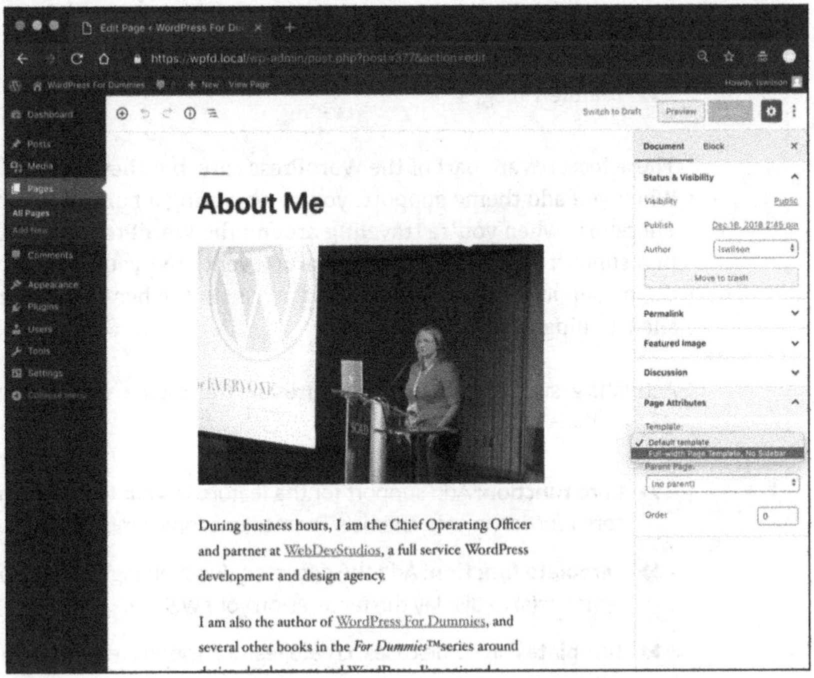

FIGURE 6-1: The Dashboard showing page attributes.

By providing a robust set of page templates, you can offer users of your theme an easy-to-use set of options for formatting their pages. These options can be used only for pages, but named header, footer, sidebar, and template parts can be used to offer users options on other site views.

Adding Theme Support for Built-In Features

The WordPress core offers several great tools that can easily be added to a theme to give the theme more customization options. WordPress provides several built-in features that enable you to enhance your site and theme. This section covers four of the most popular features:

- Custom navigation menus
- Custom post types

- Custom taxonomies
- Featured images

These features are part of the WordPress core, but they aren't activated by default. When you add theme support, you're activating a built-in feature in your theme. Therefore, when you're traveling around the WordPress community, whether it's in a support forum or at a WordCamp event, and you hear someone say that the theme supports a certain feature, you can smile because you know exactly what she's talking about.

Activating support for these features in the theme you're using involves a few steps:

- **Core function:** Add support for the feature to your theme by including the core function in your theme's Theme Functions template file (`functions.php`).
- **Template function:** Add the necessary function tags in your theme template(s) to display the features on your website.
- **Templates:** In some cases, create feature-specific templates to create enhancements to your site.

The following sections take you through these feature. You add the core function to your theme, add the function tags to your templates, and (if indicated) create a feature-specific template in your theme to handle the added features.

Adding support for custom menus

The WordPress menu-building feature is a great tool that WordPress offers to users and theme developers. Before the addition of this tool, theme developers implemented their own menu solution, creating a huge number of themes with navigation customization requiring coding and a small set of themes with very different ways of handling navigation. Creating complex, multilevel menus on your WordPress site takes just a few steps, as outlined in this section.

A *navigation menu* is a listing of links that displays on your site. These links can be links to pages, posts, or categories within your site, or they can be links to other sites. Either way, you can define navigation menus on your site with the built-in Custom Menus feature in WordPress.

It's to your advantage to provide at least one navigation menu on your site so that readers can see everything your site has to offer. Providing visitors a link, or several links, is in keeping with the point-and-click spirit of the web.

The Twenty Nineteen theme already supports menus. Looking at Twenty Nineteen's `functions.php` file, you see that the following lines of code handle registering the theme's menu:

```
// This theme uses wp_nav_menu() in two locations.
  register_nav_menus(
    array(
      'menu-1' => __( 'Primary', 'twentynineteen' ),
      'footer' => __( 'Footer Menu', 'twentynineteen' ),
      'social' => __( 'Social Links Menu', 'twentynineteen'),
    )
  );
```

This code registers three navigation areas with theme location names `menu-1`, `footer` and `social` and human-readable names of Primary, Footer Menu, and Social Links Menu. With the Twenty Nineteen theme active, click the Menus link on the Appearance menu to load the Menus page in the Dashboard, and view the different menu locations.

Core menu function and template tags

The Custom Menu feature is built into the default Twenty Nineteen WordPress theme, so you don't have to worry about preparing your theme for it. If you're using a different theme, however, adding this functionality is easy:

1. **Open the Header template (`header.php`) in a text editor.**
2. **Add the following template tag by typing it on a new line in the Header template (`header.php`):**

   ```
   <?php wp_nav_menu(); ?>
   ```

   This template tag is needed so that the menu you build by using the Custom Menu feature displays at the top of your website. Table 6-2 gives details on the parameters you can use with the `wp_nav_menu();` template tag to further customize the display to suit your needs.
3. **Save the Header template file.**

TABLE 6-2 Common Tag Parameters for wp_nav_menu();

Parameter	Information	Default	Tag Example
id	The unique ID of the menu (because you can create several menus, each with a unique ID number)	Blank	`wp_nav_menu(array ('id' => '1'));`
slug	The menu name in slug form (such as nav-menu)	Blank	`wp_nav_menu(array ('slug' => 'nav-menu'));`
menu	The menu name	Blank	`wp_nav_menu(array ('menu' => 'Nav Menu'));` or `wp_nav_menu('Nav Menu');`
menu_class	The CSS class used to style the menu list	Menu	`wp_nav_menu(array ('menu_class' => 'mymenu'));`
format	The HTML markup used to style the list (an unordered list [ul/li] or a div class)	Div	`wp_nav_menu(array ('format' => 'ul'));`
fallback_cb	The parameter that creates a fallback if a custom menu doesn't exist	wp_page_menu (the default list of page links)	`wp_nav_menu(array (' fallback_cb' => 'wp_page_menu'));`
before	The text that displays before the link text	None	`wp_nav_menu(array ('before' => 'Click Here'));`
after	The text that displays after the link text	None	`wp_nav_menu(array ('after' => '»'));`

Figure 6-2 shows the default Twenty Nineteen theme with a navigation menu (Home, Blog, About Me) below the website's name.

Create a menu called Main on the Menus page of the WordPress Dashboard. (See Book 6, Chapter 1 for details on creating menus in the WordPress Dashboard.) The template tag used in the theme to display the menu looks like this:

```
<?php wp_nav_menu( 'Main' ); ?>
```

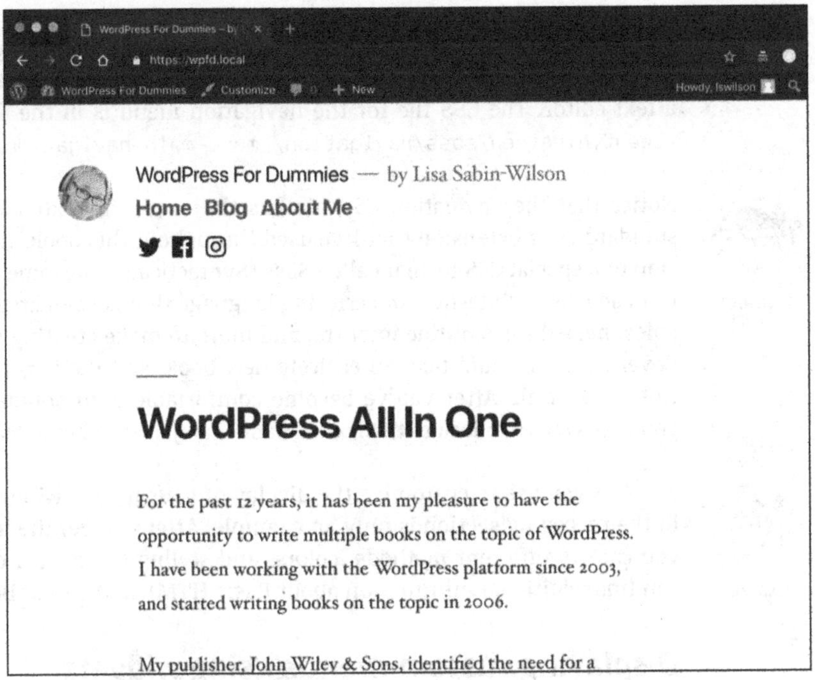

FIGURE 6-2: The Twenty Nineteen theme with a navigation menu below the header.

The HTML markup for the menu is generated as an unordered list by default and looks like this:

```
<ul id="menu-main" class="main-menu" tabindex="0">
  <li id="menu-item-412" class="menu-item menu-item-type-custom menu-item-
    object-custom current-menu-item current_page_item menu-item-home menu-item-
    412"><a href="https://wpfd.local">Home</a></li>
  <li id="menu-item-414" class="menu-item menu-item-type-post_type menu-item-
    object-page menu-item-414"><a href="https://wpfd.local/blog/">Blog</a></li>
  <li id="menu-item-413" class="menu-item menu-item-type-post_type menu-item-
    object-page menu-item-413"><a href="https://wpfd.local/about-me/">About Me
    </a></li>
</ul>
```

Notice in the HTML markup that the <ul id="menu-main" class="main-menu"> line defines the CSS ID and class.

The ID reflects the name that you give your menu. Because the menu is named Main, the CSS ID is menu-main. If the menu were named Foo, the ID would be menu-foo. By assigning menu names in the CSS and HTML markup, WordPress allows you to use CSS to create different styles and formats for your menus.

When developing themes for yourself or others to use, make sure that the CSS you define for the menus can do things like account for subpages by creating drop-down menus. You can accomplish this task in several ways. You can review the CSS for the navigation menu in the Twenty Nineteen theme by viewing it in a text editor. The CSS file for the navigation menu is in the theme folder here: `/twentynineteen/sass/navigation/_menu-main-navigation.scss`.

TECHNICAL STUFF

Notice that the navigation CSS file has the `.scss` file extension instead of the standard `.css` extension that I've used throughout this book. `.scss` is the extension of a special CSS format called Sass (Syntactically awesome style sheets). Sass is an advanced stylesheet or scripting language that developers use to create variables, nested rules, inline imports, and more to make creating stylesheets easier. Covering Sass would take an entirely new book, so I don't get into that topic in this book at all. After you've become comfortable with standard CSS, however, you may want to check out `https://sass-lang.com` to begin learning about Sass.

REMEMBER

The CSS you use to customize the display of your menus will differ; the example in the preceding section is only an example. After you get the hang of using CSS, you can try different methods, colors, and styling to create a custom look. (You can find additional information about Basic HTML and CSS in Book 6, Chapter 4.)

Displaying custom menus using widgets

You don't have to use the `wp_nav_menu();` template tag to display the menus on your site, because WordPress also provides a Custom Menu widget that you can add to your theme, allowing you to use widgets instead of template tags to display the navigation menus on your site. This widget is especially helpful if you've created multiple menus for use in and around your site in various places. Book 6, Chapter 4 provides more information on using WordPress widgets.

Your first step is registering a special widget area for your theme to handle the Custom Menu widget display. Open your theme's `functions.php` file, and add the following lines of code:

```
function my_widgets_init() {
  register_sidebar(array (
    'name'          => __( 'Menu' ),
    'id'            => 'widget-name',
    'description'   => __( 'A new widget area for my menu' ),
    'before_widget' => '<li id="%1$s" class="widget-container %2$s">',
    'after_widget'  => "</li>",
    'before_title'  => '<h3 class="widget-title">',
    'after_title'   => '</h3>',
    ) );
  }
add_action( 'widgets_init', 'my_widgets_init' );
```

These few lines of code create a new Menu widget area on the Widgets page of your Dashboard. You can drag the Custom Menu widget into the Menu widget to indicate that you want to display a custom menu in that area. Figure 6-3 shows the Menu widget area with the Custom Menu widget added.

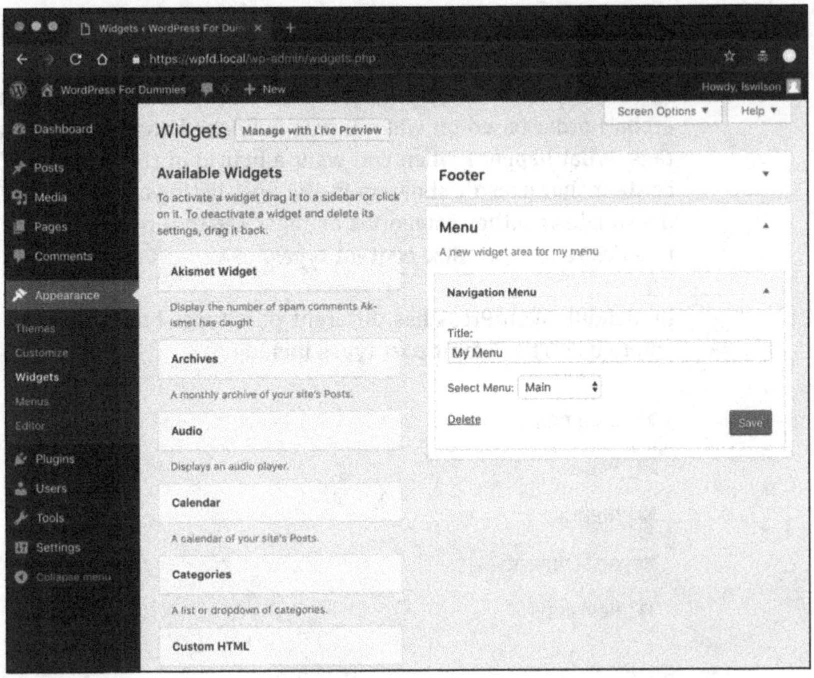

FIGURE 6-3: Widgets page displaying a Menu widget area with a Navigation Menu widget.

To add the widget area to your theme, open the Theme Editor (click the Editor link on the Appearance menu), open the `header.php` file, and add these lines of code in the area in which you want to display the Menu widget:

```
<ul>
<?php if ( !function_exists( 'dynamic_sidebar' ) || !dynamic_sidebar( 'Menu' )
   ) : ?>
<?php endif; ?>
</ul>
```

These lines of code tell WordPress that you want information contained in the Menu widget area to display on your site.

Adding support for custom post types

Custom post types and custom taxonomies have expanded the content management system (CMS) capabilities of WordPress and are likely to become a big part of plugin and theme features as more developers become familiar with their use. *Custom post types* allow you to create new content types separate from posts and pages, such as movie reviews or recipes. *Custom taxonomies* allow you to create new types of content groups separate from categories and tags, such as genres for movie reviews or seasons for recipes.

Posts and pages are nice generic containers of content. A *page* is timeless content that has a hierarchal structure; a page can have a parent (forming a nested, or hierarchal, structure of pages). A *post* is content that is listed in linear (not hierarchal) order based on when it was published and organized into categories and tags. What happens when you want a hybrid of these features? What if you want content that doesn't show up in the post listings, displays the posting date, and doesn't have either categories or tags? Custom post types are created to satisfy this desire to customize content types.

By default, WordPress has different post types built into the software, ready for you to use. The default post types include

- Blog posts
- Pages
- Menus
- Attachments
- Revisions

Custom post types give you the ability to create new, useful types of content on your website, including a smart, easy way to publish those content types to your site.

The possibilities for the use of custom post types are endless. To kick-start your imagination, here are some of the most popular and useful ideas that developers have implemented on sites:

- Photo gallery
- Podcast or video
- Book reviews
- Coupons and special offers
- Events calendar

Core custom post type function

To create and use Custom Post Types on your site, you need to be sure that your WordPress theme contains the correct code and functions. In the following steps, I create a basic Custom Post Type called Generic Content. Follow these steps to create the Generic Content basic Custom Post Type:

1. **Log in to your web server via Secure File Transfer Protocol (SFTP).**

   To see how to connect to your website via SFTP, refer to Book 2, Chapter 2.

2. **Navigate to the Twenty Nineteen theme folder.**

   On your web server, that folder is `/wp-content/themes/twentynineteen/`.

3. **Locate the `functions.php` template file.**
4. **Download the `functions.php` template file to your computer.**
5. **Open the `functions.php` file in a text editor.**

   Use Notepad if you're on a PC or TextEdit if you're using a Mac.

6. **Add the Custom Post Types code to the bottom of the Theme Functions template file.**

   Scroll to the bottom of the `functions.php` file, and include the following code to add a Generic Content Custom Post Type to your site:

```
// Add a Custom Post Type called: Generic Content
add_action( 'init', 'create_my_post_types' );
. function create_my_post_types() {
.   register_post_type( 'generic_content', array(
.     'label'          => __( 'Generic Content' ),
.     'singular_label' => __( 'Generic Content' ),
.     'description'    => __( 'Description of the Generic
  Content type' ),
.     'public' => true,
.   )
. );
}
```

7. **Save the Functions file, and re-upload it to your web server.**

Figure 6-4 shows you the WordPress Dashboard screen with a new menu item on the left menu; below the Comments link, you see a link for Generic Content. This link is the sample Custom Post Type that you added to WordPress in the preceding steps. You can see that the Generic Content post type has been successfully registered in my installation of WordPress and is ready to use.

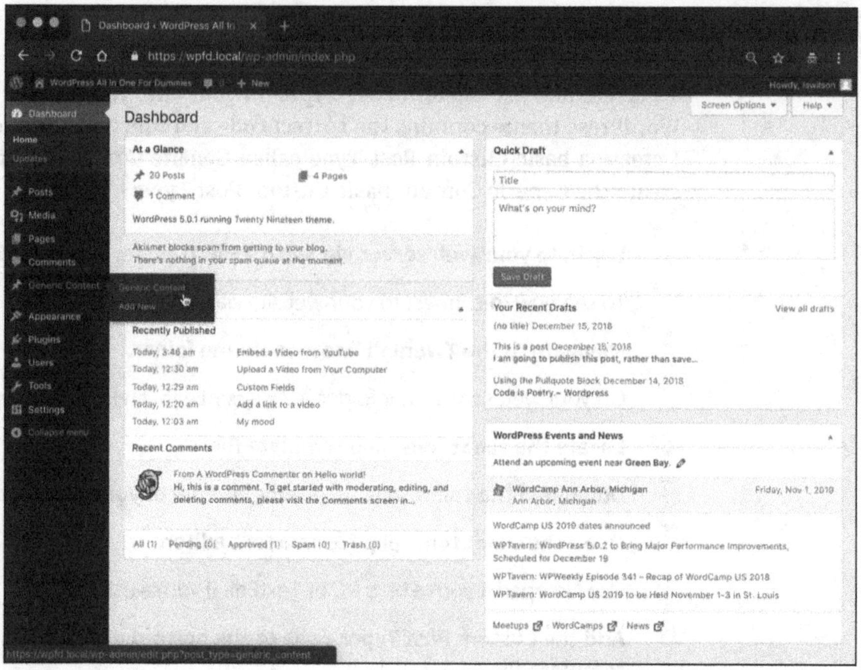

FIGURE 6-4: The new Generic Content post type.

TECHNICAL STUFF

The function `register_post_type` can accept several arguments and parameters, which are detailed in Table 6-3. You can use a variety and combination of arguments and parameters to create a specific post type. You can find more information on Custom Post Types and using the `register_post_type` function in the official WordPress Codex at `https://codex.wordpress.org/Function_Reference/register_post_type`.

TABLE 6-3 Arguments and Parameters for register_post_type();

Parameter	Information	Default	Example
`label`	The name of the post type.	None	`'label' => __('Generic Content'),`
`singular_label`	Same as `label`, but singular. If your label is `"Movies"`, the singular label would be `"Movie"`.	None	`'singular_label' => __('Generic Content'),`
`description`	The description of the post type; displayed in the Dashboard to represent the post type.	None	`'description' => __('This is a description of the Generic Content type'),`

Parameter	Information	Default	Example
public show_ui publicly_queryable exclude_from_search	Sets whether the post type is public. There are three other arguments: show_ui: whether to show admin screens publicly_queryable: whether to query for this post type from the front end exclude_from_search: whether to show post type in search results	true or false Default is value of public argument	'public' => true, 'show_ui' => true, 'publicly_queryable' => true, 'exclude_from_search' => false,
menu_position	Sets the position of the post type menu item on the Dashboard navigation menu.	Default: null By default, appears after the Comments menu on the Dashboard Set integer in intervals of 5 (5, 10, 15, 20, and so on)	'menu_position' => 25,
menu_icon	Defines a custom icon (graphic) to the post type menu item on the Dashboard navigation menu. Creates and uploads the image to the images directory of your theme folder.	Posts icon	'menu_icon' => get_stylesheet_directory_uri() . '/images/generic-content.png',
hierarchical	Tells WordPress whether to display the post type content list in a hierarchical manner.	true or false Default is false	'hierarchical' => true,
query_var	Controls whether this post type can be used with a query variable such as query_posts or WP_Query.	true or false Default is true	'query_var' => true,

(continued)

Digging into Advanced Theme Development

TABLE 6-3 *(continued)*

Parameter	Information	Default	Example
`capability_type`	Defines permissions for users to edit, create, or read the Custom Post Type.	`post` (default) Gives the same capabilities for those users who can edit, create, and read blog posts	`'query_var' => post,`
`supports`	Defines what meta boxes, or modules, are available for this post type in the Dashboard.	`title`: Text box for the post title `editor`: Text box for the post content `comments`: Check boxes to toggle comments on/off `trackbacks`: Check boxes to toggle trackbacks and pingbacks on/off `revisions`: Allows post revisions to be made `author`: Drop-down menu to define post author `excerpt`: Text box for the post excerpt `thumbnail`: The featured image selection `custom-fields`: Custom Fields input area `page-attributes`: The page parent and page template drop-down menus `post-formats`: adds Post Formats	`'supports' => array('title', 'editor', 'excerpt', 'custom-fields', 'thumbnail'),`

Parameter	Information	Default	Example
rewrite	Rewrites the permalink structure for the post type.	true or false The default is true with the post type as the slug Two other arguments are available: slug: Permalink slug to use for your Custom Post Types with_front: If you've set your permalink structure with a specific prefix, such as /blog	'rewrite' => array('slug' => 'my-content', 'with_front' => false),
taxonomies	Uses existing WordPress taxonomies (category and tag).	Category post_tag	'taxonomies' => array('post_tag', 'category'),

After you add a Generic Content Custom Post Type to your site, a new post type labeled Generic appears on the left navigation menu of the Dashboard.

You can add and publish new content by using the new Custom Post Type, just as you do when you write and publish posts or pages. (See Book 4, Chapter 1.) The published content isn't added to the chronological listing of posts; rather, it's treated like separate content from your blog (just like static pages).

View the permalink for the published content, and you see that it adopts the custom post type name Generic Content and uses it as part of the permalink structure, creating a permalink that looks like `https://`*`yourdomain.com`*`/generic-content/new-article`.

TIP

A very helpful plugin for building Custom Post Types quickly in WordPress is one called Custom Post Type UI. Written by my team at WebDevStudios, this plugin (`https://wordpress.org/plugins/custom-post-type-ui`) gives you a clean interface within your WordPress Dashboard that can help you easily and quickly build Custom Post Types on your website. It eliminates the need to add the code to your `functions.php` file by giving you options and settings so that you can configure and build the Custom Post Type that you want. Figure 6-5 shows the Custom Post Type UI options page on the Dashboard.

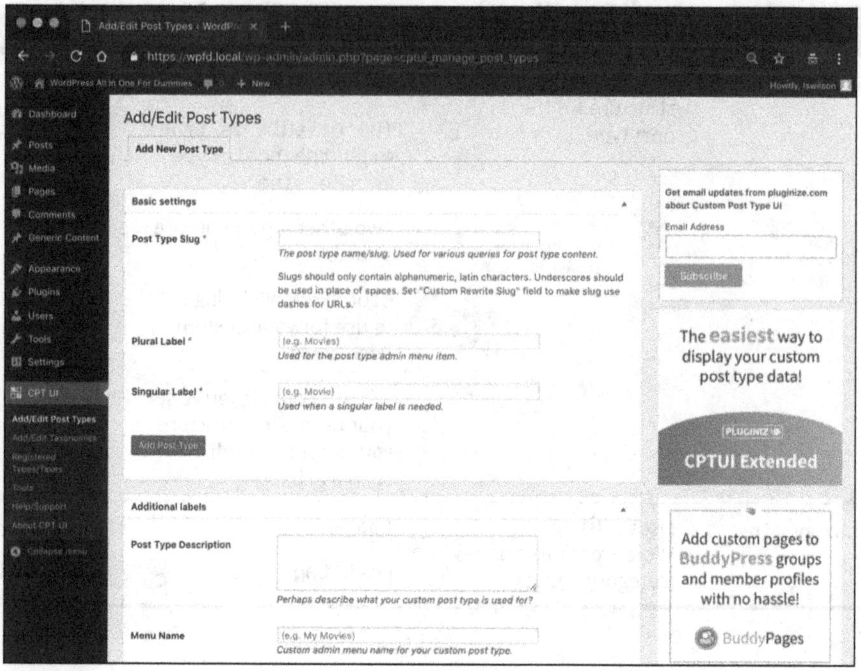

FIGURE 6-5: The options page for the Custom Post Type UI plugin.

Custom post type templates

By default, custom post types use the `single.php` template in your theme — that is, they do unless you create a specific template for your custom post type if you find the regular WordPress `single.php` template too limiting for your post type.

The preceding section has the code to build a simple Generic Content custom post. After you add that code, a Generic Content menu appears on the WordPress Dashboard. Click the Add New link on the Generic Content menu and publish a new post to add some content for testing. In this example, a new Generic Content type with a title of Test and a slug of `test` is added. Because the Generic Content type doesn't have a specific template, it uses the `single.php` template, and resulting posts look no different from a standard one.

TIP

If you get a Not Found page when you try to go to a new custom post type entry, reset your permalink settings. Click the Permalinks link on the Settings menu on the WordPress Dashboard and then click the Save Changes button. This action causes WordPress to reset the permalinks, which adds the new custom post type link formats in the process.

To build a template specific for the Generic Content post type, add a new template named `single-`*`posttype`*`.php`, where *`posttype`* is the first argument passed to the `register_post_type` function from the preceding section. For this example, the single template file specific to Sample Post Type is single-generic-content.php. Any modifications made in this template file are applied only to instances of the Generic Content post type.

Tying this material together with the section on template parts from earlier in this chapter, a basic structure for single-generic-content.php for the Twenty Nineteen theme is

```
<?php get_header(); ?>
  <section id="primary" class="content-area">
    <main id="main" class="site-main">

    <?php if ( have_posts()) {

      // Load posts loop.
      while (have_posts() ) {
        the_post();
        get_template_part( 'loop' , 'generic-content' );
        // Previous/next page navigation.
        twentynineteen_the_posts_navigation();

      } else {

        // If no content, include the "No posts found" template.
        get_template_part( 'template-parts/content/content', 'none' );

      }
    ?>

    </main><!-- .site-main -->
  </section><!-- .content-area -->
<?php get_footer(); ?>
```

When you use the template part, creating a file called loop-generic-content.php allows for easy customization of The Loop for the Generic Content post type entry.

Adding support for custom taxonomies

One of my engineers at work asks this question of every candidate who's interviewing for an engineering job: "If you were asked to design a class system for a virtual zoo, how would you architect the animal kingdom?"

There's no wrong or right answer to this question, but the answer the candidate gives tells the interviewer his or her thought process on architecting data. Does the candidate group the animals by color, for example, or by breed? One candidate started by grouping the animals based on location within the zoo; another started by grouping animals by species. These answers provide helpful insight into how a candidate would use WordPress to categorize complex data. Sometimes, though, using the built-in categories and tags aren't enough to accomplish a complex task such as architecting a virtual zoo.

On a website where content about different types of zoo animals is published, the zoo content might need a variety of new taxonomies or grouping options. Organizing zoo animals by color, breed, species, location in the zoo, and size allows visitors to the site to view different groups of animals that might interest them.

To register this new taxonomy, use the `register_taxonomy` function. Adding the following code to the bottom of your theme's `functions.php` file registers the Color taxonomy that you could use to categorize the zoo animals by color:

```
register_taxonomy( 'color', 'post', array(
  'label' => 'Color' )
);
```

This function call gives the new custom taxonomy an internal name of `color`, assigns the new taxonomy to Posts, and gives the taxonomy a human-readable name of Color. When you've successfully registered the new taxonomy, you see a link for it on the Posts menu of the Dashboard. In Figure 6-6, you see the Color taxonomy screen of the Dashboard, where you can add new terms in the same manner that you add Categories on the Category screen.

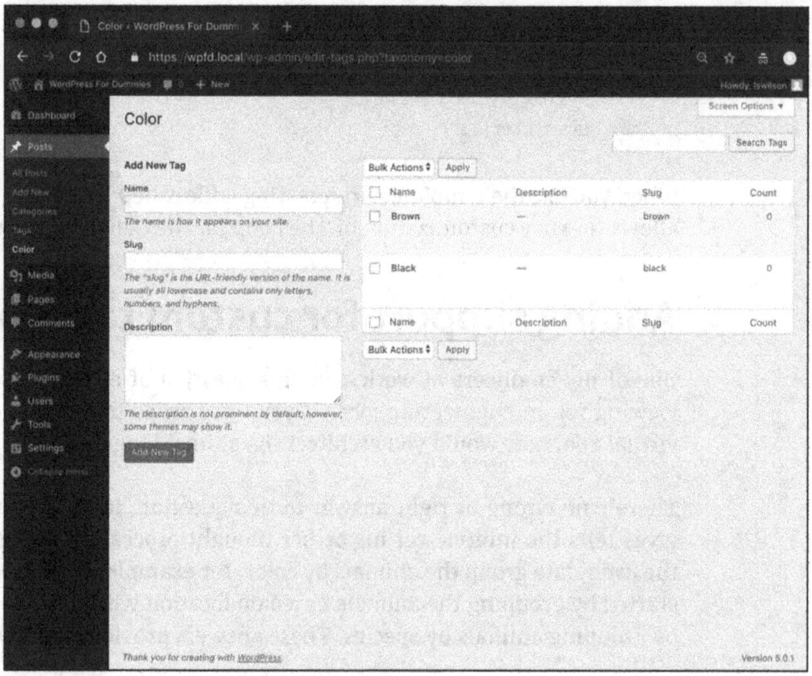

FIGURE 6-6: A new taxonomy registered in WordPress.

After adding this code to your theme, you can create and assign Colors when creating a new post or editing an existing post. For this example, you could add a color with a name of Brown to a post about a brown animal in the zoo.

With this new taxonomy (Color) added with the new term (Brown), you can visit `example.com/color/brown` to get the archive page for the new sample taxonomy.

TIP

If you get a `Not Found` page or don't get an archive listing when you try to go to a specific taxonomy entry's archive, resave your permalink settings. Click the Permalinks link on the Settings menu on the WordPress Dashboard and then click Save Changes. This action forces WordPress to reset the permalinks, which adds the new custom taxonomy link formats in the process.

Adding a new template file called `taxonomy-color.php` allows you to add a template specific to this new custom taxonomy. As you can with categories and tags, you can add a template that's specific to a single custom taxonomy entry. Therefore, a template specific to the Color taxonomy with a slug of `brown` would have a filename of `taxonomy-color-brown.php`.

REMEMBER

Custom taxonomies are a feature that appeals only to developers of specific types of sites that deal mainly in niche areas of content — sites that want to drill down navigation and grouping options for their content. You can find more about custom taxonomies in the WordPress Codex at `https://codex.wordpress.org/Function_Reference/register_taxonomy`.

Adding support for Post Thumbnails

The WordPress feature called Post Thumbnails (also known as Featured Images) takes a lot of the work out of associating an image with a post and using the correct size each time. A popular way to display content in WordPress themes includes a thumbnail image with a short snippet (excerpt) of text; the thumbnail images are consistent in size and placement within your theme. Before the inclusion of Post Thumbnails in WordPress, users had to open their images in an image-editing program (such as Adobe Photoshop) and crop and resize their image to the desired size, or use fancy scripts (which tend to be resource-intensive on web server)s to resize images on the fly, so those solutions weren't optimal. How about a content management system that crops and resizes your images for you to the exact dimensions that you specify? Yep, WordPress does that for you with just a few adjustments.

By default, when you upload an image, WordPress creates three versions of your image based on dimensions that are set on your Dashboard (click the Media link on the Settings menu):

- **Thumbnail size:** Default dimensions are 150px × 150px
- **Medium size:** Default dimensions are 300px × 300px
- **Large size:** Default dimensions are 1024px × 1024px

Therefore, when you upload an image, you end up with four sizes of that image stored on your web server: thumbnail, medium, large, and the original image. Images are cropped and resized proportionally, and when you use them in your posts, you can typically designate which size you want to use in the image options of the Image Block in the WordPress Block Editor. (See Book 4, Chapter 3 details on uploading images in WordPress.)

Within the WordPress settings panel for a post, you can designate a particular image as the featured image of the post; then, using the Featured Images function that you add to your theme, you can include template tags to display your chosen featured image with your post. This technique is helpful for creating the magazine- or news-style themes that are popular on WordPress sites. Figure 6-7 shows Post Thumbnails and featured images on my business website's blog at `https://webdevstudios.com/blog`.

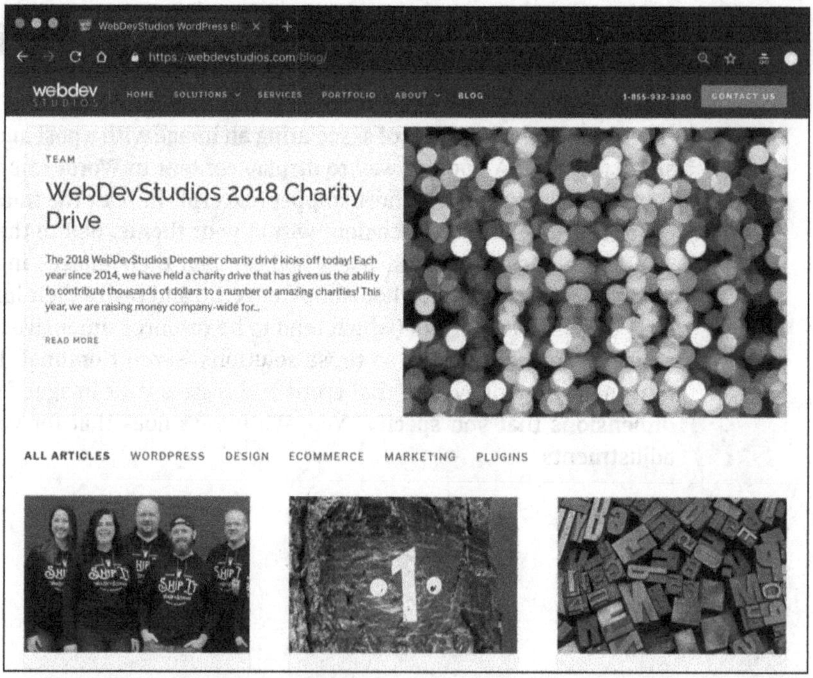

FIGURE 6-7: Post Thumbnails in use at webdevstudios.com/blog.

Also covered in the following sections is adding support for image sizes other than the default image sizes that are set on the Media Settings page of your Dashboard. This support is helpful when you have sections of your site where you want to display a much smaller thumbnail or a slightly larger version of the medium-size thumbnail. In Figure 6-7, you see two different image sizes in place: one at the top and the images along the bottom.

Core Post Thumbnails function and template tag

Adding support for Post Thumbnails includes adding one line of code to your Theme Functions template file (functions.php):

```
add_theme_support( 'post-thumbnails' );
```

After you add this line of code to your Theme Functions template file, you can use the Post Thumbnails feature for your posts. You can designate featured images in the Featured Image section of the settings panel on the Edit Post screen.

After you add featured images to your post, make sure that you add the correct tag in your template(s) so that the featured images display on your site in the area where you want them to display. Open your index.php template, and add the following line of code to include the default thumbnail-size version of your chosen featured image in your posts:

```
<?php if ( has_post_thumbnail() ) { the_post_thumbnail( 'thumbnail' ); } ?>
```

The first part of that line of code (if (has_post_thumbnail()) checks whether a featured image is associated with the post. If so, the image is attached to the post. The second part of that code snippet (the_post_thumbnail('thumbnail')) displays the thumbnail-size version of the image. If a featured image doesn't exist for the post, the second part of the code snippet is ignored, and the code returns nothing. You also can include the other default image sizes (set in the Media Settings screen of the Dashboard, as shown in Figure 6-8) for medium, large, and full-size images by using these tags:

```
<?php if ( has_post_thumbnail() ) { the_post_thumbnail( 'medium' ); } ?>
```

```
<?php if ( has_post_thumbnail() ) { the_post_thumbnail( 'large' ); } ?>
```

```
<?php if ( has_post_thumbnail() ) { the_post_thumbnail( 'full' ); } ?>
```

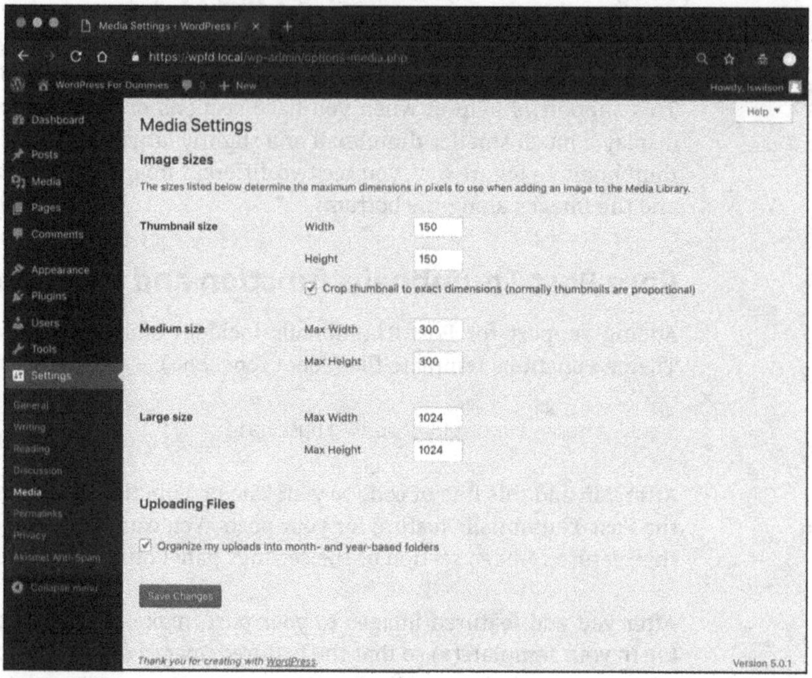

FIGURE 6-8: The Media Settings screen of the Dashboard.

Adding custom image sizes for Post Thumbnails

If the predefined, default image sizes in WordPress (thumbnail, medium, large, and full) don't satisfy you, and there's an area on your site where you want to display images with dimensions that vary from the default, WordPress makes it relatively easy to extend the functionality of the post thumbnail feature by defining custom image sizes for your images in your Theme Functions template file. Then you use the `the_post_thumbnail` function to display it in your theme.

There's no limit to what sizes you can use for your images. The following example shows how to add a new image size of 600px × 300px. Add this line to your Theme Functions template file (`functions.php`) below the `add_theme_support('post-thumbnails')` function:

```
add_image_size( 'custom', 600, 300, true );
```

This code tells WordPress that it needs to create an additional version of the images you upload and to crop and resize it to 600px × 300px. Notice the four parameters in the `add_image_size` function:

- **Name (`$name`):** Gives the image size a unique name that you can use in your template tag. The image size in this example uses the name `'custom'`.

» **Width (`$width`):** Gives the image size a width dimension in numbers. In this example, the width is defined as `'600'`.

» **Height (`$height`):** Gives the image size a height dimension in numbers. In this example, the height is defined as `'300'`.

» **Crop (`$crop`):** This parameter is optional and tells WordPress whether it should crop the image to exact dimensions or do a soft proportional resizing of the image. In this example, the parameter is set to `'true'` (accepted arguments: `true` or `false`).

Adding the custom image size to your template to display the featured image is the same as adding default image sizes. The only difference is the name of the image set in the parentheses of the template tag. The custom image size in this example uses the following tag:

```
<?php if ( has_post_thumbnail() ) { the_post_thumbnail( 'custom' ); } ?>
```


Exploring Theme Options in the Customizer

One key feature of an advanced theme adds theme options to the Customizer panel in WordPress. Theme options allow the theme user to set configurations for the theme without having to modify the theme files. Although a single-use theme could have this information hard-coded into it, this solution is inelegant. If the theme is used more than once or is managed by a nondeveloper, having an easy-to-change setting in the Customizer allows changes to be made quickly and easily. I cover the WordPress Customizer in various chapters of Book 6.

Click the Customize link on the Appearance menu to view the Customizer for the Twenty Nineteen theme, as shown in Figure 6-9.

The Twenty Nineteen theme uses the Customizer to allow its users to adjust several areas of the theme without having to touch any of the code within the template files. The Customizer options for the Twenty Nineteen theme include

» **Site Identity:** This section allows the user to upload a logo, set the website title, set the website tagline, and upload an icon for display on the browser tab.

» **Colors:** This section allows the user to set the color of design elements such as links and button colors.

- **Menus:** This section allows the user to configure the three navigation menus available in the theme.
- **Widgets:** This section allows the user to configure the widgets for the theme.
- **Home page Settings:** This section allows the user to configure the page(s) used for the home page and blog.
- **Additional CSS:** This section allows the user to add styles to the theme by using CSS.

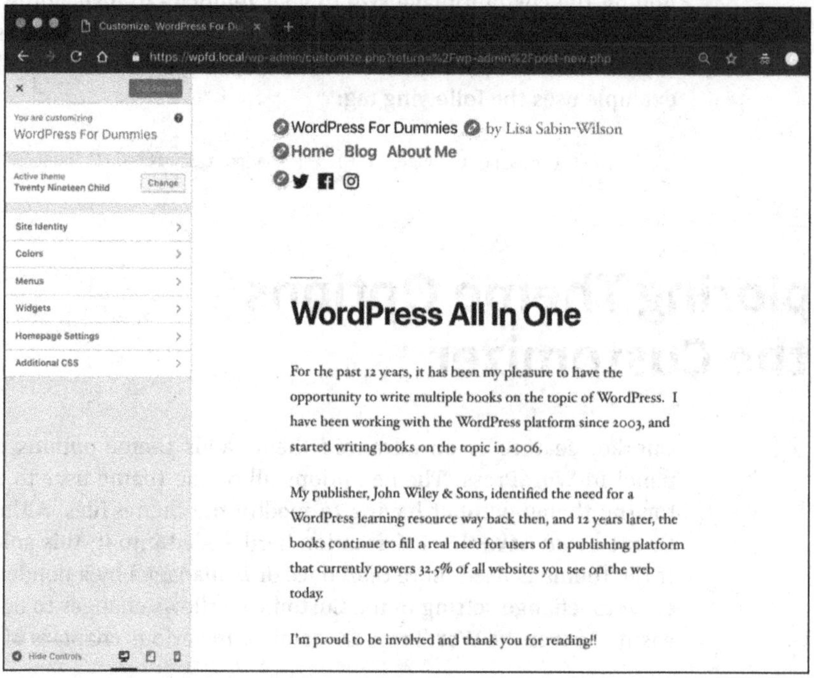

FIGURE 6-9: The Customizer panel.

Provide options in the Customizer when the information is specific to the website, not to the theme design. Web analytics code (such as visitor-tracking JavaScript from Google Analytics) is a good example of this user-specific information. Because hundreds of analytics providers exist, most analytics providers require the JavaScript code to be customized for the specific site and then added to the header or footer of the website, which requires a user to edit theme files to add the code for analytics. When you provide an option in the Customizer for the user of your theme to enter the analytics code snippet in a text field, you make the process of adding the analytics code much easier for the user.

TIP

Early in the design process, consider what a user may want to modify. Advanced uses of theme options in the Customizer vary widely and include design editors, color pickers, font options, and settings to modify the theme layout (switch a sidebar from one side of the theme to another, for example). The options offered depend on the project and the design.

Before jumping into the code, you should understand some basic concepts of theme options.

To allow the user to access the theme options, you have to offer some form of input, which means adding options to the Customizer via the WordPress Customize API. WordPress provides this API to allow developers to use the Customizer for theme options; it provides a framework for allowing users to live-preview their websites as they make changes in the Customizer.

Four types of objects can be added to the Customizer:

- **Panels:** Contain the sections and allow multiple sections to be grouped
- **Sections:** Contained within panels and control the navigation within the Customizer
- **Settings:** Handle the live preview, saving, and sanitizing of the Customizer data
- **Controls:** Contained within sections and have design inputs for the settings, such as text fields and check boxes

The Twenty Nineteen theme has already started this process for you. You can view the code in the `theme` folder in `/twentynineteen/inc/customizer.php`.

The hook, or function, that you use to initiate the Customizer option is on line 15 of the `customizer.php` file in the Twenty Nineteen theme:

```
function twentynineteen_customize_register( $wp_customize ) {
```

For any theme for which you're creating Customizer options, it's important to note that the theme folder name needs to be included in the function name. In the preceding code snippet, notice the function name: `twentynineteen_customize_register`. The `twentynineteen` part of that function corresponds with the `theme` folder, and it has to so that WordPress knows which theme to apply the options to. If the name of your `theme` folder is `mytheme`, the function to initiate the Customizer would be `mytheme_customize_register`.

Farther down in the `customizer.php` file, on line 104, you see the following line of code:

```
add_action( 'customize_register', 'twentynineteen_customize_register' );
```

Everything that exists between lines 15 and 104 in the `customizer.php` file represents the panels, sections, settings, and controls for the theme. Line 15 defines the function, and line 104 adds it to the theme Customizer. Panels, sections, settings, and controls can be added in this format, where `mytheme` is the name of my `theme` folder:

```
function mytheme_customize_register( $wp_customize ) {
 $wp_customize->add_panel();
 $wp_customize->get_panel();
 $wp_customize->remove_panel();

 $wp_customize->add_section();
 $wp_customize->get_section();
 $wp_customize->remove_section();

 $wp_customize->add_setting();
 $wp_customize->get_setting();
 $wp_customize->remove_setting();

 $wp_customize->add_control();
 $wp_customize->get_control();
 $wp_customize->remove_control();
}
add_action('customize_register','mytheme_customize_register');
```

In this code snippet, you notice a theme of add, get, and remove. The WordPress Customize API allows you to add, get, and remove panels, sections, settings, and controls as needed.

For the most part, when you're creating a theme with Customizer support, you don't need to add new panels because WordPress already has several default panels to which you can add sections. These panels are available for you to add your sections and controls to by adding the ID for the panel to the functions code. The available panels and panel IDs are

- **Site Identity:** `title_tagline`
- **Colors:** `colors`
- **Header Image:** `header_image`
- **Background Image:** `background_image`

- **Menus:** nav_menus
- **Widgets:** widgets
- **Static Front Page:** static_front_page
- **Additional CSS:** custom_css

TECHNICAL STUFF

As a rule, in the WordPress Customizer, a panel must contain at least one section, and a section must contain at least one control to be displayed in the Customizer.

In the Twenty Nineteen customizer.php, you can see the color-picker settings starting on line 40:

```
$wp_customize->add_setting(
  'primary_color',
    array(
      'default'           => 'default',
      'transport'         => 'postMessage',
      'sanitize_callback' => 'twentynineteen_sanitize_color_option',
    )
  );
```

Line 49 adds the controls for the color picker, which in this case are radio buttons for two choices: Default and Custom. Figure 6-10 shows the Color options, showing the settings and controls outlined in these code examples.

```
$wp_customize->add_control(
  'primary_color',
    array(
      'type'      => 'radio',
      'label'     => __( 'Primary Color', 'twentynineteen' ),
      'choices'   => array(
        'default' => _x( 'Default', 'primary color', 'twentynineteen' ),
        'custom'  => _x( 'Custom', 'primary color', 'twentynineteen' ),
      ),
      'section'   => 'colors',
      'priority'  => 5,
    )
);
```

The part of the code snippet that says 'section' => 'colors' is where the theme author tells WordPress that he wants the Primary Color section to appear in the Colors panel. (See the list of panels and panel IDs earlier in this section.)

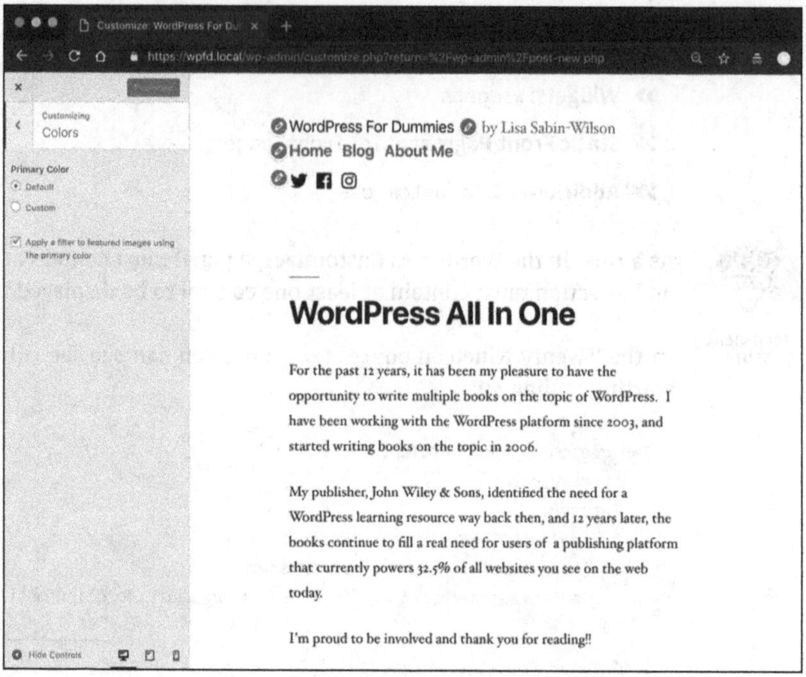

FIGURE 6-10: Twenty Nineteen theme color options in the Customizer.

The Customize API is extensive, and it's a powerful tool for providing extra design and theme functionality to users of the theme, allowing them to do things like change a background color or include a custom logo without having to edit any theme files or stylesheets.

TIP

This section gives you a brief introduction to the Customizer. If you want to dig into the Customize API, you can find full documentation, including code samples and advanced practices and techniques, at `https://developer.wordpress.org/themes/customize-api`.

7

Using and Developing Plugins

Contents at a Glance

IN THIS CHAPTER

- » Extending WordPress with plugins
- » Comparing plugins to themes
- » Finding plugins
- » Evaluating the trustworthiness of plugins

Chapter 1 Introducing WordPress Plugins

Half the fun of running a WordPress-powered website is playing with the hundreds of plugins that you can install to extend your site's functions and options. WordPress plugins are like those really cool custom rims you put on your car: Although they don't come with the car, they're awesome accessories that make your car better than all the rest.

Plugins can be very simple, such as a plugin that changes the appearance of the Dashboard menu. Or they can be very complex, accomplishing hefty tasks such as providing a complete e-commerce solution with product listings, a shopping cart, and payment processing.

In this chapter, you find out what plugins are, how to find and install them, and how they enhance your site to make it unique. Using plugins can greatly improve your readers' experiences by providing them various tools to interact and participate — just the way you want them to!

Extending WordPress with Plugins

By itself, WordPress is a powerful program for web publishing, but customizing WordPress with *plugins* — add-on programs that give WordPress almost limitless ways to handle web content —make WordPress even more powerful. You can choose any plugins you need to expand your online possibilities. Plugins can turn your WordPress installation into a full-featured gallery for posting images on the web, an online store to sell your products, a user forum, or a social networking site. WordPress plugins can be simple, perhaps adding a few minor features, or complex enough to change your entire WordPress site's functionality.

There's a popular saying among WordPress users: "There's a plugin for that." The idea is that if you want WordPress to do something new, you have a good chance of finding an existing plugin that can help you do what you want. Currently, more than 55,000 plugins are available on the WordPress website (`https://wordpress.org/plugins`), and this number is growing at a rate of a few new plugins each day. In addition, thousands of additional plugins are available outside the WordPress website for free or for a fee. So if you have an idea for a new feature for your site, you just may find a plugin for that feature.

Thousands of plugins are available for WordPress — certainly way too many for me to list in this chapter. I could, but then you'd need heavy machinery to lift this book off the shelf! Here are just a few examples of things that plugins let you add to your WordPress site:

- **Email notification:** Your biggest fans can sign up to have an email notification sent to them every time you update your website.
- **Social media integration:** Allow your readers to submit your content to some of the most popular social networking services, such as Twitter, Facebook, and Reddit.
- **Stats program:** Keep track of where your traffic is coming from; which posts on your site are most popular; and how much traffic is coming through your website on a daily, monthly, and yearly basis.

Identifying Core Plugins

Some plugins hold a very special place in WordPress in that they're shipped with the WordPress software and are included by default in every WordPress installation.

For the past few years, two plugins have held this special position:

- **Akismet:** The Akismet plugin has the sole purpose of protecting your blog from comment spam. Although other plugins address the issue of comment spam, the fact that Akismet is packaged with WordPress and works quite well means that most WordPress users rely on Akismet for their needs. Book 3, Chapter 4 covers how to activate and configure Akismet on your site.
- **Hello Dolly:** The Hello Dolly plugin helps you get your feet wet in plugin development, if you're interested. It was first released with WordPress 1.2 and is considered to be the oldest WordPress plugin. When the plugin is active, the tops of your Dashboard pages show a random lyric from the song "Hello, Dolly!"

Figure 1-1 shows the core plugins in a new installation of WordPress.

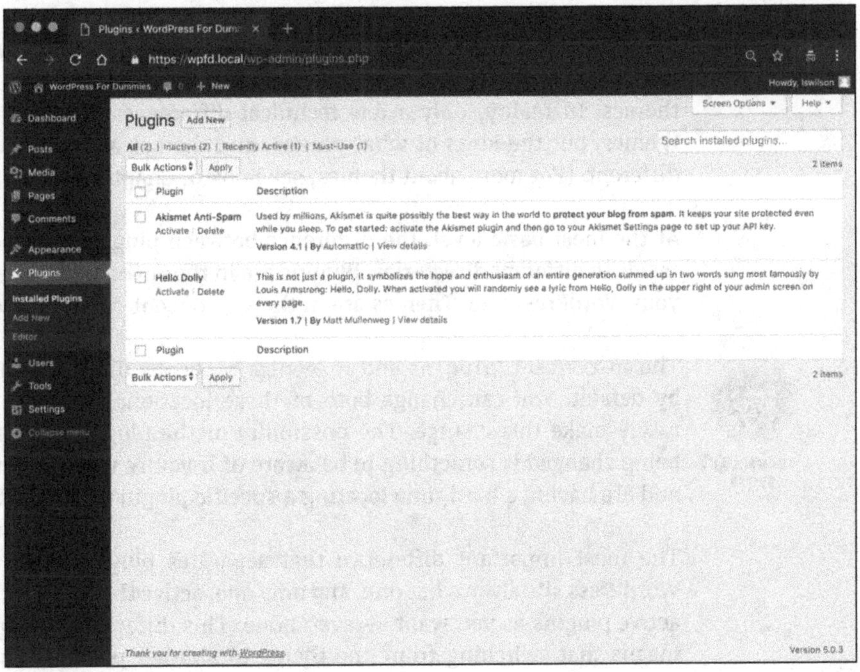

FIGURE 1-1: Core plugins in WordPress.

REMEMBER

The idea of core plugins is to offer a base set of plugins to introduce you to the concept of plugins while providing a benefit. The Akismet plugin is useful because comment spam is a big issue for WordPress sites. The Hello Dolly plugin is useful as a nice starting point for understanding what plugins are and how they're coded.

Although WordPress automatically includes these plugins, your site doesn't have to run them. Plugins are disabled by default; you must activated them manually.

You can delete core plugins, just as you can delete any other plugins, and they won't be replaced when you upgrade WordPress.

Future versions of WordPress may offer different sets of core plugins. It's possible that one or both of the current core plugins will cease being core plugins and that other plugins will be included. Although this topic has been much discussed in WordPress development circles over the past few years, at this writing, no definitive decisions have been made, so the current set of core plugins is likely to stay for a while longer.

Distinguishing between Plugins and Themes

Because themes can contain large amounts of code and add new features or other modifications to WordPress, you may wonder how plugins are different from themes. In reality, only a few technical differences exist between plugins and themes, but the ideas of what plugins and themes are supposed to be are quite different. (For more about themes, see Book 6, Chapter 1.)

At the most basic level, the difference between plugins and themes is that they reside in different directories. Plugins are in the `wp-content/plugins` directory of your WordPress site. Themes are in the `wp-content/themes` directory.

TECHNICAL STUFF

The `wp-content/plugins` and `wp-content/themes` directories are set up this way by default. You can change both of these locations, although WordPress users rarely make this change. The possibility of the plugins' and themes' locations being changed is something to be aware of if you're working on a WordPress site and are having a hard time locating a specific plugin or theme directory.

The most important difference that separates plugins from themes is that a WordPress site always has one, and only one, active theme, but it can have as many active plugins as you want — even none. This difference is important because it means that switching from one theme to another prevents you from using the features of the old theme. By contrast, activating a new plugin doesn't prevent you from making use of the other active plugins.

REMEMBER

Plugins are capable of changing nearly every aspect of WordPress. The Multiple Themes plugin, for example (available at `https://wordpress.org/plugins/jonradio-multiple-themes`), allows you to use different themes for specific parts of your WordPress site. Thus, you can overcome even the limitation of having only one active theme on a site by using a plugin.

Because WordPress can have only one theme but many plugins activated at one time, it's important that the features that modify WordPress be limited to plugins, whereas themes remain focused on the appearance of the site. For you, this separation of functionality and appearance is the most important difference between plugins and themes. (See the nearby sidebar "The difference between plugins and themes.")

TIP

This separation of plugins for functionality and themes for appearance isn't enforced by WordPress, but it's a good practice to follow. You can build a theme that includes too much functionality, and you may start to rely on those functions to make your site work, which ultimately makes switching to another theme difficult.

The functionality role of plugins doesn't mean that control of the appearance of a WordPress site is limited to themes. Plugins are just as capable of modifying the site's appearance as a theme is. The WPtouch mobile plugin, for example (available at `https://wordpress.org/plugins/wptouch`), can provide a different version of your site to mobile devices such as smartphones by replacing the functionality of the theme when the user visits the site on a mobile device.

THE DIFFERENCE BETWEEN PLUGINS AND THEMES

Other technical differences separate plugins and themes. The differences matter mostly to developers, but it could be important for you to know these differences as a nondeveloper WordPress user:

- Plugins load before the theme, which gives plugins some special privileges over themes; the result can be that one or more plugins prevent the theme from loading. The built-in WordPress functions in the `wp-includes/pluggable.php` file can be overridden with customized functions, and only plugins load early enough to override these functions.
- Themes support a series of structured template files and require a minimum set of files to be valid. By comparison, plugins have no structured set of files and require only a single `.php` file with a comment block at the top to tell WordPress that the file is a plugin.
- One final technical difference is that themes support a concept called child themes, wherein one theme can require another theme to be present to function; no such feature is available to plugins.

Finding Plugins on the WordPress Website

The largest and most widely used source of free WordPress plugins is the WordPress Plugins page (`https://wordpress.org/plugins`). As shown in Figure 1-2, this directory is filled with more than 55,000 plugins that cover an extremely broad range of features. Due to the large number of plugins freely available, the fact that each plugin listing includes ratings and details such as user-reported compatibility with WordPress versions, the Plugins page of the WordPress website should be your first stop when you're looking for a new plugin to fill a specific need.

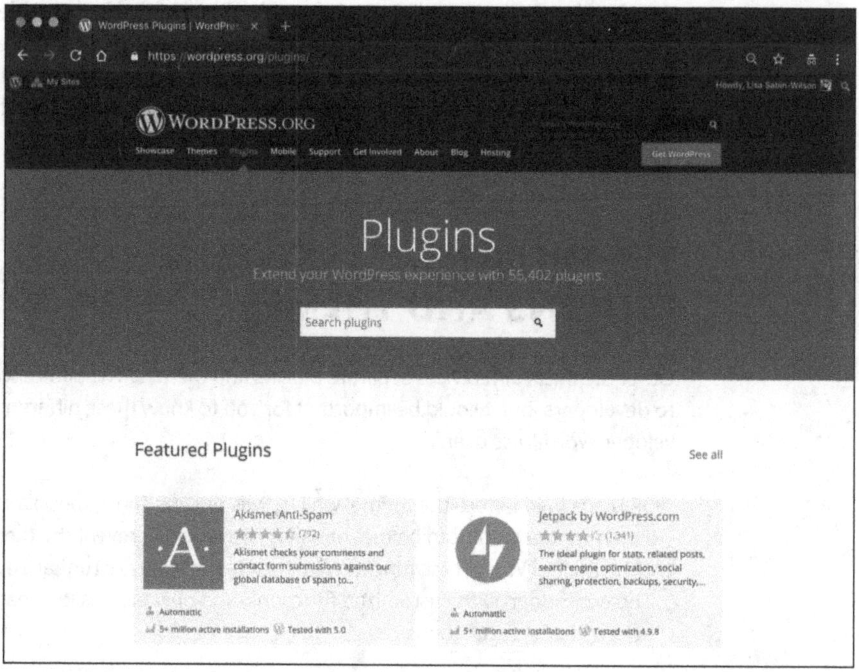

FIGURE 1-2: The Plugins page of the WordPress website.

Although you can search for plugins directly on the WordPress website, WordPress has a built-in feature for searching for plugins. This feature even allows you to easily install a plugin from WordPress without having to download it and upload it to your site.

The following sections show you how to find plugins.

Searching for plugins from the Dashboard

Before you start installing plugins on your site, it's important to explore the Plugins page of your WordPress Dashboard and understand how to manage the plugins after you install them. Click the Add New link on the Plugins menu of your WordPress Dashboard to view the Add Plugins screen, shown in Figure 1-3.

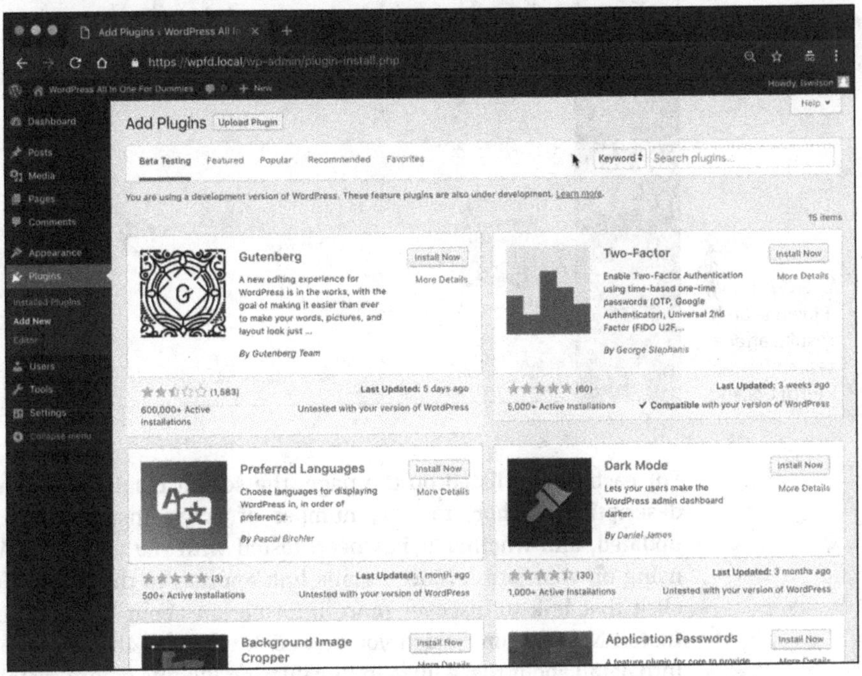

FIGURE 1-3: The Add Plugins screen.

At the top of the Add Plugins screen is a series of links and features that provide several ways to find plugins. (If you're looking to install a plugin, turn to Book 7, Chapter 2.)

Search

Figure 1-4 shows the search results screen. This screen enables you to search for WordPress plugins either by typing a search term in the Search box or by clicking one of the popular tag links to narrow the list of plugins.

After you use either search option, the screen changes to a Search Results page, which lists the plugins that match the search query. As shown in Figure 1-4, this page provides a wealth of information about each found plugin.

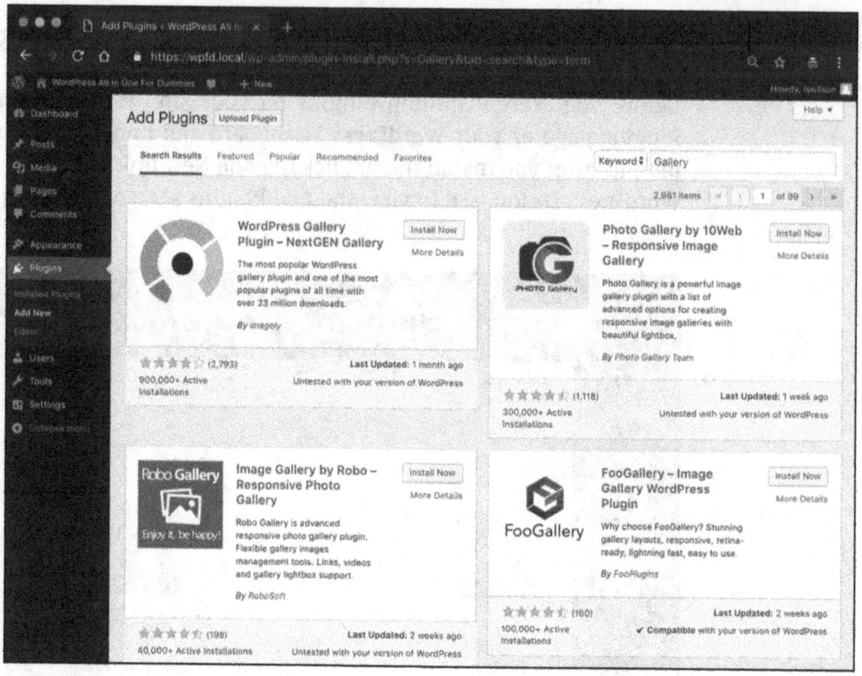

FIGURE 1-4: Plugin search results after a search for the term *Gallery*.

For each plugin listed on the page, the search results show the plugin's name, description, author, ratings, number of active installations, time it was last updated, and whether it has been tested with the version of WordPress you're using on your site A More Details link appears to the right of the plugin name; click that link to discover more information about the plugin. You also see an Install Now button, which you can click to install the plugin on your site. (I go into detail about these links in "Evaluating Plugins before Installing" later in this chapter.)

Upload Plugin

Click the Upload Plugin button on the Add Plugins screen to display the upload feature, as shown in Figure 1-5. The Upload section allows for easy installation of downloaded plugin Zip files without using SFTP or some other method to upload the files to the server. This feature makes it quick and easy to install downloaded plugin `.zip` files. Although this feature works with plugins you find on the Plugins page of the WordPress website, it's used mostly to install plugins that aren't available on the WordPress site because they can't be installed by searching for them on the Add Plugins screen.

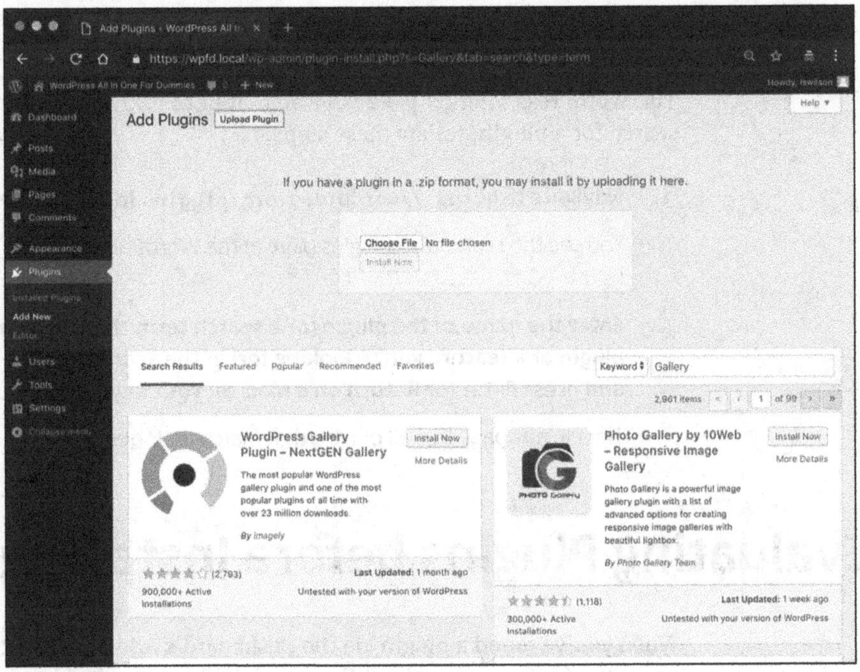

FIGURE 1-5: The upload feature in the Add Plugins screen.

After selecting the file to upload, click the Install Now button. Options to go back to the Add Plugins screen or to activate the newly installed plugin become available.

Featured, Popular, Recommended, and Favorites

The Featured, Popular, Recommended and Favorites screens are very similar. The Featured screen shows the plugins from the WordPress website that are listed as Featured. The Popular screen includes a listing of all the plugins sorted by their popularity. The Newest screen lists all the plugins, sorted with the newest plugins listed first and the oldest at the end. The Recommended screen lists plugins that WordPress recommends specifically for you, based on plugins you've already installed on your site. (If you already have a photo-gallery plugin installed, for example, the Recommended screen might recommend a plugin that helps you handle image and photo optimization.) The Favorites screen first asks you to log in to WordPress.org, if you have an account, and it lists any plugins that you've marked as favorites.

Beyond these differences, each page is identical to the Search Results page. Each listed plugin has options that let you view more details about the plugin and install it.

Finding plugins through WordPress.org

The WordPress Plugins page is located at `https://wordpress.org/plugins`. To search for a plugin, follow these steps:

1. **Navigate to `https://wordpress.org/plugins` in your browser.**

   You see the searchable Plugins page of the WordPress website. (Refer to Figure 1-2.)

2. **Enter the name of the plugin (or a search term that's relevant to the plugin or a feature you're looking for) in the Search Plugins text field, and press Enter (or Return on a Mac) on your keyboard.**

   The Plugins page lists all plugins that match your query.

Evaluating Plugins before Installing

When you've found a plugin via the Dashboard's Add Plugins screen, you can find a wealth of information about that plugin to help you decide whether to download it or go on to the next one.

The methods described here for evaluating plugins are no substitutes for testing plugins thoroughly. Testing a plugin is good practice unless you're familiar enough with the code and the developers to feel comfortable that bugs or security issues are unlikely. To test a plugin, set up a stand-alone site used just for testing, install the plugin, and check for any issues before trusting the plugin on your main site.

TIP

Look at the version number of the plugin. If the number includes the word *Alpha* or *Beta*, the plugin isn't fully ready; it's in the process of being tested and may have bugs that could affect your site. You may want to wait until the plugin has been thoroughly tested and released as a full version. Generally, the higher the version number, the more *mature* (that is, tested and stable) the plugin is.

Don't use just one of these methods of assessing trustworthiness; combine them all to get a sense of what other users think about the plugin. If the plugin has a 5-star rating given by 1,000 users but has dozens of negative comments and very little positive commentary, don't trust the plugin very much. If a plugin has a 3-star rating given by 10 users but has nothing but positive comments, the plugin may have some issues yet still works very well for some users.

REMEMBER

As with many things in life, you have no guarantees with plugins. The best you can do is find information about the plugin to determine whether it's trustworthy.

Details

Click the More Details link to the right of the plugin's name to find information taken from the plugin's page on the WordPress site. Figure 1-6 shows an example of what details are available. As on the Plugins page, Description, Installation, FAQ, Changelog, Screenshots, and Reviews tabs are available.

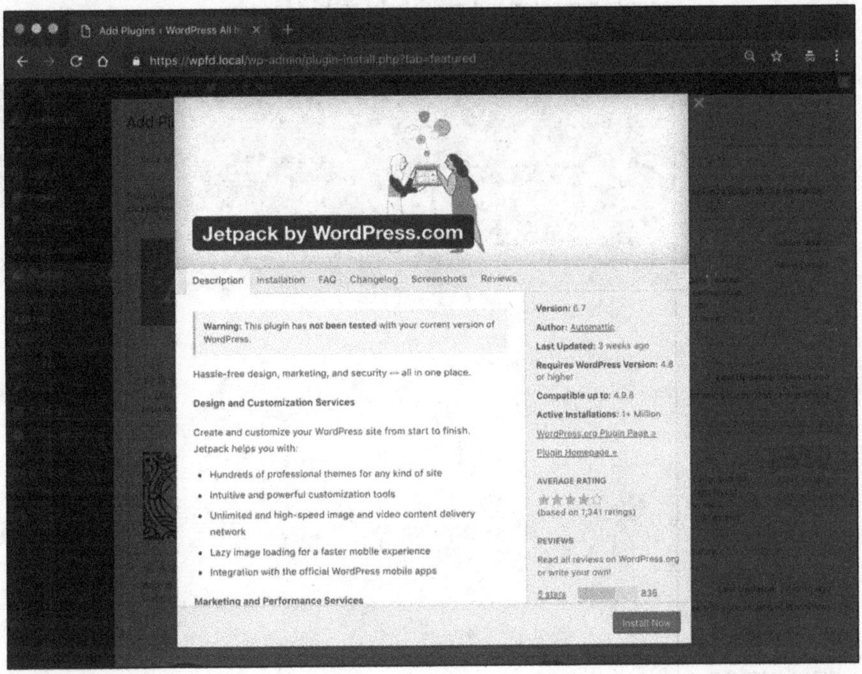

FIGURE 1-6: Details on the Jetpack plugin.

TIP Make sure to check out each plugin's Description page. You could find some very important information that aren't present on the Search Results page. When you're considering a plugin that you don't have experience with, this information can help you determine how reliable and trustworthy the plugin is.

Ratings

Consider the plugin's rating and the number of people who submitted a rating. The more people who rated the plugin, the more you can trust the rating; the fewer people who rated the plugin, the less you can trust the rating. A plugin that has fewer than 20 ratings probably isn't very trustworthy. A plugin that has more than 100 ratings is very trustworthy. Any plugin rated 20 to 100 times is acceptably trustworthy.

If a plugin has a large percentage of one- or two-star ratings, regard the plugin with suspicion. Take the extra step of visiting the plugin's page on the WordPress website to see what other people are saying about it. You can do this by clicking the WordPress.org Plugin Page link on the right side of the Description page, in the FYI box. On the plugin's page (see Figure 1-7), click the View Support Forum button or the Support link at the top of the page to see the information posted by users, both positive and negative. You can determine whether the issues that other people experienced are likely to hinder you.

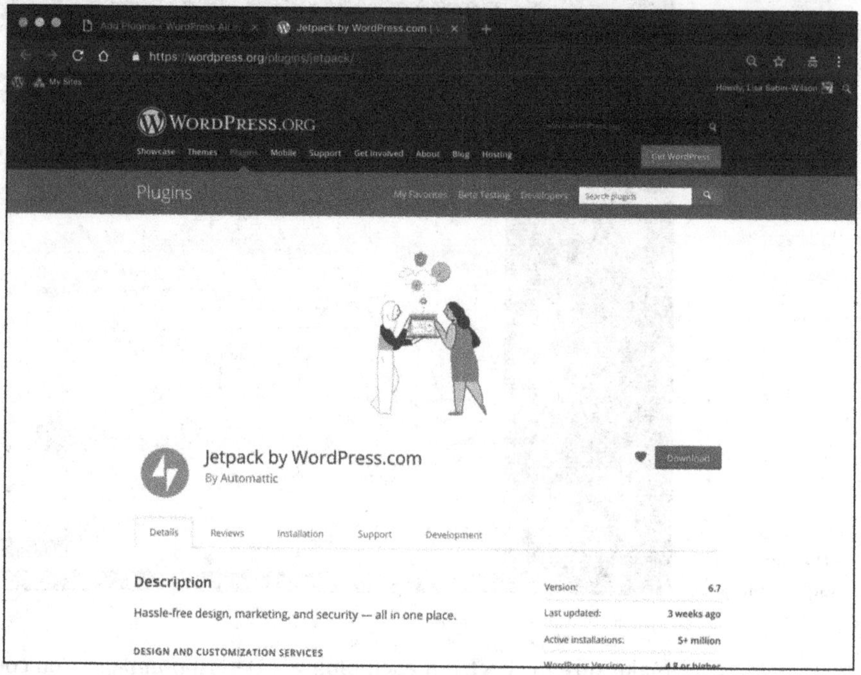

FIGURE 1-7: The Jetpack plugin's page on WordPress.org showing the Support tab.

Downloads

The next detail to consider is the number of downloads. The higher the number of downloads, the more likely the plugin is to work well; plugins that don't work very well typically don't pick up enough popularity to get many downloads. If a plugin has hundreds of thousands of downloads or more, it's extremely popular. Plugins with tens of thousands of downloads are popular and may grow even more popular.

REMEMBER

A low download count shouldn't necessarily count against a plugin. Some plugins simply provide a feature that has a limited audience. Thus, the download count is an indicator but not proof of quality or lack thereof.

The Tested Up To and the Last Updated information should be taken very lightly. If a plugin indicates that the tested-up-to version is for a very old WordPress version, it may have issues with the latest versions of WordPress. But plenty of plugins work just fine with current versions of WordPress even though they don't explicitly indicate support. Many people see an up-to-date plugin as being a sign of quality and upkeep. This reasoning is sometimes flawed, however, because some plugins are simple and don't require updating often. Plugins shouldn't be updated just to bump that number; thus, a plugin that hasn't been updated in a while may be functioning perfectly well without any updates. I check the support forum for that plugin to see whether there are any complaints that the plugin doesn't work with the latest versions of WordPress.

Advanced View

To see Advanced View information (see Figure 1-8), click the Advanced View link on the plugin's page. Active Versions and Downloads Per Day aren't fool-proof methods of getting a trusted plugin, but the Active Versions Downloads Per Day count on the graph may indicate that people are using the plugin with some success.

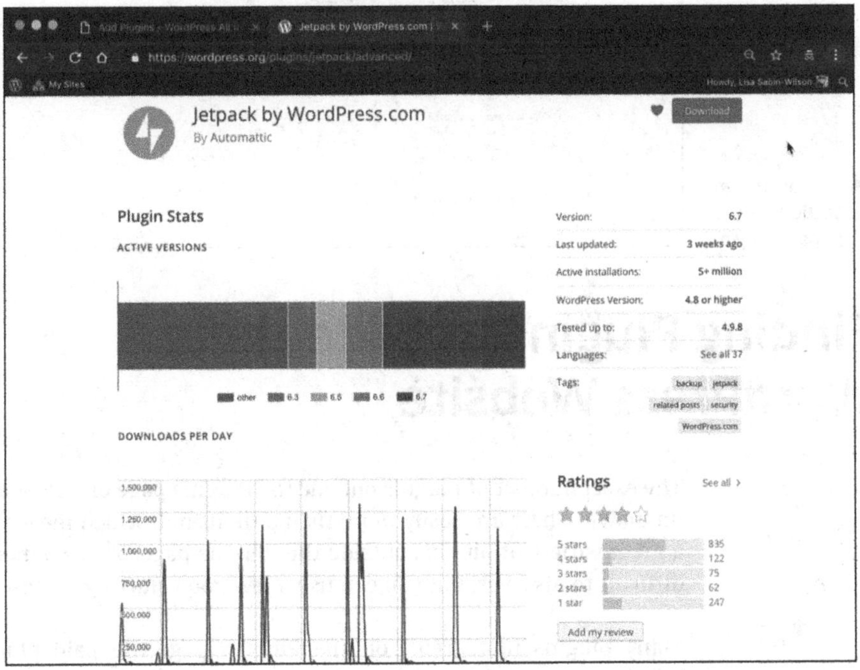

FIGURE 1-8: The download history for the Jetpack plugin on the WordPress website.

Support

Click the Support tab below the plugin's banner to view the support forum for that plugin, which is where users of the plugin request help and assistance (see Figure 1-9). By browsing the support forum for the plugin, you can get a good feel for how responsive the plugin's developer is to users, and you can see what types of problems other people are having with the plugin.

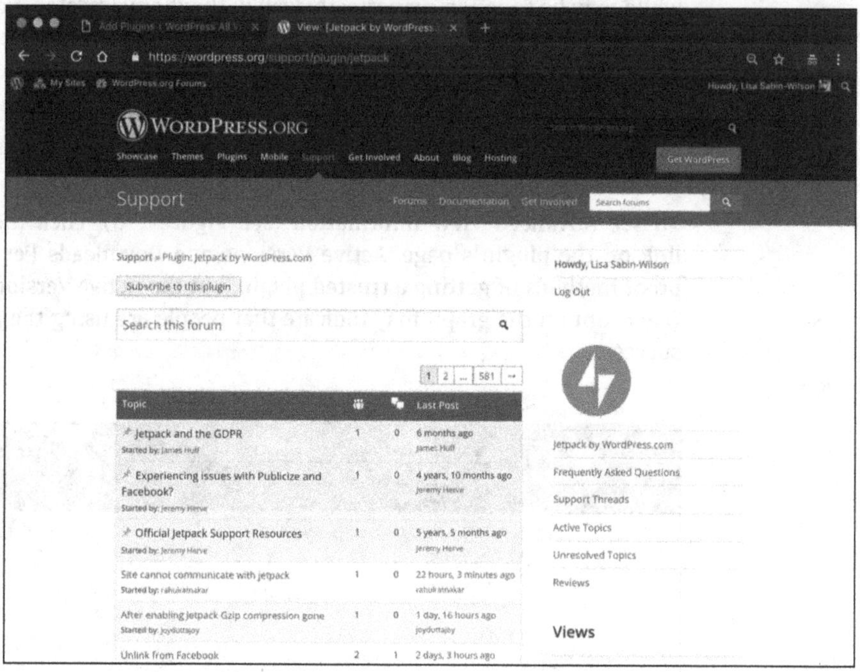

FIGURE 1-9: A support forum section for the Jetpack plugin.

Finding Plugins outside the WordPress Website

The exact number of plugins outside the Plugins page on the WordPress website is unknown. There are easily more than a thousand, which means that you can find a great variety of plugins outside the Plugins page. These outside plugins can be difficult to discover, but you can use a few good starting places.

Many plugins that aren't on the Plugins page are paid plugins. The official WordPress Plugins page lists only free plugins. If a plugin is for sale (costs more than a penny), it can't get listed in the Plugin Directory, so the author needs to find other methods of listing and promoting his or her products.

Over the past few years, the market for commercial plugins has grown tremendously. It isn't possible to list all the companies that currently offer WordPress plugins in this chapter, so the following listing is a sampling to introduce you to the world of plugins outside the Plugin Directory.

The following sites offer WordPress plugins:

- **CodeCanyon (`https://codecanyon.net`):** With thousands of plugins, this online marketplace is the paid-plugins version of the Plugin Directory. Just as the Plugin Directory contains plugins from a large number of developers, CodeCanyon is a collection of plugins from various developers rather than plugins from a single company.
- **Gravity Forms (`www.gravityforms.com`):** For many WordPress users, Gravity Forms is the plugin to pay for. Typically, it's the first and last recommendation people give someone who wants to create forms in WordPress.
- **iThemes (`https://ithemes.com`):** iThemes started with theme development but expanded to developing plugins as well. The most popular offering is BackupBuddy, a plugin for backing up and restoring your sites.
- **WooCommerce (`https://woocommerce.com`):** WooCommerce is a popular plugin with a full-featured e-commerce solution that you can integrate into your WordPress site. Essentially, this plugin turns your WordPress site into an online store.

Although these sites give you a taste of what commercial plugin sites have to offer, other sources of information about new, exciting plugins can be helpful. Many popular WordPress news sites talk about all things WordPress, including reviews and discussions of specific plugins. Check out the following sites if you want to know more about what plugins are being talked about:

- **WPBeginner (`https://www.wpbeginner.com`):** This site is dedicated to helping new WordPress users get up and running quickly. It features an active blog on a variety of topics. The site often features posts about how to use plugins to create specific types of solutions for your site.
- **WPTavern (`https://wptavern.com`):** This site is a standard WordPress news site and often publishes articles about what's being talked about in the WordPress community, including plugins.
- **Post Status (`https://poststatus.com`):** Post Status is an all-things-WordPress news site. If there's buzz on a topic in the WordPress world, you're likely to find discussions about it here.

TIP

One great thing about using a community or news site to discover new plugins is that you aren't alone in deciding whether to trust a plugin. You can get some other opinions before you take a chance on a plugin.

If you aren't finding what you want on the Plugins page of the WordPress website, don't know anyone who offers the solution you're looking for, and aren't seeing anything on community sites, it's time to go to a trusty search engine (such as Google) to see what you can find.

A good way to start is to search for the words *wordpress* and *plugin* along with one or a few words that describe the feature you want. If you want a plugin that provides advanced image-gallery features, for example, search for *wordpress plugin image gallery*. As long as your search isn't too specific, you're likely to get many results. The results often contain blog posts that review specific plugins or list recommended plugins.

WARNING

Some developers include malware, viruses, and other unwanted executables in their plugin code. Your best bet is to use plugins from the official WordPress Plugin Directory or to purchase plugins from a reputable seller. Do your research first, and read up on plugin security in Book 2, Chapter 5.

Comparing Free and Commercial Plugins

Thousands of plugins are available for free, and thousands of plugins have a price. What are the benefits of free plugins versus paid plugins? This question is a tough one to answer.

It's tempting to think that some plugins are better than others, which is why they cost money. Unfortunately, things aren't that simple. Some amazing plugins that I'd gladly pay for are free, and some terrible plugins that I wouldn't pay for have a cost.

Often, a paid plugin includes support, which means that the company or person selling the plugin is offering assurance that if you have problems, you'll receive support and updates to address bugs and other issues.

Free plugins typically list places to make support requests or to ask questions, but nothing ensures that the developer will respond to your requests within a certain period — or at all. Even though developers have no obligation to help with support requests from users, many developers work hard to help users with reported issues and other problems. Fortunately, because many free plugins are on the WordPress website, and because the Plugins page there includes a built-in support forum and rating score, you can easily see how responsive a plugin author is to support issues.

I believe that the commercial plugin model works in an environment of tens of thousands of free plugins because many WordPress users want the assurance that when they have problems, they have a place to ask questions and get help.

So if people can get paid to produce plugins, why are so many plugins free? This question is another great one.

One reason why so many plugins are available for free is that many WordPress developers are generous people who believe in sharing their plugins with the community. Other developers feel that having their plugins available to the millions of WordPress users via the Plugin Directory is a great way to market their talents, which can lead to contract work and employment. Buzzwords on a résumé are far less valuable than a plugin you wrote that was downloaded thousands or millions of times.

Another reason to release a free plugin is to entice people to pay for upgrades — a model often referred to as *freemium*. Freemium plugins often have paid plugins that add features to the free plugin. Thus, the freemium model is a mix of the free and paid plugin models — the best of both worlds. The free plugin can be listed in the Plugin Directory, giving the plugin a large amount of exposure. You can get a feel for how the plugin functions, and if you want the additional features, you can purchase the paid plugin.

An example of the freemium model is the WooCommerce plugin (`https://woocommerce.com`). The main plugin is available on the WordPress website (`https://wordpress.org/plugins/woocommerce`), yet it supports a large number of paid plugins to add more features. By itself, the WooCommerce plugin turns a site into a shopping cart. To extend this functionality, paid plugins are available to add payment processing for specific credit-card processors, shipping, download managers, and many other features.

The biggest difference between free and paid plugins is that sometimes, you won't find what you need in a free plugin and have to go with a paid plugin. In the end, what you download is up to you. Many great free plugins are available, and so are many great paid plugins. If you want the features offered by a paid plugin and are willing to pay the price, paid plugins can be very good investments for your site.

TIP

Many free plugins have links to donation pages. If you find a free plugin to be valuable, please send a donation to the developer. Most developers of free plugins say that they rarely, if ever, receive donations. Even a few dollars can really encourage the developer to keep updating old plugins and releasing new free plugins. (See the nearby sidebar "Developing plugins: A community activity.")

DEVELOPING PLUGINS: A COMMUNITY ACTIVITY

Although plugins are written and developed by people who have the skills required to do so, the WordPress user community is also largely responsible for the ongoing development of plugins. Ultimately, end users are the ones who put those plugins to the true test on their own sites. Those same users are also the first to speak up and let developers know when something isn't working right, helping the developers troubleshoot and fine-tune their plugins.

The most popular plugins are created by developers who encourage open communication with the user base. Overall, WordPress is one of those great open-source projects in which the relationship between developers and users fosters a creative environment that keeps the project fresh and exciting every step of the way.

IN THIS CHAPTER

» Installing WordPress plugins via the Dashboard

» Manually installing WordPress plugins

» Updating plugins

» Activating and deactivating plugins

» Deleting plugins

Chapter 2 Installing and Managing Plugins

With more than 55,000 plugins available, you have a huge number of options for customizing your site. Book 7, Chapter 1 details what types of plugins are available and where to find them. In this chapter, you start putting these plugins to use. This chapter is dedicated to helping you install, activate, deactivate, update, and delete plugins.

Installing Plugins within the WordPress Dashboard

When you've found a plugin in the Plugins page(see Book 7, Chapter 1) that you want to install, you can install it directly from the Dashboard. (If you've found a plugin that isn't in the Directory, you have to install it manually. See the later section "Manually Installing Plugins.")

WordPress makes it super-easy to find, install, and then activate plugins for use on your blog. Just follow these simple steps:

1. **Click the Add New link on the Plugins menu.**

   The Add Plugins screen opens, allowing you to browse official WordPress plugins from your WordPress Dashboard.

2. **Search for a plugin to install on your site.**

   Enter a keyword for a plugin you'd like to search for. For this example, you want to install a plugin that integrates your site with Twitter. To find it, select Author in the drop down to the left of the search box, then enter **Twitter** in the Search text box on the Add Plugins screen; then click the Search button.

   Figure 2-1 shows the results page for the Twitter search phrase. The first plugin listed, called simply Twitter, is a plugin developed by the developers at Twitter. This plugin is the one you want to install.

   TIP

   You can also discover new plugins by clicking any of the categories at the top of the Add Plugins screen, such as Featured, Popular, and Recommended.

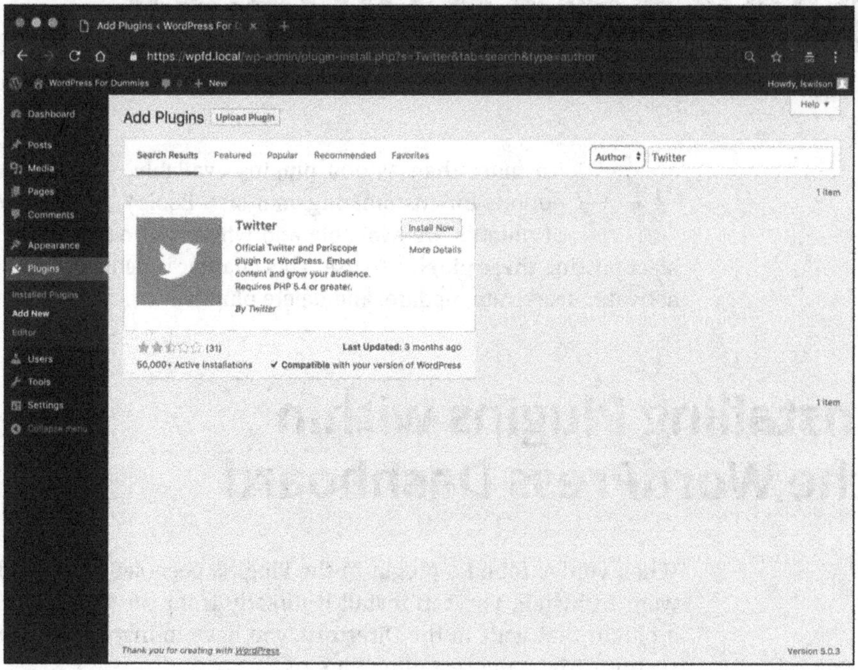

FIGURE 2-1: The Add Plugins screen's search results for the Twitter plugin.

3. **Click the More Details link.**

   A Description window opens, displaying information about the Twitter plugin (including a description, version number, and author name) and an Install Now button.

4. **Click the Install Now button.**

   The Install Now button changes to an Installing button with a spinner icon that spins until it's done installing; then the button text changes to Activate.

5. **Decide whether to activate the plugin now or later.**

   You have two methods of installing the plugin:

   - *Click the Activate button:* Click this button to immediately activate the plugin you just installed on your site.
   - *Return to the Plugins screen:* Click the Plugins link on the Plugins menu to load the Plugins screen in your Dashboard. You see the plugin listed there, but it isn't activated. When you're ready, click the Activate link below the plugin's name.

WARNING

Installation of plugins from your WordPress Dashboard works in most web-hosting configurations. Some web-hosting services, however, don't allow the kind of access that WordPress needs to complete installation. If you get any errors or find that you're unable to use the plugin installation feature, get in touch with your web-hosting provider to find out whether it can assist you.

TIP

If the Dashboard displays any kind of error message after you install the plugin, copy the message and paste it into a support ticket in the WordPress.org support forum (`https://wordpress.org/support`) to elicit help from other WordPress users about the source of the problem and the possible solution. When you post about the issue, provide as much information about the issue as possible, including a screen shot or pasted details.

Manually Installing Plugins

Installing plugins from the Dashboard is so easy that you'll probably never need to know how to install a plugin manually via SFTP. (Book 2, Chapter 2 explains how to use SFTP.) But the technique is still helpful to know in case the WordPress Plugins page is down or unavailable, or if you are installing a plugin that is not available on the WordPress website.

REMEMBER

Installing the Twitter plugin takes you through the process, but keep in mind that every plugin is different. Reading the description and installation instructions for each plugin you want to install is very important.

Finding and downloading the files

The first step in using plugins is locating the one you want to install. The absolutely best place to find WordPress plugins is the WordPress.org website at `https://wordpress.org/plugins`, where, at this writing, more than 55,000 plugins are available for download.

To find the Twitter plugin, follow these steps:

1. **Go to the official WordPress Plugins page at** `https://wordpress.org/plugins`.
2. **In the search box at the top of the page, enter the keyword** Twitter; **then click the Search Plugins button.**
3. **Locate the Twitter plugin on the search results page (see Figure 2-2), and click the plugin's name.**

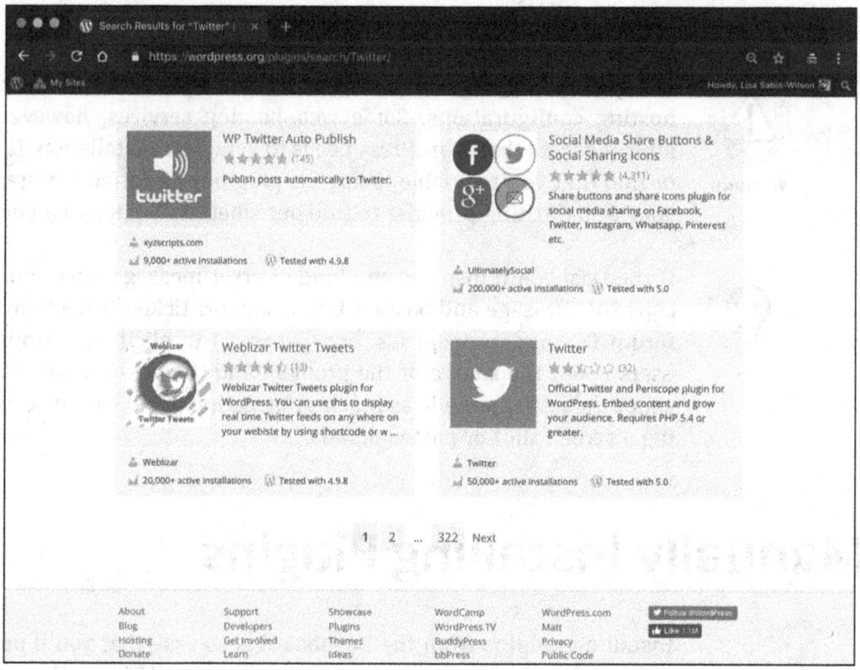

FIGURE 2-2: Use the search feature on the Plugins page to find the plugin you need.

The Twitter plugin page of the WordPress website opens, displaying a description of the plugin as well as other information about the plugin. In Figure 2-3, take note of the important information on the right side of the page:

- *Version:* The number shown in this area is the most recent version of the plugin.
- *Last Updated:* This date is when the author last updated the plugin.

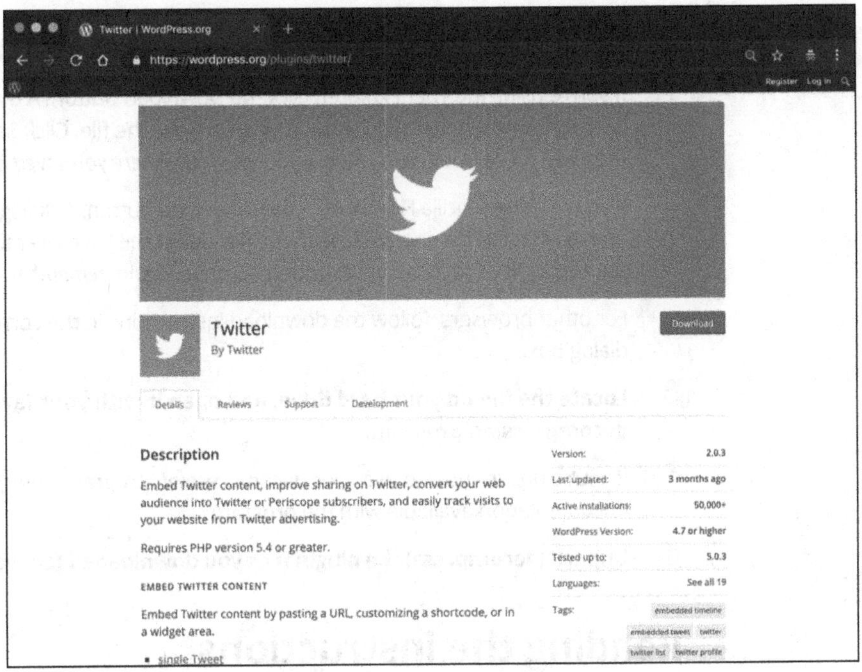

FIGURE 2-3: The download page for the Twitter plugin.

- *Active Installations:* This number tells you how many times this plugin has been downloaded and installed by other WordPress users.
- *WordPress Version:* Figure 2-3 shows that the Twitter plugin is compatible up to WordPress version 4.7 or higher.
- *Tested Up To:* This section tells you what version of WordPress this plugin is compatible up to. If it tells you that the plugin is compatible up to version 5.0, for example, you usually can't use the plugin with versions later than 5.0. I say *usually* because the plugin developer may not update the information in this section — especially if the plugin files themselves haven't changed. The best way to check is to download the plugin, install it, and see whether it works! As shown in Figure 2-3, the Twitter plugin has been tested up to WordPress version 5.0.3.
- *Languages:* A link is provided that displays the number of languages the plugin offers translations for. When you click the link, a window opens that displays the list of specific languages. The Twitter plugin provides 19 translations, as shown in Figure 2-3.
- *Tags:* This is a list of keywords that describe the plugin type. Clicking any of these words will take you to a page on the WordPress website that displays plugins that are associated with, or related to, the keyword you clicked on.
- *Ratings:* With a rating system of 1 to 5 stars (1 being the lowest and 5 being the highest), you can see how other WordPress users rated this plugin.

4. **Click the Download button for the plugin version you want to download.**

   If you're using Internet Explorer, click the Download button. A dialog box opens, asking whether you want to open or save the file. Click Save to save the `.zip` file to your hard drive, and *remember where you saved it.*

   If you're using Mozilla Firefox, click the Download button. A dialog box opens, asking what Firefox should do with the file. Select the Save File radio button and then click OK to save the file to your hard drive. Again, *remember where you saved it.*

   For other browsers, follow the download instructions in the corresponding dialog box.

5. **Locate the file on your hard drive, and open it with your favorite decompression program.**

   If you're unsure how to use your decompression program, refer to the documentation available with the program.

6. **Unpack (decompress) the plugin files you downloaded for the Twitter plugin.**

Reading the instructions

Frequently, the plugin developer includes a `readme` file inside the `.zip` file. Do what the title of the file says: Read it. Often, it contains the same documentation and instructions that are on the plugin developer's website.

Make sure that you read the instructions carefully and follow them correctly. Ninety-nine percent of WordPress plugins have great documentation and instructions from the developer. If you don't follow the instructions correctly, the best scenario is that the plugin just won't work on your site. At worst, the plugin will create all sorts of ugly errors, requiring you to start the plugin installation over.

TIP

You can open `readme.txt` files in any text-editor program, such as Notepad or WordPad on a PC or TextEdit on a Mac.

In the case of the Twitter plugin, the `readme.txt` file contains information about the requirements of the plugin and how to use it on your site.

REMEMBER

Every plugin is different in terms of where the plugin files are uploaded and what configurations are necessary to make the plugin work on your site. Read the installation instructions carefully, and follow those instructions to the letter to install the plugin correctly on your site.

Upgrading Plugins

Plugins receive updates that fix bugs, add new features, and update existing features. Some plugins are updated multiple times a week. Other plugins may never be updated. Fortunately, WordPress makes it easy to know when a new plugin version is available and also makes it very easy to update your local Plugins page from the Dashboard.

One of the easiest ways to know that plugin updates are available is to check the version number displayed on the Plugins screen on your Dashboard, directly below the plugin's description. Figure 2-4 shows that the Akismet plugin has an available update, as evidenced by the phrase below the Akismet description `There is a new version of Akismet Anti-Spam available`. Figure 2-4 also shows that the Dashboard page provides alerts about upgrades (the small circle shown next to the word *Plugins* on the left navigation menu).

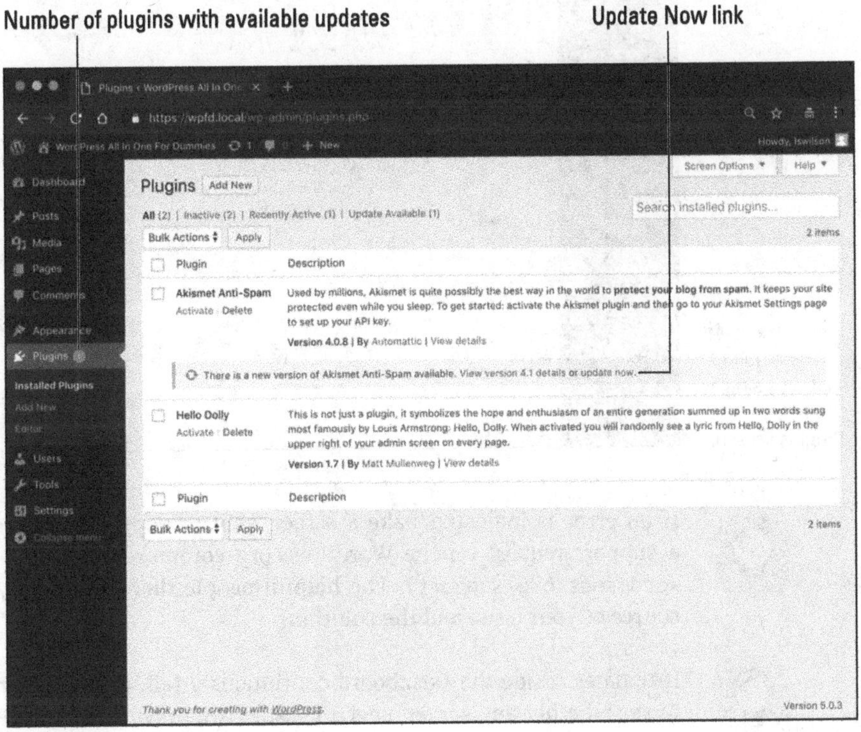

FIGURE 2-4: A WordPress plugin with an available update.

You have three ways to update a plugin: from the Plugins page, from the Updates submenu accessible on the Dashboard menu, and a manual update via SFTP.

Updating on the Plugins screen

Updating a plugin on the Plugins screen is easy. You can update plugins one at a time or update all the plugins that need updating in one fell swoop.

To update an individual plugin, click the Update Now link at the bottom of the plugin's row (refer to Figure 2-4). WordPress automatically updates the plugin with the files from the new release, displays the message `Updated`, and removes the small icon next to the Plugins-menu link (see Figure 2-5).

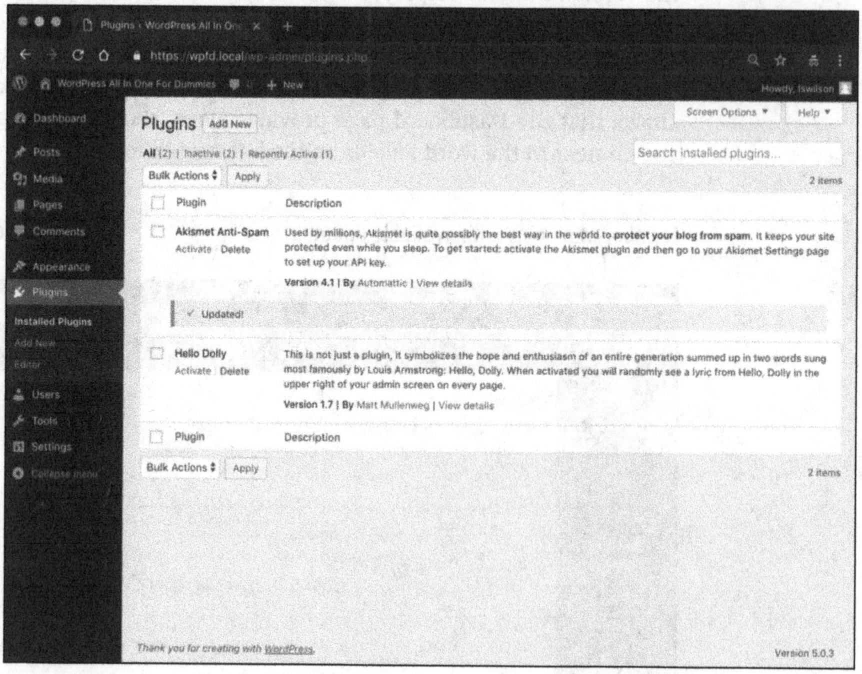

FIGURE 2-5: The result of updating a single plugin from the Plugins screen.

TIP

If an error is indicated, take a screen shot or copy the error details and create a support request on the WordPress.org community support forum (`https://wordpress.org/support`). The helpful people there can help you figure out the source of your issue and the solution.

TIP

If updates inside the Dashboard continuously fail, contact your hosting provider to see whether any server-specific issues are preventing WordPress from updating its plugins.

Although clicking the Update Now link is simple and quick, this process can get tedious if you have a large number of plugins.

To update all your plugins at the same time, click the check mark to the left of each plugin, choose Update from the Bulk Actions drop-down menu, and click the Apply button. All your plugins are updated. Figure 2-6 shows a message at the top of the screen stating that two plugins have been updated.

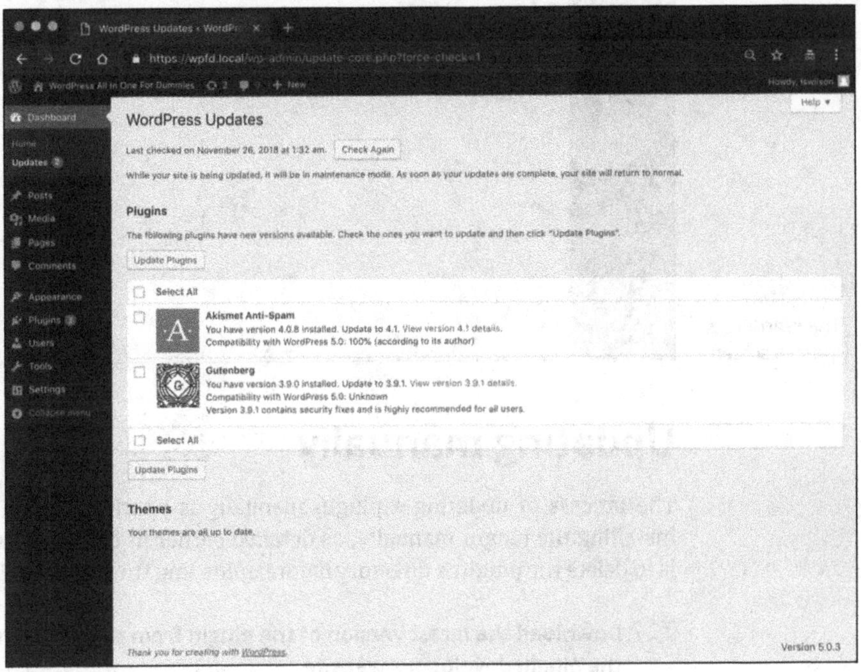

FIGURE 2-6: The results of updating multiple plugins from the Plugins screen.

Updating on the Updates screen

The WordPress Updates screen (see Figure 2-7), accessible from a submenu of the Dashboard menu, provides a quick way to update WordPress, plugins, and themes in one place. This screen is a one-stop shop for all the updates across your site.

To update all the plugins, click the check box next to the Select All header (refer to Figure 2-7) and then click the Update Plugins button. All your selected plugins are updated.

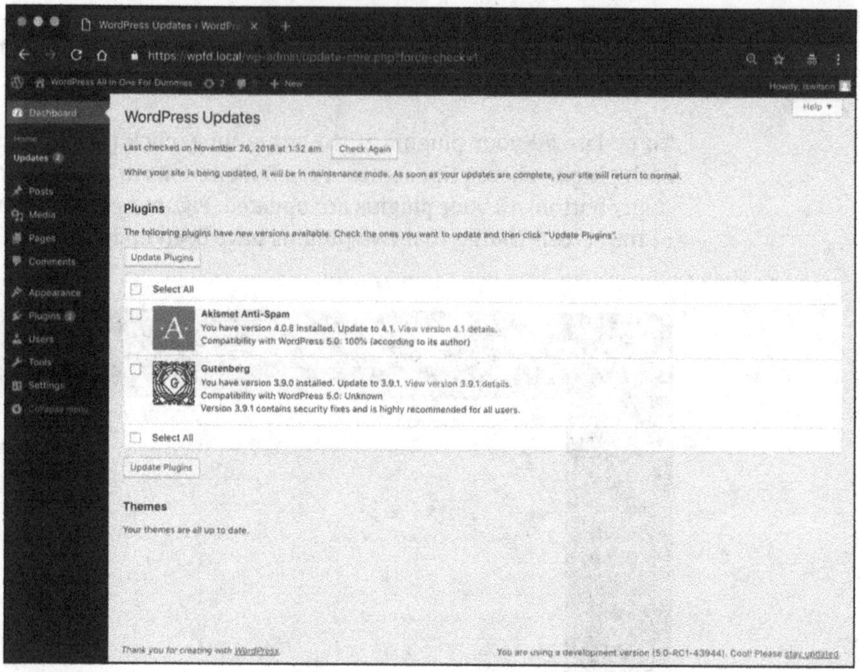

FIGURE 2-7: The WordPress Updates screen.

Updating manually

The process of updating a plugin manually is nearly identical to the process of installing the plugin manually, as detailed earlier in this chapter. The only change is to delete the plugin's directory before uploading the new files. Follow these steps:

1. **Download the latest version of the plugin from the WordPress website or the plugin developer's website.**
2. **Connect to your server via an SFTP application, and go to the `plugins` directory in the `wp-content` directory.**

   You should see a folder with the same name as the plugin you want to upgrade.
3. **Rename this folder so that you have a backup if you need it.**

   Any memorable name, such as *`plugin`*`-old`, should suffice.
4. **Upload the new version of your plugin via SFTP to your server so that it's in the `wp-content/plugins` folder.**
5. **Log in to the WordPress Dashboard, and activate the upgraded plugin.**

REMEMBER

If you made any changes in the plugin's configuration files before your upgrade, make those changes again after the upgrade. If you need to back out of the upgrade, you can delete the new Plugins page and rename the folder (*`plugin`*`-old` to *`plugin`*, for example).

Activating and Deactivating Plugins

After a plugin is on your site, activating it is extremely simple. To activate a plugin, do the following:

1. **Log in to the WordPress Dashboard.**
2. **Navigate to the Plugins screen by clicking the Plugins menu link.**
3. **Find the plugin you want to activate on the Plugins screen.**
4. **Click the Activate link just below the plugin's name in the listing.**

If everything goes well, you see `Plugin activated` at the top of the screen, which means that the plugin has been activated successfully. (See Figure 2-8.) If a long error message appears in the activation notice, the plugin has an issue that's preventing it from activating. Copy the message that appears in the notice and send the details to the plugin author for help fixing the issue.

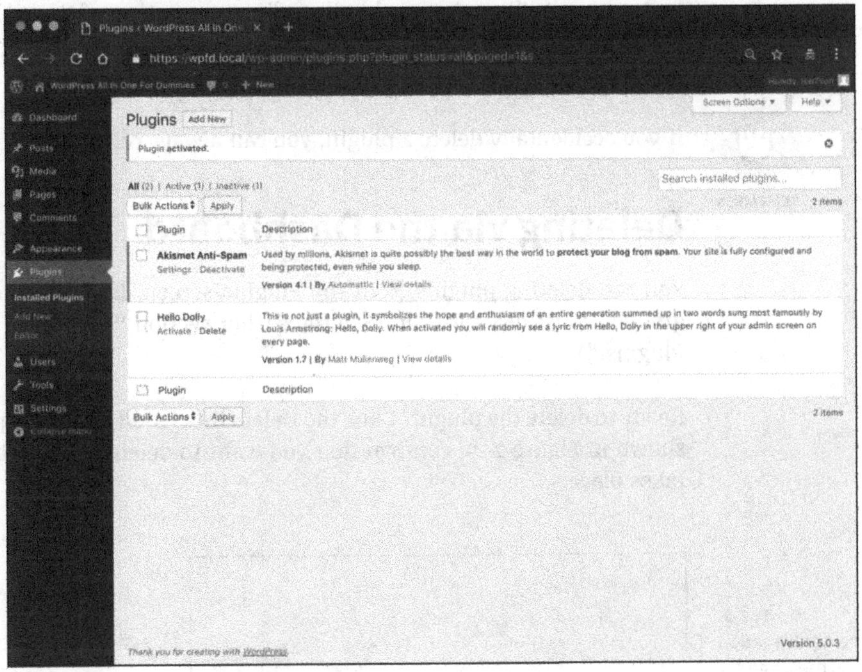

FIGURE 2-8: The Plugins screen when a plugin is activated.

The process of deactivating a plugin is nearly the same as the process of activating a plugin. Follow the same steps, but click the Deactivate link for the plugin that should be deactivated. A message at the top of your Dashboard tells you the plugin has been successfully deactivated.

Deleting Plugins

Sometimes, it's simply time to let go of a plugin and remove it from the site. You could have many reasons for deleting a plugin:

- You no longer need the feature offered by the plugin.
- You want to replace the plugin with a different one.
- You're retiring the plugin because its functionality has been replaced with features built into a new version of WordPress.
- You're removing it due to performance issues (such as the plugin required too many resources to run).

It may be tempting to deactivate undesired plugins and leave them sitting in your `plugins` directory, but take the extra step of deleting plugins that you no longer need. The PHP files of the plugin can still be run manually if someone (or some automated computer program) directly requests that PHP file. If the plugin had a security flaw that could allow direct execution of the code to compromise the security of the server, having old code lying around is a problem waiting to happen.

REMEMBER

If you accidentally delete a plugin, you can always reinstall it.

Deleting via the Dashboard

You can deleting plugins from the Plugins screen. Before you can delete a plugin, you must deactivate it. (See the earlier section "Activating and Deactivating Plugins.")

Ready to delete the plugin? Click the Delete link listed below the plugin's name. As shown in Figure 2-9, confirm that you want to delete a plugin before that action takes place.

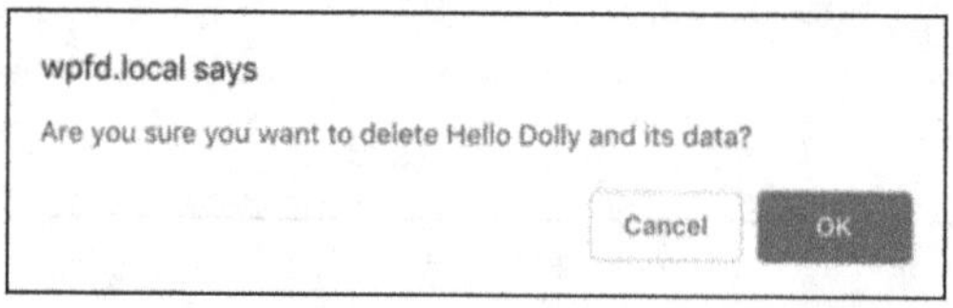
wpfd.local says
Are you sure you want to delete Hello Dolly and its data?
Cancel
OK

FIGURE 2-9: The confirmation message for deleting a plugin.

After confirming the deletion of a plugin, you return to the Plugins screen, which confirms that the plugin was deleted, as shown in Figure 2-10.

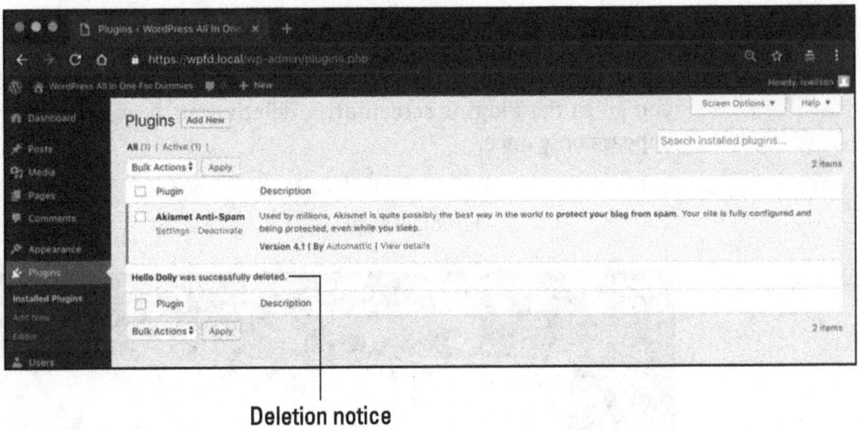

FIGURE 2-10: A notice confirming the deletion of a plugin.

Deleting manually

You can delete a plugin manually by removing its directory from the `wp-content/plugins` directory. Because the files no longer exist, the plugin simply stops running. It may be helpful to deactivate the plugin first, but doing so isn't required.

Manually deleting a plugin can be very helpful when a plugin has a fatal error that causes the site to crash. If you can't gain control of the site again, manually deleting the plugin's directory could help you regain control of your site quickly.

Because this process involves using SFTP, this process is similar to installing a plugin manually. The main difference is that rather than uploading the plugin's directory, you're deleting it.

TIP

Before deleting a plugin, download the directory to a local system so that you don't lose any data that would be difficult to get back later. If your goal is to force the plugin to deactivate, you can rename the plugin's directory rather than delete it. Renaming prevents WordPress from being able to locate the plugin, thus disabling it.

The process works as follows:

1. **Connect to your site's server, using SFTP.**
2. **Navigate to the site's directory.**
3. **Navigate to the `wp-content/plugins` directory.**
4. **Delete the plugin's directory.**

The Plugins screen shows a message confirming that the plugin is deactivated due to the missing files. (See Figure 2-11.) Note that this message appears only when you go to the Plugins screen after deleting an activated plugin manually, and it appears only once.

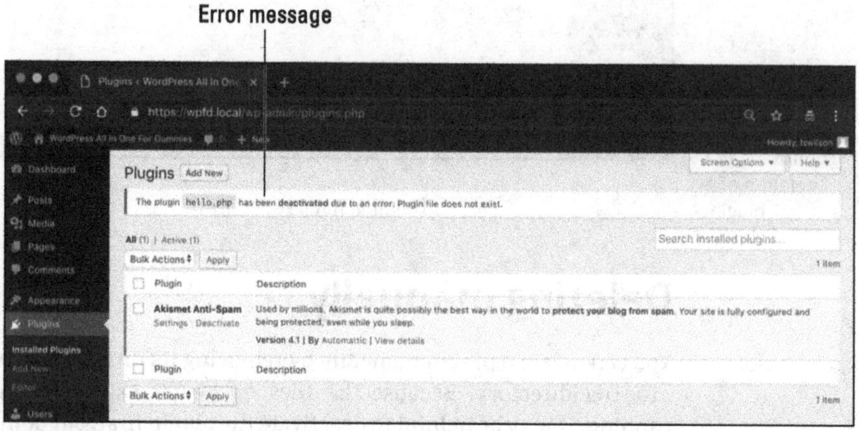

FIGURE 2-11: The error message shown after an active plugin is deleted manually.

IN THIS CHAPTER

» Exploring activate-and-go plugins

» Discovering settings screens

» Using widgets and shortcodes

Chapter 3 Configuring and Using Plugins

The types of features offered by WordPress plugins are diverse. Similarly, the ways of interacting with plugins are also diverse. Some plugins don't have an interface and can be activated or deactivated only; some provide one or more settings screens to control how the plugins behaves. Other plugins offer widgets and *shortcodes* (short, easy-to-remember codes used to execute PHP functions) used to add new features to sidebars and content.

This chapter digs into the topic of how to interact with plugins. Although this topic is a big one, the examples in this chapter prepare you for different ways of interacting with plugins.

Exploring Activate-and-Go Plugins

Certain plugins are easy to use because they don't have any settings or features to interact with. I call them *activate-and-go* plugins. You simply activate them, and they do what they're intended to do.

Like WordPress plugins as a whole, activate-and-go plugins offer a wide variety of features. The following list offers a sampling of activate-and-go plugins that you'll find useful on your website:

- **Login Logo** (`https://wordpress.org/plugins/login-logo`)**:** This plugin makes it easy to add your logo to the WordPress login page. No configuration is required; just install and activate this plugin, and then upload your logo to the `/wp-content/` directory on your web server. Make sure that your logo file is named (such as `login-logo.png`).
- **BBQ: Block Bad Queries** (`https://wordpress.org/plugins/block-bad-queries`)**:** The BBQ plugin helps protect your site against attackers who are trying to exploit specific security vulnerabilities. This plugin doesn't require any configuration; it automatically scans all requests coming to the site and protects against bad ones.
- **Disable All WordPress Updates** (`https://wordpress.org/plugins/disable-wordpress-updates`): WordPress's capability to update itself automatically has been a tremendous help to WordPress users. Keeping WordPress updated not only offers new features and enhancements, but also helps keep your site safe from attackers. For some users, the notification to update WordPress can become a distraction, especially if the site is run by many people but a single person is responsible for handling site updates. The Disable All WordPress Updates plugin disables automatic checks for new WordPress versions and also disables any notifications that a new version is available. You still can update WordPress from the Dashboard (as described in Book 2, Chapter 6), but the notifications no longer appear.

To use any of these plugins, simply install and activate them as discussed in Book 7, Chapter 2. When the plugin is activated, it starts doing its job.

REMEMBER

For some plugins, such as BBQ or Disable All WordPress Updates, the results of activating the plugin may be underwhelming. The plugins do their work behind the scenes and don't change anything that's visible to you. Just because you don't see any immediate change, however, doesn't mean that the plugins aren't doing their jobs.

Discovering Settings Screens

Many popular plugins have settings screens that allow you to tweak the functionality of the plugin and tailor it to the specific needs of your site. Often, these settings need to be configured once and updated only when the plugin changes.

The following sections explore a selection of the most popular WordPress plugins, show you how to access settings screens, and describe what you can expect from them.

Typically, you access settings screens from submenus of the Dashboard's Settings page. Another common place to access plugin settings screens (especially for plugins that provide advanced features such as site caching) is the Dashboard's Tools menu.

TIP

If you have a hard time finding the settings screen for a plugin, check the Plugins page for details on how to access the settings screen. For plugins listed on the WordPress website's Plugins page, check the Installation and FAQ tabs. If the Plugins page has a Screenshots tab, one of the screenshots usually shows the settings page.

Activating Akismet

Akismet is bundled in with WordPress and likely is already installed on your WordPress site. (See Book 7, Chapter 2 if you still need to know how to install plugins.) Akismet is the answer to comment and trackback spam.

After you activate Akismet, a notice appears saying that the plugin requires additional configuration before it will function.

TIP

Check for an activation notice after you install any plugin. Although most plugins don't offer such a notice, if one is available, it lets you know how to get started with the plugin. The Akismet plugin always has an activation notice after installation.

Follow these steps to activate and begin using Akismet:

1. **Click the Plugins link on the left navigation menu of the Dashboard to load the Plugins screen.**
2. **Click the Activate link below the Akismet plugin name and description.**

   A green box appears at the top of the page, saying `Almost done- configure Akismet and say goodbye to spam` (see Figure 3-1).

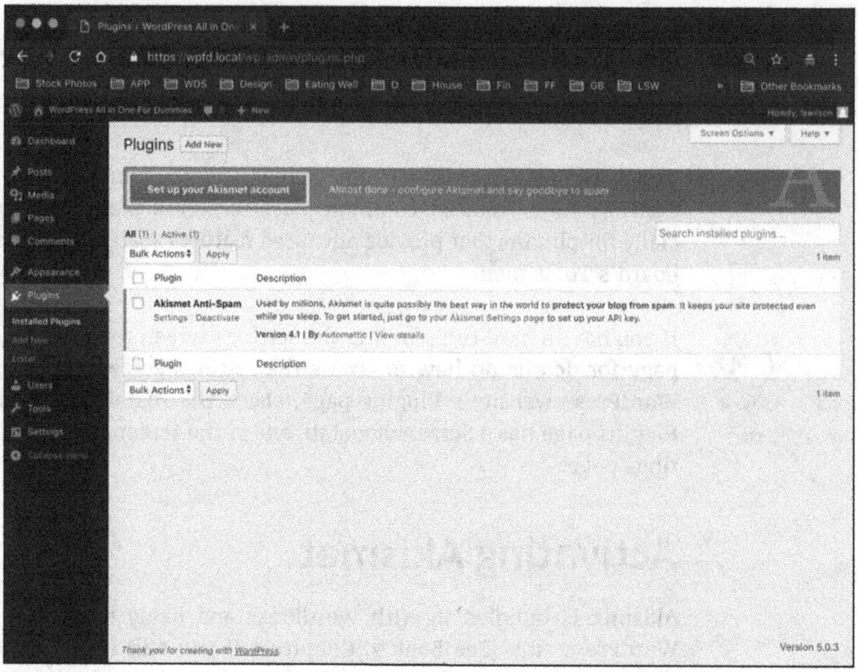

FIGURE 3-1: After you activate Akismet, WordPress tells you that the plugin isn't quite ready to use.

3. **Click the Set Up Your Akismet Account button in the green box to navigate to the Akismet configuration screen.**
4. **If you already have an API key, enter it in the Manually Enter an API Key text field; then click the Use This Key button to save your changes.**

   You can stop here if you already have a key, but if you don't have an Akismet key, keep following the steps in this section.

   An *API key* is a string of numbers and letters that functions like a unique password given to you by Akismet. This key allows your WordPress.org application to communicate with your Akismet account.
5. **Click the Get Your API key button on the Akismet configuration screen.**

   The WordPress page of the Akismet website opens.
6. **Click the Get an Akismet API Key button.**

   The sign-up page of the Akismet website opens.
7. **Enter your email address, desired username, and password in the provided text fields; then click the Sign Up button.**

   The Pick Your Plan page opens.

8. **Choose among these options for obtaining an Akismet key:**
   - *Enterprise:* $50 per month for people who own commercial or professional sites or blogs and want additional security screening and malware protection.
   - *Plus:* $5 per month for people who own a small commercial or professional site or blog.
   - *Personal:* Name your price. Type the amount you're willing to pay for the Basic plan. This option is for people who own one small, personal WordPress-powered blog. You can choose to pay nothing ($0), but if you'd like to contribute a little cash to the cause of combating spam, you can opt to spend up to $120 per year for your Akismet key subscription.
9. **Select and pay for (if necessary) your Akismet key.**

   After you've gone through the sign-up process, Akismet provides an API key. Copy that key by selecting it with your mouse pointer, right-clicking, and choosing Copy from the shortcut menu.
10. **Go to the Akismet configuration screen by clicking the Akismet link on the Settings menu of your WordPress Dashboard.**
11. **Enter the API key in the API Key text box (see Figure 3-2), and click the Save Changes button to fully activate the Akismet plugin.**

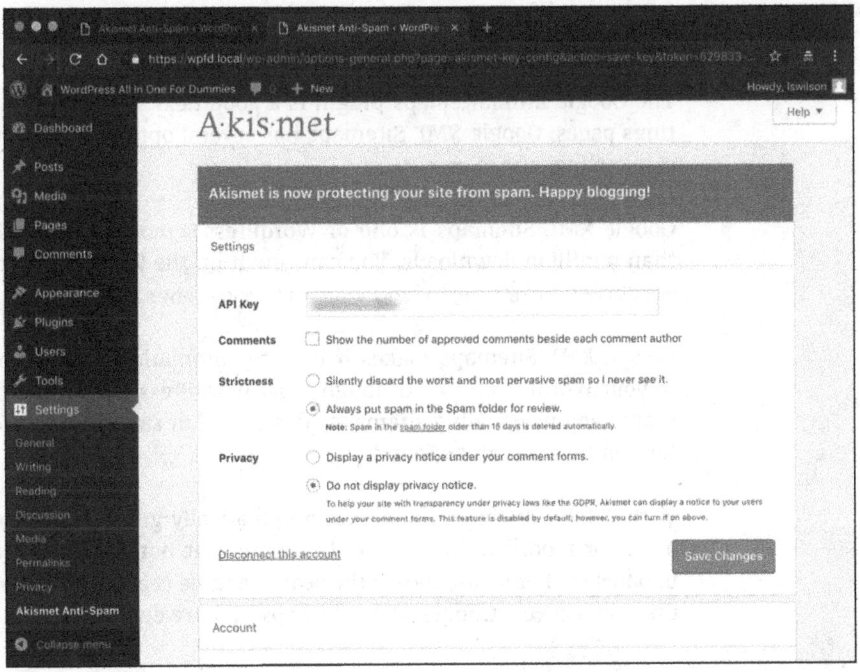

FIGURE 3-2: Akismet verification confirmation message on the Akismet configuration screen.

On the Akismet configuration screen, after you've entered and saved your key, you can select two options to further configure your spam protection:

- **Comments:** Select this option to display the number of approved comments beside each comment author.
- **Strictness:** By default, Akismet puts spam in the Spam comment folder for you to review at your leisure. If you feel that this setting isn't strict enough, you can have Akismet silently delete the worst and most pervasive spam so that you never have to see it.

Akismet catches spam and throws it into a queue, holding the spam for 15 days and then deleting it from your database. It's probably worth your while to check the Akismet spam page once a week to make sure that the plugin hasn't captured any legitimate comments or trackbacks.

REMEMBER

Check your spam filter often. I just found four legitimate comments caught in my spam filter and was able to de-spam them, releasing them from the binds of Akismet and unleashing them upon the world.

The folks at Automattic did a fine thing with Akismet. Since the emergence of Akismet, I've barely had to think about comment or trackback spam except for the few times a month I check my Akismet spam queue.

Google XML Sitemaps

The Google XML Sitemaps plugin is a good next step for diving into plugin settings pages. Google XML Sitemaps has several options and shows just how intricate settings pages can get.

Google XML Sitemaps is one of WordPress's most popular plugins, with more than 9 million downloads. You can find it on the WordPress website at `https://wordpress.org/plugins/google-sitemap-generator`.

Google XML Sitemaps makes it easy to automatically add support for sitemaps to your WordPress site. Although most WordPress sites can be scanned easily by search engines, adding sitemaps adds a level of safety to ensure that all the content on the site can be found.

With default settings, the plugin automatically generates sitemaps as content is added or modified on the site. In addition, it notifies Google and Bing of these updates so that it can update the search engine cache with this new data. (Book 5, Chapter 5 covers Google XML Sitemaps in more depth.)

The Google XML Sitemaps plugin settings screen is available from the XML-Sitemap submenu of the Dashboard's Settings menu. Notice that the menu name is different from the plugin name.

REMEMBER

Submenu names are limited in length, which means that longer plugin names are shortened to fit properly.

A portion of the Google XML Sitemaps plugin's settings screen is shown in Figure 3-3.

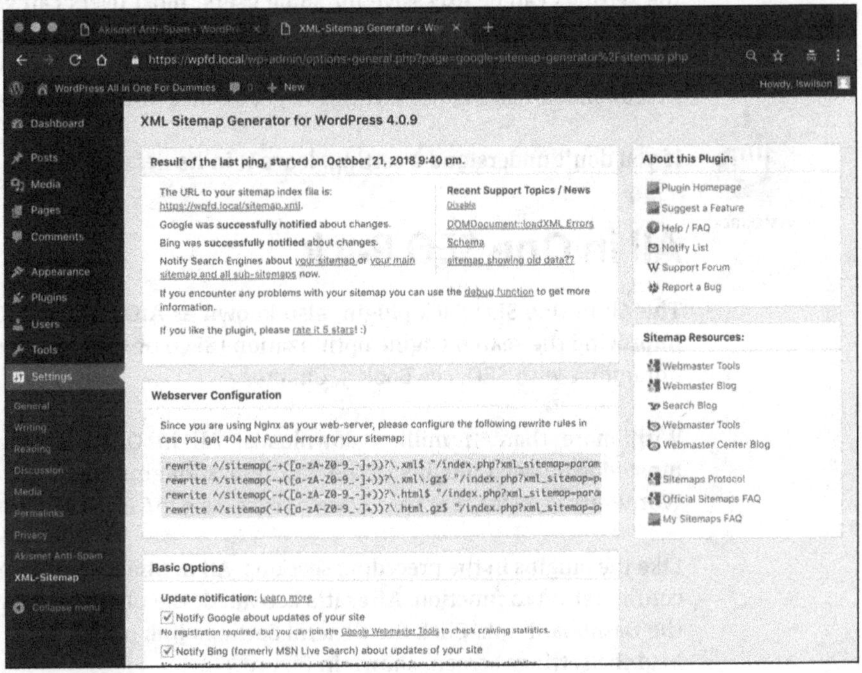

FIGURE 3-3: The settings screen for Google XML Sitemaps.

Like the Akismet plugin, Google XML Sitemaps requires an additional step to be fully functional. Unlike Akismet, Google XML Sitemaps is very quiet about how to get set up; it doesn't provide that Dashboardwide notification message. For this reason, it's important to read settings pages and plugin documentation carefully. It can be easy to miss something that's extremely important.

Below the information box used to generate and regenerate sitemaps are the settings for the plugin. Along the right side are links to information about the plugin and sitemaps. This format is common on plugin settings screens.

Scrolling through the Google XML Sitemaps screen reveals just how exhaustive the available settings are. The settings range from basic options (such as enabling or disabling automatic sitemap generation when the site's content changes) to options that control the information in the generated sitemap to advanced options that control how many server resources the plugin can consume when generating the sitemap. Nearly every aspect of the plugin's functionality is represented as an option on the settings screen, offering a large amount of flexibility in the way that the plugin functions on the site.

This type of plugin settings setup is present in many popular plugins. Although the settings can be excessive for some users, most users can get good results by using the default settings. In plugins such as Google XML Sitemaps, the settings are available for people who desire extra control of the plugin's functionality. I recommend reading the settings to get an idea of what options are available.

REMEMBER

If you don't understand a setting, leave it in its default state.

All in One SEO Pack

The All in One SEO Pack plugin, also known as AIOSEOP or AIO SEO, focuses on improving the search engine optimization (SEO) of your WordPress site. If you're unfamiliar with SEO, see Book 5, Chapter 4.

With more than 51 million downloads, All in One SEO Pack is one of the most-downloaded plugins in the WordPress Plugins page. You can find it on the WordPress website at `https://wordpress.org/plugins/all-in-one-seo-pack`.

Like the plugins in the preceding sections, All in One SEO requires some additional configuration to function. After it's activated, the plugin has its own menu below the Dashboard link. Click the General Settings link on the All In One SEO menu to load the settings screen, shown in Figure 3-4.

This screen has a variety of settings that control many features of the plugin. The portion of the screen shown in Figure 3-4 includes a large number of settings that control titles and URLs on the site. Typically, titles are controlled by the theme and are modifiable only through code changes. The ability to control titles without making code modifications is one of the primary reasons why SEO plugins such as All in One SEO are so popular.

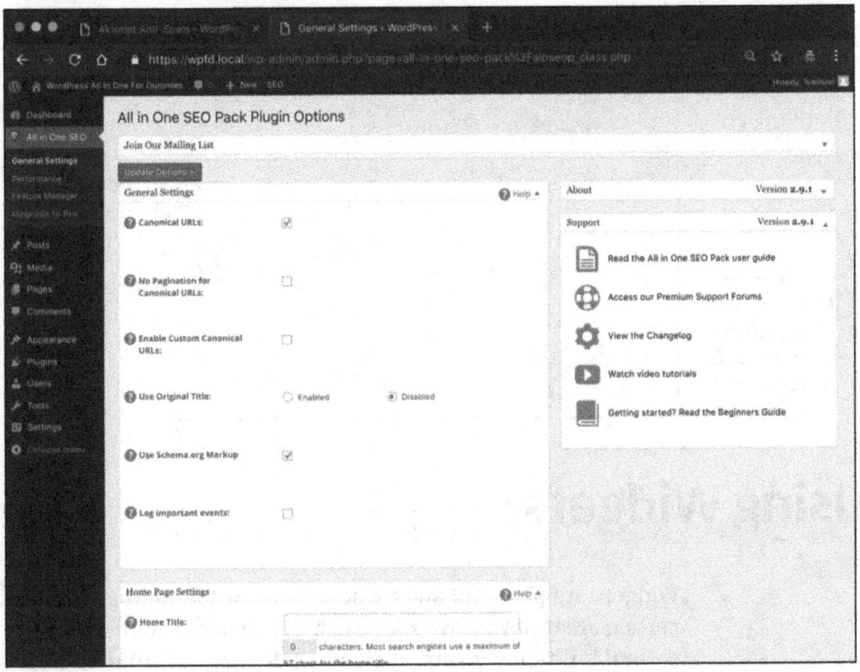

FIGURE 3-4 The settings screen for All in One SEO.

Many other settings go beyond control of titles. Some of the most commonly used settings on this screen control automatic generation of keywords and description metadata, integrate the site with Google+ and Google Analytics, and determine what content is marked as `noindex`.

TECHNICAL STUFF

When you mark a specific page with `noindex`, search engines ignore the content of the page and won't return search results that link to it.

Like the settings for Akismet and Google XML Sitemaps, the settings for the All in One SEO Pack plugin affect the site as a whole. Although some of the settings apply only to specific parts of the site, the settings screen as a whole focuses on the entire site, which is true of most plugin settings screens. If the plugin creates a stand-alone settings screen, the settings on that screen typically apply to the whole site unless the setting specifies otherwise.

Being able to customize the title, description, and keywords on each page or post is very helpful. Because customizations for the site's content would be difficult to manage in one settings screen, All in One SEO Pack provides additional settings in the editors for posts and pages. Figure 3-5 shows the settings box added to the editor by All in One SEO Pack.

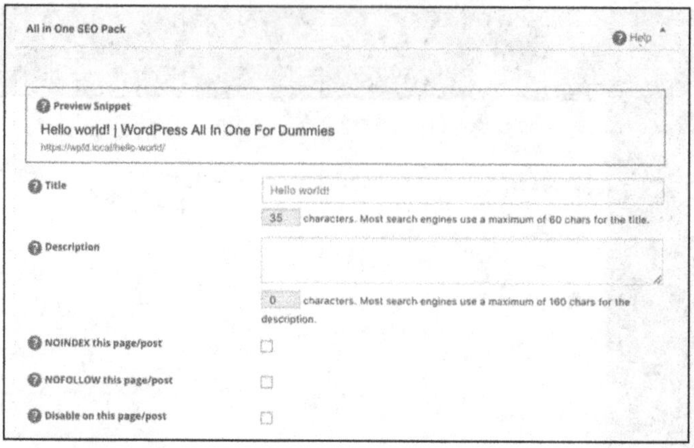

FIGURE 3-5: All in One SEO Pack settings to control SEO features for a specific post.

Using Widgets

Widgets are powerful and flexible features for adding specific kinds of content to certain areas of your website, such as sidebars and footers. WordPress comes with several built-in widgets, such as a calendar, a listing of pages on the site, a listing of recent comments, and a search tool. Plugins can expand this set of default widgets. The following sections visit plugins that add their own widgets to show you how plugin-provided widgets offer options that enhance your site.

TIP

You manage your widget management on the Widgets screen of the Dashboard. After logging in to your site's Dashboard, hover your mouse over the Appearance menu, and click the Widgets link to access the Widgets screen. You also can access widgets in the Customizer by clicking the Customize link on the Appearance menu.

Akismet

After activating and setting up a valid API key for the Akismet widget (you can find more about the API key earlier in this chapter in the Activating Akismet section), a new widget named Akismet Widget appears on your Widgets screen, as shown in Figure 3-6.

To use the Akismet widget, drag it from the Available Widgets section into one of the sidebars on the right side of the Widgets screen. As shown in Figure 3-6, after you drop the widget into the Blog Sidebar, the settings for the widget become available.

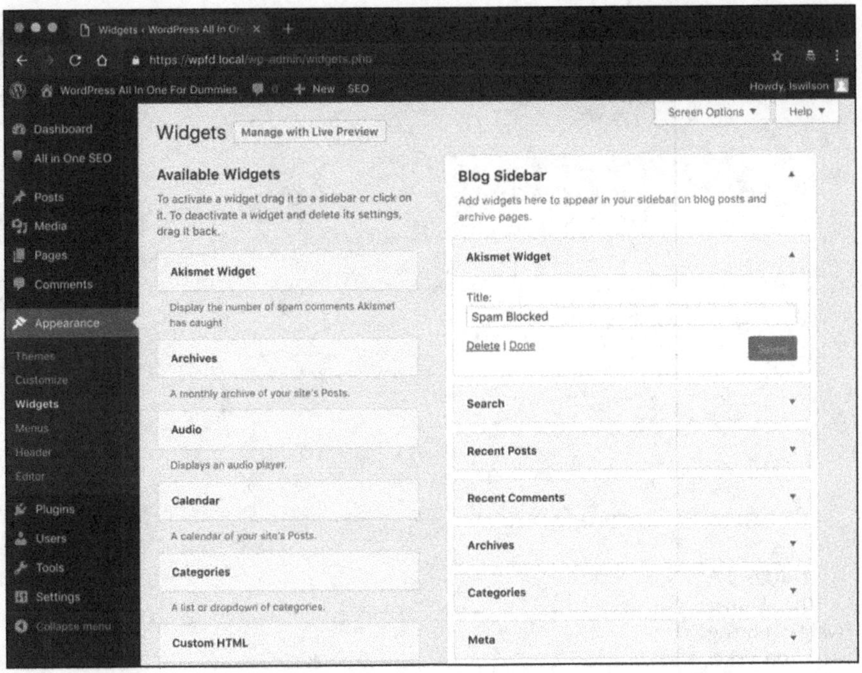

FIGURE 3-6: The Widgets screen showing the addition of the Akismet widget.

The settings are simple because you can modify only the title of the widget. At minimum, most widgets offer a title setting. Although there are exceptions, most widgets treat the title as optional and don't show a title if the setting is empty.

Now the Akismet widget appears on your site, displaying a counter that shows how many spam comments the Akismet plugin has blocked on the site. Figure 3-7 shows that the widget has blocked 300 spam comments.

Easy Twitter Feed Widget

The Easy Twitter Feed Widget serves a single purpose: making it easy to add a Twitter stream to your site. This feature takes the form of a widget, meaning that you can add the Twitter feed to any widget area on your site. The Easy Twitter Feed Widget is available on the WordPress website at `https://wordpress.org/plugins/easy-twitter-feed-widget`.

As shown in Figure 3-8, the Easy Twitter Feed Widget provides a number of settings to control the widget's output.

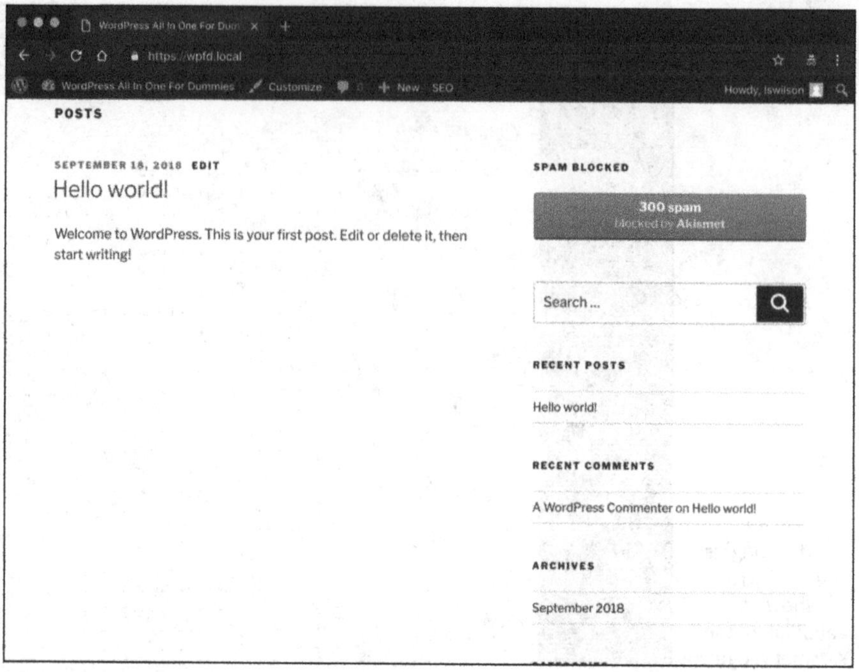

FIGURE 3-7: The Akismet widget running on a site.

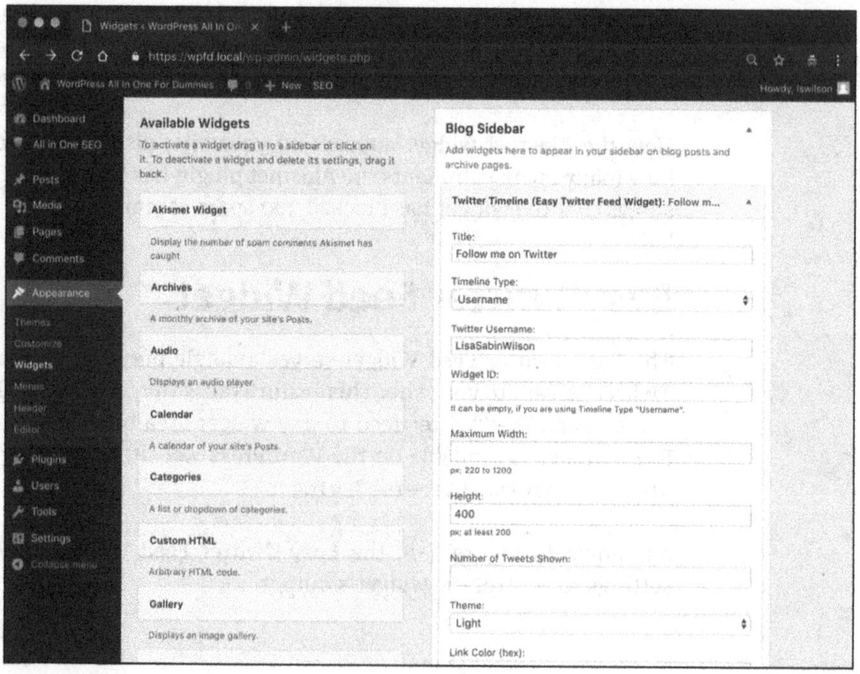

FIGURE 3-8: The settings for Easy Twitter Feed Widget.

The most important setting is Twitter Username. Without a valid Twitter username, the widget won't produce any output. If the widget fails to render anything on your site, double-check the username to ensure that the Twitter username is valid.

Figure 3-9 shows what the widget looks like in the sidebar of a website.

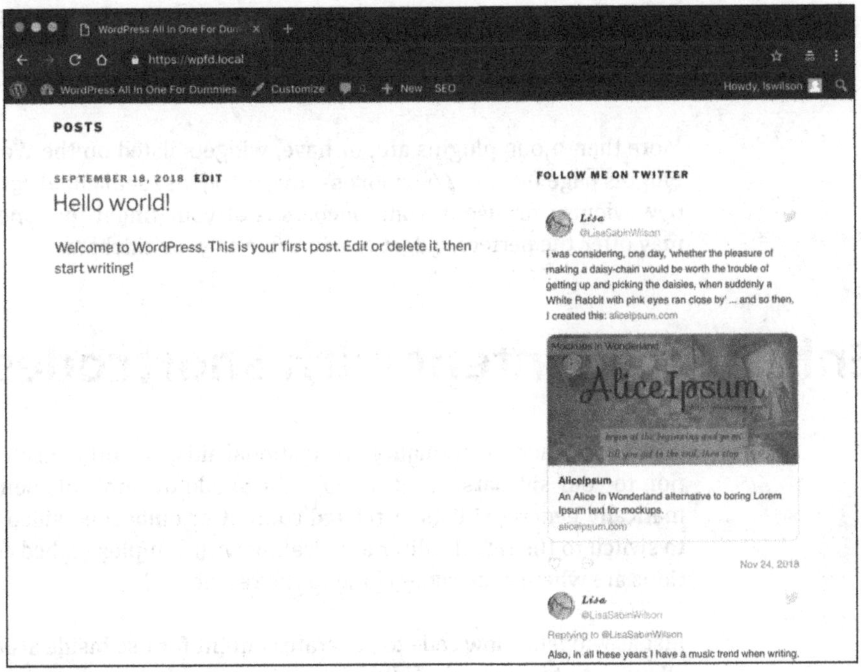

FIGURE 3-9: The Easy Twitter Feed Widget showing the latest from my Twitter feed in the right sidebar.

REMEMBER

If you're active on Twitter, using the Easy Twitter Feed Widget is an easy way to inform or remind your visitors that you can be found on Twitter.

Additional widgets to try

Akismet and Twitter Widget Pro just scratch the surface of what's possible with widgets offered by plugins. The following list shows additional plugin examples that help fill in your sidebars:

- **Facebook Widget** (`https://wordpress.org/plugins/facebook-pagelike-widget`): The Facebook Widget plugin provides a simple way to display your Facebook page likes in the sidebar of your website.

» **Image Widget:** Sometimes, you just want to add an image to a sidebar. Although the built-in Text widget and some HTML can provide this functionality, as well as the Custom HTML widget, some users don't know how to create the HTML for the image or want a simpler solution for adding images. WordPress ships with an Image Widget that allows you to upload an image to the site without writing, copying, or pasting HTML markup.

» **WP Instagram Widget:** This plugin is available on the WordPress website at `https://wordpress.org/plugins/wp-instagram-widget`. It provides an easy way to display your latest photo posts from your Instagram account on your website.

More than 9,000 plugins are, or have, widgets listed on the WordPress website's Plugins page (`https://wordpress.org/plugins/search/widget`), so a wealth of new widgets for use in your sidebars is at your fingertips. One of those plugins may offer the perfect widget to add value to your sidebars.

Enhancing Content with Shortcodes

Widgets can add functionality, navigational aids, and other useful bits of information to your sidebars. What if you want to add dynamic elements (such as automatically generated lists of related content or embedded videos) without having to switch to the HTML editor and dealing with complex embed codes? Such situations are where shortcodes come to the rescue.

Just as widgets allow code to generate content for use inside a sidebar, shortcodes allow code to generate additional content inside a post, page, or other content type. In the following sections, you find out about a few useful shortcodes.

Gallery shortcode

One of the shortcodes built into WordPress is `gallery`. (See Book 4, Chapter 3 for more about the `gallery` shortcode.)

The most basic gallery shortcode is `[gallery]`. In this format, all the default arguments are used. (Shortcodes can also support optional arguments that allow for customization.) By default, a gallery is arranged in three columns and uses thumbnail-size images. The following shortcode displays the gallery in two columns and use medium-size images:

```
[gallery columns="2" size="medium"]
```

In many ways, shortcodes are similar to HTML tags. The `gallery` shortcode looks like an opening HTML tag that swapped the ‹ and › characters for [and].

Embed shortcode

Shortcodes give you the capability to surround simple WordPress functions in an opening and closing bracket in order to execute features on your site. The `embed` shortcode, another shortcode provided by WordPress, is one such shortcode.

WordPress can automatically embed a video player on your site by using the embed shortcode with a link to a supported video, like one from YouTube. (See Book 4, Chapter 4 for details on which sites are supported.) Although this happens when supported video links are left on a line on their own, supported video links can be surrounded by the `embed` shortcode to explicitly indicate that the link is to be changed to an embedded video, as follows:

```
[embed]https://videopress.com/v/DK5mLrbr[/embed]
```

By adding the embed shortcode to a post or page using a Custom HTML block, I've embedded a video player that displays Matt Mullenweg's 2017 State of the Word video displays in place of the shortcode, as shown in Figure 3-10.

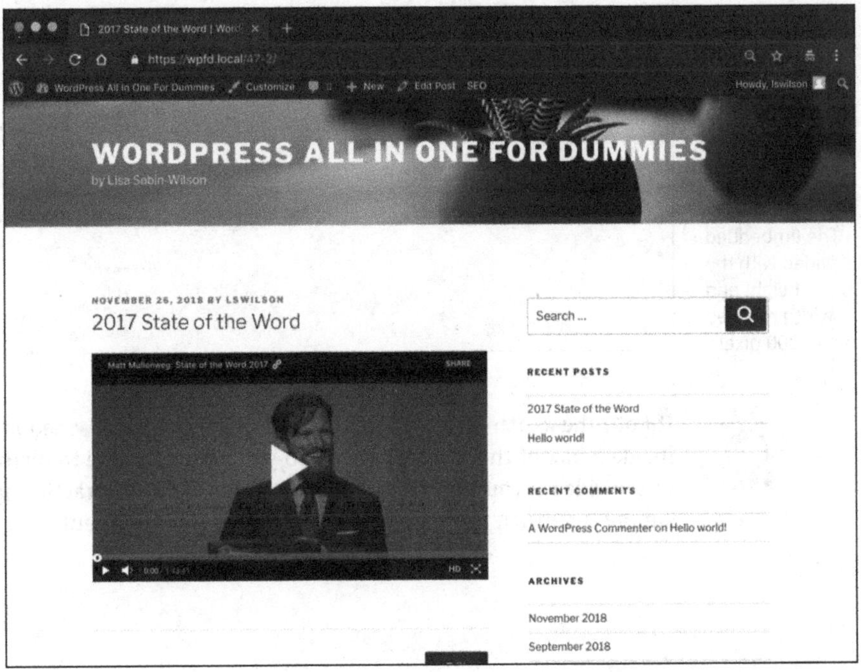

FIGURE 3-10: The embedded video replacing the embed shortcode.

You may wonder why you'd want to use the embed shortcode instead of putting the link on its own line. The reason is that like the gallery shortcode, the embed shortcode supports arguments that allow you to customize the display of the video. The supported arguments are width and height. The following shortcode modifies the embedded video to have a width of 200 pixels:

```
[embed width="200" height="200"]https://videopress.com/v/
  DK5mLrbr[/embed]
```

(I don't think you'd want a video at a width of 200 pixels; I'm doing this to show how the arguments work.) Figure 3-11 shows the result of this change. Notice that the entire video is smaller.

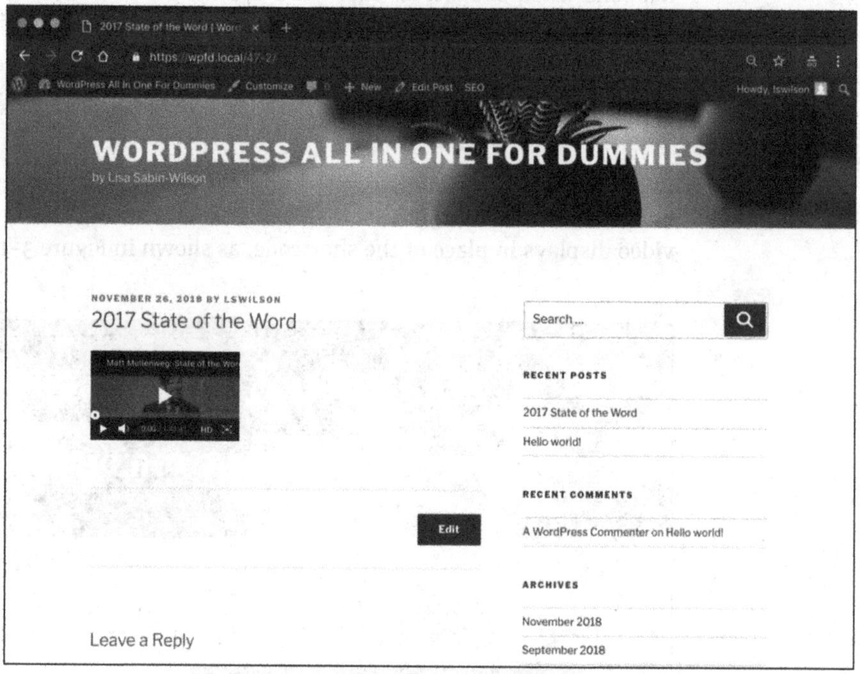

FIGURE 3-11: The embedded video with the height and width reduced to 200 pixels.

TIP If both the width and height arguments are used, the video is scaled down to fit inside a box of those dimensions, so you won't be able to distort the aspect ratio of the video if you don't get the dimensions right. In practice, it's often easiest to supply the width argument and not the height argument.

Embed Twitter Links

By default, WordPress has a feature called *oEmbed*, in which a link from a particular service or social media site automatically gets embedded in your post or page and adopts the formatting and style of the site of origin. If you paste a URL from YouTube in a WordPress post, for example, WordPress automatically embeds the video in the YouTube player. The same thing happens with links from Twitter. If you paste a Twitter link in a post, WordPress automatically formats the tweet and embeds it in your post.

For the purposes of showing off the use of the embed shortcode, following is an example of using the shortcode to embed a Twitter URL. Using a custom HTML block in the Add New Post screen, I added a Twitter link from one of my tweets:

```
[embed]https://twitter.com/LisaSabinWilson/status/1066037791249874944[/embed]
```

Figure 3-12 displays the output of this shortcode.

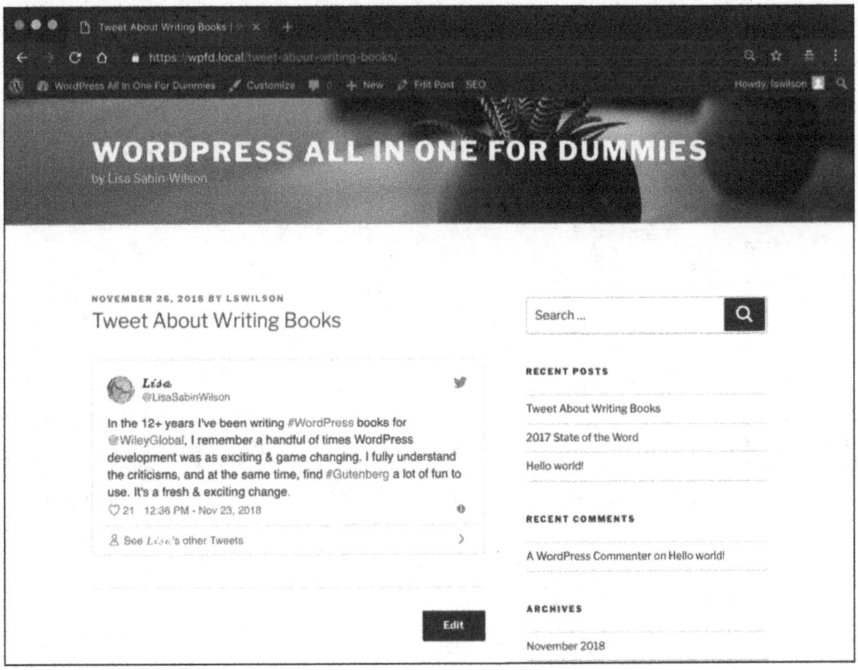

FIGURE 3-12: Using a Twitter link inside the embed shortcode.

IN THIS CHAPTER

» Avoiding problems with plugin modifications

» Removing plugin features

» Modifying plugin output

» Changing shortcode names

Chapter 4 Modifying Existing Plugin Code

WordPress has more than 55,000 plugins on its website, so you'd think that you could find a plugin to do everything you could possibly need on your WordPress website. But not even the best plugins can meet the needs of every user.

This chapter explores the idea of tweaking an existing plugin to meet your specific needs. With a little bit of programming knowledge and some determination, modifying existing plugin code is very possible. Although you won't become a full-fledged developer overnight, making changes in existing plugins can definitely get the mental gears spinning on how you can do more and more with your programming knowledge.

The examples in this chapter are simple, offering a basic introduction to modifying plugins. The next chapter goes into much more depth with regard to plugin development.

Setting the Foundation for Modifying Plugins

Before you start modifying plugins, you should do the following:

- **Set up a development site.** That way, if you accidentally break your site, no harm is done.
- **Display error messages.** By default, most WordPress sites hide error messages. You want to see those messages when developing plugins, however, because they can provide valuable feedback.

  Find the `wp-config.php` file (it's in the main WordPress installation on your web server), and change `WP_DEBUG define` (scroll to the bottom of the file) from `false` to `true` to display error-message information.

  TIP

  For more details about `WP_DEBUG`, see the WordPress Codex page on the topic: `https://codex.wordpress.org/WP_DEBUG`.
- **Set up a non-WordPress editor.** You don't want to use the editors built into WordPress. Although they're convenient, they can introduce bugs into the PHP code that can cause your entire site to break, including your ability to edit the PHP file. Thus, you should use an editor on your own computer or on the server to modify the files so that problems can be fixed quickly without large amounts of work.

REMEMBER

All code is covered by copyright. For a plugin to be added to the WordPress repository, the code needs to use the GPLv2 license or later. Any code in the plugins on the WordPress website is available for you to use, modify, and even redistribute, the only limitation being that your modified code must use the same licensing as the original code. Book 1, Chapter 2 covers licensing and the GPL.

It's important to know that when you start making changes, you're on your own. You can no longer update the plugin to gain access to bug fixes or new features. To update to a newer version of the plugin, you have to download the latest version of the code and modify it again to make your desired changes.

Because WordPress supports updating plugins automatically, you want to ensure that you don't accidentally update a modified plugin and lose your modifications. To prevent such a situation from happening, do the following:

» **Change the name of the plugin's directory.** The directory name is used as the basis for determining what to sync the plugin to for update purposes. If you change the directory name to something different, the plugin is no longer a candidate for automatic updates. Make sure that you pick a name that doesn't exist in the Plugins page. You can verify that you have a unique name by trying to go to `https://wordpress.org/plugins/`*`new-directory-name`*, where *`new-directory-name`* is replaced by the name you want to use for your directory. Note that after you change the name of the directory, the plugin needs to be activated again.

» **Modify the name of the plugin.** Although this change isn't strictly necessary, it does help ensure that the plugin stands out. Even adding *(modified)* to the name helps ensure that the modified version is kept separate from the normal version of the plugin. It also serves as a reminder to you that the plugin is modified and shouldn't be treated as a normal plugin. In other words, it's a reminder to take care when deciding to update or delete the plugin.

» **Add your name to the listing of plugin authors.** This change tells people where to send questions about the plugin. This is especially important if the modified plugin is redistributed or the plugin is used in an environment that has many users.

REMEMBER

Although I don't typically recommend editing the core files of plugins, I'm doing so in this chapter to demonstrate how plugins are built, to introduce you to the files and code, and to get you comfortable with plugin files in general.

Removing Part of a Form

One of the easiest modifications to make is removing something from an existing plugin.

The All in One SEO Pack plugin, available at `https://wordpress.org/plugins/all-in-one-seo-pack`, provides a large number of settings that control the SEO features for each post and page. Suppose that you manage this site, and several editors and authors frequently ask questions about the Preview Snippet (see Figure 4-1). Some of them complain that they don't like the snippet displayed where it is because it takes up valuable space in the Post Edit screen. You want to edit the plugin to remove the snippet.

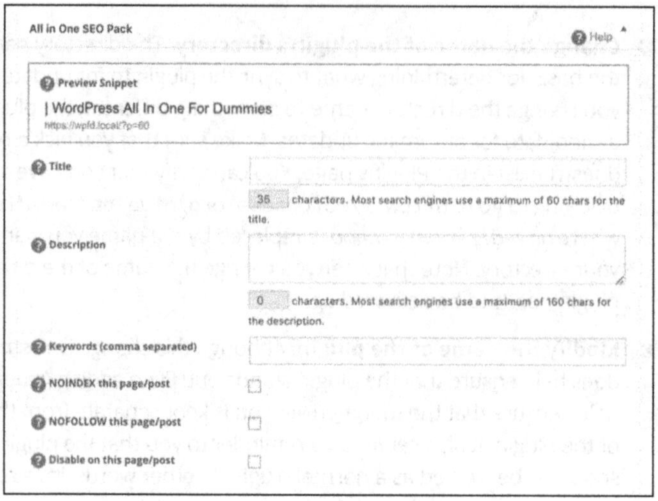

FIGURE 4-1: All in One SEO Pack post- and page-specific settings before the Preview Snippet is modified.

Follow these steps to remove the Preview Snippet:

1. **Search the plugin's files for the words *Preview Snippet*.**

   Search for this phrase because it's a unique string inside the plugin's code. After digging around in the files, you find the section responsible for this form in the plugin's `aioseop_class.php` file inside the `/all-in-one-seo-pack/` folder.

2. **Remove line 324.**

   This line (the section of the code that includes help text for the Preview Snippet) looks like this:

```
'snippet' => '#preview-snippet',
```

3. **Remove lines 944 through 960.**

```
In the section of code that adds the snippet preview setting, you can find
   the lines of code that looks like this:'snippet' => array(
'name'    => __( 'Preview Snippet', 'all-in-one-seo-pack' ),
'type'    => 'custom',
'label'   => 'top',
'default' => '<script>
jQuery(document).ready(function() {
jQuery("#aiosp_title_wrapper").bind("input", function() {
jQuery("#aiosp_snippet_title").text(jQuery("#aiosp_title_wrapper input").
   val().replace(/<(?:.|\n)*?>/gm, ""));
});
jQuery("#aiosp_description_wrapper").bind("input", function() {
```

```
jQuery("#aioseop_snippet_description").text(jQuery("#aiosp_description_
wrapper textarea").val().replace(/<(?:.|\n)*?>/gm, ""));
});
});
</script>
<div class="preview_snippet">
<div id="aioseop_snippet"><h3><a>%s</a></h3><div><div>
<cite id="aioseop_snippet_link">%s</cite></div>
<span id="aioseop_snippet_description">%s</span></div></div></div>',
),
```

To make the modification properly, you must remove all of those lines.

4. **Save the modification, and upload the change to the server.**

   The editor page looks like Figure 4-2.

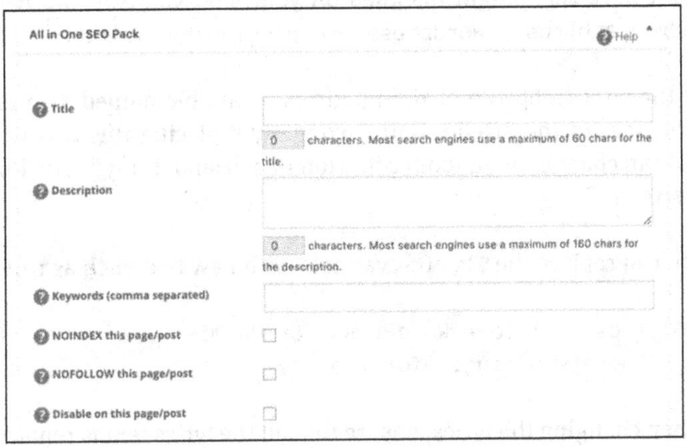

FIGURE 4-2: The All in One SEO Pack post- and page-specific settings after the Preview Snippet is removed.

After making this change, load your website in your browser to make sure that it loads with no error messages and that nothing is broken due to this modification. Save a variety of settings for the SEO feature, and ensure that the modifications still take effect after the settings are saved.

Modifying the Hello Dolly Lyrics

Matt Mullenweg, co-founder of WordPress, developed the Hello Dolly plugin. Anyone who follows the development of WordPress knows that Mullenweg is a huge jazz fan. How do we know this? Every single release of WordPress is named after some jazz great. One of the most recent releases of the software, for example, is named Tipton, after jazz great Billy Tipton Parker; another release was named Coltrane, after the late American jazz saxophonist and composer John Coltrane.

Knowing this, it isn't surprising that Mullenweg developed a plugin named Hello Dolly. Here's the description of this plugin that you see on the Plugins page of your Dashboard:

> This is not just a plugin, it symbolizes the hope and enthusiasm of an entire generation summed up in two words sung most famously by Louis Armstrong: "Hello, Dolly." When activated, you will randomly see a lyric from "Hello, Dolly" in the upper right of your admin screen on every page.

Is it necessary? No. Is it fun? Sure!

The Hello Dolly plugin is included with WordPress and is easy to modify. If you don't have this plugin installed on your site, you can find it on the WordPress website at `https://wordpress.org/plugins/hello-dolly`.

In the `hello.php` file of the plugin is a variable named `$lyrics` that stores the lyric lines of the "Hello, Dolly" song. By replacing this text with your own text, you can change the random selection of a "Hello, Dolly" lyric line to anything you desire.

You can replace the `$lyrics` variable with new text such as this, for example:

```
$lyrics = "I love WordPress For Dummies.
   There's a plugin for that.";
```

REMEMBER

When changing the lyrics, ensure that all the lyrics text is replaced; otherwise, you can accidentally introduce an error into the code.

After the modification is in place, the Hello Dolly plugin says either `I love WordPress For Dummies` or `There's a plugin for that`. Figure 4-3 shows the result of this modification. Notice the message toward the top-right corner of the screen.

When a *string* (a portion of code that's contained inside quotes) is used only for output, it's typically safe to modify the text without causing any bugs or other issues in the plugin. By changing a string's text, you can change the output of the plugin without much effort.

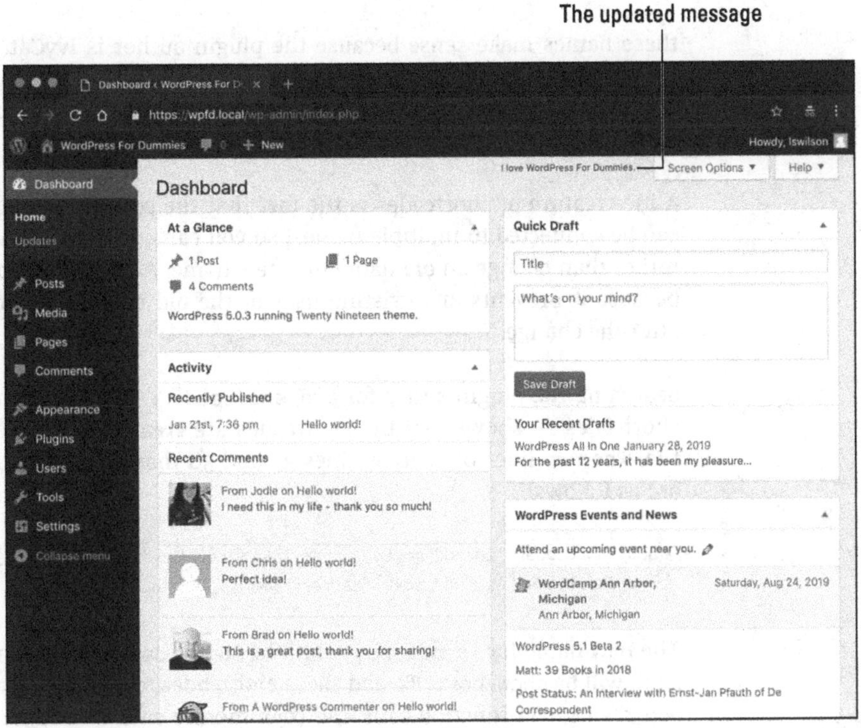

FIGURE 4-3: The modified Hello Dolly plugin declares that it loves *WordPress For Dummies.*

TIP

WordPress has a built-in mechanism for replacing strings in code with new strings. This feature, called *localization,* is typically used to change text to another language. As long as the plugin properly uses the localization functions for all its output strings, you can use this feature to change specific strings as desired, even if you simply change the words used rather than the language. This feature is discussed in Book 7, Chapter 6.

Changing a Shortcode's Name

Sometimes, shortcodes have hard-to-remember names. This problem typically occurs because the plugin author is trying to avoid creating conflicts with other plugins by using the same shortcode name. Although this practice helps prevent code conflicts, looking up a shortcode's name each time you want to use it can be annoying.

The Posts in Page plugin (available at `https://wordpress.org/plugins/posts-in-page`) shows how shortcodes can be hard to remember. It comes with two shortcodes: `ic_add_post` and `ic_add_posts`. From a developer standpoint, these names make sense because the plugin author is IvyCat. Thus, the initials ic are used to prefix each shortcode name, ensuring that the shortcode names are unique. From a user standpoint, however, the naming scheme just causes frustration.

A nice feature of shortcodes is the fact that the code that handles the shortcode can be connected to multiple names, so you can add extra names for a shortcode rather than change an old name to a new name. Adding a second name is helpful because it prevents any existing uses of the old shortcode name from breaking after the change.

Searching the plugin's files for add_shortcode — the function that creates new shortcodes — shows that the shortcodes are created in the posts_in_page.php file. The two lines of code on lines 37 and 38 that create the current shortcodes are as follows:

```
add_shortcode( 'ic_add_posts', array( &$this, 'posts_in_page' ) );
add_shortcode( 'ic_add_post', array( &$this, 'post_in_page' ) );
```

The new name for ic_add_posts will be show-posts. The new name for ic_add_post will be show-post. To add these shortcodes, copy and paste the original two add_shortcode function calls and then modify each shortcode name to the new name. After you make the changes, the section of code looks like this:

```
add_shortcode( 'ic_add_posts', array( &$this, 'posts_in_page' ) );
add_shortcode( 'show-posts', array( &$this, 'posts_in_page' ) );
add_shortcode( 'ic_add_post', array( &$this, 'post_in_page' ) );
add_shortcode( 'show-post', array( &$this, 'post_in_page' ) );
```

The functionality is exactly the same as that of the ic_add_posts shortcode; the shortcode simply has a name that's easier to remember.

TIP

It's possible to register additional names for a specific shortcode without modifying the shortcode's plugin code. You can accomplish this registration by creating a custom plugin with an add_shortcode function call that connects the new shortcode name with the callback function name (the second argument of the function). Creating new plugins is discussed in Book 7, Chapter 5.

IN THIS CHAPTER

» Creating a valid plugin

» Filtering content

» Adding shortcodes and widgets

» Creating a plugin settings page

Chapter 5

Creating Simple Plugins from Scratch

You can extend WordPress functionality through plugins and themes without modifying any of WordPress core files. This technique allows you to customize WordPress and permits easy upgrades when new versions of WordPress are released. By using the WordPress software built-in *action hooks* (placeholder functions that allow plugin developers to execute code hooked into them) and *filter hooks* (also placeholder functions that you can use to apply parameters to filter results), you can create just about any functionality you can imagine.

This chapter takes you on a crash course in creating plugins. The plugins I show you how to build start simple and iteratively introduce new concepts as the functionality gets deeper and more involved. Having a foundational knowledge of PHP is helpful for getting the most out of this chapter, but even beginner PHP developers should be able to get value out of each project.

REMEMBER

This book doesn't turn you into a PHP programmer or MySQL database administrator. Book 2, Chapter 3 gives you a glimpse of how PHP and MySQL work together to help WordPress build your website. If you're interested in finding out how to program PHP or become a MySQL database administrator, check out *PHP & MySQL For Dummies*, 4th Edition, by Janet Valade (John Wiley & Sons, Inc.).

WARNING

You may be tempted to edit the core code of WordPress rather than write a plugin to achieve the desired functionality. Doing so isn't recommended; it makes upgrading difficult and can cause various problems, including serious security issues.

To make plugin development safer, use a test site so that you don't introduce bugs that can break your site. Breaking a site that has traffic while you're developing a plugin is an easy way to annoy visitors.

When writing a plugin, use a simple text editor such as Notepad (Windows) or TextEdit (Mac). Don't use the editors built into WordPress to edit code; they can introduce bugs that can break the site.

Understanding Plugin Structure

All that's required for WordPress to see a plugin is a PHP file in the `wp-content/plugins` directory of the site with some special information at the top of the file. This information at the top of a plugin file, typically referred to as the plugin's *file header*, is what WordPress looks for when determining which plugins are installed on the site. A freshly installed WordPress site makes a good starting point for understanding how plugin file headers works in practice.

Inspecting WordPress's core plugins

As discussed in Book 7, Chapter 1, WordPress includes two core plugins: Akismet and Hello Dolly. Looking at the files for these plugins helps you understand how you can structure your own plugins.

Inside a fresh WordPress site's `wp-content/plugins` directory, you find a directory named `/akismet` and two files named `hello.php` and `index.php`. The `hello.php` file is for the Hello Dolly plugin and has the following text at the top of the file:

```
<?php
/**
 * @package Hello_Dolly
 * @version 1.7
 */
/*
```

```
Plugin Name: Hello Dolly
Plugin URI: http://wordpress.org/plugins/hello-dolly/
Description: This is not just a plugin, it symbolizes the hope and enthusiasm of an
    entire generation summed up in two words sung most famously by Louis Armstrong:
    Hello, Dolly. When activated you will randomly see a lyric from <cite>Hello,
    Dolly</cite> in the upper right of your admin screen on every page.
Author: Matt Mullenweg
Version: 1.7
Author URI: http://ma.tt/
*/
```

This section is the file header, which tells WordPress about the plugin. The Plugin Name, Plugin URI, and Description sections of the file header are referred to as *fields*. I discuss the fields and their use in Book 7, Chapter 6.

WARNING

If you remove the file header, the Hello Dolly plugin will no longer be available because WordPress will no longer recognize it as a plugin.

Open the `index.php` file in the `/wp-content/plugins/` folder, and you see the following few lines of code:

```
<?php
// Silence is golden.
?>
```

Because this file doesn't have a file header, it isn't a plugin. It's in the `plugins` directory to prevent people from going to *`domain.com`*`/wp-content/plugins` (where *`domain.com`* is your site's domain name) to get a full listing of all the plugins on your site. Because the `index.php` file doesn't output anything, people trying to get a listing of your plugins simply see a blank screen.

All that remains now in the `/wp-content/plugins` directory is the `/akismet` directory. Inside this directory are three PHP files: `admin.php`, `akismet.php`, and `legacy.php`. If you open each file, you can see that only the `akismet.php` file contains the file header.

```
<?php
/**
 * @package Akismet
 */
/*
Plugin Name: Akismet Anti-Spam
Plugin URI: https://akismet.com/
```

```
Description: Used by millions, Akismet is quite possibly the best way in the
   world to <strong>protect your blog from spam</strong>. It keeps your site
   protected even while you sleep. To get started: activate the Akismet plugin
   and then go to your Akismet Settings page to set up your API key.
Version: 4.1
Author: Automattic
Author URI: https://automattic.com/wordpress-plugins/
License: GPLv2 or later
Text Domain: akismet
*/

/*
This program is free software; you can redistribute it and/or
modify it under the terms of the GNU General Public License
as published by the Free Software Foundation; either version 2
of the License, or (at your option) any later version.

This program is distributed in the hope that it will be useful,
but WITHOUT ANY WARRANTY; without even the implied warranty of
MERCHANTABILITY or FITNESS FOR A PARTICULAR PURPOSE.  See the
GNU General Public License for more details.

You should have received a copy of the GNU General Public License
along with this program; if not, write to the Free Software
Foundation, Inc., 51 Franklin Street, Fifth Floor, Boston, MA
   02110-1301, USA.

Copyright 2005-2015 Automattic, Inc.
*/
```

Because the akismet.php file has the file header, WordPress recognizes the /akismet directory as a plugin. If the akismet.php file is removed, the Akismet plugin disappears from the listing of available plugins in your WordPress installation. (On the Dashboard, click the Plugins link to see the Plugins screen.)

Knowing the requirements

Looking at the way that the default plugins are set up gives you an idea of how to set up your plugins, but knowing all the requirements would be nice so you don't make mistakes. The reality is that there are very few requirements for how you must set up your plugin.

Requirement 1: File header

The file header allows WordPress to recognize your plugin. Without this key piece of information, your plugin won't show up as an available plugin, and you won't be able to activate it.

Although the file header has many fields, only Plugin Name is required. Following is a valid file header:

```
/*
  Plugin Name: Example Plugin
*/
```

Providing additional information can be very helpful, of course, but if you're quickly making a plugin for yourself, the plugin name is all that is required. See Book 7, Chapter 6 for more information about the file header.

Requirement 2: Correct placement of the main plugin file

The main plugin file (the one with the file header) must be in the `/wp-content/plugins` directory or inside a directory immediately inside the `/wp-content/plugins` directory.

Here are some examples of valid locations for the main plugin PHP file:

- `wp-content/plugins/plugin.php`
- `wp-content/plugins/example/plugin.php`

Here are some examples of invalid locations for the main plugin PHP file:

- `wp-content/plugin.php`
- `wp-content/plugins/example/lib/plugin.php`

WARNING

You can place the main plugin file too deep. WordPress looks only in the `/wp-content/plugins` directory and inside the first level of the directories contained in `/wp-content/plugins` but no deeper. If you place the file too deep within the `plugins` directory, it won't work.

Creating Simple Plugins from Scratch

Following best practices

The requirements are very lax and allow you to set up your plugin any way you want. You can name the main plugin file and plugin directory anything you like. You can even put multiple main plugin files inside a single directory. Just because you can doesn't mean that you should, however. Following are some best practices to help you keep some consistency.

Best Practice 1: Always use a plugin directory

Hello Dolly doesn't reside in a directory because it's simple enough to need only one file. A good rule of thumb, however, is that each plugin should reside in its own directory even if it needs only one file. This practice helps keep plugins organized in the `/plugins` directory.

When you're creating a plugin, a single file may be enough to do what you need, but further development may require adding more files. It's better to start with the plugin in a directory than to try to restructure it later.

TIP

Moving or renaming a main plugin file deactivates the plugin because WordPress stores the plugin's activation state based on the path to the main plugin file.

Do yourself and any users of your plugin a favor: Always place your plugins inside a directory.

Best Practice 2: Use meaningful, unique names

When doing any WordPress development (whether for a plugin or theme), keep in mind that your code shares space with code from other people (other plugin developers, WordPress core developers, theme developers, and so on). You should never use simple names for anything; the name of your plugin should be unique.

You may think that naming your plugin Plugin allows you to move past the boring stuff and on to development, but it just makes things difficult to keep track of. If your plugin produces a widget that displays a listing of recent movie reviews, "Lisa Sabin-Wilson's Movie Reviews Widget" is much more meaningful than "Widget Plugin."

Best Practice 3: Match the plugin and plugin directory names

Make sure that your plugin's directory name makes it easy to find the plugin in the `/wp-content/plugins` directory.

Going with the preceding example, having Lisa Sabin-Wilson's Movie Reviews Widget in a widget directory makes finding the widget difficult. The directory name doesn't have to match, but it should make sense. Some good directory names for this example are /movie-reviews-widget, /lsw-movie-reviews-widget, and /movie-reviews.

Best Practice 4: Don't use spaces in directory or filenames

Although modern desktop operating systems can handle directories and files that have spaces in the names, some web servers can't. A good practice is to use a hyphen (-) in place of a space when naming files and directories. In other words, use movie-reviews-widget rather than movie reviews widget.

Avoiding spaces in file and directory names will save you many headaches.

Best Practice 5: Consistent main plugin filenames

Although you can name the plugin's main file anything, coming up with a consistent naming scheme that you use throughout your plugins can be a good idea.

The most popular naming scheme matches the main plugin PHP filename to the plugin directory name. The main plugin file for a plugin directory called /movie-reviews, for example, is movie-reviews.php. The problem with this naming scheme is that it doesn't mean anything. Plugin filenames should always indicate that file's purpose. The purpose of the movie-reviews.php file is clear only when you know that many developers name the main plugin file the same as the plugin directory.

Another naming scheme is to use a consistent filename across all plugins. Naming the main plugin file init.php, for example, indicates that the file is used to initialize the plugin. (init is the abbreviation for *initialize.*) The name init.php makes the purpose of the file clear regardless of the plugin's name or purpose.

Creating Your First Plugin

When you're developing something new, taking very small steps is usually best. This way, if something breaks, the problem is clear. Doing multiple new things at one time makes finding where something went wrong difficult.

Sticking with this concept, the first plugin you create in this chapter is a plugin that can be activated and deactivated but doesn't do anything — in other words, a fully functional plugin shell that's ready for code to be added.

Because this plugin is an example and doesn't do anything, I named it Example Plugin: Do Nothing.

Setting up the plugin files

For this plugin, all you need is a main plugin file. Follow these steps to upload it to its own directory:

1. **Connect to your web server via Secure File Transfer Protocol (SFTP).**

   Check out Book 2, Chapter 2 for details on using SFTP.

2. **Browse to the `/wp-content/plugins` directory in your WordPress installation directory.**

   If you're unsure where your WordPress installation directory is located, see Book 2, Chapter 4, where I cover installing WordPress on your web server.

3. **Create a new directory within `/wp-content/plugins` called `/example-do-nothing`.**

   Most SFTP programs allow you to right-click in the SFTP window and choose Add New Folder or Add New Directory from the shortcut menu.

4. **Create an empty `.php` file with the filename `init.php`.**

   Use your favorite text editor, such as Notepad for PC or TextEdit for Mac, to open a new file and then save it with the filename `init.php`.

5. **Upload your blank `do-nothing.php` file to `/wp-content/plugins/example-do-nothing`.**

   Your plugin directory and plugin file are set up.

In the next section, you add code to the `do-nothing.php` plugin file.

Adding the file header

Open the `do-nothing.php` file you created in the preceding section. (Most SFTP programs have built-in text editors that allow you to right-click the file and choose Edit from the shortcut menu.) Add the following lines of code to create the file header:

```
<?php
/**
Plugin Name: Example Plugin: Do Nothing
Plugin URI: https://lisasabin-wilson.com
Description: This plugin literally does nothing. It is an example of how to
   create a valid WordPress plugin.
Version: 1.0
Author: Lisa Sabin-Wilson
Author URI: https://lisasabin-wilson.com
License: GPLv2 or later
Text Domain: nothing
*/

?>
```

TIP

Adding the closing `?>` tag at the end of a PHP file is optional at this point. Leaving it out is helpful because it prevents you from accidentally adding code after it, which may cause the PHP code to break.

Adding a plugin description isn't necessary, but it makes the purpose of the plugin clear to anyone who reads your code. Additionally, the plugin description displays on the Plugins screen on your Dashboard to give users a good idea of the purpose of your plugin. When developing, you wind up with many plugins that you used for simple tests or left unfinished. Having solid names and descriptions adds order to the chaos so that you don't forget or accidentally delete important code.

REMEMBER

Be sure to save the `do-nothing.php` file and upload it to your `/wp-content/plugins/example-do-nothing` directory on your web server.

Testing the plugin

After modifying the `init.php` file and saving it in the `/wp-content/plugins/example-do-nothing` directory, visit your WordPress Dashboard, and click the Plugins link on the navigation menu to view the Plugins screen. Your new plugin is listed with the title Example Plugin: Do Nothing, as shown in Figure 5-1.

Click the Activate link directly below the title. The Plugins page displays a `Plugin activated` message, which indicates the Example Plugin: Do Nothing plugin was activated in your WordPress installation. Although your new plugin doesn't do anything, you have a simple WordPress plugin with the correct file structure, naming conventions, and headers.

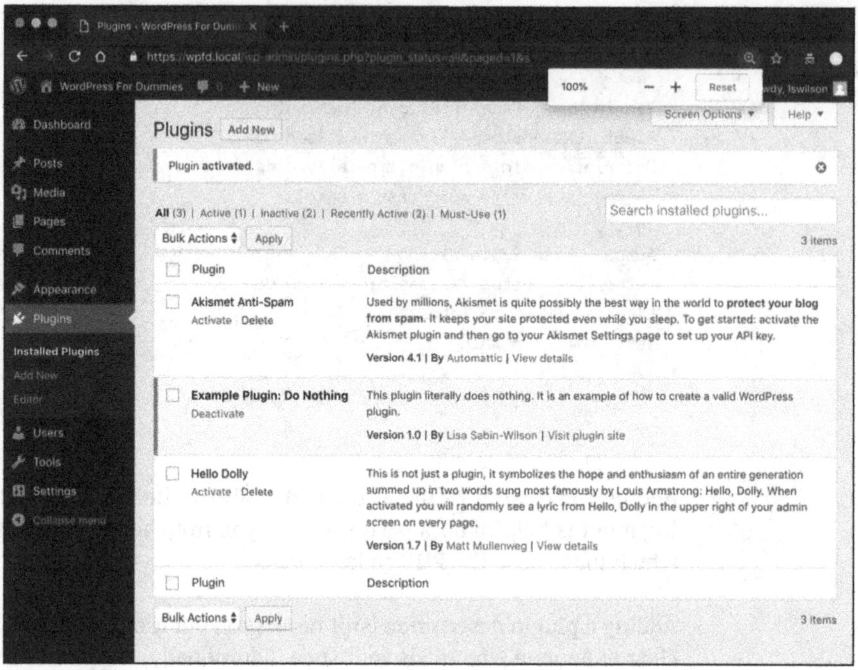

FIGURE 5-1: The Plugins page showing the sample plugin in the list.

Fixing Problems

Potentially, several things could go wrong. If you're having problems, delete the plugin file from its directory and start over. If you still have problems, the following sections cover some common issues and give you possible solutions that you can try.

White screen of nothingness

A common problem when doing plugin development is making a change and finding that every attempt to load the site in your browser window results in a blank white screen. A code error is breaking WordPress when it tries to run your plugin code.

A quick way to fix this problem is to rename your `/wp-content/plugins/example-do-nothing` plugin directory on your web server to something like `/wp-content/plugins/old.example-do-nothing`. This change causes automatic deactivation of the plugin because WordPress won't be able to locate it.

Before changing the name back, go to the Plugins screen on your Dashboard. A message at the top of the page states The plugin example-do-nothing/do-nothing.php has been deactivated due to an error: Plugin file does not exist.

This message confirms that WordPress fully deactivated the broken plugin; you should be able to load your website successfully without seeing the dreaded white screen of nothingness. After that, you can change the filename back, fix your problem, and try again. If the plugin is still broken, WordPress prevents the plugin from activating and gives you details about the error.

Unexpected output error

When you activate a plugin from your Dashboard and see an error message on the Plugins screen about unexpected output, you have code or text within the main plugin PHP file that's outside of a <?php ?> code block. Every PHP function must start with a command that tells your web server to initiate (or start) PHP. If your plugin file is missing the <?php line, an error about unexpected output occurs, and WordPress doesn't activate your plugin.

Have some fun; try to create this error so that you'll know it when you see it. You can intentionally create the error by following these steps:

1. **Connect to your web server via SFTP.**
2. **Browse to the /wp-content/plugins/example-do-nothing directory.**
3. **Open the do-nothing.php file in your text editor.**
4. **Remove the <?php line from the top of the do-nothing.php file.**
5. **Save the do-nothing.php file.**
6. **Upload the file to the /wp-content/plugins/example-do-nothing directory.**

When you try to activate the Example Plugin: Do Nothing plugin, the following message displays at the top of the Plugins page:

```
/* Plugin: Do Nothing Plugin URI: https://lisasabin-wilson.com
Description: This plugin literally does nothing. It is an example
of how to create a valid WordPress plugin. Version: 1.0 Author:
Lisa Sabin-Wilson Author URI: https://lisasabin-wilson.com License:
GPLv2 or later Text Domain: nothing */
```

WordPress also displays an error message on the Plugins page (see Figure 5-2) directly below the Plugins header:

> `The plugin generated 323 characters of` **`unexpected output`** `during activation. If you notice "headers already sent" messages, problems with syndication feeds or other issues, try deactivating or removing this plugin.`

All this fuss was because of a missing `<?php` line.

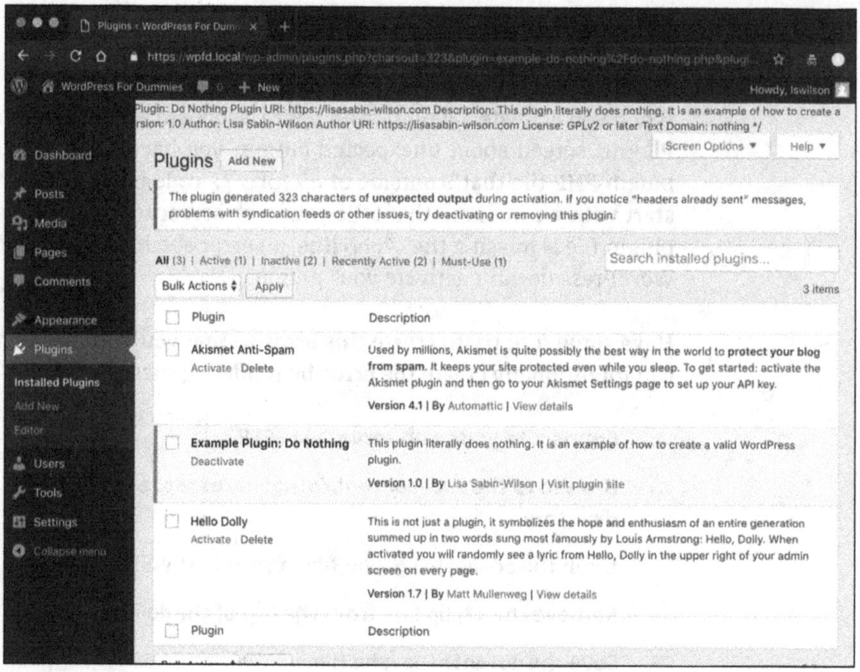

FIGURE 5-2: An unexpected-output error message displayed on the Plugins page.

Filtering Content

It's time to have some fun and create a WordPress plugin that actually does something and, in the process, discover more basics of WordPress plugin development.

A powerful feature of WordPress is its numerous filters. By latching code to a filter, you can modify information as it flows through WordPress; therefore, you can modify the information that WordPress displays or stores.

Suppose that you have a habit of using contractions far too often. Your readership mocks you and your penchant for the common practice of merging words together. At night, you worry about whether you missed an instance of *it's*, *we're*, or *I'll*.

This situation is causing you to lose sleep. You tried listening to the self-help tapes; you reviewed every word; you've been to therapy to find the deep-seated cause of your craving for contractions. Despite your best efforts and the constant ridicule, you can't help but sound like an etiquette contrarian.

Fortunately, there's a cure. With a simple filter and a bit of code, your grammatical ailment can be disguised easily with a simple WordPress plugin that you create in the next section of this chapter.

Setting up the plugin structure

The plugin that you create in this section is Example Plugin: Contraction Compulsion Correction. It resides in a directory called `/example-contraction-compulsion-correction` with a main plugin file named `contraction-compulsion.php`. Apply the same steps to create the directory and main plugin file that you did in "Creating Your First Plugin" earlier in this chapter.

Add the following file header to the top of the main plugin (`contraction-compulsion.php`) file:

```
<?php
/**
 Plugin Name: Example Plugin: Contraction Compulsion Correction
 Plugin URI: https://lisasabin-wilson.com
 Description: This plugin cannot solve your contraction issues, but it can hide
   them by fixing them on the fly.
 Version: 1.0
 Author: Lisa Sabin-Wilson
 Author URI: https://lisasabin-wilson.com
 License: GPLv2 or later
 Text Domain: contraction

  Sample plugin found in WordPress All In One For Dummies by Lisa Sabin-Wilson
  Code comments in this plugin are direct quotes from Book 7 Chapter 5.

 * Purpose: Replaces contractions with full words.
 *
 * Example:
 * Create a post on your site with this text:
    * Isn't it grand that we'll soon be sailing on the ocean blue?
    * You'll see.
```

Creating Simple Plugins from Scratch

```
    * We'll have a great time.
    * I can't wait.
  *
  * Activate this plugin and the words the contractions: Isn't, We'll, You'll,
    I'll and Can't get replaced with full words (is not, we will, you will, i
    will, cannot).
  */

?>
```

Save the `contraction-compulsion.php` file and then visit the Plugins screen of your Dashboard. The Example Plugin: Contraction Compulsion Correction plugin appears there, as shown in Figure 5-3.

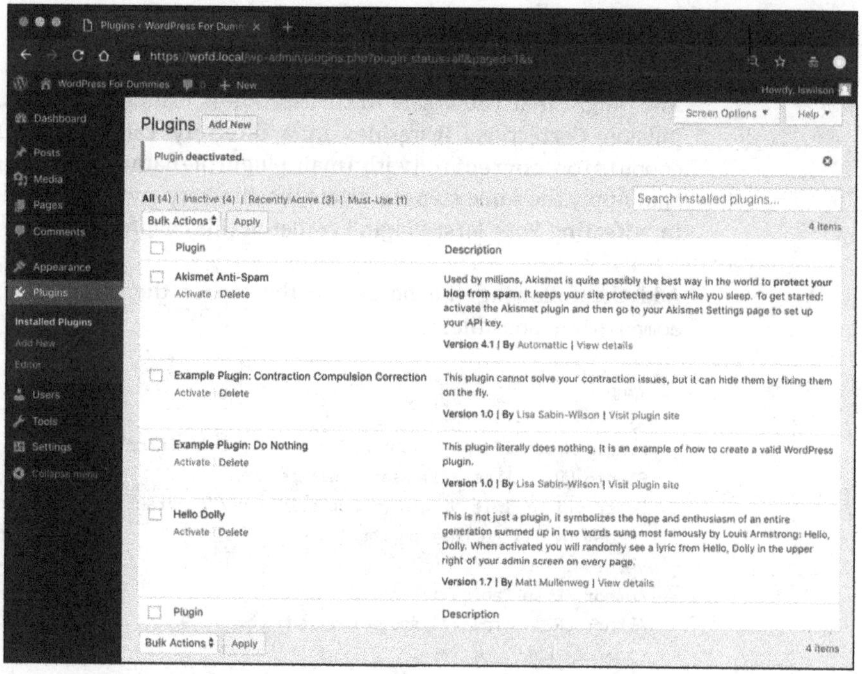

FIGURE 5-3: The Plugins page showing your new plugin in the list.

Testing the filter

The filter you use in this section is the `the_content` filter, which replaces all the content in your site posts and pages with a simple message. If the filter works as expected, you can expand it to hide the contractions that you published in your posts (or pages).

TIP

The the_content filter is one of hundreds of filters available in WordPress. You can find information about filters in the WordPress.org Codex (https://codex.wordpress.org/Plugin_API/Filter_Reference).

Follow these steps to include the the_content filter in your plugin, replacing all the content on your website (posts and pages) with a single phrase. (You change this filter in the following section to filter the contractions out of your published content.)

1. **Connect to your web server via SFTP.**
2. **Browse to this directory:**

```
/wp-content/plugins/example-contraction-compulsion-correction
```

3. **Open the contraction-compulsion.php file in your text editor.**
4. **Type the following lines of code at the end of the file (after the file header) but before the closing ?>:**

```
function my_filter_the_content( $content ) {
  $content = "Test content replacement.";
    return $content;
  }

add_filter( 'the_content','my_filter_the_content' );
```

5. **Save your contraction-compulsion.php file, and upload it to the /wp-content/plugins/example-contraction-compulsion-correction folder.**

The last line of code in step 4 tells WordPress to apply the filter after the plugin is activated. The earlier lines of code define the function (function my_filter_the_content ($content)) with a variable ($content), define the $content variable ($content = "Test content replacement.";), and tell WordPress to return $content within the body of your published posts and pages. Check out the nearby sidebar "Using curly brackets (complex syntax)" for details on using correct PHP syntax.

With the the_content filter in place in your plugin, visit the Plugins screen of your Dashboard, and activate the Example Plugin: Contraction Compulsion Correction plugin. After you activate the plugin, view any post or page on your website. The result: Test content replacement replaces the content of that entry. Your new plugin is filtering content on your website. (See Figure 5-4.) In the next section, you apply the real filter that fulfills the purpose of the plugin you're creating.

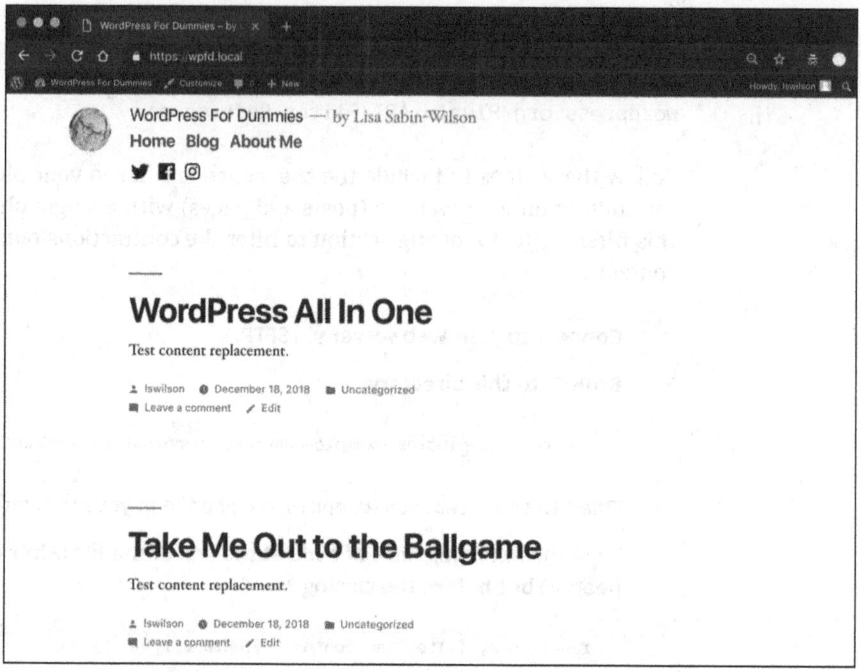

FIGURE 5-4: Filtered content on your website.

USING CURLY BRACKETS (COMPLEX SYNTAX)

You see curly brackets within code. Curly brackets (referred to as *complex syntax* in the PHP Manual; `http://www.php.net/manual/en/language.types.string.php`) serve to open and then close the function definition, or expression. The code samples in the steps in "Testing the filter" name the function `my_filter_the_content ($content)`. An open curly bracket, indicating the start of the function expression, immediately follows that line. Immediately after the lines `$content="Test content replacement.";` and `return $content`, which are the expression for the function, you see the closing curly bracket that indicates the end of the function expression. Without these curly brackets, your code won't work correctly.

Check out the entire PHP manual online at `http://php.net/manual/en/index.php` to brush up on correct PHP code syntax, including when to use single versus double quotation marks and the importance of the semicolon (;).

Replacing contractions in your content

To replace all the contractions within your content with the full phrases or words, the following steps take you through the process of changing the code in the `contraction-compulsion.php` plugin file:

TIP

To make it easier to follow along with the code in this section, you can download the code for The Example Plugin: Contraction Compulsion Correction plugin here: `https://lisasabin-wilson.com/wpfd/example-contraction-compulsion-correction.zip`.

1. **Connect to your web server via SFTP.**
2. **Browse to the `/wp-content/plugins/example-contraction-compulsion-correction` directory.**
3. **Open the `contraction-compulsion.php` file in your text editor.**
4. **Remove the following lines of code:**

```
function my_filter_the_content( $content ) {
  $content = "Test content replacement.";
    return $content;
  }

add_filter( 'the_content','my_filter_the_content' );
```

5. **Type the following lines of code at the end of the file (after the file header):**

```
function lsw_contraction_the_content( $content ) {

  // Convert any HTML entities to characters.
  $content = html_entity_decode( $content );

  // List of contractions to replace.
  $contractions = array(
    "isn't"  => "is not",
    "we'll"  => "we will",
    "you'll" => "you will",
    "can't"  => "cannot",
    "i'll"   => "i will",
  );
```

Creating Simple Plugins from Scratch

```
  // Loop through both uppercase and lowercase words and replace.
  foreach( $contractions as $search => $replace ) {
    $content = str_replace( ucfirst( $search ), ucfirst( $replace ),
      $content );
    $content = str_ireplace( $search, $replace, $content );
  }

  // Return updated content.
  return $content;
}
add_filter( 'the_content', 'lsw_contraction_the_content' );
```

6. **Save your `contraction-compulsion.php` file, and upload it to the `/wp-content/plugins/-contraction-compulsion-correction` folder.**

To make the replacement, an array holds the text to search for and to use as the replacement. The array defines the words you're replacing within your content and loops to make all the replacements. In this example, *isn't* is replaced with *is not*, *we'll* is replaced with *will not*, and so on. This example covers only a small subset of the contractions, of course. You have to modify the example to fit your specific contraction compulsions.

TIP

You may notice that much more than a simple replacement is going on in The Loop. It also uses the `str_replace` function, which replaces all occurrences of the search string with the replacement string.

The first search and replace statement (`$content = str_replace( ucfirst ($search), ucfirst($replace), $content );`) replaces content matches that have an uppercase first letter with a replacement that also has an uppercase first letter.

The second search and replace statement: (`$content = str_ireplace( $search, $replace, $content );`) does a non-case-sensitive search to replace all remaining matches with the lowercase version of the replacement.

To test your contraction replacement plugin, follow these steps:

1. **Log in to your Dashboard.**
2. **Click Add New on the Posts menu.**

   The Edit Post screen loads on your Dashboard so that you can write and publish a new post. (See Book 4, Chapter 1.)

3. **Type a title for your post in the Title text field.**

4. **Type the following text in the post editor:**

   Isn't it grand that we'll soon be sailing on the ocean blue?

   You'll see.

   We'll have a great time.

   I can't wait.

   Notice the contractions *Isn't, we'll, You'll, We'll,* and *can't.* Figure 5-5 shows an Edit Post screen with this text added.

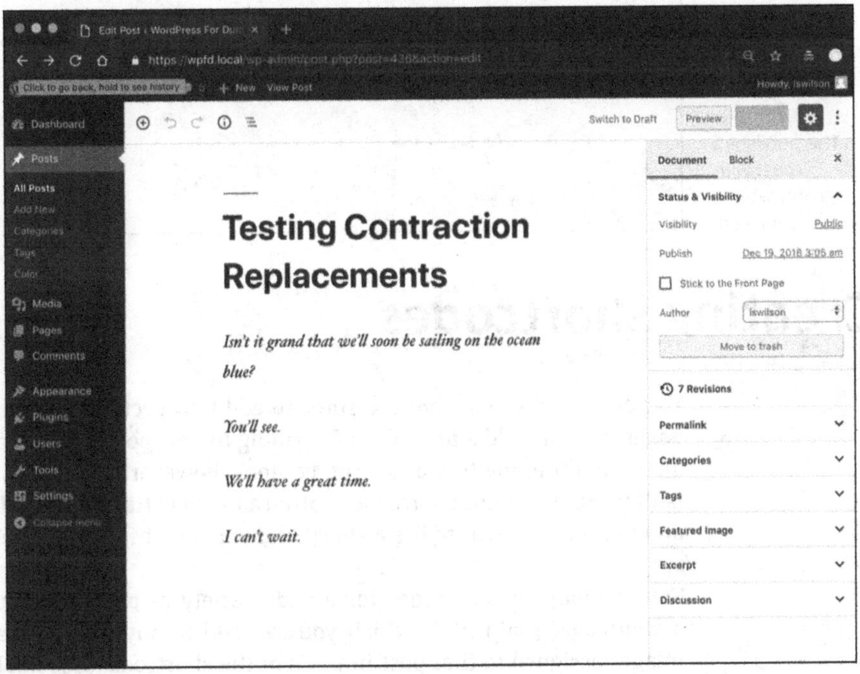

FIGURE 5-5: The Edit Post screen with the contractions in place.

5. **Publish your post by clicking the Publish button.**

   Figure 5-6 displays the post on a website with the contractions replaced by the appropriate words, as defined in the plugin function.

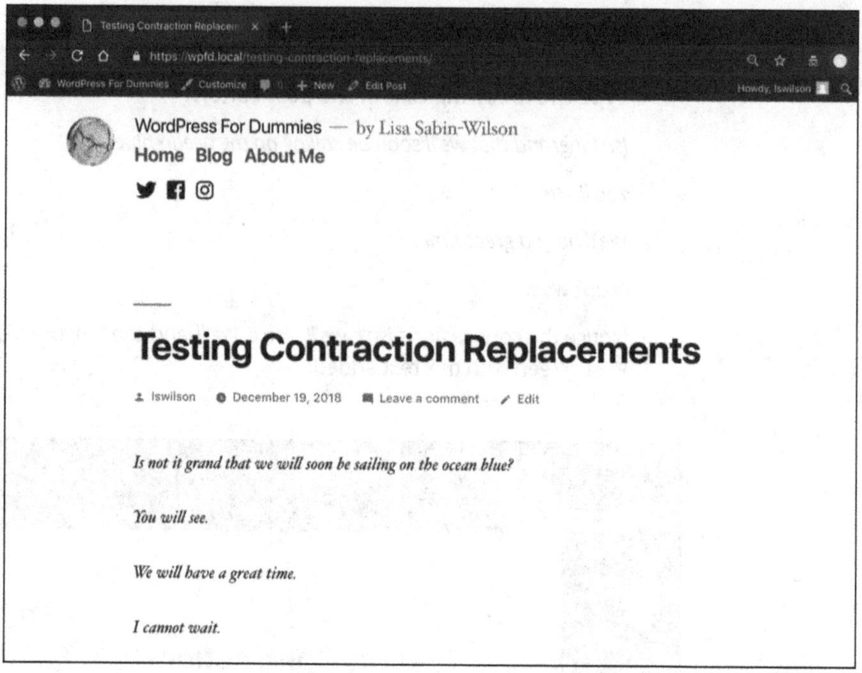

FIGURE 5-6: The published post with contractions replaced.

Creating Shortcodes

You can use the `the_content` filter to add new sections of content to posts and pages. You can add a form for subscribing to new posts, for example. This type of all-or-nothing method of adding content, however, often adds content where it isn't wanted. Using a shortcode is often a much better solution; it offers flexibility and ease of use because it's a shorthand version of fully executable code.

You can employ shortcodes for a wide variety of purposes. WordPress includes a shortcode, `[gallery]`, which you can add to any post to display a gallery of images assigned to that post in place of the shortcode. (See Book 4, Chapter 3 for details on adding photo galleries to your posts.) Many plugins (such as a forum or contact form plugin) use shortcodes to allow plugin users to designate specific pages for the plugin front end to appear. They can surround sections of content, allowing the code that powers the shortcode to modify the content.

Shortcodes can

- **Stand alone.** The `[gallery]` shortcode (built into WordPress) is a good example; simply adding `[gallery]` to the content of a page or post is all that's needed to allow the shortcode to insert a gallery of uploaded images and display them within the body of a post or page.

» **Support arguments that pass specific information to the shortcode:** This shortcode gives the default WordPress gallery a width of 400 pixels and a caption of My Venice Vacation:

```
[gallery width="400" caption="My Venice Vacation"]
```

» **Surround a section of content the way HTML tags can:** The shortcode can modify specific sections of content, such as `[code lang="php"]<?php the_title(); ?>[/code]`. (The "code" shortcode doesn't exist by default in WordPress. You build it in the upcoming section "Building a simple shortcode.")

Setting up the plugin structure

This plugin, Example Plugin: My Shortcodes, resides in a directory called `/example-my-shortcodes` with a main plugin file named `example-shortcodes.php`.

TIP

To make it easier to follow along with the code in this section, you can download the code for the Example Plugin: My Shortcodes here: `https://lisasabin-wilson.com/wpfd/example-shortcodes.zip`.

The reason for the relatively generic name is that you can use this plugin to create multiple shortcodes. To get started, add the following file header to the `example-shortcodes.php` file. (Follow the same steps you used earlier in this chapter to create the directory and main plugin file.)

```
<?php
/**
 Plugin Name: Example Plugin: My Shortcodes
 Plugin URI: https://lisasabin-wilson.com
 Description: This plugin provides the button and code shortcodes.
 Version: 1.0
 Author: Lisa Sabin-Wilson
 Author URI: https://lisasabin-wilson.com
 License: GPLv2 or later
 Text Domain: contraction
*/

?>
```

Building a simple shortcode

In many ways, shortcodes are coded like filters (similar to the content filter) except that with shortcodes, the content to be filtered is optional. For this shortcode,

Creating Simple Plugins from Scratch

you won't worry about content filtering or shortcode attributes; the shortcode is simple enough that it doesn't need either.

The shortcode you create in this section is named `example_button_shortcode`. Adding this shortcode allows you to insert a button with a URL on any page or post on your site with an easy shortcode.

Creating a shortcode requires two things:

- **Shortcode function:** This function handles the creation of the shortcode and a call to the `add_shortcode` function.
- **Shortcode arguments:** The `add_shortcode` function accepts two arguments: the name of the shortcode and the function used by the shortcode.

To get started with your shortcode, add the following code to the end of the Example: My Shortcodes plugin's `example-shortcodes.php` file, before the closing `?>`.

```
function example_button_shortcode( $atts, $content = null ) {
  $values = shortcode_atts( array(
    'url'    => '#',
    'target => '_blank',
  ),
  $atts
);

  return '<a href="'. esc_url($values['url']) .'"  target="'.
    esc_url($values['target']) .'" class="button">'. $content .'</a>';
}

add_shortcode( 'button', 'example_button_shortcode' );
```

REMEMBER

HTML links have to follow some rules because only certain characters are permitted. The `esc_url` function used for both `$values['url']` and `$values['target']` ensures that the information added to the link results in the creation of a valid link by encoding the HTML characters correctly (such as the `<`, `>`, and `"` characters and blocks XSS attacks (malicious scripts injected into your website by another user).

Save the changes, make sure that the plugin is active, and then type this shortcode in the content of a post: `[button url="https://google.com" ]Learn more >[/button]`. If everything works properly, you see a button labeled Learn More >, and when you click the button, it takes you to `https://google.com`. (See Figure 5-7.)

Shortcodes can display depending on specific criteria. It's easy to modify the `[button]` shortcode to include any URL and text that you want by modifying the text and URL within the shortcode itself.

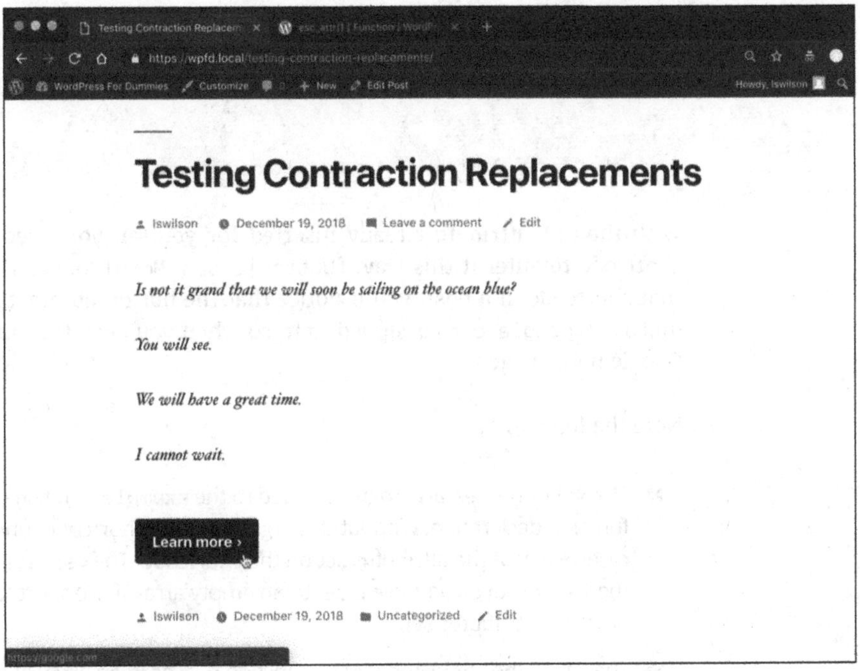

FIGURE 5-7: A button shortcode added to a post.

Using shortcode attributes

By using attributes, you can customize the shortcode output to meet specific needs without having to rewrite an existing shortcode or create a new one.

The `[button]` shortcode is a good example of how you can use an attribute to customize the shortcode output. Notice the two attributes for `url` and `target`, which allow the user to input a URL and a target for the URL, respectively. With an attribute, you can make this behavior the default while allowing the user to supply a customized description.

You can prepopulate those attributes with placeholder information. If you're going to use this shortcode on your site, you can set the `url` attribute to a URL that you know you'll use all the time. Populating the URL in the code of the plugin saves you from having to type the URL in the button shortcode over and over. Enter your desired URL for the `url` attribute:

```
function example_button_shortcode( $atts, $content = null ) {
    $values = shortcode_atts( array(
        'url'    => 'https://google.com',
        'target'=> '_blank',
    ),
    $atts );
```

```
    return '<a href="'. esc_url( $values['url'] ) .'"  target="'. esc_url(
    $values['target'] ) .'" class="button">'. $content .'</a>';

}
add_shortcode( 'button', 'example_button_shortcode' );
```

With the `url` attribute already inserted for you, all you need to do to use the shortcode to enter it this way: `[button]Learn More[/button]`. When you enter that shortcode in a post, you'll notice that the button automatically has the URL (`https://google.com`) assigned to it, so when you click the button, you visit the Google home page.

Note the following:

- The `$attributes` argument is added to the `example_button_shortcode` function declaration. Without this argument, the shortcode function can't receive any of the attributes set on the shortcode. The `=array()` ensures that the `$attributes` variable is set to an empty array if the shortcode doesn't have any attributes set.
- The call to the `shortcode_atts` function passes in an array of default attribute values and merges these defaults with the attributes used in the actual shortcode. Then it stores this resulting array back to the `$attributes` variable. Without this section, the attributes won't have a default value.

TIP

It's a good idea to set a default even if the default is an empty string.

Adding content to shortcodes

The final piece of the shortcodes puzzle is content. By wrapping a shortcode around a section of content, you can modify the shortcode function in creative ways.

Going back to the earlier example of using content with shortcodes, the example in this section creates a new shortcode called `code`. The purpose of this shortcode is to allow designated sections of content to be formatted as code.

To get the new `code` shortcode running, add the code in Listing 5-1 to the bottom of your plugin `example-shortcodes.php` file. (***Note:*** The arrows and numbers aren't part of the actual code; they're included for explanation purposes.)

LISTING 5-1: The Code Shortcode

```
function my_code_shortcode($attributes=array(),$content='') {
if(empty($content)) return '';
$attributes=shortcode_atts(
array( 'lang' => '' ),
$attributes
);
extract( $attributes );
$content=str_replace( "</p>\n<p>","\n\n",$content );
$content=str_replace( '<p>','',$content );
$content=str_replace( '</p>','',$content );
$content=str_replace( '<br />','',$content );
$content=str_replace( '<?','&lt;?',$content );
$content=str_replace( '?>','?&gt;',$content );
$style='white-space:pre;overflow:auto;';
$style.='font:"Courier New",Courier,Fixed;';
if( 'php'==$lang ) {
$style.='background-color:#8BD2FF;color:#FFF;padding: 10px';
}
else if('css'==$lang) {
$style.='background-color:#DFE0B0;color:#333;';
}
else {
$style.='background-color:#EEE;color:#000;';
}
return "<pre class='$lang' style='$style'>$content</pre>";
}
add_shortcode('code','my_code_shortcode');
```

Before digging into how everything works, save the changes to the plugin, and add the following shortcodes to a post:

```
[code]This is a basic code test[/code]

[code lang="php"]&lt?php echo "This is PHP code."; ?&gt;[/code]

[code lang="css"]p { color:#FFF; }[/code]
```

Figure 5-8 shows that these shortcodes produce some fixed-space boxes with different background colors and styling to contain the code. You see the colors on your web page, but because the figures in this book are black and white, you'll have to use your imagination when checking out the results in Figure 5-8.

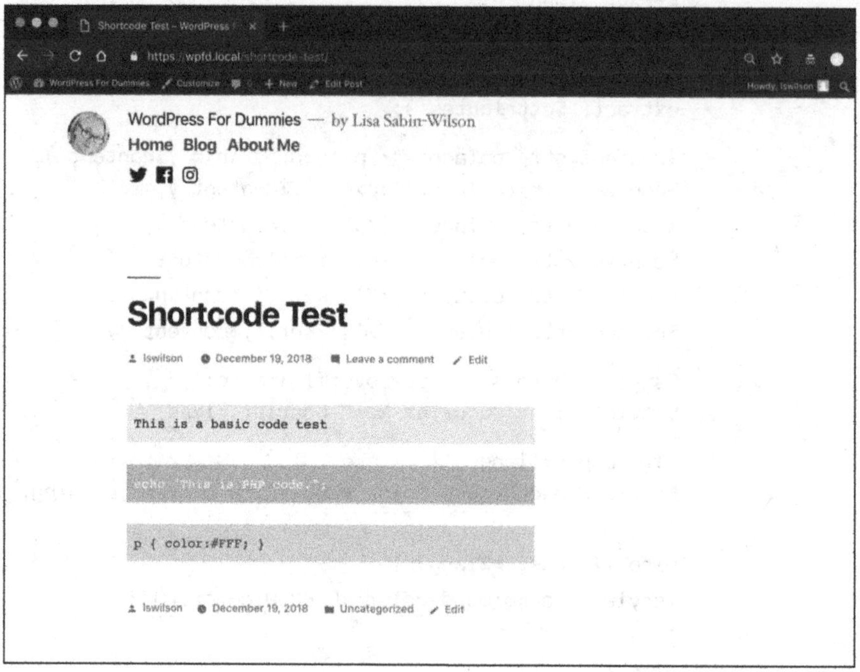

FIGURE 5-8: Code added to a post by using the code shortcode.

Now that it's clear what the shortcode is doing, you can dissect how it works.

→1 Just as it was important to add the $attributes variable to the function declaration to get access to the shortcode attributes, the $content variable is needed to access the content of the shortcode.

→2 If the $content variable is empty, the function returns an empty string because going any further with empty content is unnecessary.

→3–7 Like the [button] shortcode from the preceding section, the shortcode_atts function establishes base defaults. By default, the lang attribute is an empty string. The extract function fills out the $lang variable.

→8–11 This set of str_replace function calls allows for proper handling of multiline content by the [code] shortcode. The problem is that WordPress always tries to add the <p> (paragraph) and
 (line break) HTML markup tags even when it shouldn't. The str_replace replaces the separation of two `<p>` tag sections with two new lines (a new line is represented by the `\n` code) and then removes all the remaining `<p>` and `<br />` tags inserted by WordPress, which allows the content to display properly when it's wrapped in a `<pre>` (preformat for code) tag.

→12–13 The `$style` variable stores the basic CSS styling for the `[code]` shortcode output.

→14–21 This set of conditional code determines the background and text color based on the `lang` attribute. The php receives a blue background with white text, the css receives a khaki background with dark text, and the default is a gray background with black text. All blocks get 10px of padding.

→22 The last line of the function returns the shortcode output by wrapping the content in a `<pre>` HTML markup tag. The `<pre>` tag uses the generated style and adds the `$lang` as a class. The addition of the class allows for more customization through a stylesheet.

→24 This line adds the shortcode to the WordPress code action hook and is required for the shortcode to *fire* (execute) properly.

Adding Widgets

Widgets are individual features that you can add to theme sidebars. Widgets can add a simple site search, display a calendar, list the most recent posts, and show RSS feed updates. These features just scratch the surface of what widgets offer and what widgets are capable of.

TIP

WordPress 2.8 introduced a new widget API that makes widget creation very easy. If you tried creating widgets in the past and gave up because of the difficulty of making them work properly, it's time to try widget creation again.

Coding a simple widget

Widgets are a bit different from filters and shortcodes, which create one function and register it. Instead, widgets are a collection of functions packaged in a container called a *class*. You register the class as a widget by using the `register_widget` function.

Like shortcodes, multiple plugins can be housed in a single plugin file. Because the code for some of these widgets gets lengthy, however, each widget will be its own plugin.

The widget plugin that you build in this section creates a widget that you can use on the Widgets screen of your Dashboard to show a widget in your sidebar that displays `You are logged in as` *Name* or `Welcome Guest`, depending on whether you're logged in.

TIP

To make it easier to follow along with the code in this section, you can download the code for the Example Plugin: User Widget here: `https://lisasabin-wilson.com/wpfd/example-user-widget.zip`.

This plugin, Example: User Widget, creates a widget called User Widget. As you did in the preceding examples, create a plugin directory in the `/wp-content/plugins` directory by adding a new folder called `/example -user-widget`, add an empty `user-widget.php` file that will serve as your main plugin PHP file, and then follow these steps to create the sample plugin:

1. **Open the `user-widget.php` file in your text editor.**
2. **Add the file header to the top of the `init.php` file:**

```
<?php
/**
 Plugin Name: Example: User Widget
 Plugin URI: https://lisasabin-wilson.com
 Description: This plugin provides a  widget that shows the name of the
   logged in user
 Version: 1.0
 Author: Lisa Sabin-Wilson
 Author URI: https://lisasabin-wilson.com
 License: GPLv2 or later
 Text Domain: userwidget
*/
```

3. **Press the Enter key, and type the next line of code:**

```
class My_User_Widget extends WP_Widget {
```

This code creates a new class called `My_User_Widget`. This new `My_User_Widget` class is based on (and extends) the structure of the existing `WP_Widget` class.

A class is a way of grouping a set of functions and a set of data into a logical group. In this case, everything that's in the `My_User_Widget` class is specific to the Example User Widget. Making modifications to this class doesn't affect any other widgets on your site.

TECHNICAL STUFF

The `WP_Widget` class is the central feature of WordPress's Widget API. This class provides the structure and most of the code that powers widgets. When the `My_User_Widget` class extends the `WP_Widget` class, the `My_User_Widget` class automatically gains all the features of the `WP_Widget` class. Only the code that needs to be customized for the specific widget needs to be defined because the `WP_Widget` class handles everything else.

4. **Press Enter, and type the following lines of code in the `init.php` file:**

```
function My_User_Widget() {
  parent::WP_Widget( false,'My User Widget' );
}
```

The `My_User_Widget` function has the same name as the `My_User_Widget` class. A PHP class function that has the same name as the class is a *constructor.* This function is called automatically when the class code is run. (For widgets, WordPress automatically runs the registered widget code behind the scenes.) Constructors run necessary initialization code so that the class behaves properly.

By calling `parent::WP_Widget`, the `My_User_Widget` class can tell WordPress about the new widget. In this instance, the `My_User_Widget` says that the default base ID should be used (this is the `false` argument and defaults to the lowercase version of the class name, `my_user_widget`, in this case) and that the widget's name is User Widget.

5. **Press Enter, and type the following line of code in the `user-widget.php` file:**

```
function widget( $args, $instance ) {
```

The `widget` function displays the widget content. This function accepts two parameters: `$args` and `$instance`. For this example, only `$args` is needed. You use `$instance` when you create the next widget.

6. **Press Enter, and type the following lines of code in the `user-widget.php` file:**

```
$user=wp_get_current_user();
if( !isset( $user->user_nicename) ) {
  $message='Welcome Guest';
}
else {
  $message="You are logged in as { $user->user_nicename }";
}
```

This code finds out information about the current user and sets a message to display that's dependent on whether the user is logged in, determined by checking the $user variable. If the $user->user_nicename variable isn't set, the user isn't logged in.

7. **Press Enter, and type the following lines of code in the user-widget.php file:**

```
extract( $args );
  echo $before_widget;
  echo "<p>$message</p>";
  echo $after_widget;
}
}
```

The $args variable contains important details about how the sidebar wants widgets to be formatted. It's passed into the extract function to pull out the settings into stand-alone variables. The four main variables used are $before_widget, $after_widget, $before_title, and $after_title. Because this widget doesn't have a title, the title variables aren't used. The $before_widget variable should always be included before any widget content, and the $after_widget variable should always be included after the widget content.

8. **Press Enter, and type the following lines of code in the user-widget.php file:**

```
function register_my_user_widget() {
  register_widget( 'My_User_Widget' );
}
add_action( 'widgets_init','register_my_user_widget' );
```

To register a widget with WordPress (so that WordPress recognizes it as a widget), use the register_widget function, and pass it the name of the widget class.

Although calling the register_widget immediately after the class definition would be nice, it isn't that simple. The code of the widget that includes the different functions must run before the widget can be registered. When code needs to run at specific times, the code is placed in a function, and the add_action function is used to have WordPress run the function at a specific time.

These specific points in time are *actions*. For widget registration, you want to use the widget_init action. This action happens after WordPress finishes setting up the code necessary to handle widget registrations while being early enough for the widget to be registered in time.

REMEMBER

Don't forget to add the closing ?> tag, which tells WordPress that the PHP execution in this plugin has come to an end.

With this final piece in place, the widget is ready for use. When you're done, the entire code block looks like this:

```
<?php
/**
 Plugin Name: Example: User Widget
 Plugin URI: https://lisasabin-wilson.com
 Description: This plugin provides a widget that shows the name of the logged
   in user
 Version: 1.0
 Author: Lisa Sabin-Wilson
 Author URI: https://lisasabin-wilson.com
 License: GPLv2 or later
 Text Domain: userwidget
*/

class My_User_Widget extends WP_Widget {
  function My_User_Widget() {
    parent::WP_Widget( false,'My User Widget' );
  }

  function widget( $args, $instance ) {
    $user=wp_get_current_user();
    if( !isset($user->user_nicename) ) {
      $message='Welcome Guest';
    }
    else {
      $message="You are logged in as {$user->user_nicename}";
    }
    extract( $args );
      echo $before_widget;
      echo "<p>$message</p>";
      echo $after_widget;
    }
  function register_my_user_widget() {
    register_widget( 'My_User_Widget' );
  }
 add_action( 'widgets_init','register_my_user_widget' );
 ?>
```

With this final piece in place, the widget is ready for use. Open the Widgets page on your Dashboard (hover your pointer over Appearance, and click the Widgets link); you see a new widget called My User Widget.

Adding an options editor to a widget

Although some widgets work properly without any type of customization, most widgets need to allow the user at least to supply a title for the widget. Thanks to the `WP_Widget` class, adding options to a widget is easy.

The My User Widget example uses the `widget` function to display the widget's content. This addition to the widget code uses two functions to handle the widget options: `form` and `update`. The `form` function displays the HTML form inputs that allow the user to configure the widget options. The `update` function allows the widget code to process the submitted data to ensure that only valid input is saved.

In this example, you create a basic clone of WordPress's Text widget. Although a bit simple, this cloning allows you to focus on the process of using widget options without getting caught up in the details of a complex widget concept.

Time to start coding, so set up the plugin environment by creating a new directory in your `/wp-content/plugins` called `/example-my-text-widget` and include a blank `init.php` file as your main plugin PHP file. The plugin you're creating in this section is Example: My Text Widget, which creates a widget called My Text Widget.

TIP

To make it easier to follow along with the code in this section, you can download the code for the Example Plugin: My Text Widget here: `https://lisasabin-wilson.com/wpfd/example-text-widget.zip`.

Follow these steps to create the `my-text-widget.php` file for your Example: My Text Widget plugin:

1. **Open the `init.php` file in your text editor.**
2. **Create the file header by adding this code to the top of the `my-text-widget.php` file:**

```
<?php
/**
 Plugin Name: Example: My Text Widget
 Plugin URI: https://lisasabin-wilson.com
 Description: This plugin provides a basic Text Widget clone complete with
   widget options
 Version: 1.0
 Author: Lisa Sabin-Wilson
 Author URI: https://lisasabin-wilson.com
 License: GPLv2 or later
 Text Domain: userwidget
*/
```

3. **Press Enter, and type the following line of code in the `my-text-widget.php` file:**

```
class My_Text_Widget extends WP_Widget {
```

Like the My User Widget in the preceding section, this widget is created by extending WordPress' `WP_Widget` class. This new widget's class is `My_Text_Widget`.

4. **Press Enter, and type the following lines of code in the `my-text-widget.php` file:**

```
function My_Text_Widget() {
  $widget_ops=array( 'description'=>'Simple Text Widget
   clone' );
  $control_ops=array( 'width'=>400 );
  parent::WP_Widget( false,'My Text Widget',$widget_
   ops,$control_ops );
}
```

The constructor for this plugin is a bit different this time. The `parent::WP_Widget` function is still called to set up the widget, but two more arguments are given: `$widget_ops` and `$control_ops`. These two arguments allow a variety of widget options to be set. The `$widget_ops` argument can set two options: `description` and `classname`. The description appears below the name of the widget in the widgets listing. The `classname` option sets what class the rendered widget uses.

5. **Press Enter, and type the following line of code in the `my-text-widget.php` file:**

```
function form( $instance ) {
```

The `form` class function displays an HTML form that allows the user to set the options used by the widget. The `$instance` variable is an array containing the current widget options. When the widget is new, this `$instance` variable is an empty array.

6. **Press Enter, and type the following line of code in the `my-text-widget.php` file:**

```
$instance=wp_parse_args( $instance,array(
   'title'=>'','text'=>'' ) );
```

Remember that the shortcode plugins used the `shortcode_atts` function to merge default options with ones from the shortcode? The `wp_parse_args` in this example performs the same task by merging the existing `$instance` options with default option values.

7. **Press Enter, and type the following line of code in the `my-text-widget.php` file:**

```
extract( $instance );
```

The `extract` function is used to pull the title and text options in the `$instance` variable into the stand-alone variables `$title` and `$text`.

8. **Press Enter, and type** ?>.

By using the close PHP tag, `?>`, you can more easily display a large amount of HTML without having to echo out each line.

9. **Press Enter, and type the following lines of code in the `my-text-widget.php` file:**

```
<p>
<label for="<?php echo $this->get_field_id( 'title' ); ?>">
<?php _e( 'Title:' ); ?>
<input
  class="widefat"
  type="text"
  id="<?php echo $this->get_field_id( 'title' ); ?>"
  name="<?php echo $this->get_field_name( 'title' ); ?>"
  value="<?php echo esc_attr( $title ); ?>"
/>
</label>
</p>
```

The block of HTML displays the title input.

Notice the `$this->get_field_id` and `$this->get_field_name` function calls. These functions are provided by the `WP_Widget` class and produce the needed `id` and name values specific to this widget instance. To use these functions, simply pass in the name of the option that's used — `title` in this case.

The `_e( 'Title:' );` section prints `Title:`. It's wrapped in a call to the `_e` function because the `_e` function allows the text to be translated into other languages.

The `value` attribute of the `input` tag sets the default value of the field. Because this widget will be populated with the current title, the `$title` variable is included in this attribute. The `$title` variable is passed through the `esc_attr` function, which allows the text to be formatted properly for use as an attribute value. If the `esc_attr` isn't used, some values in the title, such as double quotes, could break the HTML.

10. **Press Enter, and type the following lines of code in the `my-text-widget.php` file:**

```
<textarea
  class="widefat"
  rows="16"
  id="<?php echo $this->get_field_id( 'text' ); ?>"
  name="<?php echo $this->get_field_name( 'text' ); ?>"
>
<?php echo esc_attr( $text ); ?>
</textarea>
```

This block of HTML displays the `textarea` input that allows the user to input the text that she wants to display. The only differences between this input and the preceding one are that the `textarea` and `text` inputs have a different format and that this input doesn't have a description.

11. **Press Enter, and type** <?php.

    The form HTML is complete, so the open PHP tag, <?php, is used to switch back to PHP code.

12. **Press Enter, and type** }.

    The `form` function closes.

13. **Press Enter, and type the following line of code in the `my-text-widget.php` file:**

```
function update( $new_instance,$old_instance ) {
```

The `update` class function processes the submitted form data. The `$new_instance` argument provides the data submitted by the form. The `$old_instance` argument provides the widget's old options.

14. **Press Enter, and type the following line of code in the `init.php` file:**

```
$instance=array();
```

A new empty array variable, `$instance`, is created. This variable stores the final options values.

15. **Press Enter, and type the following lines of code in the `my-text-widget.php` file:**

```
$instance[ 'title' ]=strip_tags( $new_instance[
   'title' ] );
$instance[ 'text' ]=$new_instance[ 'text' ];
```

Store the title and text options from the `$new_instance` variable in the `$instance` variable. The title option is run through the `strip_tags` function so that no HTML tags are stored in the title option.

16. **Press Enter, and type the following line of code in the `my-text-widget.php` file:**

```
return $instance;
```

The `update` function works like a filter function. The data is passed in, it can be manipulated as desired, and the final value is returned.

After seeing how this function works, you may wonder why it was necessary to create the `$instance` variable. Even though using `$new_instance` directly would be simpler, it also could produce unexpected results. It's possible for unexpected data to come through as part of the `$new_instance` variable, for example. By creating the `$instance` variable and assigning only known options to it, you can be assured that you know exactly what data is stored for the widget and that your code has had a chance to clean it up.

17. **Press Enter, and type }.**

    Close the `update` function.

18. **Press Enter, and type the following line of code in the `my-text-widget.php` file:**

```
function widget( $args,$instance ) {
```

    The `widget` class function is the same as before, but now it has the `$instance` argument, which stores the options set for the widget.

19. **Press Enter, and type the following lines of code in the `my-text-widget.php` file:**

```
extract( $args );
extract( $instance );
```

    Use the `extract` function on both `$args` and `$instance` to populate easy-to-use variables for each.

20. **Press Enter, and type the following line of code in the `my-text-widget.php` file:**

```
$title=apply_filters( 'widget_title',$title,$instance,$this-
  >id_base );
```

    Remember that in an earlier section, when you assembled The Example Plugin: Contraction Compulsion Correction plugin, you added the `add_filter` function to add a function to be used as a filter. The `apply_filters` in this example show how those filter functions are used. This line of code translates to "Store the result of the `widget_title` filters in the `$title` variable." Each filter is passed the `$title`, `$instance`, and `$this->id_base` variables. Every widget that has a title should have this line of code so that filters have a chance to filter all widget titles.

21. **Press Enter, and type the following lines of code in the `my-text-widget.php` file:**

```
echo $before_widget;
if( !empty( $title ) ) echo $before_title . $title .
  $after_title;
echo $text;
echo $after_widget;
```

    Like the preceding widget, the `$before_widget` variable is included before the rest of the widget content, and the `$after_widget` variable is included after all the other widget content. Because this widget supports a title, the `$before_title` and `$after_title` variables are added; like the `$before_widget` and `$after_` widget variables, they come from the $args argument passed to the function. The if statement ensures that the title displays only if the title isn't empty.

REMEMBER

! means *not*.

22. **Press Enter, and type }.**

    The widget function class closes.

23. **Press Enter, and type }.**

    The My_Text_Widget class closes.

24. **Press Enter, and type the following lines of code in the my-text-widget.php file:**

    ```
    function register_my_text_widget() {
    register_widget( 'My_Text_Widget' );
    }
    add_action( 'widgets_init','register_my_text_widget'  );
    ```

    Register the widget. Note how the My_Text_Widget argument of the register_widget function matches the name of this widget's class.

When you're finished with the preceding steps, the entire block of code looks like Listing 5-2 when it's put together in your init.php file.

LISTING 5-2: The init.php File for the Example: My Text Widget Plugin

```
<?php
/**
 Plugin Name: Example: My Text Widget
 Plugin URI: https://lisasabin-wilson.com
 Description: Provides a basic Text Widget clone with widget options
 Version: 1.0
 Author: Lisa Sabin-Wilson
 Author URI: https://lisasabin-wilson.com
 License: GPLv2 or later
 Text Domain: userwidget
*/

class My_Text_Widget extends WP_Widget {
  function My_Text_Widget() {
  $widget_ops = array( 'description' => 'Simple Text Widget clone' );
  $control_op = array( 'width'=>400 );
  parent::WP_Widget( false,'My Text Widget',$widget_ops,$control_ops );
}
```

(continued)

LISTING 5-2: *(continued)*

```
    function form( $instance ) {
      $instance=wp_parse_args( $instance,array( 'title'=>'','text'=>' ') );
      extract( $instance );
  ?>

    <p>
      <label for="<?php echo $this->get_field_id( 'title' ); ?>">
      <?php _e( 'Title:' ); ?>
      <input
        class="widefat"
        type="text"
        id="<?php echo $this->get_field_id( 'title' ); ?>"
        name="<?php echo $this->get_field_name( 'title' ); ?>"
        value="<?php echo esc_attr( $title ); ?>"
      />
      </label>
  </p>

    <textarea
      class="widefat"
      rows="16"
      id="<?php echo $this->get_field_id( 'text' ); ?>"
      name="<?php echo $this->get_field_name( 'text' ); ?>"
    >
    <?php echo esc_attr( $text ); ?>
    </textarea>

  <?php }

    function update( $new_instance,$old_instance ) {
      $instance=array();
      $instance[ 'title' ] = strip_tags( $new_instance[ 'title' ] );
      $instance[ 'text' ] = $new_instance[ 'text' ];
      return $instance;
    }

    function widget( $args,$instance ) {
      extract( $args );
      extract( $instance );

      $title=apply_filters( 'widget_title',$title,$instance,$this->id_base );

      echo $before_widget;
      if( !empty( $title) ) echo $before_title . $title . $after_title;
```

```
      echo $text;
      echo $after_widget;
    }
  }

  function register_my_text_widget() {
    register_widget( 'My_Text_Widget' );
  }

add_action( 'widgets_init','register_my_text_widget' );

?>
```

Now the widget is ready for use. Open the Widgets screen on your Dashboard (click the Widgets link on the Appearance menu); you see a new widget ready for you to use called My Text Widget. When expanded, the widget has a Title field and text box for the user to configure and add content to, as shown in Figure 5-9.

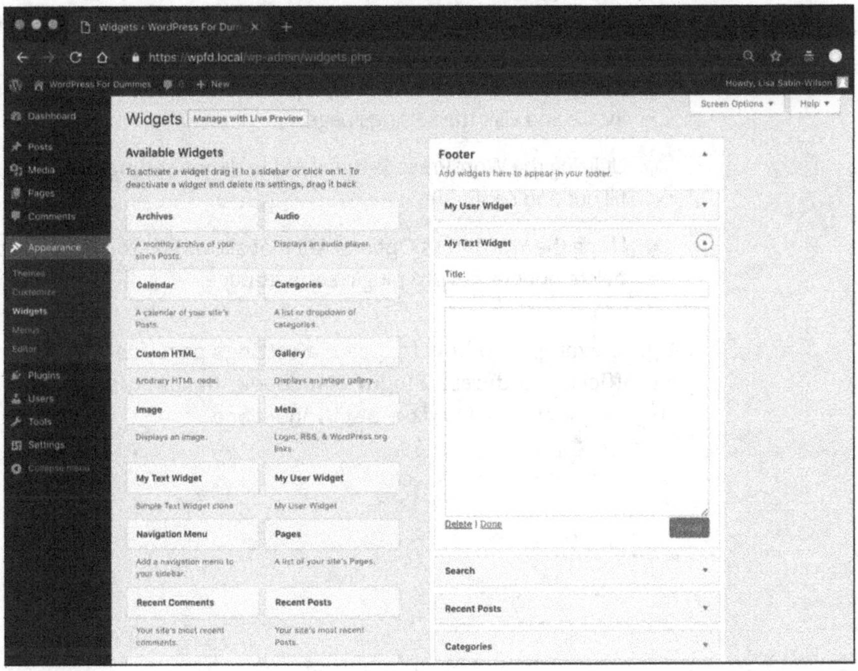

FIGURE 5-9: The My Text Widget.

TECHNICAL STUFF

The code provided for the example text widget plugin in this chapter is meant only to give you the basic mechanics of how such a plugin is constructed and put together. The plugin has input fields that a user is able to input data into, such as a text area for the text they want to enter and a text field for the title. Input fields such as this can be vulnerable to malicious scripts and can cause security flaws. If you're planning to develop plugins of your own, I strongly recommend reading about validating, sanitizing and escaping user data in the WordPress Codex: `https://codex.wordpress.org/Validating_Sanitizing_and_Escaping_User_Data`.

Building a Settings Page

Many plugins offer a settings page that allows the user to customize plugin options. The options offered by a settings page vary from a few check boxes, drop-down lists, or text inputs to multiple advanced editors that allow the user to build data sets, set up forums, or do advanced content management. Although the following sections focus on building a simple settings page, you can expand the concept to fill any type of need that your plugin has.

When reduced to a bare minimum, a basic settings page consists of code that displays the page, stores the settings, and adds the page to the WordPress admin menu. Creating a settings page involves a few different steps including:

- Creating a new menu link in the Dashboard so the users of your plugin can locate and visit the settings page.
- Utilizing the WordPress Settings API to define settings and fields for users to fill out and configure.
- Using the WordPress Options API that allows you to create, read, update, and delete options set in a plugin settings page.

A good example on how to create a settings page for your plugin can be found in the official WordPress Plugin Handbook: `https://developer.wordpress.org/plugins/settings/custom-settings-page`.

IN THIS CHAPTER

» Exploring best practices

» Naming, filing, and locating your plugin

» Internationalizing your plugin

Chapter 6

Exploring Plugin Development Best Practices

Starting to develop WordPress plugins is relatively easy. It's much more difficult to develop WordPress plugins well.

The key to doing development well is sticking with a set of standards that ensures that your plugin is well designed and implemented. A set of standards that many people can agree on is typically referred to as *best practices.* By adopting best practices as your personal development standard, you ensure that other developers can easily understand your plugin's structure and code. Doing so makes collaboration much smoother. In other words, if all WordPress plugin developers followed best practices, the WordPress development world would be a happier and more productive place.

This chapter delves deeper into best practices and is dedicated to taking your plugin quality to the next level.

Adding a File Header

The most fundamental best practice when creating WordPress plugins is to ensure that your plugin has a *file header* at the top of the main plugin file. As discussed in Book 7, Chapter 5, the file header is the part of a plugin file that identifies the file as a plugin. Without the file header, the plugin isn't a plugin and can't be enabled on the WordPress Dashboard.

TIP

Even if you don't distribute your plugin on the WordPress website (`https://wordpress.org/plugins`), take the time to fill in the file header with the name, description, author, version, and license. This info is helpful to all your plugin users.

Use the following header names to supply information about your plugin:

- **Plugin Name:** The value for this entry is listed as the name of the plugin on the Dashboard's Plugins screen. The Plugin Name is the only required entry in a plugin's file header. If it isn't present, WordPress ignores the plugin.

  When giving your plugin a name, make sure that you choose a name that is

  - *Unique:* WordPress uses the name to check for plugin updates. If you name the plugin Akismet, for example, WordPress could offer to let the user upgrade the plugin automatically, resulting in your plugin code's being replaced by the actual Akismet plugin. Starting all your plugin names with your name is a good way to achieve unique names. These are some unique plugin names: Lisa's Twitter Widget, Lisa's Amazon Affiliate Shortcodes, and Lisa's Really Cool Plugin.
  - *Descriptive:* Use a name that describes its purpose. Lisa's Twitter Widget and Lisa's Amazon Affiliate Shortcodes both describe what the plugin offers quite well, but Lisa's Really Cool Plugin doesn't help identify its purpose.

  REMEMBER

  Even if you use the plugin only on your own site, by using a nondescriptive name, you may end up having to look at the plugin's code just to remember what the plugin is doing.

- **Description:** This entry is meant to be a brief explanation of what features the plugin offers. The description entry is shown next to each plugin listed on the Dashboard's Plugins screen. Because the plugin's listing shares space with other plugins, don't add too large a description. Limit the description to one to three sentences.

  It's possible to put HTML into the description. You can add links for plugin documentation and other resources.

  WARNING

  Don't abuse this feature to make your plugin stand out among all the others. If your plugin is installed, you've already won over the user and got her to install the plugin. Don't lose the user by spamming up her plugin listing.

- **Version:** If you share the code for your plugin, the version entry of the plugin could be one of the most important entries in the plugin's file header. If the version number is updated properly, when a user reports an issue, you can quickly know exactly what code the user is running, whether the plugin is outdated, and whether the current code has a bug. The version is a simple thing but very powerful.
- **Plugin URI:** Enter the web address where you talk in depth about the plugin. At a minimum, you should provide information about what the plugin is and any necessary instructions on using it. It's a good idea to allow comments so that people can provide feedback, both good and bad. This feature works as a simple support system for your plugin.
- **Author:** List the name or names of the plugin authors. Sometimes, the name of the company behind the plugin is used instead of the name of a specific developer.
- **Author URI:** List the web address of the plugin author's website.
- **License:** List the name of the license under which your plugin is released. For most plugins, this should be GPLv2 because it matches the license that WordPress is released under. When you submit a plugin to WordPress, the plugin must be licensed under GPL version 2 or later. For more information on GPL licensing, including how it pertains to your plugin development practices, see Book 1, Chapter 2.
- **Text Domain:** This entry is part of allowing the Plugin Name, Description, Version, Plugin URI, Author, and Author URI entries to be translatable. The value of this entry is used as the domain for translating the other entries and should match the domain used in the `load_plugin_textdomain` function. For details on translating, see "Internationalizing or Localizing Your Plugin" later in this chapter.
- **Domain Path:** This entry is used together with the Text Domain entry to offer the file header translations. The value of this entry is the name of the directory inside the plugin's directory (such as `/language/` or `/translations/`) where the translation files are located. The directory must begin with a forward slash for the translation files to be found. If this entry isn't used, the plugin's directory is searched for the translation files.
- **Network:** When WordPress is running as a network (discussed in Book 8), this entry allows plugins to indicate that they must be active for the entire network rather than a single site. The only accepted value for this entry is `true`; any other value is treated the same as a blank or missing entry. If WordPress isn't running as a network, this entry is ignored.

  Using this entry is helpful if your plugin provides very low-level features, such as advanced caching. Because such a feature could create problems if only some sites on the network have it active, this entry forces an all-or-nothing activation of the plugin. Either all the sites on the network run the plugin, or no site does.

» **Site Wide Only:** This deprecated entry is superseded by the Network entry and is supported only for backward compatibility. If the Network entry is supplied, this entry is ignored. As with Network, the only recognized value is `true`. This entry shouldn't be used as support, because it may be removed in future versions.

Although you may not need all the entry options, a file header that uses all the options looks like the following. (The Site Wide Only option is left out because it's replaced by the Network option.)

```
<?php
/*
Plugin Name: Lisa's Twitter Widget
Description: Display Twitter feeds in any sidebar on your site.
Version: 1.0.0
Plugin URI: https://example.com/twitter-widget
Author: Lisa Sabin-Wilson
Author URI: http://lisasabin-wilson.com
License: GPLv2
Text Domain: lsw-twitter-widget
Domain Path: /language/
Network: true
*/
?>
```

TIP

It's customary to include a licensing statement in the header of your plugin to indicate adherence to the GPLv2 license. This statement is easy to include and is formatted as follows:

```
<?php
/*

This program is free software; you can redistribute it and/or
modify it under the terms of the GNU General Public License
as published by the Free Software Foundation; either version 2
of the License, or (at your option) any later version.

This program is distributed in the hope that it will be useful,
but WITHOUT ANY WARRANTY; without even the implied warranty of
MERCHANTABILITY or FITNESS FOR A PARTICULAR PURPOSE.  See the
GNU General Public License for more details.

You should have received a copy of the GNU General Public License
along with this program; if not, write to the Free Software
Foundation, Inc., 51 Franklin Street, Fifth Floor, Boston, MA  02110-1301, USA.
*/
?>
```

Figure 6-1 shows the Plugins screen displaying information pulled from each plugin's file header for the Akismet and Hello Dolly plugins.

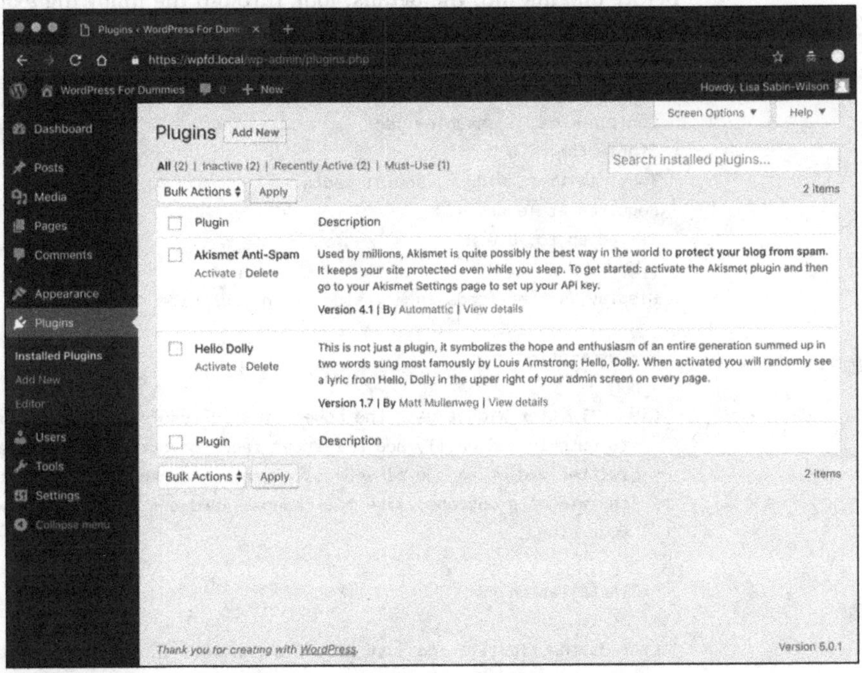

FIGURE 6-1: The WordPress Plugins screen of the Dashboard.

Creating a readme.txt File

To submit a plugin to WordPress, you must include a `readme.txt` file. The plugin won't be accepted without it. The `readme.txt` file is included with the rest of your plugin's files when a user downloads it. It should contain the information the user needs to know to use the plugin properly.

The information contained in the `readme.txt` file is much more elaborate than the information in the file header. All the plugin pages in the Plugins page are generated from information from the `readme.txt` file of each plugin. Thus, this information is very important if you want people to take your plugin seriously.

TECHNICAL STUFF

The file is formatted in a slightly modified version of the Markdown format. *Markdown* is a simple syntax for formatting content to contain headings, text styling (such as underline and bold), links, and so on. The main difference between the format used for WordPress plugin `readme.txt` files and regular Markdown is that the `readme.txt` files use a different format for headings (as you can see in the example), and is a WordPress-specific section similar to the file header of the main plugin file is at the top of `readme.txt` files.

Before digging into the details, look through the following example `readme.txt` file contents:

```
=== Lisa's Twitter Widget ===
Contributors: lisasabinwilson
Stable tag: 1.0.0
Tags: twitter, widget, social media
Requires at least: 4.0
Tested up to: 5.0.2

Display Twitter feeds in any sidebar on your site.

== Description ==

Lisa's Twitter Widget uses the power of WordPress's widget system to allow you
    to quickly and easily add a Twitter feed to your site. After adding the
    Twitter Widget to one of your sidebars, enter the desired Twitter username in
    the widget's options, save the changes, and the Twitter feed will show up on
    your site.

== Installation ==

Extract the zip file and just drop the contents in the wp-content/plugins/
    directory of your WordPress installation and then activate the Plugin from
    the Plugins screen in your WordPress Dashboard.
```

Notice that the lines with the equal signs separate the file into different sections. When the plugin's page is generated, the text at the topmost line with the three equal signs on each side (which I refer to as the *header section*) is used as the plugin's name, and the text after the Description and Installation sections is used to populate the Description and Installation tabs on the plugin's page.

You can do much more with a `readme.txt` file than what you see in this example, which is a small, simplified version of what you can see in active plugins with well-crafted `readme.txt` files.

TIP

If you're concerned about whether your plugin's `readme.txt` file adheres to the expectations of the WordPress Plugins page, use the WordPress validator tool (`https://wordpress.org/plugins/developers/readme-validator`) to validate the file. This tool tells you whether your `readme.txt` file contains all the necessary components and information. If you're still having problems, a handy `readme.txt` file generator at `https://sudarmuthu.com/wordpress/wp-readme` helps you generate a valid `readme.txt` file for your plugin by making sure that the basic requirements are met.

Setting up the header section

The header section at the top of the file is similar to the file header in the actual plugin file. This similarity occurs because, like the file header, the header section is parsed by code to format the data in specific ways. The format of the header section is as follows:

```
=== Plugin Name ===
entry: value
entry: value
entry: value

Brief description of the plugin.
```

The plugin name and short description are required and should be unique to the plugin and description. Like the description in the file header, this description should be brief (one to three sentences).

You can add entries to the header section. Table 6-1 lists the available entries for the header section. Unless otherwise noted, each entry should be considered to be required and should be included in the header section.

TABLE 6-1 Entries for the readme.txt File Header Section

Component	Description
Contributors	Comma-separated list of contributors' wordpress.org usernames. If valid usernames aren't used, the plugin page won't link properly to each contributor's other plugins.
Donation link	Web address for a page that accepts donations for the plugin. This entry is optional.
License	How the plugin is licensed, typically GPLv2.
License URI	The web address that contains the full details of the license, typically `http://www.gnu.org/licenses/gpl-2.0.html`.
Requires at least	Lowest version of WordPress that your plugin is known to be compatible with. If you haven't tested the plugin with older versions of WordPress or don't test updated versions of the plugin with older versions of WordPress, set this to be the latest version of WordPress to ensure that you don't indicate compatibility that may not be there.
Stable tag	Indicates the subversion tag of the latest stable version of your plugin. If no stable tag is provided, trunk is assumed to be stable.
Tags	A comma-separated list of descriptive tags that relate to the plugin.
Tested up to	The highest WordPress version number you've successfully tested your plugin on. Prerelease versions of WordPress (such as 5.1-beta) can be used if the plugin is compatible with the development version.

Adding other sections

After the header section, the rest of the `readme.txt` file is dedicated to providing information used to create the plugin's Plugin page on the WordPress website. This information is divided into sections that display neatly on the plugin's page as tabs. The following list describes the tabs, explains what they're meant to be used for, and provides any special details to know about them:

- **Description:** This tab is shown by default, so put the information that you want people to see when they first visit the plugin's page in this section. Focus on providing information about what features the plugin offers, what makes the plugin different from other plugins that may have similar features, and any requirements that may prevent people from using the plugin successfully.
- **Installation:** Any special instructions on how to install and configure the plugin properly should be included in this section.
- **Frequently Asked Questions:** Are users asking you the same questions over and over? Do you expect certain questions? This tab is the place for you to answer your users' questions in one place.
- **Changelog:** This section is helpful for listing the changes in each version. Be sure to include details about new features, enhancements, and bug fixes so that current users who are curious about the reason for the new release can easily find what to expect after the upgrade. It's common to remove older listings, because this section gets long. The number of listings to keep is up to you.
- **Screenshots:** This section is for listing pictures and videos that show the plugin in action. The screenshots follow a specific format:
  - Add them to the plugin's subversion repository in the `/assets` directory.
  - Name them `screenshot-1.png`, `screenshot-2.png`, `screenshot-3.png`, and so on.
  - The supported formats are PNG, JPEG, and GIF.

  TIP

  Add a description for each screenshot by using a numbered list. The description is displayed below the image with the matching number.
- **Other Notes:** The Other Notes tab is special in that it's created by merging all other sections. You can create as many custom sections as you like and have each of the custom sections appear inside the Other Notes tab.

The following example shows a `readme.txt` with each of these sections:

```
=== Lisa's Twitter Widget ===
Contributors: lisasabinwilson
Stable tag: 1.0.0
Donation link: http://example.com
Tags: twitter, widget, social media
Requires at least: 5.0
Tested up to: 5.0.3
License: GPLv2
License URI: http://www.gnu.org/licenses/gpl-2.0.html

Display Twitter feeds in any sidebar on your site.

== Description ==

Lisa's Twitter Widget uses the power of WordPress's widget system to allow you
   to quickly and easily add a Twitter feed to your site. After adding the
   Twitter Widget to one of your sidebars, enter the desired Twitter username in
   the widget's options, save the changes, and the Twitter feed will show up on
   your site.

== Installation ==

Extract the zip file and just drop the contents in the wp-content/plugins/
   directory of your WordPress installation and then activate the Plugin from
   the Plugins screen in your WordPress Dashboard.

== Frequently Asked Questions ==

= Can the widget combine the feeds from more than one username? =

Not at this time. Such a feature may be added in a future version. For now, you
   will simply have to use more than one widget.

= Can I load a feed for a hashtag? =

Yes. Rather than supplying a username, a hashtag can be used (ensure that you
   add the # before the hashtag) to show the latest feed for that hashtag.

== Changelog ==

= 1.0.0 =
* Release-ready version
* Fixed issue with feed caching not working properly, causing site slowdowns.

= 0.0.1 =
```

```
* Development version. It still has some bugs.

== Screenshots ==
1. Configuration options for the Twitter Widget.
2. The Twitter Widget showing a feed on the site.

== Thanks ==

My thanks to Twitter and its fantastic API. If it wasn't for the API, this
   plugin would not be possible.
```

TIP

The Markdown format has many options for formatting the content. Go to `https://daringfireball.net/projects/markdown/syntax` for full details on what options are available with Markdown.

Besides setting up plugin pages on the WordPress website, the `readme.txt` file serves two very important purposes: controlling the released version of the plugin and offering content to the search function WordPress site, as well as on the Dashboard.

The `readme.txt` file in your plugin's SVN trunk controls the released version of the plugin. After the plugin is updated with a new version number, the stable version value in the `/trunk/readme.txt` file needs to be updated to reflect this new version number. If you don't update this value, the new version won't be released.

Internationalizing or Localizing Your Plugin

WordPress users exist across the United States, Russia, Japan, Germany, and all points in between. Therefore, the next person to download and use your plugin may not speak the same language you do. So if you wrote and distributed your plugin in English, it may be useless to the next person if he speaks only German. The WordPress software has internationalization built into it, which means that it can be *localized*, or translated, into different languages.

REMEMBER

You aren't translating the file into different languages (unless you want to). Rather, you're providing a mechanism of support for people who want to provide translation for your plugin through the creation of `.mo` (machine object) files (discussed later in this chapter). Many people in different countries create (and have created) `.mo` files for the translation of WordPress into different languages; by providing localization for your plugin, you're enabling them to translate your plugin text as well. If you're interested in translating WordPress into a different language, check out this resource page in the WordPress Codex: `https://make.wordpress.org/polyglots/handbook`.

Using GetText functions for text strings

WordPress provides two main localization functions: `__` and `_e`. These functions use the `GetText` translation utility installed on your web server. These two functions let you wrap plain text into strings of text to be translated. You need to account for two types of text strings in your plugin file:

- **HTML:** Example: `<h1>`*`Plugin Name`*`</h1>`

  To wrap HTML text strings within the `GetText` function call, you wrap it by using the `_e` function like this:

  ```
  <h1><?php _e( 'Plugin Name', 'plugin-name' ); ?></h1>
  ```

  This code tells PHP to echo (`_e`) or display the string of text on your Web browser's screen, but it adds the benefit of using the `GetText` function, which allows that string of text to be translated.

- **PHP:** Example: `<?php comments_number( 'No Responses', 'One Response', '% Responses' );?>`

  To wrap PHP text strings with the `GetText` function, you wrap it by using the `__` function, like this:

  ```
  <?php comments_number(__( 'No Responses', 'plugin-name' ),( 'One
     Response', 'plugin-name' ),( '% Responses', 'plugin-name' ) );?>
  ```

  Unlike the echo function (`_e`), the `__` function is used when you need to add a string of text to an existing function call (in this case, `comments_number()`).

REMEMBER

Avoid slang when writing your text strings in your plugin file. Slang is significant to only a certain demographic (age, geographic location, and so on) and may not translate well into other languages.

The second argument within the `GetText` string for the PHP text string example is `plugin-name`. This argument defines the domain of the text and tells `GetText` to return the translations only from the dictionary supplied with that domain name. This second argument is the *plugin text domain*, and most plugin authors use the name of their plugin (separated by hyphens) as the definer. Use the text domain in your `GetText` functions to ensure that `GetText` pulls the dictionary you supply instead of attempting to pull the text from the core WordPress language files, because some of the text you provide in your plugin is unique and most likely won't exist within the WordPress core language files.

In a plugin file, you define the text domain in the plugin header, as discussed in "Adding a File Header" earlier in this chapter:

```
text-domain: yourplugin
```

This line in the plugin header file tells WordPress where your plugin file is located (the text domain), which in turn informs WordPress about where your .pot, or translation file, is for your specific plugin.

TIP

If the text domain is the same as your plugin slug or the name of your plugin folder, you don't need to put the text-domain in your plugin header, WordPress automatically assigns the text domain based on the folder name of your plugin if the text-domain line is missing from your plugin's header file.

Creating the POT file

After you create your plugin and include all text strings within the GetText functions of __ and _e, you need to create a .pot (portable object template) file, which contains translations for all the strings of text that you wrapped in the GetText functions. Typically, you create the .pot file in your own language, in a special format, thereby allowing other translators to create their own .po (portable object) file or an .mo (machine object) file in their language, using yours as the guide to translate by.

The .pot file is the original translation file, and the .po file is a text file that includes your original text (from the .pot) along with the translation for the text. Or you can use an .mo file, which is basically the same as a .po file. Although .po files are written in plain text to be human-readable, however, .mo files are compiled to make them easy for computers to read. Most web servers use .mo files to provide translations for .pot files.

TIP

WordPress has an extensive .pot file that you can use as a template for your own. You can download it at https://i18n.svn.wordpress.org/pot/trunk/wordpress.pot.

Additionally, .pot files can be translated into .mo files by using free translation tools such as Poedit (https://poedit.net), which is a free tool that takes the original .pot file and the provided translations in a .po file and merges them into a compiled .mo file for your web server to deliver the translated text.

The .pot file begins with a header section, which contains required information about what your translation is for. The .pot header section looks like this:

```
# Copyright (C) 2018 by the contributors
# This file is distributed under the same license as the WordPress package.
msgid ""
msgstr ""
"Project-Id-Version: WordPress 5.0.3"
"Report-Msgid-Bugs-To: https://core.trac.wordpress.org/\n"
"Last-Translator: FULL NAME <EMAIL@ADDRESS>\n"
"Language-Team: LANGUAGE <LL@li.org>\n"
"MIME-Version: 1.0\n"
"Content-Type: text/plain; charset=UTF-8\n"
"Content-Transfer-Encoding: 8bit\n"
"POT-Creation-Date: 2018-12-19T17:23:35+00:00\n"
"PO-Revision-Date: YEAR-MO-DA HO:MI+ZONE\n"
"X-Generator: WP-CLI 2.1.0-alpha-7fd4fc3\n"
```

All the capitalized terms in this code example are placeholders. Replace these terms with your own information.

The format of the .pot file is specific, and the file needs to contain the following information:

- **Filename:** The name of the file in which the text string exists. If the plugin file is wordpress-twitter-connect.php, you need to include that filename in this section.
- **Line of code:** The line number of the text string in question.
- **msgid:** The source of the message, or the exact string of text that you included within one of the GetText functions: __ or _e.
- **msgstr:** A blank string where the translation (in the subsequent .pot files) is inserted.

For your default .pot file, to format a text string by using the GetText function (<h1><?php _e('WordPress Twitter Connect'); ?></h1>), which exists on the second line in the wordpress-twitter-connect.php plugin file, you include three lines in the .pot file that look like this:

```
#: wordpress-twitter-connect.php:2
msgid: "WordPress Twitter Connect"
msgstr: ""
```

Exploring Plugin Development Best Practices

You need to go through all the text strings in your plugin file that you wrapped in the GetText functions and define them in the .pot file in the format provided. Now if anyone wants to create a .po file for your plugin in a different language, he or she simply copies the language translation of your .pot file between the quotation marks for the msgstr: section for each text string included in the original .pot file.

All .pot and .po (or .mo) files need to be included in your plugin folder for the translations to be delivered to your website. Take a look at the directory structure of the popular Gravity Forms (https://gravityforms.com) plugin in Figure 6-2: You can see the original .pot file along with the translated .mo files listed within the /wp-content/plugins/wordpress-seo/languages/ plugin folder.

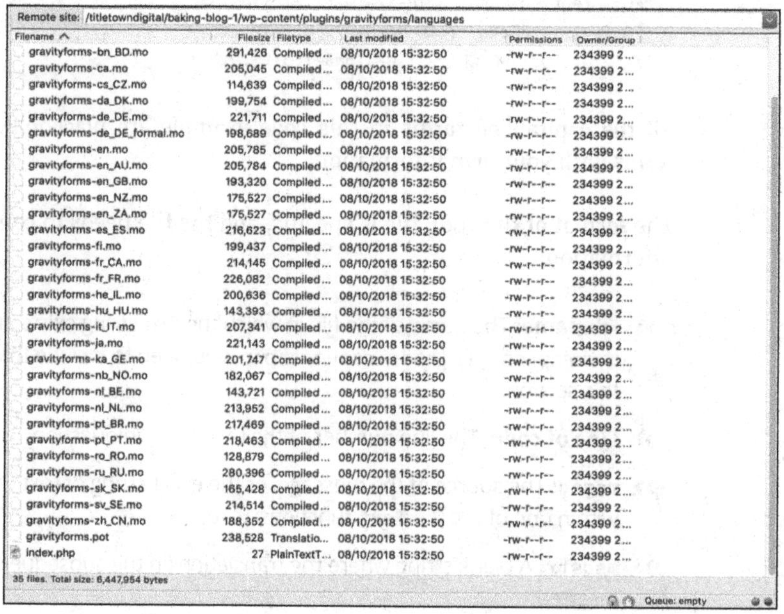

Remote site: /titletowndigital/baking-blog-1/wp-content/plugins/gravityforms/languages
Filename Filesize Filetype Last modified Permissions Owner/Group
gravityforms-bn_BD.mo 291,426 Compiled... 08/10/2018 15:32:50 -rw-r--r-- 234399 2...
gravityforms-ca.mo 205,045 Compiled... 08/10/2018 15:32:50 -rw-r--r-- 234399 2...
gravityforms-cs_CZ.mo 114,639 Compiled... 08/10/2018 15:32:50 -rw-r--r-- 234399 2...
gravityforms-da_DK.mo 199,754 Compiled... 08/10/2018 15:32:50 -rw-r--r-- 234399 2...
gravityforms-de_DE.mo 221,711 Compiled... 08/10/2018 15:32:50 -rw-r--r-- 234399 2...
gravityforms-de_DE_formal.mo 198,689 Compiled... 08/10/2018 15:32:50 -rw-r--r-- 234399 2...
gravityforms-en.mo 205,785 Compiled... 08/10/2018 15:32:50 -rw-r--r-- 234399 2...
gravityforms-en_AU.mo 205,784 Compiled... 08/10/2018 15:32:50 -rw-r--r-- 234399 2...
gravityforms-en_GB.mo 193,320 Compiled... 08/10/2018 15:32:50 -rw-r--r-- 234399 2...
gravityforms-en_NZ.mo 175,527 Compiled... 08/10/2018 15:32:50 -rw-r--r-- 234399 2...
gravityforms-en_ZA.mo 175,527 Compiled... 08/10/2018 15:32:50 -rw-r--r-- 234399 2...
gravityforms-es_ES.mo 216,623 Compiled... 08/10/2018 15:32:50 -rw-r--r-- 234399 2...
gravityforms-fi.mo 199,437 Compiled... 08/10/2018 15:32:50 -rw-r--r-- 234399 2...
gravityforms-fr_CA.mo 214,145 Compiled... 08/10/2018 15:32:50 -rw-r--r-- 234399 2...
gravityforms-fr_FR.mo 226,082 Compiled... 08/10/2018 15:32:50 -rw-r--r-- 234399 2...
gravityforms-he_IL.mo 200,636 Compiled... 08/10/2018 15:32:50 -rw-r--r-- 234399 2...
gravityforms-hu_HU.mo 143,393 Compiled... 08/10/2018 15:32:50 -rw-r--r-- 234399 2...
gravityforms-it_IT.mo 207,341 Compiled... 08/10/2018 15:32:50 -rw-r--r-- 234399 2...
gravityforms-ja.mo 221,143 Compiled... 08/10/2018 15:32:50 -rw-r--r-- 234399 2...
gravityforms-ka_GE.mo 201,747 Compiled... 08/10/2018 15:32:50 -rw-r--r-- 234399 2...
gravityforms-nb_NO.mo 182,067 Compiled... 08/10/2018 15:32:50 -rw-r--r-- 234399 2...
gravityforms-nl_BE.mo 143,721 Compiled... 08/10/2018 15:32:50 -rw-r--r-- 234399 2...
gravityforms-nl_NL.mo 213,952 Compiled... 08/10/2018 15:32:50 -rw-r--r-- 234399 2...
gravityforms-pt_BR.mo 217,469 Compiled... 08/10/2018 15:32:50 -rw-r--r-- 234399 2...
gravityforms-pt_PT.mo 218,463 Compiled... 08/10/2018 15:32:50 -rw-r--r-- 234399 2...
gravityforms-ro_RO.mo 128,879 Compiled... 08/10/2018 15:32:50 -rw-r--r-- 234399 2...
gravityforms-ru_RU.mo 280,396 Compiled... 08/10/2018 15:32:50 -rw-r--r-- 234399 2...
gravityforms-sk_SK.mo 165,428 Compiled... 08/10/2018 15:32:50 -rw-r--r-- 234399 2...
gravityforms-sv_SE.mo 214,514 Compiled... 08/10/2018 15:32:50 -rw-r--r-- 234399 2...
gravityforms-zh_CN.mo 188,352 Compiled... 08/10/2018 15:32:50 -rw-r--r-- 234399 2...
gravityforms.pot 238,528 Translatio... 08/10/2018 15:32:50 -rw-r--r-- 234399 2...
index.php 27 PlainTextT... 08/10/2018 15:32:50 -rw-r--r-- 234399 2...
35 files. Total size: 6,447,954 bytes
Queue: empty

FIGURE 6-2: The .pot and .mo files for the Gravity Forms plugin.

You, or other translators, can create unlimited .mo files for several languages. Make sure that you name the language file according to the standardized naming conventions for the different languages. The naming convention for the languages is language_*COUNTRY*.mo. The French .mo file for the wordpress-twitter-connect.php plugin, for example, is wordpress-twitter-connect-fr_FR.mo.

TIP

You can find a full list of language codes at https://www.w3schools.com/tags/ref_language_codes.asp. A full list of country codes is at https://www.nationsonline.org/oneworld/country_code_list.htm.

IN THIS CHAPTER

» Using a plugin template

» Making your plugin pluggable

» Enhancing plugins with CSS and JavaScript

» Custom post types

» Exploring little-known useful hooks

» Using custom shortcodes

Chapter 7
Plugin Tips and Tricks

When you have a WordPress plugin or two under your belt, you'll discover that you want to interact with many more parts of WordPress. WordPress is always coming out with new functionality and, with it, new API (Application Programming Interface) hooks, known as *action* and *filter hooks*, covered in Book 7, Chapter 5. This chapter discusses some of this functionality and offers you some ways to extend your use of WordPress plugins. Because this functionality involves some simple programming skills, I assume (for the purposes of this chapter) that you have some basic PHP and WordPress plugin development knowledge.

Using a Plugin Template

When you start writing WordPress plugins, you find that you spend a significant amount of time rewriting the same things. Typically, most plugins have the same basic structure and are set up the same way, meaning that they all deal with settings pages, storing options, and interacting with particular plugins, among other things. You can save hours of work each time you start a new plugin if you create a template.

Such a template varies from person to person, depending on programming styles, preferences, and the types of plugins you want to include. If you often write plugins that use your own database tables, for example, you should include tables in your template. Similarly, if your plugins almost never require options pages, leave them out of your template.

To create your own template, determine what functionality and structure your plugins usually contain and then follow these steps:

1. **Create your file structure.**

   Each plugins developer seems to have a preferred methods for organizing the files within a plugin folder. As you write more plugins, you'll find yourself repeating the same general filenames. If you find that you're including enough JavaScript and CSS in your plugins to necessitate giving the JavaScript or CSS their own files or directories, include them in your template. If you're using a lot of JavaScript or CSS, you could modify the file structure of your plugin template to look something like Figure 7-1.

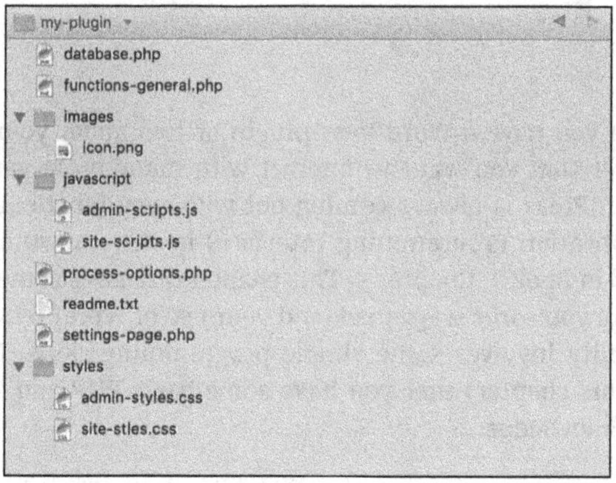

FIGURE 7-1: File structure for a plugin.

2. **Determine what functionality you generally have in your plugins.**

   If you usually have masses of code in a class, you can set up a basic class for your plugin template. Likewise, if your plugins typically have a single options page or a system of top-level and submenu pages, you can set up a general template.

3. **Create your primary plugin PHP file.**

   Usually, this file contains some general `add_action` calls, file includes, and other general initializations. (Check out Book 7, Chapter 5 for information on `add_action` calls and other plugin functions.) If you always call certain actions, set them up in your primary plugin PHP file template. If you always register a plugin function to be run when the plugin is activated (register_activation_hook) and add a menu item for the plugin in the Dashboard (admin_menu), add those calls to your primary template.

```
<?php
  $myInstance = new myPlugin();

  add_action( 'register_activation_hook','my_activation_
   plugin' );
  add_action( 'admin_menu',array( $myInstance, 'admin_
   menu' ) );

?>
```

4. **Set up the functions you use most often in the body of your primary plugin PHP file, after you add them in step 3.**

   The line of code used here — function my_activation_plugin — was added in step 3 through the use of the add_action hook. In your plugin template, you define any scripts your plugin uses by adding this function, which fires when a user activates the plugin:

```
<?php

  function my_activation_plugin(){
    //plugin activation scripts here
  }
?>
```

5. **(Optional) Create your basic class structure.**

   To do this, you might add a few lines of code that resemble the following:

```
<?php
  class myPlugin {
    var $options = ;
    var $db_version = '1';
    function myPlugin() {
      add_action( 'admin_init',array( $this,'admin_init' ) );
    }
    function admin_init(){
      //admin initializations
    }
    function process_options( $args, $data ){
      //process our options here
    }
```

```
      function admin_menu(){
        //code for admin menu
      }
      function __construct(){
        //PHP Constructor here
      }
    } //end class
  ?>
```

Obviously, your class template may be more detailed than that, depending on your particular coding styles and the types of plugins you like to write.

In addition to these steps, you may want to set up a basic plugin options page along with plugin options management scripts. Everyone uses different techniques for such things as processing plugin options, and after you determine your particular type, include the basic format in your template.

REMEMBER As your programming style, WordPress, or your interest in different types of plugins changes over time, you'll find that your template needs change too. Make sure that you update your template.

Enhancing Plugins with CSS and JavaScript

You can add functionality to a plugin in many ways. The following sections look at two methods: CSS styling and JavaScript. You may never develop a plugin that uses either method, but it's still useful to understand how to include them. Chances are good that you, as a budding plugin developer, may need this information at some point.

Calling stylesheets within a plugin

Controlling how your plugin's output looks onscreen (whether in the WordPress Dashboard or on the front end of the website or blog) is best done through a stylesheet. If you've been around web design and HTML, you're probably familiar with CSS (Cascading Style Sheets). Nearly every styling aspect for a website is controlled by a stylesheet, and WordPress is no exception. If you want to read the authoritative guide to stylesheets, visit the W3C.org website at `https://www.w3.org/Style/CSS`. (For more on CSS, see Book 6.)

You can use a single stylesheet to control how your Plugin Options screen looks on the Dashboard, how your plugin widget looks on the Dashboard, or how your plugin displays information on the front-end website.

TIP

Create and use a separate stylesheet for the plugin within the Dashboard and the plugin's display on the front end, because the stylesheets are called at different times. The back-end stylesheet is called when you're administering your site on the WordPress Dashboard, whereas the front-end stylesheet is called when a user visits the website. Additionally, this practice makes management of styling easier and cleaner.

The best practice for adding stylesheets within your plugin is to create a `/styles` directory, such as `/my-plugin/styles`. Place your stylesheets for the back end and front end inside this directory, as shown in Figure 7-1 earlier in this chapter.

To call a stylesheet from your plugin, you should use the built-in WordPress `wp_enqueue_style` function because it creates a queuing system in WordPress for loading stylesheets only when they're needed instead of on every page. Additionally, it has support for dependencies, so you can specify whether your stylesheet depends on another that should be called first. This queuing system is used for scripts, too. Moreover, the `wp_enqueue_scripts` function does the same for scripts as I discuss a little later in this section.

Suppose that you're creating a gallery plugin to display images on your website. You want your gallery to look nice, so you want to create a stylesheet that controls how the images display. Here's how to call that stylesheet in your plugin by using a simple function and action hook. (You add these lines of code to your primary plugin PHP file at the end, just before the closing `?>` tag.)

1. **Create a function in your primary plugin PHP file to register your stylesheet and invoke `wp_enqueue_style`.**

```
function add_my_plugin_stylesheet() {
   wp_register_style( 'mypluginstylesheet', '/wp-content/plugins/
    my-plugin/styles/site-style.css' );
   wp_enqueue_style( 'mypluginstylesheet' );
}
```

2. **Use the `wp_print_styles` action hook, and call your function.**

```
add_action( 'wp_enqueue_scripts', 'add_my_plugin_stylesheet' );
```

Here's a breakdown of the hooks in the function:

» **The `wp_register_style` function registers your stylesheet for later use by `wp_enqueue_style`.**

```
wp_register_style( $handle, $src, $deps, $ver, $media )
```

WARNING

The function has several parameters; the first is `$handle`, which is the name of your stylesheet.

`$handle` must be unique. You can't have more than one stylesheet with the same name in the same directory.

The second parameter, `$src`, is the path to your stylesheet from the root of WordPress. In this case, it's the full path to the file within the plugin's `styles` directory.

The remaining parameters are optional. To find out more about them, read the WordPress documentation on this function at `https://codex.wordpress.org/Function_Reference/wp_register_style`.

» **The `wp_enqueue_style` function queues the stylesheet.**

```
wp_enqueue_style( $handle, $src, $deps, $ver, $media )
```

The `$handle` parameter is the name of your stylesheet as registered with `wp_register_style`. The `$src` parameter is the path, but you don't need this parameter because you've registered the stylesheet path already. The remaining parameters are optional and explained in the WordPress documentation on this function at `https://developer.wordpress.org/reference/functions/wp_enqueue_style`.

» **The action hook that calls the function uses `wp_print_styles` to output the stylesheet to the browser.**

Figure 7-2 shows the plugin stylesheet being called in the `<HEAD>` section of the site source code.

Another example uses a stylesheet for the plugin's admin interface, which controls how your plugin option page appears within the Dashboard . These lines of code also get added to your plugin's primary PHP file (just before the closing `?>` tag):

```
add_action( 'admin_init', 'myplugin_admin_init' );

function myplugin_admin_init() {
  wp_register_style( 'mypluginadminstylesheet', '/wp-content/plugins/
    my-plugin/admin-styles.css' );
  add_action( 'admin_enqueue_scripts' 'myplugin_admin_style' );
  function myplugin_admin_style() {
      wp_enqueue_style( 'mypluginadminstylesheet' );
  }
}
```

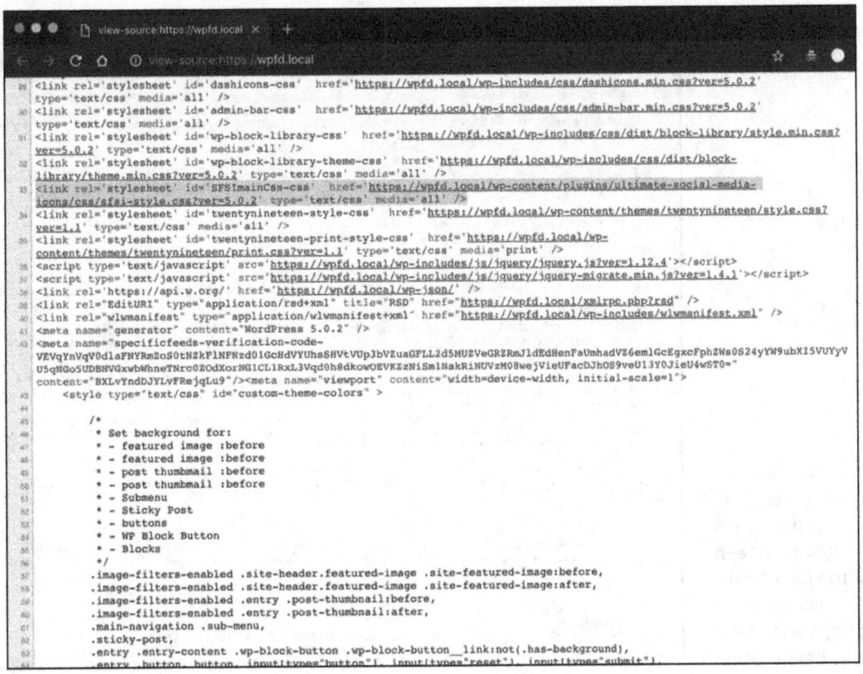

FIGURE 7-2: The source code of a website showing the plugin stylesheet being called.

This example uses some hooks that are specific to the WordPress Dashboard:

- The action hook calls `admin_init`. This hook makes sure that the function is called when the Dashboard is accessed. The callback function is `myplugin_admin_init`.
- The function registers the stylesheet, using `wp_register_style`.
- An action hook calls the `myplugin_admin_style` function. The `admin_enqueue_scripts` hook is used because it's specific to the WordPress Dashboard display.
- The function queues the stylesheet, using `wp_enqueue_style`.

Figure 7-3 shows the plugin stylesheet being called in the source code of the Plugin Options page of the Dashboard.

Calling JavaScript within a plugin

After using the `wp_register_style` and `wp_enqueue_style` functions to call stylesheets within a plugin, you can see how similar functions can call JavaScript, which has many uses within a plugin.

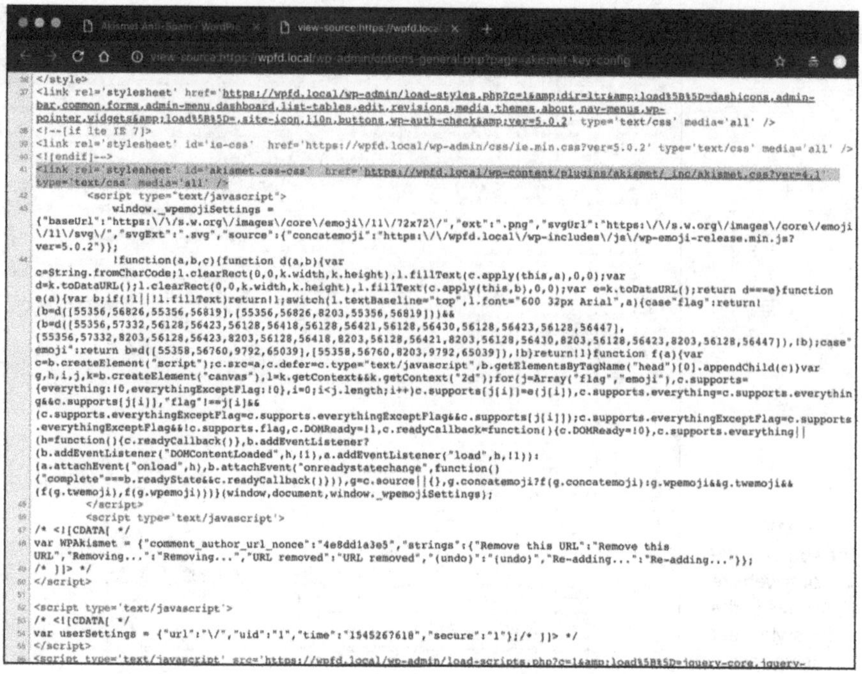

FIGURE 7-3: The source code of the Plugin Options screen of the Dashboard showing the plugin stylesheet being called.

JavaScript can control functionality within a form or display something with an effect. WordPress comes with some JavaScript in the core that you can call in your plugin, or you can write your own. As with stylesheets, it's best to store JavaScript in a separate subdirectory within your plugin, such as `/my-plugin/javascript`.

Instead of using `wp_register_style` and `wp_enqueue_style` to register and queue JavaScript, you must use `wp_register_script` and `wp_enqueue_script`, which work in much the same way and have much the same parameters. Here's an example to be added to your plugins primary PHP file, near the end before the closing `?>` tag:

```
if ( !is_admin() ) {
  wp_register_script( 'custom_script','/wp-content/plugins/
    my-plugin/javascript/custom-script.js', );
  wp_enqueue_script( 'custom_script' );
}
```

Immediately, you notice that the `wp_enqueue_script` function loads scripts in the front end of your website and on the Dashboard. Because this can cause conflicts with other scripts used by WordPress on the Dashboard display, the "if is not" (`!is_admin`) instruction tells the plugin to load JavaScript only if it's not being loaded on the Dashboard. This code loads `custom-script.js` only on the front end of the website (that is, what your site visitors see). You could add a more specific conditional `if` instruction to load JavaScript only on a certain page.

If you want to load the JavaScript in `wp-admin`, the action hook `admin_init` loads your callback function when `wp-admin` is accessed, and the `admin_print_script` function outputs the script to the browser, just like the stylesheet example.

Custom Post Types

One of the most confusing features of WordPress is custom post types. It's also a useful, powerful, and easy feature to implement and use after you understand how it works. WordPress has five default post types:

- **Post:** The most commonly used post type. Content appears in a blog in reverse sequential time order.
- **Page:** Similar to a post, but pages don't use the time-based structure of posts. Pages can be organized in a hierarchy and have their own URLs off the main site URL.
- **Attachment:** A special post type that holds information about files uploaded through the WordPress Media upload system.
- **Revisions:** A post type that holds past revisions of posts and pages as well as drafts.
- **Nav Menus:** A post type that holds information about each item in a navigation menu.

A post type is really a type of content stored in the `wp_posts` table in the WordPress database. The post type is stored in the `wp_posts` table in the `post_type` column. The information in the `post_type` column differentiates each type of content so that WordPress, a theme, or a plugin can treat the specific content types differently.

When you understand that a post type is just a method to distinguish how different content types are used, you can investigate Custom Post Types.

Suppose that you have a website about movies. Movies have common attributes such as actors, directors, writers, and producers. But suppose that you don't want to store your movie information in a post or a page because it doesn't fit either content type. This situation is where custom post types become useful. You can create a custom post type for movies and apply the common attributes of actors, directors, and so on. You can have a theme handle movies differently from a post or a page by having a custom template for the `movies` post type and creating different styling attributes and templates for the `movies` post type. You can search and archive movies differently from posts and pages.

Here's how to create a simple custom post type in WordPress by adding these lines of code to the Theme Functions template file (located in the theme file and called `functions.php`):

```
add_action( 'init','create_post_type' );                                    →1
  function create_post_type() {
    register_post_type( 'movies',                                           →3
      array(                                                                →4
        'labels'          => array (                                        →5
          'name'          => ( 'Movies' ),
          'singular_name' => ( 'Movie' ),
          'rewrite'       => array( 'slug' => 'movies' ),
        ),
        'public' => true,
      )                                                                     →11
    );
  }
```

Here's what's going on in the code:

→1 The first line is the action hook, which uses `'init'` so that it's called on the front end and on the Dashboard to display the custom post type in both.

→3 The callback function starts with the `register_post_type` function and the custom post type name. This function creates the custom post type and gives it properties.

→4 Next is an array of arguments that are the custom post type properties.

→5 The `'labels'` arguments include the name that displays on the Dashboard menu, the name that will be used (Movies), and the slug in the URL to the posts (`https://`*`yourdomain`*`.com/movies`, for example) in this custom post type.

→11 The `'public'` argument controls whether the custom post type displays on the Dashboard.

Figure 7-4 shows how the Custom Post Type page and menu item look on the Dashboard. Figure 7-5 shows a custom post type on a website.

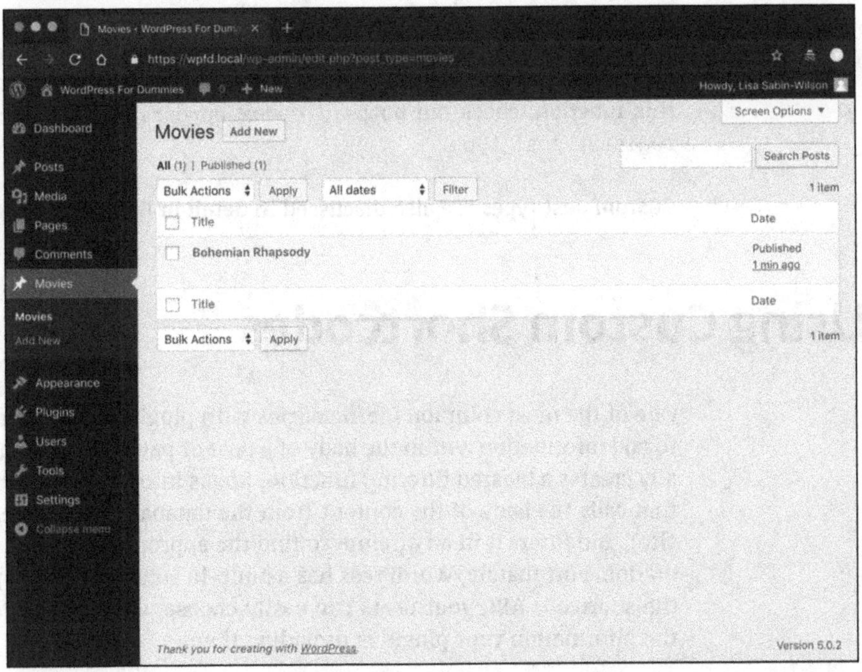

FIGURE 7-4: A custom post type on the WordPress Dashboard.

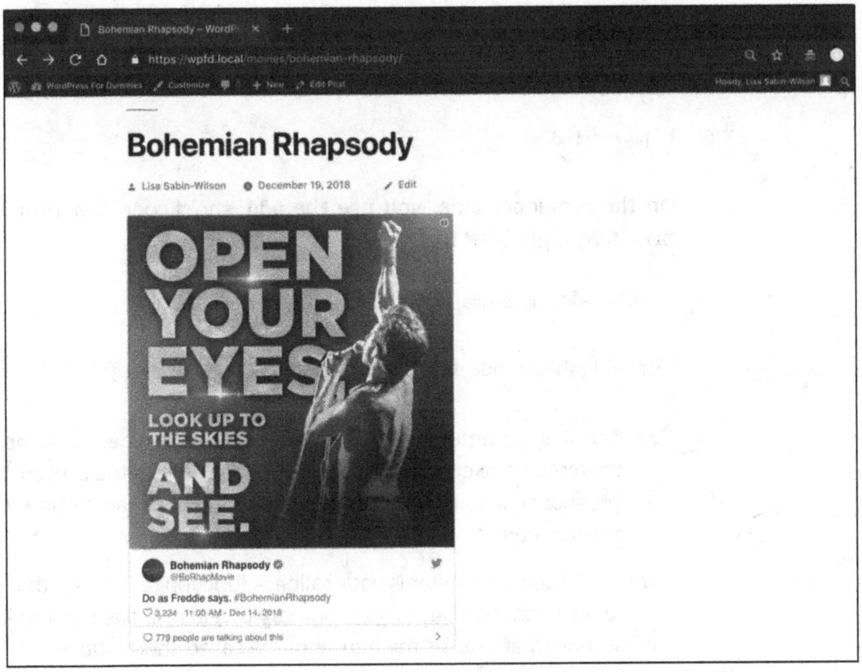

FIGURE 7-5: A custom post type shown on a website.

Many other arguments associated with register_post_type give this function its real power. For full documentation of all the arguments and the use of this function, check out https://codex.wordpress.org/Function_Reference/register_post_type.

Custom post types are also discussed in detail in Book 6, Chapter 6.

Using Custom Shortcodes

One of the most common inefficiencies with plugins occurs when a plugin wants to add information within the body of a post or page. The plugin developer manually creates a bloated filtering function, hooks into the_content (the function tag that calls the body of the content from the database and delivers it to your website), and filters it in an attempt to find the appropriate spot to display the information. Fortunately, WordPress has a built-in solution for this problem. By using the shortcode API, your users can easily choose where in a given post to display the information your plugin is providing them.

The basic premise is that you have a string of data that your plugin generates dynamically, and you want your users to determine where in each post and page that data displays. Users type a shortcode like this one within the body of their content to display information from a plugin:

```
[myshortcode]
```

On the developer side, you use the add_shortcode function and add it to your primary plugin PHP file:

```
<?php add_shortcode( $tag, $func ); ?>
```

The add_shortcode function accepts two parameters:

- » The $tag parameter is the string that users will type within the body of their content to make a call to the plugin shortcode. (In the preceding example, [myshortcode] is what the users type, so your $tag parameter would be myshortcode.)
- » The $func parameter is your callback function (a function that you still need to define in the body of your primary plugin PHP file, covered in the next section) that returns the output of the called shortcode.

The shortcode function gets added to your primary plugin PHP code, near the bottom before the closing ?> tag:

```
add_shortcode( 'myshortcode','my_shortcode' );

function my_shortcode(){
     return 'this is the text displayed by the shortcode';
}
```

In this example, you added the shortcode hook `add_shortcode( 'myshortcode','my_shortcode ');` and then defined the function (`$func`) called `my_shortcode` by telling WordPress to output the text `this is the text displayed by the shortcode`.

All your user has to do is type **[myshortcode]** somewhere in the body of his post/page editor (on the Dashboard, hover your pointer over Post and then click the Add New link), as shown in Figure 7-6. When users view the site, the shortcode that the user entered in the body of his post is translated by WordPress and displays the returned value, or *output*, of the shortcode function, as shown in Figure 7-7.

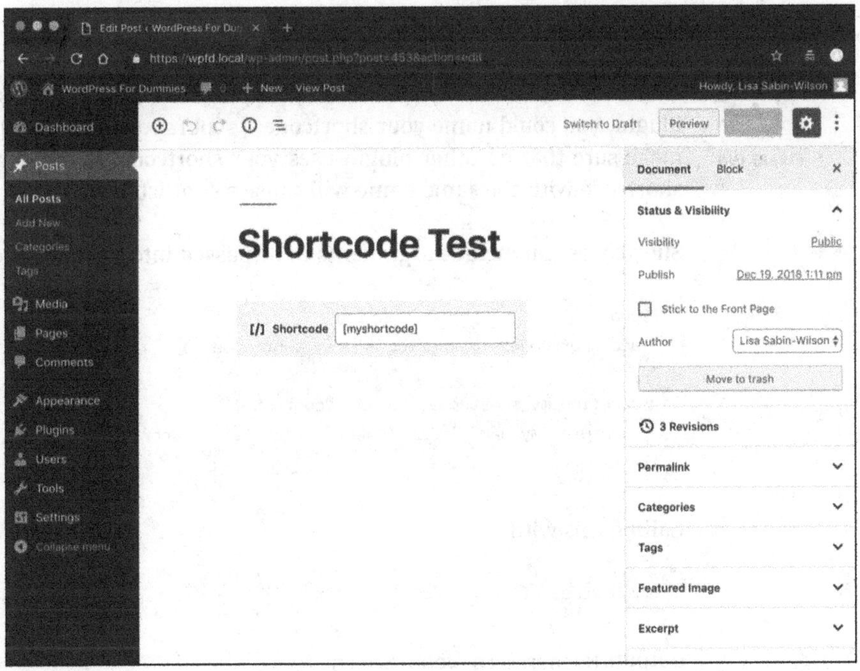

FIGURE 7-6: The post editor showing a simple shortcode.

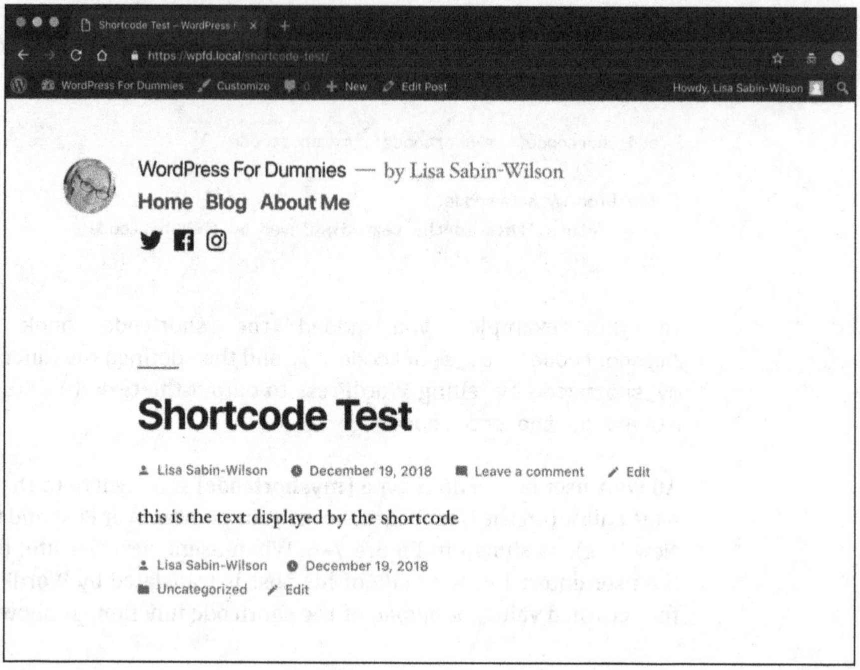

FIGURE 7-7: The shortcode is replaced by the returned value of the shortcode function.

WARNING

Shortcode names must be unique to your own plugin, so you may want to give the shortcode a name that's specific to your plugin. If your plugin is called Super SEO Plugin, you could name your shortcode: `[superseoplugincode]` in an attempt to make sure that no other plugin uses your shortcode. Another plugin that uses a shortcode with the same name will cause a conflict.

Shortcodes can include arguments to be passed into the shortcode function:

```
<?php
  add shortcode( 'myshortcode','my_shortcode' );

  function my_shortcode( $attr, $content ){
    return 'My name is ' . $attr[ 'first' ] . $attr[ 'last' ];
}
```

Calling this with

```
[myshortcode first="John" last="Smith"]
```

outputs `My name is John Smith.`

Adding Functionality to Profile Filters

Users fill out their profile data on the WordPress Dashboard by clicking the Your Profile link on the Users menu. (See Book 3, Chapter 1.) User profile fields are stored in the WordPress database in the user_metadata table; you can easily fetch them by using get_the_author_meta('description') and print them with the_author_meta('description'). If you add a Twitter Contact Info field, it appears in profiles, and you can use the_author_meta('twitter') template tags in your theme to print the account name.

Figure 7-8 shows the Twitter Contact Info field in a profile within the WordPress Dashboard.

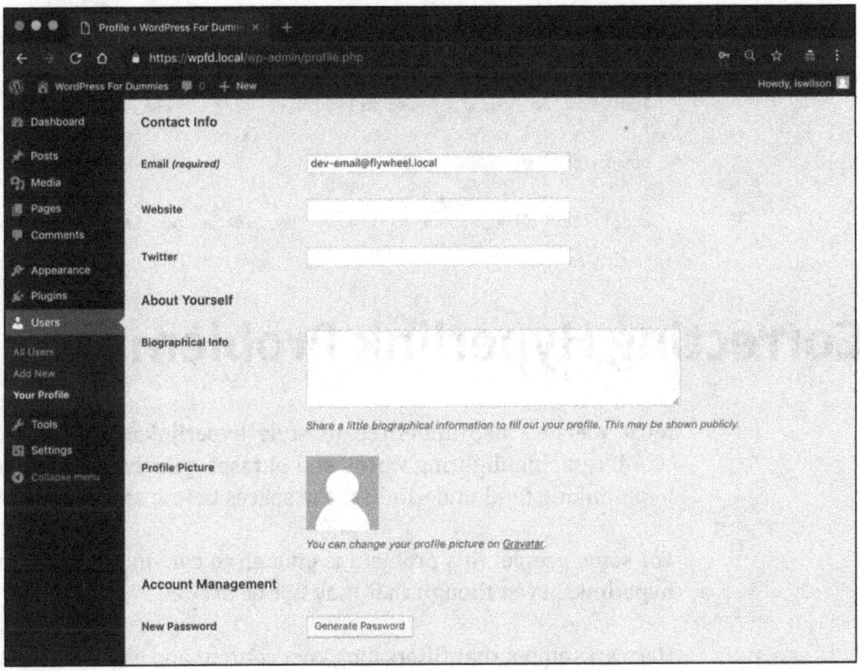

FIGURE 7-8: Custom Twitter profile field, as shown on the Dashboard.

Here, the_author_meta() template tag has a hook called the_author_{$field}, where the PHP variable $field is the requested meta field assigned to each contact type in the user profile files, such as aim in the preceding example. These dynamic hooks are powerful because they allow you to narrow your target.

In this example, I use the dynamic the_author_twitter hook to change the result from "lisasabinwilson" to <a href="http://twitter.com/lisasabinwilson">@lisasabinwilson</a>. When you call the_author_meta(

'twitter') in your theme, you get a clickable link to my Twitter profile. Start by entering the following lines of code in your Theme Functions file (functions.php) in your active theme folder. (Add this code toward the bottom of the file before the closing ?> tag.)

```
/**
 * Add Twitter to the list of contact methods captured via profiles.
 */
function my_add_twitter_author_meta( $contact_methods ) {
$contact_methods['twitter'] = 'Twitter';
return $contact_methods;
}

add_filter( 'user_contactmethods', 'my_add_twitter_author_meta' );

function my_link_author_twitter_accounts( $value ) {
if ( strlen( $value ) ) {
$url = esc_url( 'http://twitter.com/' . $value );
$value = '<a href="' . esc_url($url) . '">@' . esc_html( $value ) . '</a>';
}
return $value;
}
add_filter( 'the_author_twitter', 'my_link_author_twitter_accounts' );
```

Correcting Hyperlink Problems

Most websites use underline to style hyperlinks. When producing content in WordPress, highlighting words and phrases quickly to add hyperlinks can lead to hyperlinking (and underlining) the spaces before and after your anchor text.

For some people, this problem is enough to convince them to hide underlines for hyperlinks, even though that may not be desired.

Here's a snippet that filters blog post content and ensures that you don't have any spaces on the wrong side of the tag or between a closing tag and punctuation. Add this code to your Theme Functions (functions.php) file:

```
/**
 * Prevents underlined spaces to the left and right of links.
 *
 * @param string $content
 * @return string Content
```

```
 */

function my_anchor_text_trim_spaces( $content ) {

// Remove spaces immediately after an <a> tag.
$content = preg_replace( '#<a([^>]+)>\s+#', ' <a$1>', $content );

// Remove spaces immediately before an </a> tag.
$content = preg_replace( '#\s+</a>#', '</a> ', $content );

// Remove single spaces between an </a> tag and punctuation.
$content = preg_replace( '#</a>\s([.,!?;])#', '</a>$1', $content );

return $content;
}
add_filter( 'the_content', 'my_anchor_text_trim_spaces' );
```

REMEMBER

HTML ignores more than one space in a row (also more than one tab character and line break) unless you're using the `pre` element or nonbreaking space entities (` `). Therefore, even if your converted text contains two consecutive spaces, the browser won't show it any differently.

8

Running Multiple Sites with WordPress

Contents at a Glance

IN THIS CHAPTER

» Discovering where multiple sites began

» Exploring what you can do with multiple sites

» Configuring your web server

Chapter 1

An Introduction to Multiple Sites

In this chapter, I introduce you to the network feature that's built into the WordPress software. The network feature allows you, the site owner, to add and maintain multiple blogs within one installation of WordPress. In this chapter, you discover how to set up the WordPress network feature, explore settings and configurations, gain an understanding of the Network Administrator role, determine which configuration is right for you (do you want subdirectories or subdomains?), and find some great resources to help you on your way.

When the network features are enabled, users of your network can run their own sites within your installation of WordPress. They also have access to their own Dashboards with the same options and features covered in the chapters in Book 3. Heck, it probably would be a great idea to buy a copy of this book for every member of your network so that everyone can become familiar with the WordPress Dashboard and features, too. At least have a copy on hand so that people can borrow yours!

Deciding When to Use the Multisite Feature

Usually, for multiple users to post to one site, the default WordPress setup is sufficient. The *Multi* part of the WordPress Multisite feature's name doesn't refer to how many users have been added to your WordPress website; it refers to the ability to run multiple sites in one installation of the WordPress software. *Multisite* is a bit of a misnomer and an inaccurate depiction of what the software does. *Network of sites* is a much closer description.

Determining whether to use the Multisite feature depends on user access and publishing activity. Each site on the network shares a code base and users but is a self-contained unit. Users still have to access the back end of each site to manage options or post to that site. A limited number of general options are available networkwide, and posting isn't one of those options.

You can use multiple sites on a network to create the appearance that only one site exists. Put the same theme on each site, and the visitor doesn't realize that the sites are separate. This technique is a good way to separate sections of a magazine site, using editors for complete sections (sites) but not letting them access other parts of the network or the back ends of other sites.

Another factor to consider is how comfortable you are with editing files directly on the server. Setting up the network involves accessing the server directly, and ongoing maintenance and support for your users often leads to the network owner's doing the necessary maintenance, which is not for the faint of heart.

Generally, you should use a network of sites in the following cases:

- **You want multiple sites and one installation.** You're a blogger or site owner who wants to maintain another site, possibly with a subdomain or a separate domain, with both sites on one web host. You're comfortable with editing files; you want to work with one code base to make site maintenance easier; and most of your plugins and themes are accessible to all the sites. You can have one login across the sites and manage each site individually.
- **You want to host blogs or sites for others.** This process is a little more involved. You want to set up a network in which users sign up for their own sites or blogs below (or on) your main site and you maintain the technical aspects.

Because all files are shared, some aspects are locked down for security purposes. One of the most puzzling security measures for new users is suppression of errors. Most PHP errors (such as those that occur when you install a faulty plugin or incorrectly edit a file) don't output messages to the screen. Instead, WordPress displays what I like to call the White Screen of Death.

Finding and using error logs and doing general debugging are necessary skills for managing your own network. Even if your web host sets up the ongoing daily or weekly tasks for you, managing a network can involve a steep learning curve.

REMEMBER

When you enable the multisite feature, the existing WordPress site becomes the main site in the installation.

Although WordPress can be quite powerful, in the following situations the management of multiple sites has its limitations:

- **One web hosting account is used for the installation.** You can't use multiple hosting accounts.
- **You want to post to multiple blogs at one time.** WordPress doesn't allow this practice by default.
- **If you choose subdirectory sites, the main site regenerates permalinks with `/blog/` in them to prevent collisions with subsites.** Plugins are available to prevent this regeneration.

The best example of a large blog network with millions of blogs and users is the hosted service at WordPress.com (`https://wordpress.com`). At WordPress.com, people are invited to sign up for an account and start a blog by using the Multisite feature within the WordPress platform on the WordPress server. When you enable this feature on your own domain and enable the user registration feature, you're inviting users to do the following:

- Create an account.
- Create a blog on your WordPress installation (on your domain).
- Create content by publishing blog posts.
- Upload media files such as photos, audio, and video.
- Invite friends to view the blog or sign up for their own accounts.

Understanding the Difference between Sites and Blogs

Each additional blog in a WordPress Multisite network is a *site* instead of a *blog*. What's the difference?

Largely, the difference is one of perception. Everything functions the same way, but people see greater possibilities when they no longer think of each site as being "just" a blog. WordPress can be much more:

- With the addition of the WordPress MU Domain Mapping plugin, (`https://wordpress.org/plugins/wordpress-mu-domain-mapping`), you can manage multiple sites that have unique domain names. None of these sites even has to be a blog. The sites can have blog elements, or they can be static sites that use only pages.
- The built-in options let you choose between subdomains or subdirectory sites when you install the network. If you install WordPress in the root of your web space, you get `subdomain.`*`yourdomain.com`* (if you choose subdomains) or *`yourdomain.com`*`/subdirectory` (if you choose subdirectory). Book 8, Chapter 2 discusses the differences and advantages.

  REMEMBER

  After you choose the kind of sites you want to host and then create those sites, you can't change them. These sites are served virtually, meaning that they don't exist as files or folders anywhere on the server; they exist only in the database. The correct location is served to the browser by using rewrite rules in the `.htaccess` file. (See Book 2, Chapter 5.)
- The main, or parent, site of the network also can be a landing page of the entire network of sites, showcasing content from other sites in the network and drawing in visitors further.

Setting Up the Optimal Hosting Environment

This chapter assumes that you already have the WordPress software installed and running correctly on your web server and that your web server meets the minimum requirements to run WordPress.

Before you enable the WordPress Multisite feature, you need to determine how you're going to use the feature. You have a couple of options:

- Manage a few of your own WordPress blogs or websites.
- Run a full-blown blogging network with several hundred blogs and multiple users.

If you're planning to run a few of your own sites with the WordPress network feature, your current hosting situation probably is appropriate. If, however, you plan to host a large network with hundreds of blogs and multiple users, you should consider contacting your host and increasing your bandwidth, as well as the disk-space limitations on your account.

WARNING

Beyond the necessary security measures, time, and administrative tasks that go into running a community of sites, you have a few more things to worry about. Creating a community increases resource use, bandwidth use, and disk space on your web server. In many cases, if you go over the limits assigned to you by your web host, you'll incur great cost. Make sure that you anticipate your bandwidth and disk-space needs before running a large network on your website. (Don't say I didn't warn you!)

Checking out shared versus dedicated hosting

Many WordPress network communities start with grand dreams of developing a large and active community. Be realistic about how your community will operate to make the right hosting choice for yourself and your community.

Small Multisite communities can be handled easily by a shared-server solution, whereas larger, more active communities may require a dedicated-server solution. The difference lies in the names:

- **Shared-server solution:** You have one account on one server that has several other accounts on it. Think of this solution as apartment living. One apartment building has several apartments in which multiple people live, all under one roof.
- **Dedicated-server solution:** You have one account. You have one server. That server is dedicated to your account, and your account is dedicated to the server. Think of this solution as living in a private home where you don't share living space with anyone else.

A dedicated-server solution is a more expensive investment for your Multisite community than a shared-server solution. Your decision should be based on realistic estimates of how big and how active your community will be. You can move from a shared-server solution to a dedicated-server solution if your community gets larger than you expected, but starting with the right solution for your community is easier.

Exploring subdomains versus subdirectories

The WordPress Multisite feature gives you two ways to run a network of sites on your domain: the subdomain option and the subdirectory option. The most popular option (and recommended structure) sets up subdomains for the sites created within a WordPress network. With the subdomain option, the username of the site appears first, followed by your domain name. With the subdirectory option, your domain name appears first, followed by the username of the site.

Which one should you choose? You can see the difference in the URLs of these two options by comparing the following examples:

- A **subdomain** looks like this: `http://username.yourdomain.com`
- A **subdirectory** looks like this: `http://yourdomain.com/username`

While the network is being set up, tables that contain information about the network, including the main site URL, are added to the database. If you're developing a site or want to change the domain later, you need to change every reference to the domain name in the database. See Book 2, Chapter 3 for more about the WordPress database structure, including how data is stored in tables, as well as the use of a popular database administration tool called phpMyAdmin to manage, view, and edit database tables.

Choosing Linux, Apache, MySQL, and PHP server environments

A network of sites works best on a LAMP (Linux, Apache, MySQL, and PHP) server with the `mod_rewrite` Apache module enabled. `mod_rewrite` is an Apache module that builds URLs that are easy to read. (See the nearby "Apache mod_rewrite" sidebar for more information.) In WordPress, this Apache module is used for permalinks. If your installation uses any permalink other than the default, `?p=123`, you're okay. Your web host can help you determine whether your web server allows this practice; most servers do, and `mod_rewrite` is a requirement for setting up the WordPress Multisite feature. (You can find more information on permalink structures in Book 3, Chapter 2.)

APACHE MOD_REWRITE

Apache (`http://httpd.apache.org`) is software that's loaded and running on your web server. Usually, the only person who has access to Apache files is the web server administrator (probably your web host). Depending on your own web-server account and configuration, you may have access to the Apache software files.

The Apache module that's necessary for the WordPress network to create nice permalink URLs is called `mod_rewrite`. This module must be configured to be active and installed on your server.

You or your web host administrator can make sure that the Apache `mod_rewrite` is activated on your server by opening the `httpd.conf` file and verifying that the following line is included:

```
LoadModule rewrite_module /libexec/mod_rewrite.so
```

If it isn't, type that line on its own line and save the file. You probably need to restart Apache before the change takes effect.

For the purposes of this chapter, I stick to the LAMP server setup because it's most similar to the average web host and is most widely used.

WARNING

Remember that the Apache `mod_rewrite` module is required for WordPress multisites. If you don't know whether your current hosting environment has this module in place, drop an email to your hosting provider and ask. The provider can answer that question for you (in addition to installing the module for you in the event that your server doesn't have it).

TECHNICAL STUFF

Networks also work well on Nginx and Lightspeed servers, but many users have reported having much difficulty on IIS (Windows) servers. Therefore, I don't recommend setting up WordPress with Multisite features in a Windows server environment.

Subdomain sites work by way of a virtual host entry in Apache, also known as a wildcard subdomain. On shared hosts, your web hosting provider's support team has to enable this entry for you (or may already have done so for all accounts). It's best to ask your hosting provider before you begin. In these situations, the domain you use for your install must be the default domain in your account. Otherwise, the URLs of your subsites will fail to work properly or won't have a folder name in the URL.

WARNING

Some hosts may require you to have a dedicated IP address, but this requirement isn't a specific software requirement for a WordPress network to function.

Before proceeding with the final steps in enabling the WordPress Multisite feature, you need to get a few items in order on your web server. You also need to decide how the multiple sites within your network will be handled. You need to have these configurations in place to run the WordPress network successfully.

Adding a virtual host to the Apache configuration

You need to add a hostname record pointing at your web server in the Domain Name System (DNS) configuration tool available in your web server's administration software, such as WebHost Manager (WHM), a popular web host administration tool.

WARNING

In this section, you edit and configure Apache server files. If you can perform the configurations in this section yourself (and if you have access to the Apache configuration files), this section is for you. If you don't know how, are uncomfortable with adjusting these settings, or don't have access to configurations in your web-server software, ask your hosting provider for help or hire a consultant to perform the configurations for you. I can't stress enough that you shouldn't edit the Apache server files yourself if you aren't comfortable with it or don't fully understand what you're doing. Web-hosting providers have support staff to help you with these things if you need it; take advantage!

The hostname record looks like this: `*.`*`yourdomain.com`* (where *`yourdomain.com`* is replaced by your actual domain name).

In the `httpd.conf` file, you need to make some adjustments in the `<VirtualHost>` section of that file. If you can't find it, you can search for: VirtualHost in your editor. Follow these steps:

1. **Find the `<VirtualHost>` section in the `httpd.conf` file.**

   This line of the `httpd.conf` file provides directives, or configurations, that apply to your website.

2. **Find a line in the `<VirtualHost>` section of the `httpd.conf` that looks like this:**

   ```
   AllowOverride None
   ```

3. **Replace that line with this line:**

```
AllowOverride FileInfo Options
```

4. **On a new line, type** ServerAlias *.*yourdomain*.com.

   Replace *yourdomain*.com with whatever your domain is. This line defines the host name for your network site and is essential for the virtual host to work correctly.

5. **Save and close the `httpd.conf` file.**

You also need to add a wildcard subdomain DNS record. Depending on how your domain is set up, you can do this at your registrar or your web host. If you simply pointed to your web host's nameservers, you can add more DNS records at your web host in the web server administration interface, such as WHM (Web Host Manager).

You also should add a `CNAME` record with a value of *. CNAME stands for Canonical Name and is a record stored in the DNS settings of your Apache web server that tells Apache you want to associate a new subdomain with the main-account domain. Applying the value of * tells Apache to send any subdomain requests to your main domain. From there, WordPress looks up that subdomain in the database to see whether it exists.

Networks require a great deal more server memory (RAM) than typical WordPress sites (those that don't use the Multisite feature) because multisites generally are bigger, have a lot more traffic, and use more database space and resources because multiple sites are running (as opposed to one with regular WordPress). You aren't simply adding instances of WordPress. You're multiplying the processing and resource use of the server when you run the WordPress Multisite feature. Although smaller instances of a network run fine on most web hosts, you may find that when your network grows, you need more memory. I generally recommend that you start with a hosting account with access to at least 256MB of RAM (memory).

For each site created, nine tables are added to the single database. Each table has a prefix similar to `wp_BLOG-ID_tablename` (where `BLOG-ID` is a unique ID assigned to the site).

The only exception is the main site: Its tables remain untouched and remain the same. (See Book 2, Chapter 3 to see how the tables look.) With WordPress multisites, all new installations leave the main blog tables untouched and number additional site tables sequentially when every new site is added to the network.

Configuring PHP

In this section, you edit the PHP configuration on your web server. PHP needs to have the following configurations in place in the `php.ini` file on your web server to run WordPress Multisite on your server:

- Set your PHP to *not* display any error messages in the visitor's browser window. (Usually, this setting is turned off by default; double-check to be sure.)
- Find out whether your PHP is compiled with memory-limit checks. You can find out by looking for the text `memory_limit` in the `php.ini` file. Usually, the default limit is 8MB. Increase the memory limit to at least 64MB or even 128MB to prevent PHP memory errors when you run WordPress Multisite.

TIP

The default memory limit for WordPress is 40MB or 64MB for a Multisite setup. As an alternative to editing the `php.ini` file on your web server to increase the PHP memory limit, you can add this line to the `wp-config.php` file of your WordPress installation:

```
define( 'WP_MEMORY_LIMIT', '64M' );
```

The `64M` portion of that line of code defines the memory limit in megabytes, and you can set it to any value that doesn't exceed 512MB.

IN THIS CHAPTER

» Enabling the network

» Configuring the network installation

» Disabling the network

Chapter 2

Setting Up and Configuring Network Features

This chapter covers how to find the files you need to edit the network, how to enable multiple sites in the network, and how to remove the network should you no longer want to have multiple sites in your WordPress install.

By default, access to network settings is disabled to ensure that users don't set up their network without researching all that the setup entails. Setting up a network involves more than configuring options or turning on a feature, so before enabling and setting up a network, be sure that you read Book 8, Chapter 1.

Here's what you need:

- Backups of your site (explained in Book 2, Chapter 7)
- Access to the `wp-config.php` file for editing (Book 2, Chapter 5)
- Enabled wildcard subdomains (covered in Book 8, Chapter 1) if you're using subdomains

Enabling the Network Feature

You need to enable access to the Network menu so you can set up the network and allow the creation of multiple sites.

WARNING

It's a good idea to download a copy of the original `wp-config.php` file your web server and store it on your computer to keep it safe. That way, if you make any mistakes or experience any errors after altering it, you can easily upload the original and start over.

WARNING

If you have any plugins installed and activated on your WordPress installation, deactivate them before you proceed with the network setup. WordPress won't allow you to continue until you deactivate all your plugins.

Follow these steps:

1. **Download the file called `wp-config.php` from the WordPress installation on your web server.**

   It's easiest to use an SFTP program to download a copy of this file from your web server to your computer. If you need a refresher on SFTP, refer to Book 2, Chapter 2.

2. **Using your preferred text editor, open the `wp-config.php` file.**

   Windows users can use Notepad to edit the file; Mac users can use TextEdit.

3. **Click at the end of the line that reads `define( 'DB_COLLATE', '' );` and then press Enter (or Return on a Mac) to create a new blank line.**
4. **Type the following on the new blank line:**

   ```
   define( 'WP_ALLOW_MULTISITE', true );
   ```

5. **Save the file to your computer as `wp-config.php`.**
6. **Upload the new file to your web server in your WordPress installation directory.**
7. **Go to your WordPress Dashboard in your browser.**

   You see a new item, labeled Network Setup, on the Tools menu.

8. **Click the Network Setup link on the Tools menu.**

   The Create a Network of WordPress Sites screen displays. (It's covered in the next section and shown in Figure 2-1.) You also see a reminder to deactivate all your plugins before continuing with network setup.

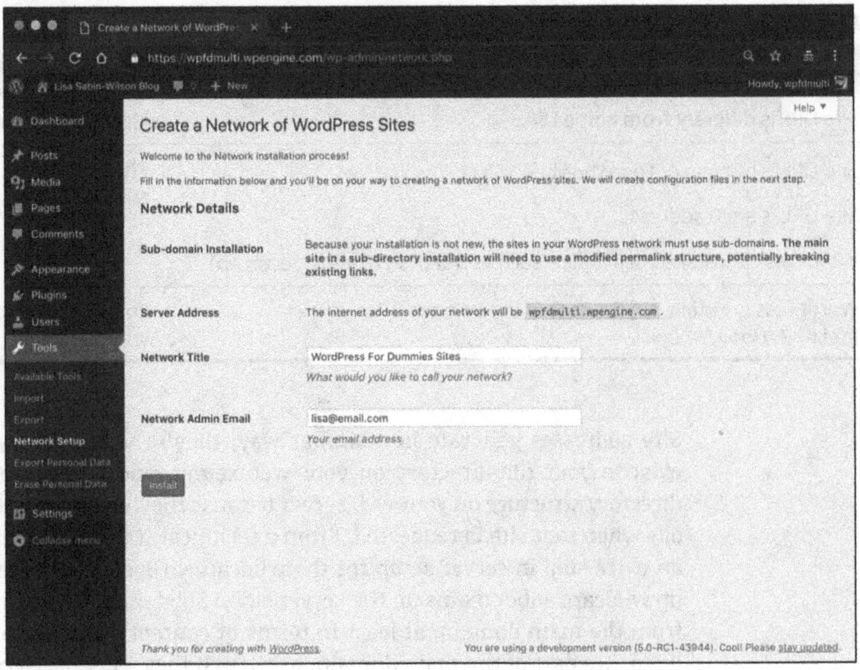

FIGURE 2-1: The Create a Network of WordPress Sites screen in your WordPress Dashboard.

Exploring the Difference between Subdirectories and Subdomains

Before you start setting up the network, the Create a Network of WordPress Sites screen informs you that your installation isn't new and that the sites in your WordPress network must use subdomains as opposed to subdirectories (refer to Figure 2-1). During the Network installation process (covered in the next section of this chapter), you can make a change in the configuration if you want to use a subdirectory setup as opposed to a subdomain.

REMEMBER

In some cases, depending on your setup, your choice may be limited. WordPress does some autodetection with information about your installation and may prevent you from choosing an option that won't work with your setup.

Table 2-1 explains some of the limitations you may encounter as you try to enable a subdomain or subdirectory format.

TABLE 2-1 Common Network Setup Situations

Situation	Format
Site URL is different from home URL.	Network can't be enabled.
Site URL is `https://localhost`. Site URL is an IP address. WordPress is installed in a folder (such as `http://`*`domain`*`.com/wp`).	The Network can use subdirectories only.
WordPress is installed in the root of the domain (`http://`*`domain`*`.com`).	Subdomains are the default, but you can choose either.

Site addresses generate in a similar way; they're virtual. They don't physically exist in your file directory on your web server, and you won't see them in the directory structure on your web server because they're served to the browser *virtually* when that site is requested. From a technical standpoint, subdomains require an extra step in server setup for the wildcards. (Book 8, Chapter 1 covers setting up wildcard subdomains on the server side.) Subdomains are somewhat separated from the main domain, at least in terms of content. Subdirectories, on the other hand, are part of the main domain, as though they were pages off the main site.

Because each site's URL is saved in its tables in the database, after you pick the subsites you want to create, you can't switch from subdirectories to subdomains (or vice versa) without reinstalling the network.

Each site format (subdomain or subdirectory) offers certain search engine optimization (SEO) benefits. Search engines read subdomains as separate sites on your web host; therefore, the subdomains maintain their page rank and authority, and search engines list multiple results for your domain. Subdirectories are read as pages or sections off your main domain. They also help the main domain's page rank and authority, and provide one result for your domain in search engines.

TIP

If you want your extra sites to have separate domain names, you still need to pick one of these options. Book 8, Chapter 6 covers top-level domains.

Installing the Network on Your Site

The Network Details section of the Create a Network of WordPress Sites page (refer to Figure 2-1 earlier in this chapter) has options that are filled in automatically. The server address, for example, is pulled from your installation and can't be edited. The network title and administrator's email address are pulled from your installation database, too, because your initial WordPress site is the main site of the network.

Follow these steps to complete the installation (and be sure to have your preferred text-editor program handy):

1. **Click the Install button at the bottom of the Create a Network of WordPress Sites screen of your WordPress Dashboard.**

   The Enabling the Network screen opens, as shown in Figure 2-2.

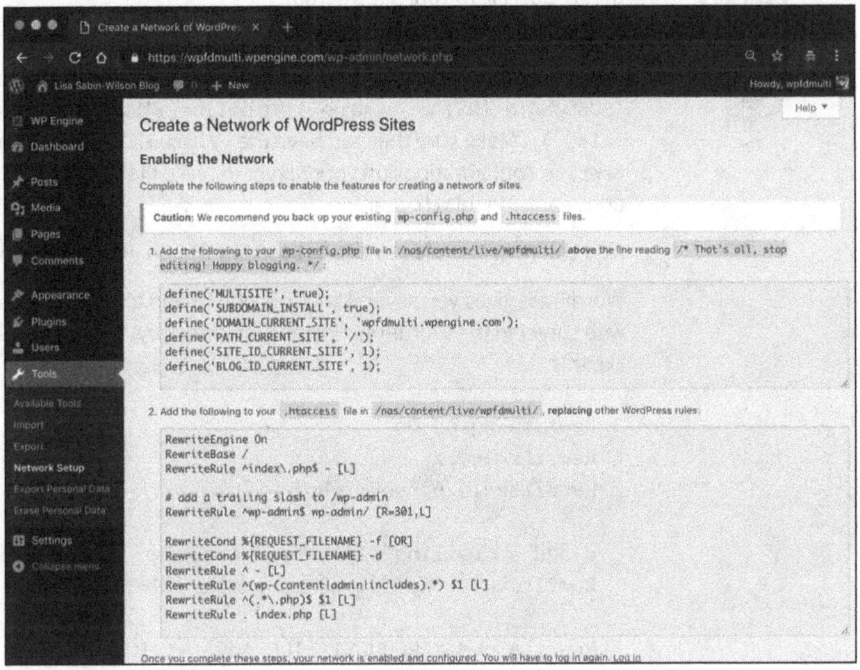

FIGURE 2-2: The Enabling the Network screen.

2. **Add the required network-related configuration lines to the `wp-config.php` file following the `define( 'WP_ALLOW_MULTISITE', true );` code you added earlier.**

   On the Enabling the Network screen, WordPress gives you up to six lines of configuration rules that need to be added to the `wp-config.php` file. The lines of code you add may look like this:

```
define( 'MULTISITE', true );
define( 'SUBDOMAIN_INSTALL', true );
define( 'DOMAIN_CURRENT_SITE', 'domain.com' );
define( 'PATH_CURRENT_SITE', '/' );
define( 'SITE_ID_CURRENT_SITE', 1 );
define( 'BLOG_ID_CURRENT_SITE', 1 );
```

These lines of code provide configuration settings for WordPress by telling WordPress whether it's using subdomains, what the base URL of your website is, and what your site's current path is. This code also assigns a unique ID of `1` to your website for the main installation site of your WordPress Multisite network.

WARNING

The lines of code that appear on the Enabling the Network screen are unique to your installation of WordPress. Make sure that you copy the lines of code on the Create a Network of WordPress Sites screen of *your* installation because they're specific to your site's setup.

TIP

My WordPress installation sets up my network to use subdomains instead of subdirectories. If you'd like to use subdirectories, change `define( 'SUBDOMAIN_INSTALL', true );` to `define( 'SUBDOMAIN_INSTALL', false );`. Make sure that you have the <VirtualHost> and Apache `mod_rewrite` configurations on your server in place first; I cover both configurations earlier in this chapter.

3. **Add the rewrite rules to the `.htaccess` file on your web server.**

   WordPress gives you several lines of code to add to the `.htaccess` file on your web server in the WordPress installation directory. The lines look something like this:

```
RewriteEngine On
RewriteBase /
RewriteRule ^index\.php$ - [L]

# add a trailing slash to /wp-admin
RewriteRule ^wp-admin$ wp-admin/ [R=301,L]

RewriteCond %{REQUEST_FILENAME} -f [OR]
RewriteCond %{REQUEST_FILENAME} -d
RewriteRule ^ - [L]
RewriteRule ^(wp-(content|admin|includes).*) $1 [L]
RewriteRule ^(.*\.php)$ $1 [L]
RewriteRule . index.php [L]
```

REMEMBER

In Book 8, Chapter 1, I discuss the required Apache module `mod_rewrite`, which you must have installed on your web server to run WordPress Multisite. The rules that you add to the `.htaccess` file on your web server are `mod_rewrite` rules, and they need to be in place so that your web server tells WordPress how to handle things like permalinks for posts, pages, media, and other uploaded files. If these rules aren't in place, the WordPress Multisite feature won't work correctly.

4. **Copy the lines of code that you entered in step 3, open the `.htaccess` file, and paste the code there.**

   Replace the rules that already exist in that file.

5. **Save the `.htaccess` file, and upload it to your web server.**

6. **Return to your WordPress Dashboard, and click the Log In link at the bottom of the Enabling the Network screen.**

   You're logged out of WordPress because by following these steps, you changed some of the browser cookie-handling rules in the `wp-config.php` and `.htaccess` files.

7. **Log in to WordPress by entering your username and password in the login form.**

With the Multisite feature enabled, you see a link to My Sites. If you hover your mouse pointer over that link, the Network Admin link appears on the drop-down menu in the top-left corner of the Dashboard. The Network Admin Dashboard is where you, as the site owner, administer and manage your multisite WordPress network. (See Book 8, Chapter 3.)

Disabling the Network

At some point, you may decide that running a network of sites isn't for you, and you may find that you want to disable the Multisite feature. Before disabling the network, you want to save any content from the other sites by making a full backup of your database. Book 2, Chapter 7 has detailed information about backing up your site.

The first step is restoring the original `wp-config.php` file and `.htaccess` files that you saved earlier. (Refer to "Enabling the Network Feature" earlier in this chapter.) This step causes your WordPress installation to stop displaying the Network Admin menu and the extra sites.

You also may want to delete the tables that were added, which permanently removes the extra sites from your installation. Book 2, Chapter 3 takes you through the WordPress database, including the use of a popular database administration tool called phpMyAdmin. You can use that tool to delete the Multisite tables from your WordPress database when you want to deactivate the feature. The extra database tables that are no longer required when you aren't running the WordPress Multisite feature include

- `wp_blogs`: This database table contains one record per site and is used for site lookup.
- `wp_blog_versions`: This database table is used internally for upgrades.
- `wp_registration_log`: This database table contains information on sites created when a user signed up if he chose to create a site at the same time.

» wp_signups: This database table contains information on users who signed up for the network.

» wp_site: This database table contains one record per WordPress network.

» wp_sitemeta: This database table contains network settings.

Additionally, you can delete any database tables that have blog IDs associated with them. These tables start with prefixes that look like wp_1_, wp_2_, wp_3_, and so on.

REMEMBER

WordPress adds new tables each time you add a new site to your network. Those database tables are assigned unique numbers incrementally.

Dealing with Common Errors

Occasionally, you may enter a configuration setting incorrectly or change your mind about the kind of network you require. If you installed WordPress, enabled the network, and then want to move it to a new location, you'll encounter errors when changing the URL. The proper method is to move WordPress first, disable the network if you installed it, and then enable the network at the new location.

To change from subdomains to subfolders, or vice versa, follow these steps:

1. **Delete the extra sites, if any were created.**
2. **Edit `wp-config.php`, changing the value of `define( 'SUBDOMAIN_INSTALL', true );` to `define( 'SUBDOMAIN_INSTALL', false );`.**

   To switch from subdomains to subdirectories, change `false` to `true`.
3. **Save the `wp-config.php` file, and upload it to your website.**
4. **Visit the Dashboard of WordPress, click the Permalink link on the Settings menu, and click the Save Changes button.**

   This step saves and resets your permalink structure settings and flushes the internal rewrite rules, which are slightly different for subdomains than they are for subdirectories.

REMEMBER

You can't perform this process if you want to keep extra sites.

IN THIS CHAPTER

» Getting familiar with the Network Admin Dashboard

» Managing your network

» Preventing spam blogs

Chapter 3
Becoming a Network Admin

After you enable the WordPress network option and become a network admin, you can examine the various settings that are available to you and go over the responsibilities you have while running a network.

As a network admin, you can access the Network Admin Dashboard, which includes several submenus, to manage the sites in your network, as well as the overall settings for your network. This chapter discusses the menu items and options on the Network Admin screen, guides you in setting network options, and discusses the best ways to prevent spam and spam blogs (splogs).

Exploring the Network Admin Dashboard

When you visit the Dashboard after activating the Multisite feature, the toolbar includes the My Sites menu, which contains the Network Admin link. (See Figure 3-1.)

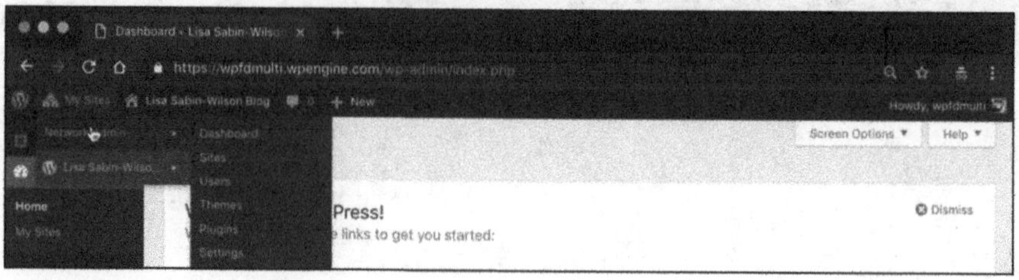

FIGURE 3-1: The Network Admin menu.

WordPress has separated the Network Admin menu features from the regular (Site Admin) Dashboard menu features to make it easier for you to know which part of your site you're managing. If you're performing actions that maintain your main website — publishing posts or pages, creating or editing categories, and so on — you work in the regular Dashboard (Site Admin). If you're managing any of the network sites, plugins, and themes for the network sites or registered users, you work in the Network Admin section of the Dashboard.

REMEMBER

Keep in mind the distinct differences between the Site Admin and Network Admin Dashboards, as well as their menu features. WordPress does its best to know which features you're attempting to work with, but if you find yourself getting lost on the Dashboard, or if you're not finding a menu or feature that you're used to seeing, make sure that you're working in the correct section of the Dashboard.

The Network Admin Dashboard (see Figure 3-2) is similar to the regular WordPress Dashboard; however, the modules pertain to the network of sites. Options include creating a site, creating a user, and searching existing sites and users. Obviously, you won't perform this search if you don't have any users or sites yet. This function is extremely useful when you have a community of users and sites within your network, however.

TIP

The Network Admin Dashboard is configurable, just like the regular Dashboard; you can move the modules around and edit their settings. Refer to Book 3, Chapter 1 for more information about arranging the Dashboard modules to suit your tastes.

The Search Users feature allows you to search usernames and user email addresses. If you search for the user *Lisa*, for example, your results include any user whose username or email address contains *Lisa*, so you can receive multiple results when using just one search word or phrase. The Search Sites feature returns any blog content within your community that contains your search term, too.

The Network Admin Dashboard has two useful links near the top of the screen:

- **Create a New Site:** Click this link to create a new site within your network. When you click the link, the Add New Site screen appears. Find out how to add a new site in the upcoming "Sites" section.

» **Create a New User:** Click this link to create a new user account within your community. When you click this link, the Add New User screen appears. Find out how to add a new user to your community in the "Users" section, later in the chapter.

Additionally, the Network Admin Dashboard gives you a real-time count of how many sites and users you have in your network, which is nice-to-know information for any network admin.

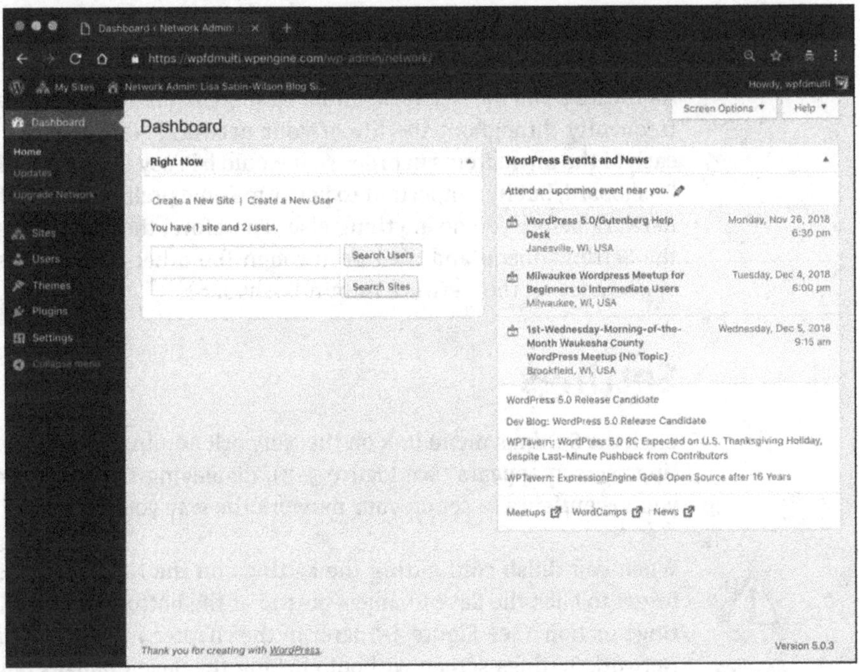

FIGURE 3-2: The Network Admin Dashboard.

Managing Your Network

As mentioned, the Network Admin Dashboard has its own set of menus separate from the regular Site Admin Dashboard. Those menus are located on the left side of the Network Admin Dashboard. This section goes through the menu items and provides explanations and instructions for working with the settings and configurations to manage your network, sites, and users.

The menus available on the Network Admin Dashboard offer these options:

- **Sites:** View a list of the sites in your network, along with details about them.
- **Users:** See detailed info about current users in your network.
- **Themes:** View all the currently available themes to enable or disable them for use in your network.
- **Plugins:** Manage (activate/deactivate) plugins for use on all sites within your network.
- **Settings:** Configure global settings for your network.

All the items on the Network Admin Dashboard are important, and you'll use them frequently throughout the life of your network. Normally, I'd take you through each of the menu items in order so it would be easy for you to follow along on your Dashboard, but it's important to perform some preliminary configurations of your network before you do anything else. Therefore, the following sections start with the Settings menu and then go through the other menu items in order of their appearance on the Network Admin Dashboard.

Settings

Click the Settings menu link on the Network Admin Dashboard. The Network Settings screen appears (see Figure 3-3), displaying several sections of options for you to configure to set up your network the way you want.

WARNING

When you finish configuring the settings on the Network Settings screen, don't forget to click the Save Changes button at the bottom, below the final Menu Settings section. (See Figure 3-7 later in the chapter.) If you navigate away from the Network Settings screen without clicking the Save Changes button, none of your configurations will be saved, and you'll need to go through the entire process again.

Operational Settings

The two options in the Operational Settings section, shown in Figure 3-3, are

- **Network Title:** This setting is the title of your overall network of sites. This name is included in all communications regarding your network, including emails that new users receive when they register a new site within your network. Type your desired network title in the text box.

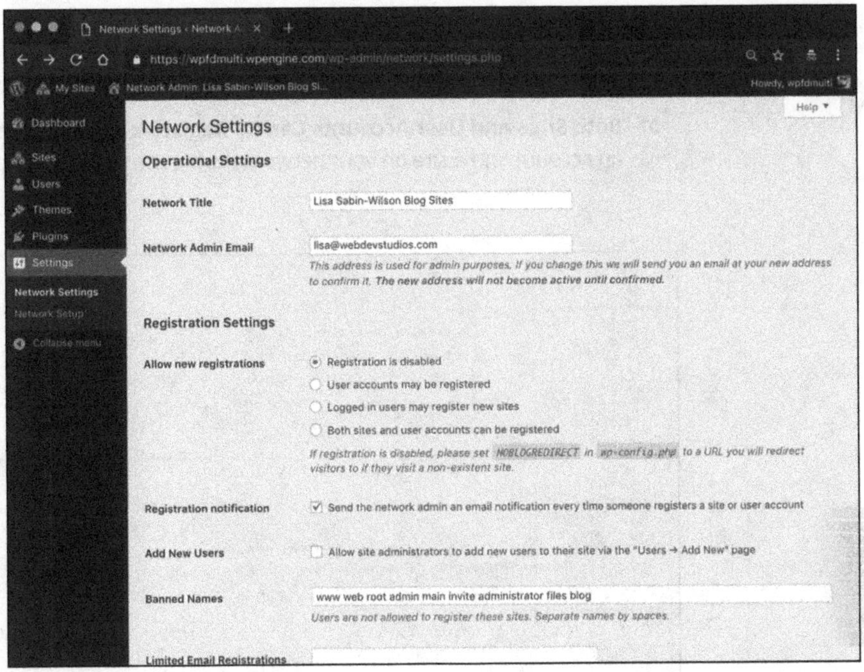

FIGURE 3-3: The Network Settings screen.

- **Network Admin Email:** This setting is the email address that all correspondence from your website is addressed from, including all registration and signup emails that new users receive when they register a new site and/or user account within your network. In the text box, type the email that you want to use for these purposes.

Registration Settings

The Registration Settings section (see Figure 3-4) allows you to control aspects of allowing users to sign up to your network. The most important option is whether to allow open registration.

To set one of the following options, select its radio button:

- **Registration Is Disabled:** Disallows new user registration. When selected, this option prevents people who visit your site from registering for a user account.
- **User Accounts May Be Registered:** Allows people to create only user accounts, not create sites on your network.
- **Logged In Users May Register New Sites:** Allows only existing users (those who are logged in) to create a new site on your network. This setting also disables new user registration. Choose this option if you don't want just

anyone registering for an account. Instead, you, as the site administrator, can add users at your discretion.

- **Both Sites and User Accounts Can Be Registered:** Allows users to register an account and a site on your network during the registration process.

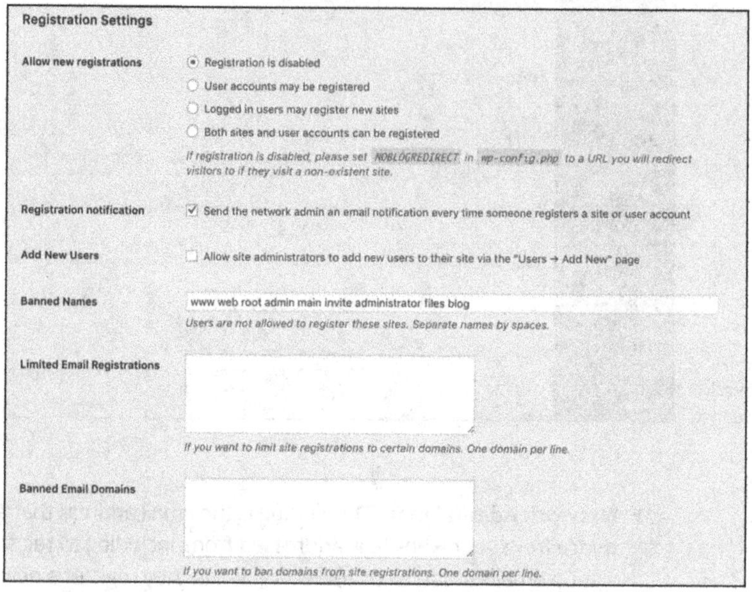

FIGURE 3-4: The Registration Settings section of the Network Settings screen.

These options apply only to outside users. As a network admin, you can create new sites and users any time you want by setting the necessary options on the Network Admin Dashboard. (For information about creating users, see the upcoming "Users" section.)

The remaining options in the Registration Settings section are as follows:

- **Registration Notification:** When this option is selected, an email is sent to the network admin every time a user or a site is created on the system, even if the network admin creates the new site.
- **Add New Users:** Select this check box if you want to allow your community blog owners (individual site admins) to add new users to their own community site via the Users page within their individual dashboards.
- **Banned Names:** By default, WordPress bans several usernames from being registered within your community, including *www, web, root, admin, main, invite,* and *administrator* — for good reason. You don't want a random user to register a username such as *admin* because you don't want that person

misrepresenting himself as an administrator on your site. You can enter an unlimited amount of usernames that you want to bar from your site in the Banned Names text box.

- **Limited Email Registrations:** You can limit sign-ups based on email domains by filling in this text box with one email domain per line. If you have open registrations but limited the email addresses, only the people who have an email domain that's on the list can register. This option is an excellent one to use in a school or corporate environment where you're providing email addresses and sites to students or employees.
- **Banned Email Domains:** This feature, the reverse of Limited Email Registrations, blocks all sign-ups from a particular domain, which can be useful in stopping spammers. If you enter **gmail.com** in the field, for example, anyone who tries to sign up with a Gmail address will be denied.

New Site Settings

The New Site Settings section (see Figure 3-5) is a configurable list of items that WordPress populates with default values when a new site is created. These values include the ones that appear in welcome emails, on a user's first post page, and on a new site's first page.

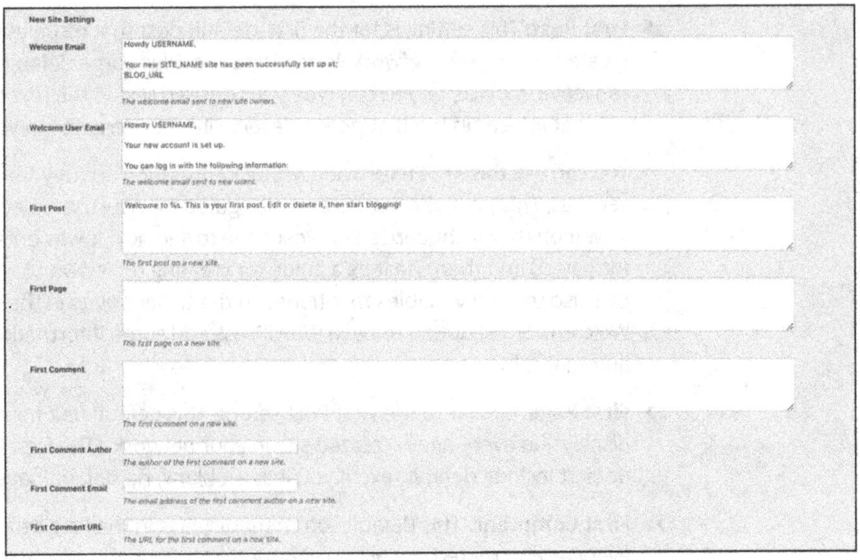

FIGURE 3-5: The New Site Settings section of the Network Settings screen.

The configurable list of items includes

- **Welcome Email:** This setting is the text of the email that owners of newly registered sites in your network receive when their registration is complete. WordPress provides a default message that you can leave in place, if you like. Or you can type the text of the email you want new site owners to receive when they register a new site within your network.

  A few variables you can use in this email aren't explained entirely on the Network Settings screen, including the following:

  - `SITE_NAME`: Inserts the name of your WordPress site
  - `BLOG_URL`: Inserts the URL of the new member's blog
  - `USERNAME`: Inserts the new member's username
  - `PASSWORD`: Inserts the new member's password
  - `BLOG_URLwp-login.php`: Inserts the hyperlinked login URL for the new member's blog
  - `SITE_URL`: Inserts the hyperlinked URL for your WordPress site

- **Welcome User Email:** This setting is the text of the email that newly registered users receive when they complete the registration process. The variables used for the Welcome Email setting apply to this email configuration as well.

- **First Post:** This setting is for the first, default post that displays on every newly created site in your network. WordPress provides some default text that you can leave in place, or you can type your desired text in the text box. This text will that appear in the first post on every site that's created in your community.

  You can use this area to provide useful information about your site and services. This post also serves as a nice guide for new users because they can view it on the Dashboard's Edit Post page to see how it was entered and formatted and then use it as a guide for creating their own blog posts. You can also use the variables mentioned in the bullet points in the earlier Welcome Email option to have WordPress add some information for you automatically.

- **First Page:** Similar to the First Post setting, this default text for a default page displays on every newly created site in your network. (The First Page text box doesn't include default text; if you leave it blank, no default page is created.)

- **First Comment:** This default comment displays in the first default post on every newly created site within your network. Type the text that you want to appear in the first comment on every site that's created in your community.

- **First Comment Author:** Type the name of the author of the first comment on new sites in your network.

» **First Comment Email**: Type the email address of the author of the first comment on new sites in your network.

» **First Comment URL:** Type the web address (URL) of the author of the first comment; this entry hyperlinks the first comment author's name to the URL you type here.

Upload Settings

Scrolling down the Network Settings screen, you get to the Upload Settings section (see Figure 3-6), which defines global values pertaining to the type of files you'll allow the site owners within your network to upload by using the file upload feature in the WordPress Write Posts and Write Page areas. (See Book 3, Chapter 3.)

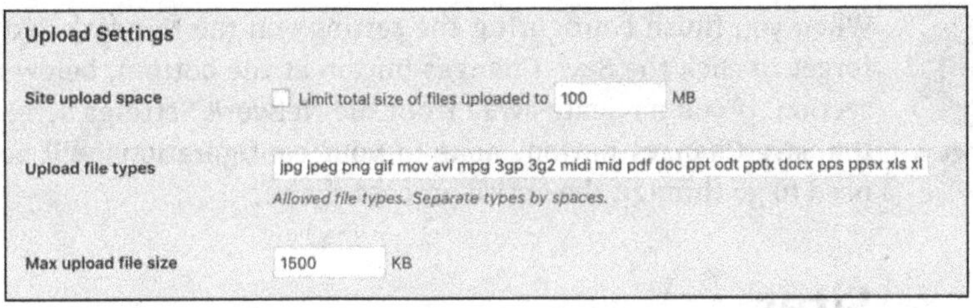

FIGURE 3-6: The Upload Settings section of the Network Settings screen=.

The fields in the Upload Settings section have default settings already filled in:

» **Site Upload Space:** If you leave this check box deselected, users are allowed to use all the space they want for uploads; they have no limits. Select the check box to limit the available space per site and then fill in the amount in megabytes (MB); the suggested, default storage space is 100MB. This amount of hard drive space is what you give users within your network for the storage of files they upload to their sites. If you want to change the default storage space, type a number in the text box.

» **Upload File Types:** This text field defines the types of files that you, as the network admin, allow site owners to upload to their sites on their Dashboards. Users can't upload any file types that don't appear in this field. By default, WordPress includes the following file types: `jpg jpeg png gif mov avi mpg 3gp 3g2 midi mid pdf doc ppt odt pptx docx pps ppsx xls xlsx key mp3 ogg flac m4a wav mp4 m4v webm ogv flv`. You can remove any default file types and add new ones.

» **Max Upload File Size:** This amount is in kilobytes (KB), and the default file size is 1500KB. This setting means that a user can't upload a file larger than 1500KB. Adjust this number as you see fit by typing a new number in the text box.

Menu Settings

The Plugins administration menu is disabled on the Dashboards of all network site owners, but the network administrator always has access to the Plugins menu. If you leave this check box unselected (see Figure 3-7), the Plugins page is visible to users on their own site's Dashboards. Select the box to enable the Plugins administration menu for your network users. For more information about using plugins with WordPress, see Book 7.

FIGURE 3-7: The Menu Settings section of the Network Settings screen.

REMEMBER

When you finish configuring the settings on the Network Settings screen, don't forget to click the Save Changes button at the bottom, below the Menu Settings section. If you navigate away from the Network Settings screen without clicking the Save Changes button, none of your configurations will be saved, and you'll need to go through the entire process again.

Sites

Clicking the Sites menu item on the Network Admin Dashboard takes you to the Sites screen, where you can manage your individual sites. Although each site in the network has its own Dashboard for basic tasks (publishing, changing themes, and so on), the Sites screen is where you create and delete sites and edit the properties of the sites within your network. Editing information from this page is handy when you have problems accessing a site's back-end Dashboard.

The Sites screen also lists all the sites within your network, displaying the following statistics for each site:

- **URL:** The site's path in your network. In Figure 3-8, you see a site listed with the username `lisa`. This path means that the site's domain is `lisa.`*`yourdomain`*`.com` (if you're using a subdomain setup) or *`yoursite`*`.com/lisa` (if you're using a subdirectory setup). I discuss subdomains and subdirectories in Book 8, Chapter 2.
- **Last Updated:** The date when the site was last updated (or published to).
- **Registered:** The date when the site was registered in your network.
- **Users**: The username and email address associated with the user(s) of that site.

» **ID**: The unique ID number assigned to the site. This ID number corresponds to the database tables where the data for this site are stored. (See Book 2, Chapter 3.)

When you hover your pointer over the pathname of a site in your network, you see a handy listing of links that help you manage the site. Figure 3-8 shows the options that appear below a site listing when you hover your mouse over a site name.

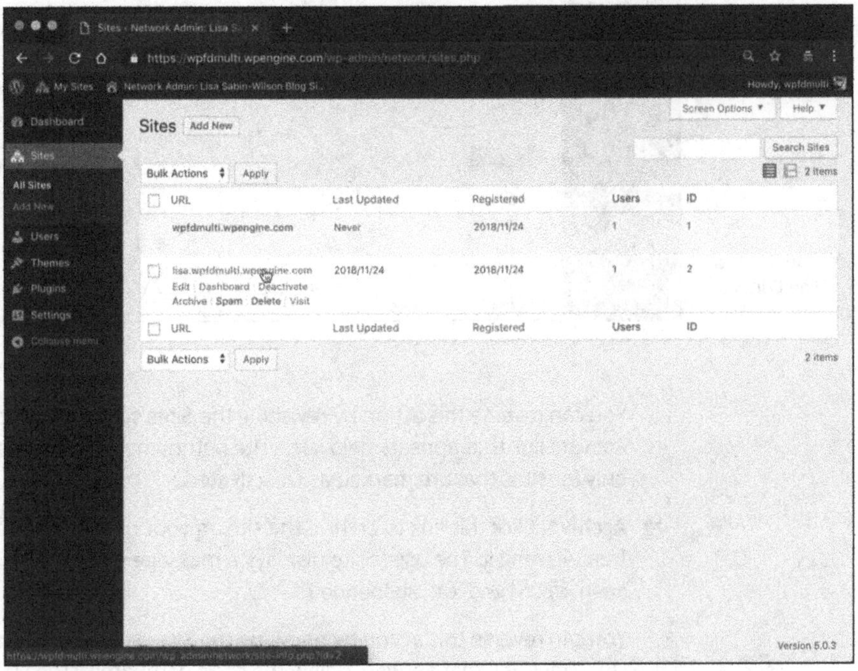

FIGURE 3-8: Site-management options on the Sites screen.

The management options for network sites, most of which are visible in Figure 3-8, are as follows:

» **Edit:** Click this link to go to the Edit Site screen (see Figure 3-9), where you can change aspects of each site.

» **Dashboard:** Click this link to go to the Dashboard of the site.

» **Deactivate:** Click this link to mark the site for deletion from your network. A message appears in a pop-up window, asking you to confirm your intention to deactivate the site. Click the Yes button to confirm. The user's site displays a message stating that the site has been deleted.

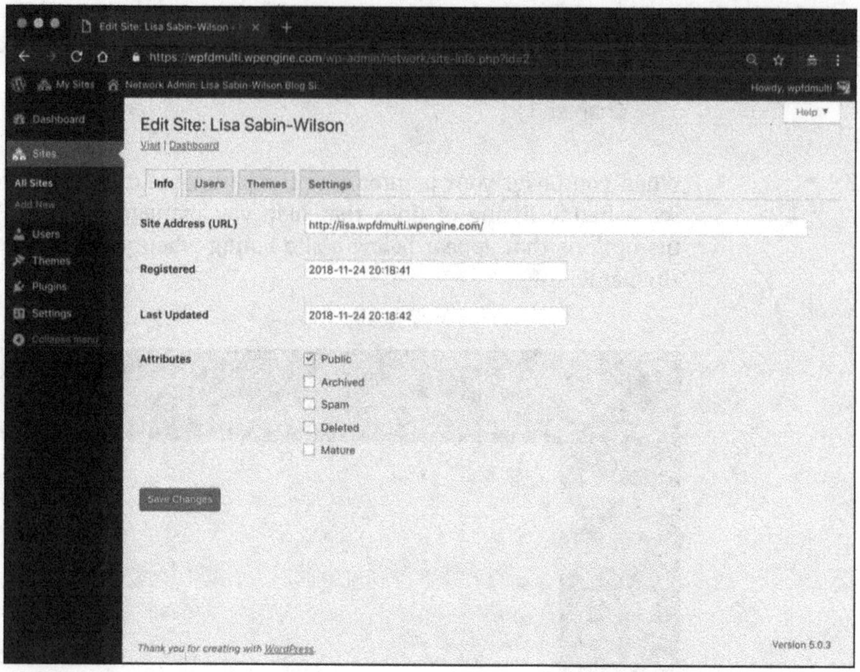

FIGURE 3-9: The Edit Site screen.

You can reverse this action by revisiting the Sites screen and clicking the Activate link that appears below the site pathname. (The Activate link appears only for sites that are marked as Deactivated.)

- **Archive:** Click this link to archive the site on your network and prevent visitors from viewing it. The user's site displays a message stating `This site has been archived or suspended.`

  You can reverse this action by revisiting the Sites screen and clicking the Unarchive link that appears below the site's pathname. (The Unarchive link appears only for sites that are marked as Archived.)

- **Spam:** Click this link to mark the site as spam and block users from accessing the Dashboard. WordPress displays the message `This site has been archived or suspended.`

  You can reverse this action by revisiting the Sites screen and clicking the Not Spam link that appears below the site's pathname. (The Not Spam link appears only for sites that are marked as Spam.)

- **Delete:** Click this link to delete the site from your network of sites. Although a confirmation screen asks you to confirm your intention to delete the site, after you confirm the deletion, you can't reverse it.
- **Visit:** Click this link to visit the live site in your web browser.

Generally, you use the Edit Site screen (refer to Figure 3-9) only when the settings are unavailable from the Dashboard of that particular site. Configure these options on the four tabs of the screen:

- **Info:** On this tab, you can edit the site's domain, path, registered date, updated date, and attributes (Public, Archived, Spam, Deleted, or Mature).
- **Users:** On this tab, you can manage the users who are assigned to the site, as well as add users to the site.
- **Themes:** On this tab, you can enable themes for the site. This capability is particularly useful if you have themes that aren't network-enabled. (I cover themes later this chapter.) All the themes that aren't enabled within your network are listed on the Themes tab, which allows you to enable themes on a per-site basis.
- **Settings:** The settings on this tab cover all the database settings for the site that you're editing. You rarely, if ever, need to edit these settings because as network administrator, you have access to each user's Dashboard and should be able to make any changes in the site's configuration settings there.

The Sites menu also includes a link called Add New. Click that link to load the Add New Site screen (see Figure 3-10) in your Network Admin Dashboard. Fill in the Site Address (URL), Site Title, Site Language, and Admin Email fields and then click the Add Site button to add the site to your network. If the Admin Email you entered is associated with an existing user, the new site is assigned to that user on your network. If the user doesn't exist, WordPress creates a new user and sends a notification email. The site is immediately accessible. The user receives an email containing a link to her site, a login link, and her username and password.

Users

Clicking the Users link on the Network Admin Dashboard takes you to the Users screen (see Figure 3-11), where you see a full list of members, or users, within your network.

The Users screen lists the following information about each user:

- **Username:** This setting is the login name the member uses when he logs in to his account in your community.
- **Name:** This setting is the user's real name, taken from her profile. If the user hasn't provided her name in her profile, this column is blank.
- **Email:** This setting is the email address the user entered when he registered on your site.

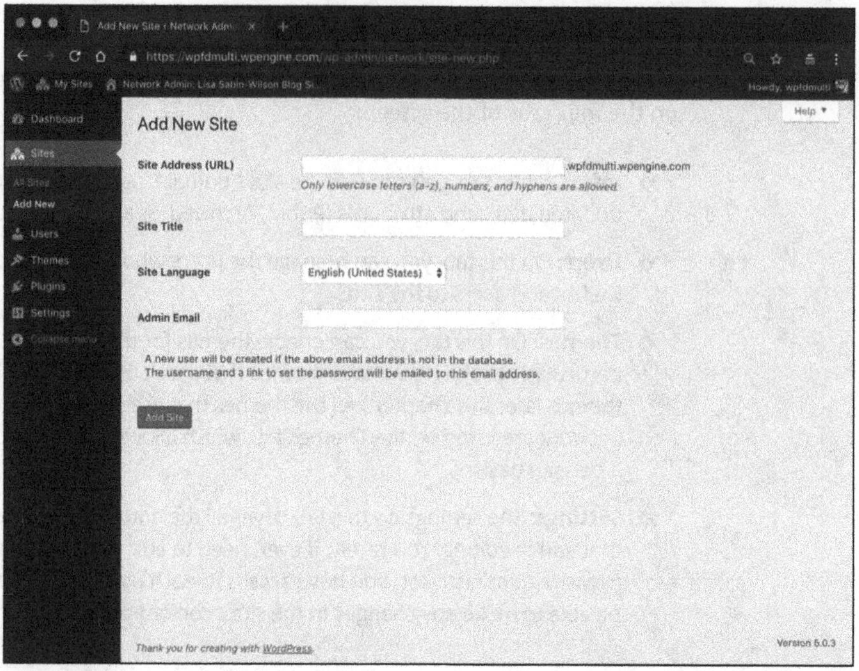

FIGURE 3-10: The Add New Site screen of the Network Admin Dashboard.

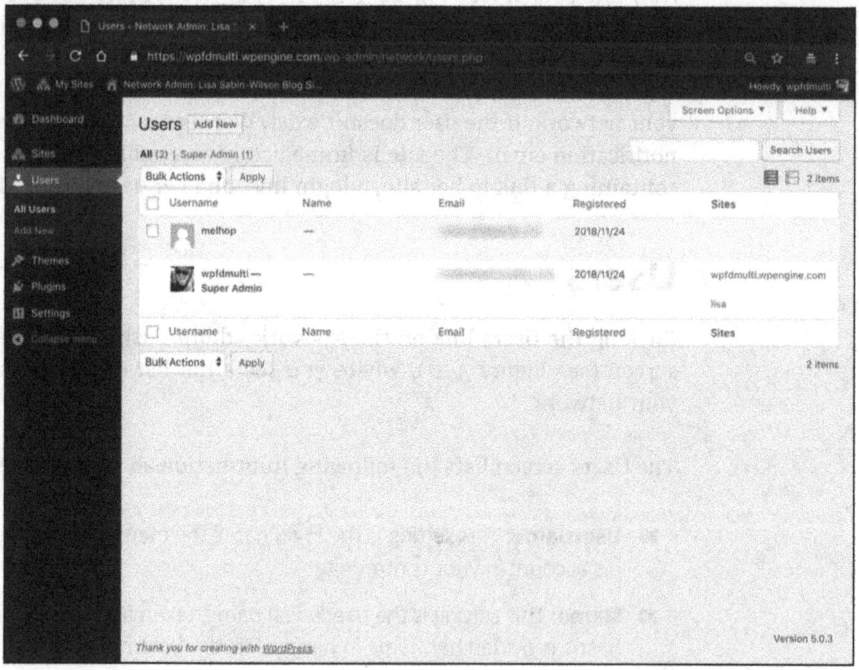

FIGURE 3-11: The Users screen.

- **Registered:** This setting is the date when the user registered.
- **Sites:** If you enable sites within your WordPress Network, this setting lists any sites where the user is a member.

You can add users to the network, manage users, and even delete users by clicking the Edit or Delete links that appear below their names when you hover over them with your mouse (the same way you do with sites on the Sites screen).

To delete a user, simply hover your mouse over the username in the list that appears on the Users screen, and click the Delete link. A new screen appears, telling you to transfer this user's posts and links to another user account (most likely, your account). Do that and then click the Confirm Deletion button. WordPress removes the user from the network.

WARNING

This action is irreversible, so be certain about your decision before you click that button!

You can also edit a user's profile information by clicking the Edit link that appears when you hover your mouse over his name on the Users screen. Clicking that link takes you to the Edit User screen, shown in Figure 3-12, which presents several options. These options happen to be (mostly) the same options and settings that you configured for your own profile information (as discussed in Book 3, Chapter 2).

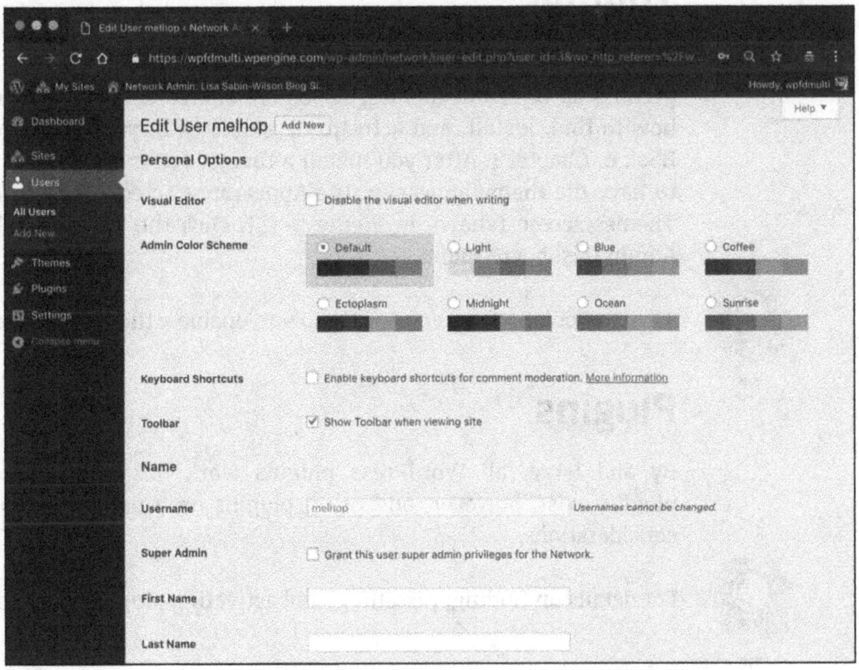

FIGURE 3-12: The Edit User screen.

The only difference with the Edit User screen within the Network Admin Dashboard is the setting labeled Super Admin, which is deselected by default. If you select this check box, however, you grant this user network admin privileges for your entire network, which means that the user has exactly the same access and permissions as you.

TIP

At this writing, the terms *super admin* and *network admin* are interchangeable. When WordPress merged the WordPress MU code base with the regular WordPress software back in 2010 (in version 3.0), the term it used to describe the network admin was *super admin*. Now *network admin* is the standard term, but areas within the Network Admin Dashboard and regular Dashboard still use the *Super Admin* label. That situation will most likely change in the near future, because WordPress will realize the discrepancy and update later versions of the software.

Also on the Users menu of the Network Admin Dashboard, you see a link called Add New. Click that link to load the Add New User page on your Network Admin Dashboard (shown in Figure 3-13).

You can add a user by filling in the Username and Email fields and then clicking the Add User button. WordPress sends the new user an email notification of the new account, along with the site URL, her username, and her password (randomly generated by WordPress when the user account is created).

Themes

When a network is enabled, only users who have Network Admin access have permission to install themes, which are shared across the network. You can see how to find, install, and activate new themes in your WordPress installation in Book 6, Chapter 1. After you install a theme, you must enable it on your network to have the theme appear on the Appearance screen of each site. To access the Themes screen (shown in Figure 3-14), click the Themes link on the Network Admin Dashboard menu.

TIP

Turn to Book 8, Chapter 5 to see how to enable a theme on a per-site basis.

Plugins

By and large, all WordPress plugins work on your network. Some special plugins exist, however, and using plugins on a network involves some special considerations.

TIP

For details on finding, installing, and activating plugins in WordPress, see Book 7.

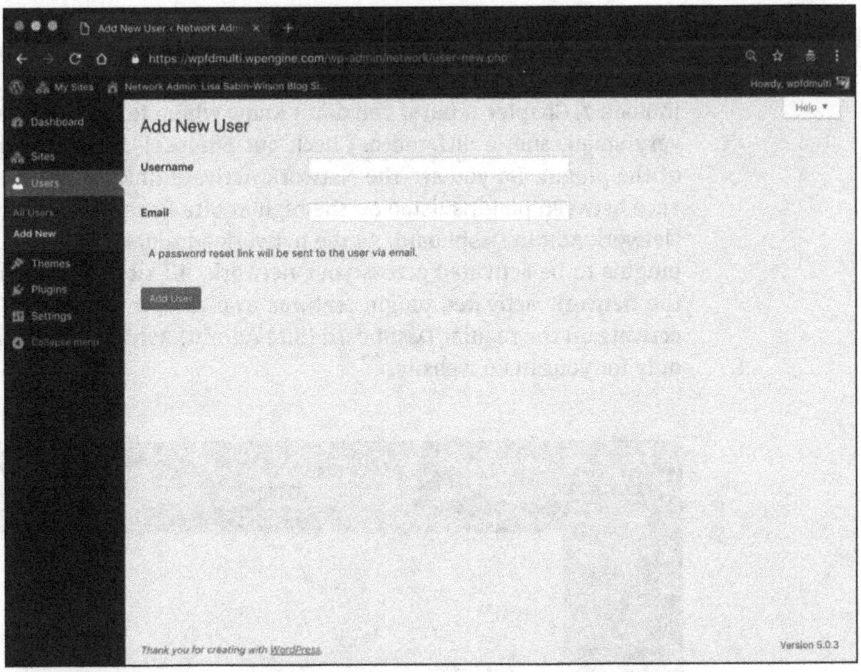

FIGURE 3-13: The Add New User screen of the Network Admin Dashboard.

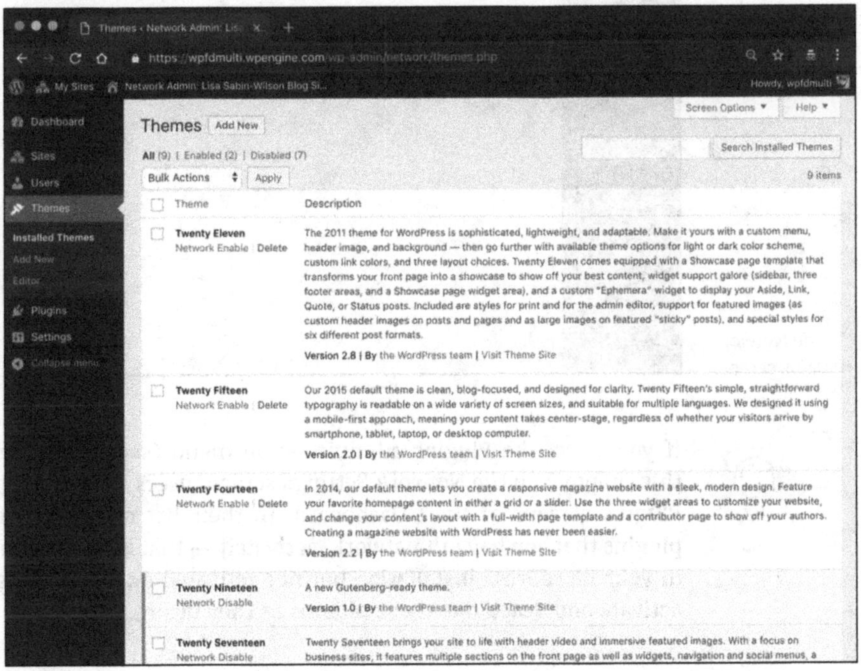

FIGURE 3-14: The Themes screen of the Network Admin Dashboard.

Browse to the Plugins screen of your WordPress Network Admin Dashboard by clicking the Plugins link. The Plugins screen is almost the same as the one shown in Book 7, Chapter 1, but if you don't know where to look, you can easily miss one very small, subtle difference. Check out Figure 3-15, and look below the name of the plugin. Do you see the Network Activate link? That link is the big difference between plugins listed on the regular Site Dashboard and those listed on the Network Admin Dashboard. As the network administrator, you can enable certain plugins to be activated across your network. All sites on your network will have the network-activated plugin features available, in contrast to plugins that you activate on the regular Dashboard (Site Admin), which are activated and available only for your main website.

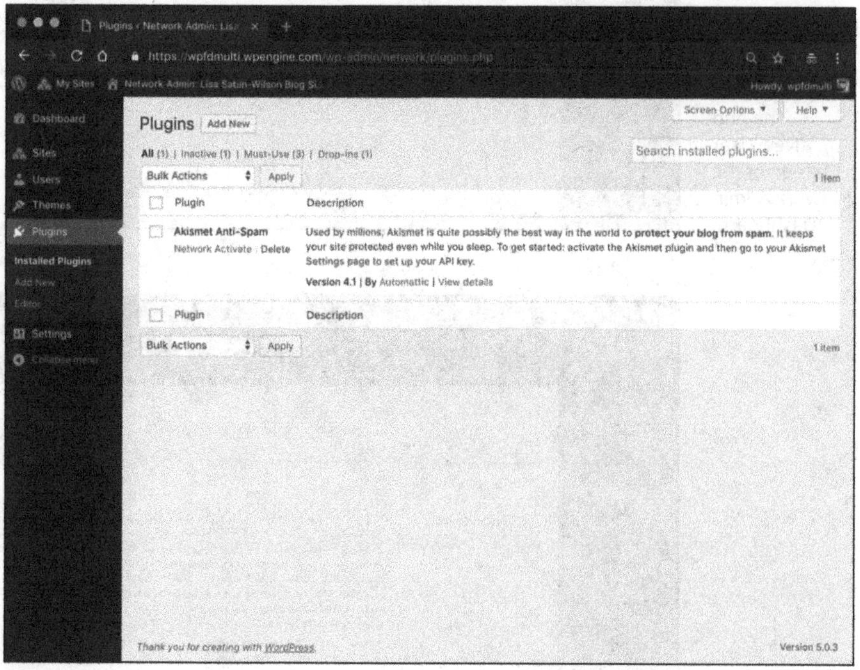

FIGURE 3-15: The Network Plugins screen.

TIP

If you select the Plugins administration menu (see "Menu Settings" earlier in this chapter) on the Network Settings screen, users see the plugins listed on their Plugins screens of their Dashboard. In their list of plugins, they see only the plugins that you haven't network-activated — that is, all the plugins you installed in your WordPress installation but not activated on those users' sites. Users can activate and deactivate those plugins as they desire.

Only network administrators can install new plugins on the site; regular users within the network don't have that kind of access (unless you've made them network administrators in their User settings).

Also located on the Plugins menu of the Network Admin Dashboard are two other links: Add New and Editor. Click the Add New link to load the Plugins screen, where you can add and install new plugins by searching the WordPress Plugins page within your Dashboard. (I cover this topic in Book 7, chapters 1 and 2.) The Editor link gives you access to the Plugin Editor (covered in Book 7, Chapter 4).

Stopping Spam Sign-Ups and Splogs

If you choose to have open sign-ups, in which any member of the public can register and create a new site on your network, at some point automated bots run by malicious users and spammers will visit your network sign-up page and attempt to create one, or multiple, sites in your network. They do so by automated means, hoping to create links to their sites or fill their site on your network with spam posts. This kind of spam blog or site is a *splog*.

Spam bloggers don't hack your system to take advantage of this feature; they call aspects of the sign-up page directly. But you can do a few simple things to slow them considerably or stop them.

In the Registration Settings section of the Network Settings screen (refer to Figure 3-4), clear the Add New Users check box to stop many spammers. When spammers access the system to set up a spam site, they often use the Add New Users feature to create many other blogs via programs built into the bots.

Spammers often find your site via a Google search for the link to the sign-up page. You can stop Google and other search engines from crawling your sign-up page by adding `rel=nofollow,noindex` to the sign-up page link. Wherever you add a link to your sign-up page inviting new users to sign up, the HTML code you use to add the `nofollow,noindex` looks like this:

```
<a href="http://yoursite.com/wp-signup.php" rel="nofollow,noindex ">Get your own
   site here</a>
```

Becoming a Network Admin

Plugins can help stop spam blogs, too. The Anti-Splog plugin prevents and limits spam bots, and also identifies humans and known spammers efficiently. You can download the Anti-Splog plugin at `https://wordpress.org/plugins/anti-splog`.

The Cookies for Comments plugin (available at `https://wordpress.org/plugins/cookies-for-comments`) leaves a cookie in a visitor's browser. If the sign-up page is visited, the plugin checks for the cookie. If no cookie exists, the sign-up fails. Be sure to check the installation directions for this plugin, because it requires editing the `.htaccess` file.

IN THIS CHAPTER

» Understanding default user management

» Changing default user behavior

» Exploring user access to site features

Chapter 4
Management of Users and Access Control

In Book 8, Chapter 3, I discuss the Network Admin menu of your Dashboard, which allows you to manage aspects of your network. In this chapter, I explain how to manage users across the network, including changing some of the default management options to suit your needs.

One of the hardest things for new network admins to understand is that although each site is managed separately, users are global. That is, after a user logs in, he's logged in across the entire network and has the ability to comment on any site that has commenting enabled. (See Book 3, Chapter 2.) The user can visit the Dashboard of the main site in the install to manage his profile information and can access the Dashboard's My Sites menu to reach sites that he administers. The user also registers at the main site — not at individual sites in the network.

Setting Default User Permissions

When you enable the Multisite feature, new site and new user registrations are turned off by default. But you can add new sites and users from the Network Admin Dashboard. To let users sign up for your network, follow these steps:

1. **Log in to the Network Admin Dashboard and then click the Settings menu link.**

   The Network Settings screen loads in your browser window.

   REMEMBER

   The Network Admin Dashboard is different from the Site Admin Dashboard. For reference, you can find your Network Admin Dashboard at this URL: `https://`*`yourdomain.com`*`/wp-admin/network/settings.php`. (Replace *`yourdomain.com`* with your actual domain name.)

2. **In the Registration Settings section, select the User Accounts May Be Registered option (shown in Figure 4-1).**

   This setting allows users to register on your network. It also assigns them to the main site as Subscribers but doesn't allow them to create new sites.

3. **Click the Save Changes button at the bottom of the page.**

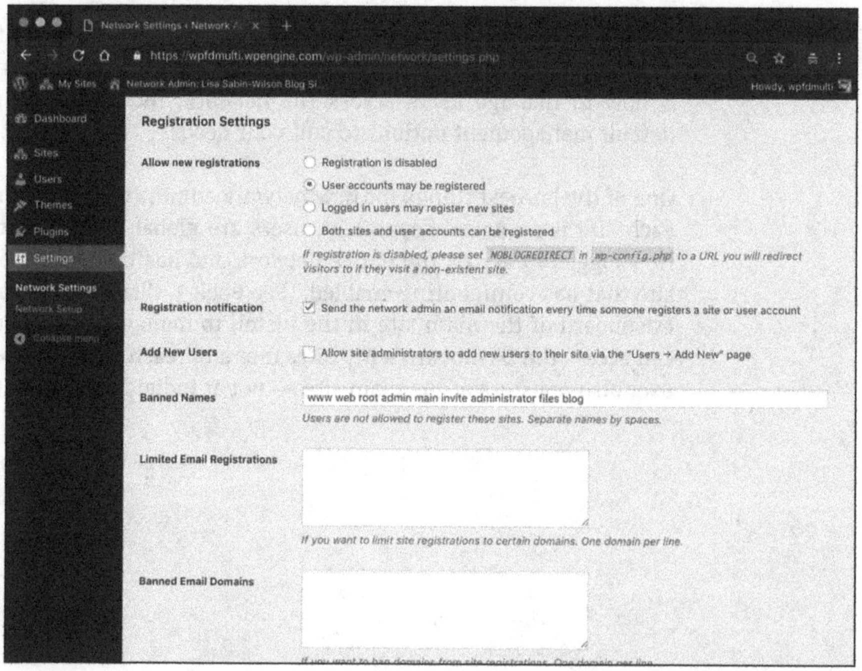

FIGURE 4-1: User registration options.

TIP

If you select the Both Sites and User Accounts May Be Registered option on the Network Admin Settings screen, you not only allow users to register a new account, but also give them the option to create a new site on your network.

Registering users

When signing up, the user is directed to the main site of the installation and then added to one of the child sites. This site may be her site (if she chose to have a site when registering) or an existing site. If it's any existing site other than the main site, you, as the network admin, must add the user to that site manually. The user who owns the site can manually add users as well if you enabled the option in Network Admin Settings that allows site admins to add users to their sites.

The registration page (see Figure 4-2) is located at `http://`*`yourdomain`*`.com/wp-signup.php`. This sign-up page bypasses the regular WordPress registration page. (See Book 3, Chapter 3.)

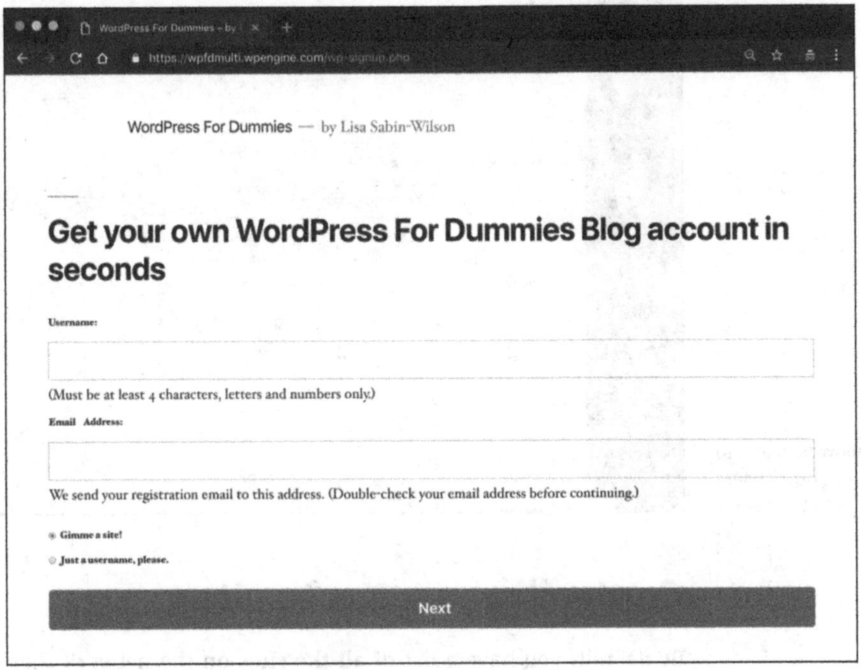

FIGURE 4-2: The network sign-up page.

After filling out the form, the user receives an email with a link to activate her account. When she does so, she can immediately log in and manage her details; she's directed to her primary site, which is the main site if she has no site to administer.

You also can add users to existing sites in the network. You can always assign users to specific sites on a per-case basis. When you set up a network and enable the option titled Allow Site Administrators to Add New Users to Their Site via the "Users⇨Add New" Page (shown in Figure 4-3), you allow site admins to add other users in the network to their sites. Although the Add New Users setting is turned off by default, you can enable it by selecting the Allow Site Administrators option on the Settings page of the Network Admin Dashboard.

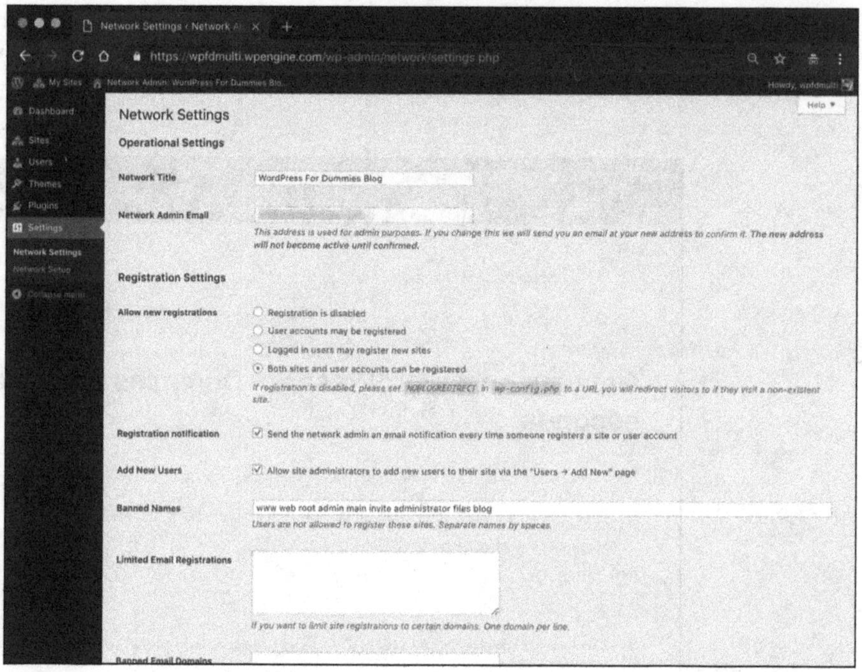

FIGURE 4-3: Allowing users to add other users to their sites.

Controlling access to sites

By default, you have a list of all the sites on the network that other users don't have access to unless they're network admins. (See Book 8, Chapter 3.) Unless you, the network admin, add such ability via plugins, a user can't navigate from one child site to the next. The only list provided to a user is on the My Sites screen, shown in Figure 4-4. You can access this screen by clicking the My Sites link on the admin toolbar menu at the top of your site.

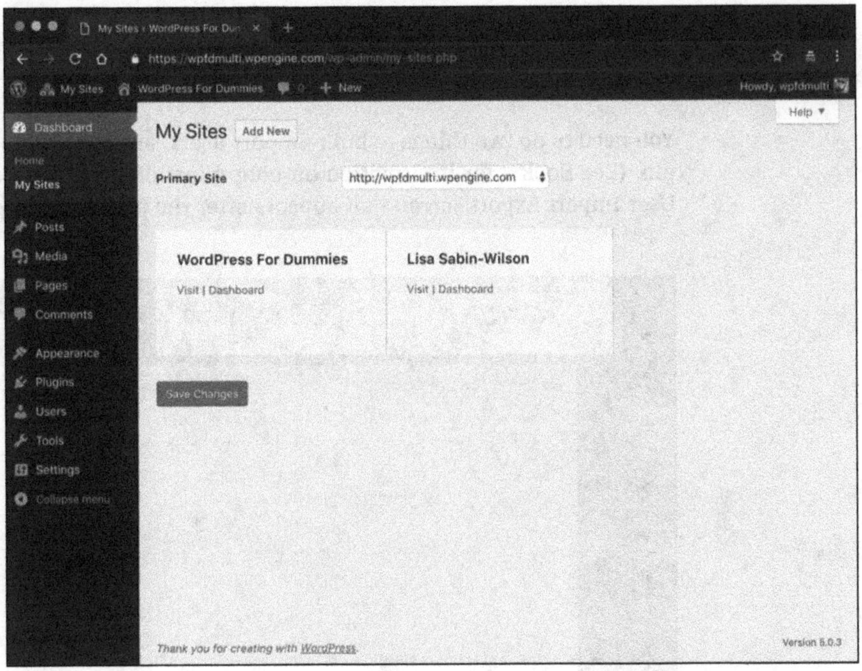

FIGURE 4-4: The My Sites screen shows sites that the user manages.

The My Sites screen lists only sites of which the user is the administrator, not sites on which the user has a lesser role. Additionally, the My Sites screen has a link that allows the user to create more sites (if the network admin allows that access via the Settings menu of the Network Admin Dashboard).

If you're running (or planning to run) a network of sites and want to display a public-facing list of sites in your network, a plugin called Multisite Site Index gives you access to a widget, or a shortcode, that you can use to display a list of sites within your network on a page of your own website. Users and visitors can click through that list to discover sites within your network easily. You can find the Multisite Site Index plugin on the WordPress site at `https://wordpress.org/plugins/multisite-site-index`.

Importing users

You may have an existing pool of users you want to add to the network if (for example) you had a website before your network existed and collected registrations or sign-ups. (Even newsletter programs give you a downloadable list of users that you can import into your network.) You can use the Import Export WordPress Users plugin, available at `https://wordpress.org/plugins/users-customers-import-export-for-wp-woocommerce`, to import a large group of users at the same time, rather than manually and one at a time. Currently, no default method is available to import users into WordPress without plugins.

You need to do two things to bulk-import users, and the first is to install the plugin. (See Book 7 for information on plugin installation.) Figure 4-5 displays the User Import Export screen that appears after the plugin is successfully installed.

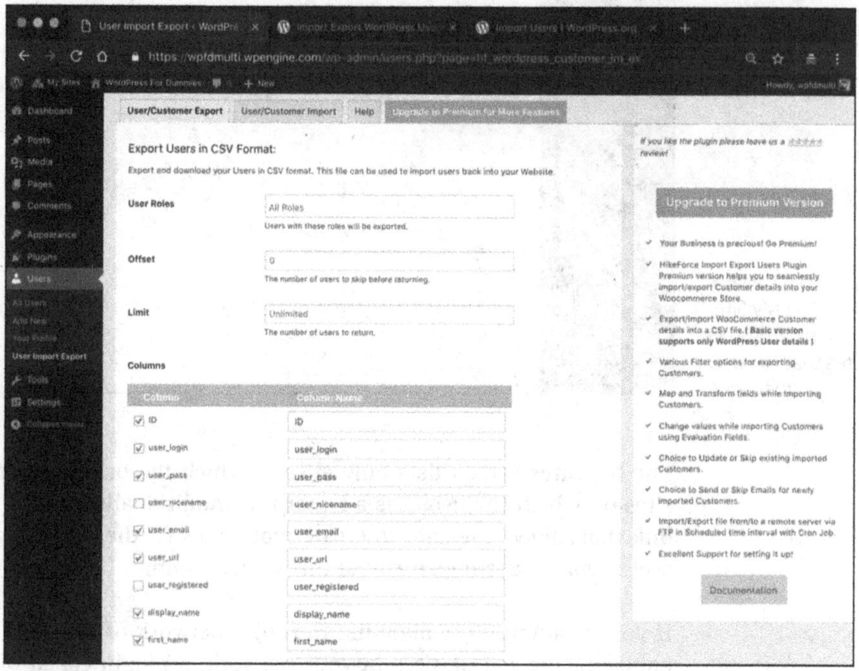

FIGURE 4-5: User Import Export screen.

After you have the plugin successfully installed, you need to get your list of users in CSV (comma-separated value) format. Figure 4-6 shows the CSV file that I created to run a test import of users. Using Microsoft Excel, I created a spreadsheet with the following columns:

- ID
- user_login
- user_pass
- roles
- user_email

- first_name
- last_name
- display_name
- user_url

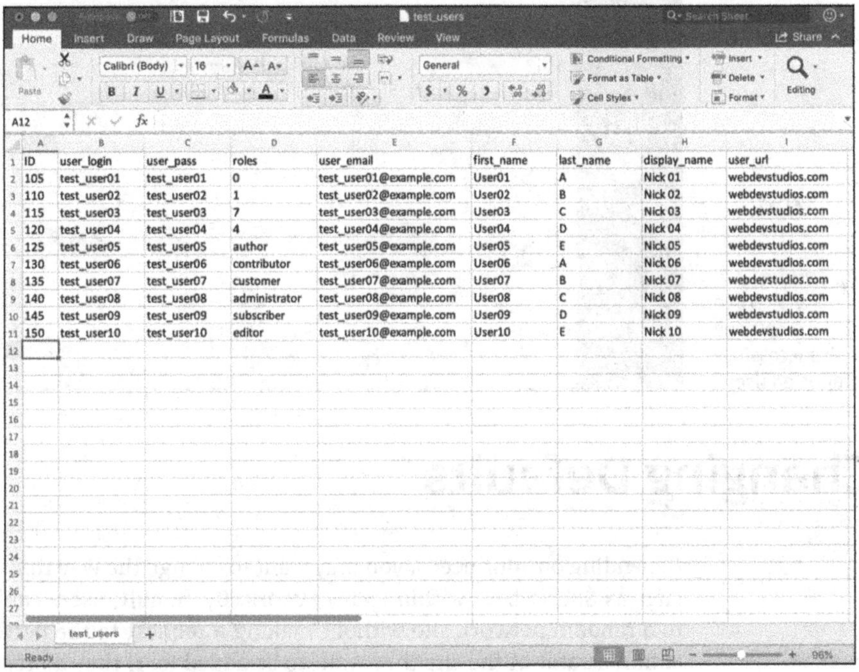

ID	user_login	user_pass	roles	user_email	first_name	last_name	display_name	user_url
105	test_user01	test_user01	0	test_user01@example.com	User01	A	Nick 01	webdevstudios.com
110	test_user02	test_user02	1	test_user02@example.com	User02	B	Nick 02	webdevstudios.com
115	test_user03	test_user03	7	test_user03@example.com	User03	C	Nick 03	webdevstudios.com
120	test_user04	test_user04	4	test_user04@example.com	User04	D	Nick 04	webdevstudios.com
125	test_user05	test_user05	author	test_user05@example.com	User05	E	Nick 05	webdevstudios.com
130	test_user06	test_user06	contributor	test_user06@example.com	User06	A	Nick 06	webdevstudios.com
135	test_user07	test_user07	customer	test_user07@example.com	User07	B	Nick 07	webdevstudios.com
140	test_user08	test_user08	administrator	test_user08@example.com	User08	C	Nick 08	webdevstudios.com
145	test_user09	test_user09	subscriber	test_user09@example.com	User09	D	Nick 09	webdevstudios.com
150	test_user10	test_user10	editor	test_user10@example.com	User10	E	Nick 10	webdevstudios.com

FIGURE 4-6: CSV file containing user data ready to import.

After I created these columns, I populated the rows with user data (in Figure 4-6, my data is dummy data used to test the functionality of the plugin) and then saved the file on my computer as a `.csv` file.

Click the User/Customer Import tab on the User Import Export screen (refer to Figure 4-5) and then click the Upload File and Import button. Figure 4-7 shows the Users screen of the WordPress Dashboard with successfully created user accounts after you perform the import by using the Import Export WordPress Users plugin.

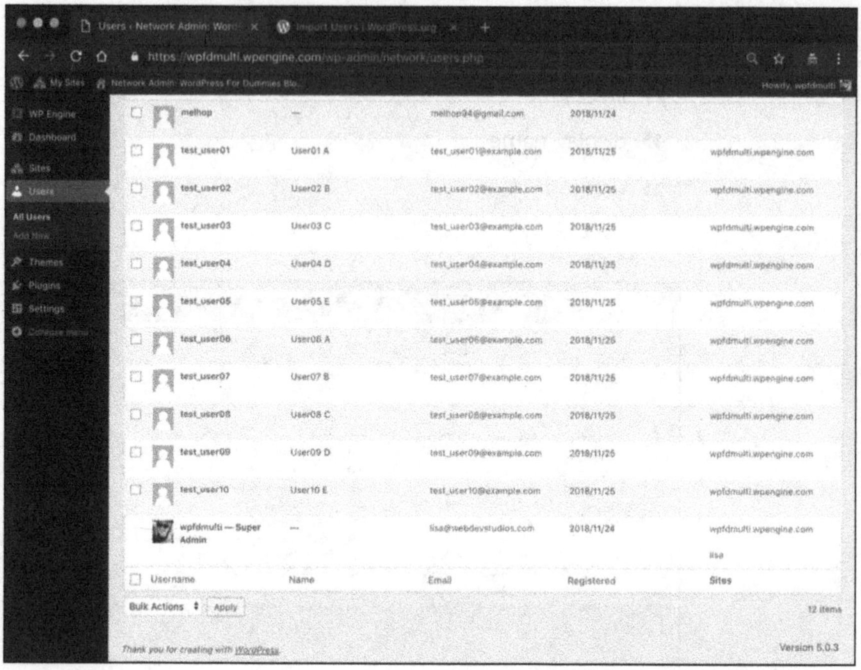

FIGURE 4-7: Users screen displaying successfully imported users.

Changing Defaults

Depending on your needs, you may want to change the way that users are added to sites as Subscribers within your network. By default, users can't add themselves to a random network site without making a request to the network admin or the administrator of the site they want to be added to. If they do register on your site, by default they're added as users only on the main site. This setup may work fine for most sites, but if you want your users to be able to register with existing sites within your network, read on, because these sections are for you.

Site-specific sign-up

For many people, signing up on the main site and then asking to be added to a subsite by a network admin can be a confusing experience. Plugins, however, can make the process easier and less confusing for everyone.

If you want existing users to be able to add themselves to existing sites on the network, the Network Subsite User Registration plugin, available on the WordPress website at `https://wordpress.org/plugins/network-subsite-user-registration`, allows users to sign up on any site within your network. Install this plugin as a regular plugin, as I outline in Book 7, chapters 1 and 2.

After the plugin is installed, choose Users⇨Registration on any site within the network to enable public registration on that site. (See Figure 4-8.)

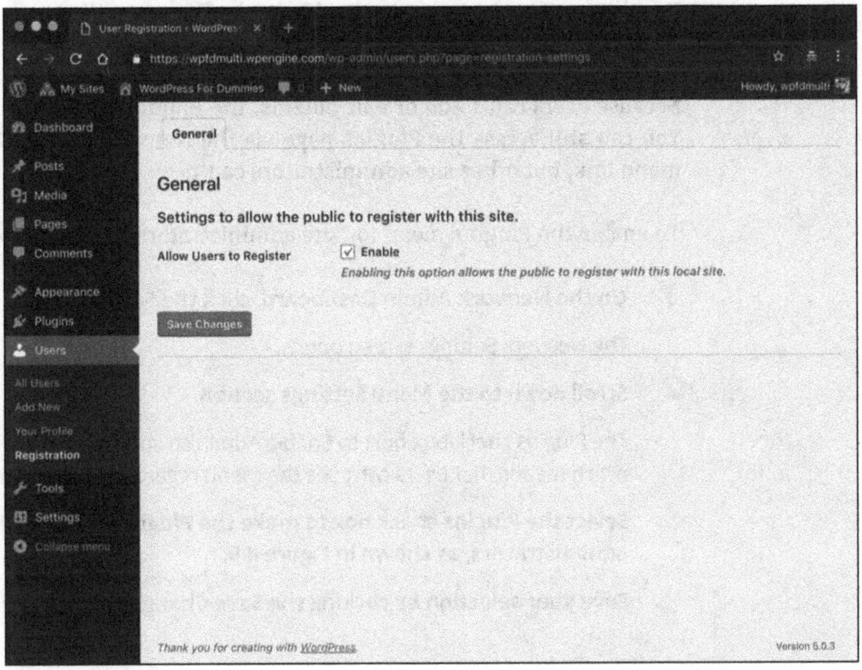

FIGURE 4-8: Enabling public registration on a network site.

User role management

When he is added to a network or a site, a user is assigned the role of Subscriber by default. You may want to assign a different role to the user and automatically add her to your other sites in the network. (Book 3, Chapter 3 explains roles and permissions.)

When a user signs up for her own site, for example, you may want to assign her a nonadministrator role. You may want to set her role to Editor, for example, to restrict the menus she can access on the Dashboard and to prevent her from using some of the functionality of WordPress. You may want to have new site owners sign up as Editors of the sites to give them fewer permissions on their Dashboards.

The Multisite User Role Manager plugin (`https://wordpress.org/plugins/multisite-user-role-manager`) allows you to manage the roles of all the users in your network from one screen, rather than on individual sites' Dashboards. This plugin saves you a lot of time in managing user roles and access in your network.

Exploring Default Site Settings

Default settings can control user access to things such as menus, themes, and the Dashboard. The next chapter in this book, Chapter 5 discusses the network settings in detail.

Because users can't add or edit plugins, the Plugins menu is disabled by default. You can still access the Plugins page via the Network Admin Dashboard Plugins menu link, but other site administrators can't.

To enable the Plugins menu for site administrators, follow these steps:

1. **On the Network Admin Dashboard, click the Settings menu link.**

   The Network Settings screen opens.

2. **Scroll down to the Menu Settings section.**

   The Plugins check box next to Enable Administration Menus is deselected, which means that users can't see the menu regardless of their user role.

3. **Select the Plugins check box to make the Plugins menu available to site administrators, as shown in Figure 4-9.**
4. **Save your selection by clicking the Save Changes button.**

FIGURE 4-9: Enabling the Plugins menu for site administrators.

REMEMBER

Similarly, you must enable any themes installed on the network before a site administrator can choose the theme from the Appearance menu. I explain how to do so in Book 8, Chapter 3.

IN THIS CHAPTER

» Understanding theme management

» Understanding networkwide plugins

» Finding networkwide and Must-Use plugins

Chapter 5

Using Network Plugins and Themes

When you add new plugins and themes to your WordPress installation, you add new functionality and aesthetics. But you don't just multiply your choices; the possibilities become endless. You can gather and display information from across the network, for example, or make the same features available to everyone. You can choose to have the same theme on all sites or different themes. You can not only manage plugins and themes on a global level but also have site-specific control.

In this chapter, I show you how certain functionality appears across the network and how certain plugins look by default on all sites for all users. I also cover controlling access to different themes for different sites.

One of the interesting features of a network is the extensive use of the `mu-plugins` folder. In this chapter, I describe exactly how this folder processes plugin code. I also cover the Network Activate link on the Plugins page, which is very similar to the Activate link but has important differences.

REMEMBER

This chapter doesn't cover installing plugins and themes. I cover installing plugins in Book 7, Chapter 2 and installing themes in Book 6, Chapter 2.

Using One Theme on Multiple Sites

In certain situations (such as when you want consistent branding and design across your entire network), each site in a network is used as a subsection of the main site. You could set up WordPress networks with a magazine-style design on your main site and populate the content with different posts from sites within your network, aggregating all the content to the main site. You can see an example on the BBC America website at `http://www.bbcamerica.com`. (See Figure 5-1.)

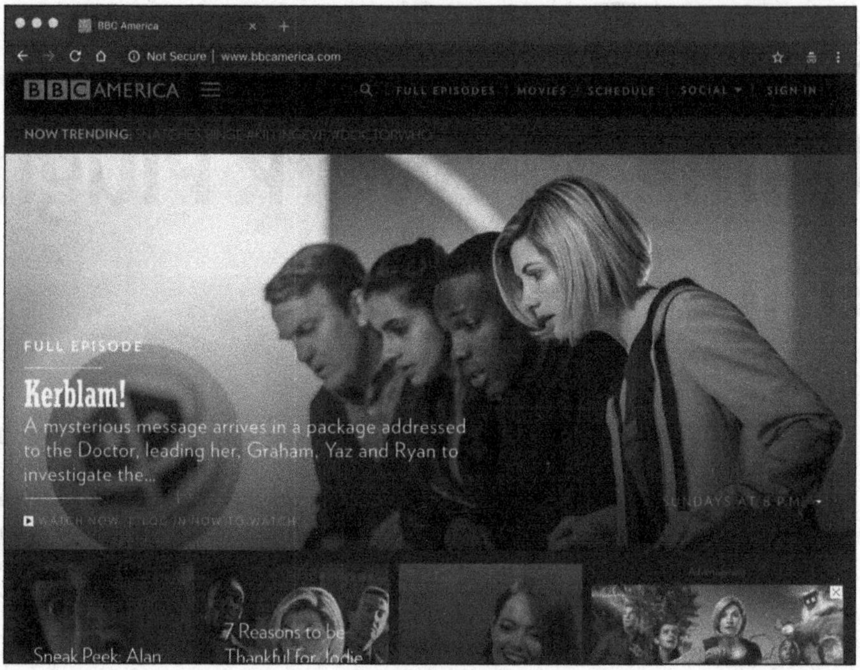

FIGURE 5-1: BBC America's WordPress network.

BBC America is a cable and satellite network that airs popular British television shows. On the main site, all the article links point to different sites within the Multisite network. Each show has its own site within the network, and the main page of the website (or the main site in the WordPress Multisite network) is a separate site that aggregates the content from all the sites within the network, making it easy for visitors to discover content on each show.

The sites within the BBC America network use the same theme to display their content, making the branding consistent across the network sites — a good example of a magazine-style theme that aggregates content from sites within a network.

Although each site in the network operates separately from the main (network admin) site, you may want each site to look the same as the main site because it ties into the main site visually, through design and branding, and provides a consistent experience for visitors to any site within the network. You may have a custom theme specially made for the main site, with added features to display networkwide content. If consistency and network branding are your goals, you may want to create a single theme to be used on all sites within your network (not just your main site).

REMEMBER

Book 6 discusses how WordPress accesses themes that are stored on the web server. When the network is enabled, these themes are shared among all sites and are available on the site administrator's Dashboard. If a theme file is changed, every site in the network that uses the theme experiences the change, because only one copy of the theme is being served. When a theme is enabled, it appears on the Manage Theme screen of the administrator's Dashboard (accessed by hovering the mouse pointer over the Appearance menu of the Network Admin Dashboard and clicking the Themes link). Users can choose to activate this theme so that it displays on the front side of the site. You must activate a theme for use across all sites in a network by clicking the Network Enable link on the Theme menu in the Network Admin Dashboard. (Access the Themes screen by clicking the Themes menu link on the Network Admin Dashboard.)

The main network site could have 20 themes installed in the main WordPress installation, but if you haven't enabled these themes for use across the entire network, site administrators can't see network-disabled themes on their Dashboards and, therefore, can't use them on their sites.

If a consistent network design is what you're after, you'll run into a few troubles with the WordPress network because by default, no matter what themes you've activated, the default WordPress Twenty Nineteen theme gets activated whenever new sites are created within your network. It would be nice if WordPress provided a global setting on the Network Admin Dashboard that allowed administrators to assign the default theme to every site that's created. Currently, however, that feature is available only by adding a small line of code to the WordPress configuration file (which I cover in "Setting the default theme for sites" later in this chapter).

Enabling themes for individual sites

You may have a customized theme for one particular site that you don't want other sites within the network to use or access. You, as network admin, can edit each site in the network. You can perform basic tasks such as enabling, disabling, or adding themes to the network without leaving your Dashboard. If you want to make a theme available for use on only one site and unavailable for other sites, follow these steps:

1. **Click the Network Admin link on the My Sites menu in the top-left corner of your Dashboard; then click the Sites link.**

   The Sites screen appears, showing a list of all sites in the network, sorted by creation date. (See Figure 5-2.)

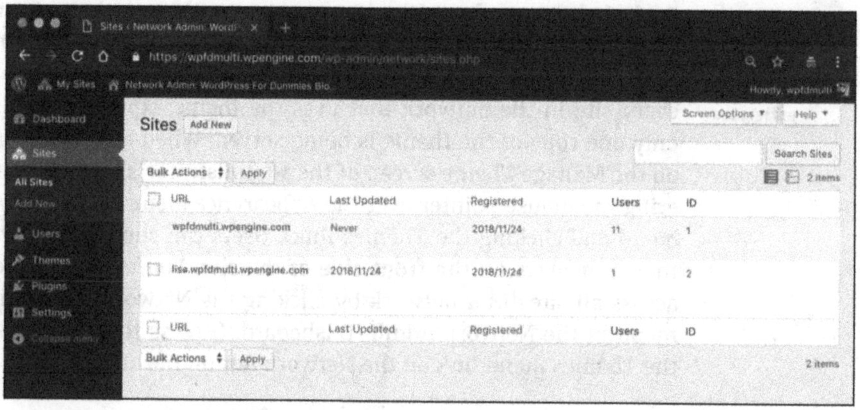

FIGURE 5-2: A list of sites in the network.

2. **Hover your mouse pointer over the site you want to enable a theme for and then click the Edit link.**

   The Edit Site screen displays on your Dashboard.

3. **Click the Themes tab of the Edit Sites screen.**

   The screen lists themes that you can enable for the site you're editing. (See Figure 5-3.)

4. **Click the Enable link for the theme you want to use for the site you're editing.**

   The Edit Site screen refreshes with the Theme tab still active and displays a message stating that the theme has been enabled.

5. **Repeat these steps for any other sites on which you want to enable a theme.**

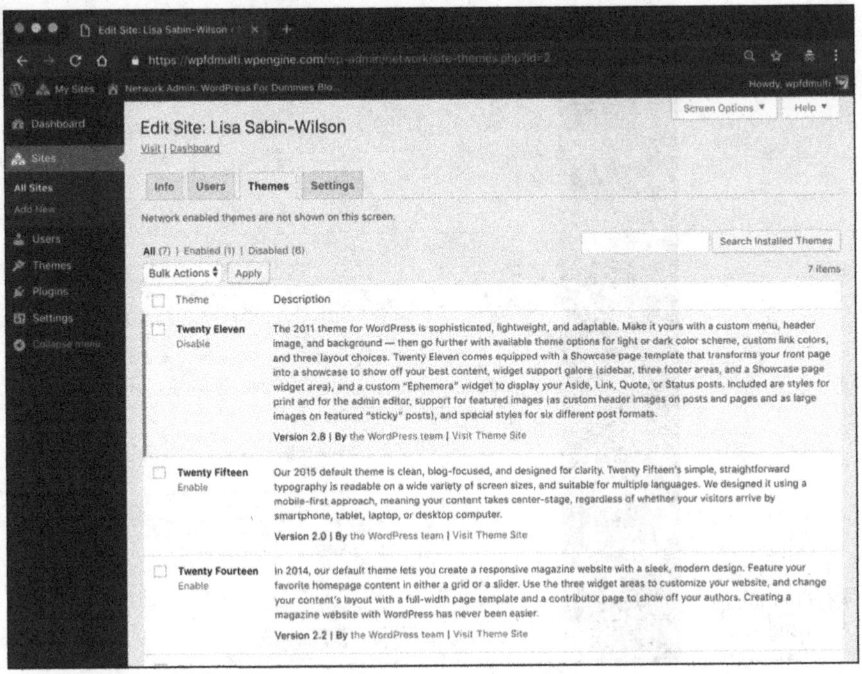

FIGURE 5-3: The Edit Site screen with the Themes tab active.

Installing themes for network use

Installing a theme for use on your network involves the same process you use to install a theme on your individual site (see Book 6, Chapter 2) but with an extra step: You have to enable each theme on the Network Admin Dashboard to activate it on the Appearance menu of the individual site administrators' Dashboards. Here's how to enable a theme so that all your site owners can use it on their sites:

1. **Click the Network Admin link on the My Sites menu in the top-left corner of your Dashboard and then click the Themes menu link.**

   The Themes screen appears, displaying a list of installed themes. (See Figure 5-4.) Each theme installed in the `/wp-content/themes` folder is listed on this screen.

2. **Click the Network Enable link for the theme you want to use.**

   Enabling a theme causes it to appear in the list of available themes on each network site's Dashboard (but doesn't change any user's active theme; it merely makes this theme available for use).

3. **Repeat these steps to enable more themes on your network.**

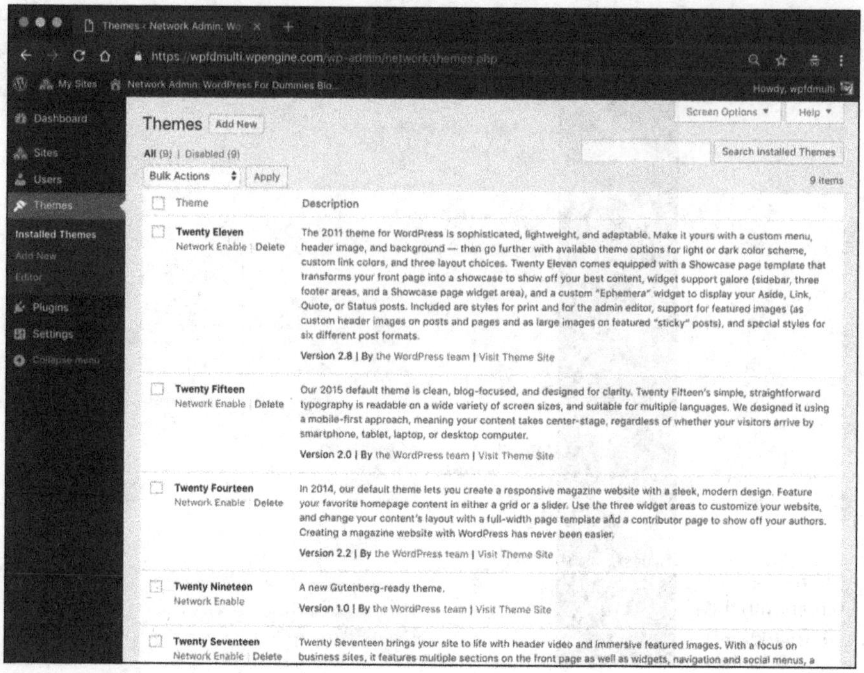

FIGURE 5-4: A list of themes used in the network.

REMEMBER

Just installing a new theme in your main WordPress installation doesn't make it available for use networkwide. As the network admin, you always have to enable a theme before your site owners can use it.

Setting the default theme for sites

When a new site is created on the network, by default it displays the Twenty Nineteen theme provided within WordPress, which is the default theme for all new WordPress installations. If you want to use a different theme for all new sites, you can add a `define` statement to the `wp-config.php` file of your WordPress installation. (Check out Book 2, Chapter 5 to familiarize yourself with the `wp-config.php` file that you're modifying.)

Install your theme on the server, as I outline in Book 6, chapters 1 and 2. You may also want to enable the theme networkwide, as outlined in "Installing themes for network use" earlier in this chapter. This step isn't necessary, but if you have other themes available, and if the active theme is disabled, a user who switches away from that theme won't be able to switch back to it.

Because the Twenty Nineteen WordPress theme is already the default, I use another popular WordPress theme (the default theme before TwentyNineteen was released) called TwentySeventeen (`https://wordpress.org/themes/twentyseventeen`). To set this theme as the default theme for all sites within a network, follow these steps:

1. **Log in to your web server via SFTP.**

   Book 2, Chapter 2 discusses using SFTP.

2. **Open the `wp-config.php` file in your favorite text editor.**

   See Book 2, Chapter 5 for details about the `wp-config.php` file.

   TIP: Save a copy of your original `wp-config.php` file to your desktop before editing it in case you make any mistakes in the next few steps.

3. **Locate the following line of code in the `wp-config.php` file:**

```
define( 'WPLANG', '' );
```

   You can find this line toward the bottom of the file; scroll until you locate it.

4. **Add a new blank line below it.**

5. **Type** define('WP_DEFAULT_THEME', 'twentyseventeen');

   This one line of code tells WordPress to use the TwentySeventeen theme as the default theme for all new sites within your network.

   TIP: The part of the line of code in step 5 that looks like this — `'twentyseventeen'` — is the name of the folder that contains the theme in the `/wp-content/themes/` folder in the file directory on your web server. The name within quotes should be identical to the name of the folder where the theme files reside.

6. **Save the `wp-config.php` file, and upload it to your web server.**

   All new sites created now display the TwentySeventeen theme.

Gathering and Displaying Networkwide Content

Depending on your needs, you may want to gather content from sites across your network to display on the front page of the main site (as the BBC America website does). Although some plugins can perform this task for you, you can accomplish the same thing by placing a few lines of code in your theme template file.

The main page of your network is controlled by the theme that's active on the Themes screen of your regular Dashboard (which you access by hovering your mouse pointer over Appearance and clicking the Themes link). You can customize this theme with the code samples provided in the next section, "Adding posts from network sites."

Adding posts from network sites

One of the best ways to pull visitors into your site is to display a short list of headlines from posts on other sites within your network. If you have a single WordPress site, the Recent Posts widget can handle this task. When you're running a network, however, you have no built-in way to pull a list of posts from across all the sites in your network. But the Network Posts Extended plugin (`https://wordpress.org/plugins/network-posts-extended`) allows you to share posts and pages from across your entire network on any given page on your main site through the use of a shortcode. The shortcode provided by the plugin has a variety of parameters you can use to customize the display of the content. You can specify the number of posts to display, for example, or display content only from certain sites. You can use several parameters and custom HTML elements with the shortcode; all the options available to you are listed at `https://wordpress.org/plugins/network-posts-extended`.

Listing network sites

To list all the sites in the network, use the Multisite Directory plugin, available for free on the WordPress website at `https://wordpress.org/plugins/multisite-directory`. You install this plugin just as you do any other plugin in WordPress; see Book 7, chapters 1 and 2 for information on installing WordPress plugins.

To display a listing of sites from your network, you must include a shortcode that the plugin developer provides within the body of a page or post published to your main site. The most common and most useful method is to create a page that includes the plugin shortcode. To list all network sites, follow these steps (which use the default TwentyNineteen theme):

1. **Log in to the WordPress Dashboard of the main site.**
2. **Hover your mouse pointer over Pages, and click the Add New link.**

   The Add New Page screen appears.
3. **Fill in a title for your page.**

   You might type something like *Network Sites List*.

4. **Click the Add Block icon.**

   This step loads the blocks you can use to create content on a page.

5. **Select the Shortcode block below the Widgets heading.**

6. **Add the `[site-directory display="list"]` shortcode in the text field.**

   This shortcode displays a list of site titles. (See Figure 5-5.)

   TIP

   The shortcode for this plugin accepts several parameters that customize the display of the sites. All the options available to you are listed on the Multisite Directory plugin's page at `https://wordpress.org/plugins/multisite-directory`.

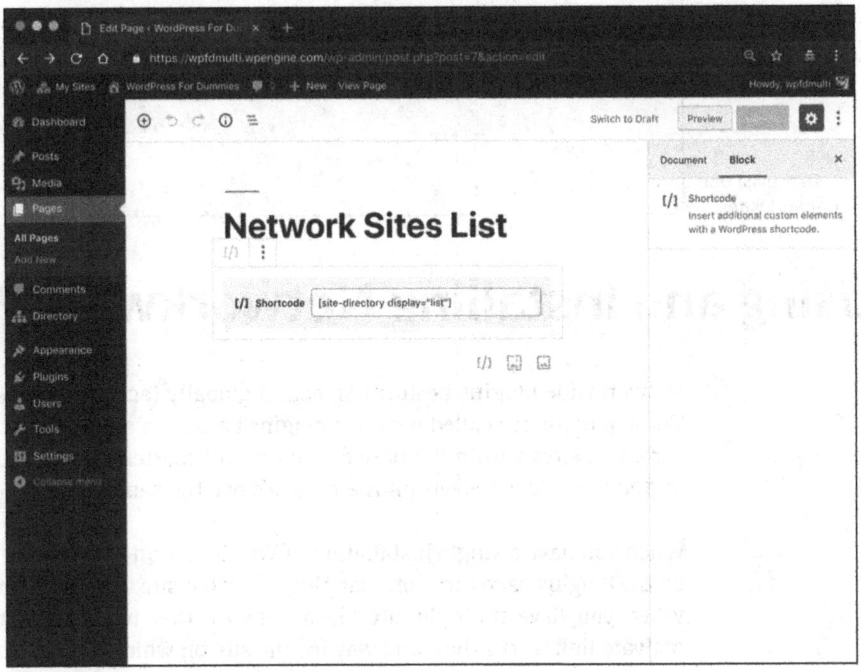

FIGURE 5-5: Adding a shortcode to a page by using the Shortcode widget block.

7. **Publish the page.**

   Now when you visit the page on your website, you see that it displays the list of sites in the network. (See Figure 5-6.)

Using Network Plugins and Themes

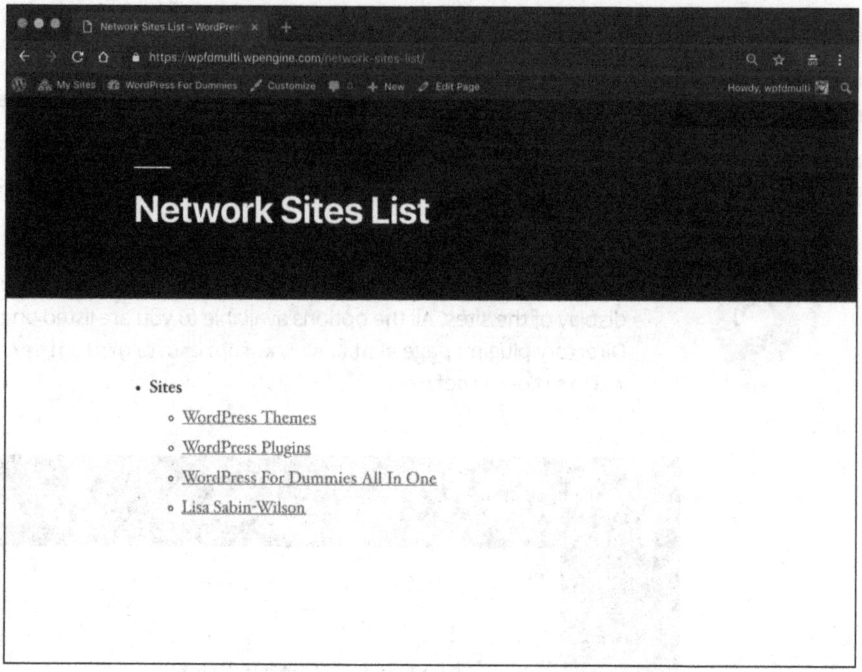

FIGURE 5-6: A page showing the list of network sites.

Using and Installing Networkwide Plugins

Networkwide plugins perform an action globally (across all sites in the network). These plugins are called network plugins because a single copy of a plugin is used across all sites within the network; it doesn't matter whether your network has 5 or 500 sites. All sites within the network use the same copy.

When you have a single installation of WordPress on a single site, the Activate link on the Plugins page turns on that plugin for that site. (See Book 7, chapters 1 and 2.) When you have multiple sites in a network that use the Multisite feature, the Activate link works the same way for the site on which you activate the plugin.

You see a Network Activate link on the Plugins screen of the Network Admin Dashboard. This link activates the plugin on all sites in the network (turns the plugin on for all network sites). You can't manage plugin options globally, however, unless the plugin itself is coded to let you do so. A list of network-activated plugins appears on the Plugins screen of the Network Admin Dashboard (which you access by clicking the Plugins menu link).

REMEMBER

Any changes made in a plugin affect every site within your network.

A special breed of plugins — Must-Use — gets installed in the `/wp-content/mu-plugins` folder on your web server. Any plugin file placed inside this folder runs as though it were part of the WordPress core installation. The plugins in this folder execute automatically without the need for activation in your Dashboard.

WARNING

You can't install or access the plugins in the `/wp-content/mu-plugins/` folder from the WordPress Dashboard. If you use the Install Plugins screen (hover your mouse pointer over Plugins, and click the Add New link) to find and install a plugin, you're required to move the plugin files from the `/wp-content/plugins` folder to the `/wp-content/mu-plugins` folder.

Generally, plugins placed in the `/wp-content/mu-plugins` folder are for networkwide features or customizations that users can't disable. An example is a custom-branded login page on each site in your network. If a plugin design adds a new menu item, the menu item appears as soon as the plugin is placed in the `/wp-content/mu-plugins` folder, without further need for activation from the Dashboard.

Not all plugins placed in the `/wp-content/mu-plugins` folder appear in the plugins list on the Plugins screen, because not all of them require activation. After you create the `/wp-content/mu-plugins` folder via SFTP or your web host's control panel, a new Must-Use link appears on the Plugins screen, as shown in Figure 5-7. This link displays the plugins that are included in the `/wp-content/mu-plugins` folder but doesn't give you the ability to activate, deactivate, or edit them.

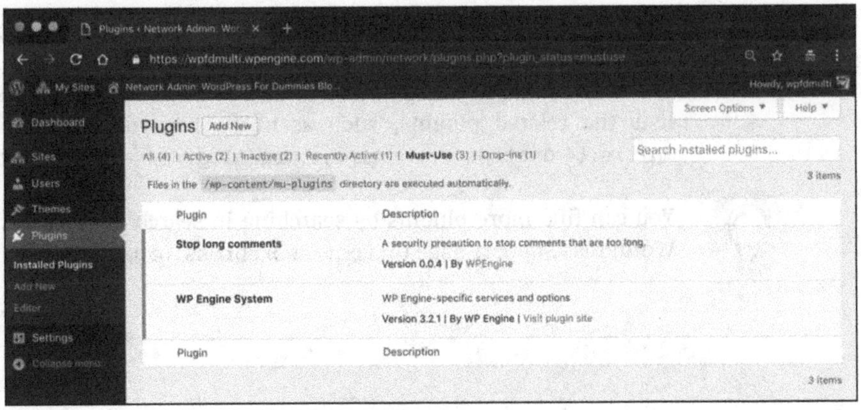

FIGURE 5-7: The Must-Use link on the Plugins screen.

REMEMBER

You still control plugin settings on a per-site basis; you must visit the back end of each site if you want to alter any settings provided by the plugin.

Here's how to create the /wp-content/mu-plugins folder and install a network-wide plugin:

1. **Connect to your web server via SFTP.**
2. **Navigate to the /wp-content folder.**

   You see the subdirectories plugins and themes.
3. **Using your SFTP program, create a mu-plugins subdirectory.**

   Most SFTP programs allow you to right-click in the SFTP window with your mouse and add a new folder from the shortcut menu.
4. **Upload the plugin file (not the plugin folder) to the /wp-content/mu-plugins folder on your web server.**

   The plugin runs in your installation immediately.

   Generally speaking, the only plugins that go in this folder are ones that have explicit instructions (typically located in the readme.txt file) to that effect.

Discovering Handy Multisite Plugins

You can find Multisite plugins that take advantage of WordPress's Multisite functionality on the WordPress Plugins page at https://wordpress.org/plugins.

Usually, Multisite plugins are tagged with certain keywords that help you find them, such as *multisite* and *network*. Use the search field on the Plugins page to search for a plugin by keyword. The WordPress website displays a page that lists the related plugins, such as https://wordpress.org/plugins/search/multisite or https://wordpress.org/plugins/search/network.

TIP

You can find more plugins by searching in search engines and by searching the WordPress Support page (https://wordpress.org/support).

IN THIS CHAPTER

» **Discovering domain mapping**

» **Understanding how to map domains**

» **Advanced usage**

Chapter 6

Using Multiple Domains within Your Network

With a network of multiple sites easily available in WordPress, many people prefer to run multiple sites on their own separate domain names through one install.

In this chapter, I discuss using multiple domains and a feature called *domain mapping*, which enables you to not only run multiple sites but also multiple sites with unique domain names that aren't tied to the main site's installation domain.

To tackle this chapter, you need to understand domains (Book 5, Chapter 1) and Domain Name System (DNS) records.

Finding Your Way with Domain Mapping

Domain mapping means telling your web server which domains you want WordPress to answer to and which site you want to be shown to visitors when they request that domain. This process is more than domain forwarding or masking because the URLs for your posts have the full domain name in them. Instead of the child site's being in `secondsite.`*`yourdomain`*`.com` format, it can be in *`myotherdomain`*`.com`.

Domain mapping isn't possible in certain cases, however. If your WordPress install is in a subfolder, and this folder is part of the URL, any mapped domain will also contain this folder name. In that case, it would be better to move the install so that it isn't in a subfolder.

You also need to access your web host's control panel (where you manage DNS records on your web server) and the control panel for your domain-name registrar, which is often a different company.

REMEMBER

By default, the network install lets you choose between a subdirectory setup and a subdomain setup. This step is still required before you can specify a domain for that site. I cover how to enable the network in Book 8, Chapter 2. Be sure to set up the network and make sure that it's functioning properly before you attempt to map domains.

Domain aliases

You need to set up your web server to accept any incoming requests for the domain you want to map and the location to send your site visitors to. I use the cPanel control panel (Book 2, Chapter 2) in this section because it's quite popular and available on many web hosts. On cPanel-based web hosts, this task is referred to as *domain parking.*

Follow these steps to park a domain on your web hosting account via cPanel:

1. **Log in to your website's cPanel.**

   The address is provided by your web host and usually is available at `http://`*`yourdomain.com`*`/cpanel`.

2. **In the Domains section, click the Aliases icon, as shown in Figure 6-1.**

   The Aliases page displays in your browser window. It lists any domains you've created aliases for (if any) and provides a form for entering a new domain.

3. **In the Create a New Alias section, enter the domain name you want to map in the Domain text box.**

   The domain is directed to the root folder of your website, which is where your WordPress install should be located. If it isn't, follow the next set of steps.

4. **Click the Add Domain button.**

   The screen refreshes and shows the domain you added in the Domains lists, shown at the bottom of the page in Figure 6-2,which indicates the successful creation of a domain alias that you entered in step 3.

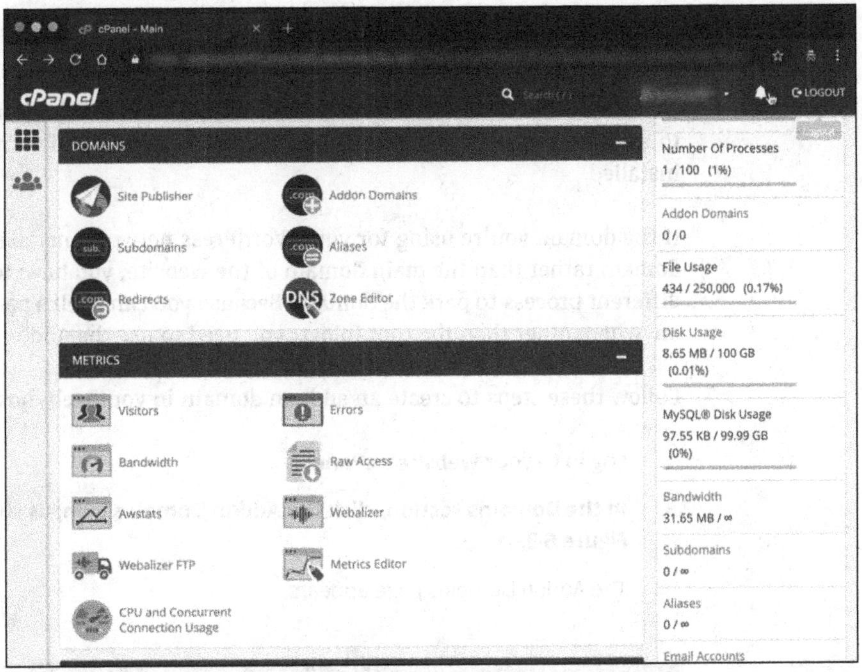

FIGURE 6-1: The Aliases icon in cPanel.

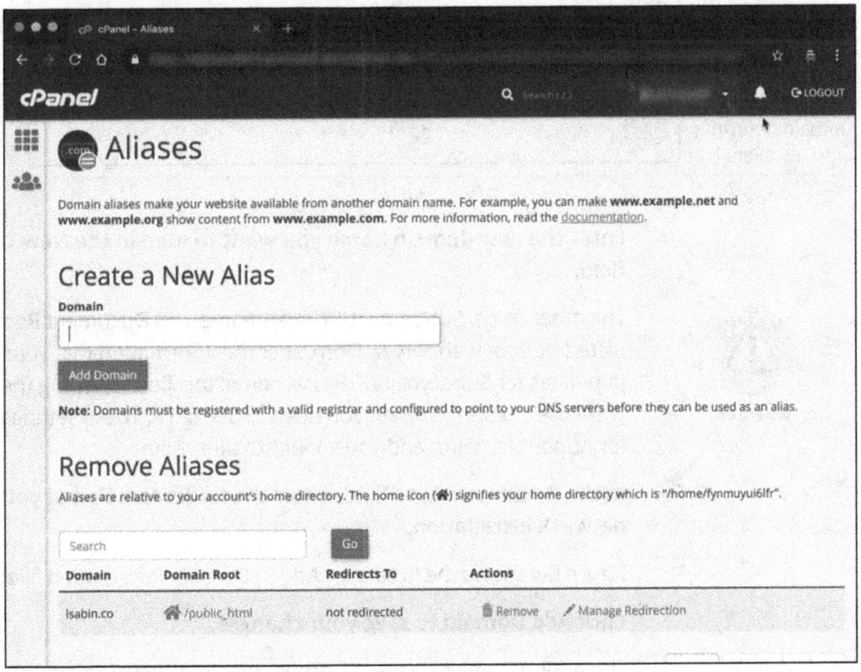

FIGURE 6-2: The Aliases page showing a domain alias.

Other web hosts may refer to a domain alias as *pointing* or *mirroring*. You may need to ask your web host's support team which area you need to do this in. You're using a `ServerAlias` directive for the mapped domains, telling the web server to send all requests for the mapped domain to the domain where WordPress is installed.

If the domain you're using for your WordPress network installation is an add-on domain rather than the main domain of the website, you have to follow a slightly different process to park the domain. Because you can't tell a parked domain to go anywhere other than the root folder, you need to use the Addon Domains feature.

Follow these steps to create an add-on domain in your web-hosting cPanel:

1. **Log in to your website's cPanel.**
2. **In the Domains section, click the Addon Domains icon, as shown in Figure 6-3.**

   The Addon Domains page appears.

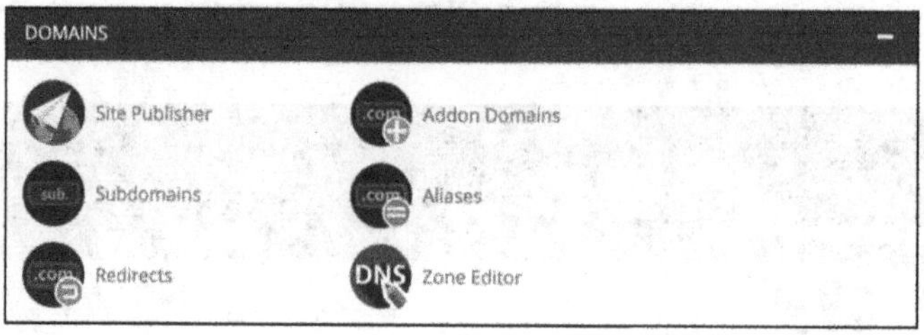

FIGURE 6-3: The Addon Domains icon in cPanel.

3. **Enter the new domain name you want to map in the New Domain Name field.**

   WARNING

   The other fields, Subdomain/FTP Username and Document Root, get autopopulated by your web server. Don't alter the information that your web server populates for Subdomain/FTP Username; this field is setting the username you'll use to connect when you need to use SFTP. These settings are defaults for Addon Domains, and you shouldn't alter them.

4. **In the Document Root field, enter the folder location of your WordPress network installation.**

   Figure 6-4 shows the Create an Addon Domain information filled in.

5. **Click Add Domain to save your changes.**

   The Addon Domains page refreshes, and your new domain appears in the Addon Domains section.

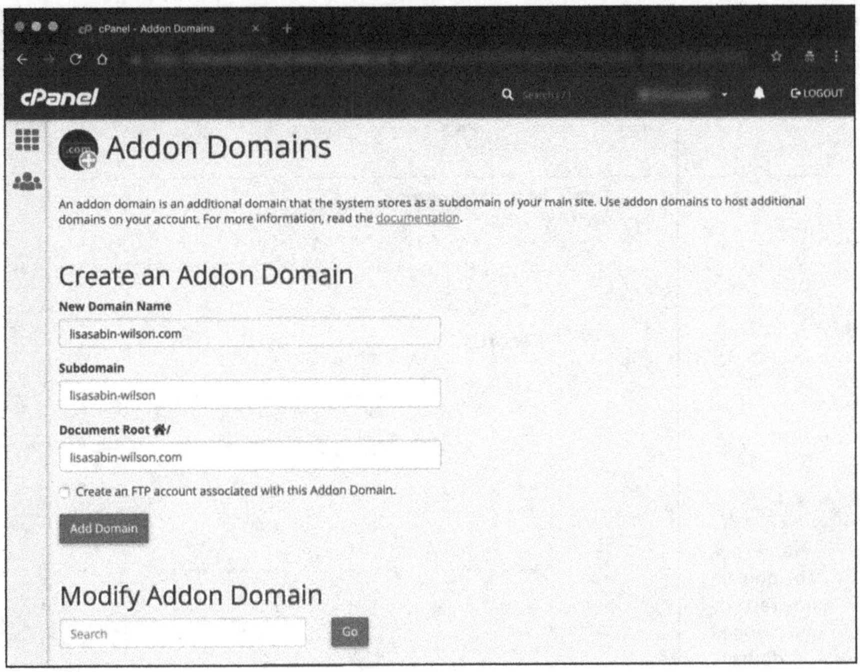

FIGURE 6-4: The Create an Addon Domain information in cPanel.

Editing DNS records

To instruct the domain name registrar where to send the domain name to, you need to edit the DNS records. GoDaddy is a common domain-name registrar, I use its domain-registration account interface in the following steps. To edit the name server records, follow these steps:

1. **Log in to your domain-name registrar.**
2. **Click the DNS management tools.**

   Figure 6-5 shows the information for the domain to map.
3. **Click the Set Nameservers link in the Nameservers section.**
4. **Type the name servers for your web host where your WordPress installation.**
5. **Click the Save Changes button.**

   Now servers around the world know that your domain "lives" at this web server location. Name server changes may take up to 24 hours to propagate across the Internet.

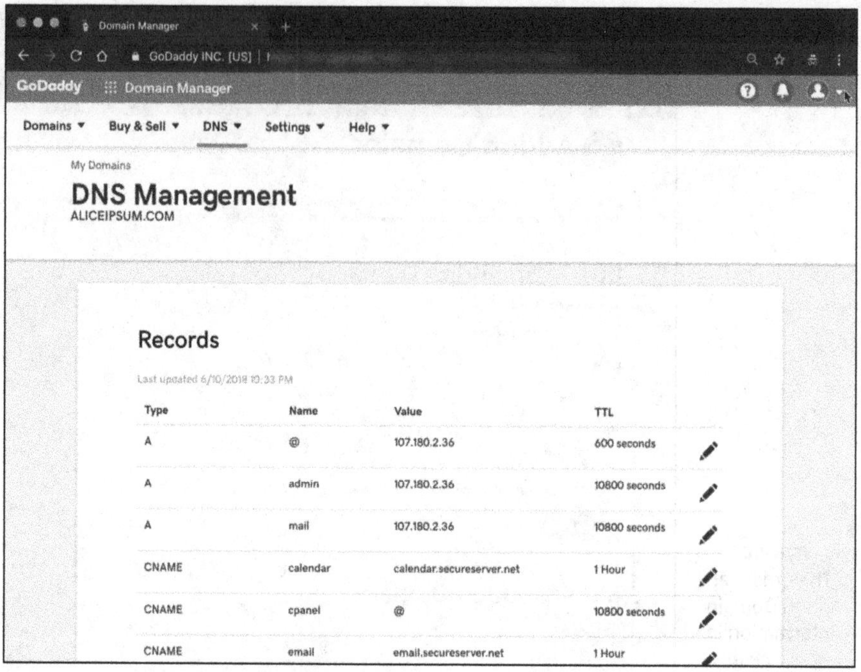

FIGURE 6-5: The domain name records of a mapped domain.

Installing the Domain Mapping Plugin

Before you can add your mapped domains to WordPress, you need to install the WordPress MU Domain Mapping plugin to help handle this task. The Domain Mapping plugin doesn't do any setup on the server side; it helps you rename the site and takes care of any login issues. To use it, follow these steps:

1. **Click the Plugins link on the Network Admin menu.**

   The Plugins screen appears.

2. **Click Add New.**

   The Add Plugin screen appears.

3. **Search for *WordPress MU Domain Mapping* in the search field.**

   A list of plugins appears.

4. **Find the plugin titled WordPress MU Domain Mapping by Donncha O Caoimh, and click its Install Now button to install it.**

5. **Click the Network Activate button.**

   This step activates the plugin for use across your entire network.

6. **Open your SFTP program, and navigate to the `wp-content/plugins/wordpress-mu-domain-mapping` folder.**

7. **Download the `sunrise.php` file to your computer.**

8. **In your SFTP program, navigate to the `/wp-content/` folder.**

9. **Upload the `sunrise.php` file to the `/wp-content` folder. (See Figure 6-6.)**

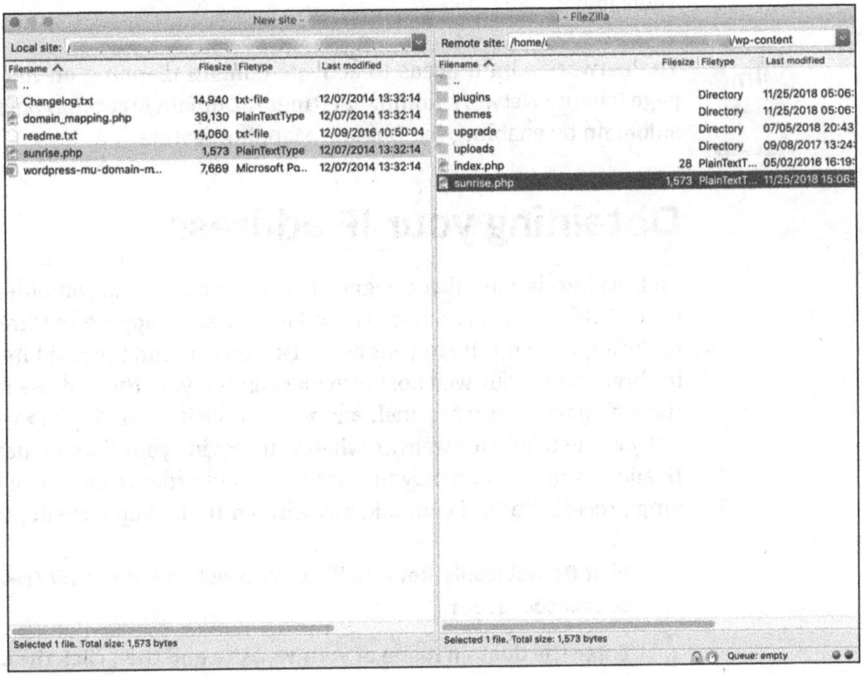

FIGURE 6-6: A look at the `/wp-content/plugins` folder that contains the `sunrise.php` file.

10. **Download a copy of your `wp-config.php` file by using your SFTP program.**

    You can find the `wp-config.php` file in the main directory of your WordPress installation.

11. **Open `wp-config.php` on your computer with a text editor, and add the following line below the `define( 'MULTISITE', true );` line:**

```
define( 'SUNRISE', 'on' );
```

12. **Save the file, and upload it to your website.**

    The plugin is available (and running) on your network immediately.

All you need to do now is set up the options and map a domain to a site. Two new items are added to the Network Settings menu: Domain Mapping and Domains. On the site administrator Dashboard, a new Domain Mapping item appears on the Tools menu.

REMEMBER

The network admin needs to activate domain mapping on the Domain Mapping page (choose Network Admin➪Settings➪Domain Mapping) before a user can map a domain by enabling the Domain Mapping feature.

Obtaining your IP address

An *IP address* is a number assigned to every website and computer that's connected to the Internet. This number is used in domain mapping to \direct Internet traffic to the appropriate site in your network. You can find the IP address of your website in three ways: Your web host provider can tell you, the address may appear within the web host's control panel, and you can visit an IP-lookup website (which can tell you the IP of your website when you provide your domain name). You need the IP address of the domain you want to map in order to complete the domain mapping process. To find your address with an IP-lookup website, follow these steps:

1. **Visit Domaintools' Reverse IP Lookup website at `http://reverseip.domaintools.com`.**
2. **Enter the domain name of your website and then click the Lookup button.**
3. **Write down the IP address displayed.**

   Figure 6-7 displays the IP address of Google.com (172.217.3.164).
4. **In your WordPress Dashboard, choose Network Admin➪Settings➪Domain Mapping.**
5. **Enter your IP address in the Server IP Address field.**
6. **Click Save.**

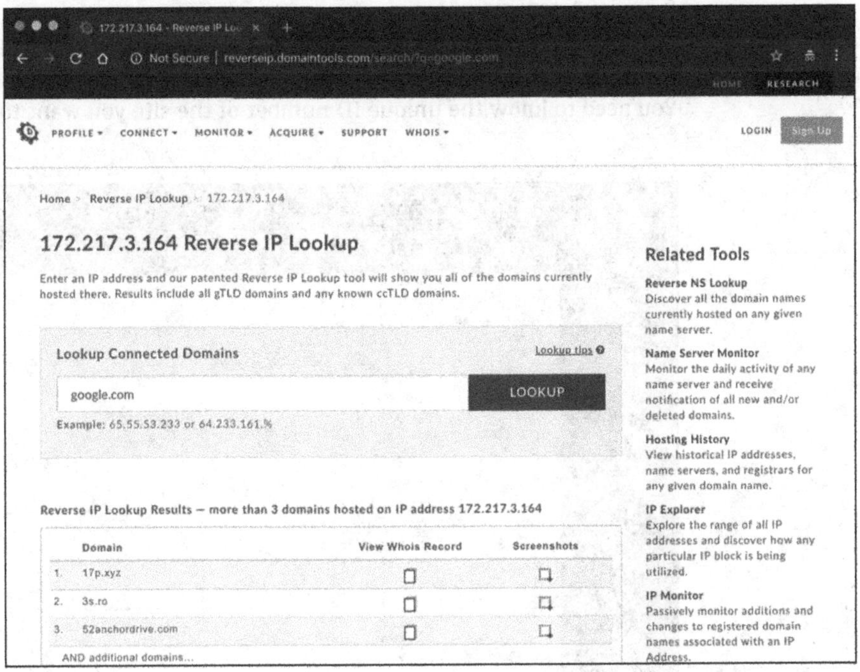

FIGURE 6-7: Reverse IP record revealing the IP address of Google.com.

Mapping a domain to a site

To map a domain to a site in your network, here's what you need to do:

1. **Navigate to the site within your network to which you want to map a domain.**
2. **Log in to that site's Dashboard.**
3. **Click the Domain Mapping link on the Tools menu.**

   The Domain Mapping screen appears.
4. **Enter the domain name you want to map to this site.**

   The check box indicates whether the domain is the primary domain for this site and is used only if you want to map multiple domains to the site. Only one domain can be the primary domain and used in the URL. Any other domains mapped to this site redirect to the primary domain.
5. **Click the Add button to save your changes.**

   The site appears when you enter the mapped domain URL in your web browser's address bar.

This plugin also lets you map a domain to a site without visiting the site's Dashboard by choosing Network Admin⇨Settings⇨Domains. (See Figure 6-8.) ***Note:*** You need to know the unique ID number of the site you want to map.

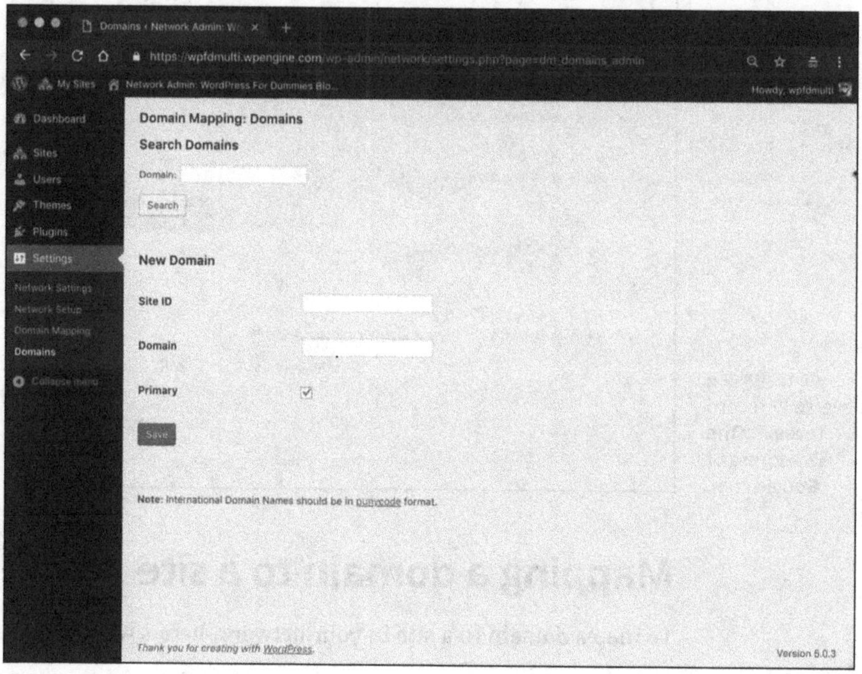

FIGURE 6-8: The Domain Mapping: Domains screen maps domains from a single location.

Mapping a Large Volume of Domains

For some enterprises, you may need to map a large volume of domains (10 or more) to the WordPress network. Adding each domain to the server with a `ServerAlias` directive is time-consuming. Also, as the list grows, the server slows while reading all the domains.

The time necessary to add these domains can be shortened considerably by using a wildcard host. To use a wildcard host, you need to access your website via a terminal or via Secure Shell (SSH) with the ability to log in with root user capabilities. The ability to add a wildcard is available only on virtual private servers or dedicated hosts. The ideal situation for using a wildcard host is when the main installation of WordPress is the default domain on the server. A quick way to check whether your WordPress main installation domain is the default domain on your web server is to type your IP address in your browser's address bar. If your main

WordPress site displays in your browser, you can proceed with using a wildcard host. If not, you need to obtain a dedicated IP address from your web hosting provider.

Configuring Apache

Adding a wildcard host to your web server requires that you access the Apache configuration files on your web server. This section assumes that you have access to those files, as well as SSH login access to your web server. If not, ask your web hosting provider to provide you the access you need or to complete the steps for you.

Here's how you set up this feature:

1. **Log in to your website as the root user via a terminal.**
2. **Navigate to the configuration files in the folder located at `/etc/httpd/` by typing**

   ```
   cd /etc/httpd/
   ```

3. **Open the `httpd.conf` file by typing**

   ```
   vi httpd.conf
   ```

   Page down in the file until you see the vhost section. Find the that contains information about your WordPress installation and the main domain of your network. (Depending on the number of domains hosted on your server, you may find several vhost entries in the `httpd.conf` file; be sure that you're editing the vhost that contains the main domain of your WordPress install.)

4. **Press the Insert key to begin editing the file.**
5. **Comment out the lines and place the wildcard as follows:**

   ```
   <VirtualHost *:80>
   ```

6. **Save the changes by pressing the Esc key, typing** :wq, **and then pressing Enter (or Return on a Mac).**
7. **On the command line, restart Apache by typing**

   ```
   /etc/init.d/apache restart
   ```

Now you can map domains in volume by following these steps:

1. **Log in to your domain-name registrar.**
2. **Click the domain-name management tools for the domain you want to map.**
3. **Click the DNS records.**

   (Refer to Figure 6-5 earlier in this chapter.)
4. **Locate the A records at the top of the page, and insert the IP address of your WordPress network.**

   (I show you how to obtain this address in "Obtaining your IP address" earlier in this chapter.)

   Figure 6-9 shows an A record and the web-server IP address to which it points. The domain is sent to that IP address regardless of name server.
5. **Choose Network Admin⇨Settings⇨Domains from your WordPress Dashboard.**

   The Domain Mapping: Domains page appears, as shown in Figure 6-10.
6. **Enter the ID of the site you want to map.**

   You can get the ID number from the Sites page (by choosing Network Admin⇨Sites). I used site ID 2 in Figure 6-10.
7. **Enter the domain name you want to map to this site.**

   In Figure 6-10, I used `myamazingdomain.com` as the domain name I want to use for the site.
8. **Click Save.**

   The page refreshes and shows you a list of mapped domains.

You no longer need to park or point domains at the web host. If you added the wildcard host in your Apache configuration, the server is instructed to take any domain-name request and send it to the WordPress network, based on the IP that you added. WordPress associates the mapped domain with the correct site.

Hiding the original installation domain

The WordPress MU Domain Mapping plugin, mentioned in "Installing the Domain Mapping Plugin" earlier in this chapter, lets you access the child site by the original location regardless of whether it's a subdomain or subfolder site. As a result, you can use domain mapping no matter which setup you chose for your network (subdomains or subdirectories). The domain mapped for the child site is also the domain used on all uploaded media files, thereby maintaining consistency for the site.

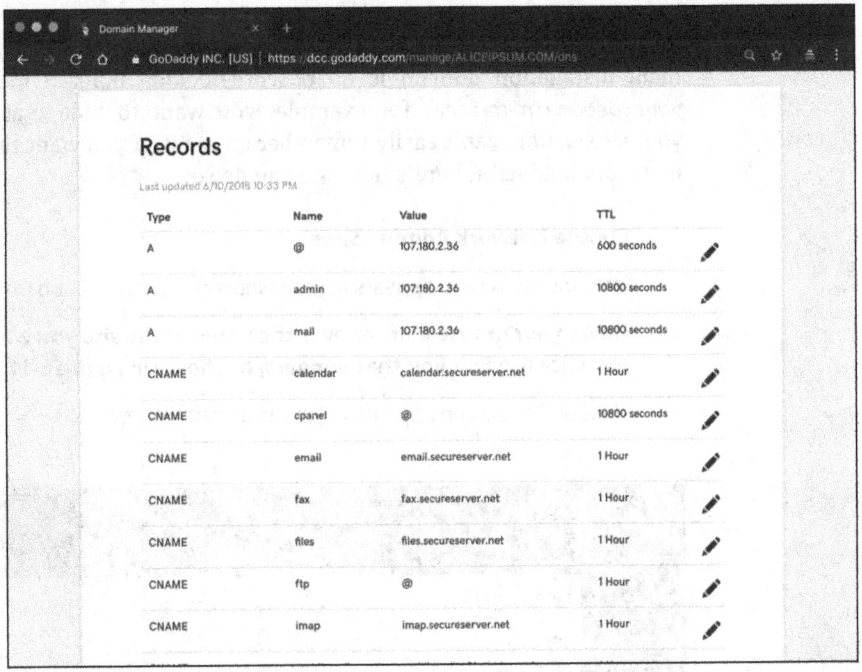

FIGURE 6-9: Domain A records.

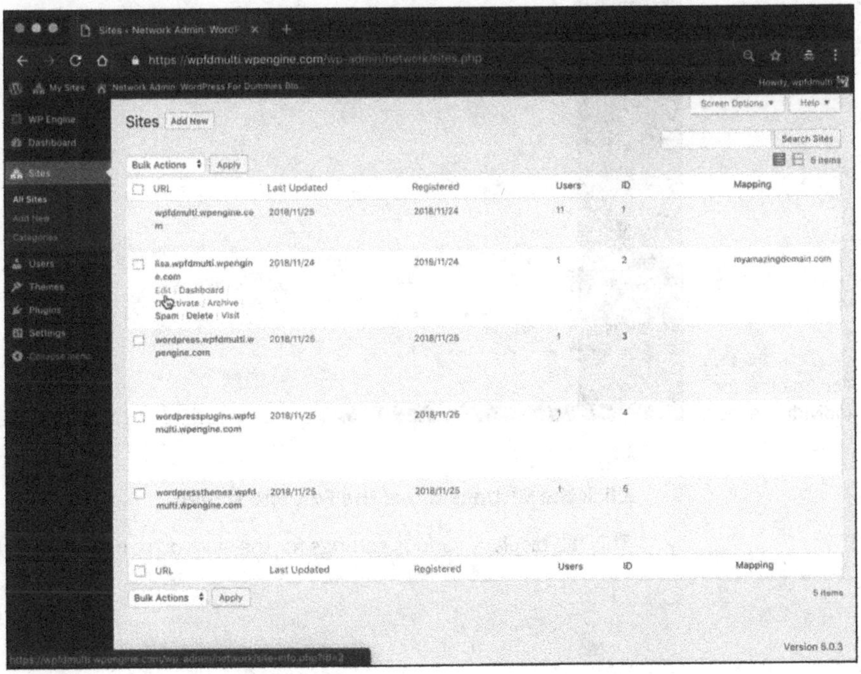

FIGURE 6-10: Mapping a domain from the Domain Mapping: Domains page.

In some cases, you may want to hide the original installation domain. If your main installation domain is an obscure-looking domain like `http://00954-yourvpsdomain-ba.com`, for example, you want to hide that domain because your site visitors can't easily remember or use it. If you want to hide the original installation domain, here's how you can do so:

1. **Choose Network Admin⇨Sites.**

   The Edit Site screen appears in your Network Admin Dashboard.

2. **Hover your mouse pointer over the name of the site you want to edit, and click the Edit link that appears, as shown in Figure 6-11.**

   The Edit Site screen appears in your browser window.

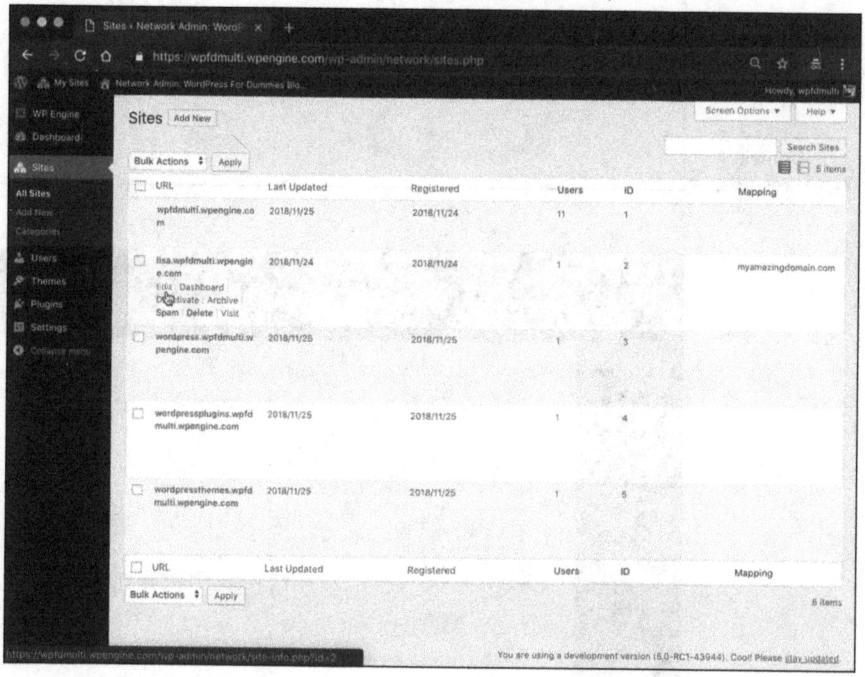

FIGURE 6-11: The Edit link for individual sites.

3. **Click the Settings tab of the Edit Site screen.**

   This tab displays various settings for the site you're editing. (See Figure 6-12.)

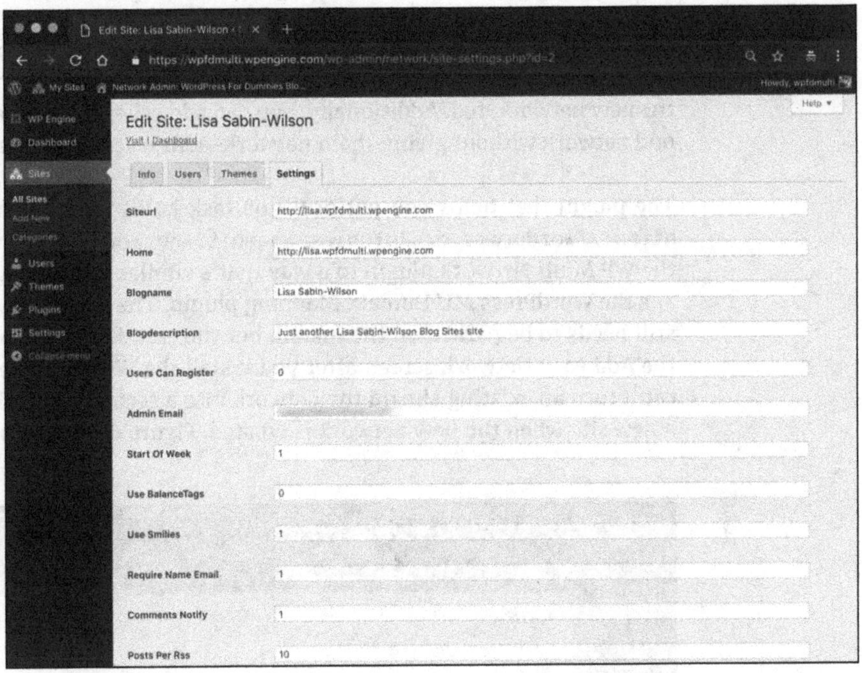

FIGURE 6-12: The Edit Site page of the Network Admin Dashboard.

4. **Find all instances of the original domain name, and change them to the new mapped domain.**

   Be sure to click each tab on the Edit Site screen (Info, Users, Themes, and Settings) to change the original domain name to the new mapped domain wherever it appears on the Edit Site screen. Keep any folder names intact.

5. **Save your changes by clicking the Save Changes button.**

Now your mapped site is inaccessible at the original child-site domain, and any references to it have been changed. Previous links within the body of posts, however, aren't updated automatically, so you need to edit the posts manually to change the links to reflect your newly mapped domain.

Setting Up Multiple Networks

Multiple networks are supported in the WordPress code base, but there's no built-in menu or interface on the Dashboard. Running multiple networks in one install is an advanced feature that allows you to have another network in the same installation acting as a second independent network of sites. That network can use its fully qualified domain name or a subdomain. The extra networks inherit the same type of sites. If your original network was installed with subdomain sites, the extra network will also have subdomain sites. The network admin carries over to the new network, too. Additionally, you can add other network admins to the second network without giving them network-admin access on the original network.

The plugin that helps you perform this task is WP Multi Network (available at `https://wordpress.org/plugins/wp-multi-network`). You install and manage the WP Multi Network plugin in a way that's similar to how you install and manage the WordPress MU Domain Mapping plugin. The domain for the new network still needs to be parked on the install, but the creation of the network is done on the Add New Network screen after you install the WP Multi Network plugin. You can't turn an existing site on the network into a second network; you must set up a new site when the new network is created. Figure 6-13 shows the

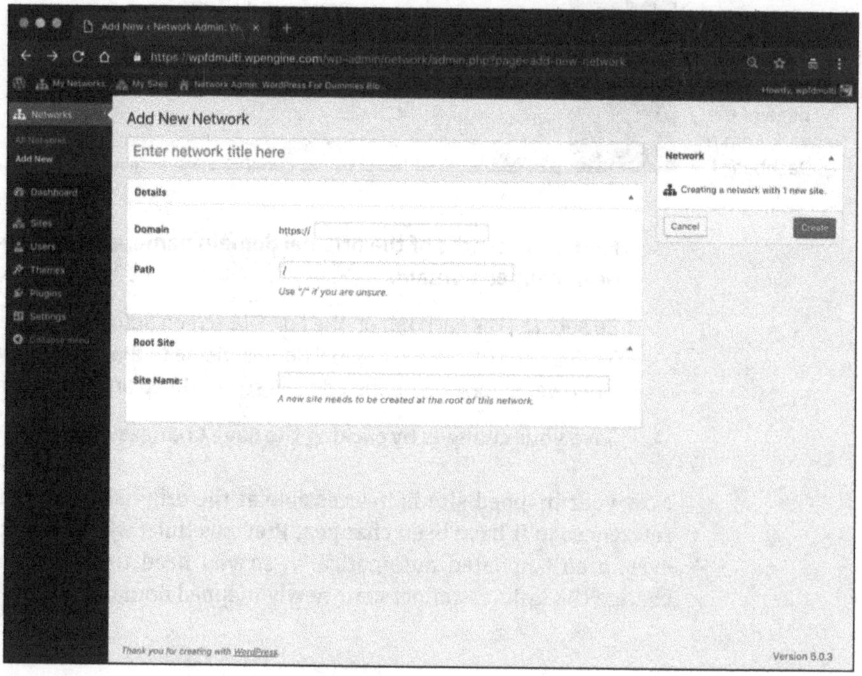

FIGURE 6-13: The Add New Network screen in the Network Admin Dashboard.

When this plugin is installed and the network is activated, you see a new menu on the Network Dashboard: called Networks. Click the Add New link on the Networks menu to load the Add New Networks screen.

To create a new network, fill in the fields on the Add New Networks screen:

- **Network Title:** The name of the network you're creating (such as My New Network)
- **Details:** The settings for the Domain and Path
- **Domain:** The domain name you'll use for this new network (such as *mynewnetwork*.com)
- **Path:** The server path your new network will use (such as /home/*mynewnetwork*/public_html/)
- **Root Site:** The settings for the Site Name
- **Site Name:** The name of the site that will serve as the main site of this network (such as Network Main Site)

When you're done, click the Create button on the right side of the Add New Network screen. WordPress creates your new network, and you can assign child sites to it.

Index

A

D

E

G

J

K

N

O

P

Q

R

S

U

V

W

X

Y

Z

About the Author

Lisa Sabin-Wilson (*WordPress For Dummies, WordPress Web Design For Dummies*) has 16 years' experience working with the WordPress platform, having adopted it early in its first year of release in 2003. Lisa is the co-owner of a successful WordPress design and development agency, WebDevStudios (`http://webdevstudios.com`), and is a regular speaker on topics related to design and WordPress at several national conferences. You can find Lisa online at her blog at lisasabin-wilson.com or on Twitter at `@lisasabinilson`.

Dedication

To WordPress . . . and all that entails from the developers, designers, forum helpers, bug testers, educators, consultants, plugin makers, and theme bakers.

Author's Acknowledgments

Every person involved in the WordPress community plays a vital role in making this whole thing work, and work well. Kudos to all of you! Also, big thanks to my wonderful husband, Chris Wilson, for his incredible support, backbone, and ability to put up with my crazy days of writing — I could *not* have done it without you!

Special thanks to the co-authors of the first edition of this book who helped form the framework of the publication and ensured its initial success: Cory Miller, Kevin Palmer, Andrea Rennick, and Michael Torbert.

Publisher's Acknowledgments

Acquisitions Editor: Ashley Barth
Project Editor: Charlotte Kughen
Copy Editor: Kathy Simpson
Technical Editor: Greg Ricksby
Editorial Assistant: Matthew Lowe
Sr. Editorial Assistant: Cherie Case
Production Editor: Magesh Elangovan
Cover Image: © pichit/Shutterstock